Literary Spaces

Literary Spaces

Introduction to Comparative Black Literature

Christel N. Temple

Associate Professor of Africana Studies
University of Maryland, Baltimore County

Carolina Academic Press
Durham, North Carolina

Library of Congress Cataloging-in-Publication Data

Temple, Christel N.
  Literary spaces : introduction to comparative Black literature / by Christel
N. Temple.
      p. cm.
  Includes bibliographical references and index.
  ISBN 978-0-89089-564-1 (alk. paper)
1. Literature--Black authors--History and criticism.   I. Title.

PN841.T46 2007
809'.8896--dc22

                                                            2007021684

CAROLINA ACADEMIC PRESS
700 Kent Street
Durham, North Carolina 27701
Telephone (919) 489-7486
Fax (919) 493-5668
www.cap-press.com

Printed in the United States of America

Dedicated to
Mr. Robert Dent, Jr.
April 8, 1931–September 11, 2005

Contents

+ Chibe Achebe things full apart

Acknowledgments

The Creator orders my steps and places special individuals along my path at perfect moments in time to help bring forth a special harvest. This collection of African writings is a tribute to the many—in the past, present, and future—whose lives, words, deeds, visions, and gifts have bloomed in my favor.

I offer my sincere gratitude to Nana Amanyi I, Abawkumahene, of Agona Swedru & Adonten Division of Agona Nyakrom Traditional Area, Ghana, also known humbly as Dr. Willie B. Lamousé-Smith, whose rich knowledge of the human spirit and potential encouraged me to pursue this project. A wise mentor, friend, and special guardian, Dr. Lamousé-Smith has helped me balance my academic journey.

I thank the Department of Africana Studies at the University of Maryland, Baltimore County (UMBC), for being a wonderful center of support, where the leadership maintains a healthy environment enabling the natural balance between sowing and reaping. Dr. Thomas N. Robinson, Jr., is a department chair from heaven: he leads with kindness and understanding in his efforts to reward hard work. I am also grateful for the administrative prowess of Mrs. Wanda S. Nottingham, who joined our department in the middle of this project and provided tremendous support for all my research. I also thank Dr. Jonathan Peters for introducing me to many African world writers, some of whom are represented in this collection.

I thank Dr. Miriam DeCosta-Willis for building my literary foundation in my early academic years and for offering unlimited feedback, support, and encouragement ever since. Her groundbreaking work in African literatures of South and Central America led me to include in this volume translations of works in the Spanish and Portuguese languages. I am also grateful beyond words for her help in introducing me to Dr. Ian I. Smart of Howard University and to the pioneering work of the Afro-Hispanic Institute. I thank Dr. Smart and his wife Juanita both for their understanding my difficulty in obtaining permission to reprint one of the works in this collection and for their help in having that most elusive request granted.

I offer a heartfelt thanks to Dr. Molefi K.Asante, his wife Ana Yenenga, the Association of Nubian and Kemetic Culture (ANKH), and the Cheikh Anta Diop Conference for continued professional support and for frequent opportunities to engage in meaningful intellectual dialogue. I also thank Dr. Mark Christian and Dr. James Naazir Conyers for their friendship and their mentoring. I appreciate their visions for the ongoing development of the discipline in both domestic and international contexts and their support for my pioneering literary pursuits. I also thank Dr. Floyd W. Hayes III and the Center for Africana Studies at the Johns Hopkins University for providing me with the opportunity to develop and refine my ideas with some of their best students. I am also grateful to my UMBC students from the spring 2006 section of Black Women: Cross-Cultural Perspectives for their help with a significant early stage of proofreading the manuscript.

Several other organizations deserve special mention. I thank the members of the College Language Association for literary support, grounding, and critique and the National Council for Black Studies for being a home and haven for innovative, groundbreaking ideas in Africana Studies. In addition, I thank the Modern Language Association, the International Comparative Literature Association, and the American Comparative Literature Association for providing ongoing debate about the worth of African world literatures—a debate that has finally given comparative Black literature uncontested space in the academy.

As always, I thank Carolina Academic Press—particularly Bob Conrow, Jennifer Whaley, and my copy editor, Lee Titus Elliott—for being the gem of a publisher that keeps magic happening in the name of Africana Studies.

Finally, I express gratitude to my family and loved ones, who released me from many commitments and familial duties during the final year of this project.

Christel N. Temple
July 26, 2006
Columbia, Maryland

Introduction

At the 1995 annual meeting of the National Council for Black Studies (NCBS), there was a debate on the floor about the direction a Black Studies curriculum should take in order to reflect an African-centered point of view. When a member suggested comparative literature as an appropriate discipline for an African-centered study of Black literatures, the suggestion was rejected. A representative from the panel explained that the discipline of comparative literature is defined from a Eurocentric framework that does not permit Black literatures to be examined in contexts most meaningful to Black cultural readers or to readers seeking an African-centered literary experience. While *Literary Spaces: Introduction to Comparative Black Literature* is not a retort to this definition, it is an attempt to offer a unique framework for a broad comparative study of Black literatures.

The African world has produced an immense body of literature, which reflects the many literatures and ideas of numerous regions where people of African descent have engaged with diverse environments and created culturally significant communities. Such communities reflect cultural and social derivations of Black experience, as well as adaptations based on interactions with stimuli beyond their African origins. *Pan-Africanism*, the broad idea of unity, commonality, and cooperation among people who are physically, culturally, consciously, geographically, psychologically, or politically of African descent, is the foundation of this text. The critical areas of inquiry introduced here, as well as the literatures grouped into the categories implied in the definition of *Pan-Africanism* above, offer readers and students opportunities to explore the similarities and differences among the agents of global African experience.

This volume has several objectives: (1) to be reader-friendly; (2) to offer a simple, common-sense approach to the art of comparison; (3) to introduce the history of comparative Black literature; (4) to present a broad description of the African world through literature; (5) to demonstrate the breadth and vitality of African world literatures, which can support a separate, unique program of comparative study; and (6) to show that students today have a greater opportunity to learn the literatures of Africa and the Diaspora than earlier celebrated writers (such as Ralph Ellison, Toni Morrison, and Charles Johnson), who were weaned largely on the richness of white European and American classics and literary traditions. Certainly there is no fault or error that earlier Black writers studied the white European and American literary classics. Any study of literature, regardless of the literature's cultural origin, is vital for broadening a reader's vision of the world.

However, in the discipline of Black Studies (also known as African-American Studies, Africana Studies, Afro-American Studies, Diaspora Studies, Pan-African Studies, and Transatlantic Studies), a discipline founded in 1968 to provide undergraduate and graduate students with immersion programs concerning topics relevant to the Black experience, there is enough literature from Africa and the Diaspora to comprise an entire course of study. The African American Studies department at the University of Maryland, Baltimore County (UMBC) proved this sufficiency when it offered a track of study in Comparative Black Literature in its master's degree program in African American Studies from 1989 to 1995. UMBC offered a pioneer immersion program in literature of the African world in a comparative context, and the program did not require students to take courses in white American or European literature. The program offered the following courses: Comparative Black Fiction, Comparative Black Drama, Comparative Black Poetry, Black Literary Theory, Black Folklore, Black Intellectual Thought, Search for African Identity, and Topics in Comparative Black Literature (for example, Black Cinema). The program thus demonstrated that Comparative Black Literature is a sustainable area of study for a graduate program. The UMBC model is a prototype for this volume.

Quincy Troupe and Rainier Schulte's edited collection, *Giant Talk: An Anthology of Third World Writings*, is also a prototype for *Literary Spaces*.[1] Troupe and Schulte place their text's selected works into six sections: "Oppression and Protest," "Violence," "A Crisis in Identity," "Music, Language, Rhythm," "The Humorous Distance," "Ritual Magic," and "The Conceptual Journey." *Literary Spaces* models itself after several ideological foundations of *Giant Talk*, even though *Giant Talk* examines not only the literatures of Africa and the Diaspora but also the literatures of the Third World. Their introductory comments about the nature of the Black writer are noteworthy:

> [I]t should be understood that the Third World writer, like any other writer, cannot create out of a vacuum. His starting point is not the celebration and elaboration of an already existing tradition or cul-

---

1. Quincy Troupe and Rainer Schulte, eds., introduction to *Giant Talk: An Anthology of Third World Writings* (New York: Random House, 1975).

ture, but the construction of a new culture as an antibody to a culture that he rejects. His position turns out to be extremely complicated, since he does not know what the exact forms of his orientation might be or should be. He only knows that he is in absolute confrontation with a culture that tried to form him but failed to do so. The cultural values that he inherited have lost their original supportive power and have left him in chaos. He must assimilate old forms and create new ones at the same time: that is his danger and his challenge as a moral, intellectual and artistic innovator.[2]

In describing the dynamics of the International Conference of Negro Writers and Artists held in Paris in 1956 and in Rome in 1959, Troupe and Schulte offer support for a distinct "Black" comparative literary endeavor:

> Richard Wright emphasized that black writers and artists were not "allowed to blend, in a natural and healthy manner, with the culture and civilization of the West." They felt that the black experience, their common bond, had its own validity and to explore that experience fully required them to separate themselves from the ideas and traditions of the Western world. One basic and historical situation, racial separatism, forced them all to start from a similar point: a clash with Western civilization.[3]

Troupe and Schulte also suggest that "Third World writers searched fastidiously for ways to distinguish their work from the dominant Western culture, and develop the beauty and strength of their culture"[4] because there was a fear at the Second International Conference "of succumbing to the sterility of the Western civilization which has been for the last few centuries basically European."[5] By the twenty-first century, with significant communities of Black writers in Europe and the Americas, the definition of *Western* and *European* literature has shifted slightly to include a representation of literature by people of African descent; yet the Black literatures appear largely on the margins of the literary canon.

Although this volume includes a section "Influence, Adaptation, and Structure," which highlights Black writing specifically modeled after previously published works (including those in European literature), writers of Black litera-

---

2. Ibid., xxx.
3. Ibid., xxv.
4. Ibid., xxvi.
5. Ibid., xxvii.

ture, unlike white European and American writers, are not constrained by a long and often burdensome tradition. Indeed, according to an analogy by Troupe and Schulte, "[w]hile the German writer may be haunted by Goethe, and the Englishman by Shakespeare, these [Third World] writers felt no such restraint, and admitted of no such measuring stick. It is exactly this freshness and vitality that now attracts the Western world to the literary productions of the Third World. The tables have been turned."[6]

Inevitably, Alioune Diop's passion as displayed at the First International Congress of Black Writers and Artists in 1956 is a challenge posed in this volume. For, during the Congress, he encouraged African scholars to "declare and assess together the wealth, the crisis and the promise of our culture ... revealing and offering to the admiration of the world varied and undoubted talents which have hitherto only been kept under a bushel by the concerted silence of the colonial powers and racism."[7]

With all of these precursors in mind, this volume offers a history of comparative Black literature, evaluates the role of Black literatures in comparative literature programs, and presents the debates, from 1969 to the present, about the placement of African-derived literatures in the universal literary canon.

---

6. Ibid., xxvii.

7. Alioune Diop, "Opening Address," *Yearbook of Comparative and General Literature* 43 (1995): 13–14. (Originally published in *Présence Africaine* 8, 9, 10 (November 1956): 10–18.)

Special Note

For artistic purposes, the author has chosen to use the many regional variations in spelling, sentence structure, punctuation, and word usage that are not considered "standard" English as it is written in the United States. In having done so, the author encourages the readers of this collection to accept such variety—and, more important, to celebrate it.

Permissions

The author gratefully acknowledges rights and permissions to use the following works:

Literary Spaces

Chapter 1

The History of Comparative Black Literature

Comparative Black literature is a new academic field that classifies and compares the ancient, traditional, modern, and contemporary literatures produced by people of African descent—both on the continent of Africa and in regions of the Diaspora. It provides conceptual approaches for critically and comparatively examining these literatures. It also acknowledges a common cultural heritage, respects and celebrates regional and cultural diversity, and portrays the ongoing struggles for agency by global populations that claim the continent of Africa as a source of identity and culture.

The 1960s is considered the decade in which the field of comparative Black literature began to emerge in colleges and universities in America. For, during that decade, Black students and faculty, as well as the Black community, advocated for a more inclusive curriculum that documented the Black experience. As a result, colleges and universities established courses in Black literature and eventually incorporated Black Studies programs as part of their curricula.

Even as early as the 1920s, scholars and writers who had been engaged in international Black literary exchange taught courses, introduced international Black literatures, participated in international Black literature conferences, and encouraged translation—efforts that comparatively documented global Black experience. One of those earlier writers was Langston Hughes, one of the most celebrated and well-known Black writers in the United States—and he was often classified as just an "American Black writer." His poems, short stories, plays, and autobiographies are frequently taught in elementary school, middle school, and high school courses, as well as in college undergraduate- and graduate-level courses. However, frequently overlooked is that Hughes's entire literary development was grounded in internationalism. His autobiographies, particularly *The Big Sea* (1940), often speak of his awareness of Black artistic sensibility on a global scale. His exchanges with French-speaking African and Caribbean writers in France and with Spanish-speaking writers in Cuba are not adequately offered by scholars as contexts for Hughes's literary classification.

His peers are Jacques Roumain (Haiti), Nicolás Guillén (Cuba), Léopold Sénghor (Senegal), and Aimé Césaire (Martinique). Thus, Langston Hughes and his international influences are a primary reason why comparative Black literature is an important area of inquiry in Black Studies programs.

The literary movement with which Hughes is associated, The Harlem Renaissance, better referred to as the "New Negro Movement" (based on Alain Locke's 1925 *The New Negro*, an edited collection of new Black writing), is studied in isolation. What would complete the study of the Harlem Renaissance, or the New Negro Movement, would be a study of the *Négritude* movement of the 1930s and 1940s—a companion movement among Black French-speaking writers and intellectuals who sought a "return to blackness" in order to counter the emptiness of the French culture that was being forced upon them as colonial subjects. Négritude's precursor was the *Indegenisme* (indigenous) movement that spread largely from Haiti, as scholars such as Jean Price-Mars began to explore and articulate the value of Black folk culture in the Caribbean. In the United States, anthropologist and writer Zora Neale Hurston was studying indigenous Black folklore on her own, and Spanish-speaking writers such as Cuban Nicolás Guillén, who acknowledged the African blood that flowed through their veins, were engaged in an *Indigenismo* movement in South and Central America as well as in the Caribbean. These few examples hardly scratch the surface in illuminating the commonalities and interrelatedness of Black peer literary activity across regions and languages.

The Négritude movement reveals a fascinating moment in the history of comparative Black literature through one of its overlooked ideological founders, Jane Nardal of Martinique. Nardal's early Pan-Africanist essay, "Black Internationalism" (1928), and her early comparative essay, "Exotic Puppets" (1928), reinforce the fact that comparative Black literature is not necessarily a phenomenon that emerged solely from the Black experience in the United States; instead, comparative Black literature is a balanced area of inquiry that does not prioritize any one region's creativity over another. Jane Nardal coined the expression *internationalisme noire* (Black internationalism) in 1928 and thus made the connection between the Black French literary endeavor and the Black literary endeavor in the United States. She writes: "Along this barely trodden path, American blacks have been the pioneers, I believe. To convince oneself of this, it suffices to read *The New Negro* by Alain Locke, which is slated to appear in French translation by Payot."[1]

---

1. Jane Nardal, "Black Internationalism," in *Negritude Women*, ed. T. Denean Sharpley-Whiting, 106 (Minneapolis: University of Minneapolis Press, 2002). (Originally published as "Internationalisme noir," *La Dépêche africaine* [February 15, 1928]: 5.)

In the essay, "Exotic Puppets," her early model of comparative Black literature, "Nardal takes on exoticism in French letters, crosses the Atlantic for a
comparative discussion of Harriet Beecher Stowe's *Uncle Tom's Cabin* and the
modernist reconfiguration in Carl Van Vechten's best seller *Nigger Heaven*, and
concludes with an acerbic critique of *indigénophile* French writer Paul
Morand's *Magie noire*."[2] Nardal is comparative and international in her analysis, and although "Exotic Puppets" does not compare authentic Black creative
productions, it is a credible model for comparative Black literature. She examines how white French and white American writers depict Black stereotypes
in their fiction. Her eclectic framework is based on ideas in Alain Locke's *The
New Negro*. Furthermore, she "prophesies the coming-into-being of Fran-
cophone New Negroes," whom she describes as Afro-Latin.[3] She made this
prophecy in the 1920s, which establishes an even earlier origin of comparative
Black literature.

The Scholarly Debate on
Comparative Black Literature

The scholarly debate on the parameters of comparative Black literature
formally emerged in the late 1960s. Although this text evaluates Black literary
history to introduce examples of comparative Black Literature, the debates are
central to understanding why the category is perceived as complex. Janheinz
Jahn's *Neo-African Literature: A History of Black Writing* appeared among the
earliest attempts at an exhaustive survey that critically addressed global Black
literature.[4] He writes:

> Africa's written literature originated in the "overlap" area of three cul-
> tures, the African, the Islamic-Arabic and the Western. The literature
> from the area where the African and Islamic cultures overlap, I shall
> call Afro-Arab; the literature from the area where the African and
> Western cultures overlap, I shall call neo-African.

---

2. T. Denean Sharpley-Whiting, ed., *Negritude Women* (Minneapolis: University of
Minneapolis Press, 2002). ("Exotic Puppets" appears on pp. 108–13 in *Negritude Women*
and was originally published as "Pantins exotiques," *La Dépêche africaine* [October 15,
1928]: 2.)

3. Ibid., 43.

4. Janheinz Jahn, *Neo-African Literature: A History of Black Writing*, trans. Oliver
Coburn and Ursula Lehrburger (New York: Grove Press, 1969).

Neo-African literature, then, is the heir of two traditions: traditional African literature and Western literature. A work which shows no European influences, including not being written down, belongs to traditional African literature, not neo-African. The boundary between the two is easy to draw: it is the boundary between oral and written literature. Conversely, a work which reveals no African stylistic features or patterns of expression belongs to Western, not neo-African literature, even if written by an African. Although theoretically simple, the distinction is hard to make in practice, for it assumes that the styles, patterns of expression and attitudes produced by Africa's traditions are well known. But they are not—for scholars have neglected this field."[5]

Jahn makes a pioneering attempt to categorize African literatures, but the distinctions he makes in his effort are not routinely embraced by Black writers and critics who prefer a more flexible, Pan-African agency in determining which people and works are considered "African." His volume was an exciting effort for the late 1960s because it provided in-depth descriptions of "The African Scene" and "The American Scene" and compared the two in great detail. Within "The American Scene"—or, more simply, *America*—a term often applied only to the United States, Jahn's work properly included Haiti, Brazil, and Cuba.

In his 1969 essay "African Literature and Comparative Literature," Charles R. Larson contends that the "study of African literature in American universities (and in most other universities throughout the world, including Africa itself) is of fairly recent development.... Indeed, so recent is this field of study that the term 'African literature' is in no way fully understood or agreed upon."[6] Part of the complexity in 1969, Larson continues, was "the lack of recognition of African literature as 'literature' by certain language departments at a number of institutions."[7] Indeed, Larson observes that African literature was "studied as something other than literature" and that anthropology and area studies departments utilized African literature for the purpose of evaluating "foreign cultures through their literatures."[8] Larson further acknowledges that a "more logical solution to the problem of where such courses belong may be found if African literature is studied as comparative literature."[9]

---

5. Ibid., 22.

6. Charles R. Larson, "African Literature and Comparative Literature," *Yearbook of Comparative and General Literature* 18 (1969): 70.

7. Ibid.

8. Ibid.

9. Ibid.

Larson relies on two accepted definitions of *comparative literature* to make his point. The first, offered by René Wellek in *Theory of Literature*, defines comparative literature as "the study of relationships between two or more literatures."[10] The other, offered by Henry H. H. Remark in an essay "Comparative Literature, Its Definition and Function," defines it as "the study of literature beyond the confines of one particular country, and the study of relationships between literature on the one hand and other areas of knowledge and belief, such as the arts, … philosophy, history, the social sciences, … the sciences, religion, etc. on the other."[11] In addressing the problem that African literature is written in "dozens of the several hundred languages and dialects spoken on the continent" as well as in colonial languages such as English, French, and Portuguese, Larson defines comparative literature more simply "as the study of the relationships between the literature of two or more ethnic groups."[12]

Larson's essay is convincing because he introduces the variables of linguistics, ethnic identity, literature-department territorialism, and competing definitions of literature that have, collectively, made the study of comparative Black literature appear complex. However, Larson does not examine comparative black literature as a global phenomenon, even though his approach can be considered international. For, as he reminds us, Africa is a continent with many nations, and African literature is affected by European colonial influences, depending on which European nation was the agent of imperialism in a particular African region.

Larson's failure to offer a global comparison is evident in several instances. While Larson does highlight the merit of viewing the effect of "voyages and trips certain writers have made and the influence of other writers" on African writers, he does not carry his analysis toward a final Pan-African conclusion.[13] First, he cites Négritude as "almost too perfect an example of one literature growing directly out of another culture [French] and its literature."[14] Larson's contention is problematic because in exclusively crediting French "negative influences" for spawning the Négritude movement, Larson never mentions Négritude's direct and positive affiliation with the Black American literary experience—according to Alain Locke's *The New Negro*, as well as through Black American jazz culture in France and other connections, as articulated by Jane

---

10. Ibid.
11. Ibid., 74.
12. Ibid., 71.
13. Ibid., 72.
14. Ibid.

Nardal, one of the ideological founders of Négritude. Nevertheless, Larson does refer to the influence of Black American writers on the South African writer, Peter Abrahams, who credits the influences of W. E. B. Du Bois, Langston Hughes, and Countée Cullen.[15]

While offering a good number of convincing observations, Larson makes a number of assumptions that appear to discredit Black literatures. Because of his lack of Pan-African sensibility, he fails to recognize that African writers in other regions—particularly the United States and the Caribbean—were in accelerated literary phases at the time he was making his observations. Since the literature of these two regions emanated from Africa, the discipline of literary criticism is necessarily cyclical, acknowledging Africa both as a core influence on literatures of the Diaspora and as a region of modern literary production.

By advocating a coherent and historical method of studying comparative Black literature, this text, in part, addresses the isolationist approach to Black literary studies found in Larson's early essay. Larson acknowledges the methodological foundations of critiquing comparative literature when he mentions the value of critiquing authors' voyages and trips, the role of "influence studies" on African writers, and the role of the themes and migrations of the oral tradition. But by 1969, when Larson's essay was published, a good number of African writers had already published excellent work. The Black American literary tradition was already broadly established. Indeed, as Daryl Cumber Dance indicates in *Fifty Caribbean Writers: A Bio-Biographical Critical Sourcebook*, "The period from 1950 to 1965 was one of such extensive and outstanding publication by West Indian writers that Edward Braithwaite has labeled it as the West Indian Renaissance."[16] The key points in Larson's essay evaluate the African novel as follows: "rarely is a character developed to any significance"; the "African novel in English has tended to be anthropological"; "rarely" is description "used to create atmosphere or mood"; and "there are very few "love" stories."[17] Thus, while this reductionist evaluation of African literature has elements of truth (at least for African literature in English, not in French, as Larson differentiates), Larson misleads the reader by presenting his evaluation in isolation, disconnected from the literary creation of the broader African world.

Another 1969 essay, "Comparative Literature," by Anthony Thorlby, offers an impression of the extent to which African-derived literatures are consid-

---

15. Ibid., 73.

16. Daryl Cumber Dance, ed., *Fifty West Indian Writers: A Bio-Biographical Critical Sourcebook* (New York: Greenwood Press, 1986), 2–3.

17. Larson, "African Literature and Comparative Literature," 74.

ered in the discipline of comparative literature. Thorlby does not mention any African literatures, but his claim of comparative literature's uniqueness and future leaves room for a dynamic interpretation of the processes involved in creating an academic program of comparative Black literature. Thorlby begins his essay by confirming that in 1969 there is broad disagreement about the definition and application of comparative literature. He then makes the favorable observation that comparative literature is "not attached to any national concept."[18] (His observation, by the way, can be seen as an important focus for comparative Black literature.) He goes on to say that unlike English, French, or German literatures, which are usually taught as national units, comparative literature "ranges across national frontiers."[19] Thorlby thus describes comparative literature as necessarily "international in its scope and purpose," a description which is appropriate for the study of African global literature whose context is transnational and attentive to diverse geographies through the notion of Diaspora.[20]

In his analysis of comparative literature, Thorlby suggests that the formal study of comparative Black literature is a wealthy literary exercise—particularly when he claims that, in the study of national literatures, "the field of research tends to appear exhausted" and that "it seems increasingly difficult to find anything that has not already been mastered."[21] Essentially, he argues in favor of invigorating the study of literature for students who may be bored or overexposed to more narrow approaches to literature.

Black global literatures have been frequently neglected and overlooked in academic curricula that prioritize national literatures (American, British, French), yet Black literatures continue to be rediscovered for deeper analysis and greater public exposure. In the past, many Black literary works were mined from an unfair social obscurity. For example, the works of the early twentieth-century Black American writer Zora Neale Hurston were rediscovered through the literary search-and-rescue missions of scholar-writers such as Alice Walker. Nevertheless, Thorlby could never claim that the study of Black global literature has come close to being exhausted or mastered, because there are too many unknown, underpublished, undermarketed, and underdistributed Black texts from around the world. *Literary Spaces* joins the efforts of noted anthologies such as *Giant Talk* that aim to make global Black litera-

---

18. Anthony Thorlby, "Comparative Literature," *Yearbook of Comparative and General Literature* 18 (1969): 75–81.
19. Ibid., 75.
20. Ibid.
21. Ibid., 75–76.

ture available and critically understood in a historical context that revitalizes the meaning of the relationship among the literatures of people of African descent. Collectively, Black writers from around the world have reacted to, responded to, and created from a geographically unique yet connected set of stimuli and circumstances associated with cultural heritage, race, politics, identity, and resistance to oppression.

According to Thorlby, another challenge to comparative literature is the belief that comparison yields "artificial surveys, where the interest of what is established is minimal."[22] However, in comparative Black literature, particularly concerning its involvement in heritage study (i.e., the realization that the literatures of Africa and its Diaspora are related because of a mutual heritage and identical systems of oppression), surveys of Black literatures are *not* artificial. Instead, they are Pan-African and informative, in a revisionist way, of the total global Black experience, and they are reflective of a historical context that relates the culture of Africa to its transnational communities throughout the world.

Thorlby's essay is useful because it establishes the fluidity of comparative literature—a flexibility that permits it to be unrestricted and capable of being tailored to modern international literary conditions. Thorlby is also an early voice that surveys the role of cultural values in the comparative literary exercise. In fact, he notes a common opposition which complains that a cultural approach to literature "distorts or neglects the truly literary qualities of a work."[23] His essay's final words are pertinent here:

> [T]his approach merely offers the possibility of making potentially (though not necessarily) illuminating comparisons with works produced in what are held to be comparable social conditions elsewhere. It thereby satisfies a fundamental desire of the comparatists: which is to discover a basis of comparison between writers working in different countries and sometimes also in different epochs.[24]

Thorlby's analysis of comparative literature does not differ structurally from that articulated in *Literary Spaces*. However, *Literary Spaces* insists that the African world has enough material and diversity to comprise an independent, exhaustive course of study in which African heritage (or even Pan-Africanism) is an initial point of reference. Thorlby notes that the structure and definition of comparative literature lead to "the cultural displacement of the European

---

22. Ibid., 76.
23. Ibid., 76–77.
24. Ibid., 77.

nations from their imagined position at the center of civilization."[25] It is ironic that, although Thorlby does not refer to Black literatures in his essay, his analysis is pluralistic and nonhegemonic—and therefore similar to Afrocentric theory.

The critical strength of Thorlby's analysis is his argument that comparative literature can reveal "deeper organic relationships and kinships"; "broaden the basis of ... experience, as an adventure"; "bring out qualities [in the literature] which might not otherwise be seen"; and "provide an opportunity for a creative openness to ideas."[26] Without referring to Black literary works, Thorlby's analysis is nevertheless a balanced one. It also anticipates new dimensions in what, in 1969, was narrowly considered comparative literature.

In 1974, Bernth Lindfors was among the earliest critics to speak freely about how the discipline of comparative literature has undermined the study of Black literatures. He writes:

> Comparative literature ... would seem the perfect refuge ... whose humanistic interests extend beyond the boundaries of a single culture. But when it becomes institutionalized, when degree programs are set up, when the discipline must prove its academic integrity by going through the ritual of formally disciplining its initiates, then it often loses its fabled elasticity and chokes off its own best liberal impulses. Like a dying dinosaur, it suddenly constricts, curls up into a relatively small ball, and petrifies. It is usually in this decadent phase of its development that arbitrary restrictions are placed on literary curiosity by designating certain areas of the world virtually off limits to scholarly inquiry. Students are discouraged from wandering too far away from the Eurocentric core of the curriculum.[27]

Lindfors is concerned with "emerging" and "neglected" literatures, and thus he confirms that in 1974 Black literatures were far from being considered mainstream. Lindfors playfully introduces three types of literary genres that might be rejected by comparative literature programs: Eskimo and Maori love songs, Chinese revolutionary theatre, and African literary criticism. But his primary focus is the academy's disregard for Black literatures.[28] He even hy-

---

25. Ibid.

26. Ibid., 79–80.

27. Bernth Lindfors, "Emerging and Neglected Literatures: Their Place in the Traditional Spectrum of Comparative Literature," *Report, Council on National Literatures* 1 (1974): 4.

28. Ibid.

pothesizes a response to a student's request to study a Black topic: " 'If you are really intent on writing a history of African literary criticism, you had better do your degree in Linguistics or Ethnic Studies.' "[29] Even now, over thirty years after the publication of Lindfors's essay, comparative literature departments still do not permit students to earn degrees based on an immersion study in global Black literatures. So where now is the curriculum that trains scholars to be experts in the complete literature of Africa and the Diaspora? *Literary Spaces* encourages the reinstatement of and the creation of programs that can guarantee such thorough literary exposure.

In his essay, Lindfors then laments: "The result is that Comparative Literature, ideally the most open-minded discipline in any university, frequently stifles creative cross-cultural research by inhibiting the outward growth of its students."[30] Furthermore, Lindfors emphatically alleges that comparative literature departments have made a fortress out of the Western literary tradition. Specifically, he asserts: "[C]omparative literature studies in North American and European universities are dangerously ethnocentric, incestuously inbred, and notoriously inhospitable to scholars seriously interested in studying 'exotic' non-Western literatures."[31] In 2005 there were approximately fifty-six universities in the United States with graduate programs in comparative literature and approximately thirty-six universities with such programs outside the United States—including fourteen in Sweden, four in Canada, and four in China.

Lindfors does not have statistical data to support his allegations. But he advocates for a study of degree programs in the United States, Europe, and Canada that would provide data revealing the percentage of non-Western courses that are either "required" or offered as electives in comparative literature programs.[32] A sampling of curricula from several major United States universities nearly corroborates Lindfors's allegations. The University of Georgia has one of the largest comparative literature programs in the world, and its program is among the most progressive in the study of Black literatures. It offers courses in three African languages—Swahili, Yoruba, and Zulu; a study-abroad program in Tanzania; and two courses on Survey of African Literature (I and II, respectively). The university offers approximately forty-two courses in comparative literature, yet only two are described as "African." And while several broad topical courses likely include the study of Black sources (e.g.

---

29. Ibid.
30. Ibid.
31. Ibid.
32. Ibid.

"The Novel"; "Literature and Cinema"; "Language, Gender and Culture"; "Seminar in Special Topics"; and "Readings in Comparative Literature") the words, or descriptions, *African American, Caribbean,* or even *Brazilian* do not appear in the titles of the courses.

In 2005, the comparative literature program at Pennsylvania State University offered thirty-nine courses. Four of them focus on Black literary topics, while six others, offered as "special topics" courses, may be used to survey Black literature. Impressively, Penn State's program offers foreign-study possibilities in Senegal, Niger, Cameroon, and Mali, although the literary focus for each possibility is unclear. The comparative literature program proudly claims over eight decades of comparative literary study, beginning in 1920, and it advertises an accurate and comprehensive definition of modern comparative literary study. According to the program at Penn State, *comparative literature* is "the discipline of studying literature transnationally, sometimes postnationally—across political boundaries, time periods, languages, genres, and across the lines of demarcation between literature and other cultural productions."[33] Modern comparative literature programs seem to fulfill at least a level of Lindfors's hope that they are "liberalizing language requirements so that Arabic may be substituted for German, Tagolog for French, and Swahili for Spanish, if these or other non-European languages happen to be more relevant to a student's major research interests than any of the standard European tongues."[34] Earlier, Thorlby insisted that comparative literature programs offer flexibility; however, Lindfors challenges programs whose degree requirements are so heavily located in Eurocentric contexts that "the student with legitimate interests in what the department might regard as 'fringe areas' is penalized."[35] Indeed, Lindfors's analysis identifies the need for and function of a graduate-degree track in comparative Black literature in which students have the opportunity for immersion studies in Black global literatures.

A final point of Lindfors's argument is that comparative literature departments seem to be training graduate students for faculty positions which seek to maintain the centrality of the Western literary tradition and that, therefore, the cycle of training and teaching systematically excludes immersion studies in Black literatures. His conclusion is worth quoting at length:

---

33. Pennsylvania State University, Department of Comparative Literature, "Welcome to Penn State's Department of Comparative Literature," http://complit.la.psu.edu/ (accessed June 6, 2005).

34. Lindfors, "Emerging and Neglected Literatures," 4.

35. Ibid., 5.

I am speaking, I admit, from the perspective of an outcast, one whose primary occupations lie outside the mainstream of Western literature and therefore do not coincide with the traditional concerns of Comparative Literature departments. Mine may be a jaundiced view, but I see no way that my students could be properly accommodated in any but the most pliable of comparative literature programs. This I regard as a great pity, for African literatures are almost custom-made for comparative study, and it would be a great advantage for anyone working in them to have some training as a comparativist. Yet I would be most reluctant to advise someone thinking of specializing in African literatures to do his degree in Comparative Literature, for I suspect he would be forced to spend far too much of his time in orthodox Western literary studies and thus would not be able to develop his competence in other equally important fields such as folklore, anthropology, and African history.[36]

Lindfors's solution is to "favor an open-ended curriculum and degree program almost devoid of specific requirements. Until it manages to evolve a structure flexible enough to serve the specialized needs of all sorts of oddballs, Comparative Literature will remain a relatively parochial discipline."[37] *Literary Spaces* poses independent immersion studies of the literature of Africa and the Diaspora as "comparative Black literature."

Lloyd Brown's essay "The Black Aesthetic and Comparative Criticism" (1974) is reproduced in the same literary bulletin as the Lindfors essay, and Brown is among the early critical voices that directly address the relationship between Black cultural theory and possibilities of comparative methodology. The primary feature of Brown's essay is his argument about whether or not the Black aesthetic is significant enough to justify distinctive criteria for analysis. This topic is beyond our immediate focus of charting a history of comparative Black literature and its debates. However, along with his primary argument, Brown's analysis of the study of comparative literature is insightful. He first analyzes the "ethno-cultural debates" of the Black aesthetic and the Black Arts Movement in order to present a three-fold analysis of "the implications of the Black aesthetic and the discipline of comparative criticism in culture and literature."[38] The process of comparative literature study involves

---

36. Ibid.
37. Ibid.
38. Lloyd Brown, "The Black Aesthetic and Comparative Criticism," *Report, Council on National Literatures* 1 (1974): 6.

the interplay between textual content and critical theories and methodologies. In his inquiry, Brown addresses both Black literary content and the function of criticism.

Brown's first objective is to argue that "the ethno-cultural thesis ... invites a comparative study of Black American culture, not only in relation to White America, but also with reference to the Black American's African antecedents."[39] Brown's argument is a seminal reference to Pan-Africanism as published among the mainstream debates on comparative literature. Brown also claims that the Black American worldview which insists on a relationship with Africa "allegedly opposes, and is irreconcilable with, the Euro-American's cultural modes."[40]

Brown's second objective (an argument quoted below) will be mentioned again in the section of this volume that introduces the rationale behind the categories used to group the anthologized works. Brown writes:

> Secondly, in dealing with claims on behalf of some unique Pan-African viewpoint, we need to establish whether or not distinctive cultural milieu—assuming that they do exist—have resulted in significantly different concepts of perceiving, producing, and using art, as we move from one culture to another. In other words, even if we are to grant the Black aesthetician's claims about historical differences between White, Western cultures, on the one hand, and African cultures, on the other, does it follow that differences between aesthetic criteria as such are always synonymous with ethno-cultural differences?[41]

Literary Spaces approaches comparative Black literature from several perspectives: (1) a presentational perspective, since students and general readers need exposure to a broad sample of Black global literary production surveyed as a collective based on a common heritage and experiential factors; (2) a critical-comparative perspective, whereby students and general readers are encouraged to evaluate the similarities and differences between the literatures; and (3) a perspective of categorization that offers insight into the extraliterary functions of global Black literatures. The volume can present only a limited survey of literary criticism since it prioritizes exposure to and awareness of global Black creative production. Thus, *Literary Spaces* mainly guides students and readers toward becoming familiar with the global Black literary tra-

---

39. Ibid.
40. Ibid.
41. Ibid.

dition in the context of its historical emergence and its resilient growth amidst ethno-cultural and curricular negligence. Nevertheless, it can also serve as a foundation upon which students may apply the skills of more complex literary criticism that they may either simultaneously study using another text or learn in future courses of study. This reiteration of the main objective of *Literary Spaces* is a disclaimer that permits a reading of Brown's essay which temporarily suspends his focus on literary criticism in favor of his contribution to the emerging definition of comparative Black literature.

Brown's third objective in his essay is to "raise crucial questions about the very nature of comparative methodology"—an inquiry which is his most important contribution to the development of comparative Black literature. His analyses are much more useful for a later section in *Literary Spaces* that explains the process of categorization. However, his broad objective to give agency to the comparative study of global Black literatures is profound. In his conclusion, Brown writes freely of the terms and conditions needed for Black literary freedom:

> [T]he Westerner has too frequently obscured and oversimplified black literature by ignoring the rich textures of cultural themes, and thematically defined structures, in favor of bland generalizations about the "human condition everywhere"—or in favor of so-called universals that are defined by Jungian and other European archetypes.[42]

Several essays published in the late 1970s paved the way for more grounded perceptions of the meaning of comparative literature in a Black global context. Students of Black literature are strongly advised to start with Christof Wegelin's "Black International Fiction" (1977) because, in spite of some of its oversights, it was an early essay that surveyed Black literature in a global context.[43] Wegelin offers a detailed introduction to readers unfamiliar with Black fiction, and he credits the Black Studies movement for the increased publication of Black literature. However, Wegelin's definition of *Black international fiction* is too narrow: it includes only the fiction written by Black American expatriates in Europe. This fiction is characterized by its treatment of interracial relationships (usually Black men and European women), by a belief that European countries offer greater racial freedom, by an ensuing revelation that Europe does indeed acknowledge the color line, and by diverse treatment of

---

42. Ibid.,8.

43. Christof Wegelin, "Black International Fiction," in *Proceedings of the 6th Congress of the International Comparative Literature Association*, ed. Michel Cadot, et al. (Stuttgart: Bieber, 1977), 351.

Black identity issues. Wegelin refers to Nella Larsen's *Quicksand* and James Weldon Johnson's *The Autobiography of an Ex-Colored Man*, both of which are excerpted in *Literary Spaces*. Finally, while Wegelin hints at the African heritage of the Black American expatriates writing in Europe, he actually refutes it in two ways. First, he suggests that these Black international fiction writers "seem to cast their lot with the West," which is a bizarre observation when one considers his survey of the fiction of so many Black American expatriate writers whose works critique meaningful racial dilemmas.[44] Second, he concludes his essay by launching an unfair attack on Pan-Africanism. He quotes Richard Wright's initial (and insecure) claim that he did not immediately feel a bolt of kinship with Africans upon his early encounters with them. If Wegelin had investigated further, he would have discovered that Wright's anti-Pan-African sentiments were vehemently protested by writers from Africa and the Caribbean at the First International Congress of Black Writers and Artists in 1956. Furthermore, in the quotation which Wegelin cites, Wright essentially asserts a *desire* for African kinship and a *disappointment* that it did not come as easily as he had expected.[45]

Inevitably, the ongoing debates about the role of Black literature in the comparative literary endeavor are concerned with evaluating and presenting a formal *literary tradition*—as defined by Arthur Wormhaudt, a scholar in Arabic literature:

> A literary tradition consists of a number of books written at various times in the past. These books display a certain continuity of thought insofar as they restate the themes from earlier books on the one hand and add original material on the other hand. Thus the old material which is carried forward ensures that the length of the tradition is not curtailed. The new material brings a fresh impetus to the effort to keep the tradition alive.
>
> If the continuity of the tradition is maintained and if the public which maintains it is sufficiently large, one can say that the tradition has a number of practical values. One of these is that readers who are familiar with the tradition have a way of carrying some of their own

---

44. Ibid., 354.

45. Ibid. [Wegelin quotes Wright: "According to some popular notions of 'race' there ought to be something of 'me' down there in Africa. Some vestige, some heritage, some vague but definite ancestral reality that would serve as a key to unlock the hearts and feelings of the African whom I'd meet ... but I could not feel anything *African* about myself, and I wonder, 'What does African mean?'"]

thoughts as far back into the past as the tradition goes. Another is that the accumulated force of the tradition serves as a guarantee that these same thoughts of the reader will be carried into the future. It is of course possible for traditions to die. But it is much less likely that a tradition that extends back for thousands of years and is the work of vast numbers of human minds will die than it is likely that the work of any single mind will manage to survive.[46]

If one compares the requirements and process of establishing a literary tradition with the frequent treatment of African-derived literatures as distinct and isolated literary genres without a common literary tradition, the need for a formally defined discipline of comparative Black literature becomes obvious. *Literary Spaces* borrows from Wormhaudt's definition of a literary tradition as it charts the relationship among global Black literatures.

In 1978, Darwin T. Turner wrote an essay, "Introductory Remarks About the Black Literary Tradition in the United States of America," in order to substantiate the existence of an African American literary tradition. Yet his essay also concerns the traditions of global Black literature—particularly in his quest to answer the question, "At what point did the Africans who were brought to America become redefined as *African Americans*?"[47] When Turner writes of "discontinuities in publication history" of African American writers, he is broadly referring to the legacy of imbalance between the development of literary traditions of the free Western world—namely, Europe and America—and the development of literary traditions of the enslaved Africans of the Western Hemisphere, who, for centuries, were denied equal access to literacy and education by either law or by racist social custom. Turner demonstrates a continuous Black literary tradition by referring to Phillis Wheatley, the first Black American woman to publish a book (poetry), as "a teen-aged Senegalese."[48] Wheatley was sold into enslavement in Boston, and her book was "the first by an African living in the American colonies."[49]

The most appealing aspect of Turner's essay is that he challenges the loosely defined Western literary tradition in order to highlight the hypocrisy of the West in denying the existence of an African American literary tradition that is

---

46. Arthur Wormhaudt, "A Place for Arabic Literature in a Tradition of World Literature," *Iowa English Bulletin* 21 (1971): 10.

47. Darwin T. Turner, "Introductory Remarks About the Black Literary Tradition in the United States of America," *Proceedings of the Comparative Literature Symposium* 9 (1978): 71–86.

48. Ibid., 71.

49. Ibid.

inextricably linked to a global Black literary tradition. Many Eurocentric scholars claim that only European literatures (for example, those of the ancient Greeks and Romans, as well as those of modern France, Germany, England, etc.) contribute to a continuous Western literary tradition. However, such scholars generally exclude from the Western canon literature of African origin and influence—beginning with the literature of the Egyptians and the Kushites. Consequently, Black literature is either routinely excluded from anthologies documenting the Western tradition or only scantily represented in such anthologies.

Turner is also aware of the "trap" of comparing Black literatures with white literatures in a way that diminishes the quality of Black literatures and "inevitably distract[s] attention from the continuity of a Black American tradition."[50] In the late 1970s, Turner knew of such instances of "the white critic's contempt for the originality and creativity of Blacks."[51] Another "trap" that weakened the Black literary tradition was racism in publishing, whereby publishers were more attentive to the tastes and preferences of the white public than they were to their commitment to Black writers.

Articulating the global Black literary tradition is a prerequisite to cementing the subdiscipline of comparative Black literature into the curriculum. One of the objectives of *Literary Spaces* is to permit Black writers around the world to have access to literatures most relevant to their heritage and culture and to have the opportunity to be nurtured on them. This objective has been interrupted for Black culture. Turner writes:

> [I]t is difficult to verify the presence or absence of a continuous tradition when proof depends upon "vanity" books. On one hand, because most privately printed books have limited distribution, one may wonder about the actual influence of such books on subsequent writers. For example, Fenton Johnson, at the beginning of the twentieth century, Frank Davis in the 1930's, and Don L. Lee in the 1960's are within the same poetic tradition. But did Davis and Lee know the work of the earlier writers, or did Davis and Lee presume they were original? … Literature unknown to scholars who depend upon the Library of Congress may be familiar to Black authors who have secured privately printed books through Black churches and bookstores, or who have heard the stories from Black teachers or other narrators in the Black American community. Consider, then, the problem of

---

50. Ibid., 76.
51. Ibid.

the literary historian who wishes to argue for a continuing tradition in Black poetry. Many readers today know the poetry of Langston Hughes, who began his career in the 1920's, and Don L. Lee, of the 1960's. Fewer have read the work of the previously mentioned Johnson or Sterling Brown in the Thirties. If one knows only the work of Hughes and Lee, one may surmise erroneously either that Lee is different from other Black American writers or that he was preceded only by Langston Hughes. If, however, Brown, Davis, and others are revealed, suddenly, one sees a fifty-year line of Black American poets who, in the Black idiom, rhythm, and style, wrote proudly, bitterly, and satirically about the masses of Black American people—the so called "common" folk.[52]

Here Turner refers only to the African American poetry tradition, but its implications reverberate throughout the global African literary tradition since bitter and satirical poems, as well as Black idioms, rhythms, and styles, appear worldwide. Turner also assesses imperatives for gender analysis and the exploration of literary periods in which Black writers "were following corresponding routes."[53] The cross-fertilization of the New Negro Movement and the Négritude movement is an early example of these "corresponding routes." But comparative studies of global Black literatures have generated and will highlight dynamic new comparisons.

Albert S. Gérard, in his brief essay "New Frontier for Comparative Literature: Africa" (1979), reminds scholars of the complexities of the study of African literature based on each region's linguistic and ethnic diversity and delivers a formal challenge to literary scholars to develop dynamic new approaches to measure literary kinship and differentiation among African literatures.[54] He lists the objectives of literary comparison in a Black global context but fails to mention Black literature in the United States—a clear oversight:

> [W]hat used to be exceptional in the world that vanished in the middle of our century [the twentieth]—the national, yet polyethnic and multilingual state—has become the rule in the new world, where Africa is bound to play an increasing role. It is not the purpose of this paper to draw upon the exhaustive inventory of the various contributions which comparatists can and should bring to our under-

---

52. Ibid., 78–79.
53. Ibid., 85.
54. Albert Gérard, "New Frontier for Comparative Literature: Africa," *English in Africa* 6, no. 2 (1979): 33–38.

standing of African literature. Such a list would include intra-African relationships between literature in the various European languages that have been put to creative use throughout the continent; the influence of the Western literary tradition, of which African writing is unquestionably an important outgrowth; and the relationships, whether factual or merely analogical, between African literatures, their evolution and their orientations, and the other literatures of the so-called Third World, that is, of the Arab world, of Asia, of the West Indies and of Latin America.[55]

In such a brief essay, Gérard provides an in-depth history of Nigerian literatures, from which he draws many examples to demonstrate methods of criticism in a multilingual state.

The last two important essays from the 1970s can be introduced together. George M. Lang's "African Inspiration and New World Nationalism" (1979)[56] and Melvin Dixon's "Toward a World Black Literature and Community" (1979)[57] are companion pieces—except for one vital distinguishing feature. Lang's essay resists a vision for comparative Black literature, while Dixon's essay, in a nearly manifesto style, embraces such a vision. Both essays describe *comparative Black literature* but without using the term; thus, it is feasible that 1979 marks the beginning of comparative Black literature identified as a *concept*.

Although Lang acquaints readers with an in-depth survey of variations of Négritude (e.g., African American Négritude and Brazilian Négritude) and with "African inspirations" of the literature of Brazil, Cuba, the Caribbean, and the United States, he does not acknowledge the basic reason why members of the African world invariably embrace notions of kinship. The obvious reason is heritage—or common African descent—which is primary enough to justify a vision for comparative Black literature. But Lang merely claims that Pan-Africanism is an "abstract ideology"—"palpable, influential, with concrete ramifications upon the societies themselves."[58]

---

55. Ibid., 34.

56. George M. Lang, "African Inspiration and New World Nationalism," in *Proceedings of the 7th Congress of the International Comparative Literature Association, I*, ed. Milan V. Dimic, et al. (Stuttgart: Bieber, 1979), 319–22.

57. Melvin Dixon, "Toward a World Black Literature and Community," in *Chain of Saints: A Gathering of Afro-American Literature, Art, and Scholarship* (Urbana, IL: University of Illinois, 1979), 175–94.

58. Lang, "African Inspiration and New World Nationalism," 322.

In contrast, Dixon's essay is unwavering in its unapologetic, uncompromising, and wholehearted embrace of the relatedness of global African-derived literatures. Dixon declares:

> Writers of the African Diaspora continually explore the idea of racial community for theme, imagery, and heroic characterization. Their works, brought to international attention through the French and English languages, define man in relation to his particular ethnic, regional and national identity and examine the universal conflict between individual and society.... [M]odern black writers have identified the broad frontiers of human need and racial progress. Their themes assess the role of the artist within society and the contribution of black peoples to world culture. This thematic concern rejects provincial colonial mentality, and expands the goals and dimensions of black life. The quest for community ... offers a point of cultural contact and *comparison* [emphasis added] in the literature and contemporary issues which shaped world black writing during the past fifty years.[59]

Through this statement about the global Black literary tradition, Dixon can reasonably be regarded as a father of modern comparative Black literature.

Dixon is a revisionist voice in the study of global Black literatures: he credits the year 1921, in which Martiniquan/French Guianan René Maran's novel *Batouala* was published, as a milestone in global Black literary history because *Batouala* "legitimized black literary expression on an international scale." He goes on to write: "The wide circulation of the book meant that a larger audience had access to Maran's work and that of other black writers in the future. It could also provide an arena for shared literary expression. *Batouala* initiated dialogue across cultural and linguistic lines."[60] Comparative Black literature is indeed the study of literatures across cultural and linguistic lines.

Dixon's mention of Jane Nardal gives his essay an authenticity based on his clearly articulated awareness of lesser-known global Black literary histories.[61] His essay is also the first work to claim that comparative Black literature originated as early as the 1920s. Dixon provides a brief summary that can be considered among the earliest historical contextualizations of what *Literary Spaces* formally terms *comparative Black literature*:

---

59. Dixon, "Toward a World Black Literature and Community," 175–76.
60. Ibid., 177.
61. Ibid.,176.

By 1935 black writers on all three continents were claiming their legitimate defense against cultural exclusion and isolation. They expressed the shared assumptions of racial progress which made ethnic and regional groups cohesive. They changed the course of modern literature by demanding that the African voice be heard. In the span of twenty-five years, 1920–1945, a *world black literature was fashioned that cemented the identity of the New Negro and an international community as his audience.*[62] (emphasis added)

To cement his analysis, he credits the "world black community" for "the moral value it sustains for the freedom of the individual *and* his race."[63]

Aside from a handful of critical and informative essays, the 1980s represented a relatively dry spell of critical examination of what had emerged as comparative Black literature. Perhaps this was a period of application rather than debate, whereby scholars and literary departments tested the possibilities of integrating Black texts into the curriculum through introduction, study, and appreciation of global African literatures. The decade was also a period of rich regional literary creation from and critical study of Africa and its Diaspora, so that the scholarship of the next decade, the 1990s, yielded criticism that measured and assessed the growth of comparative Black literature.

The first notable essay from 1980 is Willfried F. Feuser's "The Emergence of Comparative Literature in Nigeria," which proposed using comparative study for Nigerian "self-definition" and recounted how Nigerian universities and scholars were beginning to internationalize the study of global Black literature as an outgrowth of comparative literature studies.[64] Feuser begins his essay with an insightful description of the goals of comparison: "The comparative study of literature is based on the assumption that national literatures are not islands unto themselves and that border violations between the various national domains are not only inevitable but also beneficial, beneficial in the sense of a greater intellectual and aesthetic openness and an enhanced possibility of mutual understanding."[65]

Feuser introduces Nigerian literature as both universal, with respect to the commonalities between the "thought and imagery" of its oral and folkloric traditions, and as Pan-African, especially when he writes: "Nigerian literature

---

62. Ibid.
63. Ibid., 176–77.
64. Willfried F. Feuser, "The Emergence of Comparative Literature in Nigeria," *Research in African Literatures* 11 (1980): 100–07.
65. Ibid., 100.

in whatever form of linguistic expression relates to the literatures of other African countries and to those of other continents."[66] His essay is archival because he documents pioneering strides made in 1967–68 by the University of Ibadan, Nigeria, in teaching courses such as "A Comparative Study of Afro-American and West African Authors Writing in English and French" as well as in establishing an "innovative M.A. program" that "focuses on Africa and its cultural extensions in the New World."[67]

Among the earliest literature reviews that evaluate how African literatures have been regarded in a comparative context is E. C. Nwezeh's "The Comparative Approach to Modern African Literature" (1980). In his review, Nwezeh remarks on African critics' excitement about the prospect of new developments in the comparative study of modern African literatures, and he cites Charles Larson's 1969 essay as a "notable" beginning of the dialogue among non-African critics.[68] Nwezeh also criticizes the shortcomings of the standard approaches to the comparative study of African literatures, which are narrowly concerned with examining the oral beginnings of African literatures and with overemphasizing European influences on African literatures. He complains of critics like Larson who disregard the fact that "[a]ny work of African literature, like any other creative writing, is essentially a new world of the imagination transcending its constituent elements in form and meaning."[69] He also reminds readers that "[m]yths, folktales, fairy tales … are the prototypes of all narrative, the ancestors and models of later fictional developments" and that therefore the novel can no longer be claimed as an exclusively European cultural product.[70] He elaborates: "If Africa is not excluded from the realm of fictional universals which gave rise to the novel, the novel form as a genre might not be as strange to Africa as some critics would want us to believe."[71] Nwezeh's conclusion is a virtual call for a formalized study of comparative Black literature:

> Finally, an objective comparative approach to modern African literature in the above direction, which is quite distinct from the obso-

---

66. Ibid., 104.

67. Ibid., 104–105.

68. E. C. Nwezeh, "The Comparative Approach to Modern African Literature," in *Proceedings of the 8th Congress of the International Comparative Literature Association, II*, ed. Béla Köpeczi and György M. Vadja, (Stuttgart: Bieber, 1980), 321–28.

69. Ibid, 327.

70. Robert Scholes, *Structuralism in Literature* (New Haven: Yale University Press, 1974), 60–61, quoted in Newzeh, "The Comparative Approach to Modern African Literature," 325.

71. Nwezeh, "The Comparative Approach to Modern African Literature," 325.

lete, mechanical and/or chauvinistic tracing of sources and influences, is quite welcome because, among other things, "we need to know how our works stand in relation to other contemporary works throughout the world; we need to compare our works with those by past societies."[72]

Literary Spaces extends Nwezeh's conclusion with a call to compare works of the global African world not only with those of the past and the present but also with those of the future.

Isidore Okpewho makes a dynamic argument in "Comparatism and Separatism in African Literature" (1981) which does not promote comparative Black literature but highlights a prime example of its effectiveness in the name of "analogy studies" that "set out to explore, among other things, the physical, political, psychological and other contexts or backgrounds to cultural behavior across societies"[73] In introducing a comparison between Nigerian Wole Soyinka and African American LeRoi Jones (Amiri Baraka), Okpewho asks: "Why, for instance, would two artists across societies widely separated from one another in space and sometimes time and who have had no appreciable contact with each other produce similar works?"[74] He describes Chikwenye Ogunyemi's analysis of Soyinka's *The Strong Breed* and Jones's *Dutchman*:

> [T]wo black writers, with seemingly dissimilar social backgrounds and upbringing, were able, at the time they were concurrently thirty years of age (in 1964), to produce two similar works. In her discussion of the two plays Ogunyemi presses the biographical similarities of Soyinka and Jones toward an interpretation of their respective messages: at a time when these playwrights deemed it necessary to abandon the smug indifferences of their youth and become fully involved in the political ferment of the 1960s, they sought an outlet in protagonists who, as (archetypal) scapegoats, must needs pass through a painful political awareness; having each been married first to a white woman and then to a black, these chastened playwrights have put their protagonists through equally chastening experiences with women so as to convey "the necessity for complementarity between

---

72. Ibid., 328, quoting Taban lo Liyong, *The Last Word* (Nairobi: East African Publishing House, 1969), 36.

73. Isodore Okpewho, "Comparatism and Separatism in African Literature," in *Twayne Companion to Contemporary World Literature: From the Editors of World Literature Today, I,* ed. Pamela A. Genova (New York: Twayne, 2003), 300.

74. Ibid., 300.

black men and women"; and as angry young black men, Soyinka and Jones have each adopted a stridently iconoclastic tone designed to unsettle the play audience as thoroughly as it does the insensitive political establishment, for the common good of society.[75]

Okpewho is satisfied that Ogunyemi's choice to compare Black writers is informed by the two writers' similarities as well as their differences—both writers having been socialized in "two distinct societies."[76] Ogunyemi's analysis is an application of comparative Black literature, as she writes: "The African heritage speaks for itself; it permits them to take a foreign myth or a foreign idea and combine it with what is essentially African to create a new type of art."[77] Okpewho later offers a stronger, more concise statement on the usefulness of comparing Black texts with one another. He differentiates his proposal from the European literary tradition on the basis of the lack of hegemony in his argument. He writes:

> I am of course willing to admit that, in arguing a cross-cultural poetics on the basis of the African evidence, I have proposed an Afrocentric view of human cultural behavior and am therefore no less guilty of cultural chauvinism than most earlier European scholars were. But I can at least claim that I have not dissipated my energies in arguing the superiority of one group of people over the other; my inquiry has stayed safely at the level of esthetics.[78]

Thus, Okpewho is another remarkable voice in the history of comparative Black literature. He makes a case for the value of African literature when he writes: "Africa is defined by a unique set of values expressed in a language and oral tradition which is earthly, simple, unpretentious, and African writers have no business sporting with foreign sensibility when there is more than enough in the native traditions to use."[79] Okpewho's claim suggests that the vast amount of global African literature still unexamined should not be explored merely on the periphery of literary studies. Okpewho warns against "separatist poetics," which compartmentalize literary studies into sealed boxes that do not permit comparison to engage "the world as one large cultural or cognitive fam-

---

75. Ibid.

76. Ibid.

77. Chikwenye O. Ogunyemi, "Iconoclasts Both: Wole Soyinka and LeRoi Jones," *African Literature Today*, 9 (1978): 25–38, quoted in Okpewho, "Comparatism and Separatism in African Literature," 300.

78. Okpewho, "Comparatism and Separatism in African Literature," 301.

79. Ibid., 302.

ily."[80] Thus, comparative Black literature, through scholars such as Okpewho, advocates an explicit engagement in Black literature as a means of documenting the genre's vastness in an age that has never allowed global Black literature to occupy the center.

Donald Burness's candid essay, "Comparative Literature, African Literature and Critical Pitfalls" (1982), reads like a summary of the debates and scholarship from 1968 to 1980.[81] Burness frankly states the limitations of the discipline of comparative studies, and his claim that "Langston Hughes, whose international influence exceeds even that of Mr. [T. S.] Eliot, is less frequently the subject of study" has the power to shame Eurocentric scholars into giving Black writers proper credit for their internationalism and creativity.[82] Burness's objective is to formally proclaim: "It is time that the study of literature go not only beyond national boundaries, but beyond the Euro-centered world."[83]

Like Nwezeh, who critiques Charles Larson's 1969 essay, Burness critiques Willfried Feuser's 1980 essay, thus demonstrating that comparative Black literature has been formally documented for over a decade of scholarly debate and exploration. If scholars can still not comprehend what comparative Black literature involves, Burness offers liberal examples by mentioning Black literatures from the United States, Brazil, Jamaica, Nigeria, South Africa, Angola, Kenya, Cape Verde, Mozambique, the islands of Sao Tomé and Principe, Gambia, and Ghana. He also offers an extended description of the possibilities of comparative topical analysis. He suggests the following relationships that should "merit the attention of serious scholars":[84]

> [F]or instance, it would be valuable to compare Virginia Woolf's London with another London depicted in Wole Soyinka's "Telephone Conversations" or the Jamaican novelist Sam Selvon's *The Lonely Londoners*. There is a need to study the influence of Oriental poetic form and essence in the work of J. P. Clark of Nigeria, Dennis Brutus of South Africa and Arlindo Barbeitos of Angola. It would be worthwhile to examine more fully the influence of contemporary Afro-American protest poetry on black South African verse, since such

---

80. Ibid., 305.
81. Donald Burness, "Comparative Literature, African Literature and Critical Pitfalls," in *Franklin Pierce Studies in Literature*, ed. James F. Maybury and Marjorie Zerbel (Rindge, NH: Franklin Pierce College, 1982).
82. Ibid., 23.
83. Ibid.
84. Ibid., 24.

writers as Oswald Mtshali and Willi Kgotsitsile studied in the United States.[85]

Burness's expert knowledge of global African literatures would, in comparison, embarrass mainstream scholars of comparative literature who claim to conduct universally representative studies. Burness spends the remainder of his essay warning of the "star mentality" approach to the study of global African literatures, whereby only a handful of well-known writers are repeatedly selected for teaching and analysis, and of the "linguistic ignorance" of practitioners who ignore the necessity of learning African and lesser-taught world languages in order to open critical doors in the exploration of Black literatures.[86]

The decade spanning approximately 1985 through 1995 did not yield a large amount of criticism related to comparative Black literature. Albert S. Gérard's 1979 essay, "New Frontier for Comparative Literature, Africa," appears, with minor changes, as the first chapter of *Comparative Literature and African Literatures* (1993),[87] C. F. Swanepoel's edited collection of essays that assesses the state of literary production in all regions of Africa. Chapter 2 of the volume, Gérard's essay "Sub-Saharan Africa's Literary History in a Nutshell," should be required reading for students of African literatures because he provides a rarely available history of the oral and written literatures of Africa. His evenhanded, insightful essay demonstrates that the shift from oral to written expression in Africa was both a natural phenomenon and a shift similar to that which occurred among the early European civilizations as they were influenced by the Latin language transmitted throughout the Roman Empire. Gérard's essay also makes an important contribution to African literary history by showing the influence of colonialism on African writing—but without praising the colonial powers.

C. F. Swanepoel's 1993 edited collection was followed by Bernth Lindfors's collection, *Comparative Approaches to African Literatures* (1994), a volume comprised of his own previously published journal essays. The cover art for Lindfors's collection is alarming because it displays a white silhouette of Sherlock Holmes (with a pipe in his mouth) situated in the middle of the continent of Africa. The image suggests that Lindfors will merely explore the extent to which African writers have imitated the European literary canon. Fortunately,

---

85. Ibid.

86. Ibid., 25.

87. C. F. Swanepoel, ed., *Comparative Literature and African Literatures.* (Pretoria: Via Afrika, 1993).

the image is misleading, for only in a few essays does Lindfors examine the influences of Holmes, Shakespeare, and Brecht on African writers.

The volume does not contribute to defining comparative Black literature, but it is a prototype of the critical studies of African literatures that grew in publication and availability beginning in the 1980s. As a prototype, the collection offers sectional surveys of categories of African literary production: there are sections on the nation of Nigeria as well as on the regions of South Africa and East Africa. A survey of the literature of only a single African country and of the literature of only two (out of at least five) African regions is an imbalanced one. Two final sections—"Image Studies" and "Reputation Studies"—reveal the text's peripheral engagement with a broader study of comparative Black literature. In the section "Image Studies," Lindfors's essay "The Image of the African American in African Literature" (reprinted from a 1975 issue of *Literary Criterion*) provides readers with a rare treat—an assessment of African perceptions of African Americans. Black literatures were clearly getting much attention in the 1990s, but the value of comparing the literatures of Africa with those of its Diaspora was not broadly promoted. Studies written since Lindfors's original 1975 essay, such as *Literary Pan-Africanism: History, Contexts, and Criticism* (2005), address this deficiency by providing a more informed Pan-African and historical context of the relationship between African and African Americans as projected in African literatures. Nonetheless, Lindfors's assessment invites inquiry and challenge:

> The African American evidently exists on the faint outer margins of African experience, far removed from the central concerns of the creative imagination. On those rare occasions when he is summoned to make a brief appearance he usually stands as a symbol of Western decadence and degeneration, a curiously incomplete human being who has lost the hearty generosity of spirit manifested by black Africans. He may be seen as alienated or ill at ease in Africa or corrupted by materialism and his own bitter frustrations in America. But wherever he is found, he is to some degree abnormal, uncomfortable, maladjusted, confused—indeed, a different species of black man altogether. Only in the poetry of the most mystical negritudinists and the most militant black power advocates is he hailed as a racial brother. Most African writers do not regard him as kith and kin.[88]

---

88. Bernth Lindfors, "The Image of the African American in African Literature," in *Comparative Approaches to African Literatures* (Atlanta: Rodopi, 1994), 95.

Since Lindfors's essay appears in a 1994 collection, it gives the impression that his assessment is a current observation. Indeed, a reader would not realize that Lindfors's observation of stifled Pan-Africanism is almost twenty years old. Nonetheless, Lindfors's collection, which deliberately focuses on comparisons "internal to the continent of Africa," is still an attempt to broaden the discipline of comparative literature. Lindfors explains:

> Purists may desire to exclude such studies from the "literary department store" called Comparative Literature, but they may narrow their own discipline by doing so. Perhaps the field needs to be reconceived as a giant shopping mall, where a wide array of local goods can be compared as fruitfully with one another as with goods of distant manufacture. What may matter most to the selective comparative shopper is the interesting design or construction of analogous items, not the relationship discerned between the familiar and the strange, between the domestic and the foreign. Meaningful juxtapositions can begin at home, wherever that "home" might happen to be. In this book most of the comparisons are internal to the continent of Africa.[89]

Lindfors becomes close to identifying the value of comparing "home" literatures, even though he does not define *home* from a global African perspective—i.e., a worldview in which African heritage is the common denominator of people of African descent who write literature from significant cultural communities outside Africa. Comparative Black literature emerges to answer many of Lindfors's questions about heritage, similarity, difference, cultural aesthetics, and Pan-Africanism when, in his conclusion, he asks: "What is the significance of these contrasting images in African literatures?"[90]

In the section "Reputation Studies," Lindfors presents an essay on Nigerian Wole Soyinka's receipt of the 1986 Nobel Prize in Literature. The essay comments on the international scope of Black literature by exploring the meaning of the Nobel Prize in literature when it is awarded to Black writers. Lindfors's analysis revisits the underlying disparity in the discipline of comparative literature whereby Black literatures are neither as highly regarded nor as privileged as European literatures. Lindfors quotes Chinweizu at length since Chinweizu advocates that African culture have an autonomy which protects it from being viewed and treated as Europe's stepchild. According to Chinweizu, the prob-

---

89. Bernth Lindfors, introduction to *Comparative Approaches to African Literatures* (Atlanta: Rodopi, 1994), xii.

90. Lindfors, "The Image of the African American in African Literature," 102.

lem with the Nobel Prize is "namely, its role as a bewitching instrument for Euro-imperialist intellectual hegemony, and the conceit that a gaggle of Swedes, all by themselves, should pronounce on intellectual excellence for the diverse cultures of the whole wide world."[91] Lindfors highlights another important Chinweizu observation, which appeared in an unpublished paper in 1986:

> Africa does not need the cultural disorientation and subservience which western prizes promote. By its origins and operations, even the most globally prestigious of these prizes, the Nobel Prize, is a local European prize, and should go back to being just that. If it wishes to become the international prize it gives the impression of being, it should stop lending itself to hegemonic uses. Its terms of reference, its selection procedures, and its award committees should then all be internationalized[....] It is, of course, most unlikely that the West would agree to a genuine internationalisation of the Nobel Prize. That would end their control of it, and end their ability to use it for hegemonic purposes[....] It is up to the rest of the world, in a bid to stimulate a long-overdue New International Cultural Order, to publicly withdraw allegiance from the Nobel Prize, and so reduce it to its proper minitude as a local European prize.[92]

Lindfors describes Chinweizu's opinions as "the most coherent articulation of a Pan-Africanist argument that makes literature subservient to a concrete political and cultural goal—in this case, the complete intellectual liberation of Africa." Lindfors's inclusion of this argument in his collection, *Comparative Approaches to African Literatures*, is a significant ideological contribution to what has emerged as comparative Black literature.[93]

That Wole Soyinka was the first African to be awarded the Nobel Prize in Literature inevitably led to the global acknowledgment of excellence in Black writing. For after Soyinka was awarded the prize in 1986, it was awarded to St. Lucian/Trinidadian Derek Walcott in 1992 and to Black American Toni

---

91. Chinweizu, "That Nobel Prize Brouhaha," *Guardian* 3 (November 1985): 5, quoted in Lindfors, "Beating the White Man at His Own Game: Nigerian Reactions to the 1986 Nobel Prize for Literature,"143.

92. Chinweizu, "Literature and Nation Building in Africa" (paper, Second African Writers' Conference, Stockholm, April 11–17, 1986), 19–20, quoted in Lindfors, "Beating the White Man at His Own Game: Nigerian Reactions to the 1986 Nobel Prize for Literature," 147.

93. Lindfors, "The Image of the African American in African Literature," 147.

Morrison in 1993. Naguib Mahfouz of Egypt received the prize in 1988; the white South African Nadine Gordimer received the award in 1991; and Trinidadian V. S. Naipaul earned the award in 2001. The works of the latter three laureates may appear in the canon of comparative Black literature because the laureates represent Arab, white, and East Indian cultures in countries that are part of Africa and its Diaspora.

The 1990s was a period of upheaval for comparative literature as texts such as *Comparative Literature in an Age of Multiculturalism* (1995) offered a final global challenge to the hegemony of Eurocentric comparative literary design.[94] In an essay from a different text, published in 2003, Linda Hutcheon writes: "As an internationalist discipline, comparative literature could not remain untouched by the pluralistic demands for canon revision and the ethical considerations vis-à-vis minoritized groups that were part of the contested academic and intellectual climate of the 1980s."[95] The 1995 text is comprised of three state-of-the-literary-world reports from the American Comparative Literature Association (most notably, the 1993 Bernheimer Report entitled "Comparative Literature at the Turn of the Century"); three responses to the Bernheimer Report presented at the 1993 annual meeting of the Modern Language Association (MLA); and thirteen position papers on related topics. The MLA is comprised of over 10,000 members from around the world, and its attention to the 1993 Bernheimer report initiated one of the largest public debates of the decade on the discipline of comparative literature.

Following suit, the *Yearbook of Comparative and General Literature* made literary history in 1995 with a volume dedicated to the study of African literatures. The editor, Gilbert D. Chaitin, writes in his Editorial Preface:

> For the first time in its history, this volume of the *Yearbook* is devoted to African literatures. Whether we have thereby escaped from the confines of Eurocentrism is a vexed question, whose intricacies and political implications Professor Eileen Julien explores in her introduction to this number, "African Literatures in Comparative Perspective." In any case, however, we have at least shifted the focus of discussion

---

94. Charles Bernheimer, ed., *Comparative Literature in an Age of Multiculturalism* (Baltimore: Johns Hopkins University Press, 1995).

95. Linda Hutcheon, "Productive Comparative *Angst*: Comparative Literature in the Age of Multiculturalism," in *Twayne Companion to Contemporary World Literature: From the Editors of World Literature Today, I,* ed. Pamela A. Genova (New York: Twayne, 2003), 44.

from the literatures and cultures of Europe, the Americas, the Maghreb and Asia, to those of sub-Saharan Africa."[96]

According to Chaitin, the volume's contents "represent our desire to recognize the extraordinary proliferation of African literatures and African studies in the contemporary world"; however, the approach to comparative Black literature embodied in *Literary Spaces* does not concur with the liberal differentiations of African writing suggested by Chaitin's use of the word *sub-Saharan*.[97]

This volume of the *Yearbook* is a significant part of the history of comparative Black literature because it reprints key documents on Black culture from the First International Congress of Black Writers and Artists (held in 1956), thus contextualizing them as a formal part of the history of comparative Black literature. The two documents reprinted in the journal's section "Documents in the History of Comparative Literature" first appeared in the early Pan-African world journal, *Présence Africaine*, which emerged from the Négritude movement in December 1947. The reprinted essays revive the spirit of Pan-Africanism and African culture from 1956 to 1995. In "Modern Culture and Destiny," the editors of *Présence Africaine* speak of the history of Black culture and writing. This historical document of comparative Black literature conveys "two primordial tasks:"[98]

> 1. [T]o bring before the world audience the expression of our original cultures, so far as they interpret the present life of our people and our personality;
> 2. to reflect back to our own peoples the image of their aspirations, their experiences and their joys, illuminated by the experiences, joys, and hopes of the world.

> In short, to make our culture into a force of liberation and solidarity, and at the same time the hymn of our innermost personality.[99]

These words—from the founders of the 1956 Congress—express an ideology compatible with that of comparative Black literature. Their implications for comparative Black literature as a cultural endeavor are powerful because literature is a meaningful cultural product.

---

96. Gilbert D. Chaitin, editorial preface to *Yearbook of Comparative and General Literature* 45 (1995).

97. Ibid.

98. "Modern Culture and Destiny," *Yearbook of Comparative and General Literature* 45 (1995): 7.

99. Ibid.

The second reprint in the "Documents" section is Senegalese Alioune Diop's "Opening Address" from the 1956 Congress. The address is still powerful in 1995, nearly four decades after the Congress, because it reiterates the connections within the African world that justify placing comparative Black literature into a separate category and because it defines the African world as having a meaningful Diaspora. Conceptually, *Yearbook* makes a dynamic contribution even though it does not offer literary analysis beyond the domain of continental Africa. Nonetheless, Diop's powerful proclamation of Pan-Africanism gains a new audience when he writes:

> It remains, however, true that there is nothing imaginary about our sufferings. For centuries the dominant event in our history was the slave trade. That is the first link between us Congress members which justifies our meeting here. [Blacks] from the United States, the Antilles and the continent of Africa, whatever may be the distance which sometimes separates our spiritual universes, we have this incontestably in common, that we are descended from the same ancestors. The colour of our skin is a mere accident but it is none the less responsible for the events and actions, the institutions and the ethical laws which have, in indelible fashion, marked our relations with the white man.[100]

Diop explores the issues of visibility and dissemination that challenge African culture and intellectual productivity when he writes: "It is most certain that if there are any races who, as races, have so far failed to reach an international audience, they are the [Black] race."[101] The editors of the *Yearbook* reprinted Diop's observations to demonstrate, by contrast, the recent reversal of African literary invisibility on the world scene—an invisibility which had been maintained by racism and by the Western world's social predisposition to measure Black creative integrity on the basis of its commensurability to whiteness.[102] Comparative Black literature continues to permit the exhaustive study, the categorization, and the rediscovery of Black literature—all of which are a way to counter, as Diop observed in 1956, "the loss of vitality which has for some generations affected [Black] culture, not to mention all of the spir-

---

100. Alioune Diop, "Opening Address," *Yearbook of Comparative and General Literature* 45 (1995): 8.

101. Ibid., 9.

102. Natalie Melas, "Versions of Incommensurability," *World Literature Today* 69, no. 2 (1995): 275–80.

itual and social screens which prevent the acts, intentions and cultural works of our peoples from being freely communicated to the world."[103]

In the introduction to this seminal volume of the *Yearbook*, Eileen Julien first reviews the increasing global awareness of African literature after several African writers were awarded the Nobel Prize. She then verifies the global nature of African literature:

> [T]he power of the African writer may be said to be truly visible on the world stage at the end of the twentieth century.... And, of course, African literature has, for better or worse, a truly global identity: Euro-language texts are published by and large in Paris, London or New York, are read by large publics outside national and continental boundaries, and are, for a host of reasons, inaccessible to most Africans. Many writers write under censorship or in exile—all these factors suggest the complexity of the literary act in Africa and the limits of ethnic and national identities in literary matters.
>
> The term *African*, of course, also has limits. It obscures the great diversity of cultural and social realities across the continent but seems useful nonetheless in that it acknowledges the comparable histories, representations and policies that have left their mark on the array of peoples and cultures of this vast continent....[104]

Julien's African-centered introduction also criticizes the flaws of postcolonial theory and the double standard that faults Africans for literary borrowing yet praises Europeans for it. She surveys the condition of African writing and its regard on the world stage, concluding: "New notions of identity, freedom and national consciousness are needed to inspire new theorizations of African literature."[105] *Literary Spaces* begins to answer Julien's call by promoting broader comparative studies and by familiarizing readers with a global sample of Black literature.

The 1995 *Yearbook* issue on comparative literature in an African context offers one more interesting survey. It contains a section "Comparative Literature Around the World," which summarizes the curricula of comparative literature departments at two African universities—Cheikh Anta Diop University in Dakar, Senegal, and the University of Yaoundé in Cameroon.

---

103. Diop, "Opening Address," 11.
104. Eileen Julien, "African Literatures in Comparative Perspective," *Yearbook of Comparative and General Literature* 43 (1995): 15, 18.
105. Ibid., 22.

The latter has an impressive Department of Sub-Saharan Literature that offers a rare program of immersion in global Black literature. The summary, as follows, is a virtual test of one's awareness of comparative Black literature:

> The range of authors studied in the Department of Sub-Saharan African literature continues to grow with each year. First, there are the African writers, strictly speaking. Among these are the Senegalese Léopold Sénghor, Ousmane Sembène, Cheikh Hamidou Kane; Cameroonians Mongo Béti, Ferdinand Oyono, René Philombe, Guillaume Oyono Mbia, Werewere Liking, Calixthe Beyala; Nigerians Chinua Achebe, Wole Soyinka; Ivorian Amadou Kourouma; Congolese Tchicaya U'Tamsi, Henri Lopès, Sony Labou Tansi; and South Africans Peter Abrahams and Alan Paton.
>
> The Diaspora is also amply represented with authors from Martinique, Aimé Césaire, Joseph Zobel, Edouard Glissant, Daniel Maximin and Maryse Condé; Haitians Jacques Roumain, Jacques Stephen Alexis, René Depestre, Gérard Etienne, Jean Metellus and Frank Etienne; as well as African Americans Richard Wright, Langston Hughes, and Chester Himes, to name only those studied more frequently.
>
> Refusing the limits of a name that is far too reductive, the Department of Sub-Saharan African Literatures has embraced writers from the Maghreb, or North Africa. It has introduced the study of writers such as Albert Memmi, Tahar Ben Jelloun, Hédi Bouraoui, and Rachid Boudjedra because, despite the differences in race, North Africa underwent a colonial experience similar in every way to that of [S]ub-saharan Africa; this experience has profoundly marked its literature.
>
> The other distinctive feature of the Department of Sub-Saharan African Literature at the University of Yaoundé, one which contributes to its comparatist dimension, is that African oral literature occupies an important place in teaching and research.[106]

The student who can identify the majority of writers and regions on this list has made great and unusual strides toward a proficiency in comparative Black literature.

In the late 1990s, the treatment of topics related to categorizing and identifying comparative Black literature became scarce. Bernth Lindfors's 1974 essay "Emerging and Neglected Literatures: Their Place in the Traditional

---

106. André Ntonfo, "Comparative Literature at the University of Yaoundé," *Yearbook of Comparative and General Literature* 43 (1995): 134.

Spectrum of Comparative Literature" reappeared in 1998, without alteration, as "African Literatures and the Restrictive Discipline of Comparative Literature," thus indicating that the bleak and hostile situation Lindfors identified in 1974 had not much improved. However, in the same year, Guadeloupan writer Maryse Condé shifted the discussion toward a new variable that begged for an international regard of Black literatures: globalization. Her keynote address from the Twenty-Fourth Annual Meeting of the African Literature Association, "O Brave New World," is a dynamic impulse for comparative Black literatures. She confesses:

> Globalization does not frighten me. For me it means reaching out beyond national and linguistic borders in both actual exchange and transatlantic influence and in the expressive imagination of diasporic black communities. A certain message of globalization was in fact initiated after the Second World War when black America, Africa and the Caribbean came into close contact in Paris.[107]

In spite of what some may criticize as an oversimplification of globalization, in 1998 Condé reminds her listeners and readers that Black literary cross-fertilization has a long historical tradition. Condé also shows her depth as a critic of comparative Black literature when she mentions the vital role of sisters Jane and Paulette Nardal as Pan-African pioneers of the 1920s. In her remarks she inserts a Black womanist reminder: "It is a great pity that the major roles of Jane and Paulette Nardal in the globalization of black culture are unduly forgotten in literary history."[108] Condé's words echo Julien's comment that "[t]he most glaring lacuna is the absence of all reference to African women as citizens and producers of culture. Today the burgeoning literary production of women is transforming the gendered assumptions of these 'first generation' African novelists and poets, writing during the waning days of colonialism and the first years of independence."[109]

When Black writers, such as Condé and Julien, remind their audiences of the history of comparative Black literature and its African-centered and Pan-African contexts, they run the risk of sounding redundant at times. But the West's continued disregard of Black literary history and its two contexts de-

---

107. Maryse Condé, "O Brave New World," in *Multiculturalism and Hybridity in African Literatures*, ed. Hal Wylie and Bernth Lindfors (Trenton, NJ: Africa World Press, 2000). [Annual Selected Papers of the African Literature Association, 1998].

108. Ibid., 30.

109. Julien, "African Literatures in Comparative Perspective,"19.

mands repetition. Condé's remarks make the West's ongoing negligence clear as she finds it necessary to remind her audience of the value of Pan-Africanism. She says: "Back then, black people had no intention of solving individually the problems of their specific countries but looked towards the transnationalization of black culture as a solution."[110] She then asks: "What was Négritude, what was Pan-Africanism if not the forms of globalization, the implied project of a complete identity and an active solidarity among the black peoples?"[111] The strength of Condé's inquiry is that she reminds her listeners and readers that Black literary creation and global exchange have been constant in the history of twentieth and twenty-first century writing. She also clarifies how terms of the past, such as *Pan-Africanism*, are historicized, slightly modified, and embraced in contemporary terms such as *globalization*.

As a progressive thinker and a devil's advocate, Condé takes her analysis to a place unprecedented so far in the ideologies of comparative Black literature. She examines the possibilities of globalization in a world where race is decentered in favor of shifting cultural identities determined more by migrations and the mixing of races. Condé eventually admits: "I don't foresee the end of all conflicts and tensions. I don't believe naively that the world will be one." Yet her refreshing exploration of the possibilities in globalization, hybridization, and multiculturalism scatters new variables into our critical consciousness.[112] Condé's address is a realistic survey of the shifting possibilities of the global Black literary tradition. However, to limit confusion over the highly debated economic use of the term *globalization*, *Literary Spaces* interprets Condé's articulation more as *globalism* than globalization.

In 2000 the Center for African and Asian Literatures of the Arts and Humanities Research Board (AHRB) in London made strides in promoting comparative Black literature when it collaborated with the School of Oriental and African Studies and University College of London (UCL) in a venture to "promote research on literature and culture in a comparative context, with the literatures of Asia and Africa at the centre rather than at the periphery, as is usually the case in Western universities."[113] The first five projects of the initial five-year program are "'Narrating and Imagining a Nation,' 'Translation and Translation Theories East and West,' 'Literature and Performance,' 'Genre Ideologies and Narrative Transformation,' and 'Gender and Literature in Cross-

---

110. Condé, "O Brave New World," 30.
111. Ibid., 31.
112. Ibid., 35.
113. C. Andrew Gerstle, "Introduction: The AHRB Center for Asian and African Literatures," *Bulletin of the School of Oriental and African Studies, 2003* 66, no. 3 (2003): 322.

Cultural Contexts.'"[114] With these projects, the Centre's aim is to "bring the literatures of Asia and Africa into dialogue with those of the West and with each other, and through this engagement to raise questions on the predominant theories of literature and culture that have emerged out of Western literature over the last fifty years."[115]

Interpretations of globalism and globalization also appear in Earl Fitz's assessment of Portuguese-speaking, or Lusophone, Black cultures. Fitz regards Lusophone literature as a twenty-first-century issue of globalization which affects African countries such as Angola, Mozambique, the Cape Verde Islands, and Brazil. Portuguese-language literature has been neglected in comparative literature. Fitz writes: "While English departments may regard globalization as a threat to their long standing hegemony within the Academy, for Luso-Africanists and Luso-Brazilianists it represents an *abertura* of tremendous potential, an opportunity to bring our literature to the attention of the rest of the world."[116] Fitz also relates Lusophone literature to inter-American studies, African Studies, and, by application, Black Studies, which is a broader, politicized global discipline that routinely permits the teaching of Brazilian history, culture, and literature. Fitz's inquiry into the role of Lusophone African literature in African-studies curricula is worth quoting at length:

> Another question that might be taken up by Luso-Africanists has to do with the larger issues of African nationalisms and the concept of national literature in the year 2002. We know that, in the years following the fall of the regime in 1974, a great many Portuguese African writers, from José Luandino Veira to Olga Gonçalves, began to see their work published and become part of an emerging African canon. What contributions do these and other African writers of Portuguese expression make to this debate and to world literature generally? How do their positions compare to those of African writers working in French or English? What are the key similarities and differences? Why do they exist? What, comparatively speaking, is unique about Portuguese Africa and its literary production? What is its future? One could also take a look at the issues of genre and gender as they have so far related to the development of Luso-African literature. Why, for example, does it seem that so many contemporary women are writ-

---

114. Ibid.
115. Ibid.
116. Earl Fitz, "Internationalizing the Literature of the Portuguese-Speaking World," *Hispania* 85, no. 3 (2002): 442.

ing poetry rather than prose? Is it simply a coincidence, or are other factors involved? In seeking answers to these and other, related questions, scholars will begin to move the literature of Portuguese-speaking Africa forward and bring it to the attention of the rest of the world."[117]

Fitz's inquiry is a good model for the processes of comparative inquiry.

His essay also provides an updated twenty-first-century definition of *comparative literature*, which has evolved to routinely include film studies and music. Fitz observes:

> Comparative Literature as a discipline, has tended, in its commitment to the study of literature from an international perspective, to focus on such issues as theme and motif, genre and form, period and movement, literature and other (particularly humanistic) fields such as music, history, or philosophy, on issues of theory, criticism, or literary history, on translation, and more evident in our own time, on cultural studies.[118]

Though his text is not necessarily categorized as comparative literature, author and essayist Caryl Phillips, a British writer from Guyana, offers *A New World Order* (2002) as an alternative source that uniquely produces the cultural engagement objective of comparative literature.[119] Drawn from previously published reviews and writings, his universally reflective volume interprets landmarks of Black writing and culture since the eighteenth century. In its postmodern conversations on African-derived literary and cultural artifacts and legends *A New World Order* speaks from the author's geographical experiences in Britain, the Caribbean, Africa, and the U.S. The volume's authority is based on the author's comfort with pioneering a creative logic about race and colonialism in a single source. Phillips refines a *homing* impulse, whereby the modern Black author's collective narrative prioritizes the intellectual structures of his cultural, and even racial, traditions, while featuring his interpretation of, his relationship to, and his predications for the reciprocal cultural exchanges of the world at-large. The shifts in authority and cultural exposure implied by *A New World Order* are directly related to globalism.

In 2003, to once again exorcise comparative literature of either outdated modes of analysis or narrowly defined parameters, Gayatri Chakravorty Spi-

---

117. Ibid., 445.
118. Ibid., 441.
119. Phillips, Caryl. *A New World Order.* (New York: Vintage, 2002.)

vak published *Death of a Discipline*, where, among other observations, she suggests that "peripheral literature may stage more surprising and unexpected maneuvers toward collectivity," a possibility which anticipates the Pan-African literary orientation in *Literary Spaces*.[120] Spivak's discussions of collectivity and of planetarity—an alternative construction of globalization—relate mostly to the global Black literary experience. She borders on support of Pan-Africanism when she suggests: "[T]he metropolitan comparativist must imagine planetarity, displace the 'primitivism' of the colonizer into the subaltern of the postcolonial, existing now in a cultural formation historically comprised by centuries of delegitimization; through the transforming work of imagining the impossible other as that figured other imagines us."[121] This perspective also has implications for the paradigm of literary Pan-Africanism,[122] since Africans and members of the African Diaspora imagine each other through literature. Spivak offers a more concise explanation when she confesses: "I keep feeling that there are connections to be made that I cannot make, that pluralization may allow the imagining of a necessary yet impossible planetarity in ways that neither my reader nor I know yet."[123]

In response to Spivak's title, at least, Susan Bassnett suggests: "There is, of course, a case to be made for the demise of comparative literature, but … [it is] not so much a death, but a revitalized comparative literature."[124] *Literary Spaces* represents another phase of this revitalization.

---

120. Gayatri Chakravorty Spivak, *Death of a Discipline* (New York: Columbia University Press, 2003), 56.

121. Ibid., 98.

122. Christel N. Temple, *Literary Pan-Africanism: History, Contexts, and Criticism* (Durham, NC: Carolina Academic Press, 2005).

123. Spivak, *Death of a Discipline*, 92.

124. Susan Bassnett, foreword to *Bulletin of the School of Oriental and African Studies* 66, no. 3 (2003): 321.

Chapter 2

Comparative Analysis and Writing

In basic comparative writing, scholars are permitted to "cut their teeth" on analyses that explore theme. Once scholars have learned comparative thematic analysis, they are equipped for the next stage: introducing a critical framework that acts as a guide for their exploration of theme. This chapter provides instruction, guidelines, and practical, helpful hints to encourage scholars to become good analysts and writers, or good *comparativists*.

The Art of Comparative Writing

The philosophy of the comparative exercise is the understanding that there are commonalities, as well as differences, in authors' creative approaches to recording life phenomena through literature and that the process of itemizing the facets of a written work is a complex intellectual exercise that has the power to amplify the diverse meanings of collective human experience. Literature can be both fiction and nonfiction, yet the interplay between reality and hypothetical circumstance as revealed in writing expands the mind's horizons and possibilities. The comparative literary exercise enables readers to critically explore unique and diverse perspectives on the meaning of life and on the role of imagination and the written word in the construction of human existence as it varies in geography, environment, language, nationality, and era.

The classic, though complex, comparative formula is to study and then critically analyze three literary works, from three different geographical regions, that represent three different languages, and sometimes even three separate genres. This formula is an expansion of the "compare and contrast" method that students practice in a traditional literature education. Comparative literary analysis differs from the simple "compare and contrast" approach because it challenges scholars to select three works that can be categorized on the basis of a specific commonality. A categorization based on theme or topic is a minimal requirement for grouping selected texts for analysis. Scholars may discuss theme or how authors' approaches to theme differ, but the analysis gains more conceptual depth when the similarities and differences between the texts (grouped because of their treatment of an identical theme) suggest meaning based on the circumstances of character, setting, plot, conflict, narrative, and other literary devices.

The reader, who assumes the role of literary critic, plays a significant role in the process of comparative literature because the reader's background, creative imagination, familiarity with literary traditions, and skill in creating a reasonable argument are the elements that control the interpretation of a text. Inherent in the method of comparative analysis is a formula based on using three selected texts for the sake of providing a legitimate number of examples as evidence for the reader (or literary critic) to offer a reliable interpretation of the convergence and divergence of human experience, as well as an infinite number of other relationships and possibilities introduced in literary texts. However, the comparative process is still valuable when only two works are selected for comparison.

An advanced stage of the comparative literature exercise is based on complex literary analysis using paradigms, or frameworks, of literary criticism (e.g., historical-biographical analysis, Black feminist critical theory, Marxist analysis, postcolonial theory, etc.) Since *Literary Spaces* aims to introduce readers to the diverse literature of Africa and its Diaspora through categorization and sampling, it is beyond its domain and objective to offer complex information on diverse paradigms of literary criticism.

Categories of Comparative Black Literature

The categorization of selected texts is structured to guide readers, especially students, into a dynamic experience of comparative analysis. Each reader may draw different conclusions based on his or her interpretation of the meaning and contexts of the literatures—a condition which is, indeed, desirable. The categories are structured to be catalysts for the generation of dynamic ideas, discoveries, and epiphanies inspired by the levels of similarity and difference within global Black experience. This enterprise is most effectively fulfilled if readers are committed to exploring the literature with creative and open minds. Lloyd Brown candidly describes this enterprise in his 1974 essay when he warns that the issues of Black literatures can be fully examined only by those comparativists who are prepared and able to deal with cultural phenomena (language, mores, art, etc.) which lie outside the familiar borders of European languages and cultures—in short, by the critic whose notions of "civilization," "culture," and "literature," are not limited by the old Eurocentric definitions of "world" civilization, "world" culture, "world" literature, and "world" whatever else. To emphasize the desirability, and the usefulness, of a non-Eurocentric comparativism is not necessarily to prejudge the soundness, or otherwise, of Black aesthetic descriptions of art and culture. But it seems obvious enough that the kind of issues raised by the Black aesthetic are not about to vanish overnight in deference to the wish-fulfilment [sic] of the orthodox comparativists.[1]

The classic Eurocentric use of the adjective *world* to describe only a portion of the world is misleading because the European worldview does not credit Black literature on its own cultural terms. The categorizations offered reflect what Brown refers to as "a more eclectic approach to the very concept of world literature or world culture," which must include a Pan-Africanist orientation toward literary categorization and study.[2] Anthony Bogues, a theorist of Black intellectual and philosophical thought, notes:

> The idea of a *black world* is not a new one. In the early twentieth century, it found its concrete expressions in the different Pan-African congresses and the black nationalist movement of Marcus Garvey. However, the black world is no homogeneous monolith. Class, nation, and gender complicate it, and there exist different traditions peculiar to different sites. One black does not stand in for all blacks, so one has to be careful. This care would allow us to remain aware that pan-Africanism or the black world are politically constructed notions fashioned in opposition to colonialism and racism and that these constructions can mean very different things.[3]

Brown also reiterates the role of Pan-Africanism:

> The historical evidence of African and Afro-American affinities are indisputable, and the evidence continues to mount impressively with

---

1. Lloyd Brown, "The Black Aesthetic and Comparative Criticism," *Council on National Literatures Report* 1, nos. 4–5 (1974): 6.
2. Ibid.
3. Anthony Bogues, "Teaching Radical Africana Political Thought and Intellectual History," *Radical History Review: Transnational Black Studies* 87 (Fall 2003): 153.

new perspectives on Africanisms in New World Black cultures. Neither is there denying all of those massive psycho-cultural parallels which have been created by Black-White history in both Africa and the Americas. But do all of these Pan-African affinities and parallels constitute a uniform world view?[4]

Brown's question is welcomed here as a version of self-scrutiny that proves to the mainstream that Black literary theorists are not proponents of a romanticized critique of New World Black culture that denies the role of cultural adaptation based on interactions with postenslavement-trade influences. Obviously, Pan-African affinities and parallels do not make all persons of African descent, regardless of their current geographies, similar or "a homogenous whole."[5] Instead, *Literary Spaces* encourages the celebration of both similarity and difference and advocates no preconceptions. Brown's 1974 essay calls for "a more complex awareness of all the parallels, ambiguities, and conflicts inherent in these cultural relationships," and more than thirty years later, the response is the formal introduction and articulation of comparative Black literature.

In advocating that scholars seek analyses that are broader in scope and application than narrow approaches to theme, comparative Black literature follows Darwin T. Turner's warning about *saturation*. Saturation is the "writer's sensitivity to the probable reaction of a Black character to a particular act of oppression.... [I]t is an almost intuitive dependence upon allusions to and use of Black tradition, customs, heroes, heroic legend, folklore, and language or unique rhetorical devices."[6] Turner explains his skepticism of neatly packaged themes applied to Black literature:

> Many scholars and critics profess to find the most obvious tradition of Black American literature in the repetition of particular themes or subjects. Sometimes, however, scholars' fascination with exciting or significant themes has caused them to misconstrue the total picture. For example, sometimes the works of James Baldwin, Ed Bullins, and many Black Arts poets are cited as examples of the theme of violence in Black literature. A more perceptive analysis of these writings reveals the emphasis on the need for love.[7]

---

4. Brown, "The Black Aesthetic and Comparative Criticism," 6.

5. Ibid.

6. Darwin Turner, "Introductory Remarks About the Black Literary Tradition in the United States of America," *Proceedings of the Comparative Literature Symposium* 9 (1978): 83.

7. Ibid., 82.

Giant Talk, the 1975 anthology of Black and Third World literature is guilty of using such neatly packaged themes since it offers a thematic category "Violence" without an explanation of context. *Literary Spaces* uses a different approach by grouping the excerpts representing the global Black literary tradition into broad categories and offering explanations and descriptions of the categorizations that permit the explication of a variety of microthemes that may emerge from the excerpts. The categories are as follows:

I. Nationalism and Identity

II. Gender Contexts and Complementarity

III. History, Justice, and Politics

IV. Black Cultural Mythology

V. Autobiography and Personal Narrative

VI. Community, Folk Culture, and Socioeconomic Realism

VII. Speculation, Spirituality, and the Supernatural

VIII. Influence, Adaptation, and Structure

In keeping with Turner's format, "discussion of the distinguishing elements of a Black American tradition [or global African tradition] is suggestive rather than exhaustive."[8]

What Brown advises as the obvious may not be completely understood by new comparativists. He reminds students of the comparative Black literary endeavor that

> the thematic content of Black literature ought to be considered with respect to the cultural environment of that literature. And on this basis it should be axiomatic enough that a sound grasp of Tutuola's fiction depends on an understanding of his Yoruba frame of reference, that the critic who presumes to explicate LeRoi Jones' poetry and fiction without reference to the writer's sonnotative use of jazz and Afro-American language styles does so at his peril, and that a reliable exegesis of Aime Cesaire's poetry or Derek Walcott's plays demands some insights into Afro-Caribbean history and folklore.[9]

Brown's description projects an element of comparative Black literature whereby it is normal and plausible to comparatively refer to Black literatures from Nigeria, African-America, Martinique, and St. Lucia/Trinidad (Walcott

---

8. Ibid., 85.
9. Brown, "The Black Aesthetic and Comparative Criticism," 7.

is a product of both) to find something wonderful, interesting, surprising, or even disappointing to say or to write (the comparative exercise is not based on preconception). The description also demonstrates how natural and appropriate it is to think of Black literatures as a single global category whereby, regardless of the origin of a scholar of Black literature, he or she is well-informed about the global cultural products of his or her people. A person of African descent, as well as a scholar or student (of any background), who claims expertise in world literature should be able to list representative works from the global Black literary tradition while at the same time exhibiting a "kind of complex awareness which can emphasize perceptual parallels without minimizing or obliterating socio-political or ethno-cultural differences."[10]

Finally, readers are encouraged to study, beyond the pages of *Literary Spaces*, the culture and contexts of the literature excerpts. In fact, since much of the content of the volume consists of excerpts from texts, readers will likely be inspired to seek out the texts in their entirety for future or concurrent study. Also, readers should utilize the Internet to further explore the authors and countries documented in this volume.

Comparative Black Literature and the Black Studies Enterprise

An additional objective of this volume is to inspire readers to be more attentive to the role of literature, as creative production, in the Black Studies enterprise. In *Introduction to Black Studies*, Maulana Karenga theoretically places literature in the category "Creative Production" and offers the following explanation:

> As a humanities discipline, Black Studies shares with other humanities disciplines a concern for and commitment to creative production. It shares with literature, art, music, and dance a definite concern with ongoing issues of aesthetics, i.e., the nature of the artistic enterprise, art as social and personal message and meaning, standards of creativity, issues of artistic freedom and social responsibility, questions of critique, of deconstruction, of dislocation, cultural hegemony, representation, transcendence, border crossing, text,

---

10. Ibid., 8.

subtext, marginality and centrality, and recovery and reconstruction. Likewise, it shares concern about race, class and gender articulation, language use and misuse, and its ability to reveal the nature and structure of social relations, as with signs, literature and other art forms as contested terrains.[11]

Because of limited university resources, many literature courses in the Black Studies curriculum are taught through English and literature departments and by scholars who are not acutely aware of the literary methodologies that have emerged from the theoretical dimensions of the discipline of Black Studies. The discipline was created formally in 1968, and the theoretical foundations of the discipline took root in the 1980s. These foundations are often overlooked in the cross-listing process.

Black Studies is a discipline that aims to create knowledge and inspire behaviors that will increase the life chances and life experiences of people of African descent, in particular, and of humanity, in general,[12] through the critical study of at least fifteen categories of inquiry—including History, Religion, Politics, Economics, Psychology, Sociology, Creative Production, Gender, Education, Linguistics, Geography, Pan-Africanism, Philosophy, Health/Science/Technology, and Community Development. The discipline is not only an approach that views people of African descent as subjects, and not objects, of knowledge; it also requires that the academic enterprise of study and knowledge-creation that is traditionally carried out in universities be translated into a practical enterprise, whereby the knowledge is applied to and made available for use in the lives of people of African descent. Teaching global Black literature in the context of the discipline of Black Studies encourages both explication (based on structure, form, and content) as well as application.

There are other new approaches to teaching global Black literatures in an African-centered context, and they offer cultural variations on the classic Eurocentric formats of studying character, setting, plot, conflict, theme, and narrative. *Literary Spaces* encourages readers to survey and utilize various analytical tools and approaches, including the following set of Suggestions for African-Centered Literary Analysis.

---

11. Maulana Karenga, *Introduction to Black Studies* (Los Angeles: University of Sankore Press, 1993), 24.

12. This "credo" of Africana Studies is adapted from Terry Kershaw's explanation of the function of the discipline of Africana Studies in "Afrocentrism and the Afrocentric Method," *Western Journal of Black Studies* 16, no. 3 (1992): 160–68.

Suggestions for African-Centered Literary Analysis

Literature is not superior to a social-science understanding of global Black experience but should be explored in proper cultural, historical, and political contexts.

Literature that represents actual historical phenomena must be comparatively studied against primary documentation of the creatively used historical episode(s).

Conflict projected in Black literature must be contextualized within proper paradigms of Black Psychology, Black Sociology, or Black Politics, including considerations of the *Maafa*,* to ensure that literature becomes a tool to inspire solution-seeking discourse informed by available bodies of African-centered knowledge and guided by the objectives of *Ma'at*.**

Themes illuminated in Black literature should be discussed and applied to appropriate current and historical events through the unlimited use of media sources (e.g., documentaries, primary source material, and statistical reports).

Setting should include a focus on African-centered variables of environment, community, geography, and globalism and on a Pan-Africanist discussion of comparative experience.

Characterization studies should be directly associated with Black Psychology paradigms of personhood, identity, and location theory so that the static or dynamic portrayal of a character is based on the character's growth consistent with African-centered measures of consciousness and value related primarily to the process of becoming an ancestor.

Plot should be studied for its success in yielding, ordered dynamic storytelling, which may be applied to oral transmission, as well as for

---

* A Kiswahili term meaning "great suffering," "disaster," and "terrible occurrence." Marimba Ani, in *Let the Circle Be Unbroken: The Implications of African Spirituality in the Diaspora* (Trenton: Red Sea Press, 1994), offers this term to describe the nature of the Black Holocaust initiated by enslavement.

** The Ancient Eygptian (Kemetic) imperative for moral behavior based on the seven principles of order, balance, harmony, compassion, reciprocity, justice, and truth.

its value in intellectual stimulation toward creative problem solving, speculation, and narrative techniques that promote a functional Black cultural mythology.

Narrative should be studied for its creative use of models such as Shabazzian logic (based on the rhetorical skills of Malcolm X/El Hajj Malik Shabazz), whereby dialogue, communication, and rhetoric are featured for their instructional roles in transmitting skills of efficient verbal self-defense and discretion.

Content should be critiqued for its ethical and moral values based on philosophical and religious sources originating from the past (Ancient Kemet) through the present (e.g., the *Husia*,* the *Odu Ifa*,** the *Nguzo Saba*,*** the Teachings of Ptahotep, and the liberation-theology interpretations of the Koran and the Bible) and should be evaluated for its representation of survival, resistance, and empowerment, including instances of adaptation and influence.

Language use in Black literature should be evaluated for its documentation of and instructional use of African languages, proverbs, wisdom, riddles, and creative concepts that increase the reader's ability to expertly articulate the social, cultural, and political variables of the Black experience.

Literature should be a catalyst that increases a reader's skills in written and oral expression in ways consistent with both African-derived communication styles and styles that facilitate effective communication with humanity.

When readers evaluate global Black literatures as part of the Black Studies enterprise, literature serves dynamic new functions beyond art for art's sake. Using the suggestions above in Black literary critique will help scholars introduce dynamic interpretations and articulations of literary analysis, including using the Akan concept *Sankofa** as a literary paradigm; literary Pan-Africanism; the *Nzuri* model of cultural aesthetics in literature;[13] socioliterary cri-

---

* The wisdom of Ancient Egypt (or Kemet).

** The sacred text of Yoruba ancestors.

*** The seven principles that support Kwanzaa.

* *Sankofa* is an Akan word that means, "We must go back and reclaim our past so we can move forward; so we understand why and how we came to be who we are today."

13. See Kariamu Welsh-Asante, "The Aesthetic Conceptualization of *Nzuri*," in *The African Aesthetic: Keeper of the Traditions*, ed. Kariamu Welsh-Asante (Westport, CT:

tique; Black cultural mythology; and finally, dynamic modern applications of comparative Black literature.

Conclusion: *Black* versus *African*

While *Literary Spaces* can offer only a modest sampling of the literature of the Black world, it should be regarded as a prototype of the history, the culture, the character, the modes of expression, the ideologies, the points of reference, and the creative visions of the African world that cry out, because of their commonality and distinction, to be comparatively studied.

The continent of Africa contains fifty-four countries. Black literary expression in the Caribbean has emerged from over twenty-six islands, regions, or departments, including border regions such as Suriname, Guyana, and French Guyana. Many countries of South and Central America, including Brazil, Belize, and Ecuador, have active communities of African descent that maintain Black literary traditions. People of African descent in the United States and Canada, as well as in such European metropolitan countries as Britain, France, and Germany, complete the geography of Black world literature.

This volume often uses the words *Black* and *African* interchangeably, because the world has difficulty regarding globally dispersed people of African descent as collectively *African*. Such people are considered Africans "by way of," or Africans "once removed." In contrast, Ghanaian writer Ayi Kwei Armah, in the novel *Osiris Rising: A Novel of Africa Past, Present and Future*, offers one of the most political literary statements that attests to the interrelatedness of the African world—a world comprised of a collective *African* population.[14] His statement of collective African identity and his revolutionary proposal for the African literary endeavor are significant final introductory ideologies that further support the exclusivity of comparative Black literature. Regarding heritage, he enables his African American protagonist to tell her African friend, "In the end, my being born in America doesn't make a lot of difference. It means my great-great-great-grandparents were captured and transported over

---

Praeger, 1994), 1–20. Welsh-Asante introduces *Nzuri* as a paradigm of African aesthetics that features analyses of meaning, ethos, motif, mode, function, method/technique, and form as a holistic approach to critiquing African-derived creative production. In *Literary Pan-Africanism: History, Contexts, and Criticism* (Durham, NC: Carolina Academic Press, 2005), Christel N. Temple offers a seminal application of *Nzuri* to literature.

14. Ayi Kwei Armah, *Osiris Rising: A Novel of Africa Past, Present and Future* (Pompenguine, West Africa: Per Ankh, 1995).

there. Yours weren't. *I prefer not to forget several thousand years of our common history because of a few centuries of separation* [emphasis added]."[15] This dynamic, Pan-African vision is evident in the "Proposals for a New Curriculum" that Armah includes in his revolutionary novel. Two sections of this in-novel proposal are appropriate foundations for the comparative literature endeavor and serve as the final word on the function and practices associated with literature of the Black world. The sections are worth quoting at length:

Basic Assumptions of the Old Literature Syllabus

The old Literature syllabus was designed to push four main assumptions: first, that the serious study of literature was essentially the study of Western literature; second, that African literature was a recent, 20th century phenomenon; third, that oral traditions formed an inchoate background for the emergence of African literature in the 20th century; fourth, that ancient Egyptian literature had nothing to do with the continent of Africa.

The old curriculum downplayed connections between literature and the political and ideological upheavals of society, except for received metropolitan ideologies.

Literature was treated as an academic discipline with few technical or practical aspects. Teachers of literature taught students to read and appreciate books, poetry, drama, fiction and expository prose as imported commodities, not to produce their own. In sum, Literature under the colonial curriculum was a dependent consumer activity. The time has come for us to make the teaching of literature an apprenticeship in creative productivity.

Principles for a New Approach to Literature

We propose a number of guidelines designed to free Literature in African universities, colleges and schools from the narrow limits of the old curriculum:

1. Literature is the record of all humanity. The study of Literature should be the universalistic opening of minds and sense to the life and art of all the world's peoples.

2. For Africans the study of Literature should be inclusively centered on African Literature.

---

15. Ibid., 102.

3. African Literature includes the whole verbal record, written and unwritten, of all the African people throughout time.

4. The literary record of Ancient Egypt is an integral and fundamental part of African Literature.

5. The production of written literature is not a modern innovation Africa owes to the West. It is an ancient and indigenous skill once fully possessed, lost under conditions of dehumanizing distress, now retrieved in different forms, under different circumstances.

6. There is a millennia-old literary tradition in Africa, both oral and written, in which literature fulfills a definite function in the enterprise of social construction. Within that tradition literary artists were skilled, professionally trained craftspersons. It should be the vocation of university departments of Literature to revitalize this tradition.

7. This African tradition recognizes literature as a practical, necessary activity, and the study of literature as a study of skills both analytical and creative.

8. Teachers of Literature should themselves first of all be producers of literature, with sufficient skill and experience to train new generations of producers of drama, poetry, fiction, essays, etc.

9. Oral traditions, apart from being valuable in themselves, are invaluable source materials requiring collection, storage and classification for systematic use in the ongoing production of new literature.

10. Literature is not a static discipline but a dynamic activity, changing forms and techniques as technological possibilities expand. Logically then, the modern study of literature should include the practical, productive, technical and creative study of the uses of different media: print, radio, television, cinema, computerized media.[16]

While Armah's vision of the global African literary endeavor offers challenges yet to be fulfilled, Armah is both historical and prophetic is his African-centered articulation of the literary endeavor. *Literary Spaces* seeks to inspire readers to work to fulfill Armah's vision of global Black, or *African*, literatures.

---

16. Ibid., 219–221.

Chapter 3

Nationalism, Pan-Africanism, and Identity

The broad issues of nationalism, Pan-Africanism, and identity reflect distinct approaches and overlapping conditions of geography and experience for people of African descent. Nationalism is pride in one's land of birth or origin—a pride often passionate and emotional. Ethnic, tribal, and national identities of African people are documented in the historical record of pre-European contact, but people of African descent are part of a more complex system of identity because of the trans-Atlantic slave trade and the modern concept of globalism. The culturally significant communities, or *Diasporas*, that people of African descent have created since the sixteenth century reflect African-derived core culture, European influence, and diverse examples of cultural borrowing and sharing.

Black nationalism traditionally refers to self-determination, a land base, a spiritually defined destiny, an African image of God, an independent economy and means of production, and separatism from whites; however, all these variables are not necessarily present in the diverse manifestations of Black nationalism around the world. In regions where Blacks are not the majority racial population, the group can be considered as what nineteenth-century Black American scholar Martin Delany called a "nation within a nation." Black societies often reveal multiple sensibilities that are naturally addressed in the literature—sensibilities which vary according to national identity, racial or cultural heritage, and levels of institutional racism or white supremacy existing in many nations. Both African and European influences often appear in Black literatures from regions that have a history of enslavement and colonialism. This is true even for populations of African descent in seemingly unlikely places such as South and Central America. Afro-Cubans, Afro-Ecuadorians, and Afro-Brazilians base their identities on both an African heritage and their own nationalities. The layering of personal identity, group affiliation, political ideology, cultural loyalty, and patriotism makes the critical and comparative exercise both interesting and complex.

Even after the abolition of enslavement, Black writers from Africa and its Diaspora have still had a limited privilege of creating literature under conditions of relative peace and equality. However, sociopolitical systems such as colonialism have caused Black life and literature to be uniquely attentive to self-determined articulations of personhood and to processes of resisting oppression. The literature reflects a variety of articulations of the meaning of heritage, environment, and home, as well as Pan-Africanism, or transnational ideas of kinship and camaraderie based on a common African heritage. As social conditions throughout the world challenge African-centered notions of African heritage, culture, and social organization, Black writers are creative and historical in their literary responses.

Globalism is an important concept related to those of nationalism, Pan-Africanism, and identity, because travel, immigration, and advanced technological communication have initiated a process whereby individuals can selectively transplant their culture from one region to the next. For people of African descent, modern globalism is a deliberate and orderly geographical shift that contrasts to the chaotic, brutal, and culturally interruptive shifts fostered by the dispersions of African people during the trans-Atlantic enslavement trade. Black literature is a dynamic source that illuminates the choices that people of African descent make about national identity, the sociopolitical contexts of diverse Black global identities, and the role of self-determination as resistance to oppression.

To offer balance in the spectrum of analyses related to nationalism in African contexts, Eileen Julien reminds critics that "[t]he national identify of a writer, in the context of Africa, may offer little clue to the genealogy of specificity of a literary text, for the ethnic aesthetic tradition on which it draws may be far more significant that the writer's nationality."[1] Thus, the interpretive task of the comparative analyst requires precise analysis backed by strong evidence to support specific observations.

from *Desirada*

by Maryse Condé (Guadeloupe)

Chapter 1

Ranélise had described her birth to her so many times that she believed she had actually played a part—not that of a terrorized and submissive baby

---

1. Eileen Julien, "African Literatures in Comparative Perspective," *Yearbook of Comparative and General Literature* 43 (1995): 18.

whom Madame Fleurette, the midwife, wrenched out from between her mother's bloodied thighs—but that of a clear-sighted witness, a major role, her very mother, the mother in labor Reynalda, herself, whom she imagined sitting rigid, lips pursed, arms crossed, and a look of inexpressible suffering on her face. Years later, standing in from of Frida Kahlo's painting of her own birth, it had seemed to her that this woman, this stranger, must have been thinking of her.

It was three o'clock in the afternoon. The atmosphere shimmered and tingled with excitement. It was Mardi Gras, a day of jubilation when all the companies of masked dancers charged through the streets of La Pointe. The previous Sunday they had secretly plotted to converge on the Place de la Victoire from the outlying districts. The throbbing of the two *gwo-ka* drums could already be heard. Some of the masked dancers were wrapped in dried banana leaves. Others had tarred their bodies and ran through the streets cracking whips that coiled like snakes. Another group had devised buffalos' and bulls' heads for costumes and pinned to their apparel all shapes of mirrors, pieces of glass, and mica that attracted the light and glittered in the sun. These were formidable *mas'a kon* dancers, said to have come straight from the Casamance. In the meantime respectable families and their children crowded the verandas between the bougainvillea in flower and the latanias in pots. They had saved up their silver coins with holes in the middle to throw down to the crowd below. At their feet the rabble shuffled along shouting at the top of their voices.

The Vatable Canal district was deserted since everyone had gathered at the center of town. A few *moko zombis* who had strayed that way soon realized their mistake and proceeded down the rue Frébault kicking violently with their stilts at the closed wooden doors as a reminder of their presence. In Ranélise's four-room house, behind the shutters, you could hear neither the din of the *gwo-ka* drums, nor the piercing shrill of the whistles, nor the clacking of the *rara* rattles accompanying the masked dancers. You couldn't hear the screams of pleasure from the crowd either. The silence was broken only by the muffled moans of Reynalda, whose too-narrow, fifteen-year-old pelvis refused to make any concessions, and by the maternal yet exasperated berating in Creole from Mme. Fleurette: "Push, push, I'm telling you, for God's sake!" and finally, out came the frail, persistent wail of a newborn infant.

Mme. Fleurette was a handsome mulatto woman, an experienced midwife, without a diploma to her name, who was goodness herself. Rainy season come dry season she cycled through the poor neighborhoods on her "Flying Pigeon" to deliver the babies of the poor wretches who were turned away by the General Hospital and whom the sisters of the Saint-Jules Hospice could not accommodate. When Reynalda went into labor, Ranélise, who had rescued her a few months earlier after her failed attempt at drowning, recognized the bicycle parked in front of a shack, even on this day of festivities, and together with her younger sister, Claire-Alta, intercepted Mme. Fleurette. After the laborious delivery was over they were thanking Mme. Fleurette and leading her out toward the pool of clear water in the yard when Reynalda, looking like death, uttered such a mournful groan that the three women turned around in alarm. In an instant the threadbare sheet covering her had turned red and was already dripping blood. Fortunately the Saint-Jules Hospice was close by. There they bundled Reynalda into a bed still burning from the puerperal fever of a poor woman who had just passed from this life to the next, and the good sisters went to work.

When Ranélise left the Saint-Jules Hospice around midnight, the fireworks that had been set off over by the harbor were zigzagging across the sky in a multitude of colors and vanishing over Dominica way. The streets were swarming with children, women, and men yelling. Drunks were dancing their entrechats. Amid a hellish din the masked revelers were having their final fling.

Back home she found the newborn infant fast asleep, set down where they had forgotten her. Her tiny face streaked with excrement and dried blood, she smelled of rotting fish. In spite of this, rays of love beamed from Ranélise's heart and shed a glow over the tiny body. She had always wanted a child. Instead the Good Lord had sent her miscarriage after miscarriage, stillborn after stillborn, infants baptized at the very last minute, one after another. She clasped the baby to her heart, convinced that the Good Lord had finally repented for having mistreated her so. Showering her with kisses, she chose the name Marie-Noëlle, though she was born at the height of Carnival. For Marie is the name of the Holy Virgin, mother of all virtues, and Noëlle a reminder of that miraculous night when Jesus became a child to wash our sins. She prepared a bath of lukewarm water, mixed in some essence of roses, and plopped in soursop leaves as well as a pinch of sweet violets and sweet-smelling husks to soak. Then she dried the baby with a soft towel and laid her on her belly to protect her from the fear of the dark, the wind, and nightmares.

Ranélise was a tall black woman, a cook at Tribord Bâbord, a restaurant with a shabby appearance but a reputation for good food, situated at the Bas de la Source. Her specialty: conch. Nobody could match the way she extracted mollusk from its shell, left it to soak in a homemade mixture of brine and bay-rum leaves, pounded it with a pestle she had made from a piece of lignum vitae, and served it up juicy and succulent as lamb in a thick reddish sauce. Her customers came from far and wide. Sometimes from as far away as Le

Moule or La Boucan, and Gérardo Polius, the Communist mayor of La Pointe, took four meals a week at Tribord Bâbord, sitting down with his entire municipal council. A few months earlier, as she was walking down to the Carenage to meet the fisherman she usually dealt with, she saw a bundle of clothes floating on the water like a buoy. Intrigued, she went over and made out an arm, a leg, then a sliver of buttock. Her shouts had attracted passersby, and, using a pole, they had fished out a bedraggled girl whose heart was still beating unsteadily.

A young girl, almost a child. Fourteen years old. Certainly not more than fifteen. Her breasts the size of guava buds. Ranélise, who wore her heart on her sleeve, had taken her home with her. She had rubbed her with camphor oil and given her an infusion of watergrass mixed with a little rum to warm her up. Then she wrapped her in one of the flannel nightdresses she wore during the bad weather season. The first day they got little more out of her than a few reluctant words. She said her name was Reynalda Titane. Her maman, Antonine, whom everyone nicknamed Nina, hired herself out to the family of Gian Carlo Coppini. Gian Carlo Coppini was an Italian jeweler in the rue de Nozières whose shop, Il Lago di Como, was always full of customers come to buy but mainly to browse in admiration. Gian Carlo Coppini looked a little like Jesus Christ: curly, silky hair and a beard to go with it. He reigned over a host of women: first of all his own wife, always pregnant or in labor; his two sisters, always dressed in black, their heads covered with lace mantillas; and his daughters. It was thanks to him that Nina had been able to send Reynalda to the Dubouchage elementary school. Reynalda loved school. French, history, natural science. She worked hard and passed the exam for her elementary school certificate.

People advised Ranélise to send Reynalda back where she came from. Who knew whether she wasn't a thief or a good-for-nothing wanted by the gendarmes? But when Ranélise mentioned taking her back to Il Lago di Como, Reynalda had knelt down at her feet like Mary Magdalene soaked them with her tears. That was when she revealed she was pregnant and why she had thrown herself into the sea. Ranélise had stood speechless, facing her. How could she think of killing herself because someone had given her a belly? Didn't she know that a child was a blessing from the Good Lord? A sign that His elixir has enriched your heart as well as your body? A woman who sees her belly swell and grow round should throw herself on her knees, strike her breast, and cry: "Thank you, Lord!"

Reynalda did not breathe a word to anyone. Except sometimes to Claire-Alta, who was about her age. Ranélise ended up keeping her and found her a job at the restaurant Tribord Bâbord—in the kitchen, because in the dining room, customers complained she prevented them from enjoying their rum.

The second thing Marie-Noëlle imagined was her christening. It had been held right in the middle of Lent on a Saturday, the day reserved for illegitimate children, those who don't know their papa's name. The Church of Saint-Jules, adjoining the hospice of the same name, was a wooden building with a nave in the shape of a ship's hull. It had withstood the fires and earthquakes that devastated La Pointe since it was founded. At that time a good many of its louvered shutters were missing; its stained-glass windows were broken in places, while its bell tower sat askew like the madras headtie of an old woman who has seen far too much of life. Ranélise, her godmother, was carrying her in her arms like the Holy Sacrament. Ranélise was a sight to behold that day. She was radiant, dressed in her polka-dot blue satin two-piece suit with white lapels and a wide hat with a sagging brim. One of her countless good friends, dressed in a double-breasted wool suit and tie, stood in as godfather and joined her in singing: "We give thanks unto Thee, O God;/We give thanks for Thy name is near."

The font stood in front of one of the remaining unbroken stained-glass windows depicting the Annunciation. With her thumb pressed against her palate and her cheek resting against Ranélise's bosom, Marie-Noëlle was interested in neither the priest's homily nor her godfather's and godmother's well-intentioned results. She could not take her eyes off the celestial image of the archangel Gabriel, with his blue cape and great outspread wings, holding a bunch of lilies. All around her the other babies wailed or sucked on the salt of good behavior. Absorbed in her vision, she felt infinitely superior. Hadn't Ranélise proclaimed her to be the most wonderful child on earth? The day of the christening they had listened to music. Not just the usual mazurkas, *wabap* beguines, and others. Monsieur and Madame Léomidas, who worked in Senegal for the Ministry of Overseas Development, had played records on the gramophone and everyone had sat in silence listening to their explanation of the *griots* in Africa.

Curiously enough, although Ranélise must have recounted the incident fairly frequently, Marie-Noëlle had no memory of her mother leaving. All she could gather was that she had left in September. A September laden with the threat of hurricanes and storms as if the sky were flushed with anger. One or two weeks after the christening Reynalda announced that she was leaving to work in metropolitan France. In France? Yes, France! The BUMIDOM agency had found her a job, as they did for so many fellow islanders at that time—with Jean-René Duparc, who lived on the boulevard Malesherbes in the XVIIth Arrondissement in Paris. This Jean-René had a family of three small children who needed a nurse. The mayor, Gérardo Polius, did not mince his words. Nor did the neighbors, whereas Ranélise was beside herself with joy, and to show it gave Reynalda three hundred-franc notes. Before she left Reynalda had come straight to the point and told Claire-Alta that she had no intention of ending up a maid.

She intended to go to college and become somebody.

Marie-Noëlle's childhood was an enchantment. Hand in hand with Ranélise she walked in a woodland carpeted with tree ferns, milky white trumpet flowers, and heavy-petaled heliconias rimmed with yellow. Here and there blossomed the purple flower of the wild plantain. A cool wind tickled her nostrils, mingling with the scent of flowers, earth, wind, rain, and her childhood was a perfumed garden. To some people Marie-Noëlle's possessions would not have amounted to much. A chain bracelet engraved with her name. A necklace with three medallions, one of which was of the Infant Jesus, her patron saint. Some clothes at the bottom of a wicker basket. She never had a tricycle or a toy car with pedals or a Barbie doll. Merely a homemade scooter with which she whisked along the Vatable canal and the streets on the Morne Udal. But a child's joy cannot be measured in gold or expensive toys. It is measured by motions of the heart, and Marie-Noëlle was the only reason Ranélise's heart throbbed. Ranélise's hand was gentle, so gentle, even when she untangled Marie-Noëlle's thick mass of long hair. Never a slap, never a blow, never the mark of a belt on her buttocks. Never a punishment standing up or kneeling down, arms outspread under the merciless sun in the yard. Not even a word spoken louder than the next. Rather cascades of affection, with pet names and showers of kisses on the nape of her neck.

On Easter Monday they would load up a hamper with pots of conch in hot Colombo sauce and rice and set off with friends in a minibus to the beach at Grande-Anse, Deashaies. Marie-Noëlle chuckled and paddled in her Petite-Bateau panties while Rastamen with long fauve-colored dreadlocks played ball in the sand or beat the *gwo-ka*.

Marie-Noëlle's presence in the house turned Ranélise's life upside down. Until then she had been a woman who took in men. A lot of men. Inquisitive neighbors spied on those who went in at dusk to emerge only at dawn when the stars were fading. Starting with Gérardo Polius, the Communist mayor who had been a regular visitor for twenty years; and Alexis Alexius, his deputy, who slipped inside as soon as the mayor had turned his back. People did not gossip too much because Ranélise was a good soul. Always ready to help a neighbor, slip a banknote into the hands of the destitute, find a job for the unemployed or a place in the nursery school for an infant. From one day to the next, her reckless behavior changed. Except for Gérardo Polius, no man ever came to spend the night with her again. Although she abstained from taking Holy Sacrament, she had nevertheless always been on good terms with the priests of Saint-Jules and organized carol singing in her yard at Advent. Now, without going so far as to take confession and communion, she never missed a mass, vespers, or rosary. She could be seen walking in the processions of the Holy Virgin, head lowered in prayer and striking her chest as if she never stopped thanking God for all the happiness in her life.

Very early on, as soon as Marie-Noëlle started school, it was obvious that He who deals the gift of intelligence had not forgotten her. First in everything. When the prizes were handed out, she never stopped walking up to the podium. It was first prize after first prize, leather-bound books after the gilt-edge books, and Ranélise paraded around, already the proud mother of a future school-teacher. Even a midwife. For she had completely forgotten that Marie-Noëlle had not come out of her belly. Not that Reynalda did anything at all to remind her child she existed. Time passed. Days lapsed into months, months into years, and they received practically no news of her. A card at New Year's without an address. Clodomire Ludovic, a retired postman from the XIIIth Arrondissement in Paris, swore that one day he met her in the very middle of the Place d'Italie. She had looked him straight in the eye and pretended not to recognize him. In spite of the passing years, people often mentioned the name of Reynalda Titane. It's not every day you fish out a drowning girl from the waters of the Carenage. And why did she try to drown herself, come to that? If every girl who paraded around an unwanted bun in the oven did the same the earth would soon be emptied. Gradually all that was left in the people's minds was the memory of an eccentric, sullen girl who had not been content with her daily lot.

Every time they talked of her maman Marie-Noëlle sensed a feeling of danger. It was as if an icy wind blew steadily over her shoulders and she might catch pleurisy. She quickly tried to change the subject, showing off her latest composition or asking to recite a lesson. Sometimes in the middle of the night the thought of her mother gripped her and woke her up like a nightmare. She would start to cry inconsolably, and only the dawn light would dry her cheeks.

On her way to school she could not help making a detour via the rue de Nozières to look at Il Lago di Como, situated on the ground floor of a two-story wooden house that needed a fresh coat of paint. She sensed that this shop, which did not look like much, nothing more than a dark, narrow passageway, where the electric light was left on day and night, held the secret of her birth. What events so terrible occurred a few years earlier to make her barely fifteen-year-old maman throw herself into the sea and seek death?

One day—she must have been almost ten—Marie-Noëlle plucked up enough courage, pushed open the door, and mingled with the flow of customers admiring the cameo brooches and pendants and all the Florentine engraving. The wife of the owner, pallid and fatigued, sat enthroned at the cash register. The two sisters wearing mantillas were talking to customers. In a corner three or four little girls were playing with rag dolls. Gian Carlo Coppini, a jeweler's loupe inserted into his right eye, his beard and handsome silky hair, now pepper and salt, reaching almost to his shoulders, was examining a green-colored gem. A thin black skull-cap sat tightly on his head, which probably meant he was Jewish. After a while he laid the stone down on the counter and cast a look around him. He caught sight of Marie-Noëlle standing in a corner of the shop and gave her a suave, magnanimous smile, revealing a carnassial set of teeth, as if he were Our Lord Jesus Christ surrounded by his apostles. At that moment a young servant girl came out from the back of the shop carrying a small tray set with a white embroidered cloth, a gilt-edged cup, a sugar bowl, and a coffeepot. The girl poured the coffee into the cup, cautiously—like somebody fearing a reprimand—added two spoonfuls of sugar, and the penetrating aroma filled the shop.

Gian Carlo Coppini thanked her with a motion of the hand that dismissed her at the same time. Then, with the unctuousness of a priest drinking the Communion wine and yet with the theatricality of an actor, he lowered his eyes and brought the coffee cup level with his lips, which were like rosebuds set among his mass of hair. When Marie-Noëlle found herself back on the street under the sun, she leaned against a wall and almost fainted with emotion.

Yes, there was no doubt about it, this stranger had played a major role in her life.

Chapter 2

On July 5, 1970, when Marie-Noëlle had celebrated her tenth birthday and was now old enough to enter the Lycée Michelet, the postman slipped notification of a registered letter addressed to Mademoiselle Ranélise Tertullien between the shutters.

It caused a sensation.

First of all Ranélise never received any letters, apart from Reynalda's cards, the mail-order catalog from the Trois Suisses and the *billet-doux* from the tax man. Second, she didn't know how to retrieve the registered letter. Where had she placed her identity card, which she never used? Inside the drawers of her bedside table? In her bureau? In her wicker basket with the silverware? After having searched for hours she was about to strike up a prayer to Saint-Expédit, patron of lost causes, when she found it under a pile of good sheets in her chest of drawers. Then she set off for the post office that had recently opened in the Bergevin district, not far from the new bus station.

Since she could not read very well she gave the letter to Marie-Noëlle who, even before opening it and reading its contents, knew that what she had dreaded most in the world had finally arrived.

The strong brown paper envelope contained a money order, a plane ticket, some Air France forms, and a short note.

The writing on the cream-colored paper was in a firm, even elegant hand:

Sauvigny-sur-Orange, June 27

Dear Ranélise,

Contrary to what you may think I have not forgotten my daughter. The time has come when I can fulfill my duties toward her, for I am now in a position to provide her with the decent life any child deserves.

I would be grateful if you could send me by return mail her school re-port and health records. You will find enclosed some money to buy her clothes and a plane ticket for mid-October. You only have to sign the forms: she travels as an unaccompanied minor.

I don't know how to thank you for the goodness of your heart.

Reynalda Titane

P.S. I am now a welfare worker at the city hall in Savigny-sur-Orge.

Ranélise collapsed into a fainting fit. The neighbors who had rushed over had to rub her forehead and palms with camphorated alcohol. Then she re-gained consciousness and started to weep hot tears, moaning out loud and cursing fate. Had she raised and cherished a child for ten years only to bun-dle her off to a deranged individual who had done nothing less than abandon her defenseless infant on this earth? Who was the child's real maman? The one who had cared for her measles, her smallpox, and her ear infections or the one giving herself airs in France. Aren't there laws to protect people and right the wrongs in this world? No! She would never give up Marie-Noëlle. The cho-rus of neighbors nodded their approval. Then she stood up and armed her-self with a parasol to go out. She was not in the habit of disturbing Gérardo Polius at work or making a show of their relations. But on that day she felt she needed his expert advice. After all, Gérardo had studied law. He was a lawyer, even though he no longer practiced. When she arrived at Town Hall, beside herself with rage and her eyes swollen with tears, he was locked in his office with two of his councilmen and the director of garbage disposal. So she told her story to any sympathizing employee while she waited two full hours for him to finish. He carefully considered the letter she had received, listened to her patiently, then knowing how fond she was of Marie-Noëlle he said sadly: "I told you over and over again to legalize the situation by adopting her. As things stand you can't do anything. The biological mother has every right."

However much she hammered his chest with her fists and accused him of being heartless, he merely repeated what he said and she finally collapsed cursing the Good Lord. When she had calmed down somewhat, he had her driven home in his Citroën DS 19.

That evening Marie-Noëlle was gripped by a high fever. At nine o'clock her temperature was running well over a hundred, and her eyes, as red as the embers of a bonfire, seemed about to leap out of her head. Around ten she began to moan and whine like a tiny infant and utter unintelligible sounds. At times she appeared to regain consciousness and shouted in a heart-rending voice: "I want to stay with my maman!"

Then she was seized with such violent convulsions that she almost fell off her bed, and they had to tie her to bedposts with the sheets.

Mme. Fleurette, the only person who consented to leave her bed in the middle of the night, diagnosed a pernicious fever and called for her to be admitted to the emergency room at the General Hospital. There the young doctor on duty ascertained the symptoms to be nothing but a common attack of dengue fever, which he treated with sulfonamide. At four in the morning Marie-Noëlle drained herself like a sick person suffering from typhoid fever, vomiting up a thick, foul-smelling custard, after which, as stiff as a corpse, she fell into a coma. The doctors declared her a hopeless case, and people were already predicting a double funeral, for everyone knew that Ranélise would not survive her. Marie-Noëlle, however, recovered. After a week in a deep coma, her bed hidden behind a screen so as not to frighten the other patients, she opened her eyes and asked for her maman. Ranélise, who had not left her beside for one instant, went down on both knees weeping and crying Hosannah in the Highest. It should be said that the Marie-Noëlle who left the General Hospital one morning in July in the arms of Ranélise was not the same Marie-Noëlle who had gone in almost a month earlier. The chubby, mischievous little girl, temperamental and tender, who had been the delight of Ranélise's heart, was gone. In her place a great gawk of a girl, nothing but skin and bone, with a glazed look, staring at people in a way that made them feel ill at ease, for she seemed to be looking through them to pursue some personal obsession. Once so imaginative, a real chatterbox filling Ranélise's head with fantastic stories, she now said virtually not a word. She sat for hours on end without moving, staring straight in front of her; then she would rest her cheek on Ranélise's shoulder while tears streamed down her face.

Ranélise, who in her entire life had never thought about taking a vacation and had worked like a beast of burden every day the Good Lord made, borrowed some money from Gérardo and with it rented a house in Port Louis, steps from the beach at Souffleur, to give the child a change of air.

Before it was devastated by hurricanes and the demise of sugarcane, Port Louis was undoubtedly the prettiest town on Grande-Terre. Its clear blue sky knew nothing of rain; its air, nothing of miasmas. A row of tall elegant wooden houses with flower-filled balconies and deep attic windows lined the seafront. They belonged to the representatives of the financiers in the metropolitan France who had taken over from the white Creoles, the former masters of the sugar plantations. On Sundays they filled the church with their arrogance, perfume, and starched linen and placed in the collection basket the equivalent of one month's pay of one of their workers.

Port Louis was also a bustling little town. And Beauport was the focus of activity. During the cane harvest, lines of steel wagons drawn by tractors rumbled toward the factory, for the oxcart had become obsolete and was now scarcely used except by some smallholders. Furthermore it was the hub of forty kilometers of railroad track traveled daily by five locomotives and two hundred wagons.

The house Ranélise had rented was at the very end of the seafront. From the somewhat unkempt plot of garden, where a few tall canna lilies managed to grow, you could see the graves in the cemetery splashed by the red blossom of the flamboyants and the yellow clumps of allamanda. Ranélise had her own thoughts on how to cure a sick person: She knew that the sea had a healing effect on everything. Just before dawn, when the fishermen's boats were the first to sully the blue of the sea, she would wake Marie-Noëlle and take her down to the beach. Wrapped in her loose, faded dress, she cautiously stepped into the water, crossed herself twice, scooped up three mouthfuls of water in the palm of her hand, swallowed them, then went back and sat on the sand. Marie-Noëlle, however, who had taken swimming lessons at school, swam with great strokes out toward the open sea as if she wanted to reach the horizon. When the houses grew tiny in a golden arc, she stopped swimming, caught her breath, and let herself float. The slow motion of the waves comforted her, rocking her to and fro like a baby in a cradle. Her hair untangled itself. She felt herself become a seaweed towed by the whims of the current or a sea animal, a spider crab or a seahorse. The peppery scent of the water penetrated her nostrils while its gentleness washed over her, coating her like a balm. To the south was the open sea—an infinite blue. But if she looked north, the jagged blue ridge of the mountains scarred the horizon. If she looked down below the water, the great white seabed attracted her and she felt tempted to kick her way down to eternal peace. Then she thought of Ranélise waiting for her, and she swam back to the shore.

These daily swims, together with a careful diet and walks, hastened Marie-Noëlle's convalescence. Sometimes they walked as far as Massioux, Gros-Cap, and Pombiray. And the hordes of kids from the Indian families, who under the Second Empire had replaced the blacks deserting the canefields, came out on their doorsteps to take a look at this mismatched couple: a handsome, well-built black woman, followed by a puny girl with bobbing braids reddened by the seawater, who, on the contrary, gaped in wonder at everything. This was the first time Marie-Noëlle had left La Pointe and the Vatable Canal district, so everything enchanted her. She paused out of curiosity in front of the red-and-yellow-striped temples dedicated to Mariamman under the sheltering green of the trees. What went on behind those high tricolored walls? What comings and goings from the ghats of the Ganges to these limestone paths? Or else she ran until she was out of breath along the driveways lined with dwarf coconut trees and palms, remains of the sugar plantation houses that in times past had dotted the canefields. She breathed in the smell of the crushed cane juice from the Beauport factory and dreamed of clinging like the little black ragamuffins to the back of the sugarcane trains as they smoked their way across the scrubland. And so she regained a little strength, cheered, almost in spite of herself, by the hustle and bustle of her island.

She never returned to the child she once was. That time was well and truly over. Due to her sickness and long convalescence she wasn't able to leave for France until October 31 and was late for school.

Years after Marie-Noëlle still retained the sensations and images that flickered through her head while she was in a coma at the General Hospital.

At times she was cold, a cold that cut her to the bone. Other time she felt herself next to a blazing furnace. It seemed her skin was about to scorch, burn to a cinder, and leave her naked, an unwholesome heap of entrails. Daylight had been snuffed out. She remained in darkness. Behind her eyelids, shapes raveled and unraveled, taking flight or floating, like the flying ends of melancholy scarves made of silk or plastic. Then suddenly blurs of color in blue and violet hues or monochrome, here and there a red or yellow flash, emerged and grew into dazzling shapes. When she blinked, the spots burst and grew smaller. Small and menacing. They drew a constellation of tiny dots, glittering like car headlights in the distance or the eyes of a pack of animals prowling in the forest. Suddenly everything melted, clouding over again with a thick velvet folded in four, and she remained in this jet black darkness, panting and terrified.

At other times her head filled with noise. She thought she would explode and the wax of her brain ooze soft and lukewarm onto the rough pillowcase with G.H. stitched in large blue letters. It was as if a hurricane were looming up from the other side of the earth, greeted by the rustle of the cane and the screaming of the great wind. The breadfruit, mango and coconut trees fell one on top of another, preceded by an ominous cracking. The doors of the huts banged and were torn off, their hinges twisted like mere pieces of scrap iron. The louvered shutters were smashed to pieces. The roofs sliced the air with their sheets of rusted zinc. While the terrified kids crouching under the kitchen sinks never stopped squealing, she listened to the din. Until it all stopped and silence enveloped her. A silence more terrible than the noise. It was then that she traversed immense open spaces.

Some days, however, things improved. It was as if daylight broke through. She managed to distinguish the blue-and-white square of the window, the narrow bell tower of the Saint-Pierre-Saint-Paul Cathedral and the clock, which always showed one-fifteen all year round. She could make out the doctors, always in a hurry. She could see the nuns' winged coifs fluttering around the drip feed or their hands holding their syringes level with their eyes. She could see Ranélise sitting at her bedside or leaning over her or pacing up and down in her room, openly crying. Sometimes she could even hear the familiar music of Ranélise's voice, lamenting, taking stock of all the sacrifices she had made, all the tribulations she had endured during these ten years of maternity. Oh, no! The Good Lord could not take away her child! Was she talking about sickness and death or else the reunion with Reynalda? Whatever the case, for her it was nothing but grief. Marie-Noëlle would have liked to answer her. She would have liked to comfort her, assure her that wherever she was she would continue to love her more than anyone else. But she couldn't. The words got stuck in her throat and became clogged. She remained nailed to her bed, unable to respond, a prisoner of her solitude. Her eyes then filled with tears. Her suffering swelled around her and she huddled down under the threadbare sheet that was too small.

Marie-Noëlle still carried these images and sensations deep inside her. Without warning they would surge up and take possession of her. Time would stop. Right in the middle of a sentence or a gesture she appeared to fall into a trance, go numb, and her eyes glazed over.

People did not fail to notice these absences of mind. At first they remarked on them. Then they got used to them and thought her a bit cracked. Like her mother before her. Quite simply cracked.

Chapter 3

But nobody had ever described to Marie-Noëlle the day she arrived in Paris. Her memory had taken good care of that for her.

Once she had accepted the inevitable hand of fate, Ranélise acted as best she could. She dried the tears from her eyes and began to fill a suitcase full of woolen clothes. Then she asked Father Simonin to celebrate four masses for Marie-Noëlle. Four Saturdays in a row she took her to confession. For four Sundays, hands piously joined under her chin, she marched with her to the altar to receive Holy Communion. Finally, one evening after work, she opened the album she kept locked in her chest of drawers and showed her a photo of her mother taken the day when they and some close friends had celebrated the first election of Gérard Polius as mayor of La Pointe. Reynalda was almost nine months pregnant. Her protruding belly strained the checkered fabric of her shapeless dress in an unseemly way. Surrounding her, Ranélise, Claire-Alta, Gérardo Polius, and Alexis Alexius, his deputy, who was still a regular visitor to the house and Ranélise's bed, looked completely inebriated. They were raising their glasses level with the camera and grinning. Everyone looked tipsy. Except for her. Her triangular face with its somewhat sickly features did not express grief or revolt, but rather an extreme weariness. As if she had only one idea in mind: put an end to it all. Marie-Noëlle had not let herself be moved, neither by this expression nor by the sight of this mountain of flesh behind which she, the fetus, was hiding from the world. When Ranélise babbled on in a torrent of words that Reynalda should be forgiven for her ten years of neglect as Jesus had forgiven Peter his three denials, Marie-Noëlle had forcefully interrupted her and asked who her papa was, for there isn't a child on earth without a papa. You had to have a papa to make a child. It was not the first time this burning question had weighed heavily on her tongue. At the very last minute, she always managed to swallow it back. To be truthful she was afraid of the answer she might hear. Because of the color of her skin that stood out against those around her, who were decidedly black, because of her mop of hair that was the color of straw, and her eyes that were striped green or yellow by the light, depending on the hour of day. Her papa must have been a man of light skin. A mulatto? An islander from Les Saintes? A malevolent high-yellow *chaben* as red as a land crab? Perhaps even a white man? A white Creole or a French Frenchman, gendarme or officer in the riot squad? How could she bear such paternity?

Ranélise became flustered. What does it matter? Does a papa count? The only thing that counts is your maman's womb, a fortress whose door you once painfully pried open. Long, long time ago, the masters decided that the child follows its maman's womb. If she was black, the child was black.... Marie-Noëlle was no longer listening to this useless chatter. She swore to herself she would take as long as it needed, but one day she would decipher the undecipherable.

From the photos she got the impression that her mother must be ugly. Tall, whereas in fact she was quite short. Plump, whereas she must have weighed the weight of a teenager. Middle-aged, like Ranélise or her classmates' mothers at the Dubouchage school, whereas she was still a young woman. She could have been an older sister. Or a young aunt like Claire-Alta. Marie-Noëlle could not help devouring her with her eyes and, hiding her grief at having lost Ranélise, she felt like hugging her and whispering into her neck: "You're the treasure I did not know I had."

Reynalda was waiting in a corner of the airport reserved for the parents of the unaccompanied minors, leaning against a pillar like a plant against a prop. Her face betrayed nothing, as if she were wearing a mask, a wolf hiding its real emotions. She was cramped into a navy-blue, military-style coat that was buttoned up to the neck and did not suit her. But a red, green, and yellow cap provided an unexpected touch of color. She looked at Marie-Noëlle furtively, almost fearfully, forced a smile, then quickly turned her eyes away without leaning over to kiss her. While signing the forms she asked the hostess in a voice that contrasted with the loud, drawling accents of Ranélise and Claire-Alta: "Did everything go all right?"

The she grabbed Marie-Noëlle's case and preceded her to the exit.

Outside the sky shimmered gray and overcast, skimming the rooftops. It was snowing.

Was it snowing? It seldom snows in Paris. And not on November 1. In any case in Marie-Noëlle's memory big snowflakes were falling and fluttering like insects around the flame of an oil lamp. The buildings, the paving stones, the buses, and the parked cars were coated with white powder. Here and there trees brandished their stumps bandaged in white. Marie-Noëlle was shaking and did not know why. She had trouble following Reynalda as she quickly twisted and turned through the airport. Finally she stopped in front of a black car and Marie-Noëlle was amazed. Not because she was going to climb into a car. Wasn't it Gérardo Polius's DS 19, still bravely holding the road despite its aging bodywork, that had driven her to the airport? It was simply the first time she had seen a woman sit behind a wheel. At La Pointe it was always the men who occupied this seat, and Joby, Gérardo's chauffeur, swaggered officiously as he manipulated the gears, as he were handling the controls of a Caravelle. From what she had gathered from Ranélise, she was convinced her maman was poor. Was Reynalda deceiving everyone and was she, in fact rich? The car set off along the deserted streets (it was the morning of a public holiday), so dismal after the streets of La Pointe, brightened merely by the red and green lights blinking at intersections. Since Reynalda did not utter a single word, neither to ask for news about her, Ranélise, or Claire-Alta nor to enquire about the changes to La Pointe, the journey seemed endless, and Marie-Noëlle sank numbly into despair.

At that time the Jean Mermoz housing projects at Sauvigny-sur-Orge were like any other suburban apartment houses. Unattractive but calm and residential. From time to time a quarrel flared up between neighbors. A husband beat his wife. A dance ended in a brawl. The police showed up, but it was never anything serious. The housing projects consisted of a dozen buildings an architect who was a poet at heart had painted the colors of clouds. White, pale blue, dark blue, light gray, and darker gray. On the concrete squares, now padded with snow, hordes of brown-skinned children played, for the buildings housed a high percentage of Africans, West Indians, and Réunion islanders. The West Indians and Réunion islanders got along well together. They spoke Creole among themselves. They paraded together through the streets at Carnival time. They celebrated their weddings and christenings in the communal hall, whose walls were painted with frescoes by a Martinican who passed as an artist. By common accord they did not mix with the Africans. Not one. Neither from north or south of the Sahara. They were people of another race who did not mix well together.

Since the elevators were out of order Reynalda and Marie-Noëlle took the stairs, still one behind the other, in building A (pale gray). Reynalda lived in a third-floor apartment, empty in comparison to Ranélise's four-room house cluttered with low tables, pedestal tables, poufs, sofas, chests of drawers, wardrobes, cupboards, beds, with and without posts, and mirrors. Except for some reproductions on the walls, there was nothing but a few mismatched pieces of furniture scattered haphazardly over the floor strewn here and there with mats. But it wasn't the bareness that struck Marie-Noëlle. In a playpen filled with toys, a well-built little boy about one year old, standing sturdily on his bare feet, was methodically wailing for wailing's sake. At times he half-heartedly scratched his cheeks, varnished by his tears. On seeing Reynalda he stopped crying and began to stomp on the playpen mat, waving his arms. Marie-Noëlle turned to Reynalda who, barely motioning her head, said: "That's your little brother, Garvey."

Marie-Noëlle had always wanted another child in the house. She knew full well she shouldn't count on Ranélise, who had laid two or three stillborn babies in the Briscaille cemetery. Even less on Claire-Alta, who was scared to death of getting an unwanted infant. So she consoled herself with other people's children. Along the Vatable Canal she was known for this love of children. On Wednesdays, when there was no school, the women who had to run to market had no trouble entrusting her with their newborn infants. When she returned from the Tribord Bâbord it was not unusual for Ranélise to find her learning her lessons or finishing her homework with a wailing child lying in her lap. A little brother? The gift was enough to lift the veil of mourning of this first day. With a pounding heart she leaned over Garvey, who let himself be embraced. At that moment a man appeared. Very tall, all skin and bones, a tangle of unkempt reddish hair around his face. He was holding a plate full of baby cereal and a goblet. He smiled at Marie-Noëlle as if he had met up with an old acquaintance and softly said: "There you are!"

Then he drew her close and warmly kissed her. That was the second silver lining of the day.

Ludovic always hesitated a moment when asked where he was from. His father had left Haiti for Ciego de Avila in Cuba, where the caneworkers' pay was much better. There he had had three boys with a woman who also broke her back working in the cane-fields. He had lived for some time in Santa Domingo, where he fathered other children. Then he went back to Haiti, for he was homesick for the acrid smell of its burnt earth. As soon as he turned eighteen Ludovic began to wander in his father's footsteps. He put far behind him the bottomless despair of Haiti, tried his luck in the United States of America, Canada, Germany, and Africa before ending up in Belgium and striding across the border to Paris. He had been a docker in the Port of New York, an elementary school teacher at Koulikoro in Mali, a journalist at Maputo in Mozambique, and a musician on the Place de l'Horloge in Brussels. All these twists and turns had left their mark on his face, drawn crow's feet at the corners of his eyes, dug two trenches around his mouth and traced wrinkles across his forehead. A hint of melancholy permanently glimmered at the back of his eyes, as if they could not forget all the misery they had laid sight on. After elementary school he had received no other education except from life itself. But because he spoke five languages, he now worked at a municipal center for young delinquents. Ever since she was quite small, Marie-Noëlle had heard the neighbors' wives cry on Ranélise's shoulder and relate to her the bitter taste of their daily lot: abuse from their husbands, all sorts of ill treatment, and at the end of it all, abandonment. She herself had grown up without the presence or the affection of a papa, and she could clearly see she was not alone. So she had finally been convinced that men were apart and belonged to a different, somewhat malevolent species who were only concerned with their own well-being.

As soon as she arrived at Savigny-sur-Orge, this conviction began to crumble. Ludovic was the mainstay of the home. He was the one who did the shopping, the cooking, the housework—less often, it's true the laundry in the basement, hung it out to dry in front of the windows, and drove Garvey to and from nursery school after having washed and dressed him. Likewise he took full charge of Reynalda. He spoke to her only in Spanish, the language of his childhood, as if he wanted to go back to a time before enduring the stormy tribulations of his life. He put up with her constant lassitude, interpreted her silences, and, without being servile, anticipated her slightest desire, like an understanding older brother. One day while she was passing in front of their bedroom door, Marie-Noëlle saw him sitting beside Reynalda and watching over her as she slept, with the expression of a maman tending to a sick baby.

What was Reynalda suffering from?

Marie-Noëlle never stopped wondering, though she never came up with the answer. As a woman Reynalda did not concern herself with things that are a woman's lot around the house. Some days she bustled about in a frenzy, but in a selfish way. In a cubbyhole she used as an office she would type for hours on her typewriter. On those days Ludovic gaily explained to Garvey that his maman was working on her thesis and that in no way should he make any noise. Other days, back from City Hall, she drew her bedroom door over her like a tombstone. When she yielded to Ludovic's insistent calls, it was to sit at the dinner table without touching her plate and stare in sulky silence at the thousand colors of the television screen, absorbed by an obsession she shared with nobody. She had no conversation. She listened in silence to Ludovic, who provided his own call and response. In a word she did not seem to be interested in anything. Neither culture, nor politics, nor the ups and downs of Africa that fascinated Ludovic. Sometimes a book passed between her hands. Whenever this happened, Marie-Noëlle had the feeling that only her eyes registered the printed characters on the printed page, while her mind remained the prisoner of images she could not forget. Even Garvey and his little games could not capture her attention. She would hug him for a moment, then quickly set him down, wearied and once again gripped by her indifference. Marie-Noëlle understood immediately that her presence inconvenienced her more than anything else. So she asked herself the same question over and over again: Why had she broken Ranélise's heart and sent for her in Guadeloupe where she was so happy? Reynalda was not like one of the monsters whose revolting crimes you read about in the tabloids. She was worse, Marie-Noëlle decided. Neither brutal nor quick tempered, she was generous with pocket money and did not skimp on clothes and school supplies. It was simply as if her heart had no feelings for anyone.

Ludovic, on the other hand, put a lot of warmth into their lives. He was the one who taught Marie-Noëlle how to smooth her hair back with a wet brush, how to iron her jeans, and how to polish and clean her boots. He made her do her homework and work on her English, the only subject she hated at school. For her first Christmas at Savigny-sur-Orge he gave her a bicycle to ride around the squares like the other children from the projects. He let her choose the records, which she herself carefully positioned on the record player. Ludovic was a music fanatic. When he was home, the apartment vibrated with noise and commotion.

Waltzes, rumbas, boleros, operas, gospels, requiems, reggae, concertos, and symphonies merged one into the other. The LPs and singles were stored, labeled, and numbered in different-colored boxes. In La Pointe, Marie-Noëlle had only been exposed to the melodies of the beguines they played on birthdays or the rhythms of the carnival processions she followed from the Assainissement district with Claire-Alta. So she made him angry when she confused Sarah Vaughan with Bessie Smith and *The Marriage of Figaro* with *The*

Barber of Seville. To begin with she mistook his kindness for that of her lost father. Then she realized that, even in his eyes, there wasn't really any room for her in the triangle of affection he formed with Reynalda and Garvey. He pitied her, that was all. She held that against him. Reynalda and Ludovic did not have any friends. They did not go out in the evenings. Their car remained in the garage collecting dust while they spent their vacations locked in the prison of the housing project. Never a friend or a colleague from work climbed the stairs to their landing. The telephone never rang except when Ludovic's cousins called from Belgium, and the postman slipped only bills or mail-order catalogs under the door. But Marie-Noëlle soon learned through her classmates' chatter that both of them were extremely active. Ludovic was the founder of the political-cum-religious association called Muntu. The miracles he worked with the delinquents, mainly Arabs and blacks, could be attributed to the association. Guided by its principles the gangsters no longer ganged together, the robbers gave to charity, and the most rebellious became as gentle as lambs. Maire-Noëlle could not believe her ears when she learned that Reynalda too belonged to the association. That's how people explained her success at City Hall, where, together with another social worker, she was in charge of difficult cases. Her specialty was rape. But she was ruthlessly efficient at taking charge of every wretched woman who had fallen under the merciless grip of life. African women from north and south of the Sahara, West Indians from Guadeloupe and Martinique, Réunion islanders, abandoned by lovers seeking ever younger flesh, humiliated, ill treated, battered, and sexually abused. Nobody could match the way she induced the defenseless to defend themselves and the lifeless to stand up to life, the way she transformed the docile into furies and urged them to demand their rights as well as those of their children. More than one man, obliged to pay alimony and other tribulations of this sort on the basis of her family investigation and testimony before the court, swore he would teach her a lesson she would not soon forget. Marie-Noëlle thought she could see in these revelations the key to a number of small mysteries that had so intrigued her. Why the walls of every room were decorated with curious drawings. Why they never ate meat or shellfish. Why Ludovic, eyes lowered, made a silent invocation before every meal. Why neither he nor Reynalda nor Garvey went to the hairdresser, hiding their mop of hair under tam-o'shanters with three identical colors. Why they regularly disappeared every Saturday afternoon. She was not surprised at being kept away from Muntu. She knew full well she was not part of the family. What disconcerted her was imagining Reynalda as a vigilante, an activist in an association. It was beyond understanding. Reynalda sought out her victims so far away and ignored the girl who was driven to despair under her very eyes. Why heal the wounds of strangers?

Owing to her troubles Marie-Noëlle ended her childhood on a taciturn and morose note. The summers were spent at holiday camps along melancholic seashores. No friends. No boyfriends or love letters at school. She attracted nobody, not even the dirty old men who haunt the stairwells. The only things that warmed her heart were the unending letters from Ranélise, who recounted all the gossip from the Vatable Canal neighborhood in every detail, and her parcels of picked peppers, grapefruit jams, peanut nougat, and pink-topped coconut candies packed in shreds of paper that brought with them all the smells of the lost island. As for Reynalda, she never enquired about Ranélise. She never bothered to send her regrets when Marie-Noëlle was writing to her. Not a card at New Year's. Nor Christmas. Nor her birthday on April 24.

You could have sworn that her benefactor of years gone by had never existed.

A Song for the Parade

by Chudi Uwazurike (Nigeria)

Benjamin Nanah stood at the altar of St. Stephens in downtown Brooklyn as the priest administered the marriage oath. Enosa, his bride, was the first to be asked if she truly meant to take him for a husband. She said yes, her eyes sparkling, the sacred hall and its one hundred witnesses seemingly held in suspense for a fleeting moment, for the ritual response, "I do." But what if … ? What if she were to … ? For—who knows in these strange times, she could actually say the opposite, throw off the white Fifth Avenue wedding gown and, hips swinging, walk off, as in the movies, dressed only in her jeans trousers and a mini-shirt. Oh, yes, sir, be astonished at nothing. So everyone held their breath.

"I do," came the soft voice of the slender woman, stepping from spinsterhood to spouse before the whole world. Relief all around. Nanah could hardly wait for the pastor to finish before affirming this was for better or worse. Within moments, it was over and done. The two-year preparation that had ranged from the halls of Hunter College, where both had met, to the dusky villages back home in Nigeria, where family elders had hammered out the terms of marriage in nuances these two would-be New Yorkers might never fully understand. For them, it had been a whirlwind—from the courtship, the parties, and, yes, the spats to the bachelors' eve, getting the limousine, arriving at the church, wondering who would come, then getting to gasp at the packed hall, actually watching it all come to pass. Now, on to the reception.

Best man Oje Okolo was, as has been his nature, both participant and observer. He thought Ben and Enosa cut a rather striking figure—he in his tuxedo with the gold laces, waxed shoes and all; Enosa, her smile as enchanting as ever, even more radiant. Now twenty-eight, Ben knew she had become a little anxious as to where their five-year courtship was going, especially when he had been severely tempted by the Jamaican sales-woman who had, months earlier, come to sell them life insurance. Ben and Enosa had lived together for two years; in New York, that raised no eyebrows. The news, when it reached Nigeria, created a storm that hastened the pace of things. No one marries through the back door, the two cohabitants were curtly informed by her irate mother.

"Isn't it all lovely?" whispered the chief bridesmaid, Anu Mamadu, as the bridal party strolled behind the bride and groom, preceeded by the six flower girls in their lovely pink dresses strewing the path with flower petals. She wished she could break into a song right now. Indeed, she could had floated the idea of doing something different, insisting she could actually render a song at the moment the "I dos" were done with. Oje had laughed at the thought that she could sing, but he wasn't the scornful type; so she had given him a cassette of her singing for him to listen to in his car. Being a lawyer, she had assured him, did not preclude doing other interesting things. Oje always thought she meant to say: Being beautiful and sophisticated.... There was no question Anu was striking in her glossy dark skin, high forehead, and straight bearing.

But a song at the altar? No wonder most people thought her a little strange—an artist alright. The idea went nowhere; in these solemn affairs, everyone agreed, there were two sides to it—and dealing with God's portion was the pastor's to decide how. At the reception too, nothing amateurish. In a wicked moment or two, Oje had wondered if Anu really wasn't merely seeking to advertise herself, single as she was, wishing all this was for her, this gathering, all the smiles, the floating rice showers, the measured steps from the church to the waiting white limousine.

Oje Okolo and Anu Mamadu moved forward to hold open the door of the greatly elongated car. The driver, an Irish-Italian with strong, square jaws and a formal bearing borne of years of driving one of the Rockefellers, bowed as the bridal couple came up.

Ben adjusted his bride's gown as she reached out to give him a peck on the cheek; watching them, Oje knew that full-lipped kissing, which might be expected under the circumstances, was yet an unfamiliar, seemingly unhealthy, new-fangled addiction. Africans would always feel uncomfortable with this, even at this center of the Western cosmos. Yea, a few things still survive this second transplantation. But for how long? "Thanks a lot, Oje," Ben said, interrupting one of the frequent musings of his friend, whose efforts had assured today's smooth turn of events. "The pleasure's all mine," Oje assured his friend as they both gave themselves a high five, in the distinctive tradition of their college days, with finger snaps. This always ended with wagging of the long finger, symbol of deep camaraderie. Now it was off to the Matthews Ballroom in downtown New York.

It was there, at the reception, as Oje would recall later, that the idea of the parade had come to him. He had watched, sitting at the high table next to the beaming bride and groom, as drinks and condiments were served by white-jacketed waiters. People chatted animatedly. And the music was on too. From time to time, as popular tunes swept many to their feet, the dancing space would be filled. It would soon be time to ask people to go for a helping from the steaming banquet table. Everything was there: Jollof rice and peppery goat stew, ground bean *moi moi* balls, fried plantain, *foofoo* and three assortments of soup to go with it. And much more—salads of various preparation and a long array of American-inspired edibles for Non-African guests who might find the pepper a bit much.

It was fully attended, as the saying goes. Entire families—and it was suddenly clear a new generation, born this side of the Atlantic, was growing up fast. But the youngsters, he noticed, seemed a little lost. Many—and these were the ones not bored yet—instead sat through some of the highpoints of this cultural repast which each wedding had become these days. Neither the juju beats of Peter Obe, nor the *ikwokirikwo* of the Oriental Brothers, seemed to move them, not the oldest ones at least, to tap their feet. Not even the "*Afro-beat*" king, Fela Anikulakpo-Kuti, could rouse them. But Michael Jackson! The kids were on their feet in an instant. The Fat Boys, Run DMC and the rap artists! Why, they had even begun break-dancing with prize-winning gusto. Someone next to him called out to his son. Of course, they spoke in English. That reminded him of another fact of transplanted life: The old tongues were fated to die off. Most of the children would grow up speaking English. The older ones were clearly as American as apple pie. There was something definitely to think about, the larger picture.

Oje stood up and threw the folds of his *agbada* about him—he had long shed the tuxedo in an adjoining dressing room, as had Ben and his bride. They looked even more gorgeous in the matching light blue, embroidered *aso-oke* attire they now donned, he with his cap and she with her head-gear and red beaded necklace. Ambling amiably through the dancing guests, shaking proffered hands but unable to say a word that could be heard through the din of Nico Mbarga's ever-popular *Sweet Mother*, Oje sought out Asuquo Izema, a social psychologist at Fordham University. The professor, a man of medium height and wide girth, was known both for his good humor and incisive mind. That he had chosen to spend his entire career in the United States had often been a puzzle to the younger immigrants, most of whom, in contrast saw themselves as biding their time until things were resolved somewhat back home. But then their own children were growing, becoming teenagers, they themselves battling the tufts of grey hair that shot forth each month, reminding them of the steady march into middle age, even as they reminded themselves each week it was only a matter of time.

"These are no longer Nigerians," the professor explained. "No matter what you do, the younger generation, born American, is likely to stay American. Put yourself in their shoes, Oje. Despite its many shortcomings, even discounting the bogus claim of its being the mythical land of opportunity, in view of the misery it has inflicted on blacks and Indians, and on many poor whites too, there is little question that since the Civil Rights era at least, the States has indeed been the preeminent magnet for people from all corners of the world. Don't get me wrong—this is no paradise. We know better than that. But give me a better alternative, all things considered."

"In other words," observed Oje as he surveyed the hall once more, paying attention to the youngsters prancing about, laughing and fun, "they may never become fully Nigerian."

"Yep," nodded the professor, taking a sip of his champagne, "unless efforts are made to anchor them to their inheritance, they will simply drift into some amorphous mainstream. They will always belong to two worlds."

Oje, a veteran of these conversations, knew where it was all leading. Same story told by and retold by the growing community of African exiles: The corrupt governments at home; the lack of genuine opportunity; the ethnic trap that rendered one first and foremost a symbol of his group of linguistic affiliation, considered an odd person should one dare take a neutral stand on anything of public concern. But increasingly, something else, some greater threat still was in the offing—the seemingly coordinated attacks abroad that were taking its toll on the many hard-working, though self-conscious Nigerians. In the white media, from the vantage point of the black community, they seemed to hear it said: Those Nigerians, smart alecs, like the Jamaicans and the Cubans before them, are too aggressive. For the Nigerians, irritated to no end, the toll was telling. Many winced each time any drug-running brouhaha involving their countrymen was mentioned. Most went into paroxysms of pained embarrassment when the banks seemed to single them out, "tribal marks" and all, as credit card scam artists. In speaking of the two hundred and fifty, many would complain, these holier-than-thous ignored the other two hundred and fifty thousand.

Nodding, Oje felt the outlines of a project take shape in his mind. In this land of first impressions, one's image is part of one's economic well-being. Everyone knew that. Who got loans and how much? That's what makes the difference between becoming an owner or remaining owned. Then someone would raise the point best expressed in the adage of the new chicken in the yard who must need stand on one foot and survey the lay of the land. Then again someone would bring up a Western adage that said "when in Rome do as the Romans do," which was what everyone was doing, both those who worked themselves to death and those who chose the short-cut to the end result that counted material success measured in bank notes. Oje had been in enough of this sort of back and forth debate at friends' houses. A Nigerian Achievers Day, yes! Oje turned to go, but Anu, the chief bridesmaid, was already waiting to lead him to the floor where Ben and Enosa had stepped out to join their guests for a lively owa mbe group dance. The best man must always shelter the excited but tired newlyweds, for this day would mark the second stage of life's three-step journey. The children must come, they must be raised, and only then would this life cycle for Ben and his bride be done with. They would have fulfilled themselves.

* * *

The Man from D. C. put down his glass of champagne, wiped his face, and continued watching.

-II-

Two hours later, exhausted and well-fed, it was time for recollections and advice. The speeches flowed. Everyone, of course, had nice things to say about Ben—a great, bright, future in his palm. Enosa—beautiful, as indeed she was, calm, hard-working, future mother of many. The usual stuff. But Oje was still thinking. The problem with him, and he had known this to be true since his days as a student architect, once an idea seized control of his inner mind, the present tended to blur, even as he remained acutely aware of all around him. But this was important, it needed to be done. Something to say, yes. This is who we are—no matter what anyone else thought or might be thinking. Nigerian Achievers Day. It would call for an organizing committee and a lawyer or two. Endless meetings—dealing with those who would denounce the pretentious stupidity of it all. But the determination of a few would be triumphant. Then, the final day. The hall packed to capacity. The guests of honor arriving. Ambassador Hamza would arrive from Washington D. C., his limousine studded with a visible, fluttering Nigerian green-white-green. The Nigerian permanent representative to the United Nations and the Consul General in New York; a number of other African excellencies and viceroys. From the American side, Jesse Jackson would be notified—but he might be too busy with the ceaseless demands of his Rainbow Coalition. From

Atlanta, Andy Young, who with Joseph Garba, once Nigeria's foreign minister and later president of the U. N. General Assembly, had initiated an era of greater diplomatic contacts between Washington and Africa's wealthiest, if bedraggled, black nation. But General Garba had left; personal contacts in these things mattered some, he knew. Mayor Dinkins would be invited; he might choose to send his deputy, Bill Lynch. The Congressman from Upper Manhattan, Charles Rangel, might make an entrance as part of his weekend rounds to his constituency. Queen Mother Moore, bent and still vigorous in her nineties, she might be there as well. So would those Nigerians who had squeaked up the celebrity ladder in this strange land of possibilities and impediments: most notably, Olajuwon, the basketball star, and Innocent Okoye, the rising football titan. He wondered where the gifted singer Sade Adu had disappeared to. Might be possible to interest some of the Nigerian moguls with vast international connections, at home in Lagos as they were in London and New York: Arthur Nzeribe, M. K. O Abiola, Waziri Ibrahim, and many others. But for sure only those running for something or other in the Third Republic might show up—but that would be if the military barons were ever really to return power to the people. Were Pa Orlando Martins still alive today, his Hollywood past might have been thrown in as part of the solid long links since the Second World War. Someone might recall that the links were made even earlier, in the 1930s when Nnamdi Azikiwe had arranged for Kwame Nkrumah and the other Argonauts—Mbadiwe, Man of Timber and Caliber, and Mbonu "Boycott-all-Boycottables" Ojike, the cultural nationalist—to follow his path in search of the "Golden Fleece" to Lincoln University and then to Columbia. Around the semi-circular high table then, would be seated a great many interesting people. Sure.

Then there would be the honorees—a group of eleven: eight men and three women. The four-person selection panel would be seated at another table, their papers at the ready. Then would come the awards themselves, highlight of the evening. Someone from the committee would explain the ten categories—science and technology, business and management, the arts and literature, medicine, law, accounting, and other professions, the whole lot. He would go into some detail on the accomplishments of the twenty nominees in each area, how impossible it had been to select any clear winner, the several meetings of the committee. People would gasp at the number of Ivy League credentials, at how many had quietly risen through the slippery career ladders of giant corporations and universities, garnering recognition at each step. There would be talk of how this ought to silence those bank managers drafting memos on the few scam artists, tarring everyone else with the brush that ought to be reserved for the rag-tag drug peddlers the press has taken to dubbing "The Nigerian Connection." The image war needed to be declared lest the community die of image attrition.

Oh, but there would be more for that memorable evening. At some end of the hall, an all-Nigerian band, American-rooted—the African Drum Machine, most likely. Their "Flycatcher" song had made the rounds at a few parties recently, with the makings of a hit. A back-up dee jay with a stereo jukebox would be present. Two videographers would stand ready amidst their cables and wide-eyed cameras. He, Oje, would, of course, be master of ceremonies. There would be preliminaries—prayers to the Christian and Moslem God, libations to the ancestors and the Gods of Africa. The guests would have been introduced and seated. He would begin by tapping the mike to test it out, clear his voice, and announce: "And now, ladies and gentlemen, just for starters, the Igbara Dancing Girls! Give them a hand, please." And the drums would roll. A high-pitched song, in fast-tempo, arresting, would rise from the back, and the celebration of a new American presence, would have begun.

Ben nudged him in some excitement. Someone needed his attention outside. It turned out to be a deputation of Enosa's people come all the way from Nigeria—her uncle and her aunt, with a party of six who had gone to bring them from JFK. It was meant to be a surprise. Enosa's cousin from Alabama had seen to it. Arriving late, but still arriving, to give their beloved daughter away; that was important. Ben's clansmen, gathered at one end—their New York association's banner on the wall behind them—rose to give a standing ovation as the in-laws were ushered straight to the high table.

* * *

The Man from D. C. rose to leave, one more foreign guest among these new people. He was prepared for the meeting tomorrow. He had only come to check out a few things. He didn't know why the chief had asked him to handle the Nigerian official. Since New York was the center of their activities, it was logical to catch up with them here, listen to their talk, figure out some more....

-III-

Nigerian Achievers Day, New York, United States of America. The Man from D. C. watched in some amazement. He noticed the small number of white couples present, the rest being either wives or girlfriends of the Nigerians gathered here in their festive attires. Many had come dressed in assorted Nigerian fashions, eagerly gorging the food, faces beaming, glad to be living through a portion of the culture they had become part of.

The Man from D. C., the FBI man, was long seated, readier this time. Whatever happened to the Diplomat he had spoken to three months earlier, during the summer, he wondered? Thought he was supposed to be here. Sent home in chains of some sort? Could be—happened to the best, happened to Columbus the Discoverer, didn't it? Strange lot, these. He recalled how worldly the ageing Nigerian diplomat had seemed. His long stories of how as a youth he had set out to help remake the world. He had come because his embassy had sent him over with a letter of protest over the singling out of their nationals in the media as crooks. The nerve to throw stones from glass towers, the African had intoned, crossing his legs. This diplomat was a rather bulky man, but he carried himself with ease. When would the West stop its blame-the-victim tactics? First there had been the slavers, he said, then the robber barons who teamed up with imperialist carpetbaggers to run the world. Now mankind had become hostage to five nuclear warlords, the awful nuclear genie having been first released to haunt us all, by the Germans and the Americans. A glass tower comprising all sorts—Wall Street stock manipulators and business partners of the Medelín cartel drug barons, financial dupes. Wheelers and dealers always shamelessly casting the first stone at everyone else.

The Man from D. C. chuckled as he recalled his own riposte. Talk of nerves, he had shot back, fishing out a cigarette. Talk of the kettle calling the pot black. (How the African had reacted to that one!) Who didn't know corruption had become an art form in Nigeria? Oil magnates with military friends stealing quotas for the underground market. Currency counterfeiters, import-export scams. Did he wish for him to produce the thick dossier from Drawer B in Basement Office C, on his country's networks, here and in Lagos, Enugu, Calabar, and Kano? Did he? Well, maybe there is something he must see. No one must forget this country is the only one doing everyone a favor by leading the fight against drugs. No, he had wheeled in a VCR and swiftly popped in a video tape, fast-forwarding to the section he described as "apocalypse tomorrow." A man and a woman seemed to melt into one in a surreal haze of smoke and nudity. It was a narrated production in which a male baritone drawl was speaking in the first person.

Out on the ground, in the open courtyard, the neighbors over and about us. Someone in uniform too. He is in a rage, but who wants to know? I see his cap with the eagle. He is a man, he's a policeman, I know, yes I know. Ha! Ha! Ha! Fire! Do I see everyone lighting up? Yes, everyone's lighting up—lighting up their grass, why some have pipes and powdery stuff to go with it. Indeed—who says civilization says freedom! Nothing more. You in your corner, I in mine, nothing in between. Bliss it is to be alive—on the other side of hell. I know. I was there.

The camera lingers—smoke oozing everywhere; bodies gyrating, then sinking to the floor. Merry abandon. Theme music. Fade. But no credits. The end. The Diplomat had turned to the Man from D. C. "You mean—this is real?" It was obvious he was shaken.

The portly FBI man shrugged. He looked quite a contrast to the courtly Diplomat: loosened tie, rumpled jacket, a cigar stuck between his teeth—he was obviously dying to light up. "Could happen anywhere. Your people here better watch it."

"But this is a worldwide crisis. Besides, these people are not Nigerians."

"Yea, maybe not—but you Africans better keep what you have now. It's all simple at this stage, one more tropical paradise that ought to stay that way. Wait until you get your first batch of junkies. The disease will never leave. From carriers to users to addicts—that's how it all starts. I see your people on the move."

The Diplomat removed his horn-rimmed glasses and wiped them. "Exaggeration gets us nowhere. There will always be bad apples in any group of any size. It happens everywhere. Name me the exception."

The Man from the FBI stood up and walked over to the VCR. He pushed the rewind button. "One bad apple, sir, that's all it takes. One roach now, a hundred tomorrow. Keep'em down, sir, the first ones," he mumbled. "But the whole lot of ya boys here—and the girls too, they're into kooky things."

The Diplomat shrugged in his turn. "I'll pass this on to the government, I assure you. If this is the vision of tomorrow, then it's apocalypse." Here was a new war, though he wasn't sure for whose heart it was to be waged.

"You bet."

They stood for a moment in the room out there at the Embassy briefing room, two middle-aged men. "We are on the same side." The two shook hands. The Man from the FBI returned the cassette to its case, retrieved his dark, worn bag, in which the diplomat imagined, there might be listening devices as well. The man put the cassette back in the bag.

The Diplomat was already at the door, about to leave, when he remembered something. "Oh, I forgot to mention—you know there will be some sort of ceremony, some prizes, an award ceremony for deserving—"

The Man from D. C. interrupted. "You mean something called the Distinguished Nigerian Achievers Award being put up by the organizers of something called the Nigerian Pride Organization? In New York, at Columbia University, on June 3rd?"

The Diplomat was stunned. "You know about—"

The Man from the FBI permitted himself a rare smile. "We know everything."

The Diplomat forgot to ask if anyone from the FBI would be there: It was important that they see the other side of the Nigerian community, the dozens of professionals and businessmen and gifted people, the ebullience and self-assurance, the silent majority helping build the economy, provide jobs, make investments, celebrate the best of this country.

That had been weeks ago. But there were other reasons he was here, the Man from D. C. When would the kingpins arrive? He knew these Africans moved in packs. Wherever there was some good time to be had, you were bound to find the whole lot. He had the mug shots. He had never been fooled by all this talk of achievement and all that. Smart chaps, these. But too many speeches and too much dancing yet. He paused at that: Maybe they have it right; work hard, enjoy well. "Isn't it all so nice?" a woman next to him said, making him jump. "Our heritage coming alive to us after all these years." She was African-American; he wondered what she actually meant. Well, so was he. She was no more African and no less American than he was. He turned away with a thin smile for her.

As people drifted home, most agreed that aside from the heart-throbbing dancing, the debut performance of Anu Mamadu was the real treat of the evening, aside from the unsung distinctions revealed of the award recipients. Tall and elegant in her flower-patterned robes, she had strode to the accompaniment of blaring trumpets and begun to sing the national anthem. The crowd, unsure whether to stand and hold their breath, had been mesmerized. Then she stopped, looked at the African Drum Machine bandleader, then at the audience. The Machine began to throb as Nigeria's latest musical gift to the world, Anu Mamadu, broke into "A Song for the Parade." The place exploded—aware that another Sade had just been launched on her career, if only she would stay with it.

It must have been about 2 a. m. The Man from D. C. was still waiting. The party was breaking up. A child whose mother was talking animatedly with another woman, came up to him. "What's your name?" He looked past the boy, noting, waiting. "Tell me! Tell me!" The child was in a playful mood. The FBI man pursed his lips and moved away. He still had to make sense of all this, these people with their seeming joie de vivre. The kingpins had to be here, he knew. But his people had assured him about the kingpins. Were they Colombian? Jamaican? Indian? Pakistani? British? Israeli? Nigerian? Thai? Japanese Yakuza? Sicilian Mafiosi? Saudi? Russian? French? Brazilian? Irish? They would be here and he would know them from their table, their air, their gestures. Or he could dash into the bathroom and unfold the mug shots he had, pore over the forty-nine faces assigned to him. How do you tell a Nigerian from a Jamaican, a Jamaican from a Panamanian? The latter from an African-Argentine? "Tell me! Tell me!" The child had found him gain.

Oje Okolo, a little tipsy and worn out, was beaming as he and the other organizers bade the guests goodbye. Anu Mamadu, now in a killer red dress, curvaceous, charming, joined them. She and Oje held hands as they made the rounds. (An announcement of sorts, Enosa whispered to Ben, hatching a round of coaxing and nudging that would lead back, give it a year or two, to

St. Stephen's, this time roles reversed.) This has been grand enough. A better idea for next year—The Nigerian Day Parade was as good as done. Up Fifth or Madison, Lexington or Third. The community was here; it might as well start living. Tonight, this was the beginning—if only for the sake of the children who needed to know. The end of the beginning, for the rest.

The Woman from America

by Bessie Head (South Africa)

This woman from America married a man of our village and left her country to come and live with him here. She descended on us like an avalanche. People are divided into two camps. Those who feel a fascinated love and those who fear a new thing. The terrible thing is that those who fear are always in the majority. This woman and her husband and children have to be sufficient to themselves because everything they do is not the way people here do it. Most terrible of all is the fact that they really love each other and the husband effortlessly and naturally keeps his eyes on his wife alone. In this achievement he is 70 years ahead of all the men here.

We are such a lot of queer people in the southern part of Africa. We have felt all forms of suppression and are subdued. We lack the vitality, the push, the devil-may-care temperament of the people of the north of Africa. They do things first, then we. We are always going to be confederators and not initiators. We are very materialistically minded and I think this adds to our fear. People who hoard little bits of things cannot throw out and expand, and, in doing so, keep in circulation a flowing current of wealth. Basically we are mean, selfish. We eat each other all the time and God help poor Botswana at the bottom.

Then, into this narrow, constricted world came the woman from America. Some people keep hoping she will go away one day, but already her big strong stride has worn the pathways of the village flat. She is everywhere about because she is a woman, resolved and unshaken in herself. To make matters more disturbing, she comes from the West of America, somewhere near California. I gather from her conversation that people from the West are stranger than most people. They must be the most oddly beautiful people in the world; at least this woman from the West is the most oddly beautiful person I have ever seen. Every cross-current of the earth seems to have stopped in her and blended into an amazing harmony. She has a big dash of Africa, a dash of Germany, and some Cherokee and heaven knows what else. Her feet are big and her body is as tall and straight as a mountain tree. Her neck curves up high and her thick black hair cascades down her back like a wild and tormented stream. I cannot understand her eyes, though, except, that they are big, black and startled like those of a wild free buck racing against the wind. Often they cloud over with a deep, brooding look.

It took a great deal of courage to become friends with a woman like that. Like everyone here I am timid and subdued. Authority, everything can subdue me. Not because I like it that way but because authority carries the weight of an age pressing down on life. It is terrible then to associate with a person who can shout authority down. Her shouting-matches with authority are the terror and sensation of the village. It has come down to this. Either the woman is un-reasonable or authority is unreasonable, and everyone in his heart would like to admit that authority is unreasonable. In reality, the rule is: if authority does not like you then you are the outcast and humanity associates with you at its peril. So try always to be on the right side of authority, for the sake of peace.

It was inevitable though that this woman and I should be friends. I have an overwhelming curiosity that I cannot keep within bounds. I passed by the house for almost a month, but one cannot crash in on people. Then one day a dog they have had puppies and my small son chased one of the puppies into the yard and I chased after him. Then one of the puppies became his and there had to be discussions about the puppy, the desert heat and the state of the world, and as a result of curiosity an avalanche of wealth has descended on my life. My small hut-house is full of short notes written in a wide sprawling hand. I have kept them all because they are a statement of human generosity and the wide carefree laugh of a woman who is as busy as women the world over about things women always entangle themselves in—a man, children, a home. Like this:

> Have you an onion to spare? It's very quiet here this morning and I'm all fagged out from sweeping and cleaning the yard, shaking blankets, cooking, fetching water, bathing children, and there's still the floor inside to sweep, and dishes to wash and myself to bathe—it's endless.

Or again:

> Have you an extra onion to give me until tomorrow? If so, I'd appre-ciate it. I'm trying to do something with these awful beans and I've run out of all my seasonings and spices. A neighbour brought us some spinach last night so we're in the green. I've got dirty clothes galore to wash and iron today.

Or:

> I'm sending the kids over to get 10 minutes' peace in which to restore my equilibrium. It looks as if rain is threatening. Please send them

back immediately so they won't get caught out in it. Any fiction at your house? I could use some light diversion.

And, very typical …

> This has been a very hectic morning! First I was rushing to finish a few letters to send to you to post for me. Then it began to sprinkle slightly and I remembered you have no raincoat, so I decided to dash over there myself with the letters and the post key. At the very moment I was stepping out of the door, in stepped someone and that solved the letter posting problem, but I still don't know whether there is any mail for me. I've lost my p.o. box key! Did the children perhaps drop it out of that purse when they were playing at your house yesterday?

Or my son keeps getting every kind of chest ailment and I prefer to decide it's the worst:

> What's this about whooping cough! Who diagnosed it? Didn't you say he had all his shots and vaccinations? The D.P.T. doesn't require a booster until after he's five years old. Diptheria-Pertussis (Whooping cough)—Tetanus is one of the most reliable vaccinations I know all three of mine and I have had hoarse, dry coughs but certainly it wasn't whooping cough. Here's Dr. Spock to reassure you!

Sometimes, too, conversations get all tangled up and the African night creeps all about and the candles are not lit and the conversation gets more entangled, intense; and the children fall asleep on the floor dazed by it all. The next day I get a book flung at me with vigorous exasperation! 'Here's C.P. Snow. Read him, dammit! And dispel a bit of that fog in thy cranium.'

I am dazed, too, by Mr C.P. Snow. Where do I begin to understand the industrial use of electronics, atomic energy, automation in a world of mud-huts? What is a machine tool? he asks. What are the Two Cultures and the Scientific Revolution? The argument could be quaint to one who hasn't even one leg of culture to stand on. But it isn't really, because even a bush village in Africa begins to feel the tug and pull of the spider-web of life. Would Mr Snow or someone please write me an explanation of what a machine tool is? I'd like to know. My address is: Serowe, Bechuanaland, Africa.

The problem with the woman from America is that people would rather hold off, sensing her world to be shockingly apart from theirs. But she is a new kind of American or even maybe will be a new kind of African. There isn't anyone here who does not admire her—to come from a world of chicken, hamburgers, TV, escalators and what not to a village mud-hut and a life so tough, where the most you can afford to eat is ground millet and boiled meat. Sometimes you cannot afford to eat at all. Always you have to trudge miles for a bucket of water and carry it home on your head. And to do all this with loud, ringing, sprawling, laughter!

Black people in America care much about Africa and she has come here on her own as an expression of that love and concern. Through her, too, one is filled with wonder for a country that breeds individuals about whom, without and within, rushes the wind of freedom. I have to make myself clear, though. She is a different person who has taken by force what America will not give black people. We had some here a while ago, sent out by the State Department. They were very jolly and sociable, but for the most innocent questions they kept saying: 'We can't talk about the government. That's politics. We can't talk politics.' Why did they come here if they were so afraid of what the American government thinks about what they might think or say in Africa? Why were they so afraid? Africa is not alive for them. It seems a waste of the State Department's money. It seems so strange a thing to send people on goodwill projects if they are so afraid of the government of America which is a government of freedom and democracy? Here we are all afraid of authority and we never pretend anything else. Black people who are sent here by the State Department are tied up in some deep and shameful hypocrisy. It is a terrible pity because such things are destructive to them and hurtful to us.

The woman from America loves both Africa and America independently. She can take what she wants from us both and say: 'Dammit!' It is a difficult thing to do.

from *Song of Lawino & Song of Ocol*

by Okot p'Bitek (Uganda)

Song of Lawino

I

My Husband's Tongue is Bitter

Husband, now you despise me
Now you treat me with spite
And say I have inherited the
    stupidity of my aunt;
Son of the Chief,
Now you compare me

With the rubbish in the rubbish
    pit,
You say you no longer want me
Because I am like the things left
    behind
In the deserted homestead.
You insult me
You laugh at me
You say I do not know the letter
    A
Because I have not been to school
And I have not been baptized

You compare me with a little dog,
A puppy.

My friend, age-mate of my
    brother,
Take care,
Take care of your tongue,
Be careful what your lips say.

First take a deep look, brother,
You are now a man
You are not a dead fruit!
To behave like a child does not
    befit you!

Listen Ocol, you are the son of a
    Chief,
Leave foolish behavior to little
    children,
It is not right that you should
    be laughed at in a song!
Songs about you should be songs
    of praise!

Stop despising people
As if you were a little foolish man,

Stop treating me like salt-less
    ash*
Become barren of insults and
    stupidity;
Who has ever uprooted the
    Pumpkin?

My clansmen, I cry
Listen to my voice:
The insults of my man
Are painful beyond bearing.

My husband abuses me together
    with my parents;
He says terrible things about my
    mother
And I am so ashamed!

He abuses me in English
And he is so arrogant.

He says I am rubbish,
He no longer wants me!
In cruel jokes, he laughs at me,
He says I am primitive
Because I cannot play the guitar,
He says my eyes are dead
And I cannot read,
He says my ears are blocked
And cannot hear a single foreign
    word,
That I cannot count the coins.

He says I am like sheep,
The fool.

Ocol treats me
As if I am no longer a person,

---

  * Salt is extracted from the ash of certain plants, and also from the ash of the dung of domestic animals. The ash is put in a container with small holes in its bottom, water is then poured on the ash, and the salty water is collected in another container places below. The useless saltless ash is then thrown in the pathway and people tread on it.

He says I am silly
Like the *ojuu* insects that sit on
    the beer pot.
My husband treats me roughly.
The insults!
Words cut more painfully than
    sticks!
He says my mother is a witch,
That my clansmen are fools
Because they eat rats,
He says we are all Kaffirs.
We do not know the ways of
    God,
We sit in deep darkness
And do not know the Gospel,
He says my mother hides her
    charms
In her necklace
And that we are all sorcerers.

My husand's tongue
Is bitter like the roots of the
    lyonno lily,
It is hot like the penis of the bee,
Like the sting of the *kalang*!
Ocol's tongue is fierce like the
    arrow of the scorpion,
Deadly like the spear of the
    buffalo-hornet.
It is ferocious
Like the poison of a barren
    woman
And corrosive like the juice of
    the gourd.

My husband pours scorn
On Black People,
He behaves like a hen
That eats its own eggs
A hen that should be imprisoned
    under a basket.

His eyes grow large
Deep black eyes
Ocol's eyes resemble those of
    the Nile Perch!
He becomes fierce
Like a lioness with cubs,
He begins to behave like a
    hyena.

He says Black People are
    primitive
And their ways are utterly
    harmful,
Their dances are mortal sins
They are ignorant, poor and
    diseased!

Ocol says he is a modern man,
A progressive and civilized man,
He says he has read extensively
    and widely
And he can no longer live with
    a thing like me
Who cannot distinguish between
    good and bad.
He says I am just a village
    woman,
I am of the old type,
And no longer attractive.

He says I am blocking his
    progress,
My head, he says
Is as big as that of an elephant
But it is only bones,
There is no brain in it,
He says I am only wasting his
    time.

2

*The Woman With
Whom I Share My Husband*

Ocol rejects the old type.
He is in love with a modern
    woman,
He is in love with a beautiful
    girl
Who speaks English.

But only recently
We would sit close together,
    touching each other!
Only recently I would play
On my bow-harp
Singing praises to my beloved.
Only recently he promised
That he trusted me completely.
I used to admire him speaking
    in English.

Ocol is no longer in love with
    the old type;
He is in love with a modern girl.
The name of the beautiful one
Is Clementine.

Brother, when you see
    Clementine!
The beautiful one who aspires
To look like a white woman;

Her lips are red-hot
Like glowing charcoal,
She resembles the wild cat
That has dripped its mouth in
    blood,
Her mouth is like raw yaws
It looks like an open ulcer,
Like the mouth of a field!

Tina dusts powder on her face
And it looks so pale;
She resembles the wizard
Getting ready for the midnight
    dance.

She dusts the ash-dirt all over
    her face
And when little sweat
Begins to appear on her body
She looks like the guinea fowl!

The smell of carbolic soap
Makes me sick,
And the smell of powder
Provokes the ghosts in my head;
It is then necessary to fetch a goat
From my mother's brother.
The sacrifice is over
The ghost-dance drum must
    sound
The ghost be laid
And my peace restored.

I do not like dusting myself
    with powder:
The thing is good on pink skin
Because it is already pale,
But when a black woman has
    used it
She looks as if she has
    dysentery;
Tina looks sickly
And she is slow moving,
She is a piteous sight.

Some medicine has eaten up
    Tina's face;
The skin on her face is gone
And it is all raw and red,
The face of the beautiful one

Is tender like the skin of a newly
    born baby!
And she believes
That this is beautiful
Because it resembles the face of
    a white woman!
Her body resembles
The ugly coat of the hyena;
Her neck and arms
Have real human skins!
She looks as if she has been
    struck
By lightning!

Or burnt like the kongoni
In a fire hunt.
To cut yourself loose,
To be tossed by the winds
This way and that way
Like the dead dry leaves
Of the *olam* tree
In the dry season.

When you have recovered
    properly,
Go to your old mother
And ask forgiveness from her;
Let her spit blessing in your
    hands;
And rub the saliva
On your chest
And on your forehead!

And I as your first wife,
Mother of your first-born,
Mother of your son and
    daughter,
I have only one request.
I do not ask for money
Although I have need of it,
I do not ask for meat,

I can live on green vegetables
For a while yet.
Buy clothes for the woman
With whom I share you,
And buy beads for her, and
    perfume;
And shoes and necklaces, and
    ear-rings!

When you have gained your full
    strength
I have only one request,
And all I ask is
That you remove the road block
From my path.

Here is my bow-harp
Let me sing greetings to you,
Let me play for you one song
    only
Let me play and sing
The song of my youth:

> She has taken the road to
>   Nimule
> She will come back tomorrow
> His eyes are fixed on the road
> Saying, Bring Alyeka to me
> That I may see her
> The daughter of the Bull
> Has stayed away too long
> His eyes are fixed on the road

All I ask
Is that you give me one chance,
Let me praise you
Son of the chief!
Tie ankle bells on my legs
Bring *lacucuka* rattles
And tie them on my legs,
Call the *nanga* players

And let them play
And let them sing,

Let me dance before you,
My love,
Let me show you
The wealth in your house,
Ocol my husband,
Son of the Bull,
Let no one uproot the
    Pumpkin.

Song of Ocol

I

Woman,
Shut up!
Pack your things
Go!

Take all the clothes
I bought you
The beads, necklaces
And the remains
Of the utensils,
I need no second-hand things.

There is a large sack
In the boot
Of the car,
Take it
Put all your things in it
And go!

Song of the woman
Is the confused noise
Made by the ram
After the butcher's knife
Has sunk past
The wind pipe,
Red paint spraying

On the grasses;
It is a song all alone
A solo fragment
With no chorus
No accompaniment,
A strange melody
Impossible to orchestrate;

As if in echo
Of women's wailing
At yesterday's funeral,
Song of the dead
Out of an old tomb,
Stealthy cracking
Of dry bones,
Falling in of skulls
Under the weight
Of earth;
It's the dull thud
Of the wooden arrow
As it strikes the concrete
Of a wall
And falls to earth,
Extinguished
Without life
Like a bird
Hit by stone
From a boy's catapult.

Have you heard
The sigh of a monarch
In exile?

He squats on a log
In the shadow
Of a disused hut,
It is cold
The keen wind
Knifes through his
Torn trousers
Licking his bruised knee

With rough fenile tongue,

    Yesternight!
    Yesternight ah!

The smallest toe
On the left foot
Slowly weeps blood,
A fat house-fly
Drones away;

Under the arm-pit
It is sticky,
The remains of a shirt
Sticks to his back,

    Yesternight ah!
    The hot bath
    The thick purple carpet,
    The red slippers ...

His dry lips taste salty,
A ball of thirst
Is climbing up his throat
He is forcing down
Some saliva,

    Yesternight
    The water on his knees,
    The woman whispering,
    'My Lord, My husband',
    The red wine
    The soft lights,
    Woman's smile
    Inviting man to bed,
    The hot lips
    Of her younger sister
    Firm breasts
    The embrace ...

He looks at his hands
At the black finger nails,

Cold sweat ...
He is choking,
He keeps asking himself,
'But why? Why? Why?'

Song of the woman
Is the mad bragging
Of a defeated General,
Ten thousand men
Dead, dying,
The others scattered;

It is the pointless defiance
Of the condemned,
He is blindfolded,
The rough hand
Of the noose
Round his neck.

Woman
Your song
Is rotting buffalo
Left behind by
Fleeing poachers,
Its nose blocked
With house-flies
Sucking bloody mucus,
The eyes
Two lumps of green-flies
Feasting on crusts
Of salty tears,
Maggots wallowing
In the pus
In the spear wounds;

Skinny-necked
Bald head vultures
Hover above,
While aged stiff-jointed lions
And limping-hipped hyenas
Snarl over bones;

Song of the woman
Is sour sweet,
It is pork gone rancid,
It is the honeyed
Bloodied sour milk
In the stinking
Maasai gourd.

I see an Old Homestead
In the valley below
Huts, granaries ...
All in ruins,
I see a large Pumpkin
Rotting
A thousand beetles
In it;
We will plough it up
All the valley,
Make compost of the Pumpkins
And the other native vegetables,
The fence dividing
Family holdings
Will be torn down,
We will uproot
The trees demarcating
The land of clan from clan,

We will obliterate
Tribal boundaries
And throttle native tongues
To dumb death.

Houseboy,
Listen
Call the *ayah*
Help the woman
Pack her things,
Then sweep the house clean
And wash the floor,
I am off to Town
To fetch the painter.

2

What is Africa
To me?

Blackness,
Deep, deep fathomless
Darkness;

Africa,
Idle giant
Basking in the sun,
Sleeping, snoring,
Twitching in dreams;

Diseased with a chronic illness,
Choking with black ignorance,
Chained to the rock
Of poverty,

And yet laughing,
Always laughing and dancing,
The chains on his legs
Jangling;

Displaying his white teeth
In bright pink gum,
Loose white teeth
That cannot bite,
Joking, giggling, dancing ...

Stuck in the stagnant mud
Of superstitions,
Frightened by the spirits
Of the bush, the stream,
The rock,
Scared of corpses ...

He hears eerie noises
From the lakeside
And from the mountain top,
Sees snakes
In the whirlwind

And at both ends
Of the rainbow;

The caves house his gods
Or he carries them
On his head
Or on his shoulder
As he roams the wilderness,
Led by his cattle,
Or following the spoor
Of the elephant
That he has speared
But could not kill;

Child,
Lover of toys,
Look at his toy weapons,
His utensils, his hut ...
Toy garden, toy chickens,
Toy cattle,
Toy children ...

Timid,
Unadventurous,
Scared of the unbeaten track,
Unweaned,
Clinging to mother's milkless
    breasts
Clinging to brother,
To uncle, to clan,
To tribe

To blackness,

To Africa,
Africa
This rich granary
Of taboos, customs,
Traditions ...

Mother, mother,
Why,
Why was I born
Black?

from *Passing*

by Nella Larsen (USA)

ONE

IT WAS the last letter in Irene Redfield's little pile of morning mail. After her other ordinary and clearly directed letters the long envelope of thin Italian paper with its almost illegible scrawl seemed out of place and alien. And there was, too, something mysterious and slightly furtive about it. A thin sly thing which bore no return address to betray the sender. Not that she hadn't immediately known who its sender was. Some two years ago she had one very like it in outward appearance. Furtive, but yet in some peculiar, determined way a little flaunting. Purple ink. Foreign paper of extraordinary size.

It had been, Irene noted, postmarked in New York the day before. Her brows came together in a tiny frown. The frown, however, was more from perplexity than from annoyance; though there was in her thoughts an element of both. She was wholly unable to comprehend such an attitude towards danger as she was sure the letter's content would reveal; and she disliked the idea of opening and reading it.

This, she reflected was of a piece with all that she knew of Clare Kendry. Stepping always on the edge of danger. Always aware, but not drawing back or turning aside. Certainly not because of any alarms or outrage on the part of others.

And for a swift moment Irene Redfield seemed to see a pale small girl sitting on a ragged blue sofa, sewing pieces of bright red cloth together, while her drunken father, a tall, powerfully built man, raged threateningly up and down the shabby room, bellowing curses and making spasmodic lunges at her which were not the less frightening because they were, for the most part, ineffectual. Sometimes he did manage to reach her. But only the fact that the child had edged herself and the poor sewing over to the farthermost corner of the sofa suggested that she was in any way perturbed by this menace to herself and her work.

Clare had known well enough that it was unsafe to take a portion of the dollar that was her weekly wage for the doing of many errands for the dressmaker who lived on the top floor of the building of which Bob Kendry was janitor. But that knowledge had not deterred her. She wanted to go to her Sunday school's picnic, and she had made up her mind to wear a new dress. So, in spite of certain unpleasantness and possible danger, she had taken the money to buy the material for that pathetic little red frock.

There had been, even in those days, nothing sacrificial in Clare Kendry's idea of life, no allegiance beyond her own immediate desire. She was selfish, and cold, and hard. And yet she had, too, a strange capacity of transforming warmth and passion, verging sometimes almost on theatrical heroics.

Irene, who was a year or more older than Clare, remembered the day that Bob Kendry had been brought home dead, killed in a silly saloon-fight. Clare, who was at that time a scant fifteen years old, had just stood there with her lips pressed together, her thin arms folded across her narrow chest, staring down at the familiar pasty-white face of her parent with a sort of disdain in her slanting black eyes. For a very long time she had stood like that, silent and staring. Then, quite suddenly, she had given way to a torrent of weeping, swaying her thin body, tearing at her bright hair, and stamping her small feet. The outburst had ceased as suddenly as it had begun. She glanced quickly about the bare room, taking everyone in, even the two policemen, in a sharp look of flashing scorn. And, in the next instant, she had turned and vanished through the door.

Seen across the long stretch of years, the thing had more the appearance of an outpouring of pent-up fury than of an afterglow of grief for her dead father; though she had been, Irene admitted, fond enough of him in her own rather catlike way.

Catlike. Certainly that was the word which best described Clare Kendry, if any single word could describe her. Sometimes she was hard and apparently without feeling at all; sometimes she was affectionate and rashly impulsive. And there was about her an amazing soft malice, hidden well away until provoked. Then she was capable of scratching, and very effectively too. Or, driven to anger, she would fight with a ferocity and impetuousness that disregarded or forgot any danger; superior strength, numbers, or other unfavourable circumstances. How savagely she had clawed those boys the day they had hooted her parent and sung a derisive rhyme, of their own composing, which pointed out certain eccentricities in his careening gait! And how deliberately she had—

Irene brought her thoughts back to the present, to the letter from Clare Kendry that she still held unopened in her hand. With a little feeling of apprehension, she very slowly cut the envelope, drew out the folded sheets, spread them, and began to read.

It was, she saw at once, what she had expected since learning from the postmark that Clare was in the city. An extravagantly phrased wish to see her again. Well, she needn't and wouldn't, Irene told herself, accede to that. Nor would she assist Clare to realize her foolish desire to return for a moment to that life which long ago, and of her own choice, she had left behind her.

She ran through the letter, puzzling out, as best she could, the carelessly formed words or making instinctive guesses at them.

" ... For I am lonely, so lonely ... cannot help but longing to be with you again, as I have never longed for anything before; and I have wanted many things in my life.... You can't know how in this pale life of mine I am all the time seeing the bright pictures of that other that I once thought I was glad to be free of.... It's like an ache, a pain that never ceases...." Sheets upon sheets of it. And ending finally with, "and it's your fault, 'Rene dear. At least partly. For I wouldn't now, perhaps, have this terrible, this wild desire if I hadn't seen you that time in Chicago...."

Brilliant red patches flamed in Irene Redfiled's warm olive cheeks.

"That time in Chicago." The words stood out from among the many paragraphs of other words, bringing with them a clear, sharp remembrance, in which even now, after two years, humiliation, resentment, and rage were mingled.

TWO

THIS IS WHAT Irene Redfield remembered.

Chicago. August. A brilliant day, hot, with a brutal staring sun pouring down rays that were like molten rain. A day on which the very outlines of the buildings shuddered as if in protest at the heat. Quivering lines sprang up from baked pavements and wriggled along the shining car-tracks. The automobiles parked at the kerbs were a dancing blaze, and the glass of the shop-windows threw out a blinding radiance. Sharp particles of dust rose from the burning sidewalks, stinging the seared or dripping skins of wilted pedestrians. What small breeze there was seemed like the breath of a flame fanned by slow bellows.

It was on that day of all others that Irene set out to shop for things which she had promised to take home from Chicago to her two small sons, Brian junior and Theodore. Characteristically, she had put it off until only a few crowded days remained of her long visit. And only this sweltering one was free of engagements till the evening.

It was while she was on her way to a sixth place that right before her smarting eyes a man toppled over and became an inert crumpled heap on the scorching cement. About the lifeless figure a little crowd gathered. Was the man dead, or only faint? Someone asked her. But Irene didn't know and, didn't try to discover. She edged her way out of the increasing crowd, feeling disagreeably damp and sticky and soiled from contact with so many sweating bodies.

For a moment she stood fanning herself and dabbing at her moist face with an inadequate scrap of handkerchief. Suddenly she was aware that the whole street had a wobbly look, and realized that she was about to faint. With a quick perception of the need for immediate safety, she lifted a wavering hand in the direction of a cab parked directly in front of her. The perspiring driver jumped out and guided her to his car. He helped, almost lifted her in. She sank down on the hot leather seat.

For a minute her thoughts were nebulous. They cleared.

"I guess," she told her Samaritan, "it's tea I need. On a roof somewhere."

"The Drayton, ma'am?" he suggested. "They do say as how it's always a breeze up there."

"Thank you. I think the Drayton'll do nicely," she told him.

There was that little grating sound of the clutch being slipped in as the man put the car in gear and slid deftly out into the boiling traffic. Reviving under the warm breeze stirred up by the moving cab, Irene made some small attempts to repair the damage that the heat and crowds had done to her appearance.

All too soon the rattling vehicle shot towards the sidewalk and stood still. The driver sprang out and opened the door before the hotel's decorated attendant could reach it. She got out, and thanking him smilingly as well as in a more substantial manner for his kind helpfulness and understanding, went in through the Drayton's wide doors.

Stepping out of the elevator that had brought her to the roof, she was led to a table just in front of a long window whose gently moving curtains suggested a cool breeze. It was, she thought, like being wafted upward on a magic carpet to another world, pleasant, quiet, and strangely remote from the sizzling one that she had left below.

The tea, when it came, was all that she had desired and expected. In fact, so much was it what she had desired and expected that after the first deep cooling drink she was able to forget it, only now and then sipping, a little absently, from the tall green glass, while she surveyed the room about her or looked out over some lower buildings at the bright unstirred blue of the lake reaching away to an undetected horizon.

She had been gazing down for some time at the specks of cars and people creeping about in streets, and thinking how silly they looked, when on taking up her glass she was surprised to find it empty at last. She asked for more tea and while she waited, began to recall the happenings of the day and to wonder what she was to do about Ted and his book. Why was it that almost invariably he wanted something that was difficult or impossible to get? Like his father. For ever wanting something that he couldn't have.

Presently there were voices, a man's booming one and a woman's slightly husky. A waiter passed her, followed by a sweetly scented woman in a fluttering dress of green chiffon whose mingled pattern or narcissuses, jonquils, and hyacinths was a reminder of pleasantly chill spring days. Behind her there was a man very red in the face, who was mopping his neck and forehead with a big crumpled handkerchief.

"Oh dear!" Irene groaned, rasped by annoyance, for after a little discussion and commotion they had stopped at the very next table. She had been there at the window and it had been so satisfyingly quiet. Now, of course, they would chatter.

But no. Only the woman sat down. The man remained standing, abstractedly pinching the knot of his bright blue tie. Across the small space that separated the two tables his voice carried clearly.

"See you later, then," he declared, looking down at the woman. There was a pleasure in his tones and a smile on his face.

His companion's lips parted in some answer, but her words were blurred by the little intervening distance and the medley of noises floating up from the streets below. They didn't reach Irene. But she noted the peculiar caressing smile that accompanied them.

The man said: "Well, I suppose I'd better," and smiled again, and said goodbye, and left.

An attractive-looking woman, was Irene's opinion, with those dark, almost black, eyes and that wide mouth like a scarlet flower against the ivory of her skin. Nice clothes too, just right for the weather, thin and cool without being mussy, as summer things were so apt to be.

A waiter was taking her order. Irene saw her smile up at him as she murmured something—thanks, maybe. It was an odd sort of smile. Irene couldn't quite define it, but she was sure that she would have classed it, coming from another woman, as being just a shade too provocative for a waiter. About this one, however, there was something that made her hesitate to name it that. A certain impression of assurance, perhaps.

The waiter came back with the order. Irene watched her spread out her napkin, saw the silver spoon in the white hand slit the dull gold of the melon. Then, conscious that she had been staring, she looked quickly away.

Her mind returned to her own affairs. She had settled, definitely, the problem of the proper one of two frocks for the bridge party that night, in rooms whose atmosphere would be so thick and hot that every breath would be like breathing soup. The dress decided, her thoughts had gone back to the snag of

Ted's book, her unseeing eyes far away on the lake, when by some sixth sense she was acutely aware that someone was watching her.

Very slowly she looked around, and into the dark eyes of the woman in the green frock at the next table. But she evidently failed to realize that such intense interest as she was showing might be embarrassing, and continued to stare. Her demeanour was that of one who with utmost singleness of mind and purpose was determined to impress firmly and accurately each detail of Irene's features upon her memory for all time, nor showed the slightest trace of disconcertment at having been detected in her steady scrutiny.

Instead, it was Irene who was put out. Feeling her colour heighten under the continued inspection, she slid her eyes down. What, she wondered, could be the reason for persistent attention? Had she, in her haste in the taxi, put her hat on backwards? Guardedly she felt at it. No. Perhaps there was a streak of powder somewhere on her face. She made a quick pass over it with her handkerchief. Something was wrong with her dress? She shot a glance over it. Perfectly all right. *What* was it?

Again she looked up, and for a moment her brown eyes politely returned the stare of the other's black ones, which never for an instant fell or wavered. Irene made a little mental shrug. Oh well, let her look! She tried to treat the woman watching her with indifference, but she couldn't. All her efforts to ignore her, it, were futile. She stole another glance. Still looking. What strange languorous eyes she had!

And gradually there rose in Irene a small inner disturbance, odious and hatefully familiar. She laughed softly, but her eyes flashed.

Did that woman, could that woman, somehow know that here before her very eyes on the roof of the Drayton sat a Negro?

Absurd! Impossible! White people were so stupid about such things for all that they usually asserted that they were able to tell; and by the most ridiculous means, finger-nails, palms of hands, shapes of ears, teeth, and other equally silly rot. They always took her for an Italian, a Spaniard, a Mexican, or a gipsy. Never, when she was alone, had they even remotely seemed to suspect that she was a Negro. No, the woman sitting there staring at her couldn't possibly know.

Nevertheless, Irene felt, in turn, anger, scorn, and fear slide over her. It wasn't that she was ashamed of being a Negro, or even of having it declared. It was the idea of being ejected from any place, even in the polite and tactful way in which the Drayton would probably do it, that disturbed her.

But she looked, boldly this time, back into the eyes still frankly intent upon her. They did not seem to her hostile or resentful. Rather, Irene had the feeling that they were ready to smile if she would. Nonsense, of course. The feeling passed, and she turned away with the firm intention of keeping her gaze on the lake, the roofs of the buildings across the way, the sky, anywhere but on that annoying woman. Almost immediately, however, her eyes were back again. In the midst of her fog of uneasiness she had been seized by a desire to outstare the rude observer. Suppose the woman did know or suspect her race. She couldn't prove it.

Suddenly her small fright increased. Her neighbor had risen and was coming towards her. What was going to happen now?

"Pardon me," the woman said pleasantly, "but I think I know you." Her slightly husky voice held a dubious note.

Looking up at her, Irene's suspicions and fears vanished. There was no mistaking the friendliness of that smile or resisting its charm. Instantly she surrendered to it and smiled too, as she said: "I'm afraid you're mistaken."

"Why, of course, I know you!" the other exclaimed. "Don' tell me you're not Irene Westover. Or do they still call you 'Rene?"

In the brief second before her answer, Irene tried vainly to recall where and when this woman could have known her. There, in Chicago. And before her marriage. That much was plain. High school? College? Y.W.C.A. committees? High school, most likely. What white girls had she known well enough to have been familiarly addressed as 'Rene by them? The woman before her did not fit her memory of any of them. Who was she?

"Yes, I'm Irene Westover. And though nobody calls me 'Rene any more, it's good to hear the name again. And you—" She hesitated, ashamed that she could not remember, and hoping that the sentence would be finished for her.

"Don't you know me? Not really, 'Rene?"

"I'm sorry, but just at the minute I can't seem to place you."

Irene studied the lovely creature standing beside her for some clue to her identity. Who could she be? Where and when had they met? And through her perplexity there came the thought that the trick which her memory had played her was for some reason more gratifying than disappointing to her old acquaintance, that she didn't mind not being recognized.

And, too, Irene felt that she was just about to remember her. For about the woman was some quality, an intangible something, too vague to define, too remote to seize, but which was, to Irene Redfield, very familiar. And that voice. Surely she'd heard those husky tones somewhere before. Perhaps before time, contact, or something had been at them, making them into a voice remotely suggesting England. Ah! Could it have been in Europe that they had met? 'Rene. No.

"Perhaps," Irene began, "you—"

The woman laughed, a lovely laugh, a small sequence of notes that was like a trill and also like the ringing of a delicate bell fashioned of a precious metal, a tinkling.

Irene drew a quick sharp breath. "Clare!" she exclaimed, "not really Clare Kendry?"

So great was her astonishment that she started to rise.

"No, no, don't get up," Clare Kendry commanded, and sat down herself. "You've simply got to stay and talk. We'll have something more. Tea? Fancy meeting you here! It's simply too, too lucky!"

"It's awfully surprising," Irene told her, and, seeing the change in Clare's smile, knew that she had revealed a corner of her own thoughts. But she only said: "I'd never in this world have known you if you hadn't laughed. You are changed, you know. And yet, in a way, you're just the same."

"Perhaps," Clare replied. "Oh, just a second."

She gave her attention to the waiter at her side. "M-mmm, let's see. Two teas. And bring some cigarettes. Y-es, they'll be all right. Thanks." Again that odd upward smile. Now, Irene was sure that it was too provocative for a waiter.

While Clare had been giving the order, Irene made a rapid mental calculation. It must be, she figured, all of twelve years since she, or anybody that she knew, had laid eyes on Clare Kendry.

After her father's death she'd gone to live with some relatives, aunts or cousins two or three times removed, over on the west side: relatives that nobody had known the Kendry's possessed until they had turned up at the funeral and taken Clare away with them.

For about a year or more afterwards she would appear occasionally among her old friends and acquaintances on the south side for short little visits that were, they understood, always stolen from the endless domestic tasks in her new home. With each succeeding one she was taller, shabbier, and more belligerently sensitive. And each time the look on her face was more resentful and brooding. "I'm worried about Clare, she seems so unhappy," Irene remembered her mother saying. The visits dwindled, becoming shorter, fewer, and further apart until at last they ceased.

Irene's father, who had been fond of Bob Kendry, made a special trip over to the west side about two months after the last time Clare had been to see them and returned with the bare information that he had seen the relatives and that Clare had disappeared. What else he had confided to her mother, in the privacy of their own room, Irene didn't know.

But she had had something more than a vague suspicion of its nature. For there had been rumours. Rumours that were, to girls of eighteen and nineteen years, interesting and exciting.

There was the one about Clare Kendry's having been seen at the dinner hour in a fashionable hotel in company with another woman and two men, all of them white. And *dressed*! And there was another which told of her driving in Lincoln Park with a man, unmistakably white, and evidently rich. Packard limousine, chauffeur in livery, and all that. There had been others whose context Irene could no longer recollect, but all pointing in the same glamorous direction.

And she could remember quite vividly how, when they used to repeat and discuss these tantalizing stories about Clare, the girls would always look knowingly at one another and then, with little excited giggles, drag away their eager shining eyes and say with lurking undertones of regret or disbelief some such things as: "Oh, well, maybe she's got a job or something," or "After all, it mayn't have been Clare," or "You can't believe all you hear."

And always some girl, more matter-of-fact or more frankly malicious than the rest, would declare: "Of course it was Clare! Ruth said it was and so did Frank, and they certainly know when they see her as well as we do." And someone else would say: "Yes, you can bet it was Clare all right." And then they would all join in asserting that there could be no mistake about its having been Clare, and that such circumstances could mean only one thing. Working indeed! People didn't take their servants to the Shelby for dinner. Certainly not all dressed up like that. There would follow insincere regrets, and somebody would say: "Poor girl, I suppose it's true enough, but what can you expect. Look at her father. And her mother, they say, would have run away if she hadn't died. Besides, Clare always had a—a—having way with her."

Precisely that! The words came to Irene as she sat there on the Drayton roof, facing Clare Kendry. "A having way." Well, Irene acknowledged, judging from her appearance and manner, Clare seemed certainly to have succeeded in having a few other things that she wanted.

It was, Irene repeated, after the interval of the waiter, a great surprise and a very pleasant one to see Clare again after all those years, twelve at least.

"Why, Clare, you're the last person in the world I'd have expected to run into. I guess that's why I didn't know you."

Clare answered gravely: "Yes. It is twelve years. But I'm not surprised to see you, 'Rene. That is, not so very. In fact, ever since I've been here, I've more or less hoped that I should, or someone. Preferably you, though. Still, I imagine that's because I've thought of you often and often, while you—I'll wager you've never given me a thought."

It was true, of course. After the first speculations and indictments, Clare had gone completely from Irene's thoughts. And from the thoughts of others too—if their conversation was any indication of their thoughts.

Besides, Clare had never been exactly one of the group, just as she'd never been merely the janitor's daughter, but the daughter of Mr. Boby Kendry, who, it was true, was a janitor, but who also, it seemed, had been in college with some of their fathers. Just how or why he happened to be a janitor, and a very inefficient one at that, they none of them quite knew. One of Irene's brothers, who had put the question to their father, had been told: "That's something that doesn't concern you," and given him the advice to be careful not to end in the same manner as "poor Bob."

No, Irene hadn't thought of Clare Kendry. Her own life had been too crowded. So, she supposed, had the lives of other people. She defended her— their—forgetfulness. "You know how it is. Everybody's so busy. People leave, drop out, maybe for a little while there's talk about them, or questions; then, gradually they're forgotten."

"Yes, that's natural," Clare agreed. And what, she inquired, had they said of her for that little while at the beginning before they'd forgotten her altogether?

Irene looked away. She felt the telltale colour rising in her cheeks. "You can't," she evaded, "expect me to remember trifles like that over twelve years of marriages, births, deaths, and the war."

There followed that trill of notes that was Clare Kendry's laugh, small and clear and the essence of mockery.

"Oh, 'Rene!" she cried, "of course you remember! But I won't make you tell me, because I know just as well as if I'd been there and heard every unkind word. Oh, I know, I know. Frank Danton saw me in the Shelby one night. Don't tell me he didn't broadcast that, and with embroidery. Others may have seen me at other times. I don't know. But once I met Margaret Hammer in Marshall Field's. I'd have spoken, was on the very point of doing it, but she cut me dead. My dear 'Rene, I assure you that from the way she looked through me, even I was uncertain whether I was actually there in the flesh or not. I remember it too clearly. It was that very thing which, in a way, finally decided me not to go out and see you one last time before I went away to stay. Somehow, good as all of you, the whole family, had always been to the poor forlorn child that was me, I felt I shouldn't be able to bear that. I mean if any of you, your mother or the boys or—Oh, well, I just felt I'd rather not know it if you did. And so I stayed away. Silly, I suppose. Sometimes I've been sorry I didn't go."

Irene wondered if it was tears that made Clare's eyes so luminous.

"And now 'Rene, I want to hear all about you and everybody and everything. You're married, I s'pose?"

Irene nodded.

"Yes," Clare said knowingly, "you would be. Tell me about it."

And so for an hour or more they had sat there smoking and drinking tea and filling in the gap of twelve years with talk. That is, Irene did. She told Clare about her marriage and removal to New York, about her husband, and about her two sons, who were having their first experience of being separated from their parents at a summer camp, about her mother's death, about the marriages of her two older brothers. She told of the marriages, births and deaths in other families that Clare had known, opening up, for her, new vistas on the lives of old friends and acquaintances.

Clare drank it all in, these things which for so long she had wanted to know and hadn't been able to learn. She sat motionless, her bright lips slightly parted, her whole face lit by the radiance of her happy eyes. Now and then she put a question, but for the most part she was silent.

Somewhere outside, a clock struck. Brought back to the present, Irene looked down at her watch and exclaimed: "Oh, I must go, Clare!"

A moment passed during which she was the prey of uneasiness. It had suddenly occurred to her that she hadn't asked Clare anything about her own life and that she had felt a very definite unwillingness to do so. And she was quite well aware of the reason for that reluctance. But, she asked herself, wouldn't it, all things considered, be the kindest thing not to ask? If things with Clare were as she—as they all—had suspected, wouldn't it be more tactful to seem to forget to inquire how she had spent those twelve years?

If? It was that "if" which bothered her. It might be, it might just be, in spite of all gossip and even appearances to the contrary, that there was nothing, had been nothing, that couldn't be simply and innocently explained. Appearances, she knew now, had a way sometimes of not fitting facts, and if Clare hadn't— Well, if they had all been wrong, then certainly she ought to express some interest in what had happened to her. It would seem queer and rude if she didn't. But how was she to know? There was, she at last decided, no way; so she merely said again, "I must go, Clare."

"Please, not so soon, 'Rene," Clare begged, not moving.

Irene thought: "She's really almost too good-looking. It's hardly any wonder that she—"

"And now, 'Rene dear, that I've found you, I mean to see lots and lots of you. We're here for a month at least. Jack, that's my husband, is here on business. Poor dear! in this heat. Isn't it beastly? Come to dinner with us tonight, won't you?" And she gave Irene a curious little sidelong glance and a sly, ironical smile peeped out on her full red lips, as if she had been in the secret of the other's thoughts and was mocking her.

Irene was conscious of a sharp intake of breath, but whether it was relief or chagrin that she felt, she herself could not have told. She said hastily: "I'm afraid I can't, Clare. I'm filled up. Dinner and bridge. I'm so sorry."

"Come tomorrow instead, to tea," Clare insisted. "Then you'll see Margery—she's just ten—and Jack too, maybe, if he hasn't got an appointment or something."

From Irene came an uneasy little laugh. She had an engagement for tomorrow also and was afraid that Clare would not believe it. Suddenly, now, that possibility disturbed her. Therefore it was with a half-vexed feeling at the sense of undeserved guilt that had come upon her that she explained that it wouldn't be possible because she wouldn't be free for tea, or for luncheon or dinner either. "And the next day's Friday when I'll be going away for the week-end, Idlewild,* you know. It's quite the thing now." And then she had an inspiration.

"Clare!" she exclaimed, why don't you come up with me? Our place is probably full up—Jim's wife has a way of collecting mobs of the most impossible people—but we can always manage to find room for one more. And you'll see absolutely everybody."

In the very moment of giving the invitation she regretted it. What a foolish, what an idiotic impulse to have given way to! She groaned inwardly at the thought of the endless explanations in which it would involve her, of the curiosity, and the talk, and the lifted eye-brows. It wasn't she assured herself that she was a snob, that she cared greatly for the petty restrictions and distinctions with which what called itself Negro society chose to hedge itself about; but that she had a natural and deeply rooted aversion to the kind of front-page notoriety that Clare Kendry's presence in Idlewild, as her guest, would expose her to. And here she was, perversely and against all reason, inviting her.

But Clare shook her head. "Really, I'd love to, 'Rene," she said, a little mournfully. "There's nothing I'd like better. But I couldn't. I mustn't you see. It wouldn't do at all. I'm sure you understand. I'm simply crazy to go, but I can't." The dark eyes glistened and there was a suspicion of a quaver in the husky voice. "And believe me, 'Rene, I do thank you for asking me. Don't think I've entirely forgotten just what it would mean for you if I went. That is, if you still care for such things."

All indication of tears had gone from her eyes and voice, and Irene Redfield, searching her face, had an offended feeling that behind what was now only an ivory mask lurked a scornful amusement. She looked away, at the wall far beyond Clare. Well, she deserved it, for, as she acknowledged to herself, she *was* relieved. And for the very reason at which Clare had hinted. The fact that Clare had guessed her perturbation did not, however, in any degree lessen that relief. She was annoyed at having been detected in what might seem to be an insincerity; but that was all.

The waiter came with Clare's change. Irene reminded herself that she ought immediately go. But she didn't move.

---

* Idlewild, a summer resort in Michigan.

The truth was, she was curious. There were things that she wanted to ask Clare Kendry. She wished to find out about this hazardous business of "passing," this breaking away from all that was familiar and friendly to take one's chances in another environment, not entirely strange, perhaps, but certainly not entirely friendly. What, for example, one did about background, how one accounted for oneself. And how one felt when one came into contact with other Negroes. But she couldn't. She was unable to think of a single question that in its context or its phrasing was not too frankly curious, if not actually impertinent.

As if aware of her desire and her hesitation, Clare remarked, thoughtfully: "You know, 'Rene, I've often wondered why more coloured girls, girls like you and Margaret Hammer and Esther Dawson and—oh, lots of others—never 'passed' over. It's such a frightfully easy thing to do. If one's the type, all that's needed is a little nerve."

"What about background? Family, I mean. Surely you just can't drop down on people out of nowhere and expect them to receive you with open arms, can you?"

"Almost," Clare asserted. "You'd be surprised, 'Rene, how much easier that is with white people than with us. Maybe because there are so many more of them, or maybe because they are secure and so don't have to bother. I've never quite decided."

Irene was inclined to be incredulous. "You mean that you didn't have to explain where you came from? It seems impossible."

Clare cast a glance of repressed amusement across the table at her. "As a matter of fact, I didn't. I suppose under any other circumstances I might have had to provide some plausible tale to account for myself. I've a good imagination, so I'm sure I could have done it quite creditably, and credibly. But it wasn't necessary. There were my aunts, you see, respectable and authentic enough for anything or anybody."

"I see. They were 'passing' too."

"No. They weren't. They were white."

"Oh!" And in the next instant it came back to Irene that she had heard this mentioned before; by her father, or, more likely, her mother. They were Bob Kendry's aunts. He had been a son of their brother's, on the left hand. A wild oat.

"They were nice old ladies," Clare explained, "very religious and as poor as church mice. That adored brother of theirs, my grandfather, got through every penny they had after he'd finished his own little bit."

Clare paused in her narrative to light another cigarette. Her smile, her expression, Irene noticed, was faintly resentful.

"Being good Christians," she continued, "when dad came to his tipsy end, they did their duty and gave me a home of sorts. I was, it was true, expected to earn my keep by doing all the housework, and most of the washing. But do you realize, 'Rene, that if it hadn't been for them, I shouldn't have had a home in the world?"

Irene's nod and little murmur were comprehensive, understanding.

Clare made a small mischievous grimace and proceeded. "Besides, to their notion, hard labour was good for me. I had Negro blood and they belonged to the generation that had written and read long articles headed: 'Will the Blacks Work?' Too, they weren't quite sure that the good God hadn't intended the sons and daughters of Ham to sweat because he had poked fun at old man Noah once when he had taken a drop too much.* I remember the aunts telling me that that old drunkard had cursed Ham and his sons for all time."

Irene laughed. But Clare remained quite serious.

"It was more than a joke, I assure you, 'Rene. It was a hard life for a girl of sixteen. Still, I had a roof over my head, and food, and clothes—such as they were. And there were the Scriptures, and talks on morals and thrift and industry and the loving-kindness of the good Lord."

"Have you ever stopped to think, Clare," Irene demanded, "how much unhappiness and downright cruelty are laid to the loving-kindness of the Lord? And always by His most ardent followers, it seems."

"Have I?" Clare exclaimed. "It, they, made me what I am today. For, of course, I was determined to get away, to be a person and not a charity or a problem, or even a daughter of the indiscreet Ham. Then, too, I wanted things. I knew I wasn't bad-looking and that I could 'pass.' You can't know, 'Rene, how, when I used to go over to the south side, I used almost to hate all of you. You had all the things I wanted and never had had. It made me all the more determined to get them, and others. Do you, can you understand what I felt?"

She looked up with a pointed and appealing effect, and, evidently finding the sympathetic expression on Irene's face sufficient answer, went on. "The aunts were queer. For all their Bibles and praying and ranting about honesty,

---

* sons and daughters of Ham and Noah, a reference to the story in Genesis 9:20–27, which justifies the Hebrews' enslavement of the Canaanites. Ham, the progenitor of the Canaanites and one of Noah's three sons, discovers his father drunk and naked in his tent. Noah curses Ham and condemns him and his descendants to be servants to Ham's two brothers and their descendants. In the Creation legend of black slaves, in punishment for laughing at his father's nakedness, Ham and his descendants will be "hewers of wood and drawers of water" and known by their dark skin.

they didn't want anyone to know that their darling brother had seduced—ruined, they called it—a Negro girl. They could excuse the ruin, but they couldn't forgive the tar-brush. They forbade me to mention Negroes to the neighbors, or to even mention the south side. You may be sure that I didn't. I'll bet they were good and sorry afterwards."

She laughed and the ringing bells in her laugh had a hard metallic sound.

"When the chance to get away came, that omission was of great value to me. When Jack, a schoolboy acquaintance of some people in the neighborhood, turned up from South America with untold gold, there was no one to tell him that I was coloured, and many to tell him about the severity and religiousness of Aunt Grace and Aunt Edna. You can guess the rest. Afer he came, I stopped slipping off to the south side and slipped off to meet him instead. I couldn't manage both. In the end I had no great difficulty in convincing him that it was useless to talk marriage to the aunts. So on the day that I was eighteen, we went off and were married. So that's that. Nothing could have been easier."

"Yes, I do see that for you it was easy enough. By the way! I wonder why they didn't tell father that you were married. He went over to find out about you when you stopped coming over to see us. I'm sure they didn't tell him. Not that you were married."

Clare Kendry's eyes were bright with tears that didn't fall. "Oh, how lovely! To have cared enough about me to do that. The dear sweet man! Well, they couldn't tell him because they didn't know it. I took care of that, for I couldn't be sure that those consciences of theirs wouldn't begin to work on them afterwards and make them let the cat out of the bag. The old things probably thought I was living in sin, wherever I was. And it would be about what they expected."

An amused smile lit the lovely face for the smallest fraction of a second. After a little silence she said soberly: "But I'm sorry if they told your father so. That was something I hadn't counted on."

"I'm not sure that they did," Irene told her. "He didn't say so, anyway."

"He wouldn't, 'Rene dear. Not your father."

"Thanks, I'm sure he wouldn't."

"But you've never answered my question. Tell me, honestly, haven't you ever thought of 'passing'?"

Irene answered promptly: "No. Why should I?" And so disdainful was her voice and manner that Clare's face flushed and her eyes glinted. Irene hastened to add: "You see, Clare, I've everything I want. Except, perhaps, a little more money."

At that Clare laughed, her spark of anger vanished as quickly as it had appeared. "Of course," she declared, "that's what everybody wants, just a little more money, even the people who have it. And I must say I don't blame them. Money's awfully nice to have. In fact, all things considered, I think, 'Rene, that it's even worth the price."

Irene could only shrug her shoulders. Her reason partly agreed, her instinct wholly rebelled. And she could not say why. And though conscious that if she didn't hurry away, she was going to be late for dinner, she still lingered. It was as if the woman sitting on the other side of the table, a girl that she had known, who had done this rather dangerous and, to Irene Redfield, abhorrent thing successfully and had announced herself well satisfied, had for her a fascination, strange and compelling.

Clare Kendry was still leaning back in the tall chair, her sloping shoulders against the carved top. She sat with an air of indifferent assurance, as if arranged for, desired. About her clung that dim suggestion of polite insolence with which a few women are born and which some acquire with the coming of riches and importance.

Clare, it gave Irene a little prick of satisfaction to recall, hadn't got that by passing herself off as white. She herself had always had it.

Just as she'd always had that pale gold hair, which, unsheared still, was drawn loosely back from a broad brow, partly hidden by the small close hat. Her lips, painted a brilliant geranium-red, were sweet and sensitive and a little obstinate. A tempting mouth. The face across the forehead and the cheeks was a trifle too wide, but the ivory skin had a peculiarly soft lustre. And the eyes were magnificent! dark, sometimes absolutely black, always luminous, and set in long, black lashes. Arresting eyes, slow and mesmeric, and with, for all their warmth, something withdrawn and secret about them.

Ah! Surely! They were Negro eyes! mysterious and concealing. And set in that ivory face under that bright hair, there was about them something exotic.

Yes, Clare Kendry's loveliness was absolute, beyond challenge, thanks to those eyes which her grandmother and later her mother and father had given her.

Into those eyes there came a smile and over Irene the sense of being petted and caressed. She smiled back.

"Maybe," Clare suggested, "you can come Monday, if you're back. Or, if you're not, then Tuesday."

With a small regretful sigh, Irene informed Clare that she was afraid she wouldn't be back by Monday and that she was sure she had dozens of things for Tuesday, and that she was leaving Wednesday. It might be, however, that she could get out of something Tuesday.

"Oh, do try. Do put somebody else off. The others can see you any time, while I—Why, I may never see you again! Think of that, 'Rene! You'll have to come. You'll simply have to! I'll never forgive you if you don't."

At that moment it seemed a dreadful thing to think of never seeing Clare Kendry again. Standing there under the appeal, the caress, of her eyes, Irene had the desire, the hope, that this parting wouldn't be the last.

"I'll try Clare," she promised gently. "I'll call you—or will you call me?"

"I think, perhaps, I'd better call you. Your father's in the book, I know, and the address is the same. Sixty-four eighteen. Some memory, what? Now remember, I'm going to expect you. You've got to be able to come."

Again that peculiar mellowing smile.

"I'll do my best, Clare."

Irene gathered up her gloves and bag. They stood up. She put out her hand. Clare took it and held it.

"It has been nice seeing you again, Clare. How pleased and glad father'll be to hear about you!"

"Until Tuesday, then," Clare Kendry replied. "I'll spend every minute of the time from now on looking forward to seeing you again. Good-bye, 'Rene dear. My love to your father, and this kiss for him."

THE SUN HAD GONE from overhead, but the streets were still like fiery furnaces. The languid breeze was still hot. And the scurrying people looked even more wilted than before Irene had fled from their contact.

Crossing the avenue in the heat, far from the coolness of the Drayton's roof, away from the seduction of Clare Kendry's smile, she was aware of a sense of irritation with herself because she had been pleased and a little flattered at the other's obvious gladness at their meeting.

With her perspiring progress homeward this irritation grew, and she began to wonder just what had possessed her to make her promise to find time, in the crowded days that remained of her visit, to spend another afternoon with a woman whose life had so definitely and deliberately diverged from hers; and whom, as had been pointed out, she might never see again.

Why in the world had she made such a promise?

As she went up the steps to her father's house, thinking with what interest and amazement he would listen to her story of the afternoon's encounter, it came to her that Clare had omitted to mention her marriage name. She had referred to her husband as Jack. That was all. Had that, Irene asked herself, been intentional?

Clare had only to pick up the telephone to communicate with her, or to drop her a card, or to jump into a taxi. But she couldn't reach Clare in any way. Nor could anyone else to whom she might speak of their meeting.

"As if I should!"

Her key turned in the lock. She went in. Her father, it seemed, hadn't come in yet.

Irene decided that she wouldn't, after all, say anything to him about Clare Kendry. She had, she told herself, no inclination to speak of a person who held so low an opinion of her loyalty, or her discretion. And certainly she had no desire or intention of making the slightest effort about Tuesday. Nor any other day for that matter.

She was through with Clare Kendry.

from *Autobiography of An Ex-Coloured Man*

by James Weldon Johnson (USA)

There were some black and brown boys and girls in the school, and several of them were in my class. One of the boys strongly attracted my attention from the first day I saw him. His face was as black as night, but shone as though it were polished; he had sparkling eyes, and when he opened his mouth, he displayed glistening white teeth. It struck me at once as appropriate to call him "Shiny Face," or "Shiny Eyes," or "Shiny Teeth," and I spoke of him often by one of these names to the other boys. These terms were finally merged into "Shiny," and to that name he answered good-naturedly during the balance of his public school days.

"Shiny" was considered without question to be the best speller, the best reader, the best penman—in a word, the best scholar, in the class. He was very quick to catch anything, but, nevertheless, studied hard; thus he possessed two powers very rarely combined in one boy. I saw him year after year, on up into the high school, win the majority of the prizes for punctuality, deportment, essay writing, and declamation. Yet it did not take me long to discover that, in spite of his standing as a scholar, he was in some way looked down upon.

The other black boys and girls were still more looked down upon. Some of the boys often spoke of them as "niggers." Sometimes on the way home from school a crowd would walk behind them repeating:

> "Nigger, nigger, never die,
> Black face and shiny eye."

On one such afternoon one of the black boys turned suddenly on his tormentors and hurled a slate; it struck one of the white boys in the mouth, cutting a slight gash in his lip. At sight of the blood the boy who had thrown the slate ran, and his companions quickly followed. We ran after them pelting them with stones until they separated in several directions. I was very much wrought up over the affair, and went home and told my mother how one of the "niggers" had struck a boy with a slate. I shall never forget how she turned on me. "Don't you ever use that word again," she said, "and don't you ever bother the coloured children at school. You ought to be ashamed of yourself." I did hang my head in shame, not because she had convinced me that I had done wrong, but because I was hurt by the first sharp word she had ever given me.

My school-days ran along very pleasantly. I stood well in my studies, not always so well with regard to my behaviour. I was never guilty of any serious misconduct, but my love of fun sometimes got me into trouble. I remember, however, that my sense of humour was so sly that most of the trouble usually fell on the head of the other fellow. My ability to play on the piano at school exercises was looked upon as little short of marvellous in a boy of my age. I was not chummy with many of my mates, but, on the whole, was about as popular as it is good for a boy to be.

One day near the end of my second term at school the principal came into our room and, and after talking to the teacher, for some reason said: "I wish all of the white scholars to stand for a moment." I rose with the others. The teacher looked at me and, calling my name, said: "You sit down for the present, and rise with the others." I did not quite understand her, and questioned: "Ma'am?" She repeated, with a softer tone in her voice: "You sit down now, and rise with the others." I sat down dazed. I saw and heard nothing. When the others were asked to rise, I did not know it. When school was dismissed, I went out in a kind of stupor. A few of the white boys jeered me, saying: "Oh, you're a nigger too." I heard some black children say: "We knew he was coloured." "Shiny" said to them: "Come along, don't tease him," and thereby won my undying gratitude.

I hurried on as fast as I could, and had gone some distance before I perceived that "Red Head" was walking by my side. After a while he said to me: "Le' me carry your books." I gave him my strap without being able to answer. When we got to my gate, he said as he handed me my books: "Say, you know my big red agate? I can't shoot with it any more. I'm going to bring it to school for you tomorrow." I took my books and ran into the house. As I passed through the hallway, I saw that my mother was busy with one of her customers; I rushed up into my own little room, shut the door, and went quickly to where my looking glass hung on the wall. For an instant I was afraid to look, but when I did, I looked long and earnestly. I had often heard people say to my mother, "What a pretty boy you have!" I was accustomed to hear remarks about my beauty; but now, for the first time, I became conscious of it and recognized it. I noticed the ivory whiteness of my skin, the beauty of my mouth, the size and liquid darkness of my eyes, and how the long, black lashes that fringed and shaded them produced an effect that was strangely fascinating even to me. I noticed the softness and glossiness of my dark hair that fell in waves over my temples, making my forehead appear whiter than it really was. How long I stood there gazing at my image I do not know. When I came out and reached the head of the stairs, I heard the lady who had been with my mother going out. I ran downstairs and rushed to where my mother was sitting, with a piece of work in her lap. I buried my head in her lap and blurted out, "Mother, mother, tell me am I a nigger?" I could not see her face, but knew the piece of work dropped to the floor and I felt her hands on my head. I looked up into her face and repeated: "Tell me, mother, am I a nigger?" There were tears in her eyes and I could see that she was suffering for me. And then it was that I looked at her critically for the first time. I had thought of her in a childish way only as the most beautiful woman in the world; I now I looked at her searching for defects. I could see that her skin was almost brown, that her hair was not as soft as mine, and that she did differ in some way from the other ladies who came to the house; yet, even so, I could see that she was very beautiful, more beautiful than any of them. She must have felt that I was examining her, for she hid her face in my hair and said with difficulty: "No, my darling, you are not a nigger." She went on: "You are as good as anybody; if anyone calls you a nigger, don't notice them." But the more she talked, the less was I reassured, and I stopped her by asking: "Well, mother, am I white? Are you white?" She answered tremblingly: "No, I am not white, but you—your father is one of the greatest men in the country—the best blood of the South is in you—" This suddenly opened up in my heart a fresh chasm of misgiving and fear, and I almost fiercely demanded: "Who is my father? Where is he?" She stroked my hair and said: "I'll tell you about him some day." I sobbed: "I want to know now." She answered: "No, not now."

Perhaps it has to be done, but I have never forgiven the woman who did it so cruelly. It may be that she never knew that she gave me a sword-thrust that day in school which was years in healing.

Meta-Score

by Lepê Correia (Brazil)

To D'Jesus Correia

Each of your legs is a road,
Who knows a country, a city,
Black, totally black
And always increasing in size.
You are a closed, whole night
And when you come it's the roar of the seas
That carries me to our motherpeople.

Your caress is the touch of all women,
Your immense body is meadow after meadow: Afro and Brazilian.
Ah, women of the bell-songed children's laughter,
Of the tightly-curled braids,
Penetrating you I plumb the depths of negritude.
And when your body is upon mine
It's as if I were bearing
All of Africana
Dispersed throughout the world ...

The Mighty Three!

by Marcus Garvey (Jamaica/USA)

Three ancient Negroes gathered at the Old Cross Roads,
An African, West Indian and American;
They talked of separation days of slavery,
And pledged ne'er more divided be in world of bravery.

"The tricks of olden times are ended now," they said,
And they must show united front to one and all;
"No more will distance keep us down or ranks divide,"
"So help our God!" the three did swear and all decide.

A bloody slave of sire made in ignorance,
Is sure not binding now, as then, they all agreed:
To God above they looked, all three, in vision clear,
And made a vow to save the race and have no fear.

United stand the Negro man in deeds of love,
A common weal of race to urge, and then to gain;
No more the three shall be apart in actions great,
But, hand in hand, march on to glorious fate.

This is the way for you and me in conflicts drawn,
By men who dare our ranks divide with wanton rule:
Bless ye, be firm, be strong, and stand "you mighty three;"
Press on, and look to God, till you are wholly free.

—1934

Chapter 4

Gender Contexts and Complementarity

Gender is traditionally understood as the state of being male or female, but for Black cultures, race, class, nationality, religion, and culture are added variables that make the study of gender very complex. The approaches to gender analysis range from topics of biological differences between males and females, intuitive processes that determine emotional and physical behavior, hierarchies of aesthetics and beauty, unique approaches to and conditions of coming of age, differentiation of roles needed for group survival, reproduction and family organization, and ideas about love, marriage, and relationships. Gender in an African-centered context prioritizes the idea of gender complementarity, whereby the study of the relationship between males and females is approached on the basis of theories of cooperation rather than conflict. Cooperation among males and females is needed in order to support functional families, communities, societies, and nations. While there is naturally a need to assess the conflicts that arise between the genders, the African-centered approach does not view conflict as the dominant variable with respect to gender.

Gender is most frequently associated with the concept of feminism. *Feminism* is a female-centered approach to countering patriarchy, or systems of male domination in society. Black feminism responds to patriarchy by prioritizing the study of Black women based on the intersections of race, gender, and class. *Africana Womanism* is a theory that initiates the study of women's experience by first embracing cultural identity and communal existence (which jointly prioritizes male experience), including the intersections of race, class, and gender, and by then addressing gender concerns, power relationships, and areas of conflict in ways that strive for harmony between the genders. Gender studies have traditionally prioritized female experience, but in recent years scholars have initiated masculinity studies to include male experience. Black gender studies that focus more on collective male and female roles in sustaining a healthy community feature categories and concepts such as Black sexual politics, yearning, and partnership that emphasize male and female togetherness rather than cycles of debate and conflict, in the pursuit of equality.

This section is structured to provide the opportunity for sophisticated comparative analyses of multigenerational, global, individual, and collective African male and female identities and relationships. The political, cultural, and socioeconomic variables that determine the selected authors' creative treatments of gender in different regions will illuminate the heterogeneous nature of Black life around the world.

Man of All Work

by Richard Wright (USA)

—Carl! Carl!

—Hunh.

—Carl, the baby's awake.

—Yeah? Hummnn …

—Carl, the baby's crying.

—Oh, all right. I'll get up. It's time for her bottle.

—Be sure and heat it to the right temperature, Carl.

—Of course. Put on the light.

—How is she?

—Fine. Ha, ha! What a pair of lungs! She's really bawling us out. O.K. Tina. I'm getting your bottle right now. Oooowaaa … Lucy, you kind of scared me when you called me.

—I know Carl. You haven't had much sleep lately. You're jumpy. Both of us are. You want me to feed her?

—No, no. It's nothing. I'll heat the bottle now.

—I hear Henry coming.

—Papa, Papa!

—Henry, go back to bed.

—Papa, can't I see Tina? I heard her crying.

—Come in, Henry. Carl, let Henry see the baby.

—Oh, sure.

—Henry, while Papa is heating the bottle, you can look at Tina.

—But, Mama, she's still so little.

—She's as big as you were when you were a week old.

—I never looked like *that*.

—Yes, you did. Not a bit different.

—But I don't remember when I—

—Of course, you don't. And Tina won't remember either when she grows up.

—All she knows is how to eat.

—We're born with that know-how, Henry. Oh, Henry, you didn't put on your house shoes and robe. How many times must I tell you that. You'll catch cold on that bare floor.

—O.K. Mama. But why does she cry so loud?

—That's the way babies are supposed to cry. She's healthy. NOW, PUT YOUR SHOES AND ROBE ON IF YOU WANT TO WATCH PAPA.

—Yessum.

—Lucy, here's the bottle. Feel it and see if it's warm enough.

—Seems just right to me, Carl.

—Papa, don't give her the bottle. I want to see you feed her.

—Then hurry up, Henry.

—Carl, let me feed her. Hand her to me.

—No. You lie still, Lucy. You're tired. The doctor said for you to rest. I can give the baby the bottle.

—I'm coming, Papa. Lemme see you feed her.

—O.K. son. Now, watch. I lift her head up a bit, then put the nipple in her mouth. See? She's stopped crying.

—Mama, Tina's eating.

—Ha, ha! Of course, Henry. Now, go to bed.

—O.K. Good night, Mama. Good night, Papa. Good night, Tina.

—Good night, Henry.

—Good night, son.

—He sure loves his little sister.

—Yes he does. To him, she's a toy.

—How do you feel, Lucy?

—Oh, all right. You know … Sometimes I'm quite normal, then I feel faint, weak …

—Darling, don't worry. You're upset. Just let me take care of everything. Ha, ha! Good thing you married a professional cook, eh?

—Carl, I wouldn't be so worried if I knew that we weren't going to lose the house.

—Sh. Don't talk so loud. Henry'll hear you

—I'm sorry. We mustn't let him know that we've got trouble.

—Children have a way of sensing what's going on.

—Is she taking her milk all right?

—Gulping it down a mile a minute. Greedy thing.

—Oh, Carl, what're we going to do?

—Lucy, stop worrying. The doctor said—

—I can't help but worry, Carl.

—But that's the thing that's making you sick. After you had Henry, you weren't ill.

—I know. But everything was all right then. Now, all of our money's tied up in this house and we can't make the last two payments. Oh, Carl, we mustn't lose our house.

—Honey, don't worry. Something'll turn up.

—Carl, did you sleep some?

—No. I just dozed a bit. Did you?

—No.

—Lucy, the doctor said—

—I know Carl. But I can't help but worry.

—I'll think of something. You'll see.

—If we both hadn't lost our jobs at the same time. Giving birth knocked me out of my job. And your boss had to close his restaurant. Hard luck comes all at once.

—Lucy, look … She's finished her bottle.

—All of it?

—Every drop.

—Can you burp her?

—Sure.

—No. Hand her to me, Carl.

—No. Look. I'll just lift her gently and lay her across my shoulder. Like that … then I'll pat her back. Easy does it. There! Did you hear it?

—Ha, ha! You did it as well as I could.

—Why not? Burping a baby's no mystery. Ha, ha. She's gone to sleep again.

—That warm milk always knocks her out.

—Okay, Tina. To bed you go now.

—Let me take a peek at her, Carl.

—Don't get up Lucy. I'll bring her to you. Just lift yourself upon your elbow … There.

—Aw, she's a doll. Is she dry?

—I felt her diaper. It's dry. But it won't be for long.

—It never is. She looks like you, Carl.

—No. She looks like you, Lucy.

—Oh, come on. She looks like both of us.

—That's natural. She'd better not look like anybody else.

—Ha, ha. Are you jealous?

—I'll tuck her in. I think she'll be all right till morning.

—Carl, come back to bed. You've been up twice tonight.

—It's nothing. What time is it?

—It's five o'clock.

—What's that?

—That's the morning paper hitting the front door. I'll get it.

—Oh, come to bed, Carl. Get the paper later.

—No. I want to take a look at the want ads.

—Carl, don't be so nervous. Later.

—Lucy, I've got to smell out a job somehow. We've got only two fifty-dollar payments to make on this house. And, if I live, we're not going to lose this house. You go to sleep.

—Poor Carl. He does all he can. This shouldn't've happened to him.

—Darling, you won't mind if I keep the light on, will you? I want to study these ads.

—No, Carl. I'll try to sleep.

—Turn away from the light, hunh? Aw, let's see here … Yeah. MALE HELP WANTED: Machinists. Bricklayers. Pipe fitters. Masons. Bookkeepers. Salesmen. Hunh. Not a single ad for a cook.

—Carl, stop fretting and get some sleep.

—Aw, Lucy, I've *got* to get a job.

—I'm sorry, honey.

—Carl, we must try to be calm.

—Yeah. I know. No jobs for men in this paper … But there're plenty of ads for domestic workers. It's always like that.

—Oh, Carl. If I were well, I'd get a cooking job.

—Hush, Lucy.

—Well, you mentioned jobs for women and—

—I wasn't hinting that you ought to go to work. You're ill. Now, don't talk rot.

—Carl, I—

—Lucy, don't cry! Everything's going to be all right.

—I wish I could do something.

—Lucy, I'll find a job. You'll see. Aw, here's a wonderful ad. Listen:

> Cook and housekeeper wanted. Take care of one child and small modern household. All late appliances. Colored cook preferred. Salary: fifty dollars a week. References required. 608 South Ridgeway Boulevard. Mrs. David Fairchild.

—Oh Carl! That job would solve our problem.

—Yeah, but they want a woman, Lucy. Ha, ha. I'm an A-1 cook. I wish to God I could sneak in and get that job.

—Aw, Carl, stop getting so worked up. I'm turning out the light.

—Oh, O.K. Try to get some sleep, darling.

—Lucy.

—Humnnnn … Hunh?

—Look, Lucy.

—Yeah, Carl. W-what is it?

—Turn on the light, honey.

—All right. Just a sec, Carl. OHHHHHH! Who are you?

—Take it easy, Lucy. Don't tell.

—Who is that? Carl? Is that you, Carl?

—Yes, Lucy. Now, look, darling. Be calm.

—Oh, God! I thought you were somebody else. Oh, Carl, what are you doing? Those are my clothes you got on. You almost scared me to death.

—Listen, Lucy. Now I'm—

—Carl, what's the matter?

—Sh. Don't wake up the children. Darling, now I'm—

—Oh, Carl. No. Don't do that. Is this a joke? Pull off my dress!

—Lucy, listen to me. I'm—

—Carl, have you gone crazy?

—Hush and listen to me. I know how to handle children. I can cook. Don't stop me. I've found a solution to our problem. I'm an army trained cook. I can clean a house as good as anybody. Get my point? I put on your dress. I looked in the mirror. I can pass. I want that job—

—Carl! Go 'way. TAKE OFF MY DRESS! No, no!

—Lucy, I'm going for that job advertised in the paper. Nobody'll see me leave. Don't worry. I'm going out the back way across the vacant lot, see? I'll take the bus behind the church. I've got it all figured out. Trust me. I'm going to work as a maid for two months in that white family. That means two hundred dollars. Half of that money'll pay off the house. The other half will keep us eating. You just stay home. Have Henry help you a bit while I'm gone and—

—Oh, God, no! You're wild, Carl!

—Be quiet, Lucy, and listen.

—God, I'm trembling … C-c-can't you see that—Oh, no!

—Lucy, don't cry.

—Carl, you're foolish.

—I'm not. I'll get that job.

—No. They'll find out.

—How?

—Carl, people can l-look at you and s-see that you're a man.

—Ha, ha. No, Lucy. I just looked at myself in the bathroom mirror. I've got on a dress and I look just like a million black women cooks. Who looks that close at us colored people anyhow? We all look alike to white people. Suppose you'd never seen me before? You'd take one look at me and take me for a woman because I'm wearing a dress. And the others'll do that too. Lucy, colored men are now wearing their hair long, like mine. Isn't that true? Look at Sugar Ray Robinson's hair. Look at Nat King Cole's hair. Look at all the colored men in the Black Belt. They straighten their hair. It's the style.

—Y-yes, but—

—All right. I'm just about your size. Your dresses fit me. I'll take your purse. I'll wear low heeled shoes. What's more I don't need any make-up. A cook isn't supposed to be powdered and rouged. I've shaved very, very closely. I'm taking my razor with me; if my beard starts to grow, I'll sneak a quick shave, see? All I have to do is say 'Yessum, No'm,' and keep my mouth shut. Do my work. My voice is a tenor; nobody'll notice it. I'll get the money we need and we're saved.

—Oh, Carl! Have you been drinking?

—I'm not drunk. I'm going for that job.

—Oh, Carl, if they catch you, they'll put you in jail.

—They won't suspect anything.

—They will. You'll see.

—They won't.

—Suppose they get suspicious of how you walk?

—They won't. There isn't much difference between a man's walk and a woman's. Look. I'm leaving my suit in the coal house; when I come back, I'll change this dress for my suit before coming into the house, see? Nobody'll know but you. When you're cooking for a family like that, you usually stay until after dinner—to do the dishes. It's fall now; the days are getting shorter. When I leave their house, it'll be night. Nobody among our folks'll see me. Like I told you, I'll change my clothes in the coal house and come in through the kitchen … You keep Henry near you, see? He'll know nothing.

—Carl, you'll make me scream! This is crazy!

—Darling, don't shout.

—Carl, if you go out of that door like that, I'll scream.

—Lucy, let me try this.

—No, no. Of all the damnfool ideas!

—Lucy, when I was in high school, I acted in plays. When I was in the army, I was in company plays. I can act good enough to fool white folks. And it's just for two months. Then we're fixed. Think. After two months, the house is safe, is ours.

—Carl, I don't want to talk to you. Leave me alone. AND GET OUT OF MY DRESS! *Now*! You hear! *Please* …

—Lucy, listen …

—CARL, PULL OFF MY DRESS!

—Lucy, look at me. Take your face out the pillow. Be sensible. I'm taking a chance, but it'll come out all right.

—I don't want to look at you.

—Come on. Be a sport.

—The police'll catch you walking around in a dress and will put you in jail for impersonating a woman. And, if that happens, I'll leave you and the children! I'll just walk out, I swear to you. If you go out that door in that dress, I'M THROUGH!

—How will anybody know? Lift up my dress? Ha, ha. Lucy. Don't be silly. It's easy to fool 'em.

—Carl, stop it! Stop it or I'll scream! I'll get up and scratch you! PULL OFF MY DRESS!

—Oh, O.K. O.K. I give up. I'll pull off your dress. I was only joking. Now, be calm, stop crying. Turn off the light and go to sleep.

—All right, Carl. But don't ever do that again, please. Oh, God, you scared me.

—O.K.

—You're really going to pull that dress off, aren't you?

—Sure, darling. I'll be back in a sec.

—And, Carl, don't worry so much. We'll solve things somehow, hunh? Oh, God, poor Carl. What's got into him? What can I do? He's worried sick. I thought I was having a nightmare when I saw him in my dress. I almost passed out. It's a wonder I didn't scream.

—Hummnnn … Carl. Carl. *Carl!* Oh, God, where is he? He must be in the kitchen. It's almost eight o'clock. The baby needs feeding. CARL! CARL! Where's my robe? He didn't leave here. No, he wouldn't do that. But he's not in the kitchen. And he's not in the bathroom. CARL! *Oh, God, he's not in the house!* I've awakened the baby. Aw, my dress is gone. And my purse. AND MY SHOES! *Did he do that?* No, he wouldn't dare go out into the streets like that! Then where could he be? He's gone to that job, that crazy fool … He'll get into trouble. I know it. I know it.

—Mama.

—Yes, Henry.

—The baby's crying.

—Yes, I know darling. Get back to bed. I'm fixing the baby's bottle.

—I'm hungry.

—I'll get you your breakfast in minute. Just wait now.

—Where's Papa?

—He's gone out. He'll back soon.

—Mama, why are you crying?

—Henry, go back to bed till I call you, you hear?

—Okay, Mama.

—That's a good boy ... What is that crazy Carl doing? I feel I can't stand on my legs. I must lie down. THAT FOOL! Maybe I ought to try to catch him? Or tell the police? No, no. I've got to look after the children. What can I do? Poor Carl's worried sick. That's it. He's frantic.

—Who is it?

—Ma'am, I came for the job. I'm answering the ad you put in the paper. Can I speak to you for a minute?

—Oh. Just a moment. Dave! There's a colored woman outside who says she came for a job.

—My God, what time is it?

—It's a bit after eight.

—I should've been up. All right, see what she looks like. But where did she come from at this hour of the morning? We only put the ad in last night.

—Well, I guess it appeared in this morning's paper.

—I'll ask her. Anne, put on your robe and talk to her. Be stern. You picked a lemon last time. Remember?

—Who picked a lemon? She was doing all right until you started getting ideas about her.

—Aw, Anne. Don't start all that again. I'll let her in and tell her to wait for you, hunh?

—Yes, Dave.

—Good morning, sir.

—Good morning.

—Excuse me for coming so early, but I just wanted to be the first one. I really need that job, mister.

—Come in.

—Thank you, sir.

—My wife'll talk to you in a moment. What's your name?

—Lucy Owens, sir.

—How old are you?

—Thirty, sir.

—You live here in town?

—Yes, sir. Just a twenty-minute bus ride from here.

—You've done domestic work before? You can handle children?

—Oh, yes, sir. I've two children of my own.

—What ages?

—One's a year old and the other's six.

—Who looks after the young one when you work?

—My husband, sir. You see, he works at night in a lumber mill and is at home during the day.

—Have you references?

—Oh, yes, sir.

—Well, Lucy, my wife'll speak to you in a moment. This is her department. Sit down and wait a bit.

—Yes, sir. Thank you, sir.

—Anne, you'd better talk to her. She doesn't live far from here. Seems clean, strong. Knows her place. Name's Lucy Owens. Got two children.

—I'll talk to her and check her references. Dave, if she drinks, I'll not hire her.

—Use your judgment, Anne.

—How does she look? How old is she?

—Didn't ask her. Didn't notice her.

—If you didn't, it would be the first time.

—Aw, Anne, cut it out. Hire the woman if you want her.

—I'll talk to her.

—I'll shave now. If you decide to take her, you might let her try to rustle up some breakfast.

—We'll see.

—Good morning, ma'am.

—You're Lucy Owens?

—Yessum.

—Now, Lucy, do you think you can handle a child of six and do the work in the house?

—Oh, that's nothing ma'am. Give me a try. I love kiddies.

—Here's my little daughter, Lily, now Lily, come here. This is Lucy. She wants to work for us.

—Hello, Lucy.

—Hello, Miss Lily. My, you're pretty. How are you?

—Fine. Lucy, can you cook cakes?

—Ha, ha! Lucy, you'd better answer Lily. She's the boss at the table.

—Miss Lily, I can cook the best food you've ever tasted. I make fudge, cakes, ice cream—everything. I'll put some flesh on you.

—Now, run along, Lily. Lucy, what about your references?

—Well, ma'am, I have a good reference. But the trouble is that the folks I used to work for have gone to Europe and won't be back for two months. You won't be able to check on me with them. But there's Reverend Burke of the Pearl

Street Baptist Church. You can phone him any time you want and ask about Sister Lucy Owens.

—I see. How long were you with your last family?

—Five years, ma'am.

—Lucy, I want to talk frankly to you. We had a girl here. But she was a disappointment to me. She seemed so nice. But she drank. And when she did, her conduct was awful. Guess you know what I mean?

—Yessum. I think I know what you mean. But, ma'am, I don't drink. I'm a straight, God-fearing woman. I just want to give you an honest day's work. You see, ma'am, me and my husband's buying our own place. We're responsible people.

—I like that. One should own one's own place. Well, you seem clean, strong, quick.

—Oh, ma'am, you won't have any trouble from me.

—Well, Lucy, we said fifty dollars a week. You'll have to be here at seven in the morning; we're generally asleep. But by the time you get breakfast on the table, we'll be up and ready to eat. When we've gone, you take care of Lily, do the housework, do the wash when necessary, and prepare lunch and dinner. Generally, my husband's in every day for lunch. When I'm in the neighborhood, I drop in for lunch. Understand?

—Yessum. That's quite all right. You just keep to your schedule and tell me what you want done and I'll do it.

—Thank you ma'am.

—Now, Lucy, I'll show you around the house. This is the sun porch. As you see, this is the entry. There's the living room. Here's our bedroom. There's the bath. And here's Lily's room. And that's a guest room. Here's the dining room. And here's the kitchen.

—Oh, it's big ma'am.

—To save trouble, we eat breakfast in the kitchen.

—I understand. Oh, what a pretty refrigerator.

—It's the latest. And there's the washing machine.

—I can handle 'em all, ma'am.

—The food's here in the pantry. Knives and forks and dishes are here. Soap powder. Mops. Brooms. There's the backyard where you hang up clothes to dry. But your main job's looking after Lucy.

—Mama, does Lucy know about Little Red Riding Hood?

—Miss Lily, I know all about her.

—O.K., Lucy. Now, do you think you can rustle up some breakfast for us?

—I'll try, ma'am. What would you-all want?

—What do you specialize in for breakfast, Lucy?

—Reckon you all would love some pancakes? I cook 'em light as a feather. You can digest 'em in your sleep.

—Just a moment, Lucy. Dave!

—Yeah, Anne.

—Lucy wants to try her hand at some pancakes. She says she's good at 'em.

—Well, tell her to rustle some up. I haven't had any good pancakes since Heck was a pup.

—You've got your orders, Lucy.

—Ha, ha! Yessum. Pancakes coming up. Hot and with maple syrup and butter. Ha, ha!

—Breakfast is ready, everybody!

—O.K., Lucy. Come on, Lily. Lucy, Lily and I always eat breakfast together. Mrs. Fairchild's still in the bath and will eat later. She's on a strict diet and will only want a slice of toast and black coffee. She won't leave for work until a bit later.

—I understand, sir.

—Lucy, these pancakes are wonderful. Anne, you ought to try one, really. Lily, tell Mama how good they are.

—Mama, they're like cake.

—Hummmnnn … I want a stack of five of 'em.

—Dave, watch your waistline.

—Lucy, I haven't had pancakes like this in years. Hummnnn …

—Better eat your fill of 'em, Mister Dave.

—Lily, take some more.

—Sure, Papa. They're so good.

—Mister Dave, you want me to make another batch for you?

—Yeah. You'd better cook me another batch, Lucy.

—O.K. Another batch of pancakes coming up!

—Oh, Papa, she cooks real good.

—Sh. Don't talk so loud. We don't want to spoil her. That gal knows her onions. Don't know what she put in these cakes, but I'm taking a third stack of 'em. Anne!

—Yes, Dave.

—I'm downing these cakes. God, they're good.

—All right, Dave. Glad you like 'em. See you at lunch, maybe. And, Lily, I want you to be nice to Lucy, hear? You obey her. No screaming, no tantrums.

—Yes, Mama. I like Lucy. She's big and strong. Papa, may I have another pancake.

—Anne, Lily's already eating better.

—I'm sure happy about that.

—And, Anne, this coffee's good. Hummmnnn ... It's good to have a solid breakfast before hitting those streets in the morning.

—Well, Anne, I'm off. Will I see you for lunch?
—If I can make it, Dave. Good-by
—Good-by, Papa.
—Good-by, Lily. Run on back into the kitchen and stay with Lucy while Mama takes her bath.

—Hello, Lucy. What're you doing?
—Come in, Lily. I'm washing the dishes. Be through in a sec.
—Lucy, can you sing?
—Oh, yes. Why?
—Then sing something for me. Bertha used to sing all the time.
—Well, what do you want me to sing?
—Ha, ha. I know. Oh, all right. Let's see.

Swing low, sweet chariot
Coming for to carry me home ...
Looked over Jordan and what did I see?
A band of angels coming after me,
Coming for to carry me home ...

—That's pretty. Wish I could sing like that.
—You can. When you're a bit older.
—How'd you learn to sing that song?
—It was so long ago, I've forgotten, Lily.
—Lucy, your arms are so big.
—Hunh?
—And there's so much hair on them.
—Oh, that's nothing.
—And you've got so many big muscles.
—Oh, that comes from washing and cleaning and cooking. Lifting heavy pots and pans.
—And your voice is not at all like Bertha's.
—What do you mean?
—Your voice is heavy, like a man's.
—Oh, that's from singing so much, child.
—And you hold your cigarette in your mouth like Papa holds his, with one end dropping down.
—Huhn? Oh, that's because my hands are busy, child.
—That's just what Papa said when I asked him about it.

—You notice everything, don't you, Lily?

—Sure. I like to look at other people. Gee, Lucy, you move so quick and rough in the kitchen. You can lift that whole pile of dishes with one hand. Bertha couldn't do that.

—Just a lot of experience, Lily. Say, why don't you play with your dolls?

—I just like to watch you.

—Oh, Lucy!

—Mama's calling you, Lucy.

—Yessum, Mrs. Fairchild.

—That's today's wash, Lucy.

—Yessum. I understand. Lily, suppose you come with me on the porch while I put this washing in the machine, hunh? Now, we'll put this soap powder in. Then we'll run in the hot water … Now, I'll dump all the white clothes in. There. Wasn't that quick? Now, I'll throw the switch. There. The clothes are being washed.

—Gee, Lucy, you work like a machine.

—God, child, you do notice everything, don't you? But don't look too much or you might see things you won't understand.

—What do you mean? How? Why?

—Ha, ha. Nothing. Now, Lily, while I clean the house, what do you want to do? Watch me or play?

—I want to play in my sand pile.

—Where is it?

—In the backyard.

—Well, come on and show me.

—It's right by the fence. There it is.

—What a pile of sand. Child, you're lucky.

—Papa bought me a whole truck load of sand to play in.

—Suppose, I build you a sand castle?

—Oh, that'd be fun.

—Well, let's see. First, we'll make the foundation, like this … Then we start the walls. That's right. Pat the walls smoothly. Take your time. Now we'll try to make the doorway. About here, hunh?

—Oh, yes. Lucy, this is going to be a wonderful castle. I can finish it now. I know how.

—You really think so?

—Sure.

—Well, I'll get inside and start my work on the house.

—Lucy!

—Yessum. I'm coming.

—Come here, please!

—Yessum. On the way, ma'am.

—Lucy!

—Yessum. Where are you, Mrs. Fairchild?

—I'm here in the bathroom. Won't you come in? I want you to wash my back.

—Hunh?

—Come into the bathroom.

—Ma'am?

—Right here. I hear you. Open the door and come in. I want you to wash my back.

—Yessum.

—Lucy, can't you hear me?

—Yessum.

—Then open the door and come in.

—Er ... Er, yessum.

—Well, what's the matter, Lucy? Why are you poking your head like that around the door? Come in. I want you to wash my back with this brush. Come on in. I haven't got all day, Lucy.

—Yessum.

—I don't want to be late for work. Well, come on. Why are you standing there and staring like that at me?

—Er ...

—Don't you feel well, Lucy?

—Yessum.

—Them come here and wash my back.

—Yessum.

—That's it. Scrub hard. I won't break. Do it hard. Oh, Lord, what's the matter with you? Your arm's shaking. Lucy?

—Ma'am.

—What's come over you? Are you timid or ashamed or something?

—No'm.

—Are you upset because I'm sitting here naked in the bathtub?

—Oh, no, ma'am.

—Then what's the matter? My God, your face is breaking out in sweat. You look terrible. Are you ill, Lucy?

—No, ma'am. I'm all right.

—Then scrub my back. Hard. Why, your arms are like rubber. Well, I never. You're acting very strange. Do I offend you because I ask you to wash my back? Bertha always helped me with my bath ...

—It's just the first t-t-time ...

—Oh, I see. Well, I don't see why I should frighten you. I'm a woman like you are.

—Yessum.

—A bit harder, Lucy. Higher, up between my shoulder blades. That's it, that's it. Aw … Good. That's enough. Now, Lucy, hand me that towel over there. Where're you going? You're not leaving yet. I'm not through. Oh, I must be careful getting out of this tub. Tubs are dangerous things; you can have accidents by slipping in tubs … Lucy, give me the towel … WHAT IS HAPPENING TO YOU, LUCY? Why are you staring at me like that? Take a hand towel from that rack and wipe your face. Are you well? Maybe the doctor ought to take a good look at you. My brother-in-law, Burt Stallman, is a doctor. Do you want me to call him for you?

—It's just hot in here, ma'am.

—Hot? Why it's rather cold to me. I'm cold, you're hot. What's wrong with you? HAND ME THE TOWEL! Now that box of talcum … Thanks. Now, Lucy, sit here on this stool a moment. There's something I must say to you and there's no better time than now, while I'm drying myself. I want to talk frankly to you, as one woman to another.

—Yessum.

—Now, I didn't tell you when you first came here why I had to get rid of my last maid. Now, look, my husband, Dave, likes to take a drink now and then—maybe a drop more than is good for him. Otherwise, he's perfectly sober, thoughtful, and easy to get along with. You know what I mean?

—Yessum. I think I know.

—Now, Bertha too did a little drinking now and then. And, when both of 'em started drinking—well, you can imagine what happened. Understand?

—Yessum.

—Now, Lucy, tell me: do you drink?

—No Ma'am. Not a drop.

—Good. As long as you don't drink, my husband won't bother you and you can very well defend yourself. Just push him away. Now, as one woman to another, do we understand each other?

—Mrs. Fairchild, your husband isn't going to touch me.

—Well, I'm glad to hear you say it like that. Dave's not so much a problem, Lucy. He gets the way men get sometimes. Afterwards he's ashamed enough to want to go out and drown himself or something. Understand? Any strong-minded person can handle Dave when he's like that. But if you're like Bertha, then trouble's bound to come.

—Yessum. You can depend on me, Mrs. Fairchild.

—Oh, Lucy, I've just got to watch my figure. Don't you think I'm fat?

—Ma'am, some folks are naturally a bit heavy, you know.

—But my breasts—aren't they much too large?

—Maybe … a little …

—And my thighs, aren't they rather large too?

—Well, not especially, Ma'am.

—Lucy, you are too polite to tell me what you really think. I wish I were as slender as you. How do you manage it?

—Just working hard, I guess, ma'am.

—Really, Lucy, I like you very much. Ha, ha! You're like a sixteen-year-old girl. I'm surprised that you've had two children. Listen, Lucy, what I've discussed with you about my husband is just between us, see?

—Yessum. I won't open my mouth to anybody, Ma'am.

—How do you and your husband get along?

—Oh, fine ma'am.

—Oh, yes, Lucy … For lunch I want spinach, lamb chops, boiled potatoes, salad, and stewed pears. Coffee. Tonight we eat out.

—Yessum. I'll remember.

—Lucy, hand me my brassiere there …

—Yessum.

—Lord, even when I don't eat, I get fat … Give me my panties, Lucy.

—Yessum.

—Well, that's all, Lucy. You can go back to your work.

—Ma'am, the coffee's still hot. You want some toast?

—I won't touch a crumb of bread. Just black coffee.

—Yessum. I'm going to see what little Lily is up to.

—That's right, Lucy. Keep your eye on her.

—Lily! Lily!

—I'm here Lucy. Look at my castle.

—Well, you've almost finished it.

—Lucy, what's the matter? Your face is wet … You're shaking.

—Oh, nothing. I just want to sit here on the steps for a moment and get my breath. It was hot in that bathroom.

—You look scared, Lucy.

—Sometimes I'm short of breath, that's all.

—Do you really like my castle?

—It's wonderful.

—Lucy!

—Yessum, Mrs. Fairchild.

—Good-by. Good-by, Lily.

—Good-by, Mama.

—Good-by, Mrs. Fairchild.

—Oh, Lily!
—Yes.
—Your lunch's ready. You must eat and then take your nap.
—I'm coming, Lucy.
—No, Lily. You must come right now, while your food's hot.
—Oh, all right.
—Did you wash your hands?
—Yes.
—Sit down. Tuck your napkin in. Here's some nice spinach.
—I don't like spinach.
—It's good for you. Eat it. There's ice cream for dessert.
—What kind?
—Chocolate.
—I like vanilla.
—All right, now. Open your mouth and eat. Let's go.
—Lucy, your face is hard.
—Hunh?
—And very rough.
—Ha, ha. I've been working hard all my life, Lily. That's why. Why are you always staring at me so? Don't look at me. Eat.
—Papa's lunch is ready?
—Yes, lunch is ready for your papa and your mama.
—Is Mama coming to lunch?
—Don't know. Now, eat your food. Stop talking.
—Lucy, are you going to be like Bertha?
—What do you mean?
—Are you going to wrestle with Papa too?
—Hunh? Ha, ha. No, not me, Lily.
—Ha, ha. Bertha was always wrestling with Papa, running from room to room.
—What happened?
—I don't know. But it was funny. I could hear Bertha hollering. They'd make so much noise I couldn't take my nap. And Papa'd give me a dime not to tell Mama.
—I won't wrestle with your papa. You'll be able to sleep.
—Aw, but Papa is quick and strong.
—I can outrun him.
—He'll catch you like he did Bertha and make you wrestle with him.
—Stop talking, Lily, and eat your lamb chop.
—I'm eating, Lucy.

—Unless you eat faster, you won't be in bed by the time they come.

—You want me in bed, when Papa comes?

—I didn't say that.

—Bertha always made me eat fast so I would be sleeping when Papa came.

—Hummnnn ... Say, tell me a bit more about how Bertha wrestled with your papa.

—They just wrestled.

—Did it happen often?

—Almost everyday. Then Bertha left.

—Why?

—Mama said it was not nice for a lady to wrestle with a man.

—That's right, Lily.

—Lucy, don't you ever wear lipstick, like Mama?

—Oh, when I need to. Come on, Lily. Open your mouth and eat. Stop playing around. Oh, what's that whistle?

—That's the mailman.

—Now, you just eat. I'll go to the door and get the mail.

—He's Bertha's friend. He's colored, you know.

—Oh.

—Bertha used to invite him in. Are you?

—No. Now, you eat. I'll get the mail.

—Any mail, Lucy?

—Just one letter for your father.

—Did you see the mailman? Talk to him?

—No. He was leaving the door and I didn't call him.

—Bertha always did.

—I'm not Bertha.

—But isn't he your friend too?

—No.

—Don't you know his name?

—No, Lily. What is it?

—His name is Kirby Rickford.

—Oh, yeah. I've heard of him.

—Bertha used to invite him in.

—Well, I won't.

—And Bertha used to give him a drink out of Papa's bottle.

—Now, Lily, here's your dessert. While you're eating it, I'll set the table for your mother and father, hear?

—O.K., Lucy. But you're not at all like Bertha—

—Hello! Hello! Anybody in?

—Oh, Papa! Lucy, Papa's come home.

—Hello, Lily. Are you still eating?

—I'm almost through, Papa.

—I always told you to be in bed when I came—

—I was talking to Lucy, Papa.

—Oh, hello there, Lucy.

—Hello, Mr. Fairchild.

—Is everything all right, Lucy?

—Yessir. Everything's fine, sir.

—Did she eat all right, Lucy?

—Oh, so-so, Mr. Fairchild.

—Here, Lily, let me feed you this ice cream.

—I don't want it, Papa, is Mama coming to lunch?

—I don't know.

—You're going to eat by yourself?

—Maybe.

—Papa, where did Bertha go?

—I don't know. And stop talking about Bertha. Finish your ice cream.

—Ooowwa … Papa, don't be angry with me …

—Aw, come on, Lily. It's bedtime, *now*.

—You always want me to go to bed when you come home. I know. You want to talk to Lucy.

—Will you shut your mouth and eat! Now, let me see where in the hell did Anne hide my bottle. She's always trying to keep it from me. Have you seen my bottle around, Lucy?

—What kind of bottle, sir?

—You know. My bottle of whiskey. I need a little nip.

—No, sir. I haven't seen it.

—Oh, here it is. I hid it so well that I hid it from myself. Say, Lucy?

—Yessir.

—Would you like a little nip?

—Oh, no, sir. I don't drink at all.

—That's a shame. A nip never hurt anybody. There's nothing better than a good drink before lunch to get your food down.

—No, sir. It's for those who like it, sir.

—Whisky's a lot of fun, Lucy.

—I wouldn't know, sir.

—I like my whiskey, Lucy.

—Papa, did you bring me something?

—Hunh? No, darling. I never bring you anything at noon. I'll bring you something tonight. Now, finish eating.

—What'll you bring me?

—Oh, that'll be your surprise. Aw, that was a good shot ... Lily, finish eating. Say, Lucy, Lucy! Where'd she go?

—She's in the kitchen, Papa.

—Lucy!

—Yessir.

—What're you doing there in that kitchen?

—Putting the lamb chops on, sir.

—Sure you won't have a nip?

—No, sir. Thank you, sir.

—Too bad.

—I'm through now, Papa. Do I take my nap?

—Yes, right away. Lucy, come and put Lily to bed ...

—Yessir. Come on, Lily. Go right into your room and get your dress off. That's it.

—You're going to play with Papa, Lucy?

—Shut up and take off those sandals.

—O.K.

—Lucy, did Lily obey you?

—Oh, yessir. Now, Lily, climb right into bed. That's it. Pull the blanket over you lightly. That's right. Now, take a nice nap. I'm closing the door.

—You sure know how to handle people, Lucy.

—Oh, I manage, Mr. Fairchild.

—Lucy, come on and have a drink with me.

—Never drink, Mr. Fairchild.

—Where're you going now?

—I've got to tend to the lamb chops, sir.

—Lucy, you're such an A-1 cook, I want to see how you do it.

—Just ordinary cooking, sir.

—Aw, Lucy. Huumnnnn ...

—Take your hand away, Mr. Fairchild.

—Aw, come on.

—Take your hand off, Mr. Fairchild.

—Is your old man good to you, Lucy?

—Mr. Fairchild, you're going to make it impossible for me to work here.

—Lucy, I bet your old man's no good to you.

—Mr. Fairchild, don't touch me. Let me work.

—Gosh, you're cheeky. Not like Bertha, hunh? I just want to make you feel good.

—Take your hand away!

—Don't shout, Lucy. I'm only playing.

—If you touch me again, I'll grab you, Mr. Fairchild.

—Look who's threatening. You're going to grab me, hunh? Baby, that's just what I want. Aw, come on …

—I told you to stop.

—Goddamn, you're a strong bitch, eh? I can't hold you, hunh?

—Leave me alone, Mr. Fairchild!

—Goddamn, you're as strong as a man. Well, we'll see who's the stronger. I'll set my drink down and test you out, gal.

—Keep away, Mr. Fairchild.

—Damn, you've got guts. You're spry, like a spring chicken. Come here.

—I've got hold of your arm, Mr. Fairchild. If you move, I'll twist it!

—Goddamn, this nigger woman says she'll lick me. We'll see!

—Ooooow! Mr. Fairchild, it's your fault. You made me push those dishes over.

—Keep still, Lucy. You're crazy if you think you can handle me.

—I'm warning you, Mr. Fairchild!

—Damn, if you're not like steel. Let my hands go. I'll teach you.

—Stop, Mr. Fairchild. I'll pick you up and throw you.

—Godammit, I dare you, I double dare you!

—I'm asking you once more to get away from me!

—You're a sassy nigger bitch, aren't you?

—Let me go, Mr. Fairchild. Your chops are burning!

—Papa, what's happening?

—Go back to bed, Lily!

—Oh, Papa's wrestling with Lucy like he wrestled with Bertha.

—Lily, I said go back to bed.

—Yes, Papa. but—

—Get away, Mr. Fairchild.

—I'm going to teach you a lesson, Lucy.

—Oh, Papa! You knocked the table over!—Oh, Lucy, you!—

—You black bitch, you hit me!

—Papa, you're hurt? Lucy, you knocked Papa down.

—I got you, Mr. Fairchild. I'll let you up if you promise to leave me alone.

—I'll get up from here and break your neck. Turn my hands loose! Turn me loose or I'll kick you in the stomach!

—O.K., Lucy. Let me up.

—You'll let me cook?

—Yeah. Let me up.

—There, Mr. Fairchild. Now, leave me alone.

—Lily, go back to bed.
—Yes, Papa. You're hurt Papa?
—No. Goddamn, Lucy, I don't believe you're that strong. I'm coming after you.
—Mr. Fairchild, you're crazy. Stay away from me. I'll hit you!
—Haw. We'll see.
—I'm warning you. Stay away.
—Now, I got you!
—Turn me loose, Mr. Fairchild.
—Give up, Lucy.
—I'm telling you but once.
—Arrrrk! Jesus …
—Don't kill Papa, Lucy!
—I told you, Mr. Fairchild. Now, I'll hit you again if you
—No, no! Turn my leg loose! If I hit you again, I'll knock you out.
—Naw, Lucy! Goddammit, you're as strong as a mule!
—Oh, there's Mama!
—DAVE! OH, MY GOD! WHAT'S HAPPENING HERE?
—Mama, Papa's wrestling Lucy …
—Mrs. Fairchild, it's not my fault. Mr. Fairchild was drunk and he kept bothering me.
—You bitch! You're lying … Pay no attention to her, Anne.
—Mrs. Fairchild, he got drunk and kept making passes at me.
—You got drunk on my whiskey, Lucy. It was you who kept—
—That's not true, Mr. Fairchild.
—I tried to get you off me and you scratched me … Anne, I swear, it wasn't my fault.
—DAVE, OH, DAVE … YOU DRIVE ME CRAZY! EVERY TIME I TURN MY BACK THIS HAPPENS! AND YOU SWORE TO ME IT'D NEVER HAPPEN AGAIN! AND I THOUGHT I COULD TRUST YOU, LUCY! I'M SICK AND TIRED OF THIS! THIS IS THE END!
—Mama, don't cry …
—O.K., Anne. Send this bitch away, right now. Let's send her packing.
—No. Don't speak to me, Dave. I've got a better idea. Just wait.
—You see, Lucy. My wife saw what you were doing.
—You goddamn rotten white man.
—Lucy, get your damned things together and get the hell out of here. Be gone before my wife comes back in.
—O.K. I go. Let me pass—
—Aw, no! You're not getting off that lightly, Lucy.
—Aw, Mama's got a gun!

—ANNE, PUT THAT GUN DOWN!

—Get out of my way, Dave. I ought to kill both of you.

—ANNE, I SAID PUT THAT GUN DOWN! DON'T BE A FOOL!

—Get out of my way, Dave. I'll be made a fool no longer. For all I know, you might have sent this black bitch here to work … No wonder she came so early in the morning. Now, I'm going to kill her.

—Mrs. Fairchild, I didn't do anything. I swear before God. I couldn't. You don't understand.

—Yes. That Bertha did the same thing. Dave, get away. I'm going to shoot. I'll hit you, if you don't move!

—ANNE, ANNE, DON'T BE A FOOL! PUT THAT GUN DOWN!

—Stay away from me, Dave.

—ANNE, GIVE ME THAT GUN!

—No!

—I'll take it from you! Oh, God! No, no … Anne, you shot her …

—Go away, Lily! Don't go near your mama.

—Oh God … Dave, what did I do? I shot her … Oh, Dave, it's all your fault. You promised you'd never let me find you doing that again. Now, I've killed somebody. Oh, Lord! Dave, you made me do it. I'm sure I've killed her.

—Mama, there's blood on the floor …

—Anne, drop that gun.

—I want to kill myself … Dave, you've spoiled my whole life … I'll kill us all … Then my misery is over …

—Anne, drop that gun! Don't pull that trigger again. You'll hit me or Lily if you do!

—Here, Dave … Take the gun … Oh, God, Dave … Look what you made me do! You've driven me crazy with your drinking … What can I do now?

—Anne, get into your room. Take Lily with you. We've got to talk. We're in trouble now.

—Mama, don't cry. Please, Mama …

—Dave, is she dead?

—I don't know … Lily, stop crying. Listen, Anne …

—Oh, Dave … What can we do? I want to kill myself … They'll take me to jail, won't they?

—Oh, Jumping Jesus … Anne, get hold of yourself and listen. I'm sorry. Honey, I was only fooling around.

—But, Dave, you promised me …

—I started drinking this morning. I didn't know what I was doing.

—You always say that.

—Mama, is Lucy dead?

—Hush, Lily. Anne, we must call a doctor. We've got to do something.

—Oh, God. I guess so. This is the end for me. Dave, see if she's dead.

—I'll call Burt Stallman. He's your brother-in-law. He's our friend. Maybe he can advise us. A bullet wound has to be reported. Perhaps he'll find a way out for us, hunh? I'll call now. I'll dial ...

—See if she's dead first, Dave.

—No. I'll phone Burt.

—Dave, I'm so sorry, but it's all your fault. I didn't mean to shoot her.

—Hush, Anne. Sh, Lily ... That you, Burt? This is Dave speaking. Listen, Burt, you've got to get over to the house at once. Something awful has happened. I can't say it over the phone. Somebody's hurt bad. You got to come and help us. We're in trouble. Somebody's been shot, Burt. Yeah. It's a woman. A colored maid. She's bleeding. It just happened. I shot her, Burt. She's lying on the kitchen floor. I don't know if she's dead or not. Yes, Anne's all right. Sure. Lily's fine. You're coming right away? Good. Thanks, Burt. Ohhh ... Anne, he's on the way. I told him I shot her, Anne.

—No, Dave. We must tell 'im the truth. If you don't, I will.

—Honey, let me handle this. It's all a mistake.

—Mama, is Lucy dead?

—Dave, see if she's still breathing.

—O.K., stay here, both of you.

—Mama, why did you kill her?

—Oh, Lily, I'm so sorry that you have to see and hear all of this. But it's not poor Mama's fault. If I get you out of this, I'm taking you and we're going far away. Er, ooaww ...

—Anne, she seems in a bad way. She's still lying there and there's blood all over the kitchen floor.

—Oh, God ... I hope she doesn't die ... Dave, what happened to your hands?

—Oh, that gal scratched 'em. I hadn't noticed.

—Dave how could you do this to me? I want to die ... I should've shot myself, rather than that poor fool of a gal!

—Take it easy, Anne. Look, I did the shooting, see? I'll take the blame. I found her stealing and I asked to halt. She ran. I shot her.

—No, no. I won't lie, Dave. I've been lying for you for years. Now, I stop, no matter what happens.

—Anne, don't be a fool. Let's get our story straight. We can depend on Burt to help us. Now, look, I shot her, see?

—I won't lie again, Dave. I shot her, I killed her ...

—Anne, maybe one of us'll have to go to jail. I'll go. Then you look after Lily.

—Oh, God, I don't know. I want to die. You made me murder. I ought to have shot you, you fool! You rotten, low-down fool! You drunk—
—Sh. Here's Burt. Anne, remember, I shot her, see?

—Hy, Anne. Hy, Dave. Hey, what's going on?
—Come in, Burt. So glad you came. Look, we caught the maid stealing, see? I shot her ...
—My God!
—It's a lie, Burt. *I* did it.
—Shut up, Anne.
—But where's the maid?
—She's lying on the kitchen floor, Burt.
—Let's take a look at her. Stay here. I'll do it. This is serious.
—Anne, why in hell can't you let me handle this?
—I'm not going to lie, Dave.
—Mama, will we all go to jail?
—Don't talk, Lily.
—Anne, forgive me. I was drunk. I didn't know what I was doing.
—Don't talk to me, Dave.
—Mama, is Lucy dead?
—We don't know, Lily. Be quiet, darling.
—Sh. Here comes Burt.
—I'm phoning my office to bring material for a blood transfusion.
—Is she hurt bad, Burt?
—Don't really know, Anne. There's been a terrific loss of blood.
—O.K., Burt. Do what you can for her. But remember I shot her ...
—Er ... You shot *her*?
—Yeah, Burt.
—Why, Dave?
—It's a long story, Burt. I shot her. And I'll tell why in any courtroom.
—Aw, Anne, keep your mouth shut! Let me do the talking here, will you!
—Listen, you all ... Let me attend to that transfusion. Stay here. I must talk to you. I don't understand this ...
—Will she die?
—Don't know, Anne. Maybe not, if we work fast.
—Thank God. If anybody deserves to die, it's me.
—Anne, I beg you to keep quiet. I'll handle this.
—Dave, don't talk to me!

—Come in.
—Anne, Dave, the transfusion has been given.

—Is she living? Will she pull through?

—Er … The patient has a chance.

—Where is she?

—I put the patient on your living-room couch.

—Burt, what do we do now? Remember it was all my fault. Anne had nothing to do with shooting her …

—Don't lie, Dave! Burt, I shot her—

—Listen, I must ask you two a few questions.

—Yeah. I'm responsible, Burt. Not Anne.

—Where did you find this servant?

—She came in this morning in response to an ad we put in the paper.

—Had either of you ever seen her before?

—No.

—Oh, Burt … Listen, I wouldn't put it past Dave to have asked her to come here for that job. He wants a black mistress. Aw, maybe that was why she came so early.

—Anne, don't be a goddamn fool! Shut your mouth!

—Listen, Burt … It's no longer a secret. Dave has been drinking. For ever so long … We can't keep a maid because of it.

—Anne, for God's sake. Think of our child …

—Let me talk, Dave.

—Stop, both of you. This is far more complicated than you think. The bullet wound is not so serious. A flesh wound in the thigh. A great loss of blood, but, with care, the patient will be all right.

—Thank God.

—You see, Anne, everything'll be all right.

—But there's something wrong here …

—What do you mean, Burt? Give it to us straight. Anne and I can take it. I'm responsible for everything that happened.

—Well, did you, for some reason, *make him wear that dress?*

—What are you talking about, Burt?

—I don't understand, Burt.

—Didn't you know that … that … Well, hell, dammit, it's a man you shot.

—Good God, Burt! What are you talking about?

—Burt, I don't get you.

—Who shot that servant is up to you two. But what I'm trying to tell you is that your female servant is a man wearing a woman's dress.

—You're kidding.

—No, Dave. This is straight.

—Lucy is a man?

—Yes, Anne. A man.

—Ooww!

—Don't scream, Anne. Good God, Burt, is this true?

—It's true. He admits it.

—Oh, Dave … How is that possible? Aren't you mistaken, Burt?

—Ha, ha. Look, I'm a doctor. The most elementary thing I know is the difference between a man and woman. That servant lying in your living room is a man—

—Oh, that is why she was so scared this morning in the bathroom …

—What are you saying, Anne? Was he with you in the bathroom?

—She … he … She was sweating, trembling …

—Jesus! This makes it simple … Did he bother you, Anne?

—Anne, Burt, listen … I've got it solved. It's simple. This nigger put on a dress to worm his way into my house to rape my wife! Ha! *See*? Then I detected 'im. I shot 'im in self-defense, shot 'im to protect my honor, my home. That's our answer! I was protecting white womanhood from a nigger rapist impersonating a woman! A rapist who wears a dress is the worst sort! Any jury'll free me on that. Anne, that's our case.

—Anne, did this man molest you in any way in that bathroom?

—No, Burt. I'm tired of lying. No, he didn't touch me. If she is a man, she was scared to death, could barely move. Oh, I see it all now …

—What?

—That's why he was so scared … I told her to wash my back and she could scarcely—

—Then he did touch you! Burt, here's our defense!

—No, Dave. I'll not lie about this. You can't make me lie.

—Burt, can we find a way of keeping this quiet? Anne won't help me to do this thing right. Help us to get out of this. You're our friend. This scandal'll ruin me at the bank.

—I'm a doctor. Normally, I'm required to report things of this sort.

—But, Burt, this is kind of in the family, see?

—But suppose he reports that he was shot, Dave? Where does that leave you, and me, and Anne?

—Of course, Burt. You must report it.

—Anne, goddammit, keep your damned mouth shut! Burt, this nigger came into my house under false pretenses.

—That's true.

—And I defended myself against him!

—Dave, listen. I'm only a doctor. If this man talks to the police, then you're in a scandal. And I'm in trouble because I refused to report a gunshot wound. See?

—Burt, talk to 'im. Find out why he's running around in a woman's dress.

—You want me to try and make a deal with 'im?

—Right. Do that. See how he reacts.

—No, Burt. I'll not lie.

—Shut up, Anne. Let Burt see what he can do.

—O.K., you two stay right here. But, listen, this means my career if it gets out that I did not report it, see?

—Rely on us, Burt.

—Anne, for Christ's sake, stop sobbing like that. Bear up and help me to bail us out of this jam.

—Dave, it's all such a sordid mess. That's all my life's been with you. I don't want to pretend any longer.

—Mama, I'm scared. Will the police come for us?

—Hush, Lily. I wish I had somebody to take you away from all this.

—If you stopped crying, Lily'd be all right, Anne. Burt's doing all he can for us.

—Settle it any way you like, Dave. But I'm not going to lie if anybody asks me questions. I'M TIRED OF LYING!

—Anne, honey, I'll never touch another drop of whiskey.

—You've said that a thousand times, Dave.

—This time I mean it, so help me God.

—Mama, will Lucy die?

—No, thank God.

—Mama, why did you shoot her?

—Lily, don't ask poor Mama any more questions, please …

—No, Lily. The police are not coming for anybody. Lucy is all right. Papa was just playing. Anne, stop being morbid with the child.

—Papa, Uncle Burt's knocking on the door.

—Come in, Burt.

—Well, I've tried. Don't know if it will work or not. Now, you two sit down and listen to me. I don't know if I'm a good judge of character or not. Now, I've talked to this boy. He seems straight, if a man wearing a dress can be described as straight. Now, here's the story he tells me and he tells it in a way that makes me believe 'im. It seems that his wife has just had a baby. He was out of work. The wife could not work because she was sick. They were about to lose their home. He was desperate. He saw your ad. He put on his wife's dress, her shoes, took her purse, assumed her name, and came here. Then this happened.

—But he violated the law when he did that, Burt.

—True, Dave. But you said that you didn't want any publicity, didn't you? Anne says that she's not going to say he bothered her.

—O.K., Burt. I'm reasonable. Burt, what would that nigger take to forget all this?
—I've already asked him that. He says if you pay his doctor's bill and give him two hundred dollars, he'll forget it. That is, if Anne doesn't wish to prefer charges against him.
—I don't. He did not touch me.
—Burt, will that nigger sign a paper to that effect? Will he accept two hundred dollars for being shot?
—He's signed it. Here it is. But I'll not give you this paper unless you give me your check.
—Hell, yes. Right now. I'll write it out. See, Anne? It's all over.
—It's not over for me.
—Aw, honey, don't be like that … Here, Burt, give 'im that check and get 'im out of the house, quick. That settles it, hunh?
—Right. But he insists on borrowing a suit of your clothes to go home in. He can't walk. His suit is hidden in his coal house.
—Oh, O.K. give 'im something from my clothes closet. But get 'im out of here quick.
—Right. Be right back, in about an hour. I'm taking him to his house.
—Thank God, Burt. Anne, it's all over. Baby, forgive me. I'm sorry.
—Dave, I can't go on like this.
—Aw, hell, Anne. Come on; be a sport.
—I've been a sport for eight years with you. I'm tired. This is the end.
—Anne, darling. I need your sympathy now. We weathered it. Everything came out all right. Think of the danger you were in with a nigger man wearing a dress in the house.
—Nothing's all right, Dave. I'm going to my mother. I'm taking Lily.
—Anne, you just can't leave me like that.
—I can't help it, Dave.
—If you leave me, I'll get plastered and stay plastered for a month.
—Oh, Dave.
—Say you'll stay, Anne.
—Oh, God … I'll have to stay, I guess.
—Good girl. I'll change. You'll see. Sh. Look, there's Burt leading that nigger to his car. He looks pretty weak to me. Hope he doesn't die. There. They're driving off. Thank God, it's over, Anne.
—It's not over for me, Dave. Not as long as you drink, it'll never be over.
—Baby, I swear I'm on the wagon from now on.
—You always say that.

—Who is it?

—Open the door. We've got your husband here.
—Oh, God! What happened! CARL! CARL! You're sick …
—Now, Lucy, take it easy. I'm all right.
—You're hurt. What happened?
—He'll tell you about it. First, let's get him to bed.
—Come in, come in.
—Oh, Papa.
—Hi, Henry.
—You're sick, Papa?
—No, Henry. Just hurt a bit. Nothing to worry about.
—Right through that door, sir.
—O.K. Now, let's ease him onto the bed. That's it. O.K. boy?
—I'm all right.
—Have you any pain?
—No, sir.
—Now, keep in bed for at least a week. And if you get any temperature, have your wife phone me, see?
—Yes, sir.
—Now, my friends are depending upon you to do what you promised. I'll come whenever it's necessary. You'll be up and about soon.
—Yes, sir. Thank you, sir.
—If you can't sleep, then here's some pills. Take one every two hours.
—Thank you sir.
—I'll pass by and take a look at you tomorrow.
—Yes, sir. Thank you, sir.
—And, boy, never do that again. Lucy, go to the door with the doctor.
—Yes, Carl. Do we owe him anything?
—You owe me nothing. Just keep your husband quiet.
—Yes, sir.
—You feel better, Papa?
—Sure, Henry. I'm fine. How're you?
—All right, Mama was crying—
—I know. How's the baby?
—She's sleeping, Papa. Are you hurt bad, Papa?
—No. It's nothing, son. Have you been helping Mama?
—Sure. We—
—Carl, I *told* you not to do it.
—What did Papa do, Mama?
—It's none of your business, Henry. Now, Carl, what happened?

—Listen, Lucy, don't ask me any questions. I'm not going to tell you anything. I'm all right. Everything's all right. Look. Here's the money to pay for the house. Our problem's solved. Two hundred dollars.

—Oh, God! But, Carl, where'd you get it from?

—It's a gift.

—You robbed something or somebody? You can tell me …

—No, no. Lucy, for once, I'm asking you not to ask me any questions. I gave my word that I wouldn't talk. So don't ask me anything. In the morning, you can take that check to the bank and get it cashed.

—I don't understand.

—You don't need to. The house is saved. We can eat.

—What did you do?

—I said not to ask me anything!

—But the police will come for you!

—No, they won't.

—I knew something bad would happen when you left—

—Nothing bad's happened. I just hurt my leg, that's all.

—But how did you hurt it? Where? When?

—Lucy, shut up now.

—Did you really wear my dress?

—Er, yeah. But forget that.

—Then where is it?

—Oh, I don't know. I lost it—

—What happened?

—Stop hammering at me, honey. I'll buy you another dress.

—Carl, is this check real? Is it good?

—It's as good as gold. Now, what are you crying for? Aw, Lucy … Now, Henry, stop that bawling. Look, you've gone and awakened the baby and she's crying too. Goddammit, everybody's crying. Stop! I tell you, stop! Aw, Lucy … Goddammit, I can't help but cry too if all of you are crying … Oooouaw …

—I'm sorry, Carl. Henry, see about the baby and stop crying. We'll make Papa sick like that.

—Y-yessum, Mama.

—Carl, why did somebody give you two hundred dollars?

—I worked for it.

—Cooking?

—Lucy, it was all kinds of work.

—In a home?

—Yeah.

—The wife was there?

—Lucy, don't ask me any more questions!

—Was she pleased with your work?

—Oh, hell, Lucy! Yes, yes! Everybody was pleased! … That's why I got those two hundred dollars! Now, stop questioning me.

—Well, if you don't want to tell me, what can I do? But there's one thing I know: wearing that dress got you into trouble, didn't it?

—Yep. In a way, yeah.

—Carl, never—Promise me you'll never do anything like that again.

—Ha, ha, Lucy, you don't have to ask. I was a woman for almost six hours and it almost killed me. Two hours after I put that dress on I thought I was going crazy.

—But, Carl, I warned you. It's not easy for a man to act like a woman.

—Gosh, Lucy, how do you women learn it?

—Honey, it's instinct.

—Guess you're right. I didn't know it was so hard.

—Carl, never let me see you in a dress again. I almost died when I awakened and found you gone.

—You don't have to beg me, darling. I wouldn't be caught dead again in a dress.

—I was on the verge of going to the police to tell 'em.

—Oh, God! Glad you didn't do that.

—Mama, Tina's crying for her bottle.

—Carl, you could've been killed.

—Papa, why is Mama crying so?

—Henry, don't you go crying now. Aw, God! The whole bunch of you are crying … Lucy, Henry … Aw, Christ, if you all cry like that, you make me cry … Oooouuwa!

Your Handsome Captain

by Simone Schwarz-Bart (Guadeloupe)

CHARACTERS

WILNOR BAPTISTE, *a Haitian farm worker, a tall, thin man about thirty years old. The part could be played by a white actor in makeup, or wearing a mask that is flexible enough for the audience to visualize the movements of his lips; in which case the actor's body should remain white.*

A RADIO/CASSETTE RECORDER

SET

Interior of a small one-room Creole shack. There is a stool in front of a soap box, a mattress on the ground, a gas burner in a corner with some dishes and silverware, a bottle of rum, a pair of shoes. A suit hangs on the wall with a shirt and tie, and a small plastic-framed mirror. A radio/cassette recorder is on top of the soap box. The shutters are open and it is night.

STAGE DIRECTIONS

An imaginary space, like the one in the Noh theatre, for example, is created through music and dance. Traditional Haitian dances are choreographed in such a way that they become balletic. These dances have a dramatic function; they express the different moments of an individual drama rather than a collective state of mind. They can be regarded as an additional language that the main character has at his disposal. This more or less secret means of expression is common in the Caribbean. Music also plays its part. Often, the sounds that are heard in the play—human voice, drum, or band—come directly from the soul of the character. These are auditory illusions reproduced onstage and, in some cases, a synthesizer will be necessary. Sometimes the same song can be real (it comes from the cassette); sometimes imaginary.

TABLEAU I

It's nighttime. Footsteps are heard. A door opens. Someone bumps into a piece of furniture.

WILNOR: Watch out friend! This country is precious, fragile. Even the sky here is made of china; so don't go breaking these good people's furniture.

Creaking is heard. A gas lamp is lit. A black farm worker appears with a machete in his hand and a burlap sack. The man takes a large envelope from the sack, opens it slowly as if to take out a letter, and removes a cassette tape which he holds up.

The plane had a good flight, thank you. And I received the cassette the same day Brother Archibald arrived. Thank you. Thanks be to God. (*He gives a small laugh.*) Wilnor, my dear, I want to tell you that nothing belongs to you here, not even the grass on the road, not even the wind. (*He gives another small laugh.*) And if you really want to know, the only thing that is truly yours ... (*He raises the cassette up to eye level.*) is this, old friend, this.

He sits on the stool, inserts the cassette into the tape recorder and turns it on. Noises, laughter, children's voices, and a cock crow are heard. One senses there is a whole little circle of people gathered around the tape recorder. A woman's voice is heard chasing everyone out. Complete silence follows. Finally, this same female voice begins to sing.

THE VOICE:

Moin, m'aime danser, moin n'aime chanter, *(etc.)*

The song is lively and the voice happy, mischievous and high-pitched. The song stops and the woman's voice begins again.

Hello! Hello Wilnor, Wilnor Baptiste. As soon as you hear this voice, you'll know that it's Marie-Ange speaking to you. I kicked all of my people out of the shack, including the rooster, and now we're alone, you and me. You over there and me here, you here and me over there. It's all the same. Wilnor, tell me, how are you? I have so many things to tell you that my tongue has all dried up. As the old saying goes, "Man is not alone on earth; he has neighbors." So before beginning my little speech, I should first send you some greetings, shouldn't I? It's proper, the custom, the accepted thing. (*The delivery quickens.*) Your father and mother are well, thank you, (*The "thank yous" are long and ceremonious, breaking the rhythm.*) and they send their hellos. Your sisters, Lolotte, Finotte and Grenotte are well, thank you; they send their hellos. All of the relatives, friends, and in-laws here are well, thank you, and they send their hellos. Good news from all our exiled ones around the world: Grenada, the Dominican Republic, Puerto Rico, and the rest of the group; they are well and say hello. (*One clearly hears that the woman is out of breath. She begins again at a more normal rhythm.*) Yet, unfortunately … Oh God, I can't avoid telling you your friend Petrus has … drowned. He was lost at sea and vanished along with thirty other souls who were trying to reach America on a raft. Old Mama Petrus, when she heard the news, blood blocked her throat and she fell to the ground gasping like a sperm whale. We thought she was dying, completely done for, and all night long we checked her breathing and placed compresses on her. But just imagine—it would actually be funny—we'd have had a good laugh but for your poor friend at the bottom of the sea; just imagine, the next day, she was alive. Well, barely alive, but alive. And when asked how she was feeling, she replied peevishly, "I'd have slept well if I'd been left alone." (*She laughs stridently, then begins again in a normal tone.*) Wilnor, how are you? Tell me, really, how are you? In the last cassette you sent—was it three months ago? Three months already?—You say you're as fat as a prize pig and living in a large house with pillars, a big front door, and so many electric light bulbs that you're floating among the stars. I don't want to contradict you, Wilnor—may the Blessed Virgin forgive me—but the man who delivered everything to me … thank you for the money, Wilnor, thank you for the huge pile of gifts … that young man told me that our exiled brothers in Guadeloupe don't live in large houses with pillars and big front doors, with all due respect, in chamber pots. He might have been saying that to be funny; but it worried me, Wilnor, it worried me. And when I asked him how you looked, at first he didn't want to answer. Then he told me that you had changed a lot, become skinny, melted like a candle. That you now looked like a shriveled-up black man. Shriveled-up outside and shriveled-up inside. Shriveled-up, shriveled-up, (*She gives a short sob.*) shriveled-up. (*She sobs.*) He might have been saying that as a joke, too, but it worried me, Wilnor, it brought me grief. And that same night, I had a dream. First I saw myself at the river washing your flannel shirt; you know, the gray one with the red stripes, the pretty one. And suddenly I realize I'm washing your body, (*Pause.*) your living body. (*Pause.*) You are all flat inside the shirt, Wilnor. Your head and your hands stick out; your legs, everything, flat. Flat as a newspaper picture. You try to slip away and I want to hold you back—but you melt between my arms and soon there is nothing inside the shirt, Wilnor. It's empty … empty … (*The man stops the cassette and grumbles.*)

WILNOR: A woman really needs a man. I no sooner leave that even her dreams go haywire.

The man gets up, puzzled, and goes to look at himself in the mirror hanging on the wall. He puts on the white shirt and tie and reappraises himself in the mirror. Finally, he squares his shoulders.

No doubt about it, a woman really needs a man.

The man returns to the soap box, sits down and presses the play button of the cassette recorder with a confident air. At first there is silence; then, after a few long seconds, the woman's weak voice rises into crescendo, punctuated by the rhythm of light hand clapping.

THE VOICE:

Moin n'aime danser, (etc.)

This time she sings the entire first verse. Finally, the woman continues.

Wilnor, Wilnor. Today is February 2nd, 1985. It's been ages since I first sang this song for you. Remember, you often used to say that was what convinced you to tie the knot—a winged woman who sings like a dragonfly despite the tons of sorrows dragging on her skirts. And then you left; you went away to earn a wayfarer's daily bread. But you—whose soul was always full of marvels—you wanted daily bread, the whole loaf, and more. You spoke of striking it rich; you dreamed of buying land by the river and a cow. I even milked the cow. That's why I let you get on that plane, Wilnor. (*Pause.*) The years have gone by. (*Pause.*) I have wanted for nothing, nothing since you left. My stomach has not been empty and I've never gone barefoot on Sunday. No, you always have known how to come up with enough money, good money, and to send it my way. But now they tell me you're becoming all shriveled-up and that's why I beg you on my knees, come back. Come back, my dear Wilnor, even if it's without the land, without the cow.

Pause. One hears rapid breathing on the tape, then the voice continues with a small laugh.

Wilnor, I wish I were a boat sailing to Guadeloupe. Once there, you'd climb inside me, you'd walk my decks, you'd place your hands on my frame, you'd explore me from stern to stern. And then you would set sail and I would take you to a country far, far, far away. (*Pause*). On the other side of the world, perhaps, where people don't look at you as though you were less than nothing, dried-out coconuts. Wilnor, is there no country on earth where Haitians can work and send a little money home from time to time without being reduced to formless gusts of air? (*Pause.*) Wilnor, handsome captain of my ship, if my letter reaches you in the morning, I wish you good morning, and if my letter reaches you in the evening, I wish you … (*She continues in a sweeping, ceremonious tone.*) good evening. (*Pause.*) Your tape recorder wife, (*Pause.*) Marie-Ange.

She clears her throat and then continues.

By the way, you might wonder why I left you with no news for three long months. This is exactly, the very thing, I wanted to speak to you about today, and I realize it's the only thing I didn't talk about. But what do you want my dear? Sometimes there are certain words that choke you, that stick in your throat like fish bones. I'll try again tomorrow … God willing.

Black out.

TABLEAU II

The lights come back up and show the man standing in front of the soap box, paralyzed with amazement. Apparently he stopped the tape while the theater was dark and now he looks at the machine suspiciously as if he does-

n't dare restart it. His finger is poised tentatively over the play button as though it might burn him.

WILNOR: If it's bad news, waiting a bit won't matter. If it's good news, it will only be better.

He takes three steps toward a rum bottle on the ground, then suddenly seems to stumble and to catch his balance with one arm holding onto an invisible rope stretched in the air. A few measures of ti-bois music are heard which seem to come from the sky. Wilnor stumbles to the left again, then to the right in time to the ti-bois music and, while hanging onto the invisible rope, he circles around the bottle and comes to a stop with a blissful look on his face.

It seems, according to what they say at home, that the African gods invented the drums to give us consolation, while the black man invented rum, which isn't bad either, God knows! (*He brings the bottle to eye level and sizes up its contents.*) Patience is at the bottom of the bottle. (*He takes a large swig.*) At the very bottom. (*He takes another large swig.*)

With the bottle held against his chest, he returns to the box, hopping humorously in dance steps as though pursued by the light music of the ti-bois. He then sits on the stool and very carefully presses the tip of his finger down on the play button.

THE VOICE: Wilnor, about the story that stuck in my throat yesterday, you remember? I realize, finally, that there was no such point in making such a fuss about it. So much wind for so small a ship, so much mousse for so little chocolate. On thinking about it, (*She gives a small laugh.*) the story is rather funny. (*She gives a small forced laugh.*) It's about the money, the big sum you sent me three months ago with your friend from the village of Raizailles. I don't know if he's a close friend of yours, but if you see him again—which I doubt, since he left for Miami—you can tell him for me he's a big rascal. (*She gives an indignant sigh.*) One fine morning, Monsieur showed up at my door wearing a red jacket, a yellow tie and a tie pin that wasn't that bad at all and was even quite pretty. In short, a beautiful pin. He introduces himself, gives me all your gifts honestly: the blouse, the handkerchiefs, the box of goodies, all the soaps and perfumes, the perfumed soaps, everything. But then, imagine, the big good-for-nothing, as he was giving me the money—your hard-earned money—he changed his mind and let me know that he would give me nothing at all unless I gave in to his wishes. My God! As she goes through life, a woman can say that she's seen it all. Finally, he gave up, but not without trying. The animal tried everything and more. (*She laughs and laughs.*)

WILNOR: But what is this story ... ? Wait! Wait!

THE VOICE: (*playful*) Imagine—speaking of money entrusted to handsome young men who come rubbing the beautiful bills under your nose, your wives' noses—this time you won't be able to stop laughing; you'll really laugh. There's this lady from Port-au-Prince, a grand, pious lady, with a soul as pure as spring water, truly someone exceptionally moral, whose husband has been picking oranges in Florida for years. They say that from picking so many oranges, he's become an orange tree himself, he can be seen over there, standing all day long at a crossroads, holding out his branches to the passersby, his fruits up for grabs, ready to be plundered and devastated. They say this as a joke, naturally. (*She gives a small appropriate laugh.*) But, to get back to my story, one day, the woman from Port-au-Prince receives a visit on behalf of her husband: a handsome young man wearing a jacket ... but who cares how he was dressed? A young man bringing her money and the kind of gifts wives usually get from husbands who work in America's orange groves. That's where the story becomes funny. (*Pause.*) Really funny. (*Pause.*) Suddenly, she is moved, so deeply moved on seeing the young man, she has the impression that he's bringing her some of her husband's world, some of his scent. She looks at the eyes which had seen the absent one. (*She gives a small sob.*) She touches the hands which just the day before, just yesterday, had touched the absent one. My God! (*She gives a small cry.*) ... Finally, she's completely confused. (*She sighs.*) and ends up in bed with the young man. (*She sobs.*) But, in reality, it's her husband. (*Pause.*) Seemingly with the young man, but in reality lying by her husband. Do you understand, Wilnor? Do you understand? (*She gives a small sob.*)

> The man shakes his head without understanding. There is a long silence, then the woman's voice is heard again.

Do you understand, Wilnor?

> The man is bewildered. The voice continues in a whisper.

Do you understand? (*Pause.*) Wilnor, I know you. I know how sensitive you are. Nevertheless, stop shaking your head and figure it out. Take time to think. What times—what world—do you think you're living in, my poor friend? This is the earth, Wilnor, and on earth everything is whirlwind and smoke. There are none of the straight, wide lanes of heaven. So I beg you, stop shaking your head and figure it out. Take time to think, to weigh things. Don't make me say all the words. (*There is a pause and then the voice continues in a certain tone.*) Wilnor. (*She pauses again, then continues in another tone of voice.*) Wilnor. (*The voice becomes aggressive for the first time.*) The fact is that the woman from Port-au-Prince, the one who found her husband's scent on the young man, the one who became all mixed up, lost in happiness to the point of confusing everything in her head … (*The voice breaks.*) That woman is me.

WILNOR: You?

THE VOICE: He joked exactly like you, Wilnor. The same way. And his eyes reminded me of your eyes. His hands reminded me of your hands. It was you I held in my arms. It was only you that I welcomed in my bed.

WILNOR: (*cutting her off*) Enough!

THE VOICE: It was you. It was only you in my bed, enjoying my body.

WILNOR: Enough I say! Tramp! Enough said! Enough lies! Enough truth! Enough everything! Enough everybody! Leave me! Leave me alone! (*The man stops the cassette violently. Silence. He takes a few faltering steps forward.*) Enough, gods, enough! (*The faltering steps turn into a dance—small hops to the side like the Lerose. He raises his arms as though he were hovering in the air.*) Enough angels! (*A drum begins to beat, sharply at first, pulsating, then its rhythm changes with the introduction of the entire band, while a deep bass voice slowly utters the following words, with great majesty but, nonetheless, with secret melancholy.*)

BASS VOICE:

Moujé, moujé é o, (*etc.*)

The man dances now with eyes closed. Little by little, darkness falls on the stage, transforming it into night and silence.

TABLEAU III

The lights come up. The man opens his eyes, looks around him, stunned, with his mouth open. He returns to the soap box. He is out of breath as though he had been running. Halfway there, at the sound of a ti-bois, he suddenly jumps, to the left, then to the right, with arms out horizontally. Finally, he approaches the radio/cassette recorder and hesitantly turns it back on.

THE VOICE: (*strangely serene*) Wilnor, handsome captain, today is March 17, St. Valentine's day. Noon in the heavens, but more like midnight on earth, suddenly. (*Pause.*) Today is the day that our road comes to an end, that our food burns up, that the roof of our shack blows away. (*Pause.*) And since we are going to separate—don't deny it, you've already made up your mind (*The man nods his head with approval.*)—I must tell you the rest of the story ... Because there is more, Wilnor. I must tell you properly, until all things have been said, finished, wrapped up and sealed in a shroud. The first time your good friend came was Monday, January 2nd, St. Eustache's day. I thought of you on seeing him and I gave in after he threatened not to give me my money. He came back Saturday, January 7th and I thought of you again. Then I thought of you Monday, January 9th; Wednesday, January 11th; and Tuesday, the 17th, and that's all. That day your image fell like a mask from his face and I chased him away. I told him to clear out. I've seen nothing since then. (*Pause.*) I tried everything to weaken my stomach. (*Pause.*) Finally, I lost half my blood and they took me to the hospital. (*Pause.*) But the child didn't leave with my blood. It didn't leave, Wilnor; it didn't. (*Pause.*) Farewell. (*There is a long silence, from which the woman's voice emerges like a challenge, livelier than ever; very high-pitched.*)

Moin n'aime chanter, moin n'aime danser. Aye, aye, aye.

The voice breaks.
Aye, aye, aye.

WILNOR: Ha! Ha! Ha! What a woman! (*He repeats her words, still with the same surprised, almost admiring tone.*) I thought of you the 7th of January; I thought of you the 9th of January; and the 11th of January I also thought of you! Ha! Ha! ... And from thinking of me, she got a big belly! ... That's really taking a man for a jackass! ... For the king, the emperor of jackasses, since jackasses first began raining down on earth! What a woman! Ha! Ha!

He is completely stunned. Clearly he hasn't yet completely gauged what is happening to him. He gets up and takes a few steps. The sound of the tibois can be heard, very slowed, to which the man responds by an even slower, lingering attempt to dance, one step to the left, one step to the right. Then he raises his hands to his temples and says calmly, still surprised.

What a misfortune!

The ti-bois starts up again, more and more tensely; then there are three well-sounded drum beats while the man turns around as though stung by a dart and stamps in time to the drumbeats.

That tramp! All of my money went to her, all of my sweat. But now I am going to live, to live what is called the good life. Oh yes! What a relief! (*Drumbeats are heard. The man twirls around and stops with the drumbeat.*) All my money! (*More drumbeats are heard. The same movements are repeated. He speaks in a mocking tone.*) Money! Money! (*Slight pause.*) Money! Money! Money! (*The drum stops with a sharp beat.*) No, not all my money.

> *He goes to the mattress, raises a corner and frantically scratches at the ground with his hands. He removes a bowl containing a sheaf of bills and, with a somber air, places it next to the radio/cassette recorder. He removes the bills and scatters them in front of him. He speaks bitterly.*

No, not all the money.

> *Suddenly, trembling with contained violence he seizes the radio/cassette recorder and raises it as though to smash it. When he speaks again, it is in sugary tones.*

Dear Marie-Ange: When you hear this voice, you'll know that it's Wilnor speaking to you. Wilnor Baptiste answering you. O.K.? (*Pause.*) My dear, thank you for having thought so much about me, about me personally, Wilnor Baptiste, the king, the emperor of suckers. I've thought about you a great deal too. Why hide it from you any longer? Since arriving in Guadeloupe, I've thought about you a great deal. With all these beautiful black women in ruffles and flounces and all of these jazzy mulattoes buzzing around you like mosquitoes from morning til night. Gorgeous, beautiful like the rainbow, if you really want to know. That's what the women are like here, Marie-Ange. Especially since I have a house with pillars and a big front door. They like that—I can't help it—they like to come to my house even though I'm only a Haitian. I'm their black man, the black man's top black man, if you want to know, Marie-Ange. At first, I used to take sitz baths from Monday morning to Saturday night because I wanted to keep my promise to you. And then I fell into the pit; I fell under the spell just like you. Their eyes reminded me of your eyes, their scent became your scent, do you understand Marie-Ange? Do you? Ah yes, that's how it happens when separation sets in, when boats drift apart, when airplanes begin to roar, their engines full blast. A man's body cries for a woman's body, a woman's body cries for a man's and that's what the Good Lord wishes. Separation is a vast ocean and more than one person has drowned in it, O.K.? O.K. Other than that, all is well, thank you, thank the Lord. See, I have everything I need here, the only missing thing is a car, a small four-wheeled car that spits fire. Motor cars—the women here love them, there's no denying it, they love them. (*Pause.*) With a car, I would think of you even more. Farewell. (*His voice cracks.*) Wilnor. (*Dissatisfied with his tone, he shakes his head and tries another one.*) Wilnor. (*He is still dissatisfied.*) Wilnor. (*He nods his head with approval and then seems dissatisfied again. Tense, with knotted brows, he searches for inspiration then speaks, suddenly.*) What do you want my dear Marie-Ange? Man is a rat; woman is a rat. Neither one is worth a damn. O.K.? O.K.

His hands have now left the cassette; he's straightened himself up in his seat and is staring into space.

The biggest jackass ever under the stars. (*He laughs.*) But all of this is very far away. (*He gestures.*) Very far away.

As though called up by the gesture, one hears the first note of an extremely joyous Creole quadrille coming from afar. The man changes attitude. He listens and seems more relaxed. His shoulders move; his hands twitch; his teeth shine. Suddenly lively, he stands up and does a few dance steps while the quadrille takes shape under the caller's strong guiding voice.

Take your partners, (*etc.*)

He dances the quadrille with three invisible partners. Sometimes he gaily echoes the voice of the caller. At other times (five times) the music stops as though sliced by a razor and the man goes through the motions in complete silence, but at a very slow pace as though in a slow-motion tape. During those moments, he calls out a few words which are also distorted, drawn out, put through a synthesizer. The words and phrases which he will call-out successively during the five musical phrases are the following: 1) "Tramp!" 2) "Leave me alone I tell you." 3) "Life, O.K., life; but where is life, where is it?" 4) "Oh the beautiful black women in ruffles and flounces." 5) "The jazzy mulattoes." After each of these fragments, the quadrille starts up again as before. Therefore, there are five stops and five starts. But suddenly the music and dance come to a definitive stop and, cut off in mid-movement, he finds himself standing on one foot, facing the audience, his joyful features transformed into a strange mask of pain, eyes closed and mouth half open. Blackout.

TABLEAU IV

The man has stopped in a position resembling that of a winged creature. He looks at his "wings," glancing to the left and right.

WILNOR: What a beautiful quadrille! A bit more and I would have flown away.

He slowly lowers his raised foot to the ground, which he scrapes lazily once or twice.

The earth.

He turns his neck in the direction of the radio/cassette recorder. Pause.

Poor Marie-Ange, after all.

He takes a step toward the radio/cassette recorder.

Poor, poor Marie-Ange.

He sits down, shakes his head with a subtle smile, and finally makes a declaration to the cassette.

Actually, I lied to you, my little bird. (*He gives a small laugh.*) Since I've been in Guadeloupe, if you want to know, there's never—it's strange to say, funny—there's never been another woman at my house. (*He gives a small laugh.*) Every evening that the Good Lord sends, I take my cold sitz baths and sometimes I even take them during the day. I fill up my basin and sit in it. Also, when I can, I immerse myself in the stream for hours and hours. To sleep, I put compress between my thighs, and I have a basin of water ready at the side of the bed in case I wake up. Sometimes, stretched out in the darkness, like this, (*He stretches out his arms.*) I have the feeling that it's swelling. If feels like balloons between my thighs. I feel as if I'm going to fly away. And, then suddenly, it happens. I fly, I fly away, I rise up very high in the night, (*He gives a small laugh.*) attached to my two balloons.

The man is seated. Pensive, he makes a series of "philosophical" sounds in the back of his throat and, smiling, shakes his head, astonished at everything that's happened to him in the course of his life. He will continue to smile this way throughout the following monologue until the word "promptly" is first pronounced.

Actually, as for the money, about the money, I also lied to you, I didn't tell you the truth. (*Pause.*) Not the whole truth. (*Pause.*) I send you my savings, true, but I don't send you the savings from my savings. I put those in my piggybanks, in my jar.

While saying this, he seizes a bill which he holds to the flame of the lamp's gas jet. As he continues speaking, he will gradually burn all the bills spread out on the soapbox and some of the ones which have fallen on the ground.

A jar that I bury at the foot of my bed to anchor and stabilize me; (*He gives a small laugh.*) because of certain dreams, bizarre beyond belief; dreams which carry me to stranger and more foreign lands, farther and farther away; and I'm afraid that one fine morning I'll no longer be able to find the way back. That's why I sleep over my little jar of money, which I bury under my feet. (*He gives a small laugh.*) Right under my feet, so they'll get the idea and know the road back when I'm dreaming in a far-away land. (*He gives a small laugh.*) You see, it amounted to quite a few bills in the end. Some were for a veranda that I wanted to have built at the back of the house when I got back, so we could sit outside and enjoy the cool air when we would be quite old, thin as leaves, stretched out and consumed with joy. Others, maybe, might have been for the couple of goats that I'd envisioned in my head, along with the cow. Some were for enameled dishes. Some were for a white dress with matching shoes; for a radio/cassette recorder that we would own so we wouldn't have to rent one and we could listen to all the cassettes of all these years — all the years on cassette. And some were for nothing in particular, simply in expectation of a dream, a fancy, a whim that we might one day have at the end of all those years, while we would be out enjoying the cool air, for example, out on the veranda that I would have had built the day after my return, promptly.

The last bill has gone up with the word "promptly" which he repeats without smiling. He looks at his fingers full of ashes.

And now that's it?

The woman's voice can be heard coming from very far away, distorted by a synthesizer so that each syllable is infinitely drawn out, almost unrecognizable, nearly reduced to the sound of a musical saw, but still, if possible, with a poignant dramatic accent.

THE VOICE:

Moooooin n'aaaaaimmmme chaaaaaanter
Moooooin n'aaaaaimmmme daaaaaanser ...

Elbows on the soapbox, the man has covered his face with his hands as though lost in thought. One hears the woman's voice again, closer, still distorted by the synthesizer, but in an intermediate pace that is midway between the extremely slow preceding pace and the normal pace. The tonality has also changed, become "neutral" midway between the infinite sadness of the slow pace and the woman's "normal" gaiety.

Mooin n'aiime chanter
Mooin n'aiime daanser ...

This time the man raises his head slightly and spreads his fingers apart in front of his eyes. The woman's voice takes off like a rocket: lively, high-pitched, terribly alive, at the normal rhythm of the song which she sings to the end for the fist time.

Moin n'aime chanter
Moin n'aime danser, (*etc.*)

In the middle of the song, the man extends his hand hesitantly and rests it on the radio/cassette recorder. He caresses it tenderly, and continues to do so after the song ends, when he begins to speak again.

WILNOR: Marie-Ange ... (*Pause.*) When I read your cassette, for an instant, one brief instant, I almost doubted you. (*Pause.*) For one instant. (*Pause.*) Fortunately, I've always been appreciated by those in heaven. That's my good fortune, that I'm appreciated by those who live on high. And here I was be-lieving without believing, doubting and not doubting, when all of a sudden I heard your voice right here at my house, your voice coming and going just like bygone days, and suddenly I saw the light: it came to me! It may have been a kind of gesture, an act of mercy from St. Anthony of Padua. Or per-haps it was a god from Guinea, Legba, oh yes or Damballah Ouedo, or per-haps Erzulie Freda Dahomey, the good, dear, one. I don't know what it was, I don't know, but I've always been appreciated by those up there. And sud-denly I saw the light, bright and clear, oh yes, as though I had an electric bulb in the middle of my throat. (*He places his hands on either side of his throat, mimicking the radiating light.*) There. (*Pause.*) And now I see, I know, I understand. To tell you the truth, it's happened to me, to me, too. I've often been mystified, just like you, Marie-Ange. I'm watching one of the their women go by in the street and all of the sudden it's as though I had you in front of my eyes, Marie-Ange. And if that woman headed my way, it wouldn't take too much urging to put her in my bed, right in my house with the pillars and the big front door. That's it, that's exactly it. Ah yes, separa-tion is a big ocean, which muddles everything; it shakes things up like a cup-ful of dice. You start seeing with your ears, hearing with your eyes and feel-ing with your hands things that are very far away, while the things nearby that surround you, you notice no more than a puff of smoke. Marie-Ange, sometimes funny things happen to me, really funny things. Some days when I see the women trotting up the road in front of me, the cute little black women with ruffles and flounces, and all those jazzy mulattoes, I feel a blow to my stomach as though it were you; I feel a sudden painful blow and then I feel light, so light, I fly away as if I were being carried off by two balloons, ouaaye! (*He corrects himself.*) One balloon.

He seizes the bottle, takes a swig of rum and solemnly smacks his lips in a show of self-confidence. He continues with quiet majesty.

One more word, a small bit of advice. Be sure to rest now throughout the days that God gives us. Don't trouble your soul, if you want the child to come into the world with a good start. Chew your food well, keep your heart joyful, and drive all that ugliness out of your sight so that he won't be born with a crooked nose or mouth. Remember, I want that child as beautiful as an angel. (*He puffs himself up menacingly.*) Do you hear me? (*He reassumes his air of calm majesty.*) If my letter finds you in the morning, I wish you good morning; if it arrives in the evening, I wish you good evening.

He has crossed over to the little mirror hanging on the wall. He glances at himself and concludes.

Your handsome captain, Wilnor.

But something in the mirror bothers him. Hastily he removes his shirt and tie and remains bare-chested. Finally, he speaks again, in a less self-confident tone.

Your handsome captain....

He stops. The phrase seems to overwhelm him. He brings his hand to his mouth, hunching and shaking his shoulders in a smothered laugh.

Your handsome captain?

The music of the ti-bois is heard. He dismisses it with a gesture, like a temptation. But it starts up again, accompanied by a drum which shakes the man and inspires a bitter kind of dance involving desperate-looking gestures. Suddenly, the drumming and the man stop simultaneously. Feet spread apart, arms dangling, he tries again.

Your handsome captain?

The drum starts up again, more forcefully, in a faster and faster rhythm, drawing the man into a dance that's at the same time very brief and very violent. Then everything stops short, as though sliced by a razor, except that the man has his arms raised in the air and they seem to be twisting, trying to climb higher, while his face has become like a mask. Blackout. The question is heard one last time in the night.

Your handsome captain?

from *The Fisher King*

by Paule Marshall (USA/Barbados)

So far, there were a couple of things Sonny liked about the man who was the first of the relatives he had met. First, there was his big, smooth-riding American car that had ample room on the front seat to accommodate both him and Hattie, with him sitting in the middle. Second, there was the large, domed ring on the man's right hand. He'd never seen a ring that size. Or one that had writing and tiny Roman numerals inscribed on it, as well as what looked like a coat of arms on top. It was the kind of ring the laird of a castle might have used to affix his seal to the edicts that went forth from his hand.

He liked it. In the car on the way to lunch, he examined it in detail again out of the corner of his eye.

As for the man himself—his height: he appeared to be as tall sitting down as when he was standing; his voice: Sonny could feel it reverberating in his chest like the bass drum in a parade seated beside him now on the front seat; his face: a vague reminder of his grandfather's in the pictures at home; his head: bald, monumentally bald, with a wreath of pepper-and-salt hair laid at its base—this man, his great-uncle, the owner of the car and the ring and the house where he and Hattie were staying, which was on the same block of Macon Street as the two he had just visited, was too outsize, too overwhelming for him to assess as yet. He didn't even know what to call him, either out loud or in the privacy of his thoughts.

The man seemed to have anticipated his problem. When introducing himself at the airport, he had suggested that he call him Uncle Edgar. Great-Uncle Edgar was too much of a mouthful. Or even Uncle Ed would do, he'd said.

"But only when it feels right to you," he had added.

Sonny wasn't sure if it would ever feel right, and so he had taken to calling him simply "the man" to himself, or sometimes, formally, the Edgar Payne man.

The restaurant Edgar Payne chose for them to have lunch was on the long commercial avenue that bordered Macon Street to the west. Reid Avenue it was called. It was a seedy, down-at-the-heels strip where many of the small businesses and storefronts, as well as the four- and five-story walk-ups tiered above them, stood boarded up or burnt out. A thin crowd of shoppers appeared as dispirited as their surroundings. As did the loungers outside the liquor stores and the bars that were already open, and the small knots of men and women either already nodding or waiting to score on some of the corners they drove past.

"Reid Avenue, Reid Avenue, it's a hundred times worse than I remember it," Hattie exclaimed in dismay, her gaze out the passenger window.

Edgar Payne, guiding the Lincoln Continental through the noon traffic, nodded. "It is. The sixties really did it in. All the burn-baby-burn rioting. Our folks justifiably angry, but harming themselves more than anyone else, seemed like. Reid Avenue still hasn't recovered. It's got a long way to go but my group is working on it."

As proof, he presented them with the restaurant minutes later. A renovated double storefront with a striped awning outside, a bright, freshly painted interior with comfortable booths and Boston ferns hanging in the windows, it was a modest oasis amid the blight.

"For years there wasn't a decent place to have lunch around here." This as he led them inside. "But as I said, we're working on Reid Avenue."

The restaurant was owned by his Three R's Group.

"So how did the visits go?" Edgar Payne asked.

"Okay."

Hungry, Sonny was busy tackling something called a hero sandwich the man had ordered for him, as a reward, he joked, for the heroic morning he must have put in visiting the two old women. The thing was almost as long as his forearm, shaped like a submarine and crammed with enough sandwich meat and sliced cheese to last him a week had he been home. Hattie who knew how to stretch their food would have seen to that.

"And my mother … ? Were you okay with her? I hope she didn't do anything to upset you …"

"No."

"Well, he certainly made out better than me. She made it clear I wasn't welcome. Wouldn't open the basement gate till I left."

Hattie still offended by how she'd been treated.

"I apologize for my mother," Edgar Payne said. "But I'm sure you remember how difficult she can be."

"Don't I! We couldn't even jump rope outside your house. She'd come storming out and chase us away like she owned the sidewalk!"

"Well things are far worse now that her mind isn't what it used to be. There's no reasoning with her anymore …" He paused, reluctant perhaps to confide in Hattie, given the fact she had been away so long; but then clearly troubled, despairing, he was saying, "My mother shouldn't be living alone, not in her condition. But all I beg, she refuses to come stay with me and the family. And she won't hear of an adult or nursing home. She ran me out when I brought it up once. Nor can I get her to go to the doctor about the Parkinson's. Nor will she let me hire someone to look after her and the house. I make sure to keep up the exterior, so the place won't be another eyesore on the block, but inside is a disgrace and she won't let me touch it. All I'm good for is to see to it her old player piano still works.

"Ulene Payne! I can't tell you how impossible she's become!"

Someone had to defend her, so putting down the mammoth sandwich, Sonny announced once again, "She showed me how to play it, her piano, and it was fun."

"You two really got along, didn't you!" Edgar Payne turned to him, amazed. A relieved smile replaced his despair. "Let's see, I bet I know how she did it."

Before he could prepare himself, the man's arms went around him from behind, the hands—one with the great seal of a ring—took up his hands and, after arranging them as his mother had done, sent them racing under his along the edge of the table.

He laughed. The outsize hands riding piggyback on his. Colossal arms encircling him. Larger-than-life face bent close to his. The man smell. A different, more powerful aura that wasn't about creams and lotions.

Hattie looked on. When they came in, Edgar Payne had quickly seated her first, then placed Sonny and himself opposite her in the booth. Now, across from them, she sat looking on and smiling, the age lines around her mouth turned to laugh lines again. Hattie smiling, yet at the same time, unawares, frowning slightly. A faint crease of a frown had alighted like a subliminal query on the smooth mocha-colored skin of her forehead. Her skin. It had been the best feature of her otherwise ordinary, "around the block" face when she was young. And it still was now that she was in her late fifties. "*Ta peau! Merveilleuse! Pas une ride!* Your skin! Marvelous! Not a wrinkle!" "Melanin," she'd say, although the French usually didn't know what that was. "*Beaucoup, beaucoup de* melanin."

"That's the way your grandfather learned how to play," the man was saying, the demonstration over. He had withdrawn his hands, his arms. "Did you know that?"

"No."

"Well, that's how. When he was small he used to sit for hours chasing after those keys, pretending he was the one playing, with my mother an adoring audience of one. I could never understand what he got out of it. I know one thing: by the time he started taking lessons he already knew how to play.

"Did you see his picture on top the piano?"

"Yes." The boy in the old-timey suit. His grandfather, part of whose name he bore. He had figured as much. He had enlisted his help with the playing.

He turned his attention back to the sandwich.

"You don't have to eat all of that big thing," Hattie said. The faint query of a frown remained.

"And what about your other great-grandmother?"

Lunch over, they were on their way to visit Edgar Payne's office, the early afternoon sun traveling overhead at the same speed as the car, while the wind that had lost much of its force over the course of the morning struggled to keep up.

"You haven't said anything about her. I bet she talked your ears off."

"She told me to cover them so's not to hear her."

The man laughed and waited for him to go on.

He left it at that though. He didn't know why, he couldn't have given a reason, but he suddenly decided he wasn't telling on her either, the Florence Varina woman, never mind all the mean things she'd said. Let Hattie tell if she wanted to, but not him.

Which she promptly did. "You would've wanted to cover your ears too if you'd heard what she had to say about you and that group of yours. Certain practices you all go in for. She had quite a list."

"I can well imagine."

"Like pressuring people to sell."

"Sometimes," he said. "Especially when they won't keep up their property. Nothing's pure."

"And the big money you make off each deal."

"Sometimes. Nothing's wholly selfless." He shrugged, paused. Then: "Look, we're doing *some* good! You don't know it, but people who gave up on the place when things really went downhill are slowly coming back, some of them. You see it more and more. You even see a number of young people moving in, young folks who understand it's up to us to save what's ours. I tell you, it does my heart good. And I'm not being sentimental."

"You'd never know any of these things listening to Mis' McCullum-Jones."

"Look," he repeated, "don't expect a kind word about me or anything I'm associated with from that woman. As she sees it, I'm the Shylock of Central Brooklyn. Her problem is that she's still waging the American-West Indian War. As if a people in our situation can afford that kind of divisive nonsense."

Said with disgust and a hopeless shake of his head.

Minutes later, he drew up before a two-story commercial building on the same long avenue. Like the storefront restaurant, the building had been renovated and updated with a new façade of permastone and tinted glass. The entrance door, though, was a Victorian grace note, a beautifully restored, highly polished double-leaf door with carved trompe l'oeil paneling and a Tiffany glass fanlight. It easily rivaled the one at 258 Macon.

> *The Three R's Group of Central Brooklyn*
> *Reclamation. Restoration. Rebirth.*

Sonny could read only the top line of the sign above the door.

"Not bad," Hattie said, looking around the office. "Naturally yours is much bigger than the others we saw."

There was an edge to her voice.

Edgar Payne ignored it. "Naturally," he said.

He had just taken them on a brief tour of the building and along the way he had stopped to introduce them to other principal members of the group. They were middle-aged men like himself in dark business suits, and one or two women. All of them were from around the block, in the wider meaning of their part of Brooklyn. One of the men remembered Hattie. They had gone to the same high school.

Afterward, Edgar Payne brought them to his office. And it was true what she said: his was much larger than the others. The spacious room was literally three rooms, an actual office, then a sitting room complete with sofa and chairs, drapes at the windows and paintings on the walls, and beyond this, a conference area.

In the office section, Hattie immediately went over to inspect two photographs on the desk.

"Ha," she said. "Everybody always knew you'd marry Alva!"

Sonny at her side gave a look. He saw a smiling woman with glasses, a close cap of curly graying hair, and a face that looked almost as white as Madame Molineaux's. She was standing in a garden in full bloom before a two-story columned house that stretched beyond the picture's frame.

Hattie: "Little quiet Alva lived over Perlman's drugstore on Reid Avenue. You could hardly ever get a word out of her as I remember."

Edgar Payne: "Don't worry, she found her voice over the years."

"And looks like you've got yourself quite a spread."

"It's Alva's spread," he said. "I would've been perfectly content to remain on Macon Street, but she always wanted out of Brooklyn and believe me, she wasn't quiet about it. So when I got a good deal on a place through one of my contacts, she got her house on Long Island, complete with that garden you see, which is her passion, and I kept our old place on the block, renting it out except for my little pied-á-terre on the top floor where I stay when I work late and don't feel like facing that long drive out to the island. We respect each other's turf, Alva and I, which is probably why we get along so well."

The other picture on the desk was of their daughter and her children, a small boy and an older girl. His daughter, Edgar Payne said, was divorced and going to law school in Atlanta. Her children lived with him and his wife.

"Alva and I are back to being parents in our old age. But we don't mind. In fact, we're doing a much better job this time around. We didn't do so good with our daughter. But then she was a handful."

This to Hattie. And to Sonny: "Bet you didn't know you had some cousins your age, did you?"

He shook his head. He had never been told about them. About any of the relatives in America. *Pourquoi?* Why? Hattie must have her reasons.

"You'll be spending this weekend with them, so you can get in some play-time. That all right with you?"

"Yes," he said. He was already beginning to miss Jean-Jacques.

"Of course we had hoped you'd be staying longer. That way you could've spent more time with your cousins. With all of us, in fact. But that's not to be."

What he meant was that Hattie was limiting the visit to two weeks. Two weeks before the concert and perhaps—but only perhaps—a few days after it was over. They had arrived on Saturday. Today was Monday. The concert would be a week from this Friday. Two of the fourteen days were already gone.

"We're gonna keep it short and sweet," she had said once she decided not to tear up the letter and the check and consign them to the Seine.

"Anyway, we're happy to have you with us if only for a day," the man said and then both startled and pleased him by bestowing a playful little uppercut on his chin.

It was as light as a caress.

There were many other pictures in the office, and Hattie, Sonny in tow, headed for the wall behind the desk. There, on display amid a collection of plaques, framed citations, and awards, was a veritable gallery of photographs showing Edgar Payne with any number of important-looking people, nearly all of them white. Edgar Payne smiling with them, shaking hands with them, and in many instances accepting checks from them, some of the checks blown up giant size.

She came to a halt in front of the largest of the pictures which hung directly behind his desk.

"Oh-la-la! Bobby Kennedy, no less!"

The image that caused her outcry showed a younger 1960s Edgar Payne who still had most of his hair, smiling and shaking hands with Robert

Kennedy. Kennedy with the toothy grin and cowlick of a twelve-year-old and the steely, purposefully directed gaze of his calling.

"Don't tell me you actually knew him?"

"Not only knew him, but worked for him."

"Oh?"

"A long story."

Before going on, he led them around to the front of the desk and seated them there, then settled himself in the desk chair opposite. A globed light overhead shone down on the bald dome of his head and on his face below, a face whose features—broad, flared nose heavy lips, high forehead—might have been carved out of the same dark sandstone as the houses he bought and sold. And under the overhang of his brow his slightly hooded eyes also hid something as purposefully directed, and even more unyielding, in his own gaze.

"Cat don't play!" is the way they would have put it around the block.

"All right, the long story."

There had been, he said, this Marshall-type plan, spearheaded by Kennedy when he was the senator from New York, to entirely rebuild Central Brooklyn—"Or what our detractors like to call Bed-Stuy, a name I never use. I call it Central Brooklyn, the heart of the borough. That's the way I've thought of it from a kid"—and as someone already in urban planning, already trying to salvage the old neighborhood—"Florence McCullum isn't the only one who loves this place!"—he had suddenly found himself on the ground floor of the most sweeping renewal project ever undertaken anywhere.

"Ulene Payne's boychild in the right place at the right time." His laugh. He became, he said, part of the senator's inner circle on the project. He was among those who helped research and draft the proposal. And when it was finally approved by Washington, he was the one chosen to head up the huge housing program ...

"You mean you didn't hear about it over there in Paris?"

"No," said Hattie.

He went on. "As for the millions-plus needed over the years for the miracle to happen? No worry. The senator vowed to keep the pipeline from Washington open. Because apart from any rich-boy altruism on his part, there were the politics of the thing: the Central Brooklyn Renewal Plan was to be a major showpiece in his bid for the White House.

"Nothing's pure. Nothing's wholly selfless." His credo again.

"And do you know we actually got it halfway off the ground ..."

"And then they killed him too." Hattie.

"Yep. The bloodletting just wouldn't quit. And with him gone and then old LBJ gone and Nixon in charge, we soon found ourselves on our own. The pipeline all but dried up. We'd have to look elsewhere for money, we knew, if we wanted to continue even on a small scale. That's when I put that picture you see behind me up on the wall, right above my head. As collateral."

"Collateral?"

"Yep. Just that. It's helped us get many a loan. The people from the banks come in here, see me and Kennedy shaking hands—they can't miss it sitting where you are—and they're more disposed to approve the loan and hand over the check. Our reputation and track record help, of course— we've been at it a long time—but nothing quite does it like that shot of me and the senator."

Suddenly, startling him, the man's hand closed around his. He'd been sitting there thinking Big People talking again and fighting sleep, the sandwich heavy in his stomach, when the Edgar Payne man suddenly reached across his desk, swallowed up his hand in his own, and began shaking it. And he wasn't being playful as with the uppercut before. He was shaking his hand seriously, treating him almost as if he were one of the important-looking people on the wall.

And with equal seriousness, he was saying, looking him in the eye, "Sometimes shaking hands with the right folks can make a big difference in this life. Remember that, okay? It might come in handy one of these days."

"Okay," he said to accommodate him. He didn't really understand.

Edgar Payne continued to hold his hand. He had become suddenly thoughtful, abstracted.

"Not that I like it all that much—the hand shaking and smiling. Truthfully, I wish it were otherwise. That we had our own banks and loan companies, our own resources, so I wouldn't always have to be running after these people skinning my teeth, saying 'Please, massa' with my hand 'long out' as my mother would put it . . .

"By the way, did you have any trouble understanding her?"

"Sometimes."

"It's her accent. Anyway, let's hope you and my grandchildren won't have to do all the smiling and begging. That's what I'm trying my best to make happen. Right now, though, my little group doesn't have a choice. It's the only way we can find the wherewithal to get the job done, which is to take the beat-up old houses you see around here that were once beautiful and make them as close to beautiful again as possible, so people like us will have someplace nice to live. Think that's a good idea?"

He thought of Hattie's many complaints about where they lived and said yes.

Perhaps to impress all this on him, Edgar Payne kept on holding his hand across the varnished surface of the desk. He only relinquished it when Hattie, who had been silently looking on, her eye on the joined hands, abruptly stood up and said, "Jet lag. I could use a nap. So could Sonny."

from *Woman at Point Zero*

by Nawal El Saadawi (Egypt)

Let me speak. Do not interrupt me. I have no time to listen to you. They are coming to take me at six o'clock this evening. Tomorrow morning I shall no longer be here. Nor will I be in any place known to man. This journey to a place unknown to everybody on this earth fills me with pride. All my life I have been searching for something that would fill me with pride, make me feel superior to everyone else, including kings, princes and rulers. Each time I picked up a newspaper and found the picture of a man who was one of them, I would spit on it. I knew I was only spitting on a piece of newspaper which I needed for covering the kitchen shelves. Nevertheless I spat, and then left the spit where it was to dry.

Anyone who saw me spitting on the picture might think I knew that particular man personally. But I did not. I am just one woman. And there is no single woman who could possibly know all the men who get their pictures published in the newspapers. For after all, I was only a successful prostitute. And no matter how successful a prostitute is, she cannot get to know all the men. However, all the men I did get to know, every single man of them, has filled me with but one desire: to lift my hand and bring it smashing down on his face. But because I am a woman and have never had the courage to lift my hand. And because I am a prostitute, I hid my fear under layers of make-up. Since I was successful, my make-up was always of the best and most expensive kind, just like the make-up of respectable upper class women. I always had my hair done by stylists who tendered their services only to upper-class society women. The colour I chose for lipstick was always 'natural and serious' so that it neither disguised, nor accentuated the seductiveness of my lips. The skilful lines pencilled around my eyes hinted at just the right combination of attraction and rejection favoured by the wives of men in high positions of authority. Only my make-up, my hair and my expensive shoes were 'upper class'. With my secondary school certificate and suppressed desires I belonged to the 'middle class.' By birth I was lower class.

My father, a poor peasant farmer, who could neither read, nor write, knew very few things in life. How to grow crops, how to sell a buffalo poisoned by his enemy before it died, how to exchange his virgin daughter for a dowry when there was still time, how to be quicker than his neighbour in stealing from the fields once the crop was ripe. How to bend over the headman's hand and pretend to kiss it, how to beat his wife and make her bite the dust each night.

Every Friday morning he would put on a clean *galabeya* and head for the mosque to attend the weekly prayer. The prayer over, I would see him walking with the other men like himself as they commented on the Friday sermon, on how convincing and eloquent the *imam* had been to a degree that he had surpassed the unsurpassable. For was it not verily true that stealing was a sin, and killing was a skin, and defaming the honour of a woman was a sin, and injustice was a sin, and beating another human being was a sin ... ? Moreover, who could deny that to be obedient was a duty, and to love one's country too. That love of the ruler and love of Allah were one and indivisible. Allah protect our ruler for many long years and may he remain a source of inspiration and strength to our country, the Arab Nation and all Mankind.

I could see them walking through the narrow winding lanes, nodding their heads in admiration, and in approval of everything his Holiness the *Imam* had said. I would watch them as they continued to nod their heads, rub their hands one against the other, wipe their brows while all the time invoking Allah's name, calling upon his blessings, repeating His holy words in a guttural, subdued tone, muttering and whispering without a moment's respite.

On my head I carried a heavy earthenware jar, full of water. Under its weight my neck would sometimes jerk backwards, or to the left or to the right. I had to exert myself to maintain it balanced on my head, and keep it from falling. I kept my legs moving in the way my mother had taught me, so that my neck remained upright. I was still young at the time, and my breasts were not yet rounded. I knew nothing about men. But I could hear them as they invoked Allah's name and called upon His blessings, or repeated His holy words in a subdued and guttural tone. I would observe them nodding their heads, or rubbing their hands one against the other, or coughing, or clearing their throats with a rasping noise, or constantly scratching under the armpits and between the thighs. I saw them as they watched what went on around them with wary, doubting, stealthy eyes, eyes ready to pounce, full of an aggressiveness that seemed strangely servile.

Sometimes I could not distinguish which one of them was my father. He resembled them so closely that it was difficult to tell. So one day I asked my mother about him. How was it that she had given birth to me without a father? First she beat me. Then she brought a woman who was carrying a small knife or maybe a razor blade. They cut off a piece of flesh from between my thighs.

I cried all night. Next morning my mother did not send me to the fields. She usually made me carry a load of manure on my head and take it to the fields. I preferred to go to the fields rather than stay in our hut. There, I could play with the goats, climb over the water-wheel, and swim with the boys in the stream. A little boy called Mohammadain used to pinch me under the water and follow me into the small shelter made of maize stalks. He would make me lie down beneath a pile of straw and lift up my *galabeya*. We played at 'bride and bridegroom'. From some part of my body, where, exactly I did not know, would come a sensation of sharp pleasure. Later I would close my eyes and feel with my hand for the exact spot. The moment I touched it, I would realize that I had felt the sensation before. Then we would start to play again until the sun went down, and we could hear his father's voice calling to him from the neighbouring field. I would try to hold him back, but he would run off, promising to come the next day.

But my mother no longer sent me to the fields. Before the sun had started to appear in the sky, she would nudge me in the shoulder with her fist so that I would awaken, pick up the earthenware jar and go off to fill it with water. Once back, I would sweep under the animals and then make rows of dung cakes which I left in the sun to dry. On baking day I would knead dough and make bread.

To knead the dough I squatted on the ground with the trough between my legs. At regular intervals I lifted the elastic mass up into the air and let it fall back into the trough. The heat of the oven was full on my face, singeing the edges of my hair. My *galabeya* often slipped up my thighs, but I paid no attention until the moment when I would glimpse my uncle's hand moving slowly from behind the book he was reading to touch my leg. The next moment, I could feel it travelling up my thigh with a cautious, stealthy, trembling movement. Everytime there was the sound of a footstep at the entrance to our house, his hand would withdraw quickly. But whenever everything around us lapsed into silence, broken only every now and then by the snap of dry twigs between my fingers as I fed the oven, and the sound of his regular breathing reaching me from behind the book so that I could not tell whether he was snoring quietly in his sleep or wide awake and panting, his hand would continue to press against my thigh with a grasping, almost brutal insistence.

He was doing to me what Mohammadain had done to me before. In fact, he was doing even more, but I no longer felt the strong sensation of pleasure that radiated from an unknown and yet familiar part of my body. I closed my eyes and tried to reach the pleasure I had known before but in vain. It was as if I could no longer recall the exact spot from which it used to arise, or as though a part of me, of my being, was gone and would never return.

My uncle was not young. He was much older than I was. He used to travel to Cairo alone, attend classes in El Azhar, and study at a time when I was still a child and had not yet learned to read or write. My uncle would put a chalk pencil between my fingers and make me write on a slate: *Alif, Ba, Gim, Dal ...* Sometimes he made me repeat after him: 'Alif has nothing on her, Ba's got one dot underneath, Gim's got a dot in the middle, Dal has nothing at all.' He would nod his head as he recited from the thousand verse poem of Ibn Malik, just as though he was reciting from the Koran, and I would repeat each letter after him, and nod my head in the same way.

Once the holidays were over, my uncle would climb on the back of the donkey, and set off for the Delta Railway Station. I followed close behind carrying his big basket, packed full of eggs, cheese and bread cakes, topped with books and clothes. All along the way, until we got to the station, my uncle would not cease talking to me about his room at the end of Mohammad Ali Street near the Citadel, about El Azhar, Ataba Square, the trams, the people who lived in Cairo. At moments he would sing in a sweet voice, his body swaying rhythmically with the movement of the donkey.

'I abandoned ye not on the high seas
Yet on the dry land thou hast left me.
I bartered thee not for shining gold
Yet for worthless straw thou didst sell me
O my long night
O mine eyes. Oh.'

When my uncle would clamber into the train, and bid me farewell, I would cry and beg him to take me with him to Cairo. But my uncle would ask,

'What will you do in Cairo, Firdaus?'

And I would reply: 'I will go to El Azhar and study like you.'

Then he would laugh and explain that El Azhar was only for men. And I would cry, and hold on to his hand, as the train started to move. But he would pull it away with a force and suddenness that made me fall flat on my face.

So I would retrace my steps with bent head, pondering the shape of my toes, as I walked along the country road, wondering about myself, as the questions went round in my mind. Who was I? Who was my father? Was I going to spend my life sweeping the dung out from under the animals, carrying manure on my head, kneading dough, and baking bread?

Back in my father's house I stared at the mud walls like a stranger who had never entered it before. I looked around almost in surprise, as though I had not been born here, but had suddenly dropped from the skies, or emerged from somewhere deep down in the earth, to find myself in a place where I did not belong, in a home which was not mine, born from a father who was not my father, and from a mother who was not my mother. Was it my uncle's talk of Cairo, and the people who lived there that had changed me? Was I really the daughter of my mother, or was my mother someone else? Or was I born the daughter of my mother and later changed into someone else? Or had my mother been transformed into another woman who resembled her so closely that I could not tell the difference?

I tried to recall what my mother looked like the first time I saw her. I can remember two eyes. I can remember her eyes in particular. I cannot describe their colour, or their shape. They were eyes that I watched. They were eyes that watched me. Even if I disappeared from their view, they could see me, and follow me wherever I went, so that if I faltered while learning to walk they would hold me up.

Every time I tried to walk, I fell. A force seemed to push me from behind, so that I fell forwards, or a weight from in front seemed to lean on me so that I fell backwards. It was something like a pressure of the air wanting to crush me; something like the pull of the earth trying to suck me into its depths. And in the midst of it all there I was, struggling, straining my arms and legs in an attempt to stand up. But I kept falling, buffeted by the contradictory forces that kept pulling me in different directions, like an object thrown into a limitless sea, without shores and without a bed, slashed by the waters when it starts to sink, and by the wind if it starts to float. Forever sinking and rising, sinking and rising between the sea and the sky, with nothing to hold on to except the two eyes. Two eyes to which I clung with all my might. Two eyes that alone seemed to hold me up. To this very moment I do not know whether they were wide or narrow, nor can I recall if they were surrounded by lashes or not. All I can remember are two rings of intense white around two circles of intense black. I only had to look into them for the white to become whiter and the black even blacker, as though sunlight was pouring into them from some magical source neither on earth, nor in the sky, for the earth was pitch black, and the sky dark as night, with no sun and no moon.

I could tell she was my mother, how I do not know. So I crawled up to her seeking warmth from her body. Our hut was cold, yet in winter my father used to shift my straw mat and my pillow to the small room facing north, and occupy my corner in the oven room. And instead of staying by my side to keep me warm, my mother used to abandon me alone and go to my father to keep him warm. In summer I would see her sitting at his feet with a tin mug in her hand as she washed his legs with cold water.

When I grew a little older my father put the mug in my hand and taught me how to wash his legs with water. I had now replaced my mother and did the things she used to do. My mother was no longer there, but instead there was another woman who hit me on my hand and took the mug away from me. My father told me she was my mother. In fact, she looked exactly like my mother; the same long garments, the same face, and the same way of moving. But when I used to look into her eyes I could feel she was not my mother. They were not the eyes that held me up each time I was on the point of falling. They were not two rings of pure white surrounding two circles of intense black, where the white would become even whiter, and the black even blacker every time I looked into them, as though the light of the sun or the moon kept flowing through them.

No light seemed ever to touch the eyes of this woman, even when the day was radiant and the sun at its very brightest. One day I took her head between my hands and turned it so that the sun fell directly on her face, but her eyes remained dull, impervious to its light, like two extinguished lamps. I stayed awake all night weeping alone, trying to muffle my sobs so that they would not disturb my little brothers and sisters sleeping on the floor beside me. For, like most people, I had many brothers and sisters. They were like chicks that multiply in spring, shiver in winter and lose their feathers, and then in summer are stricken with diarrhoea, waste away quickly and one by one creep into a corner and die.

When one of his female children died, my father would eat his supper, my mother would wash his legs, and then he would go to sleep, just as he did every night. When the child that died was a boy, he would beat my mother, then have his supper and lie down to sleep.

My father never went to bed without supper, no matter what happened. Sometimes when there was no food at home we would all go to bed with empty stomachs. But he would never fail to have a meal. My mother would hide his food from us at the bottom of one of the holes in the oven. He would sit eating alone while we watched him. One evening I dared to stretch out my hand to his plate, but he struck me a sharp blow over the back of my fingers.

I was so hungry that I could not cry. I sat in front of him watching as he ate, my eyes following his hand from the moment his fingers plunged into the bowl until it rose into the air, and carried the food into his mouth. His mouth was like that of a camel, with a big opening and wide jaws. His upper jaw kept clamping down on his lower jaw with a loud grinding noise, and chewed through each morsel so thoroughly that we could hear his teeth striking against each other. His tongue kept rolling round and round in his mouth as though it also was chewing, darting out every now and then to lick off some particle of food that had stuck to his lips, or dropped on his chin.

At the end of his meal my mother would bring him a glass of water. He drank it, then belched loudly, expelling the air from the mouth or belly with a prolonged noise. After that he smoked his water pipe, filling the room around him with thick clouds of smoke, coughing, snorting and inhaling deeply through his mouth and nose. Once over with his pipe he lay down, and a moment later the hut would resonate with his loud snoring.

I sensed he was not my father. Nobody told me, and I was not really aware of the fact. I could just feel it deep down inside me. I did not whisper the secret to anyone but kept it to myself. Every time my uncle came back for the summer holidays, I would hang on to his *gallabeya* when the time came for him to leave, and ask that he take me with him. My uncle was closer to me than my father. He was not so old, and he allowed me to sit beside him and look at his books. He taught me the alphabet, and after my father died he sent me to elementary school. Later, when my mother died, he took me with him to Cairo.

Everything Counts

by Ama Ata Aidoo (Ghana)

She used to look at their serious faces and laugh silently to herself. They meant whatever they were saying. The only thing was that loving them all as sister, lover and mother, she also knew them. She knew them as intimately as the hems of her dresses. That is was so much easier for them to talk about the beauty of being oneself. Not to struggle to look like white girls. Not straightening one's hair. And above all, not to wear the wig.

The wig. Ah, the wig. They say it is made of artificial fibre. Others swear that if it is not gipsy hair, then it is Chinese. Extremists are sure they are made from the hairs of dead white folk—this one gave her nightmares, for she had read somewhere, a long time ago, about Germans making lampshades out of Jewish people's skins. And she would shiver for all the world to see. At other times, when her world was sweet like when she and Fiifi were together, the pictures that came into her mind were not so terrible. She would just think of the words of that crazy *highlife* song and laugh. The one about the people at home scrambling to pay exorbitant prices for secondhand clothes from America … and then as a student of economics, she would also try to remember some other truths she knew about Africa. Second-rate experts giving first-rate opinions. Second-hand machinery from someone else's junkyard.

Snow-ploughs for tropical farms.

Outmoded tractors.

Discarded aeroplanes.

And now, wigs—made from other people's unwanted hair.

At this point, tough though she was, tears would come into her eyes. Perhaps her people had really missed the boat of original thinking after all? And if Fiifi asked her what was wrong, she explained, telling the same story every time. He always shook his head and laughed at her, which meant that in the end, she would laugh with him.

At the beginning, she used to argue with them, earnestly. 'But what has wearing wigs got to do with the revolution?'

'A lot sister,' they would say. 'How?' she would ask, struggling not to understand.

'Because it means that we have no confidence in ourselves.' Of course, she understood what they meant.

'But this is funny. Listen, my brothers, if we honestly tackled the problems facing us, we wouldn't have the time to worry about such trifles as wigs.'

She made them angry. Not with the mild displeasure of brothers, but with the hatred of wounded lovers. They looked terrible, their eyes changing, turning red and warning her that if she wasn't careful, they would destroy her. And, they frightened her a lot, quite often too. Especially when she thought of what filled them with that kind of hatred.

This was something else. She had always known that in her society men and women had had more important things to do than fight each other in the mind. It was not in school that she had learnt this. Because you know, one did not really go to school to learn about Africa.... As for this, what did the experts call it? War of the sexes? Yes, as for this war of the sexes, if there had not been any at all in the old days among her people, they could not possibly have been on such a scale. These days, any little 'No' one says to a boy's 'Yes' means one is asking for a battle. O, there just are too many problems.

As for imitating white women, mm, what else can one do, seeing how some of our brothers behave? The things one has seen with one's own eyes. The stories one has heard. About African politicians and diplomats abroad. But then, one has enough troubles already without treading on big toes.

After a time, she gave up on arguing with them, her brothers. She just stated clearly that the wig was an easy way out as far as she was concerned. She could not afford to waste that much time on her hair. The wig was, after all, only a hat. A turban. Would they please leave her alone? What was more, if they really wanted to see a revolution, why didn't they work constructively in other ways for it?

She shut them up. For they knew their own weaknesses too, that they themselves were neither prepared for nor ready to face the realities and give up those aspects of their personal dream which stood between them and the meaningful actions they ought to take. Above all, she was really beautiful and intelligent. They loved and respected her.

She didn't work that hard and she didn't do brilliantly in the examinations. But she passed and got the new degree. Three months later, she and Fiifi agreed that it would be better for them to get married among a foreign people. Weddings at home were too full of misguided foolishness. She flew home, a month after the wedding, with two suitcases. The rest of their luggage was following in a ship. Fiifi would not be starting work for about three months so he had branched off to visit some one or two African countries.

Really, she had found it difficult to believe her eyes. How could she? From the air-stewardesses to the grade-three typists in the offices, every girl simply wore a wig. Not cut discreetly short and disguised to look like her own hair as she had tried to do with hers. But blatantly, aggressively, crudely. Most of them actually had masses of flowing curls falling on their shoulders. Or huge affairs piled on top of their heads.

Even that was not the whole story. Suddenly, it seemed as if all the girls and women she knew and remembered as having smooth black skins had turned light-skinned. Not uniformly. Lord, people looked as though a terrible plague was sweeping through the land. A plague that made funny patchworks of faces and necks.

She couldn't understand it so she told herself she was dreaming. Maybe there was a simple explanation. Perhaps a new god had been born while she was away, for whom there was a new festival. And when the celebrations were over, they would remove the masks from their faces and those horrid-looking things off their heads.

A week went by and the masks were still on. More than once, she thought of asking one of the girls she had been to school with, what it was all about. But she restrained herself. She did not want to look more of a stranger than she already felt—seeing she was also the one *black* girl in the whole city....

Then the long vacation was over and the students of the national university returned to the campus. O ... she was full of enthusiasm, as she prepared her lectures for the first few weeks. She was going to tell them what was what. That as students of economics, their role in nation-building was going to be crucial. Much more than big-mouthed, big-living politicians, they could do vital work to save the continent from the grip of its enemies. If only for a little while: and blah, blah, blah.

Meanwhile, she was wearing her own hair. Just lightly touched to make it easier to comb. In fact, she had been doing that since the day they got married. The result of some hard bargaining. The final agreement was that any day of the year, she would be around with her own hair. But she could still keep that thing by for emergencies. Anyhow, the first morning in her life as a lecturer arrived. She met the students at eleven. They numbered between fifteen and twenty. About a third of them were girls. She had not seen them walk in and so could not tell whether they had beautiful bodies or not. But lord, were their faces pretty? So she wondered as she stared, openmouthed at them, how she would have felt if she had been a young male. She smiled momentarily at herself for the silliness of the idea. It was a mistake to stop the smile. She should just have gone on and developed it into a laugh. For close at its heels was a jealousy so big, she did not know what to do with it. Who were these girls? Where had they come from to confront her with their youth? The fact that she wasn't really that much older than any of them did not matter. Nor even that she recognised one or two who had come as first years, when she was in her fifth year. She remembered them quite clearly. Little skinny greenhorns scuttling timidly away to do her bidding as the house-prefect. Little frightened lost creatures from villages and developing slums who had come to this citadel of an alien culture to be turned into ladies....

And yet she was there as a lecturer. Talking about one thing or another. Perhaps it was on automation as the newest weapon from the industrially developed countries against the wretched ones of the earth. Or something of the sort. Perhaps since it was her first hour with them, she was only giving them general ideas on what the course was about.

Anyhow, her mind was not there with them. Look at that one, Grace Mensah. Poor thing. She had cried and cried when she was being taught to use knives and forks. And now look at her.

It was then she noticed the wigs. All the girls were wearing them. The biggest ones she had seen so far. She felt very hot and she who hardly ever sweated, realised that not only were her hands wet, but also streams of water were pouring from the nape of her neck down her spine. Her brassiere felt too tight. Later, she was thankful that black women have not yet learnt to faint away in moments of extreme agitation.

But what frightened her was that she could not stop the voice of one of the boys as it came from across the sea, from the foreign land, where she had once been with them.

'But Sissie, look here, we see what you mean. Except that it is not the real point we are getting at. Traditionally, women from your area might have worn their hair long. However, you've still got to admit that there is an element in this wig-wearing that is totally foreign. Unhealthy.'

Eventually, that first horrid lecture was over. The girls came to greet her. They might have wondered what was wrong with this new lecturer. And so probably did the boys. She was not going to allow that to worry her. There always is something wrong with the lecturers. Besides, she was going to have lots of opportunities to correct what bad impressions she had created....

The next few weeks came and went without changing anything. Indeed, things got worse and worse. When she went home to see her relatives, the questions they asked her were so painful she could not find answers for them.

'What car are you bringing home, Sissie? We hope it is not one of those little coconut shells with two doors, heh? ... And oh, we hope you brought a refrigerator. Because you simply cannot find one here these days. And if you do, it costs so much....' How could she tell them that cars and fridges are ropes with which we are hanging ourselves? She looked at their faces and wondered if they were the same ones she had longed to see with such pain, when she was away. Hmm, she began to think she was in another country. Perhaps she had come down from the plane at the wrong airport? Too soon? Too late? Fiifi had not arrived in the country yet. That might have had something to do with the sudden interest she developed in the beauty contest. It wasn't really a part of her. But there it was. Now she was eagerly buying the morning papers to look out for the photos of the winners from the regions. Of course, the winner on the national level was going to enter for the Miss Earth title.

She knew all along that she would go to the stadium. And she did not find it difficult to get a good seat.

She should have known that it would turn out like that. She had not thought any of the girls beautiful. But her opinions were not really asked for, were they? She just recalled, later, that all the contestants had worn wigs except one. The winner. The most light-skinned of them all. No, she didn't wear a wig. Her hair, a mulatto's, quite simply, quite naturally, fell in a luxuriant mane on her shoulders....

She hurried home and into the bathroom where she vomited—and cried and cried and vomited for what seemed to her to be days. And all this time, she was thinking of how right the boys had been. She would have liked to run to where they were to tell them so. To ask them to forgive her for having dared to contradict them. They had been so very right. Her brothers, lovers and husbands. But nearly all of them were still abroad. In Europe, America or some place else. They used to tell her that they found the thought of returning home frightening. They would be frustrated....

Others were still studying for one or two more degrees. A Master's here. A Doctorate there.... That was the other thing about the revolution.

Girl

by Jamaica Kincaid (Antigua)

Wash the white clothes on Monday and put them on the stone heap; wash the color clothes on Tuesday and put them on the clothesline to dry; don't walk barehead in the hot sun; cook pumpkin fritters in very hot sweet oil; soak your little cloths right after you take them off; when buying cotton to make yourself a nice blouse, be sure that it doesn't have gum on it, because that way it won't hold up well after a wash; soak salt fish overnight before you cook it; is it true that you sing benna in Sunday school?; always eat your food in such a way that won't turn someone else's stomach; on Sundays try to walk like a lady and not like the slut you are so bent on becoming; don't sing benna in Sunday school; you musn't speak to wharf-rat boys, not even to give directions; don't eat fruits on the streets—flies will follow you; *but I don't sing benna on Sundays at all and never in Sunday school*; this is how to sew on a button; this is how to make a button-hole for the button you have just sewed on; this is how to hem a dress when you see the hem coming down and so to prevent yourself from looking like the slut I know you are so bent on becoming; this is how you iron your father's khaki shirt so that it doesn't have a crease; this is how you iron your father's khaki pants so that they don't have a crease; this is how you grow okra—far from the house, because okra tree harbors red ants; when you are growing dasheen, make sure it gets plenty of water or else it makes your throat itch when you are eating it; this is how you sweep a corner; this is how you sweep a whole house; this is how you sweep a yard; this is how you smile to someone you don't like too much; this is how you smile to someone you don't like at all; this is how you smile to someone you like completely; this is how you set a table for dinner; this is how you set a table for dinner with an important guest; this is how you set a table for lunch; this is how to behave in the presence of men who don't know you very well, and this way they won't recognize immediately the slut I have warned you against becoming; be sure to wash every day, even if it is with your own spit; don't squat down to play marbles—you are not a boy, you know; don't pick people's flowers—you might catch something; don't throw stones at blackbirds, because it might not be a blackbird at all; this is how to make a bread pudding; this is how to make doukona; this is how to make pepper pot; this is how to make a good medicine to throw away a child before it even becomes a child; this is how to catch a fish; this is how to throw back a fish you don't like, and that way something bad won't fall on you; this is how to bully a man; this is how a man bullies you; this is how to love a man, and if it doesn't work there are other ways, and if they don't work don't feel too bad about giving up; this is how to spit up in the air if you feel like it, and this is how to move quick so that it doesn't fall on you; this is how to make ends meet; always squeeze bread to make sure it's fresh; *but what if the baker won't let me feel the bread?*; you mean to say that after all you are really going to be the kind of woman who the baker won't let near the bread?

Althea from Prison

by Dolores Kendrick (USA)

> *Stone walls do not a prison make,*
> *nor iron bars a cage.*
> —Richard Lovelace,
> *"To Althea from Prison"*

Can't bear no children,
I be barren, captive.

Us slaves all be captive
in this high and mighty land.

No use pretendin',
Can't bear no children.

My body done told me so,
and all them children
I been waitin' for
all these lingerin' years
done told me, too.

They gone somewhere else.
Won't come to me,
not even for a visit.

Captive folk ain't in they blood.
Sometimes I see them
disappearin' over the horizon
in they blues and pinks and short shawls,

won't come near me.

Goodbye, y'all.
Come by here one day

before the fear starts
in my bosom, if you got
the inclination,
and birth me clean,
untethered, and comely.

Chapter 5

History, Justice, and Politics

The past, as well as its relationship to the future and the present, is one of the most consistent topics in literature, and the racial contexts of oppression in the modern era naturally inspire Black world writers to demonstrate a preoccupation with history, justice, and politics. East African critic Atieno-Odhiambo observes:

> [L]iterature and history fundamentally converge. In both disciplines, the imaginative process is important, even decisive. Thus the imaginative process can be used as a tool of analysis and as a measure of quality in both disciplines.... It can plausibly be argued that the subject matter of literature is the same as history: i.e., man in society, either in his participatory or alienated condition and role.[1]

In this sense, the literary critic or student of literature can also exist as a "historian of literature ... whose basic concern is to see literature in the wider context of the history of a people."[2]

History is redemptive, self-affirming, and full of lessons. Justice and associated concerns for equality and fairness have a long tradition both in nonfiction genres such as the speech and the essay and in fiction genres such as drama and the novel. Black writers' interest in the theme of politics, or the power relationships that control a society, is driven consistently by examples from history and by desires for justice throughout Africa and its Diaspora.

The study of comparative Black literature permits the exploration of Black literature on its own terms and permits acknowledgment of the literature's historical continuum based on cultural heritage. This philosophy is evident in the writing of Ghanaian novelist Ayi Kwei Armah who uses his

---

1. Atieno-Odhiambo, "The Historical Sense and Creative Literature," in *Black Aesthetics: Papers from a Colloquium Held at the University of Nairobi, June 1971*, ed. Andrew Gurr and Pio Zirimu (Nairobi, Kampala, and Dar es Salaam: East African Literature Bureau, 1973), 81–103.

2. Ibid., 81.

novel *Osiris Rising: A Novel of Africa Past, Present and Future* to convey a historical and political statement when his protagonist Ast says, "I prefer not to forget several thousand years of our common history because of a few centuries of separation."[3] This global unit of writing from Africa and its Diaspora is a collage of recorded experience, identity, struggle, and affirmation that exists as a vast history of global African presence. The nonfiction elements of history, justice, and politics that are infused into creative literature permit the experience of reading to be an educational and culturally affirming exercise both for the communities of African descent to which the literature is most relevant and for humanity in general. Thus, since the previous requirement is a premise of the Black Studies enterprise, which, since 1968, has been largely responsible for institutionalizing the study of Black literatures in the academy, the literature must be relevant to the community from which it emanates. Black literature that addresses history, justice, and politics often exhibits the "other," who is the agent of oppression; thus, in addition to affirming Black experience, writers offer characterizations of the enemy in order to warn Black readers and prepare them for possibilities of confrontation.

Protest and commitment are two prominent themes in Black literatures. Indeed, Aduke Adebayo claims in his "Protest and Commitment in Black American and African Literatures" (1982): "[E]ven though the social contexts of black literatures are different, the dual themes of mood of protest and commitment are their most fundamental characteristics. Black writers have similar goals and this explains why their works are directed by the same mood and controlled by similar themes."[4] Nigerian novelist Chinua Achebe suggests that the Black writer "cannot be excused from the task of re-education and regeneration that must be done.... For he is after all the sensitive point in his community."[5]

Perhaps Alioune Diop best states the political power of writing when he suggests:

> The slightest word, if it is at all felt deeply by its author, discloses an explosive power calculated to challenge not only the whole basis of

---

3. Ayi Kwei Armah, *Osiris Rising: A Novel of Africa Past, Present and Future* (Pompenguine, West Africa: Per Ankh, 1995), 102.

4. Aduke Adebayo, "Protest and Commitment in Black American and African Literatures," in *Proceedings of the Xth Congress of the International Comparative Literature Association,* ed. Anna Balakian et al. (New York: Garland, 1982), 372.

5. Chinua Achebe, "The Novelist as Teacher," in *Morning Yet on Creation Day* (London: Heinemann, 1977).

the whole colonial system, but the very structure of the Western universe and of the world. Let us be under no illusion. We live in an age in which the artists bear witness and are all more or less committed. We are bound to take sides; every major work by an African writer or artist bears witness against Western racism and imperialism. And that will go on until the tensions which are throwing the world out of balance have given place to a new order installed by the free action of peoples of all races and cultures.[6]

Black writers use history as a familiar setting or tradition from which to introduce messages to the community. Historical literature requires students to survey external sources to become familiar with a region's history before attempting a thorough analysis. Aduke Adebayo's view is central to understanding this process:

Black literatures derive very closely from social phenomena and are very closely bound with particular moments in the history of black societies. The future direction of black literatures depends on the movement of those societies. Frustration, disillusionment and anger will continue to be felt not only in real life but also in literature so long as daily humiliations, injustice, inequality, corruption and other ills are present. Questions will always be asked regarding for whom and against whom, and for what purpose black literatures are written. What must not be left out in assessing these literatures, however, is how efficiently or otherwise they have stylistically carried the weighty burden of commitment.[7]

An analysis of the presentation of themes of history, justice, and politics in global Black literatures will yield a number of unique observations in categories such as structured treatment of historical episodes, comparative integrity, cycles of prosperity (reaping and sowing), and social resistance through masking.

---

6. Alioune Diop, "Opening Address," *Yearbook of Comparative and General Literature* 45 (1995): 14.

7. Adebayo, "Protest and Commitment in Black American and African Literatures," 372.

from *The Tragedy of King Christophe: A Play*

by Aimé Césaire (Martinique)

CHARACTERS

HENRI CHRISTOPHE *former slave, former cook, former general, King of Haiti*
MADAME CHRISTOPHE *former servant, the Queen*
VASTEY *Baron, secretary to Christophe*
CORNEILLE BRELLE *Duke of the Core, first archbishop of the Cape*
MAGNY *Duke of Pleasance, general*
PÉTION *President of the Republic*
GUERRIER *General, duke*
MARIAL BESSE *French engineer*
HUGONIN *a combination of parasite, buffoon, and political agent*
RICHARD *Count of the Northern Marches*
STEWARD *Christophe's Scottish physician*
METELLUS *a conspirator*
JUAN DE DIOS *Archibishop of the Cape after the death of Corneille Brelle*

Citizens, courtiers, deputies, peasants, soldiers, workers, ladies
Scene: Haiti, 1806–1820

Prologue

THE COCK FIGHT

Six to eight PEASANTS, *standing around the arena, leaning forward. When they speak, they look up at the audience. The cocks are represented by feathers moving to and fro.*

CRIES: Here dey come!
CROWD: Sharpen yuh knuckles, fellas. De better cock mus' tell today.
THE REFEREE: Cocks mus' fight till death. No doping allowed. The battle! Pétion verus Christophe!
A VOICE: Silence!
CRIES: Go fuh yuh man, Christophe.
A VOICE: Take 'im early, Christophe.
A VOICE: Make 'im chase you, Pétion. Hit, run, and weave.
A VOICE: Dis looks to be a stalemate. Seems like dey been rubbed with snake oil.
VOICE: Lick him, Christophe, kill 'im.

VOICE: Use the ground, Pétion ... more ... more.
VOICE: He's sprawled over, he's licked.
VOICE: Ref! Make Pétion fight. He's faking. Stand 'im up.
VOICE: Wash 'is ass with nettle.
VOICE: Inject 'im. Dat will take de scare out o' 'im.
VOICE: Fake! Farce! Thief! Thieving! Pétion's an ole hen.
VOICE: Get away! He's an A-1 fighter! Rub 'im wid ginger.
CROWD: Bring 'im to 'is senses.
VOICE: Time to fight back, Pétion ... Fight ...
CROWD: Wash 'im, Christophe.
VOICE: Boy oh boy.
VOICE: Mother, what a poke in the eye!
CROWD: Hurrah! Hurra-a-a-h!

THE COMMENTATOR *enters and goes front stage. He is dressed like a European gentleman of the period. The* PEASANTS *remain on the stage, but the light shifts to* THE COMMENTATOR:

THE COMMENTATOR: Fighting cocks used to have names like Drum
Major or Peck-'is-Eye-Out; today they are named after political figures: in this corner Christophe, over there Pétion. It didn't appeal to me at first, but come to think of it, it's no more unreasonable than most fashions. A King and a President of the Republic are bound to tear each other's eyes out. And if they tear each other's eyes out, why not name fighting cocks after them? ... But, you may argue, it's all very simple with fighting cocks, relations between men are more complicated. Not necessarily. The main thing is to understand the situation and to know the men the cocks were named after. Who is Christophe? Who is Pétion? That's what I'm here to tell you.

On the island of Haiti, formerly a French colony called Saint-Domingue, there lived, early in the nineteenth century, a black general. His name was Christophe, Henri Christophe, Henri with an *i*.

No, he hadn't started out as a general. He'd been a slave, to be exact, a cook (what was known in Saint-Domingue as a "skilled black.") Well, then, this Christophe was the chef at the Sign of the Crown. (Remember that name, it was coined by fate.) The Sign of the Crown was an inn in the city of Cap Haitien, then called French Cape.

Christophe fought the French, playing an eminent part in the struggle for the liberation of his country, under the leadership of Toussaint Louverture. Once independence had been gained and

Haiti was born from the smoldering ashes of Saint-Domingue, once a black republic had been established on the ruins of the fairest of white colonies, it was only natural that Christophe should become one of the dignitaries of the new state. He became, in all his glory, General Christophe, the much feared and highly respected commander of the Northern Province. Consequently, at the death of Dessalines, of Dessalines the founder, the first Haitian chief of state, all eyes turned to Christophe. He was appointed President of the Republic. But as I have said, he was a cook, in other words, a shrewd politician, and as a cook, he felt that the dish they were offering him was short of seasoning, that his presidency was rather a hollow honor. Abandoning the city of Port-au-Prince to the mulattoes and to Pétion, their leader, he set himself up in the Northern Province. From then on, to make a long story short, two states coexisted in Haiti, and none too peacefully: in the South a republic, with Pétion as president, in the North a kingdom.

There's the situation: Christophe and Pétion, two great fighting cocks, two calojies, as they say in the islands.

Yes, Christophe was King.

King like Louis XIII, Louis XIV, Louis XVI and a few others. And like every king, every true king, every white king I mean, he created a court and surrounded himself with nobility.

But now I've said enough.

I give you Christophe, I give you Pétion.

Act 1

SCENE ONE

When the curtain rises, PÉTION *is alone on the stage, pacing back and forth. He is holding a scroll.* CHRISTOPHE *enters. They greet one another with great ceremony.*

PÉTION: Upon you as Toussaint Louverture's old companion in arms, as the highest ranking general of the Army, the Senate unanimously confers the office of President of the Republic. (*He hands* CHRISTOPHE *the scroll, which* CHRISTOPHE *sniffs at from time to time but does not unroll.*)

CHRISTOPHE: The law is explicit, I am indeed entitled to the office. But what the constitution of the Republic gives me, an amendment voted under conditions of doubtful legality takes away. The Senate appoints me President of the Republic because it might be dangerous to rub me the wrong way. But it drains the presidency of all substance and my authority of all vigor. Yes, gentlemen, I know your Constitution. Christophe would be nothing but a big harmless jack-of-the-clock, with a toy sword, entertaining the populace by striking the hours of your law on the clock of his own helplessness.

PÉTION: You are unjust to the Senate. You'll always find flies in the ointment if you look too closely. The office we are offering you still has luster and importance. It is the highest in the Republic. As to the changes the Senate has seen fit to make in the Constitution, I won't deny that they curtail the President's powers, but you can hardly be unaware that there is one danger which a people that has had to live under Dessalines fears more than any other. Its name is tyranny. The threat of it is still hanging over our heads. In my opinion it would have been unforgivable in the Senate not to take due precautions against that danger.

CHRISTOPHE: I'm not a mulatto. I don't sift my words. I'm a soldier, an old master-at-arms, and I'll speak plainly: the Senate's amendment to the Constitution is an expression of distrust in me, in my person. My dignity will not let me accept it.

PÉTION: I am sorry if I have failed to make myself clear. I've been speaking of principles, and you persist in talking about your own person. But we can't argue forever. Is this the answer you wish me to carry back to the Senate?

CHRISTOPHE: Wouldn't Pétion be glad to take me at my word?

PÉTION: What do you mean by that?

CHRISTOPHE: Because Pétion is intelligent. Very intelligent. The instant the mulatto Pétion accepts the empty power you have been offering me, a miracle will come to pass. Our friends of the Senate, the mulattoes of Port-au-Prince, will play the good fairies and then presto chango, they'll fill this bowl to the brim. Take it, Pétion, take it, you'll see, it will be a horn of plenty.

PÉTION: Then you think … ?

CHRISTOPHE: I think the amendment to the Constitution is nothing but a crude trick to keep me out of power while pretending to make me chief of state.

PÉTION: And you mean to stand aside?

CHRISTOPHE: Hell and damnation! Stand aside! (*Laughs.*) Oh no, Pétion. When you teach a monkey to throw stones, there's a good chance he'll pick one up and bash your head in. Hm. Not bad. That's my message to the Senate. They'll know what I mean.

PÉTION: The Senate will know that the sender of such a message has ceased to be anything more than a rebellious general.

CHRISTOPHE: That's neither here nor there. If you want an official answer, a noble answer, the kind that will appeal to our Solons and Lycurguses or Port-au-Prince, tell them I regret that at a time like this their spirit of animosity toward my person should blind them to the greatest need of this country, of this people which must be protected, which must be disciplined, which must be educated. And that need is ...

PÉTION: Freedom.

CHRISTOPHE: Freedom yes, but not an easy freedom. Which means that they need a State. Yes, my philosopher friend, something that will enable this transplanted people to strike roots, to burgeon and flower, to fling the fruits and perfumes of its flowering into the face of the world, something which, to speak plainly, will oblige our people, by force if need be, to be born to itself, to surpass itself. There is the message, rather too long no doubt, which I charge my obliging friend to convey to our noble friends in Port-au-Prince. (*Drawing the sword and advancing front stage, in a violent tone contrasting with his preceding calm.*)

And now: my sword and my right!

PÉTION *picks up the scroll and exits. Darkness.*

SCENE TWO

A public square in Cap Haïtien. View of the bay. Ships in the horizon. Market women. Groups of citizens, with whom mingle agents of CHRISTOPHE, *among them* HUGONIN. *As the curtain rises, a woman steps forward and sings in languid West Indian style:*

In the sea
It wasn't me
Who sank the skiff
With the police

In the sea
It wasn't you
Who sank the skiff
With the police

In the sea
The Devil did that

For you and me.

Yes, Satan
Sank the skiff
Police and all.

MARKET WOMAN: Rapadou! Sugar lumps. This way for everything your
heart desires. Tafia. Rum. Tobacco twists. Tobacco braids. Tassó!
Tassó! Strips of beef. (*Addressing* HUGONIN.) Have some sugar
candy, daddy?

HUGONIN: Hiya, honey. I'm not looking for candy, you're the sugar for
me. No strips of beef. How about stripping you?

MARKET WOMAN: Bad boy! You mind your manners. Flying fish! Kuku!
Kuku! This way, gentlemen, get your corn meal mush. Corn
mean mush!

HUGONIN: My trouble is I only want to mush with you.

MARKET WOMAN: You no-good scamp! Help, police!

FIRST CITIZEN: (*sitting on a crate off to one side. Speaks to everyone and no
one*): You'll have to admit it's curious. That ship keeps turning up
at the harbor mouth, and every time they send her back.

HUGONIN: (*comes over to him and jostles him a little*): You playing dumb?
You don't know what that ship is? (*Singing*):

That's old Mister Whale
Under that white sail
Watch out, watch out for Mister Whale
He'll bite your head off without fail.

Free translation: That ship belongs to the King of France. And I'll tell you something else: if you need whips for your lumbago they've got plenty in the hold.

FIRST CITIZEN: Sir!

HUGONIN: And if your backside want to be cut up into stewmeat, likewise.
In that ship's hold they've got just what your backside is asking for.

FIRST CITIZEN: Let's not exaggerate, sir. Perhaps they've come to suggest
an understanding. After all, why not, if it can save the country
from further commotion.

HUGONIN: Isn't that lovely! Your worship has a weak heart. Your worship
dislikes commotion. My poor friend, understandings won't help.
And neither will your caution or cowardice. Just as some women
are given to falling sickness, and it comes over them at any place
or time, there are countries given to commotion, to convulsions,

and ours is one of them. That's its nature. Do you understand? No, you don't understand. Never mind.

VASTEY: Get along, citizens. Go home. That ship is none of your business. Each man to his trade. Yours is work, free work, for you are free men, free to work for your country that is in danger. Christophe's is to protect us, our persons, our property, our freedom.

SECOND CITIZEN: Well spoken! Christophe, yes. That's a man, he's got what it takes. He's not a drag-ass like Pétion. I hear that Pétion's offered to pay the former colonials an indemnity in return for recognition by the King of France. Think of that! A Negro offering to indemnify the people whom Negroes have imprudently deprived of the privilege of owning Negroes. (*He laughs bitterly.*)

HUGONIN: What are you complaining about? You know the song:

I'll sell you my cow
Good butter, good milk
And she'll calve in the spring
For a dish of cod.
I need a meal
I need it now
Then it's a deal
You've bought my cow.

VASTEY (*casually*):   Christophe is a man, yes. All the same, he's partly to blame for the situation, though obviously not as much as Pétion.

SECOND CITIZEN: Watch your step, sir. Some comparisons are offensive ... Offensive and dangerous.

VASTEY (*patiently*):   It's you, citizen, who had better watch your step. You will agree that the French—and it makes for a dangerous situation—hold us in low esteem.

FIRST CITIZEN: Naturally, because we're black.

VASTEY: Yes and no. Listen carefully. What are the white people in France saying? That Pétion and Christophe are both weaklings. The French, you see, have no respect for republics. Napoleon proved that. And what's Haiti? It's not even one republic, but two. Two republics, sir.

FIRST CITIZEN: That's a fact ... But what can we do? Heavens alive, what can we do?

VASTEY (*raising his voice as though haranguing the crowd, which gathers around him*):   The whole world is watching us, citizens, and the nations think that black men have no dignity. A king, a court, a kingdom, that's what we've got to show them if we want to be respected. A leader at the head of our nation. A crown on the head of our leader. Believe me, that will quiet the military philanthropists who think we need their kind of order.

At this moment CHRISTOPHE *appears, preceded by a drummer and accompanied by four or five more* COURTIERS. SOLIDIERS *march in, followed by a crowd.*

THE CROWD: Long live Christophe!
HUGONIN: Long live the man Christophe!
THE CROWD: Long live King Christophe!
CHRISTOPHE: That'll do! What kind of nation is this whose only national occupation is gossiping! Haitian people! Haiti has less to fear from the French than from itself. This people's enemy is its indolence, its effrontery, its hatred of discipline, its self-indulgence, its lethargy. Gentlemen, for the honor and survival of this nation, I don't want it ever to be said, I won't have the world so much as suspect, that ten years of black freedom, ten years of black slovenliness and indifference, have sufficed to squander the patrimony that our martyred people has amassed in a hundred years of labor under the whip. You may as well get it through your heads this minute that with me you won't have the right to be tired. Very well, gentlemen. Disperse.
THE CROWD: Long live Christophe!
HUGONIN: Long live the man Christophe!
THE CROWD: Long live King Christophe!

All exit. Darkness.

SCENE THREE

At the palace. THE MASTER OF CEREMONIES *and three* COURTIERS *are wearing court trousers but are otherwise in a state of undress.*

THE MASTER OF CEREMONIES: Come, come, gentlemen. Forgive me for rushing you, but the King will be here any minute. We really have to begin our rehearsal. I shall call the roll and review the general principles of the ceremony. It is a ceremony of the utmost importance, gentlemen. The whole world has its eyes on us.

The three COURTIERS *step forward and bow to each other in a little ballet of greeting. Meanwhile* VASTEY *enters, followed by* MAGNY.

FIRST COURTIER: Your Grace!
SECOND COURTIER: Your Lordship!

THIRD COURTIER (*tittering*):   Oh, Your Excellency!

> *General laughter.*

> *Two lackeys bring in a trunk and set it down rear. During the following, until* THE MASTER OF CEREMONIES *calls the roll, some twelve* COURTIERS *enter by twos and threes, rummage in the trunk, take out festive garments, try them on and exchange them.* THE MASTER OF CEREMONIES *supervises their dressing.*

MASTER OF CEREMONIES: My goodness! This king, this kingdom, this coronation, I can't believe it.

SECOND COURTIER: You can't believe it, but you can feel it in your bones. It's backbreaking.

VASTEY: A black king! It's like a fairy tale, isn't it? This black kingdom, this court, a perfect replica in black of the finest courts the Old World has to offer.

MAGNY (*Duke of Pleasance*):   My dear Vastey, I'm an old soldier. I fought under Toussaint and Dessalines, and frankly, I can't get used to these courtly ways that you seem to find so delightful.

VASTEY (*with great dignity*):   My dear colleague! Magny! I never expected to hear such words from you, the Duke of Pleasance.

SECOND COURTIER: What do we look like with these high-sounding titles of ours, Duke of Lemonade, Duke of Marmalade, Duke of Candytown? My goodness, the French must be in stitches.

VASTEY (*ironic*):   O man of little faith! (THE MASTER OF CERMONIES *looks at* VASTEY *with approval during this speech.*) Come, come. Let the French laugh. Marmalade, why not? What's wrong with Lemonade? Those are names that tickle the palate! Gastronomic names! After all, the French have their Duke of Bouillon, the English have their Duke of Yorkshire Pudding! Are they any more appetizing? So you see, there are precedents. But seriously, Magny. Whom did Europe send us when we applied to the International Technical Aid Organization for assistance? Not an engineer. Not a soldier. Not a professor. A master of ceremonies. Form is what counts, my friend. That's what civilization is … the forming of man. Think it over. Form is the matrix of being, of substance, in short, of man himself. Of everything. It's empty, yes, but what a stupendous, generative, life-giving emptiness!

MAGNY: Sounds like pretentious rubbish to me.

> HUGONIN *enters carrying a swagger stick and goes from one to the other, listening.*

VASTEY: There's one man who understands it instinctively. That's Christophe. With his great potter's hands, kneading the Haitian clay—he may not know, but what's more important, he feels, he smells the sinuous line of the future, in a word, the form. Believe me, that's something in a country like ours.

MAGNY: Damn your esthetic foolishness! If he'd taken my advice, instead of having himself anointed with cocoa oil, instead of having a crown put on his head, he'd have buckled his sword and led us to Port-au-Prince, where there's so much fine land to take and so many scoundrels to shorten by a head.

HUGONIN (*pokes his swagger stick in Magny's chest*):   I'm not a saber rattler.... Far from it. Or a beriboned minister of state.... But all the same, I've got my ideas on the subject.... It was brilliant ... brilliant, do you hear ... inventing a nobility. Now the King can baptize anybody he likes, he can be everybody's godfather. I'll admit that if the husbands let him, he wouldn't be every Haitian's godfather, he'd be their father. If I were a minister, I'd have a little suggestion for the King.

MAGNY: That's what we've come to, Vastey. A court, a nobility ... and now the king's jester.

HUGONIN: Ho ho, it's raining titles. Upon my soul, that one's as good as another. I accept it, I welcome it. Well, here's my first try. You've heard about the baby boy that a certain portly lady has had by the King? Why not baptize him the Duke of Variety?

The COURTIERS laugh violently, some rolling on the ground. Then they pick themselves up shamefacedly and straighten their clothes.

VASTEY: Riddles may be our national sport, but that one surpasses my understanding.

HUGONIN: You see, you don't know everything. But take care! Here he is ... Hell! I've got an itch in the small of my back.

The COURTIERS improve their posture.

THE MASTER OF CEREMONIES (*catching sight of* CHRISTOPHE):   Gentlemen, I beg of you, gentlemen, be silent. I shall proceed to call the roll. (HUGONIN *stands by the trunk and hands each one a hat corresponding to his rank*):

His Grace the Duke of Lemonade
His Grace the Duke of Pleasance

His Lordship the Marquis of Downwind
His Grace the Duke of Fatso
His Grace the Duke of Marmalade
His Grace the Duke of Candytown
His Lordship the Count of Stinkhole

    Equerries:
Jean-Louis Lamour
Bobo Cemetery
Jean-Jacques Severe
Etienne Register
Hercules Cupid
Joseph Almanzor

    Offices of the Royal Dahomey:
Sir Jupiter
Sir Pierre Pompey
Sir Lolo Prettyboy

The two LACKEYS *remove the trunk and bring in an enormous chair, the back emblazoned with a sun, for* CHRISTOPHE.

    Good, we are all present. Sir Leeward, master of the storeroom, will you kindly prepare the royal ornaments ... Permit me to remind you that the order of presentation is as follows: the ring, the sword, the mantle, the hand of justice, the scepter.
    Proceed, gentlemen.

CHRISTOPHE (*enters in brilliant uniform. Looks around*):   Good, good. Splendid. But what a depressing shortage of women. Bring in the ladies, assign them their places in the ceremony. (*The* LADIES *enter: fullbodied black women, dressed fit to kill. They curtsey to* CHRISTOPHE, *who taps some of the them on their rear ends as they pass.*) Come along, ladies, come along, my dear duchesses and countesses. (*The* LADIES *take their places.*) Lady Syringe ... Lady Tidbit ... Lady Easter Parade ... my dear old friend!

After Christophe's greeting each one goes rear and returns with a CAVALIER. *The couples form a procession.*

MASTER OF CEREMONIES: Your carriage, ladies and gentlemen. Watch your carriage. Let's not have angular, spasmodic movements ... Well-rounded gestures, that's what we need. Neither the stiffness of a soldier on a drillground nor the slovenly abandon of African feet and Creole arms. Let your manner be both dignified and natural ... natural and solemn ...

CHRISTOPHE (*exploding*):   Damnation! Who cursed me with such a lot of slobs ... Good Lord, Stinkhole. Stop shuffling! It's as if you were to address me disrespectfully. (*Taking* CANDYTOWN *by the collar*) ... Is that a way to hand me the scepter? I'm not going to eat you. (*Turning to* VASTEY.) He looks as if he were giving an elephant a banana. (*General laughter.*)

MASTER OF CEREMONIES: Gentlemen, let's make a fresh start. (*The couples go back rear and come forward again.*) Remember your carriage. The carriage is all-important. (*Assuming an academic manner.*) Let me explain. To walk well, you must bear yourself erect, but without stiffness, you must advance both legs in a straight line, inclining neither to the right nor to the left of your axis; the entire body must participate imperceptibly in the general movement.

The COURTIERS *apply themselves.*

CHRISTOPHE (*quietly at first, then with mounting animation*):   It's a lofty idea, gentlemen, and I'm glad to see that you have fully understood it, that you have grasped its profound earnestness.
These new names, these titles of nobility, this
Coronation!
In the past they stole our names
Our pride
Our nobility
They, I repeat, they stole them.
Pierre, Paul, Jacques, Toussaint. Those are the humiliating brand marks with which they obliterated our real names.
I myself
your king
can you sense a man's hurt at not knowing the name he's called by, or to what his name calls him?
Only our Mother Africa knows.

Vehement.

Since we can't rescue our names from the past, we'll take them from the future.

Tender and Passionate.

With names of glory I will cover your slave names
With names of pride our names of infamy
Names of rebirth, gentlemen.

*Contemplates the royal ornaments and steps forward. HUGONIN
goes up to him, throws the royal mantle around his shoulders, and
kneels down to arrange the folds.*

Playthings, rattles, no doubt.
But thunder too.
Thousands of half-naked blacks
vomited up by the sea one night.
Come from God knows where. With their scent of hunted game.
Thunder: mystic white savannah, as my Bambara ancestors said.
Thunder: power to speak, to make, to construct, to build, to be,
to name, to bind, to remake. I'll take them, I know their weight,
I'll bear them.

*The lights go out. When they go on again, the Cathedral of Cap
Haitien.*

Prologue from **Pastrana's Last River**

by Nelson Estupiñán Bass (Ecuador)

It was just as we were going up the steps onto the aircraft that was to take us
from Quito to Esmeraldas that I got the feeling of being next to an old friend,
one to whom I had ties of heartfelt fondness that went back to our childhood.
Her eyes, sad and dull rested on mine for a moment and gave a sure jolt to
my memory. I then knew for sure, as if illumined by a violent light, that the
woman climbing the steps beside me was no stranger, she was Ana Mercedes
Lazo, and she'd been out of our city for about twelve years.

"Anita!" I said to her before getting into my seat on the airplane, in a voice
that bespoke my amazement and joy. "Anita!" I repeated, and she turned toward me, her face cold and dispassionate as if chiseled in stone.

"Juanito!" she answered me, trying to smile; I thought that as in our childhood and adolescence, we would again be communicative, full of chat; but
she stood there stiff, frozen, not knowing whether to smile or not; and I also
withdrew into myself like a river suddenly arrested in its flow.

"Good morning, Anita," was my greeting as I shook her hand.

"Good morning, Juan," she addressed me, her voice tinged with infinite bitterness. "Excuse me," she added, and took her seat.

I did the same. Then I drew back my window curtain and gazed at the runway: the sun was emptying itself into the morning. Ana Mercedes, two rows ahead of me, buried herself in a magazine.

The bright light outside penetrated into my memory, like a lamp lighting up dusty old memories. I felt the chain of life reconnecting its links, I felt the sun firing once more its crucibles. However, just a short distance away was an old friend who seemed to foreclose on any beginnings, as if life itself weren't urging her on as well. For some minutes I dwelt on the past and I smiled bitterly when I understood how much Ana Mercedes's attitude was to be expected, how there were many reasons why the few words she uttered had given me the impression of being dragged all torn up across a bed of sharp, cruel stone fragments.

She was indeed, returning from a distant time, almost like a ghost, falling and getting up, cutting herself to pieces against her own walls, returning from the experience of death and a twelve year prison sentence.

* * *

Our immaculate friendship began in our childhood, and stayed that way almost until the end of our adolescence, when, without ever ceasing to be friends, the intimacy of our earliest years came to an end. Our respective homes were opposite each other, and the children of both families played indiscriminately in one or the other house. We completed elementary school together, and we went together to secondary school. We always helped each other with our work, and, during recreation, when we got back home, or while we studied our lessons, we would tell each other everything, down to the smallest detail, that happened to us. But my father's death compelled me to drop out of school, and to seek employment, as was the case with my two older brothers. I remember Ana Mercedes's opposition and tears the morning she learnt that I was not going to be accompanying her to school any more. Then her good mother, Doña Angélica—or Mama Lenca as both her own children and we ourselves called her—begged me to accompany her to the school door one morning, so that she would not miss classes that day. We got close to the school, but she—and she had been sad all along the way—refused to go in, and we retraced our steps to go sit in the park. Once there we grieved one more time over my misfortune, it was as if we had both lost our fathers. And I wiped away her tears, and mine as well, and we went back home at midday, telling our folks that she had attended classes. In the afternoon and the next morning, and on the succeeding days, she kept her promise to me and went to school as usual. And on that first night, and many other nights, very, very many, I went to her house and we would read her lessons, and it would seem to me—a vain dream—that, all of a sudden, by some stroke of luck, I'd be going back to school. All that time I would go to sleep in sadness, thinking about the lessons I was missing, about the school books that I kept neat and tidy, and about the schoolmates from whom I could not detach myself. But my father was dead, and I learned from then on that the dead do not come back. Now we would all have to be like shields, protecting our mother and ourselves.

* * *

Don Manual Lazo, Ana Mercedes's father, was the owner of a sawmill that specialized in cedar, located at the river mouth. My mother asked him for a job for me, Mama Lenca and Ana Mercedes lent their influence, and, a few days later, I began to work as a receiver of timber. For close to six months I held this position, until one Saturday, as I picked up the envelope with my earnings, Don Manuel said to me:

"Juan, I want to promote you to assistant to the paymaster. What do you say?"

"Great, Don Manuel. You don't know how grateful I am," I told him very joyfully.

"Always do well," he added. "I want to make of you an honest hard-working man, like your father was. Strive to follow his example."

"Don't worry, my brothers and I will be like him. Thank you very much for the advice."

And the following week I was no longer, as when I first got to the sawmill, counting and recording tree trunks on the wharf or in the rafts, in sun or in rain, but rather, behind a desk, an assistant to the paymaster.

* * *

Almost a year later, the paymaster, Don Gustavo Aveiga, came to the house one night. In a hurry and nervous, he had a package wrapped in newspaper in his hand. He had already seated himself in the chair I had in my room while I took my place on the bed, then he began:

"Juan, you're a good boy, a great friend, right?"

"Ahm ... look ..." my fifteen years were not enough to furnish the right response, but he continued:

"You are; I've come to see you because I consider you a good friend. You're probably no snitch."

"No, no," I told him.

He lit a cigarette and offered me one.

"I don't smoke," I indicated to him, trying hard to figure out the reason for his visit.

"Since you're a workmate and a good friend, I'm going to tell you about this. I could leave without saying a word to you."

"Leave," I interrupted. "Why?"

"Yes, I'm leaving," he reaffirmed. "I'll tell you about it."

"Don Gustavo," I again interrupted, this time almost begging, "you shouldn't leave ..."

"Listen to me first, and afterwards you tell me if I'm doing the right thing or not. This is what's going on with me. Today I received a letter from my father, who's a teller at a bank in Guayaquil, in which he tells me that he's had he doesn't know how a shortfall of twenty thousand sucres.

"Twenty thousand?" I asked him in full astonishment.

"Twenty thousand. This is the letter." He passed it over to me, but I refused to read it; he put it away in his shirt pocket. "They've given him a week's grace period to deposit the missing amount; if not, he'll go to jail. I love my father a lot, and I'm determined to sacrifice myself for him. You know what I did?"

"No, I haven't a clue."

"I stole from the safe at the sawmill. I can't let my father be carted off to prison."

"Don Gustavo!" I exclaimed sadly.

"Don Manuel won't go bankrupt over twenty thousand sucres, which I could repay if he were to agree to lend them to me; but there's no way I can let them put my father in jail. What do you think? Answer me!" he demanded a reply as he lit another cigarette.

"I don't know," I answered in all sincerity.

"I'm going to leave him an IOU," he explained, "for the amount I've taken. I swear on my honor that I'll give Don Manuel back his money. Can I count on your silence? It's because you're a good friend that I've come to tell you this; it would really hurt to have you think I was a crook. You won't rat on me? I could have gone away without anybody knowing what I've done. Or did I make a mistake in telling you all this? Say something for God's sake!" he demanded.

I could just envisage a bent old man carted off to jail by two constables, before the eyes of astonished neighbors who had considered him a decent man. "Besides," I thought, "the truth is that Don Manuel won't go bankrupt over twenty thousand sucres, which will be returned to him. Then ..."

"Can I count on your silence?" he pressed me.

"You've got it," I replied nervously.

"Do you swear?"

"Yes," I answered even more nervously.

"On what?"

"On ... my ... honor ..."

We shook hands. He gave me an envelope which I was to deliver in two days time to Don Manuel. Then he thanked me, and we said goodbye.

I went to bed, and I couldn't fall asleep until the small hours of the morning. Could it be true, was it just a lie that business of his father's shortfall? But, what need did he have to tell me his story, if he could have gone away without confiding in me about his crime. And what if he had stolen more than twenty thousand? How would I have the nerve to give this envelope to Don Manuel? Was this the way to repay his goodness, the promotion and the kindness that he and his entire family showed me in their home? And Ana Mercedes? Why did I swear to Don Gustavo on my honor? Didn't I behave like an accomplice? Why, oh why did I swear? I felt unworthy of my home, of working in the sawmill, of being a friend of Ana Mercedes, of sitting at the table with my mother and my brothers; a bad son, a bad brother, a bad friend, unworthy of the surname our father had given us. I thought about running away as well; but that would have been worse, for they would then assume that we were both thieves. I had no choice but to stay in the city, at home and on my job, and to face whatever was to come.

* * *

Two days later, in the morning, I gave Don Manuel the envelope; he, on reading the note inside, turned red with rage. Then he took the inner key for the safe from the envelope, and banging the desk with his fist he yelled:

"Damn it, this is what I had imagined! The scamp's cleaned out my safe!"

At my desk, bent over a ledger, I felt small, and as if I were getting increasingly so with each of my boss's outbursts of anger. Scared, I pretended to be working out some figures, while Don Manuel paced up and down, uttering some swear words, that I had never before heard from him. He went over to the safe, was about to open it, when suddenly turning his tracks:

"You too!" he lashed out at me. "He did this job in cahoots with you! You too!" he yelled, pointing to me, with my officemates looking on in shock. "You! You!" he exclaimed wild-eyed and frenzied.

"No, Don Manuel, I am innocent," I countered timidly.

"Why'd you just give me the envelope, then?"

I hung my head in shame, and I lied to him:

"It got mixed up with the other stuff in the room."

Little by little he calmed down; he went over to the safe and opened it; he did an on-the-spot audit with the accountant's help. Having verified the missing amount, he said:

"It's true, the crook stole exactly twenty thousand sucres."

"In my perturbed state I felt a bit of an ease. It was true what Don Gustavo had told me, I thought.

Wrinkling his brow, he went back to his desk and took up the note that I handed him; then he passed it over to the accountant, telling him:

"Read it."

He complied and this is what we heard:

> "Most Esteemed Don Manuel:
>
> I know that this is an abuse of your trust, and that you have more than sufficient reason to come after me and have me put in prison; but you will never be able to find me. I have taken twenty thousand sucres from the safe to resolve a difficult situation, which one day, when I repay you, I will tell you about in detail. I am remitting herewith an IOU for the amount that I have taken, which I propose to repay you as soon as I am able, even though this may be in some years' time. Believe me, I will redeem myself with you, although now everyone perhaps sees me as a thief. Accept my gratitude for your countless kindnesses, for the money that I will return to you in its entirety, and for the trust I didn't know how to reciprocate.
>
> Gustavo Aveiga."

When I got home from work I sent to ask if Ana Mercedes was in, but Mama Lenca replied that she had not arrived. Her not being there was very painful for me, I so wanted to tell her in detail all that had happened. And I couldn't do so that evening either, because before going back to work they arrested me.

Now, as we rode in the aircraft and I gazed at her head of hair graying a little, all of that seemed close to me too, in spite of the crustiness that she had put up, like a wall between the two of us, or at least between the past and the minutes we were now living through.

* * *

When, after I had been taken to the common jail and, against Don Manuel's wishes and testimony, charged with being an accomplice of the ex-paymaster, I managed to explain to Ana Mercedes all that had taken place, she objected:

"Why didn't you tell papa that very night or the following morning all that you've let me know?"

"I couldn't, understand me. I told you already that I had sworn on my honor, and I had to keep my word. Don't ever tell Don Manuel what I've told you. I lied to him. Do you promise not to tell him about this conversation?"

"I promise, rest assured that it'll be a secret between the two of us."

"Thanks," I said. "Now I know I've done wrong, that I've not repaid the good your father did me, nor his trust, nor Mama Lenca's affections. I am sorry, it's just as if I'd committed the theft myself. I'm expecting my punishment, because I feel guilty, kind of stained, kind of dirty. And I'm ashamed to hold up my head to look at you, it's as if I weren't the same person, as if I could never again be your friend like before."

"Don't say that, forgive me," she declared, and taking a handkerchief from her purse she brought it up to her eyes. "You know something?"

"What?"

"My birthday ..."

"Ah!"

"I'm so sad about your not being able to come to my dance, my sweet fifteen dance."

"I'm sad about it too," I told her embarrassed.

They kept me locked up for about three months. During the first two Ana Mercedes came to see me frequently, but in the last her visits ceased completely. When, in my surprise, I asked my family members about her I noticed they said nothing. I didn't know then the reasons she had for ceasing her visits to me. When I came out I was met with an unpleasant surprise: our families had fallen out. One day mama explained to me the reason for the hostility: she told me that Don Manuel, in some circles, on talking about the facts of the theft, affirmed that I had admitted being Aveiga's accomplice. Only with the passing of time could we get to the bottom of this matter: the head of investigations—interested in winning over my friend—had made me sign a statement confessing my participation in the deed. Ana Mercedes continued as before. Our families made up later on, and in the tragedy we all had the satisfaction of feeling our old bonds of affection strengthened.

From my seat I could clearly make out all this behind her pretense of being lost in thought.

Because, a shadow of herself, stripped of her petals, she was coming back from beyond the penitentiary: from a marriage thwarted by impotence and suicide.

* * *

Exploring the distant land of our childhood, I went back to a morning which left Ana Mercedes all of a sudden smitten with a wound that would always be ready to reopen at memory's slightest stimulus.

We were in the last year of elementary school, and that Saturday we were studying a grammar lesson, when, at about nine in the morning, a serious fire broke out two blocks away. With the fire spreading quickly, people began running away, the streets, darkened by the pall of heavy smoke, were filled with their anguished cries, and Don Manuel came home in a hurry.

"It's not serious," I remember him saying, "don't be afraid. We must keep calm."

The firemen's siren suddenly filled the air, its sound assailed us and we felt it like a serpent coiling around our bodies; I can still see us, the three young Lazos and me, trembling speechless and terrified by the spine-chilling sound that morning.

Ana Mercedes, shaking like a flimsy leaf, flew to the protection of her father; he enfolded her tightly in his arms, but, when he tried to pluck up her courage, working hard, but smiling, he saw that she had fainted. I sped off to my house. From then on, every time the fire alarms sounded the same thing would happen to her in the arms of Don Manuel, Mama Lenca or her brothers.

Now, up in the air, I could see all this with crystal clarity, as if through a newly polished pane.

Because she was returning, freeing herself finally, from the tragic spiral of a siren, that, like an evil shadow, had followed or hounded her for more than ten years.

* * *

There also came to my recollection the morning of that dreadful day, when after the terrible final act, I went to a store for a black tie. Two girls were conversing as they window-shopped: Pilar, defeated two years earlier by Ana Mercedes in the provincial beauty contest, and Nela, the brand-new Miss Esmeraldas. I heard their conversation.

"Just pretending to be a sweetie pie, lovey dovey, and under it all just pure greed. You must well know who got her to win the crown when she competed against me."

"Oh yes."

"Thirty thousand sucres is what he spent on votes, that damn black man ... what am I saying! ... may he rest in peace ... thirty thousand sucres to get her to win. And she still wanted to make people believe that her supporters had put up the money, her friends from town, the battalion officers! As if all of us girls didn't know that the old man was interested in her ..."

"He thought she was very pretty."

"No, Nela, you know that there's nothing pretty about her. Can you call a girl like her pretty, no bust and with legs like noodles? The thing is that old cats like young rats, and she liked his money, not him. As you know, I'm just a half inch short of the Miss Universe measurements. Check me out, look at me good." She turned around twice so that her friend could get a better look at her, "and tell me plain, girl, do I or do I not outclass that Ana."

"You're better," the other agreed under pressure.

"If I had lost to you, I wouldn't have said anything, but I never accepted being beaten by that prude with the old man's money. That's why I hated her, and I'll hate her all my life. Maybe the curse I put on her that night has caught up with her."

"Don't say that, Pilar; we should never rejoice in the misfortune of others."

"So I mustn't be happy if God heard my plea? How I suffered that night when I found out I was beaten! You can't imagine what it is not to be able to sleep, and to count the long hours, and to toss and turn in your bed, and to cry like mad not knowing what to do! When I remember all that, and the sad months that followed, it seems to me that any punishment they get is little ..."

"Pilar, don't talk like that," Nela censured.

"Why? Do you know what they're saying now, what the friend by the corner who called me over when we were coming told me?"

"No."

"That the lovey-dovey, as they once called her, poisoned her husband ..."

"No, that can't be so, you know what kind of thing slander is."

"Slander? It's the pure truth! Can you believe there was love in that marriage? Don't be a fool, girl. What she wanted was money, not love."

"I know Ana Mercedes, and I don't think she's capable of doing what you're saying."

"You don't know her, and you don't really know any woman either. You're still a little bit dumb, I mean naive."

"You would marry a man only for his money?"

"If some fool with money came on the scene, of course I would do it, and get rich overnight; and if he were old, so much the better, because he'd give me little to do. What would it matter to me what people said!"

"I don't like to hear you talk like that, Pilar."

"What's wrong with what I'm saying? About the other stuff, I'm only repeating what everybody has begun to say, that she poisoned him to get rich. It was the punishment they both deserved! Thank you, beautiful Mother Mary! Virgin most ..."

"Pilar! Pilar! Help, sir, help me!"

I felt—although I was no friend of hers—Nela take hold of my arm violently; I helped her. We managed to hold up Pilar next to a scale, she was stiff, her teeth chattering; the store clerks went into a tizzy; they finally took her into the owner's office, and there, placed on a sofa she was attended to.

"This always happens to her," Nela explained. "She begins speaking, she raises her voice, she gets all excited and faints."

Having bought my tie, I went on my way. Now, flying over the dense forests, I remembered all this. Not the noise of the engines, not the sudden air pockets, not the coast that was bringing us its messages of warmth, nothing could interrupt the torrential flow of my memories. All of that was, to be sure, distant, and however, it seemed vivid and close, it was as if having had it evoked by the nearness of Ana Mercedes it was brought fully back to life.

Because she was returning from the flip side of our time, like a trace that the years had been unable to entomb.

* * *

One evening when I was at Alejo Muñoz's bar, José Antonio Pastrana and Alfredo Cortés came in.

"I don't know," Pastrana said to him, placing on the table a book he had been thumbing through, "if you agree with me, but the truth is that for me women are like rivers."

"Like rivers?" his companion asked in surprise.

"Yes, like rivers. I'll explain. Don't you think that a woman when she is born is almost like a river as it begins its course across the land. Just as a mother in her rupturing feels the joy, the land must have rejoiced when, after its convulsions, it managed to send forth its first rivers towards the sea. Doesn't it seem that way to you?"

"Cheers," said Cortés, avoiding an answer.

"Cheers. And let's go on. The river flows on, fertilizing the fields. The land seems more beautiful in the wash of its waters. Don't populations, streets, families, houses become more beautiful when girl children grow up? Don't you see, really, the similarity there is between a river in its beginnings and a woman in her childhood. Everything becomes prettier with a girl and a river."

"Perhaps," conceded Cortés doubtfully.

"I tell you again that they resemble, they blend into one another, they're one and the same. Sometimes the river in its early stages clambers over high ground, and then with a fatal leap, throws itself headlong, it looks like a piece of torn lace as it descends sparkling clean among the rocks. The waters splash violently only to emerge purer. In the same way a woman, at times, rises up, driven by some inexplicable fit of madness, to come crashing down and emerge purified after her fall. Have you seen women who had been lost pick themselves up to become better than they were before?"

"That's right."

"But there's more. Rivers produce energy and brighten up the fields. Don't you see, too, that women brighten up our lives, and they draw forth from us and themselves so much energy, such great capacity for struggle and suffering, that would never have flourished without their encouragement. You can be sure: a single man is an arid desert, he lives in the dumps because there's no woman in his life; the land is sick when it has no river."

"Cheers."

"Cheers. And further. Have a little patience. Have you seen a damn?"

"No."

"The river is locked up in it, it's as if it were locked up, as if there were an attempt to hold it back. Perhaps the river gets mad to begin with, but it ends up giving in, surrendering its tremendous hidden strength. So, too, a woman, for example, in the case of bad marriage or a forced one, seems to be a prisoner, like someone behind bars; but if she's decent, she, too, ends up giving in, like the rivers. Why? To give the world the harnessed energies that children represent."

"You're right."

"Yes, Alfredo, women are like rivers. Have you seen rivers which, at intervals, seem on their own to halt their flow toward the sea? Don't you find them like those women one meets from time to time who keep their good looks, who look like their daughters' sisters? It's as if everything around them were shriveling up as they remain untouched? And have you seen rivers that at some tides back up, as if they were returning for something that they had forgotten? Have you seen women who turn on their own tracks and go back to a man, with the tenderness of a homecoming?"

"Yes, yes," Cortés agreed, "I myself had such an experience. A woman came back, like a river, as you put it."

"Excuse me for going on and on with this and beating a dead horse as they say. Have you seen rivers raging in winter with their dangerous whirlpools like spirals of death? Don't you know, too, of deadly women, just like those foaming whirlpools? And have you seen how beautiful rivers become at flood tide, and how they spread out? Doesn't it seem to you that swollen rivers are like pregnant women stretched to the limit by love?"

"Yes, you've convinced me. Cheers."

"Cheers. I could continue the comparison, but I'm afraid I might tire you. Women are like rivers in almost every respect."

"You're right. That's it!" Alfredo exclaimed glad, as if he had caught something that was floating in the air. "Then you won't get upset?"

"Why?"

"When are you and Ana Mercedes getting married?"

"Day after tomorrow. Why do you ask me that, you knew when?"

"It's just that … I want to tell you something."

"Go on feel free," José Antonio encouraged him.

"Well … I want to tell you … to tell you that hearing all you've told me, it seems to me that Ana Mercedes is also … like a river," Cortés concluded with difficulty.

"Of course she is," José Antonio roundly corroborated.

"Then …"

"Yes, I know already what you want to tell me … She'll be my last river. Did I guess right?"

"Yes … yes …"

"But, why are you putting on that funeral face? Cheers."

"Cheers."

I left. They continued their conversation.

And now Ana Mercedes, José Antonio's last river, one that the wealthy man could not cross, was near to me, flying at that very moment over the tranquil bay, replete with masts of all sorts, as the pilot made his final approach. It was the return to the scene of her drama.

For she was coming back from beyond absence, like a river once diverted that finds its bed again.

* * *

Don Manuel was dead, his two sons were married and living in Guayaquil, and Mama Lenca was waiting in the airport by herself. In the terminal building, mother and daughter embraced movingly and sobbed a good while. I didn't dare interrupt them. It was in the city, as we were getting into the car that would take us home, that I managed to greet the old lady.

In the afternoon, resting in my room, more waves of recollections returned. Why were Ana Mercedes, her past and all of its ghosts stuck in my head?

Now the jury engaged my memory, that sultry day at the theatre, jam-packed with relatives, friends, and spectators. José Antonio's death had divided the town in two. Black Consuelo Quendambú—who had arrived from Quayaquil eight days after the demise of her erstwhile live-in-lover, mother of three of the magnate's children—had mobilized all her people. On the other hand Ana Mercedes's friends and sympathizers had turned out in large numbers. The black neighborhood seemed to have moved in its entirety into the theatre, in support of the Quendambú woman and her offspring. The light was faint, the air thin, and the black folks, from the gallery sent forth thunderous, cutting cries:

"Down with the murderer."

"Send her to prison."

"Give her sixteen years."

"Down with Ana Mercedes!" shouted Pilar between two black people.

On the stage, at a large table, seated in some cumbersome chairs, were the judge, the four members of the jury, the prosecutor, the lawyer for defense, the secretary and two clerks. At one side of the table, seated at a student desk, was Ana Mercedes, dressed in mourning.

"Take her away from here," thundered the Quendambú woman enraged and not understanding what was going on.

"Take her away," Pilar joined her from the gallery.

The judge enjoined silence, and asked the police to eject anyone who interrupted the proceedings.

Mama Lenca—who had attended contrary to her husband's wishes—Don Manuel, Horacio, Milton, my brothers and I were in the last row. The mother was crying tirelessly, but resisted our suggestions that she should leave.

"I have to be at my daughter's side on her most difficult day," she contended.

In the midst of our anguish, the children of both families felt somewhat pleased, experiencing a palpable togetherness at that critical moment.

Then began a tiring review of the case, the pages were read by the secretary in a monotonous voice that we could barely hear; afterwards the prosecutor pronounced a lengthy discourse, with questions and more questions for Ana Mercedes; then it was the turn of the lawyer for the defense. Ana Mercedes's cook was called to testify; the Quendambú woman also appeared, she said what we all knew already: she had lived with José Antonio for some years previously, she had returned from Guayaquil some days ago, and she had had three children with the deceased. When she tried to go beyond the question asked, the judge energetically called it to her attention; she quickly left the stage, sending the defendant a look chock-full of hatred. Five hours later the judge declared a recess. Ana Mercedes was obliged to remain seated at the desk, guarded by a constable, who advised that without any exception it was absolutely forbidden to approach her. Two hours later the jury was seated again. This time the prosecutor furiously assailed Ana Mercedes's dignity. At one point in his intervention he asked:

"Why did you get married? Did you perchance love your late husband?"

"Yes," she answered baldly.

"You're lying!" the prosecutor refuted.

"You're lying!" the Quendambú woman yelled.

"You're lying!" repeated Pilar. "Charlatan!"

"Silence!" clamored the judge.

"Did the defendant know that the deceased paid for her to be chosen as Miss Esmeraldas two years ago, and that he spent more than fifty thousand sucres on votes?"

"I didn't know that; many people helped me."

"Yes she knew!" Pilar contradicted. "Liar!"

"Silence!" roared the judge. "Constable, the next time that woman shouts, throw her out of here!"

"Would the defendant say," continued the prosecutor, "whether she knew that the deceased had a woman and three children at the time of his marriage?"

"Yes I knew, but Pepe swore to me that he had finished with her forever."

"Lies, pure lies!" the Quendambú woman shouted.

"Lies! Lies! The defendant is lying!" bellowed the gallery.

"Silence!" demanded the judge apoplectic.

"Your honor," continued the public prosecutor, "the accused is lying. The deceased could never have told her that."

"He swore it to me," Ana Mercedes reaffirmed.

"She is a schemer, your honor! And now would the defendant tell us: did you or did you not know that Don José Antonio was a rich man, a millionaire, the owner of two sawmills, of estates and houses? Answer!"

"Yes I knew!"

"Is it true that the victim, your victim!" he stretched out his tremulous hands, like hooks, right up into Ana Mercedes's face, "had been courting you for a long time, yes or no? Answer!"

"We were very good friends, we understood each other ..."

"You understood each other? You were friends, very good friends?" the prosecutor asked her scoffingly. "Did you perhaps not realize that by accepting his courtship you were undermining the home that the deceased had established with Doña Conseulo Quendambú, the worthy mother of Don José Antonio's three children? Or did you already at that time envisage the prospect of becoming a millionairess, faking a love you never felt? ..."

"Objection," shouted the defense attorney, rising to his feet. "He has no right, your honor, to ..."

"He has a right, Counsel for the Defense," the magistrate replied. "Proceed Mr. Prosecutor."

The defense lawyer sat down. Then the prosecutor struck:

"Or could it be that you had already lost your honor, that you had already been deceived by some young man, and that you tried to sell the little that was left of your honor for a high price to a decrepit old man? Answer!"

Many voices expressed approval:

"That's the way to talk!"

"Bravo Mr. Prosecutor!"

He bowed in acknowledgement of the audience's applause; then he demanded:

"Answer my question in a loud clear voice!"

"It is not true!" the defendant responded violently, rising to her feet. "I went to my marriage bed intact! I swear it by God and by my mother!" she concluded and sat back down crushed.

"I most strongly object!" counsel for the defense exclaimed, getting to his feet angrily. "It is unconscionable, ladies and gentleman of the jury, that the dignity of a lady would be dragged before the entire town, with questions of this nature that bring shame to society ..."

"Silence, Counsel for the Defense!" the judge directed. "Proceed, Mr. Prosecutor."

But the defense attorney, indignant and deaf to the judge's ruling, went on, fired with passion and raising his voice over those of the judge and the prosecutor:

" ... in this setting which should be a tribunal where at least civilized behavior should reign, the very consideration that society owes its members is being trod underfoot. How could one possibly hurl such abuse at a woman to her very face? This is an affront to society and to justice!"

"Silence, Counsel for the Defense!" demanded the judge. "You will have your own turn!"

It was at that moment that Mama Lenca collapsed. In a flash we all congregated around her. Then—and was I not, as it turned out, also perhaps responsible in part for Ana Mercedes imprisonment?—I shouted out in desperation:

"Mama Lenca! Mama Lenca! Mama Lenca is dying!"

We wept, believing she had indeed died. For a while confusion reigned in the orchestra seats, and someone cried out then:

"Doña Angélica, Ana Mercedes's mother has passed!"

The defendant stood up, and tried to go down the stage steps, but the judge cut her off:

"Constable," he commanded, "stop the prisoner."

She was pushed back to her desk; for a while she just sat there, looking on at the ruckus; suddenly she threw her head back indignantly:

"My mother! My mother! Let me give her one last kiss!"

She rose to her feet again, trying this time to throw herself into the orchestra seats, but the unflinching judge again ordered the bailiff to stop her. Crushed, she burst into convulsive sobs, with her face on the desk top, while the ensuing uproar all but caved in the theatre:

"Give her a chance to see her mother, heartless beasts!"

"Give her a chance, shit, she can't run off anywhere!"

"Give her a chance, give her a chance, don't be so wicked!" even Pilar demanded, and, to the surprise of the black folks, she went down quickly in the middle of the ruckus.

"Let the trial proceed," said the unflappable judge. "Mr. Prosecutor ..."

Mama Lenca, transfigured, without regaining consciousness, was being taken out by Don Manuel and a friend. It was then that Ana Mercedes, livid, stood up at her desk, and said in a thunderous voice, in the very faces of the jury:

"I killed him! I killed him! It was me! It was me!" all the while frantically beating her breast with her open hand. "I had lost my honor, yes, I had lost it, and that was it, and because I was greedy for Pepe's wealth, that's why I got married! And that's why I killed him! I killed him! You heard me, let the whole world hear me, I poisoned him!"

The whole theatre trembled in amazement. Her eyes bulging, she seemed to be defying the tribunal with the rage that poured forth in torrents from her words, from her hands, from her arms, from her eyes, from her hair, from her legs; she gave herself over entirely to the unprecedented explosion of rage and defiance. Then turning to face the tense audience, she continued:

"I poisoned him! Me! Me! Me!" she kept on insanely beating her breast. "Isn't that what the prosecutor, the jury and you, and everyone else wanted to hear? I alone am guilty of the crime! Kill me, imprison me, condemn me, but you have no right to kill my mother! Don't kill her, for God's sake! She is innocent! I am the murderer! Me! Me! I was always an evil person! From my childhood, I've always been perverse! I was born cursed! Now that you know, that I've said it all with my own mouth, sentence me, but let me see my mother, and don't humiliate me in front of my friends!"

"Damn you," Pilar interrupted her in a frenzy, "let her see her mother! Or did you members of the jury not have mothers?" she kept on hysterically pounding the edge of the stage with her hands. "Show some mercy, for God's sake! Or are you beasts who have no hearts?"

Mama Lenca came to at home. One month later her daughter was leaving for Quito to complete a sentence of sixteen years in the García Moreno penitentiary. By law she forfeited her share of the deceased's fortune, which went in its entirety to the children of the Quendambú woman. With Ana Mercedes's arrival all of these recollections flooded my memory, our past was made present. She was a bench mark in time, standing above all the events and things, a living bench mark, still upright.

* * *

Four days after our return to the city—a Sunday—I had lunch with Mama Lenca and Ana Mercedes. We ate merrily; mother and daughter were happy, as if life were just beginning for them, as if the ill-fated events had never occurred. We spoke about things unrelated to anything that could take us back to the past; I was pleased about all that; but, suddenly, just as I was thinking about saying goodbye:

"OK, now," declared her mother taking her leave, "tell him what you don't want to tell me."

I was astonished, but Ana Mercedes intervened:

"Don't be astonished, Juan. When you greeted me on the aircraft, and also during the trip, you must have been surprised by my behavior; but I think you must have understood and forgiven me. Now I, surely, look different to you; to tell the truth, I feel like a new person, I'm sure that here people won't look at me with the curiosity they have for criminals. You understand?"

"I understand," I told her, "this was what should have happened."

"I want you to forgive me, because I treated you in a way I shouldn't have."

"Don't worry about it."

"Now I want us to be good friends, like before."

"Delighted," I accepted her offer. "Like before."

"How happy this makes me feel!" she sighed; she paused, then added: "I have to let you in on a big secret, a horrible truth. I've kept it in for ten years, but every day I feel a greater need to shake myself loose of this weight."

"What're you saying?" I asked her laughingly, trying to overcome the somber mood that threatened to engulf us."

"A mystery that I almost don't dare talk to you about."

"Then I'm the one who will talk about it," I declared, drawing her into my trust.

"You're the same as before; you haven't changed."

"Why should I change? I wish I could always stay like this."

"You remember when you went to school with me that last morning?"

"And we didn't go in," I told her, "but here at your house we let them believe that you had gone to classes."

"Oh happy times!" she exclaimed. "Like I told you, I want to let you in on a secret, I want to confess something to you and to give you something. Listen to me well. I did not poison José Antonio."

"Who said that? Me, maybe? No, never, Ana Mercedes ..."

"No, not you, Juan; but I called myself a murderer, you remember? I said that I had poisoned him to get his wealth. You must have understood, I couldn't stand any more torture that day ..."

"I thought so. Although you refused to tell me the truth, later I guessed it."

"But, the other? Didn't many people believe I had really poisoned José Antonio? Don't they probably still keep on believing so?"

"I don't think so."

"Well," she resumed her somber air, "this is my confession; I did not kill him, but I'm not completely innocent either. I accepted my sentence as a form of expiation."

"How so?" I asked her intrigued, "An accomplice?"

"No, the cause. I still feel a little shame, but I have sworn to be a new woman. You must understand there's no one forcing me to confess this to you, that few women would have told you this once they were free; it's my conscience that's forcing me to bare myself to you. That's why I've resolved to give you ..."

"What?" I interrupted her, amazed.

"Wait ..."

She went to her room. I was lost in thought. What did all this mean? I had always considered her completely innocent, but she herself had just confessed to me that she was guilty. When she returned, she told me.

"A moment ago I told you that I was going to make a confession to you and give you something. I just made the confession; now I'm giving you the thing. Take the envelope; it's been with me for twelve years in the penitentiary. It's yours; I'm giving it to you."

I took it; it was faded and crumpled.

"Mine," I asked her still in a daze.

She smiled. She was serene, sure of herself, without any exaggeration, as if at the heart of her fullness, equidistant from the past, the present and the future. I studied her face, it seemed beautiful to me, as if youth had returned to it. Then I ran my eyes over her from head to toe, and looking closely into her eyes, I understood that she was her old self and a new woman at the same time.

"It's yours, completely yours," she insisted, instilling me with confidence.

"Can I open it?" I asked her.

"No, not here," she said lowering her head. "Open it at your house."

As I was about to say goodbye Mama Lenca came back in; then with a strong handshake:

"You will come back, as you promised," Ana Mercedes reminded.

* * *

I went back in three days time, and I found her more effusive. The old rooms were being changed up; as far as I could see they were opened up, sunlight and air could enter freely. The corridors had been scrubbed, they sparkled. Ana Mercedes was happy, totally involved in fixing up the house. I felt that her own gushing spirits, her renovation, her desires, in sum her whole being, were pouring forth merrily into the property; I had the impression that she and the house were one unit, fused together by the will to survive clear and upright. She was a mess, barefoot and her dress was damp.

"How are you?"

"As you see, trying to tidy up things, to brighten up the place. I want to air out the rooms, I want as much sunshine as possible to come into the house. You know something? I've learned to really love sunshine, air, light; I want to see everything brightened up."

She paused, looked at me and added:

"Even my very life. But, I'm not just talking foolishness, right?"

"No, I'm delighted to hear you talk like that."

"You will excuse me, since we've been friends from childhood. I want everything to be bright, like a cloudless sky. I want to live a new life, as if I've become a new person with my repentance. Otherwise the sentence wouldn't have done me any good …"

"You really do seem like a new person, or the continuation of the Ana Mercedes who used to go to school with me everyday."

"Past times!" she sighed melancholically, closing her eyes for an instant, a prisoner of her memories again. After a pause, she asked me: "You read the notes? What do you think?"

"Oh, there's so much there we could talk about! Can I tell you something?"

"Why not? Aren't we still friends like before, or do you despise me now that you know the truth?"

"No, on the contrary, I feel like our friendship's been strengthened."

"What were you going to tell me?"

"I heard it said that José Antonio was a man obsessed with money, utterly without feeling; I also heard people speak highly of his learning. That's why I wanted to tell you that much could be written on the notes he's left."

"Do you remember his library?"

"Yes."

"You knew that he read tirelessly into the early morning. That's why I began to like him. He struck me as a man very different from the rest, and I love whatever stands out, whatever seems different from the norm. Really, you read the notes already?"

"Yes."

"And …" she inquired of me as if suspended in midair.

"Was all of that true?" I asked her.

"Yes, it was all true, absolutely everything …"

She looked at me deeply, and I thought at first that her look was somewhat of a recrimination or an act of defiance, a belated outburst of insidiousness and resentment towards me, towards the world, towards everything; but I immediately understood that she had gone outside of herself and had returned in triumph, surpassing her own limitations; that she was reborn, out of the old principles, unscathed by the timeless edicts, above our time and our people, and she could feel compassion for us because she was illuminated by a light that did not reach us. Her look was becoming tender and embracing, as if she were descending some slope, like the light that softens twilight. She went on:

"Tell me frankly, don't you despise me now that you know the truth?"

"No, Ana Mercedes, my esteem for you will be greater now that you've let me in on your great secret, which perhaps could have saved you or lightened your sentence. Now that I've gotten to the bottom of things I don't find sufficient reason for you to have declared yourself the killer. Or didn't you have the notes then?"

"I had them from the time Pepe was giving his last gasps, but I was guilty, and in my own conscience I stood condemned. Our own conscience is our highest court. Now I understand that emotionally upset as I was that day of the trial, I was more myself, and that all the rest were merely the circumstances which hastened the events that inevitably were to occur as they did. The twelve years have been my expiation."

"Ana Mercedes," I interrupted her, "let's forget all that. Don't you think that once I've read them, I ought to burn the handwritten notes?"

"Burn them, you say? No, Juan, just as I want light and air to penetrate the rooms of our house, I want my tragedy to be exposed to general view, for people to know what really happened; that's why I gave you the papers."

"Exposed? You realize what that would mean?"

"Of course, I've thought about it a lot."

"What do you expect to get from this?"

"I want everyone to know the truth."

"The truth?"

"What? Are you, too, afraid of the truth?"

"No, but what're you going to achieve with this?"

"I don't know for sure, but I feel that I'm in the dark, and I want light, I swear to you."

"Are you suggesting publication, then?"

"You know more about those matters than I do. I could only help you in whatever way you think fit, if you take it on. I told you already the other day that the manuscripts are entirely yours; do whatever you want with them, but I insist that you should write this story so that people won't keep on believing that I'm a poisoner."

"OK," I consoled her, "We'll talk about it again. See you again soon."

"See you then, Juan."

* * *

I reread the manuscripts in their entirety, and I still thought that they should be burned. They contained copious information about José Antonio's life, but even so it seemed to me that it should all be kept quiet in the interest of Ana Mercedes. Why not bury all that deeper, instead of bringing it up out of the earth? She continued fixed in her idea, we couldn't come to any agreement. Things went along like this, and I thought that I would end up winning the argument, among the reasons was the fact that she was rapidly gaining back her old friends—so great was Ana Mercedes appeal that even the very Pilar Quintana figured among her close friends—until one day ...

We were at the cinema looking at a second-rate movie. The plot consisted of a set of changes the protagonist was going through to bring about the death of her husband, a millionaire; the motive of her crime, greed. Just as—could it have been a wickedly deliberate or unintentional act?—the scene was playing in which the woman, by shooting him in the back, murdered her husband, the lights in the movie theatre came on; along with the ensuing protest from the audience for the interruption, almost all eyes, like darts, fixed their gaze on Ana Mercedes; then her name was uttered in a low murmur that spread throughout the entire cinema. I was angered, but she, calmly, said to me:

"You see? People think exactly what I told you. Don't you think we ought ..."

"Yes," I cut her off, "we ought to publish it all, let them know what happened, let them know that you did not poison him."

"I've been hoping to hear you say that. Now I'm happy, and the stares and whispers don't matter to me. And what about you?"

"No, not to me either," I answered, angrily looking up at the audience.

"Really?" she inquired, checking my eyes.

"Really," I confirmed, staring straight back at her.

"How happy I am! You're becoming again the steady friend of childhood."

"We are becoming," I corrected her.

She took my hand in hers tenderly.

* * *

At that time, in support of a work stoppage by port workers, there was a strike by private-sector employees. As a result of the problem—as was the case with many co-workers—I lost my job. A friend who was clearing out a holding in an almost inaccessible jungle area, invited me to his property. I accepted with pleasure, and I set out, taking with me the notes and the information that I had gathered on José Antonio. I promised my friend that I'd return when I had finished my work.

I was back in town in two months time. On my arrival my mother gave me the crushing news: Ana Mercedes had succumbed three days earlier.

"To what?" I asked her my voice as unsteady as I was.

"The same thing as her father," she answered sorrowfully, "her heart. She went to bed, and she was found dead the next morning on the floor, by the night table."

I felt that I was going to pass out; mama held me in her arms and told me: "I too have wept over her death."

She accompanied me to my room. I locked myself in it. That day I spoke no more than a few words.

The next morning I went to give my condolences to Mama Lenca; she told me that Horacio would be coming in a little while and that he would be taking her to live with him in Guayaquil. As I was leaving, she handed me a letter, muttering:

"It's for you, it's from Anita. She wanted to send it to you, but didn't find anyone. I don't believe that the mail service reaches up to that area where you were," she concluded between sobs.

"No," I concurred sadly.

In the doorway I ripped open the envelope and read:

"Juan:

I received your letter. How are you? I hope that you are well, and there're no problems.

I'll say again that I miss you; there's no one I feel comfortable talking with as I do with you. When do you plan to return?

My girl friends have multiplied like you won't believe. Last Sunday some twelve of them were over to the house; they asked me if they could bring their friends, and before we knew if we had a nice party going; we danced until nearly midnight, or rather, they danced, for I just took two or three spins, and I preferred chatting with the girls who weren't dancing. I've forgotten how to dance; when you come back you must give me some practice so that we can go to parties. Mama was glad to see me happy.

How's your writing going? I guess you must be nearly finished. I'm very anxious to read what you've written. At times I feel the urge to go and visit you, to give you a surprise, but you know how difficult things are around here. Remember what I told you again when we were saying goodbye: I want people to know the truth about that whole affair, I don't want them to consider me a poisoner, although I know the other offense is also grave. I won't rest until your work is published; and if I were to die before that—I remember that you always say: there're no guarantees with life—promise me that you'll make public what took place, OK?

You remember Don Gustavo Aveiga, the cashier who wronged papa? Last week he was here; he's an old man now, his hair is white and he walks with a stick, with much difficulty. We almost didn't recognize him. He asked for you, and said that it really hurt his heart not finding you. He asked me to beg your forgiveness for having mixed you up in his affair, without wishing to; he sends his best wishes. He returned the twenty thousand sucres to Mama; he told us that all those years he had suffered, thinking that he might die without amassing the amount he took. He was happy to have kept his word; he was so deeply emotional that he made us cry, or rather I should say all three of us cried. He told us that he did indeed manage to save his father. As you see, there're still good and decent men, and not a few either. How I would have liked to for you to have been there at the return of the money!

Let me give you some more news: some girl friends have convinced me of the need to start up here a League of Democratic Women; they want to make me president; I'm excited; I want to do something for my people. Since these are more or less your ideas, I've accepted in principle, but I want you to give me your opinion. I want to be in agreement with you on everything. Tell me if I ought to accept or not; your word will be the deciding one.

Come back soon, Juan. Why don't you finish your work here? If you only knew how anxious I am to see you, to hear you ...

Mama sends greetings.

Reply soon.

A hug

Ana Mercedes"

That afternoon I went to the cemetery with my mother, taking flowers for her tomb; the newly turned earth was covered with withering bouquets. We placed our offering, and we returned in silence. That night, until very late, I spent time meditating on Ana Mercedes and on her wish to lay bare the truth. For some years I have battled with her idea. Like that night in the cinema, I think that she has prevailed over me—this time forever—and I ought to comply with her wishes.

I recall that she once asked me: "What? You too are afraid of the truth?"

And if you can hear me, this is my definitive reply, Ana Mercedes:

No, it's not the truth I'm afraid of, it's the lie that we live, that we're all prisoners of; I don't fear what is said or written, but what is unsaid or hidden, everything that slinks about like a serpent in the shadows.

Nineteen Thirty-Seven

by Edwidge Danticat (Haiti/USA)

My Madonna cried. A miniature teardrop traveled down her white porcelain face, like dew on the tip of early morning grass. When I saw the tear I thought, surely, that my mother had died.

I sat motionless observing the Madonna the whole day. It did not shed another tear. I remained in the rocking chair until it was nightfall, my bones aching from the thought of another trip to the prison in Port-au-Prince. But, of course, I had to go.

The roads to the city were covered with sharp pebbles only half buried in the thick dust. I chose to go barefoot, as my mother had always done on her visits to the Massacre River, the river separating Haiti from the Spanish-speaking country that she had never allowed me to name because I had been born on the night that El Generalissimo, Dios Trujillo, the honorable chief of state, had ordered the massacre of all Haitians living there.

The sun was just rising when I got to the capital. The first city person I saw was an old woman carrying a jar full of leeches. Her gaze was glued to the Madonna tucked under my arm.

"May I see it?" she asked.

I held out the small statue that had been owned by my family ever since it was given to my great-great-great-grandmother Défilé by a French man who had kept her as a slave.

The old woman's index finger trembled as it moved toward the Madonna's head. She closed her eyes at the moment of contact, her wrists shaking.

"Where are you from?" she asked. She had layers of 'respectable' wrinkles on her face, the kind my mother might have one day, if she has a chance to survive.

"I am from Ville Rose," I said, "the city of painters and poets, the coffee city, with beaches where the sand is either black or white, but never mixed together, where the fields are endless and sometimes the cows are yellow like cornmeal."

The woman put the jar of leeches under her arm to keep them out of the sun.

"You're here to see a prisoner?" she asked.

"Yes."

"I know where you can buy some very good food for this person."

She led me by the hand to a small alley where a girl was selling fried pork and plantains wrapped in brown paper. I bought some meat for my mother after asking the cook to fry it once more and then sprinkle it with spiced cabbage.

The yellow prison building was like a fort, as large and strong as in the days when it was used by the American marines who had built it. The Americans taught us how to build prisons. By the end of the 1915 occupation, the police in the city really knew how to hold human beings trapped in cages, even women like Manman who was accused of having wings of flame.

The prison yard was as quiet as a cave when a young Haitian guard escorted me there to wait. The smell of the fried pork mixed with that of urine and excrement was almost unbearable. I sat on a pile of bricks, trying to keep the Madonna from sliding through my fingers. I dug my buttocks farther into the bricks, hoping perhaps that my body might sink down to the ground and disappear before my mother emerged as a ghost to greet me.

The other prisoners had not yet woken up. All the better, for I did not want to see them, these bone-thin women with shorn heads, carrying clumps of their hair in their bare hands, as they sought the few rays of sunshine that they were allowed each day.

My mother had grown even thinner since the last time I had seen her. Her face looked like the gray of a late evening sky. These days, her skin barely clung to her bones, falling in layers, flaps, on her face and neck. The prison guards watched her more closely because they thought that the wrinkles resulted from her taking off her skin at night and then putting it back on in a hurry, before sunrise. This was why Manman's sentence had been extended to life. And when she died, her remains were to be burnt in the prison yard, to prevent her spirit from wandering into any young innocent bodies.

I held out the fried pork and plantains to her. She uncovered the food and took a peek before grimacing, as though the sight of the meat nauseated her. Still she took it and put it deep in a pocket in a very loose fitting white dress that she had made herself from the cloth that I had brought her on my last visit.

I said nothing. Ever since the morning of her arrest, I had not been able to say anything to her. It was as though I became mute the moment I stepped into the prison yard. Sometimes I wanted to speak, yet I was not able to open my mouth or raise my tongue. I wondered if she saw my struggle in my eyes.

She pointed at the Madonna in my hands, opening her arms to receive it. I quickly handed her the statue. She smiled. Her teeth were a dark red, as though caked with blood from the initial beating during her arrest. At times, she seemed happier to see the Madonna than she was to see me.

She rubbed the space under the Madonna's eyes, then tasted her fingertips, the way a person tests for salt in salt water.

"Has she cried?" Her voice was hoarse from lack of use. With every visit, it seemed to get worse and worse. I was afraid that one day, like me, she would not be able to say anything at all.

I nodded, raising my index finger to show that the Madonna had cried a single tear. She pressed the statue against her chest as if to reward the Madonna and then, suddenly, broke down and began sobbing herself.

I reached over and patted her back, the way one burps a baby. She continued to sob until a guard came and nudged her, poking the barrel of his rifle into her side. She raised her head, keeping the Madonna lodged against her chest as she forced a brave smile.

"They have not treated me badly," she said. She smoothed her hands over her bald head, from her forehead to the back of her neck. The guards shaved her head every week. And before the women went to sleep, the guards made them throw tin cups of cold water at one another so that their bodies would not be able to muster up enough heat to grow those wings made of flames, fly away in the middle of the night, slip into a slumber of innocent children and steal their breath.

Manman pulled the meat and plantains out of her pocket and started eating a piece to fill the silence. Her normal ration of food in the prison was bread and water, which is why she was losing weight so rapidly.

"Sometimes the food you bring me, it lasts for months at a time," she said. "I chew it and swallow my saliva, then I put it away and chew it again. It lasts a very long time this way."

A few of the other women prisoners walked out into the yard, their chins nearly touching their chests, their shaved heads sunk low on bowed necks. Some had large boils on their heads. One, drawn by the fresh smell of fried pork, came to sit near us and began pulling the scabs from the bruises on her scalp, a line of blood dripping down her back.

All of these women were here for the same reason. They were said to have been seen at night rising from the ground like birds on fire. A loved one, a friend, or a neighbor had accused them of causing the death of a child. A few other people agreeing with these stories was all that was needed to have them arrested. And sometimes even killed.

I remembered so clearly the day Manman was arrested. We were new to the city and had been sleeping on a cot at a friend's house. The friend had a sick baby who was suffering with colic. Every once in a while Manman would wake up to look after the child when the mother was so tired that she no longer heard her son's cries.

One morning when I woke up, Manman was gone. There was the sound of a crowd outside. When I rushed out I saw a group of people taking my mother away. Her face was bleeding from the pounding blows of rocks and sticks and the fists of strangers. She was being pulled along by two policemen, each tugging at one of her arms as she dragged her feet. The woman we had been staying with carried her dead son by the legs. The policemen made no effort to stop the mob that was beating my mother.

"*Lougarou*, witch, criminal!" they shouted.

I dashed into the street, trying to free Manman from the crowd. I wasn't even able to get near her.

I followed her cries to the prison. Her face was swollen to three times the size that it had been. She had to drag herself across the clay floor on her belly when I saw her in the prison cell. She was like a snake, someone with no bones left in her body. I was there watching when they shaved her head for the first time. At first I thought they were doing it so the open gashes on her scalp could heal. Later when I saw all the other women in the yard, I realized that they wanted to make them look like crows, like men.

Now, Manman sat with the Madonna pressed against her chest, her eyes staring ahead, as though she was looking into the future. She had never talked very much about the future. She had always believed more in the past.

When I was five years old, we went on a pilgrimage to the Massacre River, which I had expected to be still crimson with blood, but which was as clear as any water that I had ever seen. Manman had taken my hand and pushed it into the river, no farther than my wrist. When we dipped our hands, I thought that the dead would reach out and haul us in, but only our own faces stared back at us, one indistinguishable from the other.

With our hands in the water, Manman spoke to the sun. "Here is my child, Josephine. We were saved from the tomb of this river when she was still in my womb. You spared us both, her and me, from this river where I lost my mother."

My mother had escaped El Generalissimo's soldiers, leaving her own mother behind. From the Haitian side of the river, she could still see the soldiers chopping up *her* mother's body and throwing it into the river along with many others.

We went to the river many times as I was growing up. Every year my mother would invite a few more women who had also lost their mothers there.

Until we moved to the city, we went to the river every year on the first of November. The women would all dress in white. My mother would hold my hand tightly as we walked toward the water. We were all daughters of that river, which had taken our mothers from us. Our mothers were the ashes and we were the light. Our mothers were the embers and we were the sparks. Our mothers were the flames and we were the blaze. We came from the bottom of that river where the blood never stops flowing, where my mother's dive toward life—her swim among all those bodies slaughtered in flight—gave her those wings of flames. The river was the place where it had all begun.

"At least I gave birth to my daughter on the night that my mother was taken from me," she would say. "At least you came out at the right moment to take my mother's place."

* * *

Now in the prison yard, my mother was trying to avoid the eyes of the guard peering down at her.

"One day I will tell you the secret of how the Madonna cries," she said.

I reached over the touched the scabs on her fingers. She handed me back the Madonna.

I know how the Madonna cries. I have watched from hiding how my mother plans weeks in advance for it to happen. She would put a thin layer of wax and oil in the hollow space of the Madonna's eyes and when the wax melted, the oil would roll down the little face shedding a more perfect tear than either she or I could ever cry.

"You go. Let me watch you leave," she said, sitting stiffly.

I kissed her on the cheek and tried to embrace her, but she quickly pushed me away.

"You will please visit me again soon," she said.

I nodded my head yes.

"Let your flight be joyful," she said, "and mine too."

I nodded and then ran out of the yard, fleeing before I could flood the front of my dress with my tears. There had been too much crying already.

* * *

Manman had a cough the next time I visited her. She sat in a corner of the yard, and as she trembled in the sun, she clung to the Madonna.

"The sun can no longer warm God's creatures," she said. "What has this world come to when the sun can no longer warm God's creatures?"

I wanted to wrap my body around hers, but I knew she would not let me.

"God only knows what I have got under my skin from being here. I may die from tuberculosis, or perhaps there are worms right now eating me inside."

* * *

When I went again, I decided that I would talk. Even if the words made no sense, I would try to say something to her. But before I could even say hello, she was crying. When I handed her the Madonna, she did not want to take it. The guard was looking directly at us. Manman still had a fever that made her body tremble. Her eyes had the look of delirium.

"Keep the Madonna when I am gone," she said. "When I am completely gone, maybe you will have someone to take my place. Maybe you will have a person. Maybe you will have some *flesh* to console you. But if you don't, you will always have the Madonna."

"Manman, did you fly?" I asked her.

She did not even blink at my implied accusation.

"Oh, now you talk," she said, "when I am nearly gone. Perhaps you don't remember. All the women who came with us to the river, they could go to the moon and back if that is what they wanted."

* * *

A week later, almost to the same day, an old woman stopped by my house in Ville Rose on her way to Port-au-Prince. She came in the middle of the night, wearing the same white dress that the women usually wore on their trips to dip their hands in the river.

"Sister," the old woman said from the doorway. "I have come for you."

"I don't know you," I said.

"You *do* know me," she said. "My name is Jacqueline. I have been to the river with you."

I had been by the river with many people. I remembered a Jacqueline who went on the trips with us, but I was not sure this was the same woman. If she were really from the river, she would know. She would know all the things that my mother had said to the sun as we sat with our hands dipped in the water, questioning each other, making up codes and disciplines by which we could always know who the other daughters of the river were.

"Who are you?" I asked her.

"I am a child of that place," she answered. "I come from a long trail of blood."

"Where are you going?"

"I am walking into the dawn."

"Who are you?"

"I am the first daughter of the first star."

"Where do you drink when you're thirsty?"

"I drink the tears from the Madonna's eyes."

"And if not there?"

"I drink the dew."

"And if you cannot find the dew?"

"I drink from the rain before it falls."

"If you can't drink there?"

"I drink from the turtle's hide."

"How did you find your way to me?"

"By the light of the mermaid's comb."

"Where does your mother come from?"

"Thunderbolts, lightning, and all things that soar."

"Who are you?"

"I am the flame and the spark by which my mother lived."

"Where do you come from?"

"I come from the puddle of that river."

"Speak to me."

"You hear my mother who speaks through me. She is the shadow that follows my shadow. The flame at the tip of my candle. The ripple in the stream where I wash my face. Yes. I will eat my tongue if ever I whisper that name, the name of that place across the river that took my mother from me."

I knew then that she had been with us, for she knew all the answers to the questions I asked.

"I think you do know who I am," she said, staring deeply into the pupils of my eyes. "I know who *you* are. You are Josephine. And your mother knew how to make the Madonna cry."

I let Jacqueline into the house. I offered her a seat in the rocking chair, gave her a piece of hard bread and a cup of cold coffee.

"Sister, I do not want to be the one to tell you," she said, "but your mother is dead. If she is not dead now, then she will be when we get to Port-au-Prince. Her blood calls to me from the ground. Will you go with me to see her? Let us go to see her."

We took a mule for most of the trip. Jacqueline was not strong enough to make the whole journey on foot. I brought the Madonna with me, and Jacqueline took a small bundle with some black rags in it.

When we got to the city, we went directly to the prison gates. Jacqueline whispered Manman's name to a guard and waited for a response.

"She will be ready for burning this afternoon," the guard said.

My blood froze inside me. I lowered my head as the news sank in.

"Surely, it is not that much a surprise," Jacqueline said, stroking my shoulder. She had become rejuvenated, as though strengthened by the correctness of her prediction.

"We only want to visit her cell," Jacqueline said to the guard. "We hope to take her personal things away."

The guard seemed too tired to argue, or perhaps he saw in Jacqueline's face traces of some long-dead female relative whom he had not done enough to please while she was alive.

He took us to the cell where my mother had spent the last year. Jacqueline entered first, and then I followed. The room felt damp, the clay breaking into small muddy chunks under our feet.

I inhaled deeply to keep my lungs from aching. Jacqueline said nothing as she carefully walked around the women who sat like statues in different corners of the cell. There were six of them. They kept their arms close to their bodies, like angels hiding their wings. In the middle of the cell was an arrangement of sand and pebbles in the shape of a cross for my mother. Each woman was either wearing or holding something that had belonged to her.

One of them clutched a pillow as she stared at the Madonna. The woman was wearing my mother's dress, the large white dress that had become like a tent on Manman.

I walked over to her and asked, "What happened?"

"Beaten down in the middle of the yard," she whispered.

"Like a dog," said another woman.

"Her skin, it was too loose," said the woman wearing my mother's dress. "They said prison could not cure her."

The woman reached inside my mother's dress pocket and pulled out a handful of chewed pork and handed it to me. I motioned her hand away.

"No no, I would rather not."

She then gave me the pillow, my mother's pillow. It was open, half filled with my mother's hair. Each time they shaved her head, my mother had kept the hair for her pillow. I hugged the pillow against my chest, feeling some of the hair rising in clouds of dark dust into my nostrils.

Jacqueline took a long piece of black cloth out of her bundle and wrapped it around her belly.

"Sister," she said, "life is never lost, another one always come up to replace the last. Will you come watch when they burn the body?"

"What would be the use?" I said.

"They will make these women watch, and we can keep them company."

When Jacqueline took my hand, her fingers felt balmy and warm against the lifelines in my palm. For a brief second, I saw nothing but black. And then I *saw* the crystal glow of the river as we had seen it every year when my mother dipped my hand in it.

"I would go," I said, "if I knew the truth, whether a woman can fly."

"Why did you not ever ask your mother," Jacqueline said, "if she knew how to fly?"

Then the story came back to me as my mother had often told it. On that day so long ago, in the year nineteen hundred and thirty-seven, in the Massacre River, my mother did fly. Weighted down by my body inside of hers, she leaped from Dominican soil into the water, and out again on the Haitian side of the river. She glowed red when she came out, blood clinging to her skin, which at that moment looked as though it were in flames.

In the prison yard, I held the Madonna tightly against my chest, so close that I could smell my mother's scent on the statue. When Jacqueline and I stepped out into the yard to wait for the burning, I raised my head toward the sun thinking, One day I may just see my mother there.

"Let her flight be joyful," I said to Jacqueline. "And mine and yours too."

from *The Spook Who Sat by the Door*

by Sam Greenlee (USA)

Today the computers would tell Senator Gilbert Hennington about his impending campaign for re-election. The senator knew from experience that the computers did not lie.

He sat separated from his assembled staff by his massive, uncluttered desk, the Washington Monument framed by the window to his rear. They sat alert, competent, loyal and intelligent, with charts, graphs, clipboards and reports at the ready. The senator swept the group with a steely gaze, gave Belinda, his wife and chief aide, a bright smile of confidence, and said:

"All right, team, let's have a rundown, and don't try to sweeten the poison. We all know this will be the closest one yet: what I want to know is how close? Tom, kick it off."

"The campaign war chest is in excellent shape, chief: no major defectors."

"Good. I'll look over your detailed breakdown later. Dick?"

"I spent a week on Mad. Av. with both the PR boys and our ad agency. They both have good presentations ready for your approval, Senator. I think you'll be pleased."

"How do we shape up on TV, Dick? All our ducks in line?"

"Excellent, Senator. You'll be on network television a minimum of three times between now and election day—just about perfect, no danger of overexposure."

"Have you licked the makeup thing yet, Dick?" asked Belinda Hennington. "A small detail but it probably cost one man the presidency. We don't want that to happen to us."

"No sweat, Mrs. Hennington. Max Factor came out with a complete new line right after that fiasco. I think we'll be using 'Graying Temples,' in keeping with our maturity image. As we all know, the youth bit is out nowadays. Fortunately with the senator we can play it either way."

"Good show, Dick," said the senator. "Harry?"

"I've run the results of our polls through the computers, both the IBM 436 and the Remington Rand 1401. Louis Harris gave us a random pattern sampling with peer-group anchorage; Gallup a saturation vertical-syndrome personality study and NORC an ethnic and racial cross-section symbiology. The results check out on both computers, although I'm programing a third as a safety-valve check-out.

"The computers have you winning the election, Senator, but by less than three thousand votes. A small shift and there goes the ball game."

The senator, startled and troubled, glanced nervously toward his wife. She gave him a smile of reassurance.

"Do the computers indicate a possible breakthrough," he asked, "with any of the peer groups? How do we stand with the Jewish vote?"

"You're solid with the Jews, Senator. Where you're in trouble is with the Negroes."

"The Negroes!" exclaimed Senator Hennington. "Why, I have the best voting record on civil rights on Capitol Hill. Just last year I broke the ADA record for correct voting on civil rights with 97.64."

"Our polls reveal a sharp decline just after your speech requesting a moratorium on civil-rights demonstrations. If we can regain most of the lost Negro percentile, Senator, we're home free."

"No use crying about a lack of voter loyalty. This calls for a 'think session.' Perhaps we should have our special assistant on minorities and civil rights sit in; although I'm not sure how helpful he'll prove. Frankly, I'm disappointed by his performance so far."

"Judy," said the senator into his office intercom, "Think session in here. No calls, please, and cancel all morning appointments. And ask Carter Summerfield to join us, will you?"

The senator turned to his wife as they awaited the arrival of Summerfield.

"Belinda, I'm beginning to have serious doubts about Summerfield. He hasn't come up with a fresh idea since he joined us, and I don't expect anything other than tired clichés from him today."

"He's fine in a campaign, Gil, that's where he'll shine. I don't think you ought to rely on him for theory."

"Perhaps you're right. I guess it's not his brains we're looking for in him anyway."

"No," she smiled. "That's his least valuable commodity to us."

The senator swiveled his leather-covered chair half-round and gazed out at the Washington Monument.

"This question of the Negro vote could be serious. I never thought I'd ever be in trouble with those people. We have to come up with something which will remind them I'm the best friend they have in Washington, and soon."

Carter Summerfield had sat in his office all morning, worried and concerned. He sensed the senator was not pleased with his performance and could not understand why. Summerfield had sought desperately to discover what it was the senator wanted to hear in order that he might say it, and was amazed to find that the senator seemed annoyed when his own comments were returned, only slightly paraphrased. In all his career as a professional Negro, Summerfield had never before encountered a white liberal who actually wanted an original opinion from a Negro concerning civil rights, for they all considered themselves experts on the subject. Summerfield found it impossible to believe Senator Hennington any different from the others.

He had spent the morning searching for the source of the senator's displeasure until his head ached; the handwriting was on the wall and Summerfield knew his job was at stake. He must discover the source of displeasure and remove it. Perhaps he should wear ready-made clothes? Had the senator somehow seen him driving the Lincoln, rather than the Ford he always drove to the office? It was essential never to have a more impressive car than one's boss. He told all his newly integrated friends that. Had anyone discovered the encounter with the white girl in Colorado Springs when he had accompanied the senator on a trip to the Air Force Academy? He had been certain he acted with the utmost secrecy and discretion. But he had known even then that it was a stupid move which might threaten his entire career.

Summerfield took two Gelusils and a tranquilizer and reached for the phone to inquire discreetly of his fellow integrated Negro friends if there was word on the grapevine of an opening for a man of his experience. The phone rang. It was Senator Hennington's secretary summoning him to the senator's office for a think session.

Smiling, as always when in the presence of whites, Summerfield entered the senator's office, his eyes darting from face to face for some sign concerning his present status. But the looks of the other members of the staff were no longer funereal and the senator greeted him with a warm smile as he motioned Summerfield to an empty chair, briefly inquiring about his wife and children.

"It seems, Carter," said the senator, "that we're in serious trouble with the Negro vote." Summerfield frowned in sympathy and concern. "We must come up with a fresh, dramatic and headline-capturing act on my part which will prove to my colored constituents that I'm the best friend they have in Washington." He swept the room again with his steely gaze, Gary Cooper, back to the wall, but undaunted. "And we must do it today."

Summerfield nervously licked his lips. "How about calling a conference of the responsible Negro leaders to discuss our new civil-rights bill, Senator?"

The senator considered for a moment.

"I don't think so, Carter. To be perfectly frank, I don't think the bill will pass this session. White backlash."

"How about a fact-finding tour of the African countries?" said Dick.

"No. I did that last year and still haven't kicked the dysentery I picked up on safari in Tanganyika."

"How about a speech attacking apartheid at Capetown University?" asked Harry.

"I don't think South Africa would grant me a visa."

"Gil," said the senator's wife, "why don't we accuse the Central Intelligence Agency of a discriminatory hiring policy?"

"Segregation in the CIA?"

"Yes. They have no Negro officers at all; mostly menial and clerical help."

"Are you certain, Belinda? This could be what we're looking for."

"I'm positive, but I'll check it out. We have a man in personnel over there, you know."

"Couldn't a charge of that nature prove counter-productive, Mrs. Hennington?" asked Dick. "CIA's almost as untouchable as the FBI."

"Not since U-2 and the Bay of Pigs. And this should prove an irresistible combination for the press: cloak and dagger and civil rights."

"I'm inclined to agree, Belinda," said the senator, who was usually inclined to agree with his attractive wife. "What's the best way of springing this thing for maximum impact?"

"Why not at the Senate Watchdog Committee hearings?" said Tom.

"But the hearings are closed," said the senator.

"It wouldn't be the first time we've used closed hearings for a press leak, Gil. I'll brief Mark Townsend over lunch here in the office on the day of the hearings," said Belinda.

"Excellent," said Dick. "A political columnist of his stature is perfect."

"Now, how do I play it in the hearings? Indignant, angry, or do I underplay?"

"Dignified, I think, Senator," said Harry. "You're shocked and saddened that the agency in the closest grips with the forces of godless communism is shackled by the chains of racial prejudice."

"Right," said Tom. "You say that America must utilize the talents of its entire citizenry, regardless of race, color, or creed, in the cold war."

"They'll deny it at first," said Belinda, "then probably claim their personnel files are classified, but they'll back down when they get enough negative press coverage. They're very image-conscious nowadays."

Carter Summerfield sat looking interested, but carefully silent. Advising the senator how to criticize other whites was definitely not one of his functions.

"I can program one of the computers to provide statistics showing the increased efficiency of the armed forces since their integration," said Tom.

"If CIA does select a Negro, he'll be the best-known spy since 007," said Harry.

"Well, he will find it a bit difficult after all the publicity he's going to get," said the senator.

"You mean, Gil," said his wife, "the publicity you're going to get."

The senator smiled.

"General," said Senator Hennington, addressing the director of the CIA, "it has come to my attention that there are no Negroes on an officer level in CIA. Would you care to comment on that?"

The other committee members looked at Senator Hennington with some shock. They knew he faced a close election in the fall, but this gambit was below the belt. The general, fighting to control his famous temper, replied curtly.

"You know, of course, Senator, that our personnel files are highly classified."

"I'm aware of that, General, but this meeting is closed and we are all cleared for that kind of information."

"It's not true that we don't have any colored at the Agency. Our entire kitchen staff, our maintenance section and drivers are all colored."

"My question, General, concerned Negroes on an officer level."

"Well, we don't have any colored officers."

"Do you think, General, that a policy of racially selective recruiting which excludes a full 10 percent of the population is a wise one?"

"Yes. While I personally have no race prejudice, I feel Negroes are not yet ready for the highly specialized demands of intelligence work."

"Really?" said Senator Hennington, smiling a smile of patronizing pity into the face of bigotry.

"It's a question of sociology rather than prejudice; a gap simply exists between the races which is a product of social rather than racial factors."

"There are Negroes who have bridged that gap."

"If so, I would welcome them in CIA."

"I would suggest you make more of an effort to find them."

"Senator Hennington," said the committee chairman, in his rich, aristocratic southern drawl, "we all know deceit, hypocrisy, duplicity are the everyday tools of our agents in the field. Much to their credit, the childlike nature of the colored mentality is ill-suited to the craft of intelligence and espionage."

"I'm afraid, Mr. Chairman," replied the senator, once again entering into the charade concerning race he had conducted with his southern friend for well over a decade, "I don't understand what you mean by 'the colored mentality.' "

"There is a question of cover," said the general. "An agent must be capable of fading into the background, adopting the guise of the person one cannot remember minutes after meeting him. Negroes in the field would be far too conspicuous."

"General, I'd rather not carry this conversation any further. I would appreciate a report in a month's time concerning the progress of the establishment of a merit-hiring policy at CIA."

The luncheon table had been trundled away and Belinda Hennington and the famous political columnist Mark Townsend sat in the conversation corner of the senator's office, sipping brandy from large snifters.

"Both the senator and I wanted to give you an exclusive on this, Mark," said Belinda.

"Thanks, Belinda. Are you sure this checks out? The government is supposed to be at the forefront of merit hiring."

"Not CIA. We're positive."

"I have a man at CIA—mind if I check him out on this?"

"Of course not; you can use 'an undisclosed CIA source' in your lead."

"This could bring civil rights back into the headlines. It's been suffering from overexposure lately."

"You're right, Mark. The public has tired of the same old thing: fire hoses, cattle prods, dogs on the one hand and singing, marching and praying on the other. Civil rights could use a good public relations man."

"When will the senator make an official statement?"

"I should guess after the wire services and television pick up your beat. About three days, I should think."

"Sounds about right. Where will you conduct the press conference?"

"Right here. The Washington Monument makes a good backdrop for the television cameras; almost a Hennington trademark."

Townsend had left and Belinda was sipping a well-earned scotch-on-the-rocks when the senator returned. She mixed her husband a drink as he sank into the leather chair behind his big desk.

"How did it go today, dear?" she asked.

"Couldn't have gone better, honey. I'm certain this is it."

"Yes, dear, by this time next week we'll have the Negro vote wrapped up again." She handed the senator his drink and rested one sleek hip on the polished mahogany of the desk. "Never take the voters for granted. Even Negroes react eventually, you know."

"I'd have thought the CIA would have been more alert on a thing like this. If they'd had even one Negro officer, my charges would have fallen as flat as your sister's soufflés."

"If it hadn't been CIA, it would have been someone else. We're not likely to run out of institutions to accuse of segregation in our lifetime, darling."

They smiled at one another affectionately.

That November the senator won his reelection comfortably, the Negro vote accounting for more than his margin of victory.

Liberia: Its Struggles and Its Promises[*]

by Hon. Hilary Teague (Liberia)

As FAR back towards the infancy of our race as history and tradition are able to conduct us, we have found the custom everywhere prevailing among mankind, to mark by some striking exhibition, those events which were important and interesting, either in their immediate bearing or in their remote consequences upon the destiny of those among whom they occurred. These events are epochs in the history of man; they mark the rise and fall of kingdoms and of dynasties; they record the movements of the human mind, and the influence of those movements upon the destinies of the race; and whilst they frequently disclose to us the sad and sickening spectacle of innocence bending under the yoke of injustice, and of weakness robbed and despoiled by the hand of an unscrupulous oppression, they occasionally display, as a theme for admiring contemplation, the sublime spectacle of the human mind, roused by a concurrence of circumstances, to vigorous advances in the career of improvement.

The utility of thus marketing the progress of time—of recording the occurrence of events, and of holding up remarkable personages to the contemplation of mankind—is too obvious to need remark. It arises from the instincts of mankind, the irrepressible spirit of emulation, and the ardent longings after immortality; and this restless passion to perpetuate their exis-

---

[*] A speech delivered in 1846, on the anniversary of the founding of the Republic of Liberia.

tence which they find it impossible to suppress, impels them to secure the admiration of succeeding generations in the performance of deeds, by which although dead, they may yet speak. In commemorating events thus powerful in forming the manners and sentiments of mankind, and in rousing them to strenuous exertion and to high and sustained emulation, it is obvious that such, and such only, should be selected as virtue and humanity would approve; and that, if any of an opposite character be held up, they should be displayed only as beacons, or as towering Pharos throwing a strong but lurid light to mark the melancholy grave of mad ambition, and to warn the inexperienced voyager of the existing danger.

Thanks to the improved and humanized spirit—or should I not rather say, the chastened and pacific civilization of the age in which we live?—that laurels gathered upon the field of mortal strife, and bedewed with the tears of the widow and the orphan, are regarded now, not with admiration, but with horror; that the armed warrior, reeking in the gore of murdered thousands, who, in the age that is just passing away, would have been hailed with noisy acclamation by the senseless crowd, is now regarded only as the savage commissioner of an unsparing oppression, or at best, as the ghostly executioner of an unpitying justice. He who would embalm his name in the grateful remembrance of coming generations; he who would secure for himself a niche in the temple of undying fame; he who would hew out for himself a monument of which his country may boast; he who would entail upon heirs a name which they may be proud to wear, must seek some other field than that of battle as the theatre of his exploits.

We have not yet numbered twenty-six years since he who is the oldest colonist amongst us was the inhabitant—not the citizen—of a country, and that, too, the country of his birth, where the prevailing sentiment is, that he and his race are incapacitated by an inherent defect in their mental constitution, to enjoy that greatest of all blessings, and to exercise that greatest of all rights, bestowed by a beneficent God upon his rational creatures, namely, the government of themselves by themselves. Acting upon this opinion, an opinion as false as it is foul—acting upon this opinion, as upon a self-evident proposition, those who held it proceeded with a fiendish consistency to deny the rights of citizens to those whom they had declared incapable of performing the duties of citizens. It is not necessary, and therefore I will not disgust you with the hideous picture of that state of things which followed upon the prevalence of this blasphemous theory. The bare mention that such an opinion prevailed would be sufficient to call up in the mind, even of those who had never witnessed its operation, images of the most sickening and revolting character. Under the iron reign of this crushing sentiment, most of us who are assembled here to-day drew our first breath, and sighed away the years of our youth. No hope cheered us; no noble object looming in the dim and distant future kindled our ambition. Oppression—cold, cheerless oppression, like the dreary region of eternal winter,—chilled every noble passion and fettered and paralyzed every arm. And if among the oppressed millions there were found here and there one in whose bosom the last glimmer of a generous passion was not yet extinguished—one, who, from the midst of inglorious slumberers in the deep degradation around him, would lift up his voice and demand those rights which the God of nature hath bestowed in equal gift upon all His rational creatures, he was met at once, by those who had at first denied and then enforced, with the stern reply that for him and for all his race, liberty and expatriation are inseparable.

Dreadful as the alternative was, there were hearts equal to the task; hearts which quailed not at the dangers which loomed and frowned in the distance, but calm, cool, and fixed in their purpose, prepared to meet them with the watchword, "Give me liberty or give me death."

Passing by intermediate events, which, did the time allow, it would be interesting to notice, we hasten to the grand event—the era of our separate existence, when the American flag first flung out its graceful folds to the breeze on the heights of Mesurado, and the pilgrims, relying upon the protection of Heaven and the moral grandeur of their cause, took solemn possession of the land in the name of Virtue, Humanity, and Religion.

It would discover an unpardonable apathy were we to pass on without pausing a moment to reflect upon the emotions which heaved the bosoms of the pilgrims, when they stood for the first time where we now stand. What a prospect spread out before them! They stood in the midst of an ancient wilderness, rank and compacted with the growth of a thousand years.... The rainy season—that terrible ordeal of foreign constitutions—was about setting in; the lurid lightning shot its fiery bolts into the forest around them, the thunder muttered its angry tones over their head, and the frail tenements, the best which their circumstances could afford, to shield them from a scorching sun by day and drenching rains at night, had not yet been completed. To suppose that at this time, when all things above and around them seemed to combine their influence against them; to suppose they did not perceive the full danger and magnitude of the enterprise they had embarked in, would be to suppose, not that they were heroes, but that they had lost the sensibility of men. True courage is equally remote from blind recklessness and unmanning timidity; and true heroism does not consist in insensibility to danger. He is a hero who calmly meets, and fearlessly grapples with the dangers which duty and honor forbid him to decline. The pilgrims rose to a full perception of all the circumstances of their condition. But when they looked back to that country from which they had come, and remembered the degradations in that house of bondage out of which they had been so fortunate as to escape, they bethought themselves; and, recollecting the high satisfaction with which they knew success would gladden their hearts, the rich inheritance they would entail upon their children, and the powerful aid it would lend to the cause of universal humanity, they yielded to the noble inspiration and girded them to the battle either for doing or for suffering.

Let it not be supposed, because I have laid universal humanity under a tribute of gratitude to the founders of Liberia, that I have attached to their humble achievements too important an influence in that grand system of agencies which is now at work, renovating human society, and purifying and enlarging the sources of its enjoyment. In the system of that Almighty Being, without whose notice not a sparrow falls to the ground,

"Who sees, with equal eye as God of all,
A hero perish, or a sparrow fall,
Atoms or systems into ruin hurled,
And now a bubble-burst, and now a world."

"Righteousness exalteth a nation, but sin is a reproach to any people." All attempts to correct the depravity of man, to stay the headlong propensity to vice, to abate the madness of ambition, will be found deplorably inefficient, unless we apply the restrictions and the tremendous sanctions of religion. A profound regard and deference for religion, a constant recognition of our dependence on God, and of our obligation and accountability to Him; an ever-present, every-pressing sense of His universal and all-controlling providence, this, and only this, can give energy to the arm of law, cool the raging fever of the passions, and abate the lofty pretensions of mad ambition. In prosperity, let us bring orderly, virtuous, and religious conduct. In adversity, let us consider, confess our sins, and abase ourselves before the throne of God. In danger, let us go to Him, whose prerogative it is to deliver; let us go to Him, with the humility and confidence which a deep conviction that the battle is not to the strong nor the race to the swift, is calculated to inspire.

Fellow citizens! we stand now on ground never occupied by a people before. However insignificant we may regard ourselves, the eyes of Europe and America are upon us, as a germ, destined to burst from its enclosure in the earth, unfold its petals to the genial air, rise to the height and swell to the dimensions of the full-grown tree, or (inglorious fate) to shrivel, to die, and to be buried in oblivion. Rise, fellow citizens, rise to a clear and full perception of your tremendous responsibilities! Upon you, rely upon it, depends in a measure you can hardly conceive the future destiny of your race. You—you are to give the answer, whether the African race is doomed to undeterminable degradation, a hideous blot on the fair face of Creation, a libel upon the dignity of human nature, or whether it is capable to take an honorable rank amongst the great family of nations! The friends of the colony are trembling: The enemies of the colored man are hoping. Say, fellow citizens, will you palsy the hands of your friends and sicken their hearts, and gladden the souls of your enemies, by a base refusal to enter upon a career of glory which is now opening so propitiously before you? The genius of universal emancipation, bending from her lofty seat, invites you to accept the wreath of national independence. The voice of your friends, swelling upon the breeze, cries to you from afar—Raise your standard! Assert your independence! throw out your banners to the wind! And will the descendents of the mighty Pharaohs, that awed the world; will the sons of him who drove back the serried legions of Rome and laid siege to the "eternal city"—will they, the achievements of whose fathers are yet the wonder and admiration of the world—will they refuse the proffered boon? Never! never!! never!!! Shades of the mighty dead! spirits of departed great ones! inspire us, animate us to the task; nerve us for the battle! Pour into our bosom a portion of that ardor and patriotism which bore you on to battle, to victory, and to conquest. Shall Liberia live? Yes; in the generous emotions now swelling in your bosom; in the high and noble purpose—now fixing itself in your mind, and referring into the unyieldingness of indomitable principle, we hear the inspiring response—Liberia shall live before God and before the nations of the earth!

The night is passing away; the dusky shades are fleeing and even now

"Jocund day stands tiptoe
On the misty mountain top."

Ndzeli in Passage

by Dolores Kendrick (USA)

Longing

for myself in the home of myself:
Dear Sister,
    you were so brave
to jump into the waters
    rather than have
that death that I go to.

You chose
the final death, the blessed homeland:

I am a coward,
   I could not throw myself
      into the sea,

      Not me.

Listen, Sister, there is a crib-cry
     in my shaking voice:
I have just been born
     pushing through the womb of sorrow
   that is a farewell
     to my blood
  and all its heirs.

But there is a grief, Sister,
    that now beats upon my fears
    like a drum.

Remember me.
    Dead as you are, do not forget
    this parting.

Are there gratuities of death?
    One day, come and tell me,
    and I will rejoice.

Night passes over.

There are sounds and hissings.
    My heart weeps in the dark,
    I go from one land to another,
    boat to boat, sea to sea,
creature of dust,
    dying in the windbloom.

Oh, Sister! Our home is shattered!
    All I know of it, or will ever know
    is stuffed between the limbs of a Portuguese ship.
    What will I do without you, Odonga?
Somehow I feel my sanity slipping,
    what is memory is sitting beside me in the dark

(but I believe it is daylight outside,
a slip of it stole into the boat a short while ago
and it, too, now is captive).
Why have we come to this? What am I doing here?

Remember the sunset coming through
the dark, in the village, Ndzeli?
Remember eating pomegranates and figs with Odonga
under a tree at noonday?
Remember the strut of the lion?
Remember, Ndzeli, the kiss of your prince, Atezwa,
who, too, now is dead, murdered, gone?
Remember his beautiful smile
stolen from you in the dizzy night?

Now the birds sit alone on the naked limbs of the Kola tree,
Now in the bark of the lion is a whisper,
Now the griot* is silent,
Now I must go quietly into the night that brings no moon.

There is a rattle in the boat, a harder one in my breast,
a striking, a pain, a beating drum with a message of doom.

I have wanted to tell you, Sister, about this pain,
   but I couldn't; you were too close to it and to my
      hope.
   Remember me, for now I journey to the strange,
      unbidden
   land where they will call me Zeli, and my dreams
   will hang from trees like rotten fruit.

Oh, the grief, the grief!
Sister, remember me!

Yet, I am beyond the passage of this boat,
   I go on another journey
   while the cold air spins
   and the great sails pipe,
   and when this vessel finds its final harbor,
   I will not be with it. No, indeed.

---

* An African storyteller who preserves through memory the local and sometimes national mythology and history of a people.

Not even my aching breath will please the passions
   of these merchants. My body is at its end.
   The sorrow in the heart tells me
   and I so receive it willingly, joyfully.
   Oh, I celebrate these raptures.

Sister, I choose the tender way: I will be smoke.

Lifting. Risen. Gone. Free.
My litany, and natural to me.

Let me say it

by Dennis Brutus (South Africa)

Let me say it

for no-one else may
or can
or will
or dare

I have lashed them
the marks of my scars
lie deep in their psyche
and unforgettable
inescapable.

Of course there were others who served
and much that I could not have done
but I am a part of the work
and they connect it with me

they know I have done them harm

they who are artists in deprivation
who design vast statutory volumes
and spend their nights in scheming deprival

I have deprived them
that which they hold most dear
a prestige which they purchased with sweat
and for which they yearn unassuagedly
—their sporting prowess and esteem

this I have attacked and
blasted
unforgettably.

The diurnal reminders excoriate their souls

Amid a million successes
—the most valued on fronts where they were under attack—
they grimace under the bitter taste of defeat

their great New Zealand rivals
the Olympic panoply and Wembley roar
for them these things are dead
are inaccessible
unattainable

nowhere else does apartheid exact so bitter a price
nowhere else does the world so demonstrate its disgust
in nothing else are the deprivers so deprived.

And they know I will do more.

What wonder such gingerly menacing claws,
they would rend me if they could
(and perhaps will)
but I accept their leashed-in power
and the cloaked malice of their gaze
and wait

anger and resolution
yeast in me
waiting for the time of achievement
which will come if God wills
when I flog fresh lashes across these thieves.

> [2 July 1966]

My African Friend

by Paulo Colino (Brazil)

I have an African friend who travels around the world. He's a diplomat. He can discuss any issue that people do: politics, art, everything. He speaks five languages. Aside from his own. He is a great figure. But he has one defect: the vice of question. I don't know if it's from his native land or if he acquired it from the countries he's been to.

Here, we never question anything. He, meanwhile, is full of "whys". It's why this, why that—he never stops!

The other day, he asked me if I knew what democracy was. Obviously, yes! I cannot understand Greek (the origin of the Brazilian word *democracia*), but I know that democracy is the government of the people, by the people, for the people; I mean to say, it's a political regime based on the principles of popular sovereignty.

"Right," he said, laughing.

And then he came with another. Which was the actual Brazilian regime? Like this, nothing more, nothing less.

"Listen, what a question! We live in a democracy," I replied.

"Ah, we don't, no," he provoked.

And it was then added that, in a democracy, the laws that govern the relation between the state and the citizen begin always to affirm that all individuals have the right to ... They never begin with the principle that the individual cannot.... That essential to democracy is the freedom of choice, of decision, of control and authority over one's self. What liberty never can acknowledge is the word censorship.

I hurried to explain that ours is a modern democracy.

"A democracy doesn't allow adjectives! It is a fact or it is not!" he shouted.

Fine! It seems that my understandings weren't so obvious, in the end. I tried to change the subject (politics aren't my forté). My friend, however, had another question ready:

"Consequently, there is also no racial democracy here, right?"

"Calm down man"—this was all I could say.

He continued:

"In a racial democracy you can't have discrimination, right? The Afonso Arinos Law punishes discriminatory acts, correct? Where there is smoke, there is fire. If there is an active law, it is because the crime exists, am I wrong? In a racial democracy, the individuals have to have common interests and equal opportunities, do they or do they not? How many Black ministers do you have? And Diplomats? Governors? Secretaries of State? Judges? And Generals? Cite the name of just one. Just one. And Mayors? Bankers? Come on, Directors of banks. Or estates. Not even on TV? You've observed the commercials on television? I turn on the apparatus and the impression is that I'm in a Nordic country. How many Blacks go to the schools, the colleges? What is the percentage of Blacks in the Brazilian population?" He looked at his watch, slapped his palm to his kinky brow and excused himself—another engagement. He was late already.

I am Black. Not dark dye. But I am (Grammy Cota used to say past six in the afternoon, it's night). Suddenly a memory came of my discussion with a census taker, months before. In the column for color, she wrote Moreno. I corrected the act.:

"Mam, the color is wrong. It's Black."

And she, all delicately:

"But Sir, you're not Black. You're Moreno."

And I, with a furious face:

"Mrs., put it there: Black."

She corrected it. To her dislike, but she did it. It was incredible! If they rob me of color, I become invisible!

My African friend went to his engagement. Even so, he still left me with a question ping-ponging in my head: What is it that is written on our brows?

Of one thing I am sure: in this country everything ends up as Samba!

Revenge

by Marcus Garvey (Jamaica/USA)

Not yesterday, but centuries long,
The Romans hated all of Negro blood,
For Hannibal did slay the crew,
As Carthage marched to martial song.
Again Adowa made them halt,
When Menelik did crush them low:
He proved the Blacks were timely men—
The heroes still without a fault.

But Italy kept crying out,
And longed for day of victory:
With Mussolini, courage came,
To fight to win without a doubt:
They used the weapons not allowed,
And took advantage as they went:
They crushed Selassie's mighty host
With Blacks Bodoglio followed.

The Blacks shall come together now,
And they shall blast the way again:
Revenge is sweet! the Romans say;
Revenge! is on the Black Man's brow.

O sing the song of Carthage, great,
O sing the song of Afric', free:
The day will come to win again,
And pass to Italy her fate.

No man shall stop the moving throng
That goes to snatch the victory:
The world has bled the Black Man's heart,
And drowned him, too, with all the wrong.
Come now and go in vision clear,
Right up to good Adowa's mount,
And let Italians ever feel
The dash of weapons in their rear.

If not on Ethiopian land,
Go, follow them where'er they go:
Join English, French or Russian, too,
And all together strike the band—
That band of Roman renegades—
Blood-thirsty men of Fascist's creed;
With Mussolini as their head
They'll die by gas and hot grenades.
Revenge is all! it's written there,
And Blacks will ne'er forget the call:
Like gods of old, let's live on high,
And each one dream of glory, fair.
The Rome of sin shall fall again,
As Addis rise toward the sun;
So pledge your word to sacred trust
And hurl Italians to the plain.

—1937

We Wear the Mask

by Paul Laurence Dunbar (USA)

We wear the mask that grins and lies,
It hides our cheeks and shades our eyes,—
This debt we pay to human guile;
With torn and bleeding hearts we smile,
And mouth with myriad subtleties.

Why should the world be over-wise,
In counting all our tears and sighs?
Nay, let them only see us, while
      We wear the mask.

We smile, but O great Christ, our cries
To thee from tortured souls arise.
We sing, but oh the clay is vile
Beneath our feet, and long the mile;
But let the world dream otherwise,
      We wear the mask!

Chapter 6

Black Cultural Mythology

Black cultural mythology is the paradigm for reintegrating heritage practices into global Black consciousness in an age when Eurocentric education systems control and limit the extent to which knowledge of African heritage and Diaspora histories is imparted to communities of African descent. It is also a practical literary system that sustains the iconic representation of legendary figures and historical episodes of the global Black experience by the deliberate preservation of Black hero dynamics through the creation and articulation of socioliterary models of ancestor acknowledgment, immortalization theory, and Black cultural legacies. Literature, in both the written and oral traditions, plays a central role in sustaining Black cultural mythology because it is an art form that draws from history, entertains, creatively embellishes, and creates sustained images through language, or the process of *nommo*.

The African oral tradition is structured to preserve cultural memory, legend, and hero dynamics. *Sundiata: An Epic of Old Mali* is a classic example. Black cultural mythology as a deliberate creative tool to preserve history is a more pressing need in such regions of the African Diaspora as the United States because Black populations here often do not have the power to control the educational curriculum in the social institutions (schools and colleges) or in the media, which transmit primarily Eurocentric national histories. On the other hand, independent Black countries of the Diaspora, where, for example, national currencies display the faces and images of authentic Black national heroes meaningful to African people, have less of a need to deliberately engage in practices of Black cultural mythology. In these countries, the acknowledgment of Black ancestors is inherent in their cultural and national practices.

The practice of ancestor acknowledgment is central to the existence and spirituality of people of African descent. Unfortunately, however, in regions of the Diaspora created as a result of the enslavement trade, oral literary elements and practices such as the funeral dirge and annual memorial rituals were lost as formal art forms but survived in informal practices. Amazingly, however, the literature of the Diaspora proves that practices of ancestor acknowledgment, or Black cultural mythology, survive primarily through creative writing.

The speech, as a unique genre in the Black literary tradition (unique because of call-and-response, intonation, and African-derived performance aesthetics) powerfully transmits hero dynamics and contributes to Black cultural mythology. Kariamu Welsh and Molefi Kete Asante describe the speech tradition as "rhetoric" that "becomes mythological action."[1] More significantly,

> [t]hese analytical utterances, or rather utterances with embedded messages, can be found in most contemporary speeches of African Americans. Baraka's "epic memory" exercises itself in the oratory of a Jesse Jackson, Benjamin Hooks, Maulana Karenga, or Louis Farrakhan, as it did in Malcolm X, Martin Luther King, and Elijah Muhammad.
>
> Myth becomes in the language of the African American speaker an explanation for the human condition and an answer to the question of existence in a racist society.... What we notice when we examine African American myths is that they possess a kind of epistemological maturity, unlike the traditional myth, which is a sort of backward-looking explanation of reality. The idea of hope and possibility rises on the shoulders of an imaginative mythology that sees the future as bright as the present.[2]

This speech form, documented liberally in Africa and the Diaspora, summons cultural heroes in order to strengthen activism and group identity, and in literature, any roll call of leaders is a tribute to the ancestors.

There is also an antihero dynamic, whereby writers criticize individuals or political systems as a way of publicly identifying the enemy. Thus, in literature, a disliked historical figure will be named as a socioliterary villain or enemy. This dynamic is a consistent phenomenon in African culture, reminiscent of the early heroic epic *Sundiata* of the Mali Empire. While the victorious region weaves the epic narrative in honor of Sundiata as the hero, the losing region presents the same narrative to characterize Sundiata as the antihero.

The literature representing Black cultural mythology, particularly the speech and nonfiction forms, reveals embellished performance, persuasion, figurative historical descriptions and language, dynamic storytelling, captivating introductions and conclusions, inspirational narratives of well-known heroes, informative and warning examples of antiheroes, audience understanding, the offering of authoritative challenges to improve the future, shar-

---

1. Kariamu Welsh and Molefi Kete Asante, "Myth: The Communication to the African American Mind," *Journal of Black Studies* 11, no. 4 (1981): 388.

2. Ibid., 388–89, 390.

ing genius and/or conspiracy revelations, offering methods for empowerment, and demonstrating the pride and the bravery of being fearlessly outspoken. When a leader speaks out courageously about issues that ultimately lead to his assassination, giving a public speech appears as a proactively dangerous element that contributes to the development of one's hero dynamic. The list of assassinated Black leaders who promoted their culture's hero dynamic is long and painful: David Walker, Patrice Lumumba, Steve Biko, Malcolm X, Martin Luther King, Jr., Walter Rodney, Maurice Bishop, and others.

Reevaluating the role of nonfiction literature and Black literature's treatment of historical figures and episodes highlights literature's power to prepare a society for leadership. In the context of Black cultural mythology, the fiction, powerfully based on real-life examples, inspires readers to be attentive to legacies of the past and to the meaning and the power of the ancestors.

In the Spirit of Butler, Unionize! Mobilize! Educate! Democratize!

by Maurice Bishop (Grenada)

November 18, 1981

The following speech was presented at the opening of the Third Trade Union Conference for the Unity and Solidarity of Caribbean Workers, held in St. George's.

Comrades, if we were to study the history of this country, Grenada, we would find that the central theme that has characterized the lives of our people over the centuries has been *resistance.* Our people have struggled at many times and in many ways.

From the stubborn refusal of the Grenadian Caribs to accept any colonial stranglehold over their island; through the consistent pattern of slave revolts which culminated in the mass upsurge led by Julien Fedon in 1795, which for two years brought Grenada a determined, militant independence; through the years of anticolonial agitation and the eloquent leadership of T. A. Marryshow; through the two great popular uprisings of 1951 and 1973–74 to the climax of our struggle in the March 13 revolution of 1979—Grenadians have always resisted domination, injustice, and exploitation. Our great Caribbean poet, Edward Kamau Braithwaite, himself a Barbadian, has likened this spirit of permanent struggle to the dramatic and sublime peaks which tower along the spine of our island. And it is into this tradition of resistance that we must place the growth and development of our trade union movement.

We have produced here in Grenada perhaps the greatest, the most brilliant and audacious of pioneer Caribbean trade unionists. I am referring, of course, to Tubal Uriah "Buzz" Butler, that huge, monumental igniter of the spirit of the Caribbean masses, who, born in Grenada, moved to Trinidad to accomplish his great deeds of leadership of the burgeoning Caribbean working class. His volcanic influence there sent our entire region throbbing with a new will and resistance, which soon broke out through all our islands. But let it also be said that we produced Eric Matthew Gairy, perhaps the most degenerate and decadent manipulator and corruptor of the trade union movement that our islands have ever spawned.

Butler vs Gairy: To say them with the same breath makes one gasp! But we have seen both their traditions and disciples alive in our Caribbean. Our duty now is to strive to emulate the one and make certain that the other will never be recreated! Certainly we must also remember how Butler was sought, hunted, and hounded by British colonialism and the employing class that saw him as their greatest menace, how they imprisoned him, interned him, but could never smother or even dim his enormous determination and luster! And certainly we must also remember how his opposite lied, bribed, bludgeoned, and murdered in his path to power, and how the consequences of that misrule strewed hurricane wreckage through our nation and working people that he claimed to represent, so much so that nearly three years after the revolution that ended his sordidness forever in our country, we are still cleaning up the devastation he caused to our national life and economy.

So we have known only too well this type of bogus trade unionism in Grenada, and we have lived through the ghastly damage it caused to our country and people. And we also know how much our real, genuine, patriotic trade unionists fought against such deformity when its political arm came to power with the Gairy neocolonial dictatorship, which lasted for over two decades in Grenada. For right through these years of struggle, our militant, selfless trade unionists fought gallantly against Gairy's terror, squandermania, the neglect of the rights of workers, even though he could also count, through that period, upon certain sections of the trade union leadership to sell out the masses at crucial points of their struggle, as he had done himself in 1951, as the conciliators did again in April 1974.

Gairy's neocolonial dictatorship introduced several draconian laws that were clearly antiworker and were aimed at muzzling and straightjacketing any threatening action from our trade unions. The 1974 Public Order (Amendment) Act prohibited trade unions, as well as other organizations, from using public address systems. The next year he passed the Newspaper (Amendment) Act, which without just cause effectively forbade trade unionists and other workers' organizations from publishing their own newspapers. Then the Essential Services Act of 1978 was passed, particularly against the prospect of members of the Technical and Allied Workers' Trade Union taking industrial action. Significantly, the leadership of this union, notoriously inactive, did nothing to challenge the passage of a law which was designed to render them impotent. This was hardly surprising when we understand that the leadership of this union was in the hands of the same man who acted as the "research and education officer" of the American Institute of Free Labor Development in the Eastern Caribbean.

But other unions and the political leadership of the NJM fought on behalf of their brothers and sisters in this union, comrades, and when Gairy tried to extend the law to include the dockworkers—who proved to be the most militant section of the urban working class under the dictatorship—they never allowed the amendment to be implemented. For it was a common feature of those years that the workers themselves would take industrial action in the absence of or in defiance of their conciliatory leadership. This was perhaps best seen in the 1973–74 period, when the workers had to force the hand of their leaders to strike, and simultaneously resist the propaganda and persuasion techniques of the AFL-CIO.

Comrades, it is important to note that all this activity and struggle within our trade union movement was taking place against a backdrop of massive repression that was building up in our country, in all aspects and spheres of the people's lives. The dictator was making a systematic and comprehensive attack on all the rights and freedoms that our people had campaigned for and won over the years of British colonialism. The freedom to express ourselves, the freedom of assembly, in fact, the freedom to live any sort of decent life, all this was being ripped from us. The elections that were organized were rigged and farcical, a mockery of the democracy that our people truly aspired to reach. When we moved to protest or organize against the decay of life we saw against us, we were hounded by paid bandits who battered, bruised, and murdered some of our most valued and courageous comrades. Life itself was being torn away from us piece by piece in the growing fear and reality of repression.

Our youth saw desolation around them in a hopeless search for jobs. Our women faced sexual abuse and exploitation in the daily struggle to keep their dignity. A youth like Jeremiah Richardson was shot, point-blank, in the streets of Grenville because he sought to question a policeman's abuse. A boy, Harry Andrews, was killed because he climbed over a wall in a calypso tent. Harold Strachan, Alister Strachan, Rupert Bishop all heroically sought to challenge this ebbing away of freedom and the right to live, and they all fell before the horrendous rule of terror and corruption which characterized our country during those years. Our people lived in an ethos of death and tyranny, when honest people disappeared mysteriously—the fate of Inspector Bishop of the Carriacou police, or the four youths tending goats on Frigate Island. Comrades, to be an active, combative, and militant trade unionist during that portion of our history was to court this danger and violence. Militancy meant a challenge to death and an assertion of everything that was hopeful and positive and which could reconstruct life and happiness for our people.

But as the dictatorship tried to tighten its grip on the lives of the Grenadian people, more and more democratic and progressive fighters were elected to the leadership of our trade unions. By 1978 the executive of the Commercial and Industrial Workers' Union [CIWU] was demonstrating this and Gairy was answering by trying to crush the union. Resolutions were being passed by the executive against Gairy's ties with the butchers of Chile and the visit of Pinochet's torture ship, the *Esmerelda*, to our shores. The dictator realized he was not dealing with the previous pattern of pliable and opportunistic leadership. The only price of these new comrades was freedom! So he went directly to their employers, trying to persuade and bribe them to compel their workers to join *his* union, even though these employers had already signed agreements with the Commercial and Industrial Workers' Union. He also attempted to force CIWU members directly to change unions, but because of the respect they had for the consistent and principled hard work and positions of the new CIWU leadership, they were not moved.

Over the years our Caribbean trade union movement has constantly been the target of that most unscrupulous arm of imperialism: the Central Intelligence Agency. We have had rare instances of our trade union leaders consciously selling out to their silky bribes and offerings, but more usually the CIA, with its sophistication and enormous financial resources, has succeeded in manipulating and infecting unwitting trade unionists who may well have been continuing with their work with the best of intentions. In doing this, the CIA has sometimes directly infiltrated and controlled some sections of our movement, and thus forced the leadership of some of our unions to actually take antiworker positions. This has happened, we know, in Grenada, and more and more of our workers are becoming conscious of this danger to their hopes.

We saw how the CIA actually succeeded in turning back the progress of the organized workers' union in Chile, by both open and covert activity, and we in the Caribbean must be particularly vigilant in recognizing their poison and subversion of the workers' cause, for imperialism will never rest in its resolution to crush the onward march of the progress and emancipation of our struggling people.

For on the day that the revolution triumphed, March 13, 1979, trade unionists from all over the country showed direct support for and involvement in the revolutionary events. The telephone company workers, for example, were contacting and radioing our security forces to tell them of the whereabouts of Gairy's ministers, and trade unionists and workers generally all over the country left their workplaces to take up arms to end forever the power of oppression that had constantly tried to thwart the free aspirations and genuine and constructive organization of our Grenadian workers.

Since our revolution most of the old, corrupt union leadership has been thrown into the dustbin of history, for because of their growing consciousness, our workers can now contrast and see who is bringing benefits to them and who is not, who is desperately trying to maintain the old pattern of dictatorship and who is in the forefront of the struggle to bring more democracy into our trade unions.

What we are seeing more and more in Grenada is that the objectives of the revolution and the objectives of the trade union movement in our country are one in the same. Thus, any antagonisms between them are gradually lessening and disappearing, for the revolution has set free the opportunities for the trade union movement to accomplish its tasks of building the emancipation, security, and prosperity of the working people, the identical will of the revolution itself.

Let us consider the massive rise in membership since the revolution of the most militant and democratic unions. On March 13, 1979, the Bank and General Workers' Union had some hundred members. It now has about 3,000. It has spread out from its birthplace at Barclay's Bank to the banana boxing plants, the nutmeg pools, the restaurants and hotels, the factories and workshops. Its tradition of honest and consistent struggle on behalf of its members has made it the largest union in the country.

The Commercial and Industrial Workers' Union has had over 50 percent increase in membership, the Technical and Allied Workers' Union a 60 percent increase, and the Agricultural and General Workers' Union has risen from scratch to its present level of 2,300 members.

We had a huge, symbolic demonstration of our increased trade union membership and power in this year's May Day celebrations. It was the biggest-ever May Day turnout in the history of Grenada, and the seemingly endless procession of organized workers wound around the steep streets of our capital.

Along with this sudden explosion in the membership of our unions is the emphasis the new leadership is putting on their democratization. This is very much allied to the general thrust in democracy right through our society since the revolution, in all structures of mass organizations, community groups, and the other organs of our people's power. As we have seen, before the revolution there was a tradition in some unions of few or no general meetings.

Following the revolution, we have seen a massive new interest in trade unionism as Grenadians saw new hope and strength in cooperative and collective democratic solutions to their problems. At the first general meeting of the Commercial and Industrial Workers' Union after the revolution, in July 1979, there was over 100 percent increase in the attendance. Two hundred and ninety members came and voted 246 to 44 in favor of a militant, democratic leadership as against the previous conciliatory and conservative type, even though the latter had organized and conducted the elections.

What is happening now in our country is that everybody is becoming affected by the dialectic of democratic participation that is sweeping through our villages and workplaces. Involvement in one organization or meeting leads directly to involvement in another. A worker who attends a workers' parish council hears something which he wants to bring to his trade union. So he goes to the meeting of his union, although he may not have attended one for years. And when he finds, quite surprisingly, that his union is taking a vibrant, democratic direction, he involves himself on one of its new committees or structures for fundraising, sports, or planning for educational seminars. His confidence is raised through all this activity and the speaking and organizing that goes along with it, and his appetite is whetted to join one of the mass organizations—the local party support group, the militia, house repair program, or for the sisters, the National Women's Organisation. Each organization feeds strength, power, and confidence into the next, and all of them, including the trade unions, grow in real potency and democratic advancement.

And now we see workers' parish councils splitting into zonal councils, in a new sprouting of decentralized democracy right through our nation, a reflection of a similar tendency that is happening within our progressive trade unions.

The People's Revolutionary Government has been swift to take legislative action in favor of the trade unions. All Gairy's antiworker laws were repealed and two months after the revolution, in May 1979, People's Law Number Twenty-nine, the Trade Union Recognition Law, was passed.

For the fist time in Grenada's history, our workers had the opportunity to join the union of their choice, and the employer was compelled to recognize the trade union, once 51 percent of his work force were financial members. Under this law, the Ministry of Labor has to respond within seven days of the union's application for recognition, and then call a poll of workers. If the majority is shown to be members, then the union must be certified as the bargaining agent for the workers.

For apart from Barclay's, before the revolution there were other grotesque examples of nonrecognition of trade unions. The workers at the Red Spot Drinks factory had a 100 percent financial membership of the Commercial and Industrial Workers' Union in 1978, but the company still refused recognition. And it took the workers at Bata some seventeen years of struggle before they finally won recognition, so this law has changed all those old abuses and given the workers real and genuine security in making their trade unions effective bargaining agents on behalf of their workers.

For the sister trade unionists, the 1980 Maternity Leave Law has made an enormous difference to their working and personal lives. Every working woman now has the right to two months' paid maternity leave over the period of the birth of any child. And the trade unions were involved, together with mass organizations, particularly the National Women's Organisation, and the churches, in the widespread consultation conducted all over the nation before the bill was finally passed. The Equal Pay for Equal Work Decree in the state sector has also had a profound effect on improving wages of the sisters and leveling them up with those of their brother workers throughout Grenada—as well as increasing their general confidence to organize and struggle, side-by-side, with their brothers. For now both men and women are sharing equally in the improvement of wages and conditions being brought about since the revolution. The old, appalling working conditions and lack of facilities, like no drinking water or workers' amenities in workplaces, compulsory overtime without pay, and no job security, are now doomed. The recent successful strike of agricultural workers in the St. Andrew's parish, waged by members of the Agricultural and General Workers' Union, is proof of this. The comrades achieved their demands of holiday and sick-leave pay under the new democratic leadership of their new union.

At this moment, arising from a decision of a St. George's Workers' parish council, and based on requests from trade unions, the Ministry of Legal Affairs has prepared two pieces of legislation—a Rent Control Law to ease the burden of high rent costs for our people and a new Workmen's Compensation Act, both of which will be circulated to our unions for their comments before enactment.

Of course, you would know how closely higher productivity and trade union organization are connected.

More than two decades of Gairyism produced in our workers many negative attitudes. The new trade unionism in our country is now helping to transform such attitudes by helping to apply new incentives.

Before the revolution, our agricultural estates brought in absurdly low returns. They were making only a quarter of a million dollars, even though their

yearly expenditure was nearly three million. Now, from being a national liability, they have become profitable, and the workers themselves have shared
in that success, taking one-third of the profits made. This new attitude has
grown through the spirit of emulation that the workers have adopted as a result of those seminars. The age of cynicism is gone in Grenada.

Workers in a revolutionary country like ours, who are under a progressive
and democratic leadership in their trade unions, do *not* see trade unionism
solely in a narrow, economistic sense. They do not see their responsibilities
stopping only at their fundamental tasks of improving their members' wages
and working conditions. They see themselves deeply involved in *all* aspects of
the social and political life of their country, their region, and their world. Our
unionized workers have consistently shown solidarity with all other struggling
workers of the world. They see this as an internationalist duty to all trade
unionists organizing for their rights and fighting for social and political justice, be they in Chile, El Salvador, southern Africa, the Middle East, or any
part of the world where the producers of wealth are exploited and oppressed.
They see their responsibility, likewise, with other trade unionists of the Third
World, in pressing for the new international economic order that will create
more favorable terms of trade between rich and poor nations and transfer
wealth and technology for the benefit of the masses in countries such as ours.

Comrades, it is clear that the growing economic crisis in world capitalism
is having a dynamic effect in the Caribbean. Throughout our region we see
the employing class united in its attack upon trade unionism. There have been
newspaper advertisements in Barbados calling upon workers to abandon their
trade unions. There have been incidents of multinational companies in St.
Vincent forcing workers to sign documents pledging they will leave their trade
union. Clearly, the employers are trying to de-unionize their work forces to
make them more pliable and exploitable, so we, throughout the Caribbean,
must go beyond all our political and ideological differences and forge the essential unity of our regional trade union movement to combat this reactionary
offensive by the employers. This is why we have to work towards the total
unionization of our workers and the maximum democratization of our
unions, to ensure that they are vigilant and active in the struggles against the
employers, and to guarantee that the negativism and passivity that arose from
undemocratic trade union structures are forever finished in our region.

We consider that in Grenada we have a critical role to stimulate and achieve
this unity, because our revolution has emancipated our trade union movement
to fully serve the country and help to build it, along with our party, the mass
organizations, and other democratic community structures. For we are bene-
fiting, not only from increased wages and better working conditions, unlocked

freedoms, and an explosion of democracy, but also from a massively increased social wage, which makes more and more sure and profound the security of our working people, one of the prime objectives of trade unionism. Free medical treatment, pre-primary care, an eye clinic, free milk distribution, more doctors and dentists than we have ever had before, new low-cost housing and more repair schemes, free secondary education, de facto free middle-level technical and university training for all our untrained primary school teachers, a Centre for Popular Education, cheaper basic food through our Marketing and National Importing Board, loans for productive purposes through our National Commercial Bank, a vastly improved water supply system, cheaper electricity rates and less tax to pay for the poorest workers, a new international airport, a national public bus service on the way—all this has been achieved in the last thirty months. Such concrete benefits are what true trade unionists have always struggled for, and we see our trade unionists too taking a greater and greater part in this huge process of national reconstruction.

For the first time in our history, and as far as we know this step is unique in the CARICOM section of our region, our trade unions have been involved in the exercise of framing the national budget. The Public Workers' Union, the Grenada Union of Teachers, and the Technical Allied Workers' Union were all involved in this process last year, and this year and in the coming years more of our unions will be involved. Proposals for the 1982 budget will be circularized by the Ministry of Finance in a booklet, and 50,000 of these are being printed, to be given, among others, to the workers at their workplaces for them to study and add their comments and suggestions.

This, of course, is an extension of the already existing policy of our government of *opening all our books to our workers during wage negotiations* with trade unions, giving them access to all accounts and files, so that they can see for themselves what the national budget can afford to give them, and so they can make their own assessment of what could be a realistic and equitable wage demand. This is the absolute antithesis of Gairyism, a total transformation.

This process will underlie yet again that the trade union movement must be involved in *all* aspects of national development. This means planning, production, management, distribution of foods, working in the literacy campaign through the Centre for Popular Education, in the house repair program, the school repair program, the community work: democracy in all our popular and democratic programs to ensure that the benefits of the revolution reach not only its own members, but all the people of Grenada.

Finally and crucially, there is the question of national defense, particularly at this juncture when we are facing so many threats from belligerent and vulgar imperialism. Our trade unions and their members are becoming more and more involved in our people's militia, and the Trade Union Council it-self, in response to the U. S. "Amber and the Amberdines" provocation and maneuvers in Vieques Island in August, issued a call for all trade unionists to join the militia and be prepared to defend the homeland from imperialist mil-itary attack.

So, comrades, what is the way forward? What are the challenges ahead of us and how must we respond? We would not want to leave this conference without having clear ideas and proposals in our heads to secure greater bonds and solidarity between us. What concrete steps can we make as a result of our discussions?

For a start we must exchange information, insights, and experiences to make more profound the trust between us, and more unified the cause and strength that binds us. And let us pledge that in the spirit of trade union democracy we hold more regular assemblies and meetings such as this one, to combine in a more coherent and purposeful way, to consolidate our power and unity, and to coordinate our strategies to beat back the offensive against us. Our enemies are intensifying their unity, as has been seen in the recent general inter-Caribbean meetings of Chambers of Commerce, and even more pointedly, in the meetings of various army and police chiefs, with external representatives also involved.

The violence of this offensive has also been made clear in the imperialist-dominated campaign of lies, slander, and disinformation—the deliberate ma-nipulation of half-truths and fabrications—which has been principally di-rected at the revolutionary countries in our region, Cuba, Nicaragua, and Grenada, and against the progressive movement of workers generally through-out the Caribbean. This campaign intensified to a particularly blatant level in May this year, when the United States International Communications Agency, the propaganda arm of the U. S. State Department, organized a conference in Washington to which were invited the editors of all the major English-lan-guage Caribbean newspapers. The editors were counseled and lectured to by reactionary congressmen, and slick American journalists taught them tech-niques of propaganda destabilization, with "How to Deal with Grenada" as an unlisted item on the agenda.

Within two weeks of this conference we witnessed in the region signs of a coordinated approach by all of these newspapers, in their propaganda attacks against the Grenada revolution. Articles and editorials were swapped and reprinted, and this process descended into its most vulgar depths with the ap-pearance in five regional newspapers—the Jamaica *Gleaner*, the Barbados *Sunday Sun*, the Barbados *Advocate*, the Trinidad *Guardian*, and the Trinidad *Express*—of identical front-page editorials calling upon the governments, peoples and workers of the region to isolate Grenada and expel us from all regional groupings and organizations.

Comrades, this propaganda campaign continues unabated until this very day. We would therefore like to call upon all delegates here, representing as they do the most active and conscious leaders of the working-class movement in our region, to condemn this monopoly control of the Caribbean media by unprincipled press magnates in league with imperialism, and support the struggle of media workers all over the world for a *new international information order* to serve our movement and our peoples, which can only be made possible through the struggle to achieve the new international economic order, the creation of which will be of particular significance to all workers in the Caribbean and Latin America.

Comrades, very importantly, we must express that all workers of our region have a clear understanding as to why peace is in their interest and why war is such a high priority on the agenda of Reagan and the ruling circles in the USA.

At present the world capitalist system is in the midst of a serious crisis. Runaway inflation, compounded by ever-rising unemployment, has meant that for millions of workers in the industrialized capitalist economies, the cost of living keeps going up, seemingly beyond control, while job security is weakened.

Almost as daily routine, factory after factory is closed down, business after business declares bankruptcy, resulting in hundreds of thousands of workers losing their jobs. Those workers fortunate to retain jobs find that their wages remain stagnant, their unions attacked and undermined by the monopolists, their rights abused, and their hard-won gains eroded.

And as the international capitalist crisis intensifies, it generates increased imperialist aggression, spearheaded by the most reactionary circles of imperialism's military-industrial complexes, who feel that the solution to this crisis is the build-up of arms, the provocation of wars, and the creation of tension spots around the world, the Caribbean region being no exception.

The struggle carried on by the world's workers for peace is strongly linked with the effects of the crisis of capitalism on their living standards. Thus one can say that the economic and social gains won through such struggle are a contribution to the consolidation of world peace, because these gains are an expression of the change in the balance of forces against the roots of all wars: monopoly capitalism and imperialism.

Ignoring the new realities brought about by this change in the world's balance of forces, however, the military and conservative circles of imperialism are trying to return the world to the cold war period and intensification of the arms race, with the planned deployment of many more nuclear warheads in Western European countries, with mad talk of limited nuclear war, and right here in our region with stepped-up military maneuvers and exercises and preparations for military invasions of Cuba, Nicaragua, and Grenada along with massive intervention in El Salvador.

The present level of military efforts puts on the shoulders of Caribbean workers and workers all over the world a very heavy burden of sacrifice, exposing the very existence of humanity to the risk of a catastrophic disaster.

High military expenditures are damaging to economic stability, slow down the rate of development, and make unemployment more acute.

The contemporary capitalist crisis and the arms race are directly connected with each other. In many capitalist countries, arms contracts provide the motive force for the industries connected with arms manufacture.

But workers must not be intimidated or resort to pessimism in the face of this bleak scenario. Hope still exists, and it resides in the struggle of all peace-loving forces for disarmament and world peace, which will make it possible for science and technology to be put fully to work for the material and spiritual enhancement of humankind.

The working class of the world constitutes the principal force of peace. Because of its role in the crucial sphere of social life and production, the working class is also the principal force of social progress.

Thus there is a direct connection between the historical role of the working class and the struggle for peace and disarmament. The Caribbean trade union movement cannot fulfil its mission of emancipating the working people of the region in a situation where imperialism is attempting to make the Caribbean a theater of war. Genuine social and economic progress can only be achieved in an atmosphere of peaceful coexistence, cooperation, good will, mutual respect, and understanding among the region's peoples.

It is therefore an urgent imperative that the Caribbean trade union movement strongly condemn all efforts by imperialism to bring unnecessary tension to our region, and in equally strong terms support the call for the Caribbean to be declared a zone of peace.

Caribbean and Latin American workers employed by capitalist companies who do not own the means of production, because they are an exploited class, have no stake in war or in the profits derived from the manufacture of weapons as is the case with the transnational corporations.

Peace is the workers' ideal. Historical experience shows that in the imperialist wars it is the working people influenced by the ideological hegemony of imperialism who are the victims, who shed their blood and sacrifice their lives.

But it is also the working people who have always fought against wars of aggression and who now find themselves in a common front in the struggle for peace.

In fighting against monopolies, against the transnationals and the military-industrial complexes, the working people of the Caribbean and Latin America carry out a direct offensive against the roots of war.

In this context, the workers and their trade union organizations have a fundamental role to play. In defiance of the imperialist merchants of death, the Caribbean and Latin American trade union movement must make a clear and consistent response to Washington's aggression in this region by the unity and common action of all the trade union forces.

In these times there is an urgent need, comrades, for unity and coordinated action, for cooperation and direct alliance between the region's democratic trade unions, some with different ideological tendencies but all with the same class interests and with similar economic and social aspirations.

Warmongering in our region can only be stopped by a united and decisive workers' struggle for peace and disarmament.

Workers of our region can be heartened and even inspired by the forthright resistance demonstrated by millions of workers who have taken to the streets of European capitals in recent weeks to say a loud "no" to the war policies of the Reagan administration.

So our message today, comrades, to all our workers in our island and throughout the Caribbean, is: In the Spirit of Butler, Unionize! Mobilize! Educate! Democratize! Dynamize the trade union movement throughout our region! Let the spirit of Butler fire and inspire us! Let us seek to emulate his cause and dedication to the most sacred commitment of all—the emancipation and freedom of our working people.

We in Grenada pledge to continue to put our trade union movement at the center of the process in our country, to link all our workers in an organized relationship with democratic structures and practices, and so pump with ever-increasing vigor the vibrant blood that runs through all the organs of our revolution.

Long live the working class of Grenada, the Caribbean, and the world!
Long live the unity and solidarity of working people of the world!
Long live the spirit of Tubal Uriah "Buzz" Butler!
Forward ever, backward never!

Prologue from *Dreamer: A Novel*

by Charles Johnson (USA)

"The Pauper has to die before the Prince can be born."

MEISTER ECKHART

"But unto Cain and to his offering the Lord had not respect. And Cain was very wroth, and his countenance fell."

GENESIS 4:5

"If you sow the seeds of violence in your struggle, unborn generations will reap the whirlwind of social disintegration."

MARTIN LUTHER KING JR., *Strength to Love*

"Behold, this dreamer cometh. Come now therefore, and let us slay him, and cast him into one of the pits, and we will say: Some evil beast hath devoured him; and we shall see what will become of his dreams."

GENESIS 37:19–20

PROLOGUE

In the Upsouth cities he visited, violence followed him like a biblical curse, but one step ahead of his assassins. Despite his clerical vows, or perhaps because of them (I am come to send fire on the earth, Luke 12:49), he walked through a world aflame. Chicago in the hundred-degree summer heat of 1966 was the site for the special form of crisis his wing of the Movement produced: families divided, fathers at the throats of their sons, brothers spilling each other's blood. Unhappily I have the eloquence of neither Guido the Angelic nor Teresa of Avila, and so with each halting sentence I pray for the words to demonstrate how this was the beginning of his northern crusade to undo the work of the Devil. This was the battlefield, a modern plain of Kurukshetra, where in the midst of a shooting war between Richard Daley's police and black snipers on the West Side (two were dead, hundreds were in detention), he composed that electrifying speech, "A Knock at Midnight," read for him by friends of St. Peter's Cathedral, seeing how he was stretched so thin, there in Chicago, that he couldn't fly as scheduled to Geneva and instead spent three hellish nights rushing from one burning slum to another, pleading until 4 A.M. with both armed camps for peace. It is ... midnight in our world, and the darkness is so deep that we can hardly see which way to turn.

He was tired by the time the Movement reached the North. His life had always belonged to others. For ten years he'd been God's athlete, traveling nearly eight million miles (one-fourth the distance to Mars) back and forth across a country as divided as it had been during the Civil War, giving thousands of speeches in churches where he was celebrated as the heir of Thoreau—or better as the North American mahatma (Great Soul), meeting with presidents and heads of state, performing more eulogies for the Movement's martyrs than he cared to remember, leading his generals in the siege of one southern town after another; flying to Africa, then to India, and five years before to Oslo to accept the Nobel Peace Prize with a team of federal agents right on his heels, as they always were, closer even than his own heartbeat, he sometimes felt, though you had to wonder where they were and what the devil they were doing when that Harlem madwoman, Izola Curry, plunged a Japanese letter opener into his chest. Or when his Montgomery home was bombed, nearly killing his young wife and baby Yolanda.

More tired, acclaimed, hated, gaoled, and hunted than any other Negro in history, but living this close to death was as inevitable as his being ordained a minister when he was eighteen. No matter how he looked at it, his calling meant that from the moment he donned his robe the laws governing his life were different from those of the vast majority of men; indeed, it was no longer his life to do with as he pleased. The world owned him long before he could own himself. As it is with candles, so it was with him: the more light he gave, the less there was of him. Moreover, since the First World War the Army had sniffed something dangerous in his family, some blood-gift for subversion more radical than anything Lenin dreamed up in Moscow; they had watched his father and his grandfather closely, and interfered with their lives just as they did his, as devoted to shaming him, discrediting him, and driving him from public life as he was to bringing his ever expanding congregation a bit closer to the Kingdom of God on earth. People always thought he was older than his thirty-seven years. In point of fact, he felt old. Centuries old, and looked over fifty in some photographs: washed by all waters. Sometimes late at night, when he couldn't sleep before yet another early morning flight, and his leather suitcase from Paris lay packed on the table in yet another unfamiliar hotel room, and the memories came washing over him in waves—the poor living like chattel, children dynamited in a church, Watts burning for six days, the death threats spewing through the telephone at his wife—on those nights he wept for the blood spilled by his enemies, for his own life's lost options, for the outrageous fragility of what he hoped to achieve in a world smothering in materialism, in the propaganda of sensation, in scientific marvels unmoored from any sense of morality, and he wondered, there in the darkness before the dawn of what might be his last day on earth, if he'd ever been young at all.

"Don't go to Chicago," his closest advisor said. "You can't win there. You don't know cities. Stay on your own turf."

The enemy was more elusive, said Hosea Williams and the city's famed pastor, Joseph H. Jackson. Not crude country sheriffs like "Bull" Connor, who fell tail over tin cup before the world's cameras into the bully-buffoon role they scripted for him, or heavy-browed bigots like George Wallace, whose reactions made outstanding copy for the cause. In Chicago, the villains were faceless institutions: banks, real estate agents, insurance companies, and landlords hardly better off, in some cases, than their ghetto tenants. But this town, he knew, was the Up North equivalent of Birmingham. If they could triumph here, establishing a beachhead for satyagraha (truth force) in a brutal city with a murder rate of slightly more than two people per day, here in balkanized ethnic enclaves that spawned Al Capone and hardened street gangs like the Cobras, the Vice Lords, and the Black Stone Rangers, here in a city where Stokely Carmichael's poorly timed but inevitable cry for Black Power during their Mississippi march to support one of the South's wounded heroes, James Meredith, opened a Pandora's box of rage and rang deeper into black hearts than any appeal for love (he knew betrayal, a stab in the back when he saw it, but told Carmichael, "I've been used before"), then they could conquer any citadel of inequality in the world.

Yet no one thought he could win.

A decade after his Montgomery victory, and spiraling successes throughout the South, nigh Hegelian in the mysterious way the Movement kept changing as he chased it, and changing him, pushing him higher and higher, beyond anything he'd dreamed possible in college, from local bus boycotts to unqualified calls for integration, and finally to grander dreams of global peace and equality—a decade after his finest triumphs for nonviolence, the press, and even people who'd joined hands with him singing "We Shall Overcome," now saw his methods as outmoded, his insistence on loving one's enemies as lunacy, his opposition to Black Power as outright betrayal. Oh, he needed a victory here. The Chicago crusade was costing as much as $10,000 some months. In the spirit of Martin Luther four centuries earlier, he taped his demands for the poor on the door of City Hall after marching three miles with five thousand men and women of goodwill from Soldier Field; but despite money spent and speeches delivered, the mayor's office maneuvered, matching his call for jobs and open housing with promises and claims for progress that his critics dismissed as smoke and mirrors, mere Band-Aids aimed at making the problem (and him) go away. Never a day passed when he did not read that his stature was diminished, his day of leadership done, and he could not ignore his critics if he was, as he so often claimed, committed to the truth. Twelve times he'd been imprisoned in Alabama and Georgia jails, stabbed once, spat upon, and targeted for death so many times he could say, like the Apostle Paul, "I bear in my body the marks of the Lord." Yet for all his sojourning on the Jericho Road, his long journey through the valley of the shadow of death, his deeper, esoteric message about freedom had barely been heard. The gleaming keys he offered to the Kingdom made men and women who accepted his exoteric, surface-

skimming political speeches shrink back once they saw the long-sealed door he was asking them to enter; they could not pass through that portal and remain as they were: white and black, male and female, Jew and Gentile, rich and poor—these were ephemeral garments, he knew, and could no more clear that entrance than a camel through a needle's eye. To gain the dizzying heights of the mountaintop the self's baggage had to be abandoned in the valley. Little wonder, then, that so few grasped the goal he pointed to, or that on the Mississippi march and then in Chicago he was booed, and would have wept over this but instead thought back with thanksgiving (and was not all thought, as Heidegger pointed out, a form of thanksgiving?) to his professor at Morehouse, Benjamin Mays, who impressed upon him the importance of learning Henley's poem "Invictus" (It matters not how strait the gate ...). After his twelve years of sacrifice, the young people in the Mississippi crowd called him a traitor, an Uncle Tom (How charged with punishments the scroll ...). *In the cities, they sang "We Shall Over-Run."* (I am the master of my fate:/ I am the captain of my soul.)

But somehow their rejection and resistance to his vision fit well into the way he then understood the world. He was a tightrope walker straddling two worlds. One of matter. One of spirit. Every social evil he could think of, and every "ontological fear," as he was fond of saying lately, arose from that mysterious dichotomy inscribed at the heart of things: self and other, I and Thou, inner and outer, perceiver and perceived. It was a schism that, if not healed, would consume the entire world. Martyrdom held no appeal for him, but for every sorcerer named Jesus there was a Judas; for every bodhisattva called Gandhi, a Poona Brahmin named Nathuram Godse. The way to the crown was, now and forever, the cross. And it made no sense to carry the cross unless one was prepared to be crucified.

He sensed how close he was to the end, this Christian boy from Atlanta, this product of three generations of black preachers, this theistic idealist, and sometimes he wished he was two people, or perhaps three. One to co-pastor each Sunday beside his father at Ebenezer Baptist Church. Another to spend more time with his family, especially with his children; catch up on his reading (especially Tillich, Fromm, and Buber, who interested him now more than when he was in college); listen to opera, take his wife dancing, play basketball with the Southern Christian Leadership Council's staff, leave his blue suits in the closet, dress more casually, and perhaps one day pursue the simple, ascetic life similar to that of Thich Nhat Hanh, Zen master, and chairman of the Vietnamese peace delegation whom he was currently promoting as a candidate for the Nobel. As he'd told his Montgomery congregation the day he resigned as pastor in 1959, he longed to escape "the strain of being known ... I've been faced with the responsibility of trying to do as one man what five or six people ought to be doing ... What I have been doing is giving, giving, giving, and not stopping to retreat or meditate like I should—to come back. If the situation is not changed, I will be a physical and emotional wreck. I have to reorganize my personality and reorient my life. I have been too long in the crowd, too long in the forest ..."

And a third person to direct the Chicago campaign from the foul-smelling flat the SCLC and the Coordinating Council of Community Organizations leased at 1550 South Hamlin Street in the heart of "Slumdale." From a security standpoint its location was a nightmare. The neighborhood was notorious for crime. Saturday-night shootings and streetwalkers. Establishing a perimeter was impossible. Any rooftop across the street would tempt a rifleman. Noises from downstairs, loud, braying conversations from other apartments, could not be kept out. When a sanitation truck rolled by, the floor shuddered and pictures fell off the wall. Even so, he insisted that not a blessed thing in this soulless place be changed. They had come to Chicago to dramatize the fact that for $90 per month slumlords gave poor blacks—who on the average earned $4,700 yearly—the opportunity to dwell, some families packed ten to a flat, in wretched dumps of such advanced rot and decay that each crumbling unpainted wall, each untiled floor, each broken-down radiator, each crisp roach egg in the cabinets, each dishrag curtain on the windows, and each rusted faucet reinforced the free-floating despair that if you lived here, where every particle of your physical surroundings induced shame and was one step up from trash, was a throwaway, was substandard, then the country must regard you as a throwaway too.

The hallway leading to his third-floor rooms was black-dark. The stairs trembled under his feet. He couldn't lock the front door, so winos were free to piss in the entryway. In other words, the place where he'd brought his family was a urinal. And he, even he, hated the climb up the rickety steps to the top of the stairs. High above his door a single tungsten bulb buzzed in a halo of swirling dust motes the last few seconds before its filament flimmered out. Inside, their four rooms— hollow rinds filled with secondhand furniture—were arranged boxcar style (one for sitting, two for sleeping, and a miserable little kitchen) and were blisteringly hot and claustrophobic in the summer of 1966, even when his wife threw open the windows, for whatever breezes came through the rooms carried as well petroleum fumes and loud conversations and the roar of traffic from the streets below. Was this worth ninety dollars a month? Moreover, was proving his point by living here worth the toll he saw it taking on his family? The drain, the darkening of their spirits. "There's nothing green in sight," Coretta said, and for a moment he'd felt panicky, afraid, wondering if his work for his people, which he knew would kill him ("This is what is going to happen to me," he'd told her as they sat solemnly watching the news of John Kennedy's murder)—wondering if it would destroy his beautiful wife and four children as well.

In the last forty-eight hours, he'd survived a meeting with Richard Daley, from whom he'd won a few precious concessions (sprinklers attached to fire hydrants,

swimming pools shipped to the West Side) that might defuse the potential for
more rioting; then he'd gathered with gang members to sway them to the side of
nonviolence, meetings so torn by conflict and shouting and hatred of police that
he had to make himself appear to be the person at fault in order to calm the oth-
ers down. Having come through these crises, and with more to face, the man from
whom the world expected everything, who sometimes went for days on four hours
of sleep and rested fully only when he checked into a hospital, tried for a moment
to nap, to step back from the severe discipline that black manhood called for in
the twentieth century for just one precious moment in the sweltering heat of his
Lawndale flat.

Toussaint L'Ouverture and the Haytian Revolutions[*]

by James McCune Smith (USA)

Ladies and Gentlemen:
WHILST THE orgies of the French revolution thrust forward a being whose
path was by rivers of blood, the horrors of Santo Domingo produced one who
was preeminently a peacemaker—Toussaint L'Ouverture.

In estimating the character of Toussaint L'Ouverture, regard must be paid,
not to the enlightened age in which he lived, but to the rank in society from
which he sprang—a rank which must be classed with a remote and elementary age of mankind.

Born forty-seven years before the commencement of the revolt, he had
reached the prime of manhood, a slave, with a soul uncontaminated by the
degradation which surrounded him. Living in a state of society where worse
than polygamy was actually urged, we find him at this period faithful to one
wife—the wife of his youth—and the father of an interesting family. Linked
with such tender ties, and enlightened with some degree of education, which
his indulgent master, M. Bayou, had given him, he fulfilled, up to the moment of the revolt, the duties of a Christian man in slavery.

At the time of the insurrection—in which he took no part—he continued
in the peaceable discharge of his duties as coachman; and when the insurgents
approached the estate whereon he lived, he accomplished the flight of M.
Bayou, whose kind treatment (part of this kindness was teaching this slave to
read and write) he repaid by forwarding to him produce for his maintenance
while in exile in these United States.

---

[*] Extracts from a lecture [speech] delivered at the Stuyvesant Institute, New York, for
the benefit of the Colored Orphan Asylum, February 26, 1841.

Having thus faithfully acquitted himself a slave, he turned towards the higher destinies which awaited him as a freeman. With a mind stored with patient reflection upon the biographies of men, the most eminent in civil and military affairs; and deeply versed in the history of the most remarkable revolutions that had yet occurred amongst mankind, he entered the army of the insurgents under Jean François. The chief rapidly promoted him to the offices of physician to the forces, aid-de-camp, and colonel. Jean François, in alliance with the Spaniards, maintained war at this time for the cause of royalty.

Whilst serving under his chief, Toussaint beheld another civil war agitating the French colony. On one side, the French Commissioners, who had acknowledged the emancipation of the slaves, maintained a war for the Republic; on the other side, the old noblesse, or planters, fought under the royal banner, having called in the aid of the British forces in order to re-establish slavery and the ancient regime.

In this conflict, unmindful of their solemn oaths against the degree of the 15th of May, 1791, the whites of both parties, including the planters, hesitated not to fight in the same ranks, shoulder to shoulder, with the blacks. Caste was forgotten in the struggle for principles!

At this juncture Jean François, accompanied by his principal officers, and possessed of all the honors and emoluments of a captain-general in the service of his Catholic Majesty, retired to Spain, leaving Toussaint at liberty to choose his party. Almost immediately joining that standard which acknowledged and battled for equal rights to all men, he soon rendered signal service to the Commissioners, by driving the Spaniards from the northern, and by holding the British at bay in the eastern part of the island. For these services he was raised to the rank of general by the French commander at Port aux Paix, General Laveaux, a promotion which he soon repaid by saving that veteran's life under the following circumstances: Villate, a mulatto general, envious of the honors bestowed on Toussaint, treacherously imprisoned General Laveaux in Cape François. Immediately upon hearing this fact, Toussaint hastened to the Cape at the head of 10,000 men and liberated his benefactor. And, at the very moment of his liberation, a commission arrived from France appointing General Laveaux Governor of the Colony; his first official act was to proclaim Toussaint his lieutenant. "This is the black," said Laveaux, "predicted by Raynal, and who is destined to avenge the outrages committed against his whole race." A remark soon verified, for on his attainment of the supreme power, Toussaint avenged those injuries—by forgiveness!

As an acknowledgment for his eminent services against the British, and against the mulattoes, who, inflamed with all the bitterness of *caste*, had maintained a sanguinary war under their great leader Rigaud, in the southern part of the colony, the Commissioners invited Toussaint with the office and dignity of general-in-chief of Santo Domingo.

From that moment began the full development of the vast and versatile genius of this extraordinary man. Standing amid the terrible, because hostile, fragments of two revolutions, harassed by the rapacious greed of commissioners upon commissioners, who, successively dispatched from France, hid beneath a republican exterior a longing after the spoils; with an army in the field accustomed by five years' experience to all the license of civil war, Toussaint, with a giant hand, seized the reins of government, reduced these conflicting elements to harmony and order, and raised the colony to nearly its former prosperity, his lofty intellect always delighting to effect its object rather by the tangled mazes of diplomacy than by the strong arm of physical force, yet maintaining a steadfast and unimpeached adherence to truth, his word, and his honor.

General Maitland, commander of the British forces, finding the reduction of the island to be utterly hopeless, signed a treaty with Toussaint for the evacuation of all the posts which he held. "Toussaint then paid him a visit, and was received with military honors. After partaking of a grand entertainment, he was presented by General Maitland, in the name of His Majesty, with a splendid service of plate, and put in possession of the government house which had been built and furnished by the English."

* * *

Buonaparte, on becoming First Consul, sent out the confirmation of Toussaint as commander-in-chief, who, with views infinitely beyond the short-sighted and selfish vision of the Commissioners, proclaimed a general amnesty to the planters who had fled during the revolutions, earnestly invited their return to the possession of their estate, and with a delicate regard to their feelings, decreed that the epithet "emigrant" should not be applied to them. Many of the planters accepted the invitation, and returned to the peaceful possession of their estates.

In regard to the army of Toussaint, General Lacroix, one of the planters who returned, affirms "that never was a European army subjected to a more rigid discipline than that which was observed by the troops of Toussaint." Yet this army was converted by the commander-in-chief into industrious laborers, by the simple expedient of *paying them for their labor*. "When he restored many of the planters to their estates, there was no restoration of their former property in human beings. No human being was to be bought or sold. Severe tasks, flagellations, and scanty food were no longer to be endured. The planters were obliged to employ their laborers on the footing of hired servants." "And under this system," says Lacroix, "the colony advanced, as if by enchantment towards its ancient splendor; cultivation was extended with such rapidity that every day made its progress more perceptible. All appeared to be happy, and regarded Toussaint as their guardian angel. In making a tour of the island, he was hailed by the blacks with universal joy, nor was he less a favorite of the whites."

Toussaint, having effected a bloodless conquest of the Spanish territory, had now become commander of the entire island. Performing all the executive duties, he made laws to suit the exigency of the times. His Egeria was temperance accompanied with a constant activity of body and mind.

The best proof of the entire success of his government is contained in the comparative views of the exports of the island, before the revolutions, and during the administration of Toussaint. Bear in mind that, "before the revolution there were 450,000 slave laborers working with a capital in the shape of buildings, mills, fixtures, and implements, which had been accumulating during a century. Under Toussaint there were 290,000 free laborers, many of them just from the army or the mountains, working on plantations that had undergone the devastation of insurrection and seven years' war."

* * *

In consequence of the almost entire cessation of official communication with France, and for other reasons equally good, Toussaint thought it necessary for the public welfare to frame a new constitution for the government of the island. With the aid of M. Pascal, Abbe Moliere, and Marinit, he drew up a constitution, and submitted the same to a General Assembly convened from every district, and by that assembly the constitution was adopted. It was subsequently promulgated in the name of the people. And, on the 1st of July, 1801, the island was declared to be an independent State, in which *all men*, without regard to complexion or creed possessed *equal rights*.

This proceeding was subsequently sanctioned by Napoleon Buonaparte, whilst First Consul. In a letter to Toussaint, he says, "We have conceived for your esteem, and we wish to recognize and proclaim the great services you have rendered the French people. If their colors fly on Santo Domingo, it is to you and your brave blacks that we owe it. Called by your talents and the force of circumstances to the chief command, you have terminated the civil war, put a stop to the persecutions of some ferocious men, and restored to honor the religion and the worship of God, from whom all things come. The situation in which you were placed, surrounded on all sides by enemies, and without the mother country being able to succor or sustain you, has rendered legitimate all articles of that constitution."

Although Toussaint enforced the duties of religion, he entirely severed the connection between Church and State. He rigidly enforced all the duties of morality, and would not suffer in his presence even the approach to indecency of dress or manner. "Modesty," said he, "is the defense of woman."

The chief, nay the idol of an army of 100,000 well-trained and acclimated troops ready to march or sail where he wist, Toussaint refrained from raising the standard of liberty in any one of the neighboring islands, at a time when, had he been fired with what men term ambition, he could easily have revolutionized the entire archipelago of the west. But his thoughts were bent on conquest of another kind; he was determined to overthrow an *error* which designing and interested men had craftily instilled into the civilized world,—a belief in the natural inferiority of the Negro race. It was the glory and the warrantable boast of Toussaint that he had been an instrument of demonstrating that, even with the worst odds against them, this race is entirely capable of achieving liberty and of self-government. He did more: by abolishing caste he proved the artificial nature of such distinctions, and further demonstrated that even slavery cannot unfit men for the full exercise of all the functions which belong to free citizens.

"Some situations of trust were filled by free Negroes and mulattoes, who had been in respectable circumstances under the old Government; but others were occupied by Negroes, and even by Africans, who had recently emerged from the lowest condition of slavery."

But the bright and happy state of things which the genius of Toussaint had almost created out of elements the most discordant was doomed to be of short duration. For the dark spirit of Napoleon, glutted, but not satiated with the gory banquet afforded at the expense of Europe and Africa, seized upon this, the most beautiful and happy of the Hesperides, as the next victim of its remorseless rapacity.

With the double intention of getting rid of the republican army, and reducing back to slavery the island of Hayti, he sent out his brother-in-law, General Leclerc, with 26 ships of war and 25,000 men.

Like Leonidas at Thermoplylæ, or the Bruce at Bannockburn, Toussaint determined to defend from thralldom his sea-girt isle, made sacred to liberty by the baptism of blood.

On the 28th of January, 1802, Leclerc arrived off the bay of Samana, from the promontory of which Toussaint, in anxious alarm, beheld for the first time in his life so large an armament. "We must all perish," said he, "all France has come to Santa Domingo!" But this despondency passed away in a moment, and then this man, who had been a kindly-treated slave, prepared to oppose to the last that system which he now considered worse than death.

It is impossible, after so long a tax on your patience, to enter on a detailed narration of the conflict which ensued. The hour of trial served only to develop and ennoble the character of Toussaint, who rose, with misfortune, above the allurements of rank and wealth which were offered as the price of his submission; and the very ties of parental love he yielded to the loftier sentiment of patriotism.

On the 2d of February, a division of Leclerc's army, commanded by General Rochambeau, an old planter, landed at Fort Dauphin, and ruthlessly murdered many of the inhabitants (freedmen) who, unarmed, had been led by curiosity to the beach, in order to witness the disembarkation of the troops.

Christophe, one of the generals of Toussaint, commanding at Cape François, having resisted the menaces and the flattery of Leclerc, reduced that ill-fated town to ashes, and returned with his troops into the mountains, carrying with him 2,000 of the white inhabitants of the Cape, who were protected from injury during the fierce war which ensued.

Having full possession of the plain of the Cape, Leclerc, with a proclamation of liberty in his hand, in March following re-established slavery with all its former cruelties.

This treacherous movement thickened the ranks of Toussaint, who thenceforward so vigorously pressed his opponent, that as a last resort, Leclerc broke the shackles of the slave, and proclaimed, "Liberty and equality to all the inhabitants of Santo Domingo."

This proclamation terminated the conflict for the time. Christophe and Dessalines, general officers, and at length Toussaint himself, capitulated, and giving up the command of the island to Leclerc, he retired, at the suggestion of that officer, to enjoy rest and the sweet endearments of his family circle, on one of his estates near Gonaives. At this place he had remained about one month, when, without any adequate cause, Leclerc caused him to be seized, and to be placed on board of a ship of war, in which he was conveyed to France, where, without trial or condemnation, he was imprisoned in a loathsome and unhealthy dungeon. Unaccustomed to the chill and damp of this prison-house, the age frame of Toussaint gave way, and he died.

In this meagre outline of his life, I have presented simply facts, gleaned, for the most part, from the unwilling testimony of his foes, and therefore resting on good authority. The highest encomium on his character is contained in the fact that Napoleon believed that by capturing him he would be able to re-enslave Hayti; and even this encomium is, if possible, rendered higher by circumstances which afterward transpired, which showed that his principles were so thoroughly disseminated among his brethren, that, without the presence of Toussaint, they achieved that liberty which he had taught them so rightly to estimate.

The capture of Toussaint spread like wild-fire through the island, and his principal officers again took the field. A fierce and sanguinary war ensued, in which the French gratuitously inflicted the most awful cruelties on their prisoners, many of whom being hunted with bloodhounds, were carried in ships to some distance from the shore, murdered in cold blood, and cast into the sea; their corpses were thrown by the waves back upon the beach, and filled the air with pestilence, by which the French troops perished in large numbers. Leclerc having perished by pestilence, his successor, Rochambeau, when the conquest of the island was beyond possibility, became the cruel perpetuator of these bloody deeds.

Thus it will be perceived that treachery and massacre were begun on the side of the French. I place emphasis on these facts in order to disabuse the public mind of an attempt to attribute to emancipation the acts of retaliation resorted to by the Haytians in *imitation* of what the enlightened French had taught them. In two daily papers of this city there were published, a year since, a series of articles entitled the "Massacres of Santo Domingo."

The "massacres" are not attributable to emancipation, for we have proved otherwise in regard to the first of them. The other occurred in 1804, twelve years after the slaves had disenthralled themselves. Fearful as the latter may have been, it did not equal the atrocities previously committed on the Haytians by the French. And the massacre was restricted to the white French inhabitants, whom Dessalines, the Robespierre of the island, suspected of an attempt to bring back slavery, with the aid of a French force yet hovering in the neighborhood.

And if we search for the cause of this massacre, we may trace it to the following source: Nations which are pleased to term themselves civilized have one sort of faith which they hold to one another, and another sort which they entertain towards people less advanced in refinement. The faith which they entertain towards the latter is, very often, treachery, in the vocabulary of the civilized. It was treachery towards Toussaint that caused the massacre of Santo Domingo; it was treachery towards Osceola that brought bloodhounds to Florida!

General Rochambeau, with the remnant French army, having been reduced to the dread necessity of striving "to appease the calls of hunger by feeding on horses, mules, and the very dogs that had been employed in hunting down and devouring the Negroes," evacuated the island in the autumn of 1803, and Hayti thenceforward became an independent State.

Ladies and Gentlemen, I have now laid before your eyes a concise view of the revolutions of Hayti in the relation of cause and effect; and I trust you will now think, that, so far from being scenes of indiscriminate massacre from which we should turn our eyes in horror, these revolutions constitute an epoch worthy of the anxious study of every American citizen.

Among the many lessons that may be drawn from this portion of history is one not unconnected with the present occasion. From causes to which I need not give a name, there is gradually creeping into our otherwise prosperous state the incongruous and undermining influence of *caste*. One of the local manifestations of this unrepublican sentiment is, that while 800 children, chiefly of foreign parents, are educated and taught trades at the expense of all the citizens, colored children are excluded from these privileges.

With the view to obviate the evils of such an unreasonable proscription, a few ladies in this city, by their untiring exertions, have organized an "Asylum for Colored Orphans." Their zeal in this cause is infinitely beyond all praise of mine, for their deeds of mercy are smiled upon by Him who has declared, that "Whosoever shall give to drink unto one of these little ones a cup of cold water, shall in no wise lose her reward." Were any further argument needed to urge them on in their blessed work, I would point out to them the revolutions in Hayti, where, in the midst of the orgies and incantations of civil war, there appeared, in the spirit of peace, the patriot, the father, the benefactor of mankind—Toussaint L'Ouverture, a freedman, who had been taught to read while in slavery!

Bicentennial Blues

by Gil Scott-Heron (USA)

Some people think that America invented
    the blues
and few people doubt that America is the home
    of the blues
And the bluesicians have gone all over the world
    carrying the
blues message and the world has snapped its
    fingers and tapped
its feet right along with the blues folks, but
the blues has always been totally American.
As American as apple pie.
As American as the blues.
As American as apple pie.
The question is why …
why should the blues
    be so at home here?
Well, America provided the atmosphere
America provided the atmosphere for the blues
and the blues was born.
The blues was born on the American wildnerness,

The blues was born on the beaches where the
    slave ships docked,
born on the slave man's auction block
The blues was born and carried on the howling
    wind.
The blues grew up a slave,
The blues grew up as property.
The blues grew up in Nat Turner visions.
The blues grew up in Harriet Tubman courage.
The blues grew up in small town deprivation.
The blues grew up in the nightmares of the
    white man.
The blues grew up in the blues singing of
Bessie and Billie and Ma.
The blues grew up in Satchmo's horn, on Duke's
piano
in Langston's poetry, on Robeson's baritone.
The point is … that the blues is grown.
The blues is grown now—fully grown and you
    can trace/
The evolution of the blues on a parallel line
with the evolution of this country.
From Plymouth Rock to acid rock.
From 13 states to Watergate,
The blues is grown, but not the home.
The blues is grown, but the country has not.
The blues remembers everything the country
    forgot.

It's a Bicentennial year and the blues is
celebrating a birthday, and it's a Bicentennial
    blues.
America has got the blues and it's a Bicentennial
    edition.
The blues view may amuse you but make
no mistake—it's a Bicentennial year.
A year of hysterical importance
A year of historical importance:
ripped-off like donated moments
from the past.

Two hundred years ago this evening.
Two hundred years ago last evening, and what
    about now?
The blues is now.
The blues has grown up and the country has not.
The country has been ripped-off!
Ripped-off like the Indians!
Ripped-off like jazz!
Ripped-off like nature!
Ripped-off like Christmas!
Manhandled by media over-kill,
Goosed by aspiring Vice Presidents.
Violated by commercial corporations—A
    Bicentennial year
The year the symbol transformed into the B-U-Y-
    centennial.
Buy a car.
Buy a flag.
Buy a map ... until the public en masse has been
    bludgeoned into
Bicentennial submission
or Bicentennial suspicion.
I fall into the latter category ...
It's a blues year and America
has got the blues.
It's got the blues because of
partial deification of
partial accomplishments over a
partial period of time.
Half-way justice.
Half-way liberty.
Half-way equality.
It's a half-ass year
and we would be silly in all our knowledge,
in all our self-righteous knowledge
When we sit back and laugh and mock the
    things
that happen in our lives;
to accept anything less than the truth
about this Bicentennial year.

And the truth relates to two hundred years of
people and ideas getting by!
It got by George Washington!
The ideas of justice, liberty and equality got cold
by George Washington
Slave owner general!
Ironic that the father of this country
should be a slave owner.
The father of this country a slave owner
having got by him
it made it easy to get by his henchmen,
the creators of this liberty,
who slept in bed with the captains of the slave
    ships,
Fought alongside Black freed men in the Union
    Army,
and left America a legacy of hypocrisy.
It's blues year.
Got by Gerald Ford!

Oatmeal Man.
Has declared himself at odds with people
on welfare ... people who get food stamps,
day care children, the elderly, the poor, women
    and
people who might vote for Ronald Reagan.
Ronald Reagan—It got by him. Hollyweird!
Acted like an actor
acted like a liberal
acted like General Franco, when he acted like
Governor of California.
Now he acts like somebody might vote for him
    for President.
It got by Jimmy Carter,
"Skippy."
Got by Jimmy Carter and got by him and his
    friend
the Colonel ... the creators of southern fried
    triple talk,
A blues trio.

America got the blues.
It got Henry Kissinger
the international Godfather of peace.
A Piece of Vietnam!
A Piece of Laos!
A Piece of Angola!
A Piece of Cuba!

A blues quartet and America got the blues.
The point is that it may get by you
for another four years
for another eight years ... you stuck playing
    second fiddle
in a blues quartet.
Got the blues looking for the first principle
which was justice.
It's a blues year for the San Quentin Six, looking
    for
justice.
It's a blues year for Gary Tyler, looking for justice.
It's a blues year for Rev. Ben Chavis, looking for
    justice.
It's a blues year for Boston, looking for justice.
It's a blues year for babies
on buses,
It's a blues year for mothers and fathers with
    babies on buses.
It's a blues year for Boston and it's a blues year
all over this country.
America has got the blues and the blues is
in the street looking for three principles—
justice, liberty, equality
We would do well to join the blues looking for
justice, liberty, and equality.
The blues is in the street.
America has got the blues but don't let it get by
us.

For Chief

by Dennis Brutus (South Africa)

A Tribute
to
Albert John Luthuli
died
July, 1967

1

So the old leonine heart is stilled

the grave composure of the carven face
matched at last by a stillness overall

the measure of bitterness, totally filled
brims to the tautness of exhausted space

and he who sustained a faith in grace
believing men crippled could still walk tall
in the thorn-thickets of corrupting power

and more dear the central humanity
than any abstractions of time or place
daring to challenge, refusing to cower

mangled even at the end, he lies quiet
his stillness no less an assertion of faith
and the indestructible stubbornness of will.

2

So the machine breaks you
and you fall
still fighting grimly

the years epitomize
in this harsh act
of many:

Should one despair
knowing how great the power
how unavailing opposition?

Yet your great soul
asserts a worth—
transcendant humanity.

There is a valour
greater than victory:
        Greatness endures.

    3

And the people mourn
the millions mourn,
the sorrowing land
is plunged in deeper sorrow:

When will the soft rains dissolve the entire landscape
        at dusk?

Sorrow and anger stir,
Dull pain and truculent woe,
and bitterness slowly seethes
till fury cauldrons from pain—

Oh when will the blind storms rampage the landscape in
        the dark?

    4

Return to us

when sunset smoulders on the smooth horizon,
when the trees are starkly black
and beautiful
against the red and mauve of the sky

Return to us

when woodsmoke comes sweet and poignant
from the fields at dusk
after the winds of our fury have breathed
on the smouldering coals of our anger
and our fierce destruction has raged

O great patient enduring spirit
return to us.

5

O grave and statuesque man
stand along our paths,
overlook our ways

goad us by your calm regard
fire us with your desire,
steel us with your will.

Spirit of freedom and courage
guard us from despair
brood over us with your faith.

Fire the flagging and the faint,
spur us to fierce resolve,
drive us to fight and win.

6

And you
my friends
my allies
cosily chaired in London
or terminating in a thousand towns
or treadmilling the arid round
of protest, picket, pamphlet—
for as long as fervour lasts:
what shall I say of us?

O let Chief's reflected splendour
and the aura resistance sometimes brings—
except to the jaded, jaundiced, cynic—
o let us catch a little of this fire
and let us burn and steadily assert
our faith, our will to freedom and our love
for freedom and our dear unhappy land:
of inextinguishable and hungry fire
of love and hunger and imperishable resolve.

7

And the men
the dear lonely men

gaunt, and with a hunger around the eyes.
and the busy women
friendly strangers in a hundred lands:
ah these, my comrades and my friends!
how long, oh how much longer must it be?
how long still the wrench at throat
the pluck at eyes
at mention of some small forgotten word—
Fietas or Woodstock or Gelvandale—?
how much longer must we doggedly importune
in the anterooms of governors of the world
or huddle stubborn on the draughty frontiers of
       strange lands?
how long must we endure?
and how shall I express my gratitude and love?

[*Kitwe, Lusaka, Nairobi, London July 1967*]

Nanny: A Poem for Voices

by Marguerite Curtin (Jamaica)

[Passage to be read to background of haunting folk songs of the Blue Mountains—almost plaintive, with echo effect, e.g. "Hill & Gully Rider," "Gal &
Boy," "The Mountain Breeze A Blow," "A Know A Follie Man." At intervals,
very faintly, there should be the sound of the *abeng*.]

Blue Mountains, what secrets do you hold?
Cloud enveloped, swathed in swirling mists—
What have you seen
among soft slanting sunlight shafts
on your slopes,
swift, racing cloud-shadows,
icy, crystal mountain-water
and windblown, wynne grass on
mountain-top?

Beautiful hill country, moody and
majestic
mighty magnificence
summits

of Soul joy.

Blue Blue Mountains, what have
you watched
Among wind-twisted trees,
bromeliad clad,
Tall tree fern, cool moss and
silvery blue mahore?
What do your silent banksides of
lead and life and fragile Spanish
needle know?

Pure, heady mountain air,
Earthy smell of fern,
silver-backed
And pungent wild ginger,
Remind us of the past-shadows of
the past.
Pervading music of many waters
mingles with
Bird calls of the wood-land—
Ground doves, bald pates and solitaire.
Did harsh death-struggle once penetrate
this landscape of serenity?
Maroon shadows elude
And crimson redcoats fire?

[music of birdsounds—flute etc.
abeng and bugle intermingle.]

The helpless of the earth,
The wretched of the earth,
The hunted of the earth,
Look to you, woman of Ashanti blood
Princess of stately bearing and
noble dignity.
Fear conqueror
With fear-dismissing,
Fear-despising
Eyes.
Save us from Indians of Mosquito
Coast

And from blood hungry, blood-hounds
with curdling cry.
Find for us a mountain fastness,
A refuge.
Save us!

[Working songs, digging songs, etc.]

Dawn in the Blue Mountains
Dawn for a brave Maroon people
Busy people, building houses,
making homes.
Deep in dank coffee walk, red
berries are appearing among
Deep green coffee leaves.
Down in the gullies, the yam hills
flourish,
Corn leaves wave in sweet mountain
breeze
While plantains unfurl purple
blossom-shields
And in the wild cane the wild pig
grunts and squeals.
Happiness is come to Nanny Town.
Happiness pervades all Nanny Town.
Rejoice!

Night falls on the Blue Mountains
Evening star, whistling frogs,
firefly dance
And shrill "critch" owl cry,
Smell of pig roasting, yam and
green plantain.
Maroon watchers, foliage hidden,
Guard the secret of the mountain
gaps.
Keep the secret of the mountain passes.

[Faint sound of abeng]

Flickering firelight
And storyteller's tales

Rich legends of the homeland
Of mighty warriors of a mighty
empire,
Ancestors of an ancient kingdom.

Elegies of a journey through the
Great Gulf of suffering
To Latin conquered
Amerindian lands.
With eyes, heavy-lidded with sleep
But large
With excitement
Enraptured children listen.
Suspense filled, child eyes speak:

Teller of stories, break your
silence;

Spin your tale of the Anancy Man,
the "ginnal" man;

And how he spun his trap to catch
that "nyams," Brer Tacama.
Deep night: children slumber.
Full moon and celebration.
Calabash guitar and plaintive notes
of melancholy, bamboo flutes
Give way to soft drum throbs.

Listen.
Maroon Mountains throb.
Throb with the drum rhythms of the
Cimarrones,
Dwellers of the peak.
Swelling sound. Powerful sound.
Penetrating barriers of the
conscious.
Listen
In the inner silence to the language
of the other world.
Mysterious phenomenon
Unleashing unseen forces.

Mystic communication
Unleashing unseen forces.
Mystic communication
Unleashing unseen forces.
Setting in motion an invisible
universe. [DRUMOLOGY]

Presence.

Oh ecstasy
Of goodness   [SILENCE … drums
Outpouring   and background]
Joy
Overwhelming joy
Baptism of the drums.
Sweet mystery
Mystifying serenity
Peace
Power

War, War
War for rugged mountain warriors.
Mercilessly sharpen the cutlass
blade,
Sound the abeng,
Make ready for lowland raids.
Slaughter the English enemies
on lowland plains.
Like melting shadows, merge with
tropic landscape, and
Sabotage.

        [SOUNDS OF STEEL & ABENG]

Victoriously we return
Oh chieftaness of the Mountain
Passes.
Success in ambush.
Ambush of the bloodhounds,
Ambush of the redcoats.
Praise to you, defiant Maroon
Daughter, brave, warrior queen.

Intuitively knowing,
Confidence inspiring,
Possessor of the supernatural,
Woman of deep, deep sources.

What?

Bloodshot eyes of foaling calf seen
in noonday heat?

Ratbats leave dark caves and circle
round midday sun?

Sun hot and the patoo calls?

What portends these for Nanny Town?

     [NANNY'S MEDITATION]
     Blue, Blue Mountains
     I sorrow over Kufu,
     I sorrow over Brother Quashie
     Mountains of blue, deep blue,
     Where is Sido?

     Brave Sido.
     Oh Great Onyame help me.
     Help a woman's sorrow,
     Human sorrow,
     A woman's pain and knowing.

     PRAYER
     Great Anyame,
     You are changing me—
     I, the born frightened one.
     Like fire in the cane piece,
     Courage ignites.
     Now, near at hand is the great test.
     How shall I face the final defeat?
     How shall I bear it and not lose heart?

     Oh Great Onyame, keep me from the
     ruthless cruelty
     of the coward's panic.
     Give me grace in danger,

To be gracious under pressure
With the battle of my torn heart,
Let me listen to the inner voice
in meekness.
Tramp, tramp of the redcoats' boots,
English boots.
Fire, pistol fire, fire.
English fire and buglenote.
Anguished cries and leaps of death
Too late
To sound the abeng
Agony and children's cries.
Fire, fire, redcoat fire.
Captured Sideo has the place revealed.
Tortured Sido has given way.
Sorrow comes to Nanny Town
Only sorrow is left in Nanny Town,
Grief and lamentation.

Maroons dispersed
Desolate Nanny Town lies derelict
Broken Maroon homes, house night—
creatures;
And mournful mountain winds howl
through their dwellings.

Maroons of Accompong, mourn for us.
Cudjoe of St. James, weep for us.
Brothers of the Cockpit Country
lament for us.
Abeng of blue, Blue Mountains,
Sound for us.
Send your sad echoes to Portland
and St. Thomas in the East.

[Use Jamaican folk music that expresses the
courage of the Jamaican woman in bearing the
main brunt of life]

Great Woman of the blue, Blue
Mountains
Your spirit has not died.

Rejoice! Rejoice!
Your spirit lives on.
Rejoice!

Fairy Tales for a Black Northeast

by Lepê Correia (Brazil)

I want a new story
Not this tale of white and ordinary fairies
Owners of our achievements.
I want an ancient right
Hidden in the drawers of speeches
Meant to contain and palliate
(Full of apples and pears)
Embroidered with guilt and crimes.

What I want back, right now,
Are the keys to those drawers
Of the imprisoned archives
Where my heroes lie
A "new" old story
Full of thick-lipped fairies
Making *auê*, shouting
With rings in their ears
And kinky hair,
Choking white princes
With pineapple stems.

George S. Schuyler Again

by Marcus Garvey (Jamaica/USA)

George S. Schuyler is a joke;
His brain must be like sausage pork,
Or he must be a "nutty" ass
To bray at those he cannot pass:
The man, if man he is, is crude;
His very look is mighty rude,
He feeds on what his masters say,
And acts like monkey all at play.

He writes his soppy stuff each week,
The stuff of journalistic freak:
No one would worry over him,
But pass him with a good "boof, bim,"
A Negro man he claims to be,
And that puts us up on a tree:
If he should look at his old face,
He'd see the libel of his race.

—1934

Were U There When They Crucified My Lord

by Laini Mataka (USA)

if we rounded up all the men in the Nation
and scrutinized them to the nth degree
we still wldnt find one malcolm.
if we took all the speeches spoken by all the blk leaders since
1965, they cld not illuminate our reality more than the words left
by malcolm.
if we combined all
the post-garvey fears of wite people and laid them down
at the feet of the one
whose truths terrorized them the most,
it wld have to be malcolm.

for malcolm was our lord of liberation.
he was the alpha & omega of blk manhood. the answer
to the mystery of the sphinx. the uncontested paradigm
of metamorphosis. the first pharaoh to unite upper and lower self.
the buddha of ebony consciousness.
the christ of analytical persuasion.

did he walk on water, no, he walked on fire.
did he feed the masses with seven loaves & seven fish, no,
he fed hungry minds with facts & figures.
did he make the lame walk, no,
he made the challenged realize their power.
did he suffer the little children to come unto him, no,
he took healing to the streets and embraced all ages.
did he challenge the scribes & the pharisees, no,

he debated with all of racist amerika, & trapped them in the nets
of their own lies.
did he raise lazarus from the dead, no,
he raised a million lazarus's from a million ghetto graves.
did he teach people to love their enemies, no,
he showed his people
how to luv themselves.
did he rise from the dead after the third day, no,
he stripped death of its power & stepped into the gloryfield
of his peerless ancestors.

were u there when they crucified my lord?

were u in the house when uncle tomism came full circle
to surround our prince of peace.
were u on yr way to the ballroom when the low-lifed,
punk-ass pistolers took their seats. where was security when
our lord entered his final hours.
where were the police
when time & circumstance descended upon
our anointed one. where was elijah when his real son
was being lined up on the cross.

were u there when they crucified my lord?

were u behind the stage when destiny lured him out
into the open.
were u sitting near his children
when fatherlessness claimed them.
did u smell the fear in his stomach as he pressed forward
into infinity.
were his eyes glassy.
were his movements jerky.
when he as-salaam-alaikum'd, did he stutter.
when somebody screamed, get yr hand outa my pocket,
did u jump.
when the steel thunder of shotguns filled the audubon ballroom,
did u hit the floor.
did u run towards him or away.
when his blood burst forth from the various holes,
did u go into shock, did u throw up, or were u too paralyzed
to move. when his body

went limp & slid to the floor
where were the cpr trainees. where was the f.o.i.
where was the o.a.a.u., where was farrakhan, where was shorty,
where were the warriors! where was n.y.'s finest, where were the
fbi infiltraters, where was elijah, where was justice,
where was allah.

were u there when they crucified our lord?

when all the poems have been perpetrated. when all the dirges
have been sung.
the memory of our steel-boned warlord, will come to us in our
darkest hour & make us try ourselves for his murder.
for we are guilty of having been too human to save him.
we are guilty of letting his killers live.
we are guilty of paying tribute to those who executed him
not by pulling the trigger, but by giving the final order
& creating the atmosphere to make it so.
we are guilty of allowing amerika to
downplay his legacy.
we are guilty of not supporting his wife & children.
we are guilty of not honoring his sistah ella.
we are guilty of
allowing farrakhan to profane mosque #7 by
letting one of malcolm's convicted murderers take over
the very temple he built into prominence.
we are guilty of
letting amerika badmouth him
& then put his face on a postage stamp.
we are guilty of not making his birthday
a universal holiday.
we are all guilty of not loving him half as much as he
passionately luv'd us.

& if anybody out there thinks that malcolm was not one of the
greatest, most fearless, warrior-scholars of this century
my friend, u've been misled, bambuzzled, hoodwinked.

George

by Laini Mataka (USA)

this poem does not commemorate ghosts
ghosts being a white mans conception of a
universal entity.
this poem will key the unlocked spirit of
george jackson
         (jonathan being a whole otha testament)
this poem
is a demonstration; designed to re-expose the
primitiveness of white people who still dont kno that it's
time to come outa that cro-magnon shit.

         they laid for him.
forced him to play the victim for the last time
and even after they filled his body with lead
and was sure he had to be dead. dead. dead.
they handcuffed him
afraid even of his spirit
that it might fly up outa his body
and avenge it.
they tried to capture his soul in death,
since they were never able to do it in life.
and they left his body bakin
away in the sun for six hours
to be sure he was no longer a threat.
but little did they kno
that his people had feasted on his dreams
and drank deep the blood in his eye,
to later go out into the nite
lookin for something white
         to mutually sacrifice.

freedom's divas should always be luv'd

by Laini Mataka (USA)

(for H. Tubman and Dr. Welsing)

i like to think
that somewhere between the bodacious flights
and unbelievable weariness
a quilted cloud was laid out on the ground
and a big, sudanese-looking war-lord
dropped his weapons and a fragile creature
of living ebony fell into his arms laughing
as she imagined the look on ole marse tom's face
when he realized his ten best field niggahs were gone.

i like to think,
that history just never got his name,
but that when harriet came in from off the road
(underground, that is)
there was food on the table,
a fire in the hearth,
and the general understanding
that he wld reverse her aches
and turn them into derringers
that she cld stuff in her clothes
for protection on her next trip.

becuz freedom was & shld always be the goal
of every Black person on the planet

i like to think
that when harriet was gearing up
for her next rescue mission
that he argued to go with her,
to help her, to hold her if
a sleeping fit came.
to protect her from possible capture or betrayal.
i like to think
that in the end she always left
with as much of him as he cld part with

and still stay alive.
that he gave his blessings and did spiritual
somersaults
to gain God's attention
to make secure harriet's tenacious back.
i like to think that he left every pore open
to try and gauge
even from a distance.
if harriet was alright.
that sleep rejected his advances
as long as absence left her side of the bed empty
and his nuller than void.

i already know that her love of God
and race were impetus enuff to send her out
into the ignominious night
to emancipate her people
from the festering bowels of slavery.
this i know w/out a doubt!
and i like to think that
he licked her wounds, and washed her hair,
and placed wild-flowers on the table before her,
and picked her up to put her to bed
and made her infinitely know
that she was the only one.
                    and when she stayed away
                        one night longer than estimated,
                 i like to think
             he cried
          not wanting to live,
      if she died.

becuz i love harriet,
i had to speculate this pome.
becuz i love harriet, and
i've been planning
some midnight raids of my own.
becuz i love harriet
for showing me how to actively love Black people,
until i agreed to
letting that one principle rule my life.

i love harriet
for pointing me towards freedom
& making me fight for it myself.

i adore harriet and when it comes
to being loved by a Blackman
i like to think she had it like that
and if she didn't
  she shldve!

Chapter 7

Autobiography and Personal Narrative

Individuals tell their life stories in first-person narratives through autobiography, and although nonfiction, this literary genre boasts of unique forms of testimony that mimic the function of other literary forms, such as the novel and the short story. Indeed, Troupe and Schulte suggest: "[W]riting is not entertainment, it is survival. Through the power of the word and its associations, the writer hopes to create a world that reflects his human and intellectual dilemma."[1] Storytelling is an element of autobiography's value, as it reminds readers of the beauty of shared human experience. The self is not prioritized above the community in traditional African philosophy, and the genres associated with autobiography always emphasize the role of the community in the individual's development and conscience. Autobiography and personal narrative are testimonials, or eye-witness accounts, of the Black experience over time and space.

Personal narrative describes the written, shared life experiences of lesser-known or unknown persons. This genre is equally inspirational because it highlights the often overlooked merit of the lives of average people. A memoir is similar to an autobiography but differs because it narrates the author's relationships with a specific set of companions or acquaintances during a certain period of the author's life.

In the ancient Kemetic (Egyptian) tradition, the elaborate tombstone engravings of a leader's life story emerged as a sort of autobiography. In broader contexts of the African oral tradition, the epic narrative, retained as a formal ancestral record and transmitted by the hereditary role of *djeli*, chronicled the life stories of great individuals in the community. However, the story is told as a celebration of an individual and as a testament to the community from which he emerged.

---

1. Quincy Troupe and Rainer Schulte, eds., introduction to *Giant Talk: An Anthology of Third World Writings* (New York: Random House, 1975), xxxvii.

The genre of published autobiography in the Black literary tradition is a descendant of the enslavement narrative, which is the life story of an African who endured enslavement or the enslavement trade. The enslavement narrative chronicles the author's unbelievable struggles and degradation in bondage, and in addition to validating a challenging life experience, the enslavement narrative was also propaganda supporting the abolitionist movement. Some autobiographies, such as South African singer-activist Miriam Makeba's *My Story* (1987), served as much-needed antiapartheid propaganda. Propaganda, as suggested in W. E. B. Du Bois's and Amiri Baraka's claims that "all art is propaganda," is not a tool of exploitation; it can be effectively used as a tool of persuasion for a greater good.

Ideally, individuals who publish autobiographies have interesting and climactic real-life stories to tell, and readers may get satisfaction from the narrative because the autobiography chronicles authentic human experience. An autobiography often reflects the author's sense of destiny and narrates examples of defeating incredible odds and the trials and successes that transmit invaluable life lessons. It is interesting to notice who is worthy of mention by name and how the inclusion of peripheral characters varies in function and importance from one author's narrative to another's. Nationalism, racial identity, cultural identity, African heritage and kinship, and articulations of the kinds of racism in the world are among the many topics explored in autobiographies, but they are not the only noteworthy categories of analysis. Also, the idea of "home," sometimes in the context of "exile," looms large in the attentions and affections of the writers selected in this chapter.

Autobiography and personal narrative are also significant for the relationships they illuminate between the author and his or her ancestors, family, friends, lovers, and the community. Thus autobiography and personal narrative offer liberal sketches of life and relationships that validate both the author's exceptional circumstances and his or her universal human qualities. Authors uniquely blend topics of religion and spirituality, community, crisis, growth and development, racial identity and consciousness, parents, children, siblings, naming, history and heritage, historical context, and wars with both emphasis and understatement. Without delving into psychoanalysis (which biographies tend to do), autobiography and personal narrative reveal information about the author's motives, character, and even subconsciousness.

The autobiography of a famous person of African descent helps to increase the individual's status as a *mythoform*, or a legendary figure whose image is part of Black cultural mythology. The narrative is a tool of documentation, preservation, inspiration, and imitation that supports the hero dynamics of people of African descent. An amazing power of autobiography and personal narrative is that they share stories of a past that predates the author. Readers learn of the life stories of ancestors whose voices were not recorded during their own lifetimes. Such stories include those of previously voiceless earlier generations of enslaved Africans, pioneering ancestors, and diligent mothers and fathers. Autobiography and personal narrative show the similarities and differences between diverse communities of African descent, and most Black sources reveal at least a moment of Pan-African awareness.

When comparatively analyzing autobiography and personal narrative, it is always of interest to assess the amount of bias that appears in the author's style of self-depiction. These genres of testimony and confession are sometimes difficult for authors to write and publish because it is not an easy task to bare one's soul to the general public by sharing incidents that may not always be admirable. Readers assume that authors convey absolute truth, but "truth" is a more abstract notion than most readers realize. Truth can be complicated by bias, interpretation, personal denial, and lapses in memory. In contrast, a biography generally offers a different angle and interpretation of a person's life because the author is not emotionally attached to or overly protective of the private details of the biographical subject. This chapter also includes Albert Memmi's autobiographical novel, *The Pillar of Salt*, which challenges readers to be critically aware of where autobiography ends and fiction begins.

Nadine

recorded by Rebecca Carroll (Haiti/USA)

Nadine
Fifteen
Roxbury, Massachusetts

When I was thirteen years old, I decided that I'd like to do some experimenting with makeup. So I went to this huge CVS, which had a fairly decent-sized cosmetics section, and looked for some makeup to try on. None of the foundations, blushes, or eyeshadows matched my skin tone. I thought for a moment about asking one of the salespeople for help, but it didn't take long before I realized that there was no makeup for black people there. I didn't pursue it further.

My parents fled from Haiti when I was three or four. My father was Lucien Mallebranch. He was very involved in the political climate during the time that Duvalier was in office. And my mother was Jacqueline Adrien. They are both deceased. My father died of a cancer-related disease and my mother died of causes unknown. My social worker has told me that she has some new information on my mother's death, but I'm not ready to hear it yet. I have two older sisters who stayed in Haiti, and a younger brother and sister who live in a foster home in Florida. When my parents brought our family to the States, they moved us to Florida. We lived in an all-black, poverty-stricken neighborhood in a town called Immokaly, which wasn't at all what we had been accustomed to in Haiti. When we moved here, my father was not prepared for what he faced. His expectations of making a happy life for us here came crashing down. Because he didn't have a degree or a document testifying his work and high-standing position in Haiti, he ended up having to get a job as a dishwasher at a hotel. We had to eat.

I went to kindergarten through fourth grade at a school where there were kids from all ethnic backgrounds: Asian, Hispanic, white, black. But I had a very difficult time feeling comfortable with any of the kids at school. I felt upheaved and I wasn't a very trusting child. The neighborhood we were living in was so foreign to me that I think I carried that same sense of the unfamiliar with me to school. Also, our family life had changed in the way we all related to each other. In Haiti, I remember my father and I as being very close, which was unusual for a Haitian father. Normally in Haiti fathers are not especially close with their daughters. When we moved to the Sates, I sometimes didn't see my father for weeks at a time. He would be at work until long after I had gone to bed, asleep when I left for school, and gone again when I got home. I was no longer his "little princess" as I had been in Haiti, which deeply affected me.

At that time, my brother, who is four years younger than me, and I didn't really have any kind of sibling relationship because he was so much younger. My baby sister hadn't even been born yet. I haven't seen my brother in five years and have no contact at all with my sister. It's not that I don't want to see them, but between moving around from foster home to foster home and focusing on getting through school, I don't think it's a good idea right now for us to be in close contact. My situation is too unstable.

After my father died, my mom also became sick. She was pregnant with my little sister when she first became ill, and her illness eventually became so bad that she couldn't care for my brother and me. She gave birth to my sister and then put her and my brother in foster care while arranging for me to move up north to live with my aunt in Boston. I lived with my aunt for a while, but it was not the best situation. She was both emotionally and verbally abusive, and I knew enough to know that I would not be able to move forward with my life if I stayed with her. So then I moved into a shelter-type place for thirty days until a foster home became available. And that's where I've lived up until about three days ago when I moved into another foster home with a woman I feel more comfortable with.

As you can see, there was a lot going on for me before I could afford the time to think about being black and female in America. The irony is that when I did start thinking about it, I didn't exactly know what I was supposed to think. I mean, being from Haiti and having a sense of its history as the first independent black nation in the Western hemisphere, I *knew* that I was black. It was not an issue in Haiti, where everyone was black and there was integrity in that fact. When we moved here, I very quickly realized that in America, being black was another story. It hit me hard, too. Because here, it is an issue that far exceeds just being in the minority; there are serious power differentials and excruciatingly painful historical facts to reconcile.

When I was still in Florida growing up in my neighborhood there, I remember wondering why I had to be black. Like, *Why me?* My complexion seemed too dark and my nose seemed too wide. I wished desperately that I could be white so that I could go back to the lifestyle we had known in Haiti. Being black in America meant being poor. It wasn't until one of my teachers in the fourth grade, Mrs. Brown—oh, I loved her!—she said to me, "Girl, there is nothing wrong with you, there never was, and I pray to God there never will be! Take a good look in the mirror, chile, you are beautiful!" And I started looking in the mirror a little more and slowly began to reach a point where I could tell myself that I wasn't horrible looking anyway.

When I moved to Boston, I attended a public junior high school, which was predominantly black, with a few whites and Cambodians. My first year was a lot of peer pressure, just like any junior high experience: a lot of hype, trend-setting and -following, stuff like that. I never got the feeling that the school had any particular concern about academics; it was more about social activities and making friends. I couldn't see getting all worked up about trends, although I did have straightened hair. This natural hair that I have now is only a year old. It keeps me more focused, at least in the sense of being 100 percent black and female, not some watered-down, assimilated version. When I had my hair straightened, it was more of an issue of management, according to the adults in my life. And I just kept it that way until a year ago when I got tired of my hair breaking off from the damage caused by continuous processing.

Because I am from Haiti, I think it is interesting to contemplate whether or not I have a stronger, and perhaps more peaceful, sense of my African heritage than most African-Americans do. I think that I am more at ease with the part of me that claims my Haitian history than I am with the part of me that claims my American history. Haitians are a do-for-self culture, and coming to America and finding out the horror and submission of slave history has sort of gnawed around the edges of my soul. Seeing so clearly that black Americans are still not considered as "beautiful" or "smart" or "good" as white Americans is completely unsettling. As a fifteen-year-old black girl in society, I can flip through page after page of any major fashion magazine and not once see myself. What I do see is women who look nothing like me. After I have bought the magazine and flipped through it, I feel cheated and humiliated for paying the money and for believing that I might see an image I could relate to. And why do I have to buy *Essence* and *Ebony* in order to see an image of celebrated blackness? It's unfair. By default, I feel compelled to go and work for one of those mainstream fashion magazines, on behalf of black girls and women everywhere, to try and make some changes. But I really resent having to be pushed to that point.

A couple of years after my ill-fated search for makeup is when I happened upon *Essence* and *Ebony* for the first time. I was probably thirteen at the time, and I remember feeling this strange and very new feeling of hope about the way I looked. I was so thrilled to see black women on the cover, but I was angry that I had waited so long. The pain and insecurity I endured prior to this discovery made my awakening bittersweet.

Fortunately for me, my father, when he was alive, was very interested in feeding the mind history and literature. So my early years were filled with Haitian cultural philosophies. When I came here, all I learned about black culture in America was that black people were slaves, and then Martin Luther King showed up and single-handedly freed us all! So I had to self-educate. I spent a lot of time at the library and found out about people like Malcolm X, Nat Turner, Sojourner Truth, and Denmark Vesey. I realized how hard black people had fought against the nature of the grain in this country. That was my renaissance, which left me with a sense of wanting to fight. And I have, every step of the way.

Sometimes I think about what my father accomplished in Haiti and what his family accomplished—his family is scattered throughout France now, but they were all part of Haiti's hierarchy—and I worry endlessly about living up to those accomplishments. I haven't been back to Haiti because I haven't had the means and because I haven't wanted to. I feel firmly rooted in this country right now and feel that I have a lot of work to do here. I've taken on a lot of issues that plague black America, such as the "plight of the black male." Despite the hyped-up term, I am sincerely concerned about black men in this society and the ways in which they deal with black women. I think there's a lack of understanding between black men and black women that is unnecessary, but because there are so many myths and struggles to deal with, neither black men nor black women end up getting the support they need. I think the issue is partly because black women want to be appreciated by, but not mythologized by, black men. We know we're tough, be we'd like to be pretty and soft, too. Black men have fragile egos, so they often interpret women's needs as infringing upon their own needs. Ever since black men set foot on American soil, this country has been grinding at the black man's ego, trying to tear him down. It's all well and good to tell black men to move on, but when you're in the mire, you're breathing the stench.

I do think that young black men are far worse off than young black women because we young women have the strength of knowing that black culture has been throughout history and still is today a matriarchal one. We know that we will survive because we have. I'm also very interested in feminism and how it relates or doesn't relate, as the case may be, to black women. There is the common denominator of us all being women, which is a natural given. But from what I have read, it seems to me that when feminism began, white women wanted to get away from white men or to be equal to them. It has always been very much about these white women being given the opportunity to enter the workplace, which up until then had been a foreign concept. See, black women have *been* working. Matter of fact, we could use a vacation, come to think of it. One of the richest qualities about black culture is that when black women and black men do get along, we're not trying to be as good as each other, we're trying to be good *to* each other.

I don't spend much time thinking about my image or my body right now, but when I was younger (a little while after arriving in the States), I did have a hard time feeling okay, if you know what I mean. It has been and probably always will be to some extent an instant reflex to feel self-conscious as a black woman in this society. As I've said, there is no evidence on a consistent basis that we are beautiful, and it is not at all surprising or unrealistic to think that a character like Toni Morrison's Pecola Breedlove would go insane from wanting blue eyes. I think Pecola's character can represent young black girls in America as a whole, although perhaps on a less harsh level. It is a struggle, though, and a fine line between coming out the other side and going completely crazy.

It is bizarre when people talk about blackness as just a color and that there is no difference between black people and white people. It is precisely our skin color that fortifies and perpetuates racism in this society and, at our best moments, what makes us proud. We have to be. Without our black skin, we would be naked and our history would be more invisible that it already is.

Whether or not America wants to deal with me, I exist. And in memory of Zora: "I love myself when I am laughing."

from *All God's Children Need Traveling Shoes*

by Maya Angelou (USA)

The breezes of the West African night were intimate and shy, licking the hair, sweeping through cotton dresses with unseemly intimacy, then disappearing into the utter blackness. Daylight was equally insistent, but much more bold and thoughtless. It dazzled, muddling the sight. It forced through my closed eyelids, bringing me up and out of a borrowed bed and into brand new streets.

After living nearly two years in Cairo, I had brought my son Guy to enter the University of Ghana in Accra. I planned staying for two weeks with a friend of a colleague, settling Guy into his dormitory, then continuing to Liberia to a job with the Department of Information.

Guy was seventeen and quick. I was thirty-three and determined. We were Black Americans in West Africa, where for the first time in our lives the color of our skin was accepted as correct and normal.

Guy had finished high school in Egypt, his Arabic was good and his health excellent. He assured me that he would quickly learn a Ghanaian language, and he certainly could look after himself. I had worked successfully as a journalist in Cairo, and had failed sadly at a marriage which I ended with false public dignity and copious secret tears. But with all crying in the past, I was on my way to another adventure. The future was plump with promise.

For two days Guy and I laughed. We listened to the melodious languages and laughed. We looked at each other and laughed out loud.

On the third day, Guy, on a pleasure outing, was injured in an automobile accident. One arm and one leg were fractured and his neck was broken.

July and August of 1962 stretched out like fat men yawning after a sumptuous dinner. They had every right to gloat, for they had eaten me up. Gobbled me down. Consumed my spirit, not in a wild rush, but slowly, with the obscene patience of certain victors. I became a shadow walking in the white hot streets, and a dark spectre in the hospital.

There was no solace in knowing that the doctors and nurses hovering around Guy were African, nor in the company of the Black American expatriates who, hearing of our misfortune, came to share some of the slow hours. Racial loyalties and cultural attachments had become meaningless.

Trying utterly, I could not match Guy's stoicism. He lay calm, week after week, in a prison of plaster from which only his face and one leg and arm were visible. His assurances that he would heal and be better than new drove me into a faithless silence. Had I been less timid, I would have cursed God. Had I come from a different background, I would have gone further and denied His very existence. Having neither the courage nor the historical precedent, I raged inside myself like a blinded bull in a metal stall.

Admittedly, Guy lived with the knowledge that an unexpected and very hard sneeze could force the fractured vertebrae against his spinal cord, and he would be paralyzed or die immediately, but he had only an infatuation with life. He hadn't lived long enough to fall in love with this brutally delicious experience. He could lightly waft away to another place, if there really was another place, where his youthful innocence would assure him a crown, wings, a harp, ambrosia, free milk and an absence of nostalgic yearning. (I was raised on the spirituals which ached to "See my old mother in glory" or "Meet with my dear children in heaven," but even the most fanciful lyricists never dared to suggest that those cavorting souls gave one thought to those of us left to moil in the world.) My wretchedness reminded me that, on the other hand, I would be rudderless.

I had lived with family until my son was born in my sixteenth year. When he was two months old and perched on my left hip, we left my mother's house and together, save for one year when I was touring, we had been each other's home and center for seventeen years. He could die if he wanted to and go off to wherever dead folks go, but I, I would be left without a home.

The man who caused the accident stood swaying at the foot of the bed. Drunk again, two months later, still drunk. He, the host of the motor trip and the owner of the car, had passed out on the back seat leaving Guy behind the steering wheel trying to start the stalled engine. A truck had careened off a steep hill and plowed into Richard's car, and he had walked away unhurt.

Now he dangled loosely in the room, looking shyly at me. "Hello, Sister Maya." The slurred words made me hate him more. My whole body yearned for his scrawny neck. I turned my face from the scoundrel and looked at my son. The once white plaster that encased his body and curved around his face was yellowing and beginning to crumble.

I spoke softly, as people do to the very old, the very young, and the sick. "Darling, how are you today?"

"Mother, Richard spoke to you." His already deep voice growled with disapproval.

"Hello, Richard," I mumbled, hoping he couldn't hear me.

My greeting penetrated an alcoholic fog, and the man lumbered into an apologetic monologue that tested my control. "I'm sorry, Sister Maya. So sorry. If only it could be me, there on that bed ... Oh, if only it could be me ..."

I agreed with him.

At last he had done with his regrets, and saying good-bye to Guy, took my hand. Although his touch was repulsive, Guy was watching me, so I placed a silly grin on my face and said, "Good-bye, Richard." After he left, I began to quickly unload the basket of food I had brought. (The teenage appetite is not thwarted by bruises or even broken bones.)

Guy's voice stopped me.

"Mother, come so I can see you."

The cast prevented him from turning, so visitors had to stand directly in his vision. I put the basket down and went to stand at the foot of the bed.

His face was clouded with anger.

"Mother, I know I'm your only child, but you must remember, this is my life, not yours." The thorn from the bush one has planted, nourished and pruned, pricks most deeply and draws more blood. I waited in agony as he continued, eyes scornful and lips curled, "If I can see Richard and understand that he has been more hurt than I, what about you? Didn't you mean all those sermons about tolerance? All that stuff about understanding? About before you criticize a man, you should walk a mile in his shoes?"

Of course I meant it in theory, in conversation about the underprivileged, misunderstood and oppressed miscreants, but not about a brute who had endangered my son's life.

I lied and said, "Yes, I meant it." Guy smiled and said, "I know you did, Mother. You're just upset now." His face framed by the cast was beautiful with forgiveness. "Don't worry anymore. I'm going to get out of here soon, then you can go to Liberia."

I made bitterness into a wad and swallowed it.

I puckered and grinned and said, "You're right, darling. I won't be upset anymore."

As always, we found something to laugh about. He fumbled, eating with his unbroken left hand and when he did have the food firmly in his grasp, he pretended not to know how to find his mouth. Crumbs littered his gown. "I'll figure it out, Mom. I promise you I won't starve to death." We played word games, and the visiting hours went by quickly.

Too soon I was back on the bright street with an empty basket in my hands and my head swimming in the lonely air.

I did know some people who would receive me, but reluctantly, because I had nothing to offer company save a long face and self-pitying heart, and I had no intention of changing either. Black Americans of my generation didn't look kindly upon public mournings except during or immediately after funerals. We were expected by others and by ourselves to lighten the burden by smiling, to deflect possible new assaults by laughter. Hadn't it worked for us for centuries? Hadn't it?

On our first night in Ghana, our host (who was only a friend of a friend) invited Black American and South American expatriates to meet us. Julian Mayfield and his beautiful wife Ana Livia, who was a medical doctor, were known to me from New York and the rest were not. But there is a kinship among wanderers, as operative as the bond between bishops or the tie between thieves: We knew each other instantly and exchanged anecdotes, contacts and even addresses within the first hour.

Alice Windom, a wit from St. Louis, and Vicki Garvin, a gentle woman from New York City, were among the Americans laughing and entertaining in the small living room. In the two years which had passed since Guy had been in the company of so many Black Americans, he had grown from a precocious adolescent into an adept young man. He bristled with pleasure, discovering that he could hold his own in the bantering company.

Each émigré praised Ghana and questioned my plans to settle in Liberia. There was no need to tell them that I hungered for security and would have accepted any promised permanence in Africa. They knew, but kept up the teasing. One asked, "You remember that Ray Charles song where he says, 'When you leave New York, you ain't going nowhere'?"

I remembered.

"Well, when you leave Ghana, going to Liberia, you ain't going to Africa, in fact you ain't going nowhere."

Although I knew Liberians who were as African as Congo drums, I honored the traditional procedure and allowed the raillery to continue.

Alice advised, "Honey, you'd better stay here, get a job and settle down. It can't get better than Ghana and it could be a lot worse." Everyone laughed and agreed.

The fast talk and jokes were packages from home and I was delighted to show the group that I still knew how to act in Black company. I laughed as hard as the teasers and enjoyed the camaraderie.

But Guy's accident erased all traces of their names, their faces and conviviality. I felt as if I had met no one, knew no one, and had lived my entire life as the bereft mother of a seriously injured child.

Tragedy, no matter how sad, becomes boring to those not caught in its addictive caress. I watched my host, so sympathetic at the outset, become increasingly less interested in me and my distress. After a few weeks in his house, his discomfort even penetrated my self-centeredness. When Julian and Ana Livia Mayfield allowed me to store my books and clothes in their house, I gave my host only perfunctory thanks, and moved into a tiny room at the local YMCA. I focused my attention on myself, with occasional concentrations on Guy. If I thought about it I was relieved that no one anticipated my company, yet, I took the idea of rejection as one more ornament on my string of worry beads.

One sunny morning Julian stood waiting for me at the YWCA lobby. His good looks drew attention and giggles from the young women who sat on the vinyl chairs pretending to read.

"I'm taking you to meet someone. Someone you should know." He looked at me without smiling. He was tall, Black, tough and brusque.

"You need to have someone, a woman, talk to you. Let's go." I withdrew from his proprietary air, but lack of energy prevented me from telling him that he wasn't my brother, he wasn't even a close friend. For want of resistance, I followed him to his car.

"Somebody needs to tell you that you have to give up this self-pity. You're letting yourself go. Look at your clothes. Look at your hair. Hell, it's Guy whose neck was broken. Not yours."

Anger jumped up in my mouth, but I held back the scorching words and turned to look at him. He was watching the road, but the side of his face visible to me was tense, his eyes were unblinking, and he had pushed his full lips out in a pout.

"Everybody understands … as much as anyone can understand another's pain … but you've … you've forgotten to be polite. Hell, girl, everybody feels sorry for you, but nobody owes you a damn thing. You know that. Don't forget your background. Your mother didn't raise you in a dog house."

Blacks concede that hurrawing, jibing, jiving, signifying, disrespecting, cursing, even outright insults might be acceptable under particular conditions, but aspersions cast against one's family call for immediate attack.

I said, "How do you know my business so well? Was that my daddy visiting your mother all those times he left our home?"

I expected an explosion from Julian. Yet his response shocked me. Laughter burst out of him, loud and raucous. The car wobbled and slowed while he held tenuously to the steering wheel. I caught his laughter, and it made me pull his jacket, and slap my own knee. Miraculously we stayed on the road. We were still laughing when he pulled into a driveway and let the engine die.

"Girl, you're going to be all right. You haven't forgotten the essentials. You know about defending yourself. All you have to do now is remember … sometimes you have to defend yourself from yourself."

When we got out of the car Julian hugged me and we walked together toward The National Theatre of Ghana, a round, white building set in an embrace of green-black trees.

Efua Sutherland could have posed for the original bust of Nefertiti. She was long, lean, Black and lovely, and spoke so softly I had to lean forward to catch her words. She wore an impervious air as obvious as a strong perfume, and an austere white floor-length gown.

She sat motionless as Julian recounted my dreadful tale and ended saying that my only child was, even as we spoke, in the Military Hospital. When Julian stopped talking and looked at her pointedly, I was pleased that Efua's serene face did not crumble into pity. She was silent and Julian continued. "Maya is a writer. We knew each other at home. She worked for Martin Luther King. She's pretty much alone here, so I have to be a brother to her, but she needs to talk to a woman, and pretty soon she'll need a job." Efua said nothing, but finally turned to me and I had the feeling that all of myself was being absorbed. The moment was long.

"Maya," she stood and walked to me. "Sister Maya, we will see about a job, but now you have need of a Sister friend." I had not cried since the accident. I had helped to lift Guy's inert body onto the x-ray table at the first hospital, had assisted in carrying his stretcher to an ambulance for transfer to another hospital. I had slept, awakened, walked, and lived in a thick atmosphere, which only allowed shallow breathing and routine motor behavior.

Efua put her hand on my cheek and repeated, "Sister, you have need of a Sister friend because you need to weep, and you need someone to watch you while you weep." Her gestures and voice were mesmerizing. I began to cry. She stroked my face for a minute then returned to her chair. She began speaking to Julian about other matters. I continued crying and was embarrassed when I couldn't stop the tears. When I was a child, my grandmother would observe me weeping and say, "Be careful, Sister. The more you cry, the less you'll pee, and peeing is more important." But the faucet, once opened, had to drain itself. I had no power over its flow.

Efua sent Julian away with assurances that she would return me to the hospital. I looked at her, but she had settled into herself sweetly, and I was freed to cry out all the bitterness and self-pity of the past days.

When I had finished, she stood again, offering me a handkerchief. "Now, Sister, you must eat. Eat and drink. Replenish yourself." She called her chauffeur, and we were taken to her home.

She was a poet, playwright, teacher, and the head of Ghana's National Theatre. We talked in her car of Shakespeare, Langston Hughes, Alexander Pope and Sheridan. We agreed that art was the flower of life and despite the years of ill-treatment Black artists were among its most glorious blossoms.

She knew the president and called him familiarly "Kwame."

She said, "Kwame has said that Ghana must use its own legends to heal itself. I have written the old tales in new ways to teach the children that their history is rich and noble."

Her house, white as chalk and stark, had rounded walls which enclosed a green lawn. Her three children came laughing to greet me, and her servant brought me food. Efua spoke in Fanti to the maid, and a mixture of Fanti and English to the children.

"This is your Auntie Maya. She shall be coming frequently. Her son is ill, but you shall meet him, for he will soon be released from the hospital."

Esi Rieter, the oldest, a girl of ten, Ralph, seven, and the five-year old, Amowi, immediately wanted to know how old my son was, what was his illness, did I have other children, what did I do. Efua sent them away assuring them that time would answer all questions.

I ate as I had cried, generously. After the meal, Efua walked me to the car.

"Sister, you are not alone. I, myself, will be at the hospital tomorrow. Your son is now my son. He has two mothers in this place." She put her hand on my face again. "Sister, exercise patience. Try."

When the driver stopped at the hospital, I felt cool and refreshed as if I had just gone swimming in Bethesda's pool, and many of my cares had been washed away in its healing water.

The hospital acquired color, there was laughter in its halls and Guy's good humor stopped being contrived. He and the doctors, surprisingly, had been right. Recovery was evident in the ways of his hands and in his lumbering, cast-top-heavy lurching up and down the corridors.

Outside, the sun, which had pounced, penetrating and hostile, now covered me with beneficial rays, hoisting me out of depression and back on my feet, where my new mood told me I deserved to be.

I smiled at strangers and took notice of buildings and streets. Weeks passed before I was conscious that I had let go of misery.

The visit to Efua, and Julian's reluctant but sincere offer to be my brother had been very strong medicine.

I was impatient to get my life in order. Obviously, I wouldn't go to Liberia, so ... I had to find a job, a car and a house for Guy to come to while he continued recuperating. I needed to get my hair cut, a manicure, a pedicure. My clothes were disgraceful.

Flashes of panic occurred and recurred. Was it possible that during the two-month depression, I had damaged my determination? The only power I had ever claimed was that I had over myself. Obviously, I had come perilously close to giving it away to self-pity.

I thought about Julian's harsh words. "Your mother didn't raise you in a dog house." His intuition had come understated.

My mother, that pretty little woman with a steel chest, had taught me and my brother Bailey that each person was expected to "paddle his own canoe, stand on his own feet, put his shoulder to the wheel, and work like hell." She always added, "Hope for the best, but be prepared for the worst. You may not always get what you pay for, but you will definitely pay for what you get." Vivian Baxter had axioms for every situation, and if one didn't come to mind when she needed it, she would create a better one on the moment.

I had been a pretty good student, ingesting and internalizing her advice, so now I pushed away the gnawing fear that I might have lost some of my vital willfulness.

I looked at the disheveled mess I had been living in and at my nearby neighbors. To my surprise, many of the women who had been at that first-night party and who had faithfully attended Guy's hospital room, lived down the hall from me. I was also amazed to learn that mops, brooms, pails and other cleaning implements were available for the free use of the center's guests.

Alice and Vicki watched me emerge from the bonds of my chrysalis and accepted me with no comment, save an easy teasing. While I swabbed my small floor and washed my clothes Alice said, "I would offer to help you Maya, but somehow I didn't inherit any of the race's domestic talents."

Vicki offered, but I knew the work was cathartic, so I washed walls, polished door knobs and the tiny window. The scales and stench of defeat floated into the pail's dirty water.

The YWCA residents forgave me my drunken spree with hopelessness and we began to spend time together in the building's cafeteria and on the streets filled with views I had not seen. Alice took me to Black Star Square to see the monumental arch, named in part for the newspaper founded in the United States by the ex-slave and abolitionist, Frederick Douglass.

Vicki and Sylvia Boone rode with me to Flagstaff House, the seat of government. Seeing Africans enter and leave the formal building made me tremble with an awe I had never known. Their authority on the marble steps again proved that Whites has been wrong all along. Black and brown skin did not herald debasement and a divinely created inferiority. We were capable of controlling our cities, our selves and our lives with elegance and success. Whites were not needed to explain the working of the world, nor the mysteries of the mind.

My visits to the hospital diminished to one daily appearance and Guy's gladness made me young again.

Efua introduced me to the chairman of the Institute of African Studies at the university and pleaded with him to hire me. She had told him that I had been on my way to a job in Liberia until my seventeen-year-old son had been involved in an accident, adding that I had to stay in Ghana until he fully recovered. She smiled at him and said I was already trying to hear Fanti, and would make a good Ghanaian.

Professor J. H. Nketia, one of Ghana's leading scholars, was so unpretentious as to be unsettling. He listened with patience to Efua, then asked me, "Can you type?" When I said only a little, but that I could file and write, he gathered his chin in a stubby brown hand and smiled. "Can you start on Monday?" He told me I would be paid on the Ghanaian scale and he would arrange for me to get a small car. I knew that the proffered job spoke more of his own compassion and his affection for Efua than of a need for my services.

Foreign employees at the university earned high salaries, compared to the national average wage, and very liberal compensations. They were given housing allowances, tuition or aid for their offspring's education, transportation allowances and a perk charmingly referred to as dislocation allowance. They had been recruited in their own countries, and hired for their academic credentials and experience. Save for two youthful years at night school, I had only a high school education.

I challenged myself to do whatever job assigned to me with intense commitment and a good cheerfulness.

A professor went on leave and I moved into his house for three months. When Guy was released from the hospital he settled into our furnished, if temporary, home.

The community of Black immigrants opened and fitted me into their lives as if they had been saving my place.

The group's leader, if such a collection of eccentric egos could be led, was Julian. He had three books published in the United States, had acted in a Broadway play, and was a respected American-based intellectual before an encounter with the CIA and the FBI caused him to flee his country for Africa. He was accompanied in flight and supported in fact, by Ana Livia, who was at least as politically volatile as he.

Sylvia Boone, a young sociologist, had come to Africa first on a church affiliated tour, then returned with sophistication, a second Master's degree and fluent French to find her place on the Continent. Ted Pointiflet was a painter who argued gently, but persistently that Africa was the inevitable destination of all Black Americans. Lesley Lacy, a sleek graduate student, was an expert on Marxism and Garveyism, while Jim and Annette Lacy, no relation to Lesley, were grade school teachers and quite rare among our group because they listened more than they talked. The somber faced Frank Robinson, a plumber, had a contagious laughter, and a fierce devotion to Nkrumah. Vicki Garvin had been a union organizer, Alice Windom had been trained in sociology. I called the group "Revolutionist Returnees."

Each person had brought to Africa varying talents, energies, vigor, youth and terrible yearnings to be accepted. On Julian's side porch during warm black nights, our voices were raised in attempts to best each other in lambasting America and extolling Africa.

We drank gin and ginger ale when we could afford it, and Club beer when our money was short. We did not discuss the open gutters along the streets of Accra, the shacks of corrugated iron in certain neighborhoods, dirty beaches and voracious mosquitoes. And under no circumstances did we mention our disillusionment at being overlooked by the Ghanaians.

We had come home, and if home was not what we had expected, never mind, our need for belonging allowed us to ignore the obvious and to create real places or even illusory places, befitting our imagination.

Doctors were in demand, so Ana Livia had been quickly placed in the Military Hospital and within a year, had set up a woman's clinic where she and her platoon of nursing sisters treated up to two hundred women daily. Progressive journalists were sought after, so Julian, who wrote articles for American and African journals, also worked for the *Ghana Evening News*. Frank and his partner Carlos Allston from Los Angeles founded a plumbing and electric company. Their success gave heart to the rest. We had little doubt about our likability. After the Africans got to know us their liking would swiftly follow. We didn't question if we would be useful. Our people for over three hundred years had been made so useful, a bloody war had been fought and lost, rather than have our usefulness brought to an end. Since we were descendants of African slaves torn from the land, we reasoned we wouldn't have to earn the right to return, yet we wouldn't be so arrogant as to take anything for granted. We would work and produce, then snuggle down into Africa as a baby nuzzles in a mother's arms.

I was soon swept into an adoration for Ghana as a young girl falls in love, heedless and with slight chance of finding the emotion requited.

There was an obvious justification for my amorous feelings. Our people had always longed for home. For centuries we had sung about a place not built with hands, where the streets were paved with gold, and were washed with honey and milk. There the saints would march around wearing white robes and jeweled crowns. There, at last, I would study war no more and, more important, no one would wage war against us again.

The old Black deacons, ushers, mothers of the church and junior choirs only partially meant heaven as that desired destination. In the yearning, heaven and Africa were inextricably combined.

And now, less than one hundred years after slavery was abolished, some descendants of those early slaves taken from Africa, returned, weighted with a heavy hope, to a continent which they could not remember, to a home which had shamefully little memory of them.

Which one of us could know that years of bondage, brutalities, the mixture of other bloods, customs and languages had transformed us into an unrecognizable tribe? Of course, we knew that we were mostly unwanted in the land of our birth and saw promise on our ancestral continent.

I was in Ghana by accident, literally, but the other immigrants had chosen the country because of its progressive posture and its brilliant president, Kwame Nkrumah. He had let it be known that American Negroes would be welcome to Ghana. He offered havens for Southern and East African revolutionaries working to end colonialism in their countries.

I admitted that while Ghana's domestic and foreign policy were stimulating, I was captured by the Ghanaian people. Their skins were the colors of my childhood cravings: peanut butter, licorice, chocolate and caramel. Theirs was the laughter of home, quick and without artifice. The erect and graceful walk of the women reminded me of my Arkansas grandmother, Sunday-hatted, on her way to church. I listened to men talk, and whether or not I understood their meaning, there was a melody as familiar as sweet potato pie, reminding me of my Uncle Tommy Baxter in Santa Monica, California. So I had finally come home. The prodigal child, having strayed, been stolen or sold from the land of her fathers, having squandered her mother's gifts and having laid down in cruel gutters, had at last arisen and directed herself back to the welcoming arms of the family where she would be bathed, clothed with fine raiment and seated at the welcoming table.

I was one of nearly two hundred Black Americans from St. Louis, New York City, Washington, D.C., Los Angeles, Atlanta, and Dallas who hoped to live out the Biblical story.

Some travelers had arrived at Ghana's Accra Airport, expecting customs agents to embrace them, porters to shout—"welcome," and the taxi drivers to ferry them, horns blaring, to the city square where smiling officials would cover them in ribbons and clasp them to their breasts with tearful sincerity. Our arrival had little impact on anyone but us. We ogled the Ghanaians and few of them even noticed. The newcomers hid disappointment in quick repartee, in jokes and clenched jaws.

The citizens were engaged in their own concerns. They were busy adoring their flag, their five-year old independence from Britain and their president. Journalists, using a beautiful language created by wedding English words to an African syntax, described their leader as "Kwame Nkrumah, man who surpasses man, iron which cuts iron." Orators, sounding more like Baptist southern preachers than they knew, spoke of Ghana, the jewel of Africa leading the entire continent from colonialism to full independence by the grace of Nkrumah and God, in that order. When Nkrumah ordered the nation to detribalize, the Fanti, Twi, Ashanti, Ga and Ewe clans began busily dismantling formations which had been constructed centuries earlier by their forefathers. Having the responsibility of building a modern country, while worshipping traditional ways and gods, consumed enormous energies.

As the Ghanaians operated an efficient civil service, hotels, huge dams, they were still obliged to be present at customary tribal rituals. City streets and country roads were hosts daily to files of celebrants of mourners, accompanied by drums, en route to funerals, outdoorings (naming ceremonies), marriages or the installations of chiefs, and they celebrated national and religious harvest days. It is small wonder that the entrance of a few Black Americans into that high stepping promenade went largely unnoticed.

The wonder, however, was neither small nor painless to the immigrants. We had come to Africa from our varying starting places and with myriad motives, gaping with hungers, some more ravenous than others, and we had little tolerance for understanding being ignored. At least we wanted someone to embrace us and maybe congratulate us because we had survived. If they felt the urge, they could thank us for having returned.

We, who had been known for laughter, continued to smile. There was a gratifying irony in knowing that the first family of Black Americans in Ghana were the Robert Lees of Virginia, where the first Africans, brought in bondage to the American Colonies in 1619, were deposited. Robert and Sarah Lee were Black dentists who had studied at Lincoln University in Pennsylvania with the young Kwame Nkrumah, and had come in 1957 to Ghana to celebrate its just won independence. They returned a year later with their two sons to become Ghanaian citizens.

The Lees and the presence of W. E. B. Du Bois and Alphaeus Hunton nearly legitimized all of us.

Dr. Du Bois and his wife Shirley Graham had been personally invited by the President to spend the rest of their lives in Ghana. Dr. Hunton had come from the United States with his wife Dorothy to work with Dr. Du Bois on the ambitious Encyclopedia Africana.

The rest of the Black Americans, who buzzed mothlike on the periphery of acceptance, were separated into four distinct groups.

There were over forty families, some with children, who had come simply and as simply moved into the countryside hoping to melt onto the old landscape. They were teachers and farmers.

The second group had come under the aegis of the American government and were viewed with suspicion by Ghanaians, and Black Americans stayed apart from them as well. Too often they mimicked the manners of their former lords and ladies, trying to treat the Africans as Whites had treated them. They socialized with Europeans and White Americans, fawning upon that company with ugly obsequiousness.

There was a miniscule business community which had found a slight but unsure footing in Accra.

Julian's circle had stupendous ambitions and thought of itself as a cadre of political émigrés. Its members were impassioned and volatile, dedicated to Africa, and Africans at home and abroad. We, for I counted myself in that company, felt that we would be the first accepted and once taken in and truly adopted, we would hold the doors open until all Black Americans could step over our feet, enter through the hallowed portals and come home at last.

from *The Pillar of Salt*

by Albert Memmi (Tunisia)

Part Two

1

The City

My name is Benillouche, Alexandre Mordekhai.

How galling the smiles of my classmates! In our alley, and at the Alliance School, I hadn't known how ridiculous, how revealing, my name could be. But at the French lycée I became aware of this at once. From then on, the mere sound of my own name humiliated me and made my pulse beat faster.

Alexandre: brassy, glorious, a name given to me by my parents in recognition of the wonderful West and because it seemed to them to express their idea of Europe. My schoolmates sneered and blared "Alexandre" like a trumpet blast: Alexan-ndre! With all my strength, I then hated them and my name. I hated them, but I believed they were right, and I was furious with my parents for having chosen this stupid name for me.

Mordekhai (colloquially, I was called Mridakh) signified my share in the Jewish tradition. It had been the formidable name of a glorious Maccabee and also of my grandfather, a feeble old man who never forgot the terrors of the ghetto.

Call yourself Peter or John, and by simply changing your clothes you can change your apparent status in society. But in this country, Mridakh is as obstinately revealing as if one shouted out: "I'm a Jew!" More precisely: "My home is in the ghetto," "my legal status is native African," "I come from an Oriental background," "I'm poor." But I had learned to reject these four classifications. It would be easy to reproach me for this, and I have not failed to blame myself. But how is it possible not to be ashamed of one's condition when one has experienced scorn, mockery, or sympathy for it since childhood? I had learned to interpret smiles, to understand whispers, to read the thoughts of others in their eyes, to reconstruct the reasoning behind a casual phrase or a chance word. When anyone speaks about me, I feel provoked in advance: my hair stands up on end and I am ready to bite. One can, of course, ultimately learn to accept anything at the cost of an enormous effort and a vast weariness. But, before this happens, one resists and hates oneself; or else, to defy the scorn of others, one asserts one's own ugliness and even exaggerates it so as to grin and bear it.

At the lycée, I very quickly got into the habit of dropping "Mordekhai" from my lesson headings, and before long I forgot the name as if I had shed it like an old skin. Yet it dragged on behind me, holding fast. It was brought back to my attention by all official notices and summonses, by everything that came from beyond the narrow frame of daily routine. When commencement-time came, on the day diplomas were to be awarded, I knew I would be one of the triumphant scholars; in the midst of a nervous crowd, I waited undisturbed, certain of success. When the usher climbed onto a chair, my name was the first to be called out; in the tense silence, the exact order of my legal status was re-established:

"Alexandre, Mordekhai, Benillouche!"

I didn't move. Surprised by the silence, the crowd looked around for the happy candidate, astonished to hear no explosion of joy, no throwing of notebooks into the air; no one was surrounded or kissed by a delighted family. (I never cared to have my parents present at the public events of my life, so they hadn't been told when the diplomas were to be awarded.) I merely smiled to those of my classmates who congratulated me with a look; and I was soon forgotten because everyone was concerned with his own fate.

Alexandre, Mordekhai, Benillouche. Benillouche or, in Berber-Arabic dialect, the son of the lamb. From what mountain tribe did my ancestors descend? Who am I, after all?

I sought—in everything from official documents to my own sharply defined features—some thread which might lead me to the knowledge of who I am. For a while, I believed my forebears had been a family of Berber princes converted to Judaism by Kahena, the warrior-queen and founder of the Jewish kingdom in the middle of the Atlas Mountains. It pleased me to think that

I came from the very heart of the country. But then, another time, I found I was descended from an Italian Renaissance painter. I tore the article from the big Larousse encyclopedia and displayed reproductions of my ancestor's paintings to all my friends. Philology could explain away what changes the name had undergone, and my friend Sitboun, the star Latin student, backed me up and even discovered that the patron of a Latin poet had had a similar name. But philology is a fragile science, and the past is much too far away. Could I be descended from a Berber tribe when the Berbers themselves failed to recognize me as one of their own? I was Jewish, not Moslem; a townsman, not a highlander. And even if I had borne the painter's name, I would not have been acknowledged by the Italians. No, I'm African, not European. In the long run, I would always be forced to return to Alexandre Mordekhai Benillouche, a native in a colonial country, a Jew in an anti-Semitic universe, an African in a world dominated by Europe.

Had I believed in signs, might I not have said that my name holds all the meaning of life? How is it possible to harmonize so many discords in something as smooth as the sound of a flute?

My native city is after my own image. Through Tarfoune Street, our alley led to the Alliance School; and between home and the schoolyard, the atmosphere remained familiar, all of a piece. We were among Jews of the same class, and we had no painful awareness of our situation, no pretenses. At school, we persisted in speaking our own dialect despite the director's posters which demanded French. Sometimes I crossed a Moslem quarter as if I were fording a river. It was not until I began attending the lycée that I really became acquainted with the city. Until then, I had believed that, by some special privilege, the doors of the world were being opened to me and that I need only walk through them to be greeted with joy. But I discovered I was doomed forever to be an outsider in my own native city. And one's home town can no more be replaced than one's mother.

A man may travel, marvel at the world, change, become a stranger to his relatives and friends, but he will always retain within him the hard kernel of his awareness of belonging to some nameless village. Defeated, blind, his imagination will bring him back to that landmark, for his hands and feet know its contours and his nerves are wonderfully attuned to it. And I—well, I am my city's illegitimate son, the child of a whore of a city whose heart has been divided among those to whom she has been a slave. And the list of her masters, when I came to know some history, made me giddy: Phoenicians, Romans, Vandals, Byzantine Greeks, Berbers, Arabs, Spaniards, Turks, Italians, French—but I must be forgetting some and confusing others. Walk five hundred steps in my city, and you change civilizations: here is an Arab town, its houses like expressionless faces, its long, silent, shadowed passages leading suddenly to packed crowds. Then, the busy Jewish alleys, so sordid and familiar, lined with deep stalls, shops and eating houses, all shapeless houses piled as best they can fit together. Further on, little Sicily, where abject poverty waits on the doorstep, and then the *fondouks*, the collective tenements of the Maltese, those strange Europeans with an Arab tongue and a British nationality. The Russian Orthodox church too, its illuminations and domes surely conceived in a night of Muscovite dreams; and the clean little eclectic street-car line from Belgium, as neat as a Flemish interior. We have Standard Oil buildings too, and an American airport and cemetery, with improved U. S. equipment, jeeps and trucks at the exclusive disposal of the dead; the Shell Company or British Petrol; the residence of Her Britannic Majesty's Ambassadors, and finally the little homes of retired French *rentiers*, cottages with red-tiled roofs and gardens, cabbages—all in a row, just as in French songs.

And within this great variety, where everyone feels at home but no one at ease, each man is shut up in his own neighborhood, in fear, hate, and contempt of his neighbor. Like the filth and untidiness of this stinking city, we've known fear and scorn since the first awakening of our consciousness. To defend or avenge ourselves, we scorned and sneered among ourselves and hoped we would be feared as much as we ourselves experienced fear. This was the atmosphere in which we lived at mealtimes, in school and in the streets. If any youthful ingenuousness or skepticism allowed us still to hope, we were promised nothing but treachery and blood-red dawns. Slowly, as if a poison administered drop by drop had at last had its effect, my sensibility, my sentiments, my entire soul was permeated with it and reshaped; I learned to check the odious inventory of it all. Beyond a ceremonious polite-ness, everyone remained secretly hostile and was finally horrified by the image of himself that he discovered in the minds of others.

One can make a mess of one's childhood or of one's whole life. Slowly, painfully, I understood that I had made a mess of my own birth by choosing the wrong city.

Bissor was a strong boy, all muscles and big bones, like a ploughhorse. Healthy as a peasant, robust, vigorous, thickset—he was a miracle within the ghetto's rotten heart. A mop of jungle-wild red hair stressed his primitive appearance. Yet, for all this, he had within him the fears, humiliations, and resentments of all those born and still living in the ghetto. At the age of eleven, he had begun to deliver evening newspapers after school and had thus come to know the city.

I was not self-conscious in his presence, and once I even told him about my father's terrors and hatreds. But he interrupted me at once:

"Your father's right. You don't yet know what it's like."

His own father's store, he explained, had been burned in a pogrom, and his old man had then died of grief. Although Bissor's schooling was paid for by the community, he worried constantly about his mother and sisters, fearing that they might not be able to support themselves without his help. (He was right about this, for even though he left school before graduating, he was unable to prevent one of his sisters from becoming a prostitute.) He used to describe to me his daily rounds: the distrust and innuendoes, the perfect imperviousness of others. In Bissor, I caught echoes of my father's despair, but I still refused to accept it. Constantly, I heard him talk of his hatred of the city, of his horror of having been born there, of the impossibility of ever finding normal opportunities there. I was ironical when the city seemed to stir but he would then race home, put up a supply of food, and barricade the doors and windows, terrified by the unpredictable. Other people's misfortunes could force me to retreat, but could never convince me; they had bungled the situation, I thought, through awkwardness or prejudice. If the same thing happened to me, I was sure I would come out better.

But I had to confess I was wrong. Sometimes with Bissor—who was the only one of the lycée boys whose standard of living was not beyond my own means—I went to the movies on Saturdays. More than anything else, it was the way we spent our leisure time that showed up the difference between ourselves and our schoolmates; we used to go to the Kursaal which they considered a dive, having never set dainty foot there. Certainly, they were not altogether wrong. In order to get in there for the three o'clock show, we had to queue up at one, be jostled and elbowed and attacked by kids of our own age, older boys, and even adults, until the box office opened. Often the queue grew too long and dissolved into sudden confusion; by the time things had straightened out, we had lost our places. Once, our tickets were torn out of my hand before I could identify the thief; Bissor in his rage couldn't refrain from railing at me while I burst into tears. So we went to complain to the manager and he allowed us into the theater despite his mistrust.

On one of our movie Saturdays, Bissor was unexpectedly called in for an additional assignment on his newspaper route. We decided that I'd go alone to buy the tickets and leave one with the cashier for Bissor to pick up as soon as he was free to join me. It was anguish for me to stand in line without Bissor; I was a weakling, and I don't know how many humiliations his presence saved me.

I got to the Kursaal long before the box office opened, but there was already a big crowd. To my delight, a policeman was there lording it over the whole square. The Sicilian laborers who composed our aristocracy, with slicked-down hair and bright ties; the ragged bootblacks who were its lowest class and had gathered the price of a ticket by collecting cigarette butts; the fritter-vendors in their greasy fezzes; the Maltese cabbies with their cap visors coquettishly broken; the porters with professional ropes thrown over their shoulders; all these people, so brutal and dishonest in past weeks, were now miraculously orderly, almost polite, waiting under the eyes of the Mohammedan policeman, an enormous fellow with a pock-marked face and a pointed black mustache. I felt happy being where I was: the façade of the Kursaal, built to look like a dragon's head, spat out its flames; there were colored posters glued to the monster's cheeks, and the crowd itself was disturbing but full of living joy; all this contributed to give me each time the same glow of happiness. On this particular day, there was also the promise of security.

The posters on the dragon's cheeks announced two Tom Mix films and one Rin-Tin-Tin. We were used to this, but we never tired of exulting in the triumphs of our wonderful cowboy. We joined him in his pursuit of the stagecoach that contained the gold and the exquisite blond heroine and was being driven away by bandits. How could one remain a passive spectator when faced with such sublime excitements? We threw ourselves into the scuffles and added to the rhythm of the galloping horses by stamping our feet on the floor; we pulled at the reins with our hero and roared with joy or disappointment. For a few minutes, we all forgot our individual fears and hatreds and became a single unity in the noisy expression of our emotions.

We entered the hall slowly, quietly. I was sorry the policeman had not come in with us, because the crowd's savagery soon revealed itself again. My seat was in the second row and so close to the screen that I would certainly come away with an aching back, a headache, and a stiff neck. The Kursaal, in spite of its majestic name, smelled of wine. But the magic of its silver screen, brightened by a frame of darkness, and the mystery of its little blue lights, even its odor—a special mixture of disinfectant, damp, and human emanations—made me ecstatic.

The impatient audience was already overexcited, stamped rhythmically on the floor and began to whistle. But the projecting staff was used to their outbursts and ignored the cries of: "Come on! Let's go! We want the picture! Give us our money back!" Soon, however, the fickle occupants of the reserved stalls lost interest in shouting and turned their energy on us, the Jews, who sat crowded together. A shower of beans and gourd seeds began to fall on my head.

Because humiliation was my daily bread, I believed for a long time that all stories which tell of heroic action resulting from humiliation were either exaggerated or completely false. Our skin was thick and, if we weren't stung too deeply, we could bear it: we could manage to continue enjoying ourselves, as people can who are pestered by flies. But, that day, the show was delayed and the ingenuity of our tormentors became excessively inventive and went beyond a mere sting. In the gloom, they had the bright idea of striking matches and tossing them over us. Our real fears delighted them and they roared with joy each time they threw a match. Meanwhile, we tried to save ourselves by ducking down in our seats and heard them call: "Kiki! Kiki!"—which is, for them, the nickname of all Jews. Sickened by my own impotence, crushed under the weight of blind and anonymous injustice, I could have burst into tears from disgust and rage.

Then, in the impressive semidarkness of the safety lights, I saw Bissor's square silhouette. Never before had physical strength given me such joy; I stood up and waved to him despite the risk of offering a target for a flaming match. Bissor sat down beside me in very bad spirits because his newspaper route had been reduced by one third since he began his round too late; except on Tuesdays and Thursdays, he could not begin his deliveries before four o'-clock. I tried, in spite of the noise, to hear what he was saying. Suddenly, as he spoke, a lighted cigarette butt streaked through the blue air and landed on Bissor's head. I smelled the burning hair and, since he didn't seem quite aware of what was happening, I began to grope for the butt. Then, understanding, he rose with clenched teeth and began looking around for the villain who was easily identified: a Sicilian worker who, with his friends, was shrieking with delight at having hit the jack pot. The Sicilian, ready for battle, shouted:

"*Cosa vole?*" (What do you want?)

Without reply or warning, Bissor lifted his arm and rammed his fist at the man's nose. Blood began to flow over his lips and chin, and there was a moment of stupefaction before the loud and indignant response. No one dared to touch Bissor, but the Sicilians all yelled, surrounded their beaten friend, pushed his head back to stop the blood and, forgetting their pride, argued all at once. Watching them, one might have concluded that we had all been playing a harmless game together and that our side had taken it badly. The rest of the audience was curious, couldn't figure out what had happened, and reacted, as always, by screaming as if a fire had broken out.

The uproar increased and someone went for the policeman who came in at once and saw the injured man, head thrown back, clothes covered with blood. The avenging Sicilians pointed Bissor out to him and the whole audience had risen to its feet and was screaming. The cop felt that no explanation was necessary and moved toward Bissor, who was now returning to his own seat. My heart pounded with fear, as I was terrified of all cops. What was going to happen to Bissor, and perhaps to myself? Grabbing the boy's arm, the officer pushed him toward the exit; I followed them to the door and joined Bissor outside.

"Let's go to the harbor," he said.

That was one of our favorite walks, and although Bissor tried to be bold I knew he was heavyhearted, just as I was. Not only had we lost our money, but we had been cruelly disappointed.

"You see how they hate us?" said Bissor, hopelessly convinced.

They: the young Sicilians, the Arab policeman, the French newspaper owner, our classmates at the lycée, the whole city in fact. And it was true that our native city was as hostile to us as an unnatural mother. We had been disappointed at one blow; it was final and couldn't be healed.

I admired Bissor and often asked myself if his reaction wasn't the best. For a year I forced myself to go along with him and practice boxing in the same gym. I managed to acquire some skill, but I remained weak because I was undernourished. Nor did I ever manage to overcome the nausea that I experienced whenever I struck an opponent's eyes, nose, or mouth. I was already suspicious of my body and disgusted whenever it affirmed its presence, for I knew that no amount of animal self-assertion could ever heal the wound my native city had inflicted upon me.

Later, I began to experience a strange new fear whenever I found myself in the bowel-like maze of the covered bazaar. I would feel a sudden nausea and that I must reach an open space as fast as possible, because otherwise I might knock my head against walls that were too close to me.

from *Here I Stand*

by Paul Robeson (USA)

Prologue

A HOME IN THAT ROCK

THE GLORY OF MY BOYHOOD years was my father. I love him like no one in all the world. His people, among whom he moved as a patriarch for many years before I was born, loved him, too. And the white folks—even the most lordly of aristocratic Princeton—had to respect him.

Born a plantation slave in Martin County, North Carolina, my father escaped at the age of fifteen, in 1860, and made his way North up on the Underground Railroad. In 1876, after working his way through Lincoln University, he married my mother, Maria Louisa Bustill, a school teacher in nearby

Philadelphia. Following a brief pastorate in Wilkes-Barre, Pennsylvania, he was called to be pastor of the Witherspoon Street Presbyterian Church in Princeton, New Jersey, where I was born on April 9, 1898.

I was the youngest of Reverend Robeson's children, and there were four others living at the time of my birth: William D., Jr., age 17; Reeve, 12; Benjamin, 6; and Marian, my only sister, who was 4.

In later years my father was pastor of A. M. E. Zion churches in the nearby towns of Westfield and Somerville, until his death in 1918, at the age of seventy-three. An editorial in the Somerville newspaper made this comment at the time:

> "The death of Rev. W. D. Robeson takes from this community one who has done a quiet but successful work among his own people for the past eight years. Mr. Robeson was a man of strong character ... he was very familiar with the characteristics of his race and was always interested in their welfare. He quickly resented any attempt to belittle them or to interfere with their rights. He had the temperament which has produced so many orators in the South and he held his people together in the church here with a fine discernment of their needs. He has left his impress on the colored race throughout the State and he will be greatly missed here."

Go today to the towns in that part of New Jersey and you will find his memory still warm in the communities he served. As you drive down on the highway past New Brunswick you may see the William D. Robeson Houses, a government project named for him. In Princeton, the Witherspoon Street Presbyterian Church still stands, with one of the stained-glass windows glowing "In Loving Remembrance of Sabra Robeson" who was my father's slave mother on the Carolina plantation. Many of the older church members and other longtime residents you might meet on shady lanes of the Negro community nearby—Green Street, Hulfish Street, Quarry, Jackson, Birch, John—will tell you with quiet pride of my father's devoted labors, his wisdom, his dignity. And they will tell you, too, about my mother, Maria Louisa: how she moved, so strong and tender, in their midst—comforting the sick, mothering the orphaned, collecting food and clothing for the hungry and ragged, opening to many the wonders of book learning.

I cannot say that I remember her, though my memory of other things goes back before her tragic death. I was six years old when she, a near-blind invalid at the time, was fatally burned in a household accident. I remember her lying in the coffin, and the funeral, and the relatives who came, but it must be that the pain and shock of her death blotted out all other personal recollections.

Others have told me of her remarkable intellect, her strength of character and spirit which contributed so much to my father's development and work. She was a companion to him in his studies; she helped compose his sermons; she was his right hand in all his community work.

Maria Louisa Robeson, born on November 8, 1853, in Philadelphia, was a member of the noted Bustill family. The history of the Bustills, who are of mixed Negro, Indian and white Quaker stock, goes back to the earliest days of America. My great-great-grandfather, Cyrus Bustill, who baked bread for Washington's troops, became a leader of the Negroes in Philadelphia; and in 1787 he was a founder of the Free African Society, first mutual aid organization of American Negroes. Through the years the Bustills produced many teachers, artists and scholars, and, in the Quaker tradition, took part in running the Underground Railroad by which so many, like my father, escaped from bondage.

I don't know if the custom is still observed, but when I was a boy the Bustill Family Association held annual reunions to which all of the relatives from far and near would come. I find in my college scrapbook a printed program of the reunion of 1918, held at Maple Grove in Philadelphia. My aunt, Gertrude Bustill Mossell, is listed as vice-president of the association; and on the program of the day was a reading of the family history by my cousin, Annie Bustill Smith, and speeches by various other members, including an address by "Mr. Paul Roberson." (Though this spelling of my name was a printer's error, it is likely that "Roberson" was the ancestral name of the slave-holding Robesons from whom my father got his name. The county seat of his birthplace, Martin County, N. C., is Robersonville; and one of the earliest Negro freedom petitions on record is that of a slave, Ned Griffin, who, in 1784, from Edgecombe County which adjoins Martin County, urged the state government to grant him the freedom that was promised him for his services in the Revolutionary Army and which was being denied him by his owner, one Abner *Roberson*.)

I cannot recall anything I said in my speech on that occasion, though I did jot down in my scrapbook its title — "Loyalty to Convictions." That I chose this topic was not accidental, for that was the text of my father's life-loyalty to one's convictions. Unbending. Despite anything. From my youngest days I was imbued with that concept. This bedrock idea of integrity was taught by Reverend Robeson to his children not so much by preachment (for by nature Pop was restrained of speech, often silent at home, and among us Robesons the deepest feelings are largely unexpressed in words) but, rather, by the daily example of his life and work.

Though my father was a man of ordinary height, he was very broad of shoulder and his physical bearing reflected the rock-like strength and dignity of his character. He had the greatest speaking voice I have ever heard. It was a deep, sonorous basso, richly melodic and refined, vibrant with the love and compassion which filled him. How proudly, as a boy, I walked at his side, my hand in his, as he moved among the people! There was a wide gap in years between us—he was fifty-three when I was born, near sixty when my mother died—but during many of his years as a widower I was the only child at home and his devoted care and attention bound us closely together. It was not like him to be demonstrative in his love, nor was he quick to praise. Doing the right thing—well, that was something to be taken for granted in his children. I knew what I must do—when to come home from play, my duties in the household, my time for study—and I readily yielded to his quiet discipline. Only once did I disobey him.

I was ten years old at the time, and we were then living in Westfield. My father told me to do something and I didn't do it. "Come here," he said; but I ran away. He ran after me. I darted across the road. He followed, stumbled and fell. I was horrified. I hurried back, helped Pop to his feet. He had knocked out one of his teeth. I have never forgotten the emotions—the sense of horror, shame, ingratitude, selfishness—that overwhelmed me. I adored him, would have given my life for him in a flash—and here I had hurt him, disobeyed him! Never did he have to admonish me again; and this incident became a source of tremendous discipline which has lasted through the years.

I have said that the white families who dominated Princeton recognized my father's dignity and accorded him respect. How remarkable that was, and what a tribute to his character, can be appreciated fully only when one recalls that the Princeton of my boyhood (and I don't think it has changed much since then) was for all the world like any small town in the deep South. Less than fifty miles from New York, and even closer to Philadelphia, Princeton was spiritually located in Dixie. Traditionally the great university—which is practically all there is in town—has drawn a large part of its student body and faculty from below the Mason-Dixon Line, and along with these sons of the Bourbons came the most rigid social and economic patterns of White Supremacy. And like the South to which its heart belonged, Princeton's controlling mind was in Wall Street. Bourbon and Banker were one in Princeton, and there the decaying smell of the Countinghouse. The theology was Calvin: the religion—cash.

Rich Princeton was white: the Negroes were there to do the work. An aristocracy must have its retainers, and so the people of our small Negro community were, for the most part, a servant class—domestics in the homes of the wealthy, serving as cooks, waiters and caretakers at the university, coachmen for the town and laborers at the nearby farms and brickyards. I had the closest of ties with these workers since many of my father's relatives—Uncle Ben and Uncle John and cousin Carraway and Cousin Chance and others— had come to this town and found employment at such jobs.

Princeton was Jim Crow: the grade school that I attended was segregated and Negroes were not permitted in any high school. My oldest brother, Bill, had to travel to Trenton, eleven miles away—to attend high school, and I would have had to do the same had we not moved to another town. No Negro students were admitted to the university, although one or two were allowed to attend the divinity school.

Under the caste system in Princeton the Negro, restricted to menial jobs at low pay and lacking any semblance of political rights or bargaining power, could hope not for justice but for charity. The stern hearts and tight purses of the master class could on occasion be opened by appeals from the "deserving poor," and then philanthropy, in the form of donations, small loans or cast-off clothing might be looked for. The Negro church, center of community life, was the main avenue through which such boons were sought and received, and, in fact, the Witherspoon Street Presbyterian Church was itself largely built by white philanthropy. The pastor was a sort of bridge between the Have-nots and the Haves, and he served his flock in many worldly ways—seeking work for the jobless, money for the needy, mercy from the Law.

In performing these Christian duties my father came to know and be known by all of the so-called "Best People" of the town. But though the door of the university president might be open to him, Reverend Robeson could not push open the doors of that school for his son, when Bill was ready for college. The pious president, a fellow Presbyterian, said: No, it is quite impossible. That was Woodrow Wilson—Virginian, graduate of Princeton, professor there for a decade, college president from 1902 to 1910, then Governor of New Jersey, elected President of the United States in 1912, re-elected in 1916 because "he kept us out of the war" into which he led the nation one month after his second inaugural, Nobel Peace Prize winner, apostle of the New Liberalism, advocate of democracy for the world and Jim Crow for America!

He who comes hat-in-hand is expected to bow and bend, and so I marvel that there was no hint of servility in my father's make-up. Just as in youth he had refused to remain a slave, so in all the years of his manhood he disdained to be an Uncle Tom. From him we learned, and never doubted it, that the Negro was in every way the equal of the white man. And we fiercely resolved to prove it.

That a so-called lowly station in life was no bar to a man's assertion of his full human dignity was heroically demonstrated by my father in the face of a grievous blow that came to him when I was a baby. After more than two decades of honored leadership in his church, a factional dispute among the members removed him as pastor. Adding to the pain was the fact that some of his closet kin were part of the ousting faction. A gentle scholar and teacher all his adult life, my father, then past middle age, with an invalid wife and dependent children at home, was forced to begin life anew. He got a horse and a wagon, and began to earn his living hauling ashes for the townsfolk. This was his work at the time I first remember him and I recall the growing mound of dusty ashes dumped into our backyard at 13 Green Street. A fond memory remains of our horse, a mare named Bess, whom I grew to love and who loved me. My father also went into the hack business, and as a coachman drove the gay young students around town and on trips to the seashore.

Ash-man, coachman, he was still the dignified Reverend Robeson to the community, and no man carried himself with greater pride. Not once did I hear him complain of the poverty and misfortune of those years. Not one word of bitterness ever came from him. Serene, undaunted, he struggled to earn a livelihood and see to our education. Soon after the tragedy that took his wife from him, Pop sent my brother Ben away to prep school and Biddle University (now Johnson C. Smith) in North Carolina, and my sister Marian to Scotia Seminary, a school for colored girls in the same state. Bill, the oldest, was then at Lincoln University—the school my father had attended—and for a time Reeve (or Reed, as we called him) was at home, working as a hack driver.

Some might say that Reed did not turn out as well as the other Robeson children, and it is a fact that my father was sorely disappointed in this son and disapproved of his carefree and undisciplined ways. Yet I admired this rough older brother and learned from him a quick militancy against racial insults and abuse. Many was the time that Reed, resenting some remark by a Southern gentleman-student, would leap down from his coachman's seat, drag out the offender and punish him with his fists. He always carried for protection a bag of small, jagged rocks—a weapon he used with reckless abandon whenever the occasion called for action.

Inevitably there were brushes with the Law, and then my father, troubled in heart, would don his grave frock-coat and go down to get Reed out of trouble again. But this happened once too often, and one day I stood sadly and silently as Pop told Reed he would have to leave—he must live his life elsewhere because his example was a dangerous one for his young brother Paul.

Reed is dead now. He won no honors in classroom, pulpit or platform. Yet I remember him with love. Restless, rebellious, scoffing at conventions, defiant of the white man's law—I've known many Negroes like Reed. I see them every day. Blindly, in their own reckless manner, they seek a way out for themselves; alone, they pound with their fists and fury against walls that only the shoulders of the many can topple. "Don't ever take low," was the lesson Reed taught me. "Stand up to them and hit back harder than they hit you!" When the many have learned that lesson, everything will be different and then the fiery ones like Reed will be able to live out their lives in peace and no one will have cause to frown on them.

Because I was younger, my own days in Princeton were happier ones. Mostly I played. There were the vacant lots for ball games, and the wonderful moments when Bill, vacationing from college where he played on the team, would teach me how to play football. He was my first coach, and over and over again on the weed-grown lot he would put me through the paces—how to tackle a man so he stayed tackled, how to run with the ball. Then there were the winter evenings at home with Pop: he loved to play checkers and so we two would sit for hours in the parlor, engrossed in our game, not speaking much but wonderfully happy together.

My father never talked with us about his early years as a slave or about his parents, Benjamin and Sabra, though long afterward I learned from others that before his mother died, Pop made at least one, and possibly two, dangerous trips back to the plantation to see her. I'm sure that had he ever spoken about this part of his life it would have been utterly impossible for me as a boy to grasp the idea that a noble human being like my father had actually been owned by another man—to be bought and sold, used and abused at will.

(I might mention here, in passing, that many years later in New York I met one of the family that had held my father in bondage. I had gone to a downtown night club to hear a friend who was singing in the place, and there I was accosted by a man who introduced himself as one of the Robesons of North Carolina. He said he was sure that I'd be pleased to hear that his mother was quite proud of my accomplishments in life, and that she had carefully kept a scrapbook on the various honors that I had won for the family name. Then the stranger went on to say that he would like to get together with me for a chat some day soon. "You see," he confided proudly, "your father used to work for my grandfather." As politely as was possible under the circumstances I assured that Southern gentleman that it was undoubtedly true that the Negroes who had come by his family's name had added a bit more distinction to it than did any of the original owners or their descendants. "You say my father 'used to work' for your grandfather. Let's put it the way it was: *Your grandfather exploited my father as a slave!*"—That ended it; and *this* Robeson never did have a chummy get-together with *that* one.)

Not old enough to work for them, I had very little connection with the white people of Princeton; but there were some white children among my playmates. One of these was a boy, about my age, whose father owned a neighborhood grocery a few doors down from our house. We could not go to school together, of course, but during the long summer days we were inseparable companions at play. Once—and I don't remember why—the two of us got into a small-boy fight. After much crouching and circling and menacing gestures, we each got up enough courage to land a blow on the other's nose and then, wailing loudly, we ran away to our homes. Next day we were friends again.

There must have been moments when I felt the sorrows of a motherless child, but what I most remember from my youngest days was an abiding sense of comfort and security. I got plenty of mothering, not only from Pop and my brothers and sister when they were home, but from the whole of our close-knit community. Across the street and down each block were all my aunts and uncles and cousins—including some who were not actual relatives at all. So, if I were to try to put down the names of all the folks who helped raise me, it would read like a Negro roster of Princeton. In a way I was "adopted" by all these good people, and there was always a place at their tables and a place in a bed (often with two or three other young ones) for Reverend Robeson's boy when my father was away on one of his trips to the seashore or attending a church conference.

Hard-working people, and poor, most of them, in worldly goods—but how rich in compassion! How filled with the goodness of humanity and the spiritual steel forged by centuries of oppression! There was the honest joy of laughter in these homes, folk-wit and story, hearty appetites for life as for the nourishing greens and black-eyed peas and cornmeal bread they shared with me. Here in this little hemmed-in world where home must be theatre and concert hall and social center, there was a warmth of song. Songs of love and longing, songs of trials and triumphs, deep-flowing rivers and rollicking brooks, hymn-song and ragtime ballad, gospels and blues, and the healing comfort to be found in the illimitable sorrow of the spirituals.

Yes, I heard my people singing!—in the glow of parlor coal-stove and on summer porches sweet with lilac air, from choir loft and Sunday morning pews—and my soul was filled with their harmonies. Then, too, I heard these songs in the very sermons of my father, for in the Negro's speech there is much of the phrasing and rhythms of folk-song. The great, soaring gospels we love are merely sermons that are sung; and as we thrill to such gifted gospel singers as Mahalia Jackson, we hear the rhythmic eloquence of our preachers, so many of whom, like my father, are masters of poetic speech.

There was something else, too, that I remember from Princeton. Something strange, perhaps, and not easy to describe. I early became conscious—

I don't quite know how—of a special feeling of Negro community for me. I was no different from the other kids of the neighborhood—playing our games of Follow the Leader and Run Sheep Run, saying "yes ma'am" and never sassing our elders, fearing to cross the nearby cemetery because of the "ghosts," coming reluctant and new-scrubbed to Sunday School. And yet, like my father, the people claimed to see something special about me. Whatever it was, and no one really said, they felt I was fated for great things to come. Somehow they were sure of it, and because of that belief they added an extra measure to the affection they lavished on their preacher's motherless child.

I didn't know what I was supposed to be when I grew up. A minister like my father? A teacher like my mother? Maybe. But whatever the vocation might be, I must grow up to be a "credit to the race," as they said. "You got something, boy, something deep down inside, that will take you to the top. You'll see—sure as I'm sitting here!" I wondered at times about this notion that I was some kind of child of destiny and that my future would be linked with the longed-for better days to come, but I didn't worry about it. Being grown up was a million years ahead. Now was the time for play.

Though we moved away from Princeton in 1907, when I was nine, I was back and forth between the other towns and this community until I finished college at twenty-one. Visiting Princeton was always being at home.

Westfield, where we moved first, was thirty-odd miles away in the direction of New York. For years in Princeton, after he lost his church, friends had told my father that he must return to preaching. And so, at the age of sixty-two, when he got the chance, he eagerly set out to begin all over again. Now he joined a different denomination, the African Methodist Episcopal Zion church. The Negro community of Westfield was even smaller than in Princeton and there were at the start not more than a dozen members in Reverend Robeson's new congregation to help him dig the foundation for the Downing Street A.M.E. Zion Church. There were too few Negro children for the town to have a separate school "for colored only," so the grade school I attended during the three years we lived there was mixed.

Westfield, and later Somerville, were quite unlike Princeton. Barriers between Negro and white existed, of course, but they were not so rigid; and in the ordinary way of small-town life there were more friendly connections between the two groups. And here there were white workingmen, too, many of them foreign-born, who, unlike the Princeton blue-bloods, could see in a workingman of a darker skin a fellow human being (a lower-paid worker, of course, and perhaps a competitor for a job, but not a person of a totally different caste).

In these towns I came to know more white people. I frequently visited the homes of my schoolmates and always received a friendly welcome. I wasn't conscious of it at the time, but now I realize that my easy moving between the two racial communities was rather exceptional. For one thing, I was the respected preacher's son, and then, too, I was popular with the other boys and girls because of my skill at sports and studies, and because I was always ready to share in their larks and fun-making. Observing my manner of respectful politeness and courtesy, in which Pop had trained us, some of the white parents encouraged their children's friendship with me, hoping, I suppose, that I might have a favorable influence on them. A good boy studied hard, helped with chores, gladly ran errands, tipped his hat to ladies, always said "No thank you" when offered a piece of cake (at the first offer, that is), never puffed a cigarette or said bad words, would never in all his years touch a drop of hard liquor, never told lies, never played hookey, never missed Sunday School, and got nothing but A's on his report card.

Well, I was a good boy, sure enough—but I wasn't *that* good! Not all the time, at any rate. For my father gave my teachers permission to paddle me for any waywardness, and though I don't recall the misdeeds, this permission was firmly (and memorably) exercised on a couple of occasions.

In 1910 we moved to Somerville, a larger town midway between Westfield and Princeton, where Reverend Robeson served as pastor of St. Thomas A.M.E. Zion Church until his death eight years later. I attended eighth grade in Somerville (here again the school was all colored) and graduated at the head of my class. Pop was pleased by that, I guess, though it was only what he expected of me and his attitude never allowed for feelings of exaggerated self-esteem.

I have often told how he was never satisfied with a school mark of 95 when 100 was possible. But this was not because he made a fetish of perfection. Rather it was that the concept of *personal integrity*, which was his ruling passion, included inseparably the idea of *maximum human fulfillment*. Success in life was not to be measured in terms of money and personal advancement, but rather the goal must be the richest and highest development of one's own potential.

A love for learning, a ceaseless quest for truth in all its fullness—this my father taught. His own schooling had been along the classic pattern which today has been largely displaced by an emphasis on technology. I do not know, in political terms, what stand my father took in the debate then raging in Negro life between the militant policy of W. E. B. Du Bois and the conservative preachments of Booker T. Washington—that clash of opposing ideas as to the path for Negro progress which was so largely expressed in terms of educational goals. But in practice Reverend Robeson flatly rejected Washington's concept that Negro education be limited essentially to manual training; he firmly believed that the heights of knowledge must be scaled by the freedom-seeker. Latin, Greek, philosophy, history, literature—all the treasures of learning must be the Negro's heritage as well.

So for me in high school there would be four years of Latin and then in college four more years of Latin and Greek. Closely my father watched my studies, and was with me page by page through Virgil and Homer and the other classics in which he was well grounded. He was my first teacher in public speaking, and long before my days as class orator and college debater there were the evenings of recitations at home, where his love for the eloquent and meaningful word and his insistence on purity of diction made their impress.

High school in Somerville was not Jim Crow, and there I formed close friendships with a number of white classmates. One of these was Douglas Brown, a brilliant student who was in my class through the four years and who later became the dean of Princeton University. I was welcomed as a member of the glee club (unlike later at college) and the dramatic club and into the various sports and social activities around the school. The teachers were also friendly and several of them are especially remembered.

Miss Vosseller, the music teacher who directed our glee club, took a special interest in training my voice. Anna Miller, English teacher, paid close attention to my development as a speaker and debater; and it was she who first introduced me to Shakespeare's works. Many years were to pass before the American theatre would permit a Negro to play Othello, but the idea seemed eminently right to Miss Miller and she coached me in the part for a high-school dramatic performance. Nervous and scared, I struggled through the lines on that solemn occasion (mindful of my father's ear for perfect diction and my teacher's patient direction) and no one in the world could have convinced me then that I should ever try acting again.

Miss Vandeveer, who taught Latin, seemed to have no taint of racial prejudice; and Miss Bagg, instructor in chemistry and physics, made every effort to make me feel welcome and at ease in the school's social life of which she was in charge. Miss Bagg urged me to attend the various parties and dances, and when I did so, it was she who was the first to dance with me. But despite her encouragement, I shied away from most of these social affairs. There was always the feeling that—well, something unpleasant might happen; for the two worlds of white and Negro were nowhere more separate than in social life. Though I might visit the homes of white classmates, I was always conscious that I belonged to the Negro community.

From an early age I had come to accept and follow a certain protective tactic of Negro life in America, and I did not fully break with the pattern until many years later. Even while demonstrating that he is really an equal (and, strangely, the proof must be *superior* performance!) the Negro must never appear to be challenging white superiority. Climb up if you can—but don't act "uppity." Always show that you are *grateful*. (Even if what you have gained has been wrested from unwilling powers, be sure to be grateful lest "they" take it all away.) Above all, *do nothing to give them cause to fear you*, for then the oppressing hand, which might at times ease up a little, will surely become a fist to knock you down again!

Well, as a boy in high school I tried my best to "act right." I would make the best of all of my opportunities. I would measure myself only against my own potential and not see myself in competition with anyone else. Certainly I had no idea of challenging the way things were. But courtesy and restraint did not shield me from all hostility: it soon became clear that the high school principal hated me. Dr. Ackerman, who later rose to higher positions in the New Jersey school system, made no effort to hide his bitter feelings. The better I did, the worse his scorn. The cheers of my fellow students as I played fullback on the football team—"Let Paul carry the ball! Yay—Paul!"—seemed to curdle the very soul of Dr. Ackerman; and when the music teacher made me soloist of the glee club it was against the principal's furious opposition.

He never spoke to me except to administer a reprimand; and he seemed constantly to be looking for an excuse to do so. One fault I had was occasionally being late to class in the morning—probably because our house was only a few hundred yards from the school! "Early to bed and early to rise" was always a hard rule for me to keep, and sometimes I misjudged the few minutes needed to get up and get to class. Then, like a watchful hawk, Dr. Ackerman would pounce on me, and his sharp words were meant to make me feel miserably inferior as he thought a Negro was. One time he sent me home for punishment. Usually Pop preferred that the teacher's hand rather than his own should administer the proper penalty, but this time I had something to say about that. "Listen, Pop," I said, "I'm bigger now. I don't care what *you* do to me, but if that hateful old principal ever lays a hand on me, I swear I'll try my best to break his neck!" I guess Pop understood. He let it go at that.

Of lasting value during these formative years was the devoted help of my brothers and sister in the periods when they were home.

There was Bill, the oldest, to whom the other children of Reverend Robeson gave first place as far as "brains" were concerned. Though I have met many other brilliant persons in the years since then, time has not lessened the marveling regard I had for Bill's mental powers. Like Reed, he is dead; and his potential was never fulfilled. He seemed always to be going to school—at Lincoln and Penn, in Boston and at Howard—except for interludes when his money was exhausted and he went to work at such jobs as were open to Negroes. At various times he got work "running on the road" as a Pullman porter, and for a while he was a redcap at Grand Central Station in New York where his fellows, impressed by his erudition, bestowed on him the nickname "Deep Stuff."

More formal recognition of his scholarship came to Bill: his field was medicine and he earned his degree. But by temperament Bill was not meant to be a practicing physician. I'm sure that if faced with the workaday task of setting a broken bone, Bill's mind would be concentrating on Lord knows what. (Maybe the history of bone-setting going back to the ancient Egyptians, or wondering about the molecular structure of bones in general—or, more likely, grappling with some problem of medical theory not even remotely related to the job at hand.) Bill should have found a place in some scientific laboratory where his restless, searching mind might have been applied to the finding of deep-hidden answers (with someone else around to see to it that some test tubes were at hand and to jot down a finding before Bill forgot about it in his zest for discovering something else.)

Though his gift for theory and analysis had such little practical effect on his own life, for me Bill was the principal source of learning how to study. During my high school years in Somerville, Bill was often at home, between colleges and railroad runs, and he spent much time directing my studies. He was never satisfied when I came up with a correct answer. "Yes, but *why?*" he would insist sharply. What was the relationship of one fact to another? What was the system, the framework, of a given study? When I couldn't explain, Bill would quickly and clearly demonstrate the mystery to me; and to my constant amazement he could do that, after a very short inquiry, even in subjects he himself had not previously studied. Often nowadays, when I am struggling with some difficult question in language or music study, trying to "break down" the particular system involved, I think of this brother and tutor and say to myself: "I'll bet if Bill were here he'd lick this problem in no time!"

It was my older brother Ben who most inspired my interest in sports. Ben was an outstanding athlete by any standards, and had he attended one of the prominent colleges I'm convinced he would have been chosen All-American. Certainly he ranked in ability with many of the famous stars I later encountered in college games and professional football. Ben was also a remarkable baseball player, fleet of foot and a power at bat; and had Negroes then been permitted to play in the major leagues, I think that Ben was one of those who could have made the grade.

Closer to me in age than my other brothers, Ben was my favorite. It was he who first took me out into the world beyond our small-town life. When I was about fourteen, and in high school, Ben got a job for the summer as a waiter at Narragansett Pier, in Rhode Island, where many Negro students found vacation-time employment in the resorts of the rich. I went along with Ben, to serve as a kitchen boy. My work—and I'm sure I have never again in all my life worked quite so hard—began at 4:00 A.M. and it was late evening before I emerged from the mountains of pots and pans I scrubbed, the potatoes I peeled, the endless tasks ordered by the chef, the second cooks and helpers, all of whom outranked the kitchen boy and who were finished long before he had mopped up for the last time and put everything away in gleaming splendor. But always there was the comforting presence of brother Ben, around somewhere, keeping a watchful eye out for the kid brother in the kitchen who was bewildered by the rush and clatter of his first job, innocent among the other, more worldly-wise, workers. Later, in college days, I would go back again to Narragansett, and there, among the waiters, bus boys and kitchen help, I made many friendships which last until today. From among these student-workers came many of the leading Negro professionals whom I meet around the country today.

My sister Marion was not at home as much as Ben, but the thought of Sis always brings an inner smile. She lives now in Philadelphia, with her husband, Dr. William Forsythe. If it turned out that it was to be Ben who followed my father's calling as a minister, it was Marion who continued the teaching traditions of my mother's family. As a girl she brought to our household the blessing of laughter, so filled is she with warm good humor. When she was at home from school, Sis did the cooking, but firmly believing that a woman's place was not in anybody's kitchen—at least not for long—she always left the big stack of dishes ... for me! (We laugh about that, too, when we get together.)

With all her happy ways, Marion was earnestly resolved to stand on her own feet and make a way for herself, aware, more keenly than the rest of us, of the double burden that a Negro woman bears in striving for dignity and fulfillment in our boasted "way of life." As a young woman she became a school teacher in Philadelphia and remained in that vocation until recently. I recall with pride her dedication to work with so-called backward children, and her zeal to prove that devoted attention can bring these along with the others.

Marion and Ben—the two of them so much like my father in temperament. Reserved of speech, strong in character, living up to their principles—and always selflessly devoted to their youngest brother who cannot express in words his gratitude for their love. But in his heart there is a song, the most tender of songs—for them!

When I was seventeen and in my final semester at high school, I still had no vocation in mind. Singer? No, that was just for fun. Dramatics? Not I! There was the lingering thought, never too definite, of studying for the ministry; and though my father would have liked that choice, he never pressed it upon me. Perhaps in college I'd come to a decision about a career. The choice of a college had long been settled—Lincoln University, of which Pop and Bill were alumni.

But then, in my senior year at Somerville High, I learned about a competitive examination open to all students in New Jersey; the prize—a four-year scholarship to Rutgers College. Now a state university with an enrollment of over 12,000, Rutgers was then a private school with fewer than a thousand students. I knew about the college, for it was only fifteen miles away, in New Brunswick. One of the oldest colleges in America (founded in 1766), it was considered rather exclusive; and while one or two Negroes had once been admitted, none had attended Rutgers for many years.

Pop said I should take the examination, which for our county would be held in the Somerville Courthouse. Lincoln was our preference, but if I managed to win this scholarship the financial strain on my father's income would be eased. There was one big hitch: I should have taken a preliminary test the previous years, covering the subjects studied in the first three years of high school. Somehow I had not known about it then, and so now I was faced with an examination embracing the entire four-year course, in the same three-hour period during which the other competitors would cover only their senior year's work. Still, even with this handicap, we decided the prize was worth trying for, and I set to work getting ready for the big day. The extra hurdle called for extraordinary effort, and I studied hard until late at night. The good wishes of classmates and teachers and the ill-will of Dr. Ackerman, the principal, were spurs; and most of all Pop's quiet confidence had to be justified.

Well, I won the scholarship—and here was a decisive point in my life. That I would go to Rutgers was the least of it, for I was sure I'd be happier at Lincoln. The important thing was this: *Deep in my heart from that day on was a conviction which none of the Ackermans of America would ever be able to shake.* Equality might be denied, but I *knew* I was not inferior.

Soon after the scholarship examination, in the spring of 1915, I took part in a state-wide oratorical contest of high school students that was held at Rutgers. Prize debater at Somerville High, diligent student of my father's artistry of speech, I shared the high hopes of my family and classmates that I might win first place. I didn't. First prize was won by Hilmar Jensen, a Negro student from Asbury Park (his father, too, was a minister); second place went to a white girl; and I was third.

The speech I declaimed on that occasion was Wendell Phillips' famous oration on Toussaint L'Ouverture. I don't know why I picked that material for the contest (I guess it was my brother Bill's idea), but now I marvel at the selection for I had no real appreciation of its meaning, nor did I have any idea of the significance of a Negro reciting it to an audience that was mostly white. But there I was, voicing, with all the fervor and forensic skill I could muster, Wendell Phillips' searing attack on the concept of white supremacy! His eulogy of the great Haitian revolutionary was made in New York and Boston during the first year of the Civil War, before Emancipation, and he had challenged his audience of *"blue-eyed Saxons, proud of your race,"* to show him *"the man of Saxon lineage for whom his most sanguine admirers will wreathe with a laurel such as embittered* foes *have placed on the brow of this Negro!"*

Here was the fiery Toussaint speaking to the blacks whom he had led in a victorious rebellion and against whom Napoleon was sending General Leclerc with 30,000 troops:

> *"My children, France now comes to make us slaves. God gave us liberty; France has no right to take it away. Burn the cities, destroy the harvests, tear up the roads with cannon, poison the wells, show the white man the hell he comes to make!"*

(Strong meat for a babe! But I was concentrating on getting the phrasing and diction just right and gave no thought to the meaning of the flaming words.)

True, there were softening touches in the speech where Wendell Phillips assured the good white people listening to him that Toussaint L'Ouverture had not only spared his former master and mistress but had benevolently provided for their future welfare, and that every one of his black generals had been equally magnanimous with the household that owed him. ("Loud cheers" were indicated in the printed record of Phillips' address and perhaps this thought was also happily received by the audience that heard me.)

Yet relentlessly the Abolitionist orator had hammered away at his theme: the Negro, still enslaved in the South and despised in the North, was in every respect the equal of the white man; and Toussaint, *"a pure-blooded African,"* was not only the First of the Blacks, as he was known, but peerless among all men. And so I went through it all, to the great, soaring climax—giving it all I had in voice and gesture:

> *"You think me a fanatic tonight, for you read history not with your eyes but with your prejudices. But ... the Muse of History will put Phocion for the Greek, Brutus for the Roman, Hampden for England, Fayette for France, choose Washington as the bright, consummate flower of our earlier civilization, and John Brown the ripe flower of our noonday, then, dipping her pen in the sunlight, will write in the clear blue,*

above them all, the name of the soldier, the statesman, the martyr—
Toussaint L'Ouverture!"

(If I ever enter another oratorical contest, I'd like to try that one again.)

Wendell Phillips—the best kind of American Fighter for Negro liberation, white comrade of our great Frederick Douglass, speaker in countless towns across the land—"on a literary subject, fee one hundred dollars; if on slavery, free." On that occasion I paid tribute only to his powers of rhetoric, but I would come to learn, in my own way, the great truth he spoke of when, after chattel slavery was abolished, he joined the fight for Labor's emancipation: *"When I want to find the vanguard of the people I look to the uneasy dreams of an aristocracy and find what they dread most."*

I knew little of such matters that fall of 1915 when I entered college to learn more Latin and Greek, more Physics and Math, more History which included neither Toussaint nor Phillips—and to play a little more football, too. As I went out into life, one thing loomed above all else: I was my father's son, a Negro in America. That was the challenge.

In the pages which follow I do not tell the story of my life since childhood, because that is not the purpose of this book. Although many later personal experiences are related in the succeeding chapters, I have sought to present my ideas about a subject that is infinitely more important than any personal story—the struggle of my people for freedom. All which came later, after Rutgers and Columbia Law School—my career as an artist in America and abroad, my participation in public life, the views which I hold today—all have their roots in the early years recalled in this prologue.

from *Soul to Soul: A Black Russian Jewish Woman's Search for Her Roots*

by Yelena Khanga (Russia)

CHAPTER ONE

DISTANT WORLD

"Ba-a-aby," sings my mama, drawing out the syllable in a low voice that combines the smoky intonations of a black American blues singer with her classical Russian accent. "Baby, won't you please come home." Her fingers move over the piano keys in our Moscow apartment as she imitates the sounds she has heard on recordings by Billie Holiday and Ella Fitzgerald. I sing along happily—"I have tried in vain, never no more to call your name...."

I'm only eight, but I already know and love these songs from the faraway America of our ancestors—just as I love the classical Russian melodies Mama plays, with verses by Pushkin. One thing every Russian schoolchild knows is that our country's greatest poet was descended from Blacks—just like Mama and me. I'm proud to know that Pushkin's great-grandfather, Hannibal, was born in Abyssinia and grew up, through a strange destiny, to become a general in the army of Tsar Peter the Great. *"O krasavitsa"* (Oh, beautiful girl), I sing in my true, childish soprano as Mama plays one of Pushkin's romantic songs.

Even as a small girl, I understood that all of this music, all of this culture, somehow belonged to me. Today, as a woman of thirty, I know my heart will always be in thrall both to the blues and to the great Russian composers.

When I was growing up in Moscow, I never heard the American expression "melting pot." This description might have been invented for me—even if the pot now looks more like a stew with distinct chunks.

I am a black Russian, born and raised in the Soviet Union (at least that's what we used to call it) and shaped by an extraordinary mixture of races and cultures.

I am descended from American idealists, black and white, who came to the new Soviet state in the 1930s with high hopes of building a more just society through communism. Although time proved them tragically wrong about the revolutionary experiment, there was nothing wrong with their heartfelt dream of racial and economic justice. Thanks to the unforeseen, unprecedented political changes in my native land, it has now become possible for me to explore the dreams and realities that shaped my ancestors—those who remained in America as well as those who journeyed back across the ocean in search of yet another New World. In seeking out those old dreams, I am trying to reclaim lost parts of myself.

One of my great-grandfathers was born an American slave, while another was a Polish Jew who left Warsaw for the United States just before World War I. Hilliard Golden became of the largest black landowners in Yazoo County, Mississippi, after the Civil War, while Isaac Bialek taught Hebrew school and worked in a New York garment factory. My great-grandfathers had one important thing in common, though they probably wouldn't have recognized any common ground at the time: They were both religious men. Hilliard was a Methodist preacher, and Isaac was a rabbi in Warsaw before immigration transformed his settled existence.

I believe it's fair to say that 'only in America' would the children of two such different families and backgrounds have been drawn together in the 1920s.

Those children—my black grandfather and white grandmother—joined the newly established American Communist Party and met in a New York jail after a union demonstration in 1928. Oliver Golden and Bertha Bialek soon fell deeply in love, defying both my grandmother's family (most of whose members never spoke to her again) and the larger American taboo against interracial marriage.

In 1931, Oliver and Bertha left the United States to pursue their common dream of building a new, more equitable society in the Soviet Union. They could not have known then what we know now, that the dream would turn into a nightmare as countless millions perished under the tyranny of Joseph Stalin.

My grandfather, an agronomist who studied under George Washington Carver at Tuskegee Institute, was sent to the Soviet republic of Uzbekistan, in central Asia, to help develop a cotton industry in what was then a primitive agricultural society. This move was never meant to be permanent. My grandparents intended to return to the United States—they had signed ordinary work contracts with the Soviet government—but changed their minds after my mother was born in 1934.

Oliver and Bertha named their daughter Lily. It has always seemed to me that Tiger-lily might have been more appropriate for this forceful child of an interracial love match spanning three continents. My mother is a tall, striking woman with a café-au-lait complexion and hazel eyes. In America half a century ago, her black ancestry—and her ambiguous status as the child of an interracial couple—would have severely limited her opportunities, in very different ways, in both black and white communities.

My grandparents saw no place for a family like theirs in segregated, pre-World War II America. Of course, there were havens where interracial couples were tolerated—in the bohemia of Greenwich Village and in certain open-minded segments of Harlem society. But how would my grandfather have supported his family? He was an agricultural specialist, not an artist or poet who might have carved an economic niche for himself in a cosmopolitan environment. The places where he could have worked—in farming areas of the South and Midwest, for instance—would not have tolerated a black man married to a white woman. This was a time when an African-American man could be lynched simply for looking the wrong way at a white woman. In these places, local blacks could hardly have extended a warm welcome to my grandparents or their child.

So my grandparents stayed in the Soviet Union, and my family took its place in a complicated, painful national history extending from the fear-filled depths of Stalinism, through the rebuilding that began when Mikhail Gorbachev inaugurated the *glasnost* era in 1985, and, finally, to the collapse of the system under which I grew up. Gorbachev's reforms signaled the beginning of the end for the fear that dominated Soviet society and cut off my family's contacts with America for fifty years.

In the Russia of my childhood, not to mention the terror-ridden country of my mother's girlhood, it was unimaginable that we would live to see young men and women impose their bodies in front of tanks and successfully defend the concept of government by the consent of the governed.

At the time of my birth, my mother's main goal was to bring up her child with integrity and individuality in a society that demanded conformity. This wasn't easy for any Russian parent, but Mama's task was especially hard because the color of our skin told everyone we were different. Our foreign connections were literally written on our faces.

My father was Abdullah Khanga, an African independence leader who spent years studying in Moscow before returning to his native Zanzibar (where he was murdered by political opponents in the mid-sixties). My mother met my father in Moscow as a result of her own African connections; she is a historian specializing in African music and culture.

Long before I was old enough to remember him, Abdullah Khanga left the Soviet Union for the last time. I was born on May Day, 1963. Mama was excited that day, because my father, whom the Soviets treated as a future government leader, had been invited to view the traditional May Day parade from atop Lenin's tomb. Mama intended to accompany him to the celebration, where thousands of Young Pioneers and adult Party stalwarts, in the years before *glasnost*, always carried gigantic portraits of Lenin and Marx through Red Square. Instead, my mother went into labor and had to dodge unruly drunks, celebrating in their own fashion, as she made her way to the maternity hospital

After my mother managed to detach herself from the crowds, I came into the world without untoward incident. I am the first native *Moskovichka* in my far-flung family (Mama having been born in the Uzbek capital of Tashkent).

In spite of the many strands in my heritage, I am also Russian to the core. Russian was my first language, though my mother and grandmother often spoke English at home. My schooling was Soviet, beginning with the kindergarten where I was taught to love *Dedushka* (Grandpa) Lenin. My mind and soul have been shaped by the compassionate irony of Chekhov, the poetry of Pushkin, the romantic music of Tchaikovsky.

Yet there was always a shade of difference; I had only to look in the mirror to see it. I was black—to be more precise, deep burnished copper—in a world where nearly everyone was white. My favorite song was "We Shall Overcome," which I learned in English as a small child. Those black American voices, resonant with a world of sorrow and joy, came to us on records, gifts from a steady stream of black American visitors who passed through our home. I was raised on tales of my grandparents' friendships with such great black Americans as the singer Paul Robeson, the poet Langston Hughes, and the father of pan-Africanism, W. E. B. Du Bois. In fact, Dr. Du Bois was responsible for the creation of the African Institute of the Soviet Academy of Sciences, where my mother worked. Dr. Du Bois was a friend of my grandfather, and he was talking with twenty-two-year-old Lily about her future on the day before he was scheduled to drop by the Kremlin for a chat with Premier Nikita Khrushchev. The year was 1958—a time when a dictator could still get something done in Russia!—and all Dr. Du Bois had to do was mention the need for an African studies institute to the impetuous Khrushchev. In as little time as it takes to say "It always pays to deal with the man at the top," my mother was ensconced as the institute's first scholar.

When Americans ask whether there is racism and discrimination in Russia, my answer can never be a simple one. The story of Pushkin isn't beside the point. His great-grandfather came to the court of Peter the Great in the early eighteenth century after being held hostage by the Turks. Peter immediately recognized the boy's intellectual gifts, sent him to France to study, and eventually made him a general after he returned to Russia as a mathematician and engineer. In portraits of Pushkin, it's easy to discern traces of his black ancestry—in spite of his very light skin—after three generations of intermarriage. He occupies the same position in Russian culture as Shakespeare does in the English-speaking world. As a black girl growing up in Moscow, it mattered to me that Russians considered Pushkin a purely Russian poet. In America, I suspect his ancestry would have led whites to consider him a marginal black rather than a purely "American" writer.

In Russian culture, I never felt like a stranger in my black skin. Unlike many African-Americans, I was never made to feel less intelligent, less likely to achieve than my white schoolmates.

Was my family, by virtue of its descent from one of the few American blacks who came to the Soviet Union in the thirties, a special case? Yes and no. In many ways, I was insulated from the kind of prejudice experienced not only by African students but also by mixed-race children of unions between Africans and Russians. Anti-black prejudices are not institutionalized in Russia; racism feeds on visible targets, and there are too few of us to attract the kind of bigotry directed toward larger minorities. (According to Western sources, there are only 5,000 to 10,000 native black citizens in the former Soviet Union, plus some 40,000 African students. But this estimate of native blacks is probably too low, not only because the law allows children to choose the nationality of either parent but because many blacks are officially registered under a "white" nationality on their internal passports.)

When I was growing up, I thought of my color not as a target for discrimination but simply—and not so simply—as a mark of separateness. No racist taunts were aimed at me, but I did attract persistent, usually polite curiosity. When I was very small, playmates would ask why my skin didn't turn white, since my family no longer lived in Africa but in cold, snowy Russia. This kind of curiosity does not draw blood, but it does leave microscopic pinpricks. No one else could see the tiny jabs, but I always felt them. They didn't really hurt but left a prickly sensation, a reminder that I wasn't like everyone, or anyone, else.

And there was another difference, much less obvious to me and to the outside world. One of my earliest memories is the voice of my beloved grandmother, singing me to sleep with a Yiddish lullabye: *Lommir, Lommir, 'le zing'n a liddeleh vus dus maydel vil*—"Let's sing a little song, whatever the little girl wants."

Until last year, when my mother and I found our second- and third-generation Jewish cousins in the United States, I never knew that my grandmother spoke Yiddish or that it had, in fact, been her first language. I did know she immigrated to the United States from Warsaw in 1920 and her father was some sort of scholar, but she never discussed her Jewish heritage with me.

That part of her identity may have seemed less and less meaningful to her as time passed, but my grandmother also lived through a period of Soviet history when it was dangerous to be a Jew, especially one with indisputable foreign connections. In the late forties, when Stalin launched his campaign against "rootless cosmopolitans" (code for Jews and foreigners), my grandmother lost her job as a professor of English at the Institute of Foreign Languages in Tashkent. She must have thought it wouldn't do her daughter and granddaughter any good to emphasize what in Soviet terms was yet another liability.

But there was one time—and I have never forgotten it—when she made herself crystal-clear on the subject of Jewishness. I was just five years old when I came home from kindergarten talking about something "this *zhid*" had done. The Russian *zhid* is the equivalent of the American "kike" or "yid," but I didn't understand that at the time. To me, *zhid* was just a word used by schoolchildren, a bit of ordinary playground slang—and that, of course, says a good deal about the prevalence of anti-Semitism in ordinary Soviet life.

I was stunned when my grandmother slapped my face—the only time she ever hit me in my life—and said, "Every time you call a Jewish person a bad word, you're calling me and your mother and yourself bad. To hate them is to hate yourself. Because I am Jewish, and that means your mother is Jewish, and that means you are also Jewish."

My grandmother never explained further about Jews or Judaism. It was many years before I understood what she meant, that in traditional religious law, Judaism is inherited through the mother. But I clearly understood her real point. What she intended to impress upon me was that it's morally wrong to classify or stigmatize groups of people according to their race, nationality, or religion. Since that time, I have experienced an almost physical pain whenever Russians make derogatory remarks about Jews, Armenians, Gypsies, or any other group. For the most part, I don't hear slurs about blacks—not because no one makes them, but because no one I know would make them to my face. But I have heard anti-Semitic remarks from Russians, most of whom have no idea my grandmother was Jewish. Whenever I hear such comments—based, of course, on the assumption that I too will enjoy a good laugh at the expense of a dirty *zhid*—real friendship with the speaker becomes impossible for me.

I cherish the memory of my grandmother's voice today, especially as I try to come to grips with different forms of prejudice in the United States. It hurts when I hear certain white Americans talk about "lazy blacks," as if my being a Soviet citizen somehow renders me less black or less likely to feel pain and humiliation, and it hurts just as much to hear some black Americans describe all Jews as greedy or all whites as bigots. *To hate them is to hate yourself.*

In 1985, I would have laughed in disbelief if anyone had told me I would ever have the chance to discover America and to explore the American part of my family history on my own. A year after graduating from Moscow State University, I was an editorial assistant for *Moscow News*—then a stupefying dull publication noted mainly for putting readers to sleep in Russian, English, and several other languages. Although Gorbachev had just taken over leadership of the government, it was impossible for most Soviets to foresee the changes—involving everything from censorship to foreign travel—that would sweep away the rules we had all taken for granted. Like most Russians, I had known about these restrictions since I was old enough to understand the meaning of *nyelzya* (it's impossible, no way).

One rule—even more powerful because it was unwritten—decreed that no one with a foreign background would be allowed to travel outside the "fraternal socialist" countries of eastern Europe. If that seems crazy, think about it from a secret policeman's point of view: A Soviet citizen who spoke good English (both my mother and I do) was likely to meet people, learn more, and enjoy more in English-speaking countries than she would if she spoke only Russian. As for an English-speaking Russian with live American relatives: God only knows what might happen! Such an unreliable person might have decided to become a spy, or at the very least to defect to the West.

Thanks to this paranoid thinking, my mother never managed to travel to any of the African countries where her scholarly articles had been widely published and appreciated. (From Africa, after all, one may telephone freely and take a plane to any country in the world. The pre-*glasnost* Soviet system couldn't tolerate such a possibility.)

As a fledgling journalist. I had even less hope of getting permission to travel. In the first place, foreign assignments were reserved for men: for men, for party members (which neither my mother nor I were), and for people with spotless (usually meaning Russian or Ukranian) ethnic backgrounds. With luck, I might hope to turn the modest column I was writing about tourists into a real reporting job. Whenever I interviewed American tourists at that time, I was careful not to get too close, not to give them my home phone number or go out with them in the evening. That's the way things were; that's the way I assumed they would be for the rest of my life. I had no premonition that I was about to embark on a journey resembling nothing so much as Alice's fall through the looking glass.

I was hired for *Moscow News* in 1984, in the twilight of the old regime, by Gennadi Ivanovich Gerasimov. Gerasimov's face and voice would eventually become known to millions around the world when he became Gorbachev's personal spokesman. Looking back, I wonder if Gennadi Ivanovich may have sensed that a black Russian with American connections would soon be regarded in a far more positive light.

I owe a great deal to my first boss; many years later, I learned he had to fight hard, sticking out his neck with his own superiors, to hire me. Without his help, I might well have wound up working for a trade-union newspaper in some dismal backwater, far from the exciting political changes in the capital.

As *glasnost* gathered steam, Gennadi Ivanovich was succeeded as editor of *Moscow News* by Yegor Vladimirovich Yakovlev, who set about transforming the once-stolid publication into a voice for democratization. Even for the young—and I was only twenty-four when Yegor Vladimirovich took over the editorship of the paper—it was a wrenching experience to change the passive habits of a lifetime. In the journalism department of Moscow State University, I was trained not to investigate real news but to produce whatever stories were demanded by my bosses and, ultimately, by the political authorities. Individual initiative comes hard when it has always been discouraged.

But I did change; the freedom to say and write what you think is an addiction. The experience is not mine alone but the story of an entire generation of Russians; we have learned, in Chekhov's famous phrase, to squeeze the slave out of ourselves "drop by drop."

Part of the change in me is connected with America. In 1987, the unimaginable happened: I was chosen as the first Soviet journalist to visit the United States on an exchange program. Before *glasnost*, there was no possibility that someone like me—young, female, a non-Party member, and, horror of horrors!, the granddaughter of Americans, would ever have been selected to represent her country abroad.

I could hardly believe my good luck when I found myself on a plane headed for the land my grandparents left behind more than half a century earlier. I was to spend several months working at the *Christian Science Monitor* in Boston.

As a Soviet citizen and a journalist, one of my proudest moments came when I found myself attending the first Washington summit meeting between Gorbachev and President Reagan. I even became something of a hot story myself, as American reporters discovered a black Russian in their midst. This was more interesting than boring arms control—a young black woman talking casually about "we Russians."

"You've got to be kidding," said the American correspondent in the next seat. "There aren't any blacks in Russia."

"Well, you can see for yourself I'm not white," I replied.

Surrounded by hundreds of reporters from every country in the world, listening to Gennadi Ivanovich, announce a tentative agreement on strategic arms control, I glowed with the knowledge that I was fulfilling several of my grandparents' dreams in ways they could scarcely imagine.

Oliver and Bertha had dreamed of Soviet-American cooperation, and here were two leaders moving beyond the rhetoric of "evil empire" and "capitalist imperialism" in order to make the fragile world a slightly safer place.

They dreamed of a life in which their children and grandchildren would not be crippled by bigotry—and here I was, functioning in my profession at a level impossible for a black woman in the America they left behind (though not, I was beginning to understand, in the America of the eighties).

On that first trip to the United States, I made no effort to find either my black or white relatives. But I did speak to a number of community groups and gave several interviews about my unusual family history. As a result of the publicity, some of my relatives began looking for me.

On the black side of the family, my Golden relations began tracking me down after I was interviewed in the ABC newsmagazine program "20/20." In

Chicago, my grandfather's aged niece, Mamie Golden, cried out in recognition when Oliver's picture flashed across the screen. "That's my Uncle Buck," she said with tears in her eyes. Mamie, who lived with my grandfather and his parents in Memphis when she was a girl, remembered her uncle as a smiling young man, always handing out silver dollars to children (hence, the nickname "Uncle Buck"). Delores Harris, Mamie's niece, was able to track down our Moscow address and phone number through ABC. A week later, the phone rang in Moscow, and my mother listened in amazement as Delores introduced herself and explained that her grandmother, Rebecca, had been my grandfather's oldest sister. My grandmother, Mama, and I always thought of ourselves as an isolated family of three. In the span of one phone call, Mama and I started to see ourselves as two Russian offshoots of a large family tree. Mamie and Delores informed us that we had at least a hundred Golden cousins in the United States.

Finding my black relatives was an uncomplicated joy, but I experienced great ambivalence when I started looking into the white side of my family. My grandmother's pain at her old estrangement from her relatives was never far from my mind. With the exception of one brother, Jack, no one in the Bialek family maintained contact with Bertha after she left for the Soviet Union with my grandfather. Jack was considered the most liberal member of the family; he'd drawn his younger sister into the Communist Party during the twenties. But he wasn't able to come to terms with his sister's love for a black man and told his son that Bertha married a Russian in Russia.

By the time I got to the United States, only one person in Jack's branch of the Bialek family—his widow, Minnie—knew the real story. Most of the family lives in Los Angeles, and in 1988 an article about me—in which I mentioned my grandmother's maiden name—appeared in the Los Angeles *Times*. At that point, Minnie decided it was time to tell her son about his aunt's long-ago marriage to a black American, since it seemed likely the secret would come out anyway.

When they finally learned their aunt Bertha had married not a Russian but a black man, neither Jack's son Eugene, nor his grandchildren could understand the reasons for the long secrecy. My cousin Nancy, just a year older than I—her warm, sparkling brown eyes remind me of my grandmother—can't imagine being upset by the existence of a black cousin.

As it turns out, my mother and I weren't a total family secret. Although Jack didn't tell his children about us, my grandmother's older brothers, Marcus and Sidney, didn't keep the secret from their families. But it seems the brothers had their own disagreements, so information didn't travel from one branch of the family to the other.

After more than seventy years, who can know of all the explanations for family feuds and family secrets in the older generation? I do know that I have many second- and third-generation Bialek cousins who are pleased and fascinated to have reconnected with the two black Russians in the family. Black Bialeks! In fact, my relatives have pointed out a marked resemblance between my mother's features and those of the Hebrew poet Chaim Nachman Bialik. Like the poet, my great-grandfather's family originally came from Odessa, and Bialek family tradition maintains that Chaim Nachman and my great-grandfather Isaac were distant cousins.

My grandmother died in Moscow on the same day her brother Jack died in Los Angeles in 1985. I'm sad she didn't live long enough to see her young relatives in America move beyond the prejudices and fears that cut her off from her own generation. Even though she rarely talked about her pain, I felt it and to some degree still do. When I returned to the United States in 1990 to investigate my family history on a Rockefeller Foundation fellowship, I probably would not have looked for my white relatives were it not for the insistence of my supervisor at the foundation. I was still afraid—afraid my living relatives would reject me as the dead had denied my grandmother. A part of me is still surprised that my white cousins are pleased rather than dismayed to have found me.

Americans talk a great deal about "putting the past where it belongs—in the past." Raised in a country that has suffered so much by lying about its past, I cannot leave history behind. I prefer the concept embodied in a quotation, passed on to me by an American friend, from the international lawyer and Holocaust survivor Samuel Pisar: "We may not have to live in the past, but the past lives in us."

Only by confronting history courageously, by uncovering wounds most of us would rather forget, does it become possible truly to put the past "where it belongs." That is what I have tried to do during the last five years. My journey has taken me from Tashkent to Tanzania, from London to Los Angeles, from Chicago to the Mississippi cotton fields where my grandfather was born and raised. I am searching for the past that lives not only in me but in the two great countries lodged deep in my heart.

from *Aké: The Years of Childhood*

by Wole Soyinka (Nigeria)

The sprawling, undulating terrain is all of Aké. More than mere loyalty to the parsonage gave birth to a puzzle, and a resentment, that God should choose to look down on his own pious station, the parsonage compound, from the profane heights of Itoko. There was of course the mystery of the Chief's stable with live horses near the crest of the hill, but beyond that, this dizzying road only sheered upwards from one noisy market to the other, looking down across Ibàràpa and Ita Aké into the most secret recesses of the parsonage itself.

On a misty day, the steep rise towards Itoko would join the sky. If God did not actually live there, there was little doubt that he descended first on its crest, then took his one gigantic stride over those babbling markets—which dared to sell on Sundays—into St Peter's Church, afterwards visiting the parsonage for tea with the Canon. There was the small consolation that, in spite of the temptation to arrive on horseback, he never stopped first at the Chief's who was known to be a pagan; certainly the Chief was never seen at a church service except at the anniversaries of the Alake's coronation. Instead God strode straight into St Peter's for morning service, paused briefly at the afternoon services, but reserved his most formal, exotic presence for the evening service which, in his honour, was always held in the English tongue. The organ took on a dark, smoky sonority at evening service, and there was no doubt that the organ was adapting its normal sounds to accompany God's own sepulchral responses, with its timbre of the egúngún,* to those prayers that were offered to him.

Only the Canon's residence could have housed the weekly Guest. For one thing, it was the only storey-building in the parsonage, square and stolid as the Canon himself, riddled with black wooden-framed windows. BishopsCourt was also a storey-building but only pupils lived in it, so it was not a house. From the upper floor of the Canon's home one *almost* looked the top of Itókò straight in its pagan eye. It stood at the highest lived-in point of the parsonage, just missing overlooking the gate. Its back was turned to the world of spirits and ghommids who inhabited the thick woods and chased home children who had wandered too deeply into them for firewood, mushrooms and snails. The Canon's square, white building was a bulwark against the menace and the siege of the wood spirits. Its rear wall demarcated their territory, stopped them from taking liberties with the world of humans.

Only the school-rooms of the primary school shared this closeness to the woods, and they were empty at night. Fenced by rough plastered walls, by the windowless rear walls of its houses, by tumuli of rocks which the giant trees tried vainly to obscure, Aké parsonage with its corrugated roofs gave off an air of fortifications. Secure within it, we descended or climbed at will into

---

* Ancestral masquerade.

overlapping, interleaved planes, sheer rock-face drops, undergrowths and sudden hideouts of cultivated fruit groves. The hibiscus was rampant. The air hung heavy with perfumes of lemon leaves, guavas, mangoes, sticky with the sap of *boum-boum* and the secretions of the rain-tree. The school-compounds were lined with these rain-trees with widespread shade filled branches. Needle-pines rose above the acacia and forests of bamboos kept us permanently nervous; if monster snakes had a choice, the bamboo clumps would be their ideal habitation.

Between the left flank of the Canon's house and the School playing-fields was—the Orchard. It was too varied, much too profuse to be called a garden, even a fruit-garden. And there were plants and fruits in it which made the orchard an extension of scripture classes, church lessons or sermons. A leaf-plant, mottled white-and-red was called the Cana lily. As Christ was nailed to the Cross and his wounds spurted blood, a few drops stuck to the leaves of the lily stigmatizing it for ever. No one bothered to explain the cause of the abundant white spots which also appeared on every leaf. Perhaps it had to do with the washing of sins in the blood of Christ, leaving even the most mottled spots in a person's soul, snow-white. There was the Passion fruit also, born of another part of that same history, not however a favourite of any us children. Its lush green skin was pleasant to fondle in one's palm, but it ripened into a dessicated yellow, collapsing like the faces of the old men and women we knew. And it barely managed to be sweet, thus failing the infallible test of a real fruit. But the queen of the orchard was the pomegranate which grew, not so much from a seed of the stone church, as of the lyrical Sunday School. For it was at the Sunday School that the real stories were told, stories that lived in the events themselves, crossed the time-border of Sundays or leaves of the Bible and entered the world of fabled lands, men and women. The pomegranate was most niggardly in producing. It yielded its outwardly hardy fruit only once in a while, tended with patience by the thick-veined hands and face which belonged to someone we only knew as Gardener. Only Gardener could be trusted to share the occasional fruit among the small dedicated band of pomegranate watchers, yet even the tiniest wedge transported us to the illustrated world of Biblical Tales Retold. The pomegranate was the Queen of Sheba, rebellions and wars, the passion of Salome, the siege of Troy, the Praise of beauty in the Song of Solomon. This fruit, with its stone-hearted look and feel unlocked the cellars of Ali Baba, extracted the genie from Aladdin's lamp, plucked the strings of the harp that restored David to sanity, parted the waters of the Nile and filled our parsonage with incense from the dim temple of Jerusalem.

It grew only in the Orchard, Gardener said. The pomegranate was foreign to the black man's soil, but some previous bishop, a white man had brought the seeds and planted them in the Orchard. We asked if it was *the* apple but Gardener only laughed and said No. Nor, he added, would that apple be found on the black man's soil. Gardener was adjudged ignorant. It was clear that only the pomegranate could be the apple that lost Adam and Eve the joys of paradise. There existed yet another fruit that was locally called apple, soft yet crisp, a soft pink skin and reasonably juicy. Before the advent of the pomegranate it had assumed the identity of the apple that undid the naked pair. The first taste of the pomegranate unmasked that impostor and took its place.

Swarms of bats inhabited the fig tree, their seed-pocked droppings would cake the stones, lawns, paths and bushes before dawn. An evergreen tree, soft and rampant bordered the playing-field on the side of the bookseller's compound, defying the Harmattan; it filled the parsonage with a tireless concert of weaver birds.

An evil thing has happened to Aké parsonage. The land is eroded, the lawns are bared and mystery driven from its once secretive combs. Once, each new day opened up an unseen closure, a pocket of rocks, a clump of bush and a colony of snails. The motor-hulk has not moved from its staging-point where children clambered into it for journeys to fabled places; now it is only a derelict, its eyes rusted sockets, its dragon face collapsed with a progressive loss of teeth. The abandoned incinerator with its lush weeds and glistening snakes is marked by a mound of mud. The surviving houses, houses which formed the battlements of Aké parsonage are now packing cases on a depleted landscape, full of creaks, exposed and nerveless.

And the moods are gone. Even the open lawns and broad paths, bordered with whitewashed stones, lilies and lemon grass clumps, changed nature from season to season, from weekday to Sunday and between noon and nightfall. And the echoes off the walls in lower Parsonage acquired new tonalities with the seasons, changed with the emptying of the lawns as the schools dispersed for holidays.

If I lay across the lawn before our house, face upwards to the sky, my head towards BishopsCourt, each spread-out leg would point to the inner compounds of Lower Parsonage. Half of the Anglican Girls' School occupied one of these lower spaces, the other half had taken over BishopsCourt. The lower area contained the school's junior classrooms, a dormitory, a small fruit-garden of pawpaws, guava, some bamboo and wild undergrowth. There were always snails to be found in the rainy season. In the other lower compound was the mission bookseller, a shrivelled man with a serene wife on whose ample back we all, at one time or the other slept, or reviewed the world. His compound became a short cut to the road that led to Ibarà, Lafenwá or Igbèin and its Grammar School over which Ransome-Kuti presided and lived with his family. The bookseller's compound contained the only well in the parsonage; in the dry season, his place was never empty. And his soil appeared to produce the only coconut trees.

BishopsCourt, of Upper Parsonage, is no more. Bishop Ajayi Crowther would sometimes emerge from the cluster of hydrangea and bougainvillaea, a gnomic face with popping eyes whose formal photograph had first stared at us from the frontispiece of his life history. He had lived, the teacher said, in BishopsCourt and from that moment, he peered out from among the creeping plants whenever I passed by the house on an errand to our Great Aunt, Mrs. Lijadu. BishopsCourt had become a boarding house for the girls' school and an extra playground for us during the holidays. The Bishop sat, silently, on the bench beneath the wooden porch over the entrance, his robes twined through and through with the lengthening tendrils of the bougainvillea. I moved closer when his eyes turned to sockets. My mind wandered then to another photograph in which he wore a clerical suit with waistcoat and I wondered what he really kept at the end of the silver chain that vanished into the pocket. He grinned and said, Come nearer, I'll show you. As I moved towards the porch he drew on the chain until he had lifted out a wholly round pocket-watch that gleamed of solid silver. He pressed a button and the lid opened, revealing, not the glass and face-dial but a deep cloud-filled space. Then he winked one eye, and it fell from his face into the bowl of the watch. He winked the other and this joined its partner in the watch. He snapped back the lid, nodded again and his head went bald, his teeth disappeared and the skin pulled backward till the whitened cheekbones were exposed. Then he stood up and, tucking the watch back into the waistcoat pocket, moved a step towards me. I fled homewards.

BishopsCourt appeared sometimes to want to rival the Canon's house. It looked a house-boat despite its guard of whitewashed stones and luxuriant flowers, its wooden fretwork frontage almost wholly immersed in bougainvillaea. And it was shadowed also by those omnipresent rocks from whose clefts tall, stout-boled trees miraculously grew. Clouds gathered and the rocks merged into their accustomed grey turbulence, then the trees were carried to and fro until they stayed suspended over BishopsCourt. This happened only in heavy storms. BishopsCourt, unlike the Canon's house, did not actually border the rocks or the woods. The girls' playing fields separated them and we knew that this buffer had always been there. Obviously bishops were not inclined to challenge the spirits. Only the vicars could. That Bishop Ajayi Crowther frightened me out of that compound by his strange transformations only confirmed that the Bishops, once they were dead, joined the world of spirits and ghosts. I could not see the Canon decaying like that in front of my eyes, nor the Rev. J. J. who had once occupied that house, many years before, when my mother was still like us. J. J. Ransome-Kuti had actually ordered back several ghommids in his life-time; my mother confirmed it. She was his grand niece and, before she came to live at our house, she had lived in the Rev. J. J.'s household. Her brother Sanya also lived there and he was acknowledged by all to be an òrò, which made him at home in the woods, even at night. On one occasion however, he must have gone too far.

'They had visited us before,' she said, 'to complain. Mind you, they would-n't actually come into the compound, they stood far off at the edge, where the woods ended. Their leader, the one who spoke emitted wild sparks from a head that seemed to be an entire ball of embers—no, I'm mixing up two occa-sions—that was the second time when he chased us home. The first time, they had merely sent an emissary. He was quite dark, short and swarthy. He came right to the backyard and stood there while he ordered us to call the Reverend.'

'It was as if Uncle had been expecting the visit He came out of the house and asked him what he wanted. We all huddled in the kitchen, peeping out.'

'What was his voice like? Did he speak like an egúngún?'

'I'm coming to it. This man, well, I suppose one should call him a man. He wasn't quite human, we could see that. Much too large a head, and he kept his eyes on the ground. So, he said he had come to report us. They didn't mind our coming to the woods, even at night, be we were to stay off any area beyond the rocks and that clump of bamboo by the stream.'

'Well, what did Uncle say? And you haven't said what his voice was like.'

Tinu turned her elder sister's eye on me. 'Let Mama finish the story.'

'You want to know everything. All right, he spoke just like your father. Are you satisfied?'

I did not believe that but I let it pass. 'Go on. What did Grand Uncle do?'

'He called everyone together and warned us to keep away from the place.'

'And yet you went back!'

'Well, you know your Uncle Sanya. He was angry. For one thing the best snails are on the other side of that stream. So he continued to complain that those òrò were just being selfish, and he was going to show them who he was. Well, he did. About a week later he led us back. And he was right you know. We gathered a full basket and a half of the biggest snails you ever saw. Well, by this time we had all forgotten about the warning, there was plenty of moonlight and anyway, I've told you Sanya is an òrò himself....'

'But why? He looks normal like you and us.'

'You wouldn't understand yet. Anyway, he is òrò. So with him we felt quite safe. Until suddenly this sort of light, like a ball of fire began to glow in the distance. Even while it was still far we kept hearing voices, as if a lot of people around us were grumbling the same words together. They were saying something like, "You stubborn, stiff-necked children, we've warned you and warned you but you just won't listen....'"

Wild Christian looked above our heads, frowning to recollect the better. 'One can't even say, "they". It was only this figure of fire that I saw and he was still very distant. Yet I heard him distinctly, as if he had many mouths which were pressed against my ears. Every moment, the fireball loomed larger and larger.'

'What did Uncle Sanya do? Did he fight him?'

'Sanya wo ni yen? He was the first to break and run. Bo o ló o yă mi, o di kítìpà kítìpà!* No one remembered all those fat snails. That iwin** followed us all the way to the house. Our screams had arrived long before us and the whole household was—well, you can imagine the turmoil. Uncle had already dashed down the stairs and was in the backyard. We ran past him while he went out to meet the creature. This time that iwin actually passed the line of the woods, he continued as if he meant to chase us right into the house, you know, he wasn't running, just pursuing us steadily.' We waited. This was it! Wild Christian mused while we remained in suspense. Then she breathed deeply and shook her head with a strange sadness.

'The period of faith is gone. There was faith among our early christians, real faith, not just church-going and hymn-singing. Faith. Igbàbó. And it is out of that faith that real power comes. Uncle stood there like a rock, he held out his Bible and ordered, "Go back! Go back to that forest which is your home. Back I said, in the name of God". Hm. And that was it. The creature simply turned and fled, those sparks falling off faster and faster until there was just a faint glow receding into the woods.' She sighed. 'Of course, after prayers that evening, there was the price to be paid. Six of the best on every one's back. Sanya got twelve. And we all cut grass every day for the next week.'

I could not help feeling that the fright should have sufficed as punishment. Her eyes gazing in the direction of the square house, Wild Christian nonetheless appeared to sense what was going on in my mind. She added, 'Faith and Discipline. That is what made those early believers. Psheeaw! God doesn't make them like that any more. When I think of the one who now occupies that house ...'

Then she appeared to recall herself to our presence. 'What are you both still sitting here for? Isn't it time for your evening bath? Lawanle!' 'Auntie' Lawanle

---

* If you aren't moving, get out of my way!
** A 'ghommid'; a wood sprite which is also believed to live in the ground.

replied 'Ma' from a distant part of the house. Before she appeared I reminded Wild Christian, 'But you haven't told us why Uncle Sanya is òrò?'

She shrugged, 'He is. I saw it with my own eyes.'

We both clamoured. 'When? When?'

She smiled. 'You won't understand. But I'll tell you about it some other time. Or let him tell you himself next time he is here.'

'You mean you saw him turn into an òrò?'

Lawanle came in just then and she prepared to hand us over, 'Isn't it time for these children's bath?'

I pleaded, 'No, wait Auntie Lawanle', knowing it was a waste of time. She had already gripped us both, one arm each. I shouted back, 'Was Bishop Crowther an òrò?'

Wild Christian laughed. 'What next are you going to ask? Oh I see. They have taught you about him in Sunday school have they?'

'I saw him.' I pulled back at the door, forcing Lawanle to stop. 'I see him all the time. He comes and sits under the porch of the Girls School. I've seen him when crossing the compound to Auntie Mrs Lijadu.'

'All right,' sighed Wild Christian. 'Go and have your bath.'

'He hides among the bougainvillaea....' Lawanle dragged me out of hearing.

Later than evening, she told us the rest of the story. On that occasion, Rev. J.J. was away on one of his many mission tours. He travelled a lot, on foot and on bicycle, keeping in touch with all the branches of his diocese and spreading the Word of God. There was frequent opposition but nothing deterred him. One frightening experience occurred in one of the villages in Ijebu. He had been warned not to preach on a particular day, which was the day for an egúngún outing, but he persisted and held a service. The egúngún procession passed while the service was in progress and, using his ancestral voice, called on the preacher to stop at once, disperse his people and come out to pay obeisance. Rev. J.J. ignored him. The egúngún then left, taking his followers with him but, on passing the main door, he tapped on it with his wand three times. Hardly had the last member of his procession left the church premises than the building collapsed. The walls simply fell down and the roof disintegrated. Miraculously however, the walls fell outwards while the roof supports fell among the aisles or flew outwards—anywhere but on the congregation itself. Rev. J.J. calmed the worshippers, paused in his preaching to render a thanksgiving prayer, then continued his sermon.

Perhaps this was what Wild Christian meant by Faith. And this tended to confuse things because, after all, the egúngún did make the church building collapse. Wild Christian made no attempt to explain how that happened, so that feat tended to be of the same order of Faith which moved mountains or enabled Wild Christian to pour ground-nut oil from a broad-rimmed bowl into an empty bottle without spilling a drop. She had the strange habit of sighing with a kind of rapture, crediting her steadiness of hand to Faith and thanking God. If however the basin slipped and she lost a drop or two, she murmured that her sins had become heavy and that she needed to pray more.

If Rev. J.J. had Faith however, he also appeared to have Stubborness in common with our Uncle Sanya. Stubborness was one of the earliest sins we easily recognized, and no matter how much Wild Christian tried to explain the Rev. J.J. preaching on the *egúngún's* outing day, despite warnings, it sounded much like stubborness. As for Uncle Sanya there was no doubt about his own case; hardly did the Rev. J.J. pedal out of sight on his pastoral duties than he was off into the woods on one pretext or the other, and making for the very areas which the *òrò* had declared out of bounds. Mushrooms and snails were the real goals, with the gathering of firewood used as a dutiful excuse.

Even Sanya had however stopped venturing into the woods at night, accepting the fact that it was far too risky; daytime and early dusk carried little danger as most wood spirits only came out at night. Mother told us that on this occasion she and Sanya had been picking mushrooms, separated by only a few clumps of bushes. She could hear his movement quite clearly, indeed, they took the precaution of staying very close together.

Suddenly, she said, she heard Sanya's voice talking animatedly with someone. After listening for some time she called out his name but he did not respond. There was no voice apart from his, yet he appeared to be chatting in friendly, excited tones with some other person. So she peeped through the bushes and there was Uncle Sanya seated on the ground chattering away to no one that she could see. She tried to penetrate the surrounding bushes with her gaze but the woods remained empty except for the two of them. And then her eyes came to rest on his basket.

It was something she had observed before, she said. It was the same, no matter how many of the children in the household went to gather snails, berries or whatever, Sanya would spend most of the time playing and climbing rocks and trees. He would wander off by himself, leaving the basket anywhere. And yet, whenever they prepared to return home, his basket was always fuller than the others'. This time was no different. She came closer, startling our Uncle who snapped off his chatter and pretended to be hunting snails in the undergrowth.

Mother said that she was frightened. The basket was filled to the brim, impossibly bursting. She was also discouraged, so she picked up her near empty basket and insisted that they return home at once. She led the way but after some distance, when she looked back, Sanya appeared to be trying to follow her but was being prevented, as if he was being pulled back by invisible hands. From time to time he would snatch forward his arm and snap, 'Leave me alone. Can't you see I have to go home? I said I have to go.'

She broke into a run and Sanya did the same. They ran all the way home.

That evening, Sanya took ill. He broke into a sweat, tossed on his mat all night and muttered to himself. By the following day the household was thoroughly frightened. His forehead was burning to the touch and no one could get a coherent word out of him. Finally, an elderly woman, one of J.J.'s converts, turned up at the house on a routine visit. When she learnt of Sanya's condition, she nodded wisely and acted like one who knew exactly what to do. Having first found out what things he last did before his illness, she summoned my mother and questioned her. She told her everything while the old woman kept nodding with understanding. Then she gave instructions:

'I want a basket of *àgìdi*, containing 50 wraps. Then prepare some *èkuru* in a large bowl. Make sure the *èkuru* stew is prepared with plenty of locust bean and crayfish. It must smell as appetizing as possible.'

The children were dispersed in various directions, some to the market to obtain the *àgìdi*, others to begin grinding the beans for the amount of *èkuru* which was needed to accompany 50 wraps of *àgìdi*. The children's mouths watered, assuming at once that this was to be an appeasement feast, a *sàarà** for some offended spirits.

When all was prepared however, the old woman took everything to Sanya's sick-room, plus a pot of cold water and cups, locked the door on him and ordered everybody away.

'Just go about your normal business and don't go anywhere near the room. If you want your brother to recover, do as I say. Don't attempt to speak to him and don't peep through the keyhole.'

She locked the windows too and went herself to a distant end of the courtyard where she could monitor the movements of the children. She dozed off soon however, so that mother and the other children were able to glue their ears to the door and windows, even if they could not see the invalid himself. Uncle Sanya sounded as if he was no longer alone. They heard him saying things like:

'Behave yourself, there is enough for everybody. All right you take this, have an extra wrap ... open your mouth ... here ... you don't have to fight over that bit, here's another piece of crayfish ... behave, I said ...'

And they would hear what sounded like the slapping of wrists, a scrape of dishes on the ground or water slopping into a cup.

---

* An offering, food shared out as offering.

When the woman judged it was time, which was well after dusk, nearly six hours after Sanya was first locked up, she went and opened the door. There was Sanya fast asleep but, this time, very peacefully. She touched his forehead and appeared to be satisfied by the change. The household who had crowded in with her had no interest in Sanya however. All they could see, with astonished faces, were the scattered leaves of 50 wraps of *àgìdì*, with the contents gone, a large empty dish which was earlier filled with *èkuru*, and a water-pot nearly empty.

No, there was no question about it, our Uncle Sanya was an *òrò*; Wild Christian had seen and heard proofs of it many times over. His companions were obviously the more benevolent type or he would have come to serious harm on more than one occasion. J.J.'s protecting Faith notwithstanding. Uncle Sanya was very rarely with us at this time, so we could not ask him any of the questions which Wild Christian refused to answer. When he next visited us at the parsonage, I noticed his strange eyes which hardly ever seemed to blink but looked straight over our heads even when he talked to us. But he seemed far too active to be an *òrò*; indeed for a long time I confused him with a local scoutmaster who was nicknamed Activity. So I began to watch the Wolf Cubs who seemed nearest to the kind of secret company which our Uncle Sanya may have kept as a child. As their tight little faces formed circles on the lawns of Aké, building little fires, exchanging secret signs with hands and twigs, with stones specially placed against one another during their jamboree, I felt I had detected the hidden companions who crept in unseen through chinks in the door and even from the ground, right under the aggrieved noses of Wild Christian and the other children in J.J.'s household, and feasted on 50 wraps of *àgìdì* and a huge bowl of *èkuru*.

The Mission left the parsonage just a vicar and his catechist; Aké was no longer worth a bishop. But even the Vicar's 'court' is a mere shell of itself. The orchard has vanished, the rows of lemon grass have long been eaten by goats. Lemon grass, the cure of fevers and headaches—an aspirin or two, a cup of hot lemon grass tea and bed. But its effusion was really fragrant and we drank it normally as a variant of the common tea. Stark, shrunk with time is that white square monument which, framed against the rocks dominated the parsonage, focussing the eye on itself as a visitor entered the parsonage gate. The master of that house was a chunk from those rocks, black, huge, granite head and enormous feet.

Mostly, they called him Pastor. Or Vicar, Canon, Reverend. Or, like my mother, simply Pa Delumo. Father's choice was Canon and this also became my own, but only because of a visit to Ibara. We made several of those outings; visit to relations, accompanying Wild Christian on her shopping expeditions or for some other purpose which we could never grasp. At the end of such outings however, we were left with a vague notion of having been taken out to see something, to experience something. We were left with exhilaration—and of course exhaustion, since we walked most of the way. But sometimes it was difficult to recall what concrete things we had seen, what had been the purpose of our setting out, specially dressed and neatly combed. And with much bustle and preparation.

We had climbed a steep road and come on the imposing entrance—the white pillars and plaque which said: THE RESIDENCY. Some white man clearly lived there, the gate was patrolled by a policeman in baggy shorts who stared over our heads. The house itself was set well back up a hill, part hidden by trees. But the objects on which my eyes were fastened were two black heavy-snouted tubes mounted on wooden wheels. They stood against the pillars, pointed at us, and beside each one was a pile of round metallic balls, nearly as big as footballs. They are guns, my mother said, they are called cannons, and they are used to fight wars.

'But why does Papa call Pa Delumo a cannon?'

She explained the difference but I had already found my own answer. It was the head, Pa Delumo's head was like a cannon ball, that was why father called him Canon. Everything about the guns recalled the man's presence, his strength and solidity. The cannons looked immobile, indestructible, and so did he. He seemed to overwhelm everything; when he came to visit us he filled the front room completely. Only the parlour appeared to suit him, once he was sunk in one of the armchairs he became easier to contain. I felt sorry for his catechists, junior vicar or curate—his assistants seemed to have different names also—they appeared insipid, starved parodies of himself, so seemingly poor in spirit that I would later think of them as church mice. Of the men who came to our house wearing a round collar, only our uncle Ransome-Kuti—whom everyone called Daodu—matched and even exceeded his personality. Pa Delumo's presence awed me, he dominated not merely the parsonage but Aké itself, and did this more effectively than Kabiyesi, our Oba at whose feet I often saw men fall prostrate. Occasionally I met far more mysterious clerics, elusive, with their own very private awesomeness, such as Bishop Howells who lived in retirement not far from our house. But the Canon was the vicar of St Peter's and he filled the paths and lawns completely as he strode downhill to visit his flock and deliver his booming sermons.

The Canon came often for discussion with father. Sometimes the talk was serious, other times his laughter resounded throughout the house. But they never argued. Certainly I never heard them argue about God the way my father carried on with the bookseller or his other friends. It was frightening at first to hear them discuss God in this way. The bookseller especially, with his shrill voice and turkey neck, he seemed to be poorly equipped, physically, for such flippant statements about such a Power. The Canon sometimes seemed to be that Power, so the contest, conducted though it was indirectly, seemed very unequal and risky for the bookseller. My father of course I assumed to be specially invulnerable. Once, the Canon was walking across the parsonage while they argued on something which had to do with the birth of Christ. They spoke at the top of their voices, sometimes all at once. The Canon was separated from them by no further than the lawn outside and I wondered, when he stopped suddenly, if he had overheard and was about to come and rebuke them.

But he had only stopped to talk to a little boy held by the hand by a woman, perhaps his mother. He stooped to pat him on the head, his large mouth opened in an endless smile and the corners of his eyes broke into wrinkles. His forehead creased—sometimes it was difficult to tell whether he was pleased at something or he had a sudden headache. His jacket was far too small, the trousers stopped some distance above his ankles and his round collar seemed about to choke him. The broad-brimmed clerical hat squashed his giant figure—I glanced quickly to see if he had suddenly diminished in size and was reassured by his enormous shoes which, I learnt from a cousin, were called No-Size-in-London. I obtained a last flash of his vast bottom before he straightened up and the woman's hand vanished totally from sight as he encased it in his own. These alternations between superhuman possibilities and ordinary ill-fitting clothes unsettled me, I wished he would remain permanently in his cassock and surplice.

Essay's favourite position in all arguments was the devil's advocate—he was called S. A. from his initials, HM or Headmaster, or Es-Ay-Sho by his more rumbustious friends. For some reason, few called him by his own name and, for a long time, I wondered if he had any. It did not take long for him to enter my consciousness simply as Essay, as one of those careful stylistic exercises in prose which follow set rules of composition, are products of fastidiousness and elegance, set down in beautiful calligraphy that would be the envy of most copyists of any age. His despair was real that he should give birth to a son who, from the beginning, showed clearly that he had inherited nothing of his own handwriting. He displayed the same elegance in his dressing. His eating habits were a source of marvel to mother, who by contrast I soon named The Wild Christian. When Essay dissected a piece of yam, weighed it carefully, transferred it to his plate, paused, turned it around, sliced off a piece and returned it to the dish, then commenced the same ritual with the meat and stew, she would shake her head and ask,

'Does that extra piece really matter?'

Essay merely smiled, proceeded to chew methodically, slicing off each piece of meat, yam, like a geometric exercise, lifting a scoop of stew with the edge of his knife and plastering the slice of yam like a master mason. He never drank between mouthfuls, not even a sip. At debate time however, he soon grew as excitable as the bookseller, the shrillest of them all with his tiny twinkling eyes. He appeared to have the sun permanently beamed in his eyes. The bookseller brought into the house that aura of guinea-fowl, turkeys, sheep and goats all of which he raised in his abundant compound. The sheep were always being rounded up; either the gates had been left carelessly open by a visitor or the stubborn animals had found yet another gap in the stone-and-mud walls. Thin and peppery, leather-taut cheekbones thrust out restlessly, he punctuated his discourse with bird-like gestures. Even at his most aggressive his shoulders slouched, his fingers refused to release the cloth-cap which, outside, never left his head, perhaps because he was completely bald. We could tell his laughter apart, shrill and raspy, revealing gapped teeth which imparted to his face, finally, the look of an old wicker-chair.

The bookseller's wife was one of our many mothers; if we had taken a vote on the question, she would be in the forefront of all the others, including our real one. With a bovine-beauty, jet-black skin and inexhaustible goodness, she nevertheless put disquieting thoughts in my head, and all because of her husband. By contrast to him, she was ample, and sometimes when the bookseller disappeared for days, I felt certain that she had just swallowed him up. It was with great relief that I would encounter his bald head bobbing about in animation somewhere in his house or in the bookshop. Of all the women on whose backs I was carried, none was as secure and comfortable as Mrs B's. It was capacious, soft and reassuring, it radiated the same repose and kindliness that we had observed in her face.

We slept often at the bookseller's. Mrs B would send a maid to inform our house that we would eat and sleep at their house for the night, and that was that. When we got into trouble we ran behind her and she shielded us:

'No no, I take the beating on myself....'

Wild Christian tried to reach round her with the stick, but there was simply too much of her. Unless the offence was particularly serious, that was the end of the matter.

Her only daughter, Bukola, was not of our world. When we threw our voices against the school walls of Lower Parsonage and listened to them echo from a long distance, it seemed to me that Bukola was one of the denizens of that other world where the voice was caught, sieved, re-spun and cast back in diminishing copies. Amulets, bangles, tiny rattles and dark copper-twist rings

earthed her through ankles, fingers, wrists and waist. She knew she was
*àbikú.** The two tiny cicatrices on her face were also part of the many coun-
ters to enticements by her companions in the other world. Like all *àbikú* she
was privileged, apart. Her parents dared not scold her for long or earnestly.

Suddenly her eyes would turn inwards, showing nothing but the whites.
She would do it for our benefit whenever we asked her. Tinu stood at a distance ready to run away, somehow she expected terrible things to follow. I
asked Bukola:

'Can you see when you do that with your eyes?'

'Only darkness.'

'Do you remember anything of the other world?'

'No. But that is where I go when I fall into a trance.'

'Can you fall into a trance now?'

From her safe distance Tinu threatened to report to our parents if I encouraged her. Bukola merely replied that she could, but only if I was sure I
could call her back.

I was not very sure that I could do that. Looking at her, I wondered how
Mrs B. coped with such a supernatural being who died, was re-born, died
again and kept going and coming as often as she pleased. As we walked, the
bells on her anklets jingled, driving off her companions from the other world
who pestered her incessantly, pleading that she should rejoin them.

'Do you actually hear them?'

'Often.'

'What do they say?'

'Simply that I should come and play with them.'

'Haven't they got anyone to play with? Why do they bother you?'

She shrugged. I felt resentful. Bukola was after all our own playmate. Then
I had an idea.

'Why don't you bring them over here? Next time they call you, invite them
to come and play with us in our own compound.'

She shook her head. 'They can't do that.'

'Why not?'

'They cannot move as we do. Just as you cannot go over there.'

She was so rare, this privileged being who, unlike Tinu and me, and even
her companions in that other place, could pass easily from one sphere to another. I had seen her once during her fainting spell, her eyes rolled upwards,
teeth tightly clenched while her body went limp. Mrs B. kept wailing:

---

* A child which is born, dies, is born again and dies in a repetitive cycle.

'Egbà mi, ara è ma ntutu! Ara è ma ntutu!'* desperately chafing her limbs to bring her back to life. The bookseller ran from the shop through the adjoining door and forced her teeth open. The maid had already snatched a bottle from the cupboard and together some liquid was forced down her throat. The àbikú did not immediately regain consciousness but I could tell, after a little while, that the danger had passed. The household grew less tense, they stretched her on the bed and she relaxed totally, her face suffused with an unnatural beauty. We sat beside her, Tinu and I, watching until she woke. Her mother then made her drink some light fish soup which she had busied herself preparing while she slept. Normally we would all eat from the same bowl but this time, Mrs B. transferred some of the soup to a smaller pot to which she then added some thick liquid from a bottle. It was brackish and had a pungent smell. While we spooned our soup from a separate bowl, Mrs B. held her daughter's head back and made her drink her own soup in one go. Bukola evidently expected it; she drank her potion without any complaint.

Afterwards we went out to play. The crisis was completely over. Mrs B. however insisted that we remain within their compound. I reminded Bukola of that spell. 'Was it your other playmates who called you then?'

'I don't remember.'

'But you can do it any time you want.'

'Yes, especially if my parents do something to annoy me. Or the maid.'

'But how do you do it? How do you actually *do* it? I know your eyes first turn all white....'

'Do they? All I know is that if ... let us say I want something, and my mother says No. It isn't all the time mind you, but sometimes my father and mother will deny me something. So then I may hear my other companions saying, "You see, they don't want you there, that is what we've been telling you." They may say that and then I get a feeling of wanting to go away. I really *want* to go away. I always tell my parents, I will go, I will go if you don't do so and so. If they don't, I just faint.'

'What happens if you don't come back.'

'But I always come back.'

It made me uneasy. Mrs B. was too kind a woman to be plagued with such an awkward child. Yet we knew she was not being cruel; an àbikú was that way, they could not help their nature. I thought of all the things Bukola could ask for, things which would be beyond the power of her parents to grant.

---

* Help me, she is getting cold all over!

'Suppose one day you ask for something they cannot give you. Like the Alake's motor-car.'

'They have to give me what I ask,' she insisted.

'But there are things they don't have. Even a king doesn't have everything.'

'The last time it happened I only asked for a *sàarà*. My father refused. He said I had one not so long ago, so I fainted. I was really going.'

Tinu protested, 'But one cannot have a *sàarà* every day.'

'I don't have a *sàarà* every day,' she persisted. 'And the *sàarà* I asked for that time was not for me, it was for my companions. They told me that if I couldn't come to play with them just yet, I should make them *sàarà*. I told my mother and she agreed, but father refused.' She shrugged. 'That is what happens when grown-ups refuse to understand. Papa had to kill an extra fowl because it took longer than usual for me to come back.'

Her oval, solemn face changed from innocence to authority as she spoke. I watched her intently, wondering if she was scheming another departure. Natural as it all seemed, there was also a vague disquiet that this was too much power for a child to wield over her parents. I went over all the faces at the *sàarà*, the movement of food and drinks, the sudden disputes that rose as we ate, and the peace-making voices of the grown-ups; nothing unusual appeared to have happened. It had been a *sàarà* like any other. We sat in groups on mats spread out in the garden, all in outing dresses, Bukola especially gorgeously dressed. Her eyes were deeply marked in antimony and her face powdered. She ate at our mat, from the same dish, there was nothing other-worldly about her; certainly I had not seen her giving food secretly to other companions, yet the *sàarà* was for them.

I wondered sometimes if Mr B. took refuge in our house to escape the tyranny of this child. Fond of arguments as father was, on any subject on earth or in heaven, it was the bookseller who usually prolonged their disputations far into the night. He would worry the dead flesh of an argument with hawk-like talons, conceding a point with the greatest reluctance, only to return to a position long discarded or overtaken by new arguments. Even I could tell that, and the exaggerated patience in Essay's voice only served to confirm it.

And sometimes their arguments took frightening turns. One day the bookseller, Fowokan the junior headmaster of the primary school, the catechist and one other of Essay's cronies followed him home from church service. Osibo the pharmacist enjoyed sitting on these sessions but took little part in them. Their voices had long preceded them into the house, they were all hotly wrapped in the debate, talking all at once and refusing to yield a point. It went on right through bottles of warm beer and soft drinks, exhausted Wild Christian's stock of chin-chin and sweet biscuits and carried over into lunch. Even as she shook her head in despair at 'these friends of your father', wondering why he always managed to attract to himself friends with such stomachs for arguments and food, it was obvious that Wild Christian enjoyed the rôle played by the Headmaster's house as the intellectual watering-hole of Aké and its environs.

Towards late afternoon, tea and sandwiches or cakes refueled their vocal powers for the final rally, for by then it was approaching the hour of evening service and they all had to return home for a change of clothing. It was usually at this time that Bukola's father seemed in the greatest danger. The arguments would take a physical turn with the bookseller, always the bookseller, about to be made the sacrificial proof of some point of disagreement. My loyalty to his wife created a terrible dilemma. I felt it was my duty to run and warn her that her husband was about to be sold into slavery, banished from Abeokuta, dropped from an aeroplane, hurled from the church tower, tied to a tree in the dead of night alone with evil spirits, sent on an investigatory mission to hell or on a peace mission to Hitler ... always some dangerous consequence of a going argument, and the only way, they would all decide, in which it could be resolved. That day, these friends actually wanted to cut off one of Mr B's limbs.

'All right, shall I tell Joseph to sharpen the cutlass?'

The argument had started from that morning's sermon. It had gone a hundred different ways at different times and, as usual, the bookseller's gesticulating arms had fanned the embers back to life when every point had been exhausted. Now he seemed about to lose the arm. Still, he fought back. He always did.

'Did I tell you that my right arm had offended me?'

Amidst laughter—and this was the strangest part, they always laughed—Essay called out to Joseph to bring the cutlass.

Mr Fowokan offered. 'Or an axe. Whichever is sharper.'

Mr B's hands flapped out even more desperately, 'Wait, wait. Did I tell you that my arm had offended me?'

'Are you now saying that you are without sin?' the Catechist countered.

'No, but who is to say definitely that it was my hand which committed the sin? And which arm are you going to cut off, left or right?'

'Well ...' My father gave the matter some thought. 'You are left-handed. So the probability is that your left hand committed the sin. Joseph!'

'Not so fast. Let's go over God's injunction again ... if thine right hand offendeth thee ... note, *offended thee* ... it says nothing about committing a sin. My right hand may commit a sin, or my left. That makes it an offence against God. But that does not mean that *I* am offended. God may be offended, but it is up to him to take whatever action he pleases.'

Essay looked shocked. 'You are now claiming that an offence against God is not to be regarded as an offence against man? You refuse to take God's side against sin?'

Hastily, the bookseller reassured God. 'No, don't put words into my mouth. I never said such a thing....'

With one accord they shouted, 'Good. In that case let's waste no more time.'

Joseph had already arrived and was waiting in the wings. My father took the cutlass, the others seized the bookseller.

'Wait, wait,' the man pleaded. I turned to Tinu with whom I eavesdropped from the corner of the parlour: 'One of us had better run and fetch Mrs B'. But then she was never really interested in the discussions, so she could not see when an argument had to be put to a dangerous test.

Essay tested the edge of the cutlass with the tip of his thumb. The bookseller shouted: 'But I tell you neither my left nor right hand has offended me.'

My father sighed. 'Today is a Sunday, God's own day. Imagine you're standing before him. You are his servant, a respected sides-man in his church at St Peter's. You insist that Christ's injunctions are meant to be taken literally. All right, God is now asking you, has your right hand *ever* offended thee? Yes or no.'

It was the sort of language which frightened me even more than the violence about to be visited on the bookseller. My father had the habit of speaking as he was on first-name terms with God. Why should he suggest that God would come into our front-room just to prosecute the bookseller! I expected any moment a Visitation worse than the bookseller would ever experience from this unequal contest.

Tinu slipped away. The crowd in the front room were laughing at the bookseller who struggled furiously, especially with his voice. Their laughter made it all the more wicked. Essay scraped the cutlass along the concrete floor and advanced one step. The bookseller suddenly wriggled free, flung open the door and escaped. Yelling 'After him! Catch him' they all dispersed, remembering to fling back their thanks to Wild Christian for the Sunday feast. I dashed through the dining-room and the backyard to our gate so I could watch the chase through the parsonage. It ended where the paths separated, one towards the bookseller's compound, the other to the parsonage gate through which the others would regain their own homes. Their laughter rang through the compound as they waved good-bye to one another. I did not appreciate their levity in the least, feeling too deeply thankful that Mrs B. would not have to cope with a one-armed husband in addition to that wilful *àbikú*.

Chapter 8

Community, Folk Culture, and Socioeconomic Realism

Categorizing the topics of community, folk culture, and socioeconomic realism as one unit is an attempt to present Black literature's response to various sociological environments, which is consistent with Donatus Ibe Nwoga's observation: "All literatures arise from specific interactions of social forces within a sociological environment. They express the environment, reflect upon it, and are in turn impacted upon the environment. The process involved is a cycle—or, more exactly, a spiral."[1] A socioliterary approach to Black literature is appropriate for texts that creatively chronicle the *ethos*, or the character and disposition of Black communities. The *folk*, or members of the community whose ways of life (including language and speech patterns, religious practices, beliefs, superstitions, rhetoric, philosophies, art forms, humor, and intergenerational communication), are representative of an unadulterated version of Black culture. The value of folk culture is measured by its function within the Black community, and it represents philosophies of proactive self-love and self-affirmation, as well as behaviors and ideologies of resistance to the outside oppressive hegemonic society that lies beyond the domain of the community. The resistance is based on the tug-of-war between the community and the larger society that competes for ideological and physical control of the folk through governing, media, technology, and work options.

Folk culture, existing within bona fide Black communities, is a sort of counterculture to the mainstream, Eurocentric society. The folk community creates and practices unique strategies for survival as a matter of circumstances (e.g., poverty, limited employment and opportunities, segregation, low income, and limited access to social services), and its separatism from mainstream society is a healthy, deliberate Black nationalistic choice. As another

---

1. Donatus Ibe Nwoga, "Bilingualism and Literary Creativity," in *English: New Perspectives* (Frankfurt: Peter Lang, 1990), 106.

comparative variable in literary analysis, capitalism (and class analysis) can be interpreted as socioeconomic realism. Black writers approach the topics of money and material assets in a range of contexts that demonstrate the consequences of how different communities respond to their wealth and assets, or lack thereof. The literary treatment of socioeconomic realism can yield complex and informative analyses of human relationships, identity, institutions, and change. Issues such as community leadership, group identity versus individual identity, cultural hierarchies of power, and sustained progress over time are also introduced in the Black literatures that address community, folk culture, and socioeconomic realism. Considering these three topics in synthesis can highlight how literature, though mostly fiction, can transmit common sense. Experiencing folk realism in literature encourages readers to approach life in a way that permits them to embrace the good but also appreciate the lessons that can come from adversity. The folk response is essentially a *blues* aesthetic, as the human spirit prevails and survives by using humor, irony, camaraderie, and creative philosophies to strategically respond to life.

The Lesson

by Toni Cade Bambara (USA)

Back in the days when everyone was old and stupid or young and foolish and me and Sugar were the only ones just right, this lady moved on our block with nappy hair and proper speech and no makeup. And quite naturally we laughed at her, laughed the way we did at the junk man who went about his business like he was some big-time president and his sorry-ass horse his secretary. And we kinda hated her too, hated the way we did the winos who cluttered up our parks and pissed on our handball walls and stank up our hallways and stairs so you couldn't halfway play hide-and-seek without a goddamn gas mask. Miss Moore was her name. The only woman on the block with no first name. And she was black as hell, cept for her feet, which were fish-white and spooky. And she was always planning these boring-ass things for us to do, us being my cousin, mostly, who lived on the block cause we all moved North the same time and to the same apartment then spread out gradual to breathe. And our parents would yank our heads into some kinda shape and crisp up our clothes so we'd be presentable for travel with Miss Moore, who always looked like she was going to church, though she never did. Which is just one of things the grown-ups talked about when they talked behind her back like a dog. But when she came calling with some sachet she'd sewed up or some gingerbread she'd made or some book, why then they'd all be too embarrassed to turn her down and we'd get handed over all spruced up. She'd been to college and said it was only right that she should take responsibility for the young ones' education, and she not even related by marriage or blood. So they'd go for it. Specially Aunt Gretchen. She was the main gofer in the family. You got some ole dumb shit foolishness you want somebody to go for, you send for Aunt Gretchen. She been screwed into the go-along for so long, it's a blood-deep natural thing with her. Which is how she got saddled with me and Sugar and Junior in the first place while our mothers were in a la-de-da apartment up the block having a good ole time.

So this one day Miss Moore rounds us all up at the mailbox and it's puredee hot and she's knockin herself out about arithmetic. And school suppose to let up in summer I heard, but she don't never let up. And the starch in my pinafore scratching the shit outta me and I'm really hating this nappy-head bitch and her goddamn college degree. I'd much rather go to the pool or to the show where it's cool. So me and Sugar leaning on the mailbox being surly, which is a Miss Moore word. And Flyboy checking out what everybody brought for lunch. And Fat Butt already wasting his peanut-butter-and-jelly sandwich like the pig he is. And Junebug punchin on Q.T.'s arm for potato chips. And Rosie Giraffe shifting from one hip to the other waiting for somebody to step on her foot or ask her if she from Georgia so she can kick ass, preferably Mercedes'. And Miss Moore asking us do we know what money is, like we a bunch of re-tards. I mean real money, she say, like it's only poker chips or monopoly papers we lay on the grocer. So right away I'm tired of this and say so. And would much rather snatch Sugar and go to the Sunset and terrorize the West Indian kids and take their hair ribbons and their money too. And Miss Moore files that remark away for next week's lesson on brotherhood, I can tell. And finally I say we oughta get to the subway cause it's cooler and besides we might meet some cute boys. Sugar done swiped her mama's lipstick, so we ready.

So we heading down the street and she's boring us silly about what things cost and what our parents make and how much goes for rent and how money ain't divided up right in this country. And then she gets to the part about we all poor and live in the slums, which I don't feature. And I'm ready to speak on that, but she steps out in the street and hails two cabs just like that. Then she hustles half the crew in with her and hands me a five-dollar bill and tells me to calculate 10 percent tip for the driver. And we're off. Me and Sugar and Junebug and Flyboy hangin out the window and hollering to everybody, putting lipstick on each other cause Flyboy a faggot anyway, and making farts with our sweaty armpits. But I'm mostly trying to figure how to spend this money. But they all fascinated with the meter ticking and Junebug starts laying bets as to how much it'll read when Flyboy can't hold his breathe no more.

Then Sugar lays bets as to how much it'll be when we get there. So I'm stuck. Don't nobody want to go for my plan, which is to jump out at the next light and run off to the first bar-b-que we can find. Then the driver tells us to get the hell out cause we there already. And the meter reads eighty-five cents. And I'm stalling to figure out the tip and Sugar say give him a dime. And I decide he don't need it bad as I do, so later for him. But then he tries to take off with Junebug foot still in the door so we talk about his mama something ferocious. Then we check out that we on Fifth Avenue and everybody dressed up in stockings. One lady in a fur coat, hot as it is. White folks crazy.

"This is the place," Miss Moore say, presenting it to us in the voice she uses at the museum. "Let's look in the windows before we go in."

"Can we steal?" Sugar asks very serious like she's getting the ground rules squared away before she plays. "I beg your pardon," say Miss Moore, and we fall out. So she leads us around the windows of the toy store and me and Sugar screamin, "This is mine, that's mine, I gotta have that, that was made for me, I was born for that," till Big Butt drowns us out.

"Hey, I'm going to buy that there."

"That there? You don't even know what it is, stupid."

"I do so," he say punchin on Rosie Giraffe. "It's a microscope."

"Whatcha gonna do with a microsope, fool?"

"Look at things."

"Like what, Ronald?" ask Miss Moore. And Big Butt ain't got the first notion. So here go Miss Moore gabbing about the thousands of bacteria in a drop of water and the some-thinorother in a speck of blood and the million and one living things in the air around us is invisible to the naked eye. And what she say that for? Junebug go to town on that "naked" and we rolling. Then Miss Moore ask what it cost. So we all jam into the window smudgin it up and the price tag say $300. So then she ask how long'd take for Big Butt and Junebug to save up their allowances. "Too long," I say. "Yeh," adds Sugar, "outgrown it by that time." And Miss Moore say no, you never outgrow learning instruments. "Why, even medical students and interns and," blah, blah, blah. And we ready to choke Big Butt for bringing it up in the first damn place.

"This here costs four hundred eighty dollars," say Rosie Giraffe. So we pile up all over her to see what she pointin out. My eyes tell me it's a chunk of glass cracked with something heavy, and the different-color inks dripped into the splits, then the whole thing put into a oven or something. But for $480 it don't make sense.

"That's a paperweight made of semi-precious stones fused together under tremendous pressure," she explains slowly, with her hands doing the mining and all the factory work.

"So what's a paperweight?" asks Rosie Giraffe.

"To weigh paper with, dumbbell," say Flyboy, the wise man from the East.

"Not exactly," say Miss Moore, which is what she say when you warm or way off too. "It's to weigh paper down so it won't scatter and make your desk untidy." So right away me and Sugar curtsy to each other and then to Mercedes who is more the tidy type.

"We don't keep paper on top of the desk in my class," say Junebug, figuring Miss Moore crazy or lying one.

"At home, then," she say. "Don't you have a calendar and a pencil case and a blotter and a letter-opener on your desk at home where you do your homework?" And she know damn well what our homes look like cause she nosys around in them every chance she gets.

"I don't even have a desk," say Junebug. "Do we?"

"No. And I don't get no homework neither," say Big Butt.

"And I don't even have a home," say Flyboy like he do at school to keep the white folks off his back and sorry for him. Send this poor kid to camp posters, is his specialty.

"I do," say Mercedes. "I have a box of stationery on my desk and a picture of my cat. My godmother bought the stationery and the desk. There's a big rose on each sheet and the envelopes smell like roses."

"Who want to know about your smelly-ass stationery," say Rosie Giraffe fore I can get my two cents in.

"It's important to have a work area all your own so that ..."

"Will you look at this sailboat, please," say Flyboy, cuttin her off and pointin to the thing like it was his. So once again we tumble all over each other to gaze at this magnificent thing in the toy store which is just big enough to maybe sail two kittens across the pond if you strap them to the posts tight. We all start reciting the price tag like we in assembly. "Handcrafted sailboat of fiberglass at one thousand one hundred ninety-five dollars."

"Unbelievable," I hear myself say and am really stunned. I read it again for myself just in case the group recitation put me in a trance. Same thing. For some reason this pisses me off. We look at Miss Moore and she lookin at us, waiting for I dunno what.

"Who'd pay all that when you can buy a sailboat set for a quarter at Pop's, a tube of glue for a dime, and a ball of string for eight cents? "It must have a motor and a whole lot else besides," I say. "My sailboat costs me about fifty cents."

"But will it take water?" say Mercedes with her smart ass.

"Took mine to Alley Pond Park once," say Flyboy. "String broke, Lost it. Pity."

"Sailed mine in Central Park and it keeled over and sank. Had to ask my father for another dollar."

"And you got the strap," laugh Big Butt. "The jerk didn't even have a string on it. My old man wailed on his behind."

Little Q.T. was staring hard at the sailboat and you could see he wanted it bad. But he too little and somebody'd just take it from him. So what the hell. "This boat for kids, Miss Moore?"

"Parents silly to buy something like that just to get all broke up," say Rosie Giraffe.

"That much money it should last forever," I figure.

"My father'd buy if for me if I wanted it."

"Your father, my ass," say Rosie Giraffe getting a chance to finally push Mercedes.

"Must be rich people shop here," say Q.T.

"You are a very bright boy," say Flyboy. "What was your first clue?" And he rap him on the head with the back of his knuckles, since Q.T. the only one he could get away with. Though Q.T. liable to come up behind you years later and get his licks in when you half expect it.

"What I want to know is," I says to Miss Moore though I never talk to her, I wouldn't give the bitch that satisfaction, "is how much a real boat costs? I figure a thousand'd get you a yacht any day."

"Why don't you check that out," she says, "and report back to the group?" Which really pains my ass. If you gonna mess up a perfectly good swim day least you could do is have some answers. "Let's go in," she say like she got something up her sleeve. Only she don't lead the way. So me and Sugar turn the corner to where the entrance is, but when we get there, I kinda hang back. Not that I'm scared, what's there to be afraid of, just a toy store. But I feel funny, shame. But what I got to be shamed about? Got as much right to go in as anybody. But somehow I can't seem to get hold of the door, so I step away for Sugar to lead. But she hangs back too. And I look at her and she looks at me and this is ridiculous. I mean, damn, I have never ever been shy about doing nothing or going nowhere. But then Mercedes steps up and then Rosie Giraffe and Big Butt crowd in behind and shove, and next thing we all stuffed into the doorway with only Mercedes squeezing past us, smoothing out her jumper and walking right down the aisle. Then the rest of us tumble in like a glued-together jigsaw done all wrong. And people lookin at us. And it's like the time me and Sugar crashed into the Catholic church on a dare. But once we got in there and everything so hushed and holy and the candles and the bowin and the handkerchiefs on all the drooping heads, I just couldn't go through with the plan. Which was for me to run up to the altar and do a tap dance while Sugar played the nose flute and messed around in the holy water. And Sugar kept givin me the elbow. Then later teased me so bad I tied her up in the shower and turned it on and locked her in. And she'd be there till this day if Aunt Gretchen hadn't finally figured I was lyin about the boarder takin a shower.

Same thing in the store. We all walkin on tiptoe and hardly touchin the games and puzzles and things. And I watched Miss Moore who is steady watchin us like she waitin for a sign. Like Mama Drewery watches the sky and sniffs the air and takes note of just how much slant is in the bird formation. Then me and Sugar bump smack into each other, so busy gazing at the toys, 'specially the sailboat. But we don't laugh and go into our fat-lady bump-stomach routine. We just stare at that price tag. Then Sugar run a finger over the whole boat. And I'm jealous and want to hit her. Maybe not her, but I sure want to punch somebody in the mouth.

"Watcha bring us here for, Miss Moore?"

"You sound angry, Sylvia. Are you mad about something?" Givin me one of them grins like she tellin a grown-up joke that never turns out to be funny. And she's lookin very closely at me like maybe she plannin to do my portrait from memory. I'm mad, but I won't give her that satisfaction. So I slouch around the store bein very bored and say, "Let's go."

Me and Sugar at the back of the train watchin the tracks whizzin by large then small then gettin gobbled up in the dark. I'm thinkin about this tricky toy I saw in the store. A clown that somersaults on a bar then does chin-ups just cause you yank lightly at his leg. Cost $35. I could see me askin my mother for a $35 birthday clown. "You wanna who that costs what?" she'd say, cocking her head to the side to get a better view of the hole in my head. Thirty-five dollars could buy new bunk beds for Junior and Gretchen's boy. Thirty-five dollars and the whole household could go visit Granddaddy Nelson in the country. Thirty-five dollars would pay for the rent and the piano bill too. Who are these people that spend that much for performing clowns and $1,000 for toy sailboats? What kinda work they do and how they live and how come we ain't in on it? Where we are is who we are, Miss Moore always pointin out. But it don't necessarily have to be that way, she adds then waits for somebody to say that poor people have to wake up and demand their share of the pie and don't none of us know what kind of pie she talkin about in the first damn place. But she ain't so smart cause I still got her four dollars from the taxi and she sure ain't gettin it. Messin up my day with this shit. Sugar nudges me in my pocket and winks.

Miss Moore lines us up in front of the mailbox where we started from, seem like years ago, and I got a headache for thinkin so hard. And we lean all over each other so we can hold up under the draggy-ass lecture she always finishes us off with at the end before we thank her for borin us to tears. But she just looks at us like she readin tea leaves. Finally she say, "Well, what did you think of F.A.O. Schwartz?"

Rosie Giraffe mumbles, "White folks crazy."

"I'd like to go there again when I get my birthday money," says Mercedes, and we shove her out the pack so she has to lean on the mailbox by herself.

"I'd like a shower. Tiring day," say Flyboy.

Then Sugar surprises me by sayin, "You know, Miss Moore, I don't think all of us here put together eat in a year what that sailboat costs." And Miss Moore lights up like somebody goosed her. "And?" she say, urging Sugar on. Only I'm standin on her foot so she don't continue.

"Imagine for a minute what kind of society it is in which some people can spend on a toy what it would cost to feed a family of six or seven. What do you think?"

"I think," say Sugar pushing me off her feet like she never done before, cause I whip her ass in a minute, "that this is not much of a democracy if you ask me. Equal chance to pursue happiness means an equal crack at the dough, don't it?" Miss Moore is besides herself and I am disgusted with Sugar's treachery. So I stand on her foot one more time to see if she'll shove me. She shuts up, and Miss Moore looks at me, sorrowfully I'm thinkin. And somethin weird is goin on, I can feel it in my chest.

"Anybody else learn anything today?" lookin dead at me. I walk away and Sugar has to run to catch up and don't even seem to notice when I shrug her arm off my shoulder.

"Well, we got four dollars anyway," she says.

"Uh hunh."

"We could go to Hascombs and get half a chocolate layer and then go to the Sunset and still have plenty money for potato chips and ice-cream sodas."

"Uh hunh."

"Race you to Hascombs," she say.

We start down the block and she gets ahead which is O.K. by me cause I'm goin to the West End and then over to the Drive to think this day through. She can run if she want to and even run faster. But ain't nobody gonna beat me at nuthin.

from *Xala*

by Ousmane Sembene (Senegal)

The 'businessmen' had met to mark the day with a celebration worthy of the event. Never before in the history of Senegal had the Chamber of Commerce

and Industry been headed by an African. For the first time a Senegalese occupied the President's seat. It was their victory. For ten long years these en-
terprising men had struggled to capture this last bastion of the colonial era
from their adversaries.

They had come together from different sectors of the business community
to form the 'Businessmen's Group' in order to combat the invasion of foreign
interests. It was their ambition to gain control of their country's economy.
Their anxiety to constitute a social clan of their own had increased their com-
bativity, tingeing it with xenophobia. Over the years they had managed—with
some help from the politicians—to obtain a foothold in the wholesale trade,
and to a lesser extent in the import and export field. They had become more
ambitious and had tried to acquire a stake in the administration of the banks.
In their public statements they had specified those branches of the economy
which they felt were theirs by right: the wholesale trade, public works contracts, the pharmacies, the private clinics, the bakeries, the manufacturing industry, the bookshops and cinemas; but their exclusion from the banks had
first stimulated then sharpened a nationalist feeling from which expectations
of improved social status were not entirely absent.

The appointment of one of their number as President of the Chamber of
Commerce and Industry gave them renewed hope. For the men gathered together on this auspicious day, the road was now open that led to certain
wealth. It meant access to the heart of the country's economy, a foothold in
the world of high finance, and of course, the right to walk with head held
high. Yesterday's dreams were beginning to come true. The full significance of
what was happening today would be felt in the days to come. Its importance
fully justified this celebration.

The Group's President paused in his speech. His eyes shone with satisfaction as they came to rest on each member of his audience in turn: ten or so
expensively dressed men. The cut of their made-to-measure suits and their
immaculate shirts were ample evidence of their success.

Smiling and relaxed, the President resumed his speech: 'Friends, this is a
great occasion. Since the beginning of foreign occupation no African has ever
been President of the Chamber' (Perhaps because of their megalomania, they
always referred to the 'Chamber of Commerce and Industry' as 'the Chamber'.) 'In appointing me to this post of great responsibility our government has
acted with courage and shown its determination to achieve economic independence in these difficult times. This is indeed an historic occasion. We owe
a debt of gratitude to our government and to the man at its head.'

They broke into applause, congratulating themselves on their victory. Calm
returned amid coughing and scraping of chairs.

'We are the leading businessmen in the country, so we have a great responsibility. A very great responsibility indeed. We must show that we can measure up to the confidence the government has placed in us. But it is time now to bring this memorable day to a close by reminding you that we are invited to the wedding of our colleague El Hadji Abdou Kader Beye. Although we are anxious to belong to the modern world we haven't abandoned our African customs. I call upon El Hadji to speak.'

El Hadji Abdou Kader Beye, who was seated on the President's right, rose to his feet. His close-cropped hair was streaked with white but he carried his fifty odd years well.

'Friends, at this precise moment (looking at his gold wrist-watch) the marriage has been sealed at the mosque. I am therefore married.'

'Re-married. How many times does that make it?' flung out Laye, the Group's humorist, sarcastically.

'I was coming to that, Laye. I have now married my third wife, so I'm a "captain" as we Africans say. Mr. President, will you all do me the honour of being my guests?'

'A fitting way to end the day. Gentlemen, the women are waiting for us. Shall we go?'

The meeting was over.

Outside a line of expensive cars was waiting for them. El Hadji Abdou Kader Beye drew the President to one side: 'Take the head of the convoy. I must go and collect my other two wives.'

'All right.'

'I won't be long,' said El Hadji, climbing into his black Mercedes.

Modu his chauffeur drove off.

El Hadji Abdou Kader Beye had once been a primary-school teacher, but he had been dismissed from the service because of his involvement in trade-union activity during the colonial period. After his dismissal he had acquired business experience in the grocery trade and had then set himself up as the middleman in property transactions. He had made an increasing number of friends among the Lebanese and Syrian businessmen, one of whom became his associate. For nearly a year they had held a monopoly on the sale of rice, a staple commodity. This period of success had placed him way ahead in the ever-growing field of small middlemen.

Then came Independence. By now he had capital and connections, so he was able to set up on his own. He turned his attention to the south, especially the Congo, concentrating on the importation of dried fish. It was a gold mine, until a competitor with better ships and more solid business connections forced him out. He turned his energies toward Europe, with shell-fish. Lack of funds and inadequate financial backing obliged him to abandon this scheme. However, because he was well-known and had a certain standing in the business community, overseas investors paid him to act as a front. He was also on the boards of two or three local companies. He played his various roles well but, although the law was fooled, everyone knew what was really happening.

He was a good, albeit a non-practising Muslim, so on the strength of his growing affluence he took his first wife on the pilgrimage to Mecca. Hence his title of 'El Hadji', and 'Adja' for his wife. He had six children by this wife, the eldest of whom, Rama, was a student at the university.

El Hadji Abdou Kader Beye was what one might call a synthesis of two cultures: business had drawn him into the European middle class after a feudal African education. Like his peers, he made skillful use of his dual background, for their fusion was not complete.

His second wife, Oumi N'Doye, had given him five children. So, to date El Hadji had two wives and a string of progeny. Eleven in all. Each of his families had its own villa. Being a practical African, he had provided a minibus for their domestic use and to take the children to their various schools in town.

This third marriage raised him to the rank of the traditional notability; it represented a kind of promotion.

* * *

The reception for the third marriage was being held at the home of the young girl's parents. In this, ancient custom was being more than just respected, it was being revived. The house had been invaded since early morning. Male and female griots welcomed the guests—family, friends, acquaintances—who proceeded to gorge themselves with food and drink. Those among them who claimed royal or noble ancestry spent freely, rivaling one another in generosity, and made great display of their clothes and—among the women—of their head-dresses and jewelry. Boubous spangled with silver and gold thread, gold and silver pendants and bracelets glittered in the sunlight. The wide necklines of the women revealed the shimmering, velvety aubergine of their shoulders. The laughter, the clapping of hands, the soft, melodious accents of the women and the thick tones of the men created an atmosphere of noisy well-being, like the gentle roar from inside a sea shell.

In the middle of the main room of the house the husband's gifts were displayed in sets of a dozen each on a trestle-table: lady's underwear, toiletries, shoes in various fashions and colours, wigs from blonde to jet black, fine handkerchiefs and scented soaps. The centre-piece was a red casket inside which lay the keys of a car.

The guests clustered round the table, admiring and commenting on these proofs of love. A young woman wearing a heavy gold bracelet turned to her neighbour and remarked: 'As well as the car, El Hadji has promised her 2,500 gallons of five-star petrol.'

'There are strings attached, my dear,' retorted the neighbour, lifting the wide sleeves of her embroidered silk boubou with a gesture of her hand.

'Strings or not, I'd marry el Hadji even if he had the skin of a crocodile.'

'Ah! But you're no longer a virgin, my dear!'

'You think so?'

'What about your children?'

'And what about the Virgin Mary?'

'Don't blaspheme!' the woman objected sulkily, waving a finger in the other's face. For a moment they glared at each other in silent confrontation.

'I was only joking,' said the first woman, in reluctant conciliation.

'I should hope so,' replied the other, who was a Catholic. She smiled in triumph. Then she spoke, gesturing towards the gifts.

'Personally I'd hate to be one of El Hadji's wives.'

'You can make good soup in an old pot,' murmured the other. She ran her fingers over a skirt to see if it was made of silk or terylene.

'Not with new sweet-potatoes,' replied the second.

They shook with laughter and moved off towards another group of women.

Yay Bineta, the 'mistress of ceremonies', otherwise known as the Bayden (the bride's aunt and her father's sister) was keeping a wary eye on things. A dumpy woman with a large behind, a flabby black face and spiteful eyes, she made sure the guests kept their places according to the rank in this welter of individuals. It was she who had given 'her' daughter in marriage for according to traditional law the brother's child is also his sister's daughter.

Some months previously when they had met at a family gathering, the girl's mother had unburdened herself to her sister-in-law (the Bayden is equal in status to the husband). She had told the Bayden quite frankly of her fears. Her daughter had twice failed the elementary certificate; she was now nineteen years old and her parents could not afford to go on paying for her schooling.

'If she cannot find a job,' said the mother, 'it's Yalla's will. (But deep down she thought her daughter had enough education to be a secretary.) She will have to get married. We must find her a husband. She is at the right age. There have never been any unmarried mothers in our family, although these days it is no exaggeration to say that to be an unmarried mother is the height of fashion.'

Old Babacar, the head of the family who had retired from work, agreed with his wife's arguments for he was finding it impossible to keep his large brood of seven children on his tiny quarterly pension.

'Do you have anyone in mind?' Yay Bineta had asked, fixing her narrow, bean-like eyes on her brother.

Old Babacar lowered his eyes with that feigned modesty of men of religion. Nothing had been ... His wife's authority was limitless. Friends of his own age-group all said that it was Babacar's wife who wore the trousers in the home. The fact too that he had never taken a second wife made him particularly vulnerable to male criticism.

'Yalla is my witness, if N'Gone our daughter had a husband I'd be very happy. But it is all a question of chance, and only Yalla provides that,' he said, speaking with circumspection.

'Yalla! Yalla! You must plough your own field!' retorted his wife angrily as she turned to face Yay Bineta (and in so doing effectively silenced her husband). 'I won't try and hide what kind of young men she goes about with. Until today's sun not a single well-bred, serious, worthwhile man has been to this house. The only ones that come are the sort who don't have a pocket handkerchief and wear clothes only fit for a scarecrow. N'Gone spends all her time going out with them to the cinema and dances. None of them has a job. They're just a lot of loafers. I dread the month when she won't be washing her linen at nights.'*

'I understand,' said Yay Bineta. 'There's a queue of girls waiting for husbands that stretches from here to Bamako. And it is said that the lame ones are in the front.'

Her irony made Babacar laugh, but his laughter stung Mam Fatou, his wife.

'This is women's business,' she said harshly to her husband. Anger began to show at the end of her chin and gathered in her eyes.

Old Babacar meekly withdrew, full of apologies, saying it was time to go and pray. When they were alone Mam Fatou begged the Bayden:

'Yay Bineta, N'Gone is your daughter. You know so many people in N'-Dakaru. People who could help us. Look how we live, like animals in a yard. And if N'Gone or her younger sister brings us bastard children, what will become of us? The way things are these days chance has to be helped along a little.'

Weeks, then months passed. One morning Yay Bineta dressed N'Gone in her best clothes and they went to El Hadji Abdou Kader Beye's shop, where he also had his office. Yay Bineta and El Hadji had known each other for a long time. Yay Bineta immediately set to work to explore the lie of the land.

---

* The menstrual period; the linen is never dried in the daytime so as to keep it out of sight of the men.

'El Hadji, this is my daughter N'Gone. Take a good look at her. Could she not be a kind of measure? A measure of length or a measure of capacity?'

'She is gentle. A drop of dew. She is ephemeral too. A pleasant harbour for the eyes,' replied El Hadji, who had been accustomed to using this kind of language since attaining manhood.

'You say "for the eyes". You speak in the plural. I am talking of the singular. One owner only.'

'One-eyed then!' the man laughed, relaxed.

'You don't tell a person with one eye to close it.'

'No more than you need to show the hand how to find the mouth.'

'You have to prepare something for the hand to take to the mouth.'

This was a game in which Yay Bineta was well versed. She did battle with the man in the ancient, allegorical language preserved by custom. N'Gone, the child of national flags and hymns, understood nothing of what they were saying. The contest was interrupted by the ringing of the phone. The Bayden pretended she was looking for a job for her daughter. The man promised to see what he could do. Careful of his reputation for generosity he gave them a thousand francs to pay for a taxi home.

Other visits followed. Conversations that were all the same, with nothing special about them. The Bayden would bait the man: 'You're afraid of women! Your wives make the decisions, wear the trousers in your house, don't they? Why don't you come and see us? Hey? Why don't you?' El Hadji Abdou Kader Beye was wounded in his pride. His honour as an African in the old tradition was being called into question. He was at last stung into taking up the challenge. 'No woman is going to tell me what to do,' he said to himself. And so, to prove that he was master in his own house, he accompanied them to the home of the girl's parents.

And then what happened? N'Gone began to visit him by herself, especially in the afternoon. She said she had come to see if El Hadji had found her a job, an excuse thought up by the Bayden. The man had slowly succumbed. A change in his feelings began to take place. He became used to her. He felt a growing desire for her. As her visits continued and settled into regularity, El Hadji took her out to tea shops, occasionally to a restaurant. Once or twice they attended the 'businessmen's' cocktail parties.

He had to admit it, N'Gone had the savour of fresh fruit, which was something his wives had long since lost. He was drawn by her firm, supple body, her fresh breath. With his two wives on the one hand and the daily demands of his business life, N'Gone seemed to him like a restful oasis in the middle of the desert. She was good for his pride too—he was attractive to a young woman!

Yay Bineta, the Bayden, kept discreetly out of sight, all the better to direct events. El Hadji Abdou Kader Baye was received in princely style at the girl's home. The food was exquisite and the scent of incense filled N'Gone's small wooden room. Nothing was omitted in the careful process of conditioning the man. The Bayden spun her web as painstakingly as a spider. All the neighbours knew—chiefly from gossip round the public tap—that El Hadji Abdou Kader Beye was courting N'Gone with the most honourable intentions. Skillfully the Bayden got rid of the young men in her daughter's circle. Then the engagement was officially announced.

The fruit was ripe. The Bayden was going to pluck it.

On the day in question El Hadji was to take N'Gone with him to an important reception. The day before he had fitted her out from head to foot in new clothes. Her father, her mother and the Bayden greeted him when he arrived. While they waited for N'Gone to get ready Yay Bineta opened the discussion:

'El Hadji Abdou Kader Beye, you have been to Mecca, the home of the prophet Mohammed—peace be on him and on the whole world. You are a respectable man and we all know your honourable intentions towards N'Gone. We can tell you with certainty that our daughter sees only with your eyes, hears only with your ears. But you know how young she is. The neighbours are gossiping. We are not rich in money, that we cannot deny; but we are decent people, rich in our pride. No one in our family has ever acted dishonourably. We want you to know today that it depends on you alone for N'Gone to be yours for the rest of her life.'

El Hadji was trapped. The thought of marriage had until now never crossed his mind. He had been caught off his guard by the Bayden and could only splutter a reply in the vaguest terms. He must talk to his wives. Yay Bineta realized she had the upper hand. She goaded him. Was he not a Muslim? The son of Muslim? Why did he try to evade Yalla's obvious wishes? Was he a whiteman that he must consult his wives? Had the country lost its men of yesterday? Those brave men whose blood flowed in his veins?

As always in this kind of exchange, the less aggressive of the two contestants eventually gave in. El Hadji Abdou Kader Beye surrendered out of weakness. There was no way he could use the law of the Koran for his own justifications. As for his wives, why should he explain himself to them? All he had to do was tell them.

In the weeks that followed, Yay Bineta speeded up the preparations. Mam Fatou, the girl's mother, seeing the way things were going and the urgency that seemed to possess the Bayden, had certain misgivings. She was deeply opposed to polygamy and wanted El Hadji to repudiate his two wives.

The Bayden was angry at her sister-in-law for her attitude. 'Mam Fatou, get this clear,' she told her, 'El Hadji is a polygamist, but each of his wives has her own house in the best part of town. Each of these houses is worth fifty or sixty times this hovel. And he is such a good match from your point of view! N'-Gone's future and the future of her own children are assured.'

'I admit that I hadn't thought of that,' agreed the mother, giving in.

So, from that day until this the wedding day, all the arrangements had been in the Bayden's hands.

There was an outburst of cries, mingled with applause. A group of female griots was clustered around a woman who was handing out money.

'It's the best marriage of the year,' said one female griot. Bank-notes were pinned to her fulsome chest like decorations.

Her companion was enviously calculating her haul.

'I'm out of luck today. Everyone I meet seems to be broke,' she said.

'The day is not yet over,' the first said encouragingly, as she moved off towards another victim.

Above the heads and the head-dresses, in and out among the chanting griots, roamed the dishes of food: bowls of fritters, pails and plastic dishes full of ginger, flavoured with various kinds of herbs. In groups of six, seven, eight, or even as many as ten or twelve, people were regaling themselves with meat and rice.

The men who had united the couple at the mosque in their absence—the 'marriers'—now made their entrance. There were ten or more of them, all notables, in ceremonial dress. The Bayden welcomed them and made sure they were given comfortable seats. Then they were served liberally with refreshments—kola nuts, dishes of food and for each of them a large packet of fritters.

'Alhamdoulillah!' exclaimed one of their number, who seemed to be the spiritual leader of the community. 'Yalla's will has been done. These two people have been united before Yalla.'

'Which is something we don't often see these days in this country,' pronounced the neighbor sententiously.

Isolated from the other guests the elders discussed the present times.

The young people, who had attended the ceremony dressed in European clothes, were in another, smaller room, anxious to escape.

'The marriage is over. What are we waiting for now?' complained a bridesmaid seated near the door.

'It's stifling in here! It's time we went,' grumbled a young man adjusting his black bow-tie.

'What about some records?'

'I told you before, there's to be a band.'

'And what about the bride? Where has she got to?'

'She's at her mother's house with the marabouts, for the gree-grees.'

All together they began drumming on the walls, whistling and shouting.

At last when there was no more advice to be given and there were no more prayers to be said for a happy married life, N'Gone, in her white crêpe de Chine wedding dress, with its crown and white veil, was handed over by her parents, the Bayden and the elders to her escort of young people. As if from a single pair of lungs there rose a great cry. The Bayden's joy knew no bounds. She intoned the praises of the family lineage, backed by the female griots, who took up the chorus. Expensive cloths were laid in a carpet of honour from the bedroom to the front door. The bride and her large escort made their way along it.

In the street fifteen or so cars were waiting. At the rear, on a trailer, a two-seater car with a white ribbon tied in a bow like an Easter egg symbolized the 'wedding gift'. The horns sounding a mechanical serenade, the cortège set off through the streets of Dakar. People clapped and called out their good wishes to the bride as the cars passed by, with the trailer and its two-seater car following on behind like a trophy.

* * *

The villas were named after the wives. The first wife's villa, 'Adja Awa Astou' was situated on the eastern periphery of the residential suburb. Flame trees lined its tarred roads. A calm reminiscent of the first morning of creation pervaded this part of the town, where the officers of the peace patrolled in pairs without any sense of urgency. A well kept bougainvillæa hedge surrounded the house, and the wrought-iron front door bore an enamel plaque inscribed with the words 'Villa Adja Awa Astou'. The doorbell had the muffled tones of an oriental gong.

The first wife and her two eldest children were waiting in the over-furnished sitting-room. In spite of her age—she was between thirty-six and forty—and in spite of having borne six children, Adja Awa Astou had kept her slim figure. Her colouring was a soft black; she had a prominent forehead above the delicate line of her nose which flattened very slightly at the sides; her face was alive with subdued smiles and there was frankness in her almond-shaped eyes. There emanated from this deceptively fragile woman great strength of will and determination. Since her return from the Holy Place she dressed only in white. She had been born on the island of Gorée and had given up her Christian faith so as to enjoy more fully the pleasures of married life. At the time of their marriage, El Hadji Abdou Kader Beye was still a primary-school teacher.

Speaking in a restrained voice, with an intense gleam in her eyes, Adja Awa Astou repeated what she said a few moments before:

'My co-wife and I should attend the ceremony. It's your father's wish. So …'

'Mother you can't expect Mactar and me to believe that you are happy about this third marriage and that it is taking place with your agreement.'

Rama, her eldest daughter, with her face thrust forward and her short hair plaited, was consumed with anger and reproach.

'You are young still. Your day will come if it pleases Yalla. Then you will understand.'

'Mother, I am not a child. I'm twenty. I will never share my husband with another woman. I'd rather divorce him.'

There was a long silence.

Mactar, who admired his eldest sister, looked away out of the window into the distance beyond the flowers. He avoided his mother's eyes. The sharp pangs he felt in his heart grew worse. In spite of her directness, Rama was anxious to be tactful. She had grown up during the upheavals of the struggle for Independence, when her father and others like him had fought for freedom for everyone. She had taken part in street battles and pasted up posters at night. With the evolution of African society she had joined political associations, been a university student and a member of the Wolof language group. This third marriage of her father's had taken her by surprise and deeply disappointed her.

'It's easy to talk about divorce, Rama,' her mother began slowly. What she was about to say was the product of much careful reflection. 'You think I should get a divorce. Where would I go at my age? Where would I find another husband? If I left your father and with luck and Yalla's help found a husband, I would be his third or fourth wife. And what would become of you?'

As she finished speaking, she smiled, just a little, to soften the impact of her words. Had she convinced Rama? She did not ask herself this question. Adja Awa Astou kept no secrets from her children.

Angry with impotence, Rama rounded on her mother:

'Don't you realize, mother, that this villa belongs to you? Everything in it is yours. Father owns nothing here.'

'Rama, I know that too. But it was your father who gave it to me. I cannot turn him out.'

'I won't go to his wedding.'

'I will. I must put in an appearance. If I don't it will be said that I am jealous.'

'Mother, that wife of my father's, that N'Gone, is my age. She's just a whore. You are only going because you're afraid of what people will say.'

'Don't talk like that!' her mother interrupted her. 'It's true N'Gone is your age. But she is only a victim.…'

The gong gave its oriental sound.

'It's your father.'

El Hadji Abdou Kader Beye came into the sitting-room with a sprightly step. 'Greetings!' he said to the two children. 'Are you ready?' he asked his wife. 'Yes.'

'And you, Rama?'

'I'm not going, father.'

'Why not?'

'Father, can you give me some money for school?' asked Mactar, approaching his father. El Hadji took out a bundle of notes and counting five gave them to his son.

Rama stood where she was. She caught her mother's eye and said:

'I'm against this marriage, father. A polygamist is never frank.'

El Hadji's slap struck her on her right cheek. She stumbled and fell. He moved towards Rama to repeat the blow. Quickly Mactar stepped between them.

'You can be a revolutionary at the university or in the street but not in my house. Never!'

'This is not your house. Nothing here belongs to you,' retorted Rama. A trickle of blood ran from the corner of her mouth.

'Come, el Hadji. Let us go,' said the girl's mother, pulling her husband towards the door.

'You should have brought that child up properly,' El Hadji shouted at his wife.

'You are right. Come, they are waiting. It's your wedding day.'

When their parents had left, Mactar ventured:

'Father is becoming more and more reactionary.'

Rama got up and went to her room.

As the Mercedes drove slowly away the man and his first wife sat silent, looking in opposite directions, anxious.

The second wife's villa was identical with the first's except for the hedge. Trees provided shade at the front. The front door had an enamel plaque with the words 'Villa Oumi N'Doye' in black lettering.

Modu the chauffeur drew up at the entrance and opened the door of his employer's car. El Hadji Abdou Kader Beye climbed out and stood for a moment on the pavement. Then he put his head through the window and said to Adja Awa Astou:

'Come on, get out!'

Adja Awa Astou glanced at her husband and shook her head. Her eyes were lifeless, they had a deep inscrutability that seemed like a total absence of reaction. But there was the strength of controlled inertia burning in them.

El Hadji could not sustain her look. He turned away. Then, as if he were addressing someone else, he pleaded with her:

'Adja, either you get out or you return home. What will Oumi N'Doye think?'

Adja Awa Astou had not lowered her eyes. Etiquette? She struggled to keep her temper. Deep inside her like an angry sea, her resentment welled up. But since she was sincerely religious she controlled herself and tamed her fury, imploring to Yalla to help her. Restraining the urge to speak out, she said:

'El Hadji, I beg you to forgive me. You seem to forget that I am your *Awa*.* I will not set foot in that house. I'll wait here.'

El Hadji Abdou Kader Beye knew his first wife's pride very well. As soon as she finished speaking her bearing became rigid again and she turned her face away from him. Her husband crossed the garden and pushed open the front door of the villa. He entered the sitting room, full of expensive French furniture and artificial flowers. As soon as he appeared the youngest daughter, Mariem, flung her arms joyfully around his neck. She was fifteen years old, big for her age, and wore a mini-skirt.

'Shouldn't you be at school?' asked her father.

'No, I've got permission to stay away today. I'm coming to the wedding with some of my friends from school. Father, can you give me some money?'

'All right. Where's your mother?'

Mischievously Mariem indicated where she was with her thumb. Her father gave her three bank-notes and crossed the room.

Oumi N'Doye saw El Hadji in her mirror. She was securing her black wig with the aid of pins.

'I'll be with you in a minute,' she said in French.

'Who's with you in the Mercedes?'

'Adja Awa. She's waiting in the car.'

'Why doesn't she come in?' asked Oumi N'Doye immediately, turning towards the man. 'Mariem! Mariem!' she called.

Mariem arrived and stood with her hand on the door-knob.

'Mother?'

'Tell Adja Awa to come inside. She's in the car. Tell her I'm having my shower.'

Mariem went out.

'Is she angry?'

---

* '*Awa*' is the Arabic name for the first woman on earth and the title given to the first wife.

'Who?' asked El Hadji, sitting on the bed.

'Adja Awa Astou.'

'Not that I know of,' he replied, leafing through a woman's magazine.

'She persuaded you to marry this third wife purely out of jealousy. Just because I'm younger than she is, the old cow.'

Had her shaft gone home? El Hadji did not react. She had spoken with heavy sarcasm, gritting her teeth. There was still no reply so she went on:

'She's playing games now, your old woman. She's waiting outside just to see how I will take it, isn't she? Your old piece of dried fish-skin thinks I'm her rival. I bet you she'll gang up with that N'Gone to annoy me. But we'll see about that.'

'Listen, Oumi, I don't want any quarrelling, here or at the wedding. If you don't want to come that's your affair. But please stop talking like that.'

'What was I saying then? Now you're threatening me. If you don't want me at the wedding say so. That's what she said, didn't she? Your third, N'Gone, is no different from us.'

She stood facing the man, menace in her voice.

'Believe me, I'm not going to your third's to pick a fight. You needn't worry.'

'Get me something to drink. I'm very thirsty,' said El Hadji to change the subject.

'There is no mineral water in the house.' (El Hadji only drank mineral water.) 'Will you have tap water?' asked Oumi N'Doye in a mocking tone of voice and with an air of defiance that wrinkled the corners of her mouth.

El Hadji Abdou Kader Beye left the room. Outside he called his chauffeur Modu.

'Sir?'

'Bring me some mineral water.'

Beside the Mercedes Mariem was trying her best to cajole Adja Awa Astou from the car into the house.

'Mariem, tell your mother I'd rather wait here.'

'Mother Adja, you know how long my mother takes to get ready. She's having a shower,' said the child.

Defeated by Adja Awa Astou's smile Mariem returned in dejection to the house, followed by Modou carrying the portable ice hamper.

As they came out of the front door Oumi N'Doye whispered to El Hadji:

'Which of us is to sit in back with you?'

Before El Hadji could reply she continued: 'All three of us then. After all it isn't her *moomé*.'*

---

* *Moomé*, or *ayé*, is the period the polygamist spends with each of his wives in turn.

Settling herself in the Mercedes Oumi N'Doye asked after the health of her co-wife's children. The conversation between the two women was distant and full of courtesy. Each complimented the other on her clothes.

'So you don't want to come into my house?'

'You mustn't misunderstand me. I was comfortable in the car. I didn't get out because I still have those attacks of dizziness,' said Adja Awa Astou by way of apology.

El Hadji Abdou Kader Beye, seated in the back between his two wives, let his mind wander, only half listening to what they were saying.

They could hear the band—playing modern music—from some way off. A crowd of youngsters were dancing among themselves on the pavement. Stewards stood guard on the entrance, examining the guests' invitations before letting them in. Couples were dancing on the cement floor of the courtyard. Under the verandah a *kora*-player with two women accompanists took advantage of breaks in the band's playing to show what he could do, singing at the top of his voice.

The third wife's villa, which was of recent construction, stood outside the more heavily populated residential area in a new suburb intended for people of means.

The Mercedes pulled up.

Walking two paces ahead of his wives El Hadji crossed the courtyard amid the acclamations of the guests and the frenzied playing of the band, which completely drowned the efforts of the *kora*-player.

Yay Bineta reached the wives before the bride and in her role of mistress of the house she welcomed them and escorted them to a room where all the most distinguished women guests were congregated. Urbane as ever the Bayden abounded in civilities towards the co-wives.

'You will give a good example to the young ones, won't you? Good co-wives should be united.'

'Don't worry, we are used to it. We are one family. The same blood flows in our children's veins,' parried Oumi N'Doye, not giving Adja Awa Astou a chance to say anything. 'I take Adja our senior as my example. I thank Yalla for putting me to the test so that in my turn I too can show that I am not jealous or selfish.'

'Your presence here today speaks in your favour. All N'Dakaru knows you both. Your reputations are well established.'

The co-wives and Yay Bineta knew they were only playing to the gallery. They resorted to euphemism in preparation for the real hostilities which would come later. The Bayden left them and went to look for El Hadji in the bridal chamber. The room was decorated completely in white. A mattress laid on the floor in a corner, an upside-down mortar and a woodcutter's axe-handle were for the moment the only furnishings.

'It is time for you to change, El Hadji,' the Bayden told the man.

'Change? What for?'

'You must put on a caftan without trousers and sit there on the mortar, with the axe-handle held between your feet, until your wife's arrival is announced.'

'Yay Bineta, you don't really believe in all that! I have two wives already and I did not make a fool of myself with this hocus-pocus on their account. And I am not going to start today!'

'You're not a European, although I can't help wondering. Your two wives are somehow too nice today; it troubles me. My little N'Gone is still innocent. She isn't old enough to cope with rivalry. Go and take your trousers off and sit down! I'll come back and tell you when your wife arrives.'

Being ordered about by a woman was not in the least to El Hadji's liking and he was sufficiently Westernized not to have faith in all this superstition.

'No!' he replied curtly and walked out, leaving the Bayden standing by herself.

Adja Awa Astou and Oumi N'Doye had realized what the Bayden's game was when she had led their husband away. The same thought had occurred to both of them. Oumi N'Doye's courage abandoned her and she spoke what was on her mind:

'What are we doing here in this house?'

Because of the noise Adja Awa Astou leaned over towards her. 'What did you say?'

Oumi N'Doye looked around to make sure that no one was listening or watching them.

'What are we doing here, you and I?'

'We are waiting for our *weje** to arrive,' replied Adja, her eyes fixed on the base of the second wife's neck.

'Are you, the *awa*, going to do nothing? You must be in favour of this third marriage then. You gave El Hadji your blessing, didn't you?

Oumi N'Doye stuck out her chin. The light from the doorway lit up her face animated by jealousy. She pursed her lips.

'You want us to leave?' asked Adja confidentially.

'Yes, let's get away from here,' replied Oumi N'Doye, making to rise to her feet.

Adja Awa Astou held her by the knee, as if to rivet her to her seat. Oumi N'Doye followed her eyes. Standing in the doorway opposite Yay Bineta was

---

* *Weje* means co-wife.

watching them. Intuition told the Bayden that the co-wives were discussing her goddaughter. She moved off.

After a moment Adja Awa Astou went on:

'It is Yay Bineta who is your rival. I have never entered the fray. I am incapable of fighting or rivalry. You know that yourself. When you were a young bride you never knew I existed. I have been the *awa* for nearly twenty years now, and how many years have you been his wife, my second?'

'Seventeen years, I think.'

'Do you know how many times we have met?'

'To tell the truth I don't,' admitted Oumi N'Doye.

'Seven times! During the fifteen or so years you have been the second wife that man, that same man, has left me every three days to spend three nights with you, going from your bedroom to mine. Have you ever thought about it?'

'No,' said Oumi N'Doye.

'And you have never been to see me!'

'Yet you have come to see me several times. I really don't know why I have never visited you.'

'Because you regarded me as your rival.'

The Bayden interrupted them. 'You have eaten nothing! Come on, help yourselves. You must act as if you were at home.' She placed a tray of drinks beside them.

Adja Awa Astou drank. Before raising the glass to her mouth Oumi N'Doye dipped her little finger into the liquid and scattered a few drops on the floor. Scandalized, Yay Bineta hurried off.

'The bride! The bride!'

The rest of the sentence was drowned in the general uproar that followed. A fanfare of car horns reverberated through the air. A thick-set woman with a shoe in her hand rushed towards the door. She was knocked over and fell to the floor. Her tight-fitting dress split, a long, horizontal tear which exposed her behind. She was helped back to her feet by a couple of women and roundly abused the male guests for their lack of manners and consideration for women.

Yay Bineta, the Bayden, pushed the crowd aside. In keeping with their usual exhibitionism the President of the 'Businessmen's Group' led El Hadji forward to meet his bride.

El Hadji Abdou Kader Beye's head had been covered in a cloth.

The two co-wives went to the top of the stairs. From this vantage point they followed the enthronement. They too, at the start of their own marriages, had lived that moment, their hearts full of promise and joy. As they watched someone else's happiness the memory of their own weddings left a nasty taste.

Eaten up with a painful bitterness they shared a common sense of abandonment and loneliness. Neither spoke.

Already El Hadji was on the dance-floor with his bride, inaugurating the festivities that were to last all night. The band played the inevitable *Comparsita*. After the tango came a rock-'n-roll number and the young people invaded the floor.

Things had got off to a good start.

Twelve men, each carrying a spit-roasted lamb, made their entrance. In their enthusiasm some guests beat the furniture with any object they could lay their hands on, while others simply applauded.

Adja Awa Astou hid her chagrin with a show of forced laughter.

'Oumi,' she called softly, 'I am going to slip away.'

'Stay a little longer.... Don't leave me alone.'

'I've left the children by themselves at the villa.'

Adja shook her co-wife's hand and went down the stairs. She walked along the edge of the dance floor and reached the street, which was lined with parked cars.

'Take me home.'

Back at the villa Adja Awa Astou felt unwell. She hid it from her children as they assailed her with questions about the festivities. She had thought jealousy was banished from her heart. When long ago her husband had taken a second wife, she had hidden her unhappiness. The suffering had been less then, for that was the year when she had made the pilgrimage to Mecca. She was completely absorbed in her new religion. Now that she was an *adja*, she wanted to keep her heart pure, free of any hatred or meanness towards others. By an act of will she had overcome all her feelings of resentment towards the second wife. Her ambition was to be a wife according to the teachings of Islam by observing the five daily prayers and showing her husband complete obedience. Her religion and the education of her children became the mainstays of her life. The few friends she still kept and her husband's friends all spoke of her as an exemplary wife.

When she had given the children their supper she took her beads and prayed fervently. She thought of her parents. She longed to see her father again. He was still alive and living on the island of Gorée. After her conversion to the Muslin faith she had gradually stopped seeing her family. Then when her mother died she had broken with them completely.

Her father, Papa John as the islanders called him, was an intransigent Christian, born into the third generation of African Catholicism. He attended Mass regularly with all his household and enjoyed a reputation for piety which had given him a certain ascendancy over his colleagues. During the colonial period he had been a member of the municipal council for a number of years. When he discovered that his daughter was being courted by a Muslim from the mainland, he had decided to have it out with her. He had asked her to accompany him on his daily walk and together they had climbed the steep path up to the fort. Beneath them the angry, foam-covered sea battered the sides of the cliff.

'Renée.' He said.

'Father?'

'Is this Muslim going to marry you?'

Renée lowered her eyes. Papa John could see he would get no reply. He knew a lot about this Muslim and his trade-union activities. He had heard about his speeches at political meetings criticizing French colonialism and its allies as *assimilés*. He could not visualize this man as his son-in-law and suffered in anticipation at the thought that he might one day be associated with his family.

'Will you become a Muslim?'

This time his voice had hammered out the question firmly.

Renée was flirting with the teacher, who was something of a hero with the young generation; nothing more. She had certainly given no thought to the conflict of religions.

'Do you love him?'

Papa John had watched his daughter out of the corner of his eye as he waited for a reply. Deep down he had hoped it would be 'no.'

'Renée, answer me!'

* * *

Rama's arrival broke the thread of her memories.

'I thought you were asleep,' said Rama, sitting on a chair.

'Have you eaten?' asked her mother.

'Yes. Were there a lot of people at father's wedding?'

'With all that he spent on it! You know what the people of this town are like!'

'And Oumi N'Doye?'

'I left her there.'

'I supposed she was unpleasant?'

'No. We were together.'

Rama was sensitive to her mother's least suffering. The atmosphere did not encourage conversation. The light from the wall-lamp and the white scarf wound round her head made her mother's face look thin. Tiny bright dots shone in her eyes. Rama thought she could see tears on the edge of her lashes.

'I'm going to work a bit before I go to bed,' announced Rama, getting to her feet.

'What have you got to do?'

'I have a Wolof translation to finish. Pass the night in peace, mother.'

'And you too.'

The door closed, leaving Adja Awa Astou alone again. As others isolate themselves with drugs she obtained her daily dose from her religion.

Village People

by Bessie Head (South Africa/Botswana)

Poverty has a home in Africa—like a quiet second skin. It may be the only place on earth where it is worn with an unconscious dignity. People do not look down at your shoes which are caked with years of mud and split so that the toes stick out. They look straight and deeply into your eyes to see if you are friend or foe. That is all that matters. To some extent I think that this eye-looking, this intense human awareness, is a reflection of the earth all about. There is no end to African sky and to African land. One might say that in its vastness is a certain kind of watchfulness that strips man down to his simplest form. If that is not so, then there must be some other, unfathomable reason for the immense humanity and the extreme gentleness of the people in my village.

Poverty here has majority backing. Our lives are completely adapted to it. Each day we eat a porridge of millet in the morning; a thicker millet porridge with a piece of boiled meat at midday; and at evening we repeat breakfast. We use our heads to transport almost everything: water from miles and miles, bags of corn and maize, and fire wood.

This adaptation to difficult conditions in a permanently drought-stricken country is full of calamity. Babies die most easily of starvation and malnutrition: and yet, within this pattern of adaptation people crowd in about the mother and sit, sit in heavy silence, absorbing the pain, till, to the mother, it is only a dim, dull ache folded into the stream of life. It is not right. There is a terrible mindlessness about it. But what alternative? To step out of this mindless safety, and face the pain of life alone when the balance is heavily weighted down on one side, is for certain to face a fate far worse. Those few who have, are insane in a strange, quiet, harmless way: walking all about the village, freely. Only by their ceaseless muttering and half-clothed bodies are they distinguishable from others. It is not right, as it is negative merely to strive for existence. There must be other ingredients boiling in the pot. Yet how? We are in the middle of nowhere. Most communication is by ox cart or sledge.

Poverty also creates strong currents of fear and anxiety. We are not outgoing. We tend to push aside all new intrusions. We live and survive by making as few demands as possible. Yet, under the deceptive peace around us we are more easily confused and torn apart than those with the capacity to take in their stride the width and reach of new horizons.

Do we really retain the right to develop slowly, admitting change only in so far as it keeps pace with our limitations, or does change descend upon us as a calamity? I merely ask this because, anonymous as we are, in our favour is a great credit balance of love and warmth that the Gods somewhere should count up. It may be that they overlook desert and semi-desert places. I should like to remind them that there are people here too who need taking care of.

The old woman

She was so frail that her whole body swayed this way and that like a thin stalk of corn in the wind. Her arms were as flat as boards. The flesh hung loosely, and her hands which clutched the walking stick were turned outwards and knobbled with age. Under her long dress also swayed the tattered edges of several petticoats. The ends of two bony stick-legs peeped out. She had on a pair of sand-shoes. The toes were all sticking out, so that the feet flapped about in them. She wore each shoe on the wrong foot, so that it made the heart turn over in amusement.

Yet she seemed so strong that it was a shock when she suddenly bent double, retched and coughed emptily, and crumbed to the ground like a quiet sigh.

'What is it, Mmm? What is the matter?' I asked.

'Water, water.' she said faintly.

'Wait a minute. I shall ask at this hut here if there is any water.'

'What is the matter?' they asked.

'The old lady is ill.' I said.

'No.' she said curtly. 'I am not ill. I am hungry.'

The crowd laughed in embarrassment that she should display her need so nakedly. They turned away; but old ladies have no more shame left. They are like children. They give way to weakness and cry openly when they are hungry.

'Never mind.' I said. Hunger is a terrible thing. My hut is not far away. This small child will take you. Wait till I come back, then I shall prepare food for you.'

Then, it was late afternoon. The old lady had long passed from my mind when a strange young woman, unknown to me, walked into the yard with a pail of water on her head. She set it down outside the door and squatted low.

'Good-day. How are you?' I said.

She returned the greeting, keeping her face empty and carefully averted. It is impossible to say: what do you want? Whom are you looking for? It is impossible to say this to a carefully averted face and a body that squats quietly, patiently. I looked at the sky, helplessly. I looked at the trees. I looked at the ground, but the young woman said nothing. I did not know her, inside or out. Many people I do not know who know me, inside and out, and always it is this way, this silence.

A curious neighbour looked over the hedge.

'What's the matter?' she asked.

I turned my eyes to the sky again, shrugging helplessly.

'Please ask the young woman what she wants, whom she is looking for.'

The young woman turned her face to the neighbour, still keeping it averted, and said quietly:

'No, tell her she helped our relative who collapsed this morning. Tell her the relatives discussed the matter. Tell her we had nothing to give in return, only that one relative said she passes by every day on her way to the water tap. Then we decided to give a pail of water. It is all we have.'

Tell them too. Tell them how natural, sensible, normal is their human kindness. Tell them, those who judge my country, Africa, by gain and greed, that the gods walk about her barefoot with no ermine and gold-studded cloaks.

Summer sun

All day I lie asleep under the thorn tree, and the desert is on this side of me and on that side of me. I have no work to do. We are all waiting for the rain, as we cannot plough without rain. I think the rain has gone away, like last year. We had a little rain in November, but December has gone, and now it is January; and each day we have been sitting here, waiting for rain: my mother, my grandmother and my grandfather, my cousin Lebenah, and my sister and her little baby. If it were to rain my grandfather would push the plough and my cousin Lebenah would pull the oxen across the great miles of our land. We women would follow behind, sowing maize, millet, pumpkin and watermelon seed. I feel great pity for my family, and other families. I wonder why we sit here like this. Each day the sun is hot, hot in the blue sky. Each day the water pool of November rain gets smaller. Soon we will have to leave the land and return to the village.

In the village we have a politician who takes the people on the hill to pray for rain. He wears a small suit and has a big black car and a beautiful deep African voice. His mind is quick and moves from one thing to another. He can pray, and cry, and speak politics all at once. People always expect the rain to fall the minute after he has stopped praying and crying. They call him the one who has shaken God loose.

Actually, I have not been sleeping the whole day. I am trying to learn English. My cousin Lebenah tells me that things are changing in Africa, and that it is necessary for women to improve themselves. I love my cousin Lebenah so much that I do anything he tells me to do. He tells me that English is the best language to learn, as many books have been written in English; and that there is no end to the knowledge that can be gained from them. He gave me a geography book and I have read it over and over. I am puzzled and afraid. Each year the sun is more cruel. Each year the rain becomes less and less. Each year more and more of our cattle die. The only animal that survives is the goat. It can eat anything and we eat the goat. Without the goat, I do not know what we would do. It is all about us, like the family. It has the strangest eyes. They are big and yellow, and the pupil is a black streak right across the yellow ball of the eye.

I am trying to improve myself too, as I am very afraid that I may have an illegitimate baby like my elder sister. My family will suffer much. And the child too. It may die. There is never enough food and we are always hungry. It is not so easy for a woman to have too many babies when she has improved her mind. She has to think about how she will feed the baby, clothe it, and wash it. My sister's baby is lovely, though. He laughs a lot for no reason at all.

My geography book makes me wonder and wonder. It tells me that water is formed by hydrogen and oxygen. I wonder so much about that. If we had green things everywhere, they might help to make the oxygen to make the rain. The soil is very fertile. If there is only a little rain, green things come out everywhere, and many strange flowers. How can we live like this? Here are our bags with the seeds of maize, and millet, and the land is hard as stone.

Tomorrow the sun will rise, quietly. The many birds in the bush will welcome it. I do not. Alone, without the help of the rain it is cruel, killing and killing. All day we look on it, like on death. Then, at evening, all is as gentle as we are. Mother roasts goat meat over the coals of the wood fire. Sister feeds her baby. Grandfather and cousin Lebenah talk quietly to each other about little things. The stars spread across the sky and bend down at the horizon. The quiet talk of grandfather and cousin Lebenah seem to make earth and heaven come together. I do not know what we would do if we all did not love one another, because tomorrow the sun will rise again.

The green tree

This small hill of my village in Africa abounds with the song of birds. The birds are small and brown and seem bound up in the thick profusion of dark brown branches. The green leaves of the trees are so minute that the eye can hardly see them. Everything that is green in my country is minute and cramped, for my country is semi-desert.

From this hill you may think the village below a fertile valley. It is shrouded and hidden in tall greenery. But that greenery is unproductive, contained and drawn into itself, concerned alone with its silent fight for survival. We call it the green tree. It came here as a stranger and quickly adapted itself to the hardness of our life. It needs no water in the earth but draws into itself the moisture of the air for its life. We use it as a hedge. It also protects us from the sandstorms that blow across our desolate and barren land.

If you tell my people that there are countries with hills and hills of green grass where no cattle graze, they will not believe you. Our cattle graze on parched grass that is paper-dry. Our goats eat the torn shreds of wind-scattered papers and thrust their mouths into the thorn bushes to nibble at the packed cluster of leaves that look like pin-points of stars farflung in the heavens. That is our life. Everything is jealously guarded. Nothing is ever given out. All strength and energy must be contained for the fight to survive tomorrow and tomorrow and tomorrow.

Many strangers traverse our land these days. They are fugitives from the south fleeing political oppression. They look on our lives with horror and quickly make means to pass on to the paradise of the north. Those who are pressed by circumstances and forced to tarry a while, grumble and complain endlessly. It is just good for them that we are inbred with habits of courtesy, hospitality and kindness. It is good that they do not know the passion we feel for this we love which cannot be touched by them. The powdery dust of the earth, the heat, the cattle with their slow, proud walk—all this has fashioned our way of life. Our women with their tall thin hard bodies can drive a man to the depth of passion. All this is ours. Few are they, strangers, who like the green tree are quickly able to adapt themselves to our way of life. They are to be most feared for the adaptation is merely on the surface, like a mask, while underneath they are new and as strange as ever. They cause a ripple on the smooth pond of life that cannot be stopped from spreading from one thing to another.

None can be more sure of this than I. For thirty-eight years of my life I have lived in full control of myself. Now, I am full of conflict due to unaccustomed feelings that have taken possession of me. I am weakened and confused and no longer recognise myself as the man I once was. I am at one moment enraged to the point of blind destruction and the next overcome by a terrifying and utterly foreign feeling of tenderness.

With women a man must be direct, blunt, and brutal. If not, he soon finds that he loses his pride and becomes dependent on her. It is not necessary to control the passions but it is necessary to be in full control of the heart.

This strange obsession crept in on my life unaware. I do not know where I first saw her. I have not even spoken to her but now my eyes seek her out in every corner of the village and I am pursued by a thousand devils of restlessness if I do not see her. Deceitful stranger, she has put on the mask of her adaptability and assumed our ways and manners but to her, the woman, all gates are closed. It is just as well that she fears me. Sometimes I could destroy her with the thunderbolt of violence that is within me and I see the shock and terror reflected in her eyes. Then, when I am not able to control the feelings that obsess me, it is I in turn who tremble at her sharp daring look of gloating power and indifference. It is I who stand unmanned, drained of strength and will and my rage and hatred at the loss of my pride and independence drive me beyond the bounds of sanity.

Everything I have wanted I have had through force, cunning or calculation. Now, I lie awake at night, craving something I fear to possess. Just as our cattle would go insane at the unaccustomed sight of a hill covered with greenery; so do I live in fear of the body of a woman that has been transplanted by upheaval and uncertain conditions into harsh and barren soil. Sometimes I feel it beneath me; cool, like the depths of the night when the moon brings the pale light of heaven to earth and makes the dust shimmer like gold. Then my hands reach out to crush the life out of the thing that torments me.

Tao

A desert has a strange effect on human life. As long as you search for outward things like underground water and possible new grazing ground for your cattle, all is well. But should an inward longing awaken in you then your life becomes very unsafe. There is no possible way of fulfilling these longings when the fight for survival is so intense. We desert people are in some way cruel. We are too much like the starkness and desolation that surround us. Sometimes you cannot tell where man ends and nature begins. The pattern of his hard, gnarled brown body is repeated in the pattern of the hard, dry, dark and leafless trees. We are a complement to the earth. Nature is extreme and violent. We are gentle and conciliatory as though making up to her for the mercilessness she lacks. We tolerate no violent eruptions of feeling; no quarrelling. Any dispute between neighbour and neighbour, husband and wife is thoroughly and openly discussed in the village courts. We are passionately addicted to long speeches and in that way rid ourselves of all passion. Really, I do not think we understand the inward life at all. We are always suppressing it. The weight of group thinking and group feeling always suppresses individual thought and initiative. In that way it is hard to change us. Our country is the poorest on the continent of Africa and at least five hundred centuries behind the rest of the world. Even our political independence is a reflection of our life. It moves against the trend of politics in Africa. People in the North, who won their independence with prison terms, blood and tears, find us very amusing.

'Where have you ever heard of an African government defending British imperialism', they say.

'But we are not like you', we say. 'We were never subjects under colonialism. We were protected people. Our fathers and grandfathers ...' and then we make a long speech justifying ourselves.

The political refugees and busy men of these days look at us aghast.

'Don't you people know there is a war on? Don't you know about the Great White Conspiracy? They want us to use this country as a buffer to stem the tide of African nationalism that is sweeping the continent! You people are playing right into the hands of the settler government! This place is dynamite! It's going to blow up sky high! You're all sitting on a keg of dynamite!'

'A keg of dynamite?'

'Just you wait and see', they hint darkly. 'You people think a tide doesn't reach a backwater?'

We defend ourselves. We make a long speech about how our country has always been peaceful and a refuge for those in trouble. We tell them the ancient story about the Kalanga tribe who fled from the persecution of the Matabele tribe and for three centuries have lived in peace here, though being a different nation with different customs.

'There is only peace here', we say, spreading our hands eloquently.

Somehow we will never grasp the meaning of the word intrigue. Somehow we will never grasp the meaning of any of the dark torments and anxieties that ravage the human soul. All that is suppressed so deep within us that it would take an upheaval of gigantic proportions to release it. Maybe that is our greatest weakness. We who are so careful, conservative and conformist find ourselves the non-conformists of Africa. We who have only looked at life in straight lines find that there are twistings and turnings about which we know nothing. Thus, we are vulnerable and open to everything. The old people who judge everything are already uneasy.

'Miracles are happening these days', they say unhappily.

For all the peace here we really live very unsettled lives. Desert people are migratory people. At very little provocation a whole village of cousins, aunts, parents, children will move off with goats, sheep, cattle and all; overnight. A teacher who had a class of sixty on one day finds she has no class to teach. School buildings are makeshift and equipment almost nil. Teachers never know where they will be the next day, the next term. They are always migrating after the children. In the very large villages and small towns, life is more permanent and settled so that teachers are unashamedly happy if by hook, crook or good luck they can be transferred to the towns and large villages. A large number of my teaching years had been spent drifting from one remote bush outpost to another where all that could be seen by day were the sand dunes and the rough grey stubble of the thorn trees; and at night, the stars hanging large, low and glowing in a deathly silence; so silent that it melts into hollow cavities of loneliness, making tolerable and bearable all the unfulfilled longings. It seemed impossible that I should ever leave it, that I should be transferred to a place with a different pace of life, with a few shops, a cinema and cars tearing up and down the dusty roads the day long. Cars fascinate me. They are a strange contrast to the unchanging desert. They are shocking and defiant and new. The people who drive them are shocking and defiant and new too and hide behind dark sunglasses. It seems as though they see every-thing and yet their faces are remote, impassive.

The principal, for some reason a much harassed man, who spoke and walked in a jerky manner said: 'Look, there's no accommodation for teachers. You'd better see one of the officials. I don't know why they keep sending me teachers who have no relatives here.'

You never bother about accommodation. I have slept many nights in the open veld and watched the stars whirl, tumble and explode above me.

Some people are a great trouble to themselves. They are overpossessed by violent extremes of feeling that allow them no rest but drive them on endlessly, restlessly. More than others, they draw down the anger, hatred, envy and out-rage of their fellow-men upon their heads. Oppose me and I'll knock you down at all costs, their fierce intent expressions seem to say. Such a man is so rare among my people that I gazed at the official to whom I had come to apply for accommodation with a startled curiosity. He looked up as I entered and right through me with blind eyes. I might have been the wall—which was also very rare. Our men have a facile kind of charm and they delight in turning it on whenever a woman appears, making some idiotic, playfully provocative joke. His face was grim and set and closed with many harsh lines etched by pain, sorrow, rage, excesses and abuses.

'I'm looking for accommodation', I said mildly, pretending I did not see all these things.

He stood up. It was effortless the way in which he held his body upright. His arms were short, powerful in strange contrast to his long, thin, slender, supple fingers. Altogether too many extremes. It seemed impossible that such an intensely masculine man should be so entirely unaware of it!

He hid his face behind the dark sunglasses and drove at tearing speed amid the twisting, dusty circular paths of the village. Goats scattered in all directions, outrage in their yellow gleaming eyes. I wish I could ride in a car like that every day. It is a wonderful feeling yet I do not know how to adequately explain it. The car stopped abruptly before one of the numerous, anonymous mud huts that seem to grow up out of and cling squatly and pathetically to the earth. A tall woman with twinkling, mischievous eyes darted out. He smiled briefly and it was like a flash of lightning across a dark and brooding sky.

'My God, Kate', he said. 'Are you still alive?'

'Of course I am, Tao', she replied with cheeky gaiety. 'I don't know why you think I should be dead when you're far older than me. Don't tell me this woman will have to stay with me. Women never live peacefully together. It looks as though I shall have to share my supper with her too. Why don't you people give us teachers increased salaries? We are such a necessary commodity but we have to live on a wage that's an old age pension.'

He smiled, again briefly.

'All you think about is food and money. You know things happen too slowly here.'

Then, he turned abruptly and drove off churning up the dust road like a furious windstorm.

'He is a strange man', I said, breaking the momentary silence between the tall woman and myself.

She shook her head.

'No, he is quite simple', she said. 'We used to play together when young. Now he is unhappy because he has a wife who loves him more than necessary; who turns the lock on the door as soon as he gets home. It offends us because she has to march about the whole village saying, 'He is my husband, dark or blue.'

'Yes. Then he became a speaker for the political party and everybody says he preaches politics like a mad man. It is the straw the drowning man clutches. What may be your name, madame?'

'Lorato', I said.

'You're much of a dignity mistress but never mind, we shall be friends.'

Between the few who have and the majority who have not is a great gulf fixed. The few who have become the thing they have till man can no longer separate himself from his possessions. Without them he would be a shaken, frail, shrunken, lifeless skeleton for he has put all of himself into his possessions. To have and yet not to lose the self in the possessions; to know that there is no possibility of fulfillment of the insatiable cravings of the human soul is to know that the life of man is an ever-expanding horizon. Those who seek to constrict that horizon to possessions and things condemn themselves to a living death and a dread emptiness. The laugher and gaiety of the poor are because for them life is an expanding horizon of unattained and seemingly un-attainable desires. Blessed are the poor, for they do inherit the earth.

Women of my country are faced with a strange dilemma. It is hard to see how the situation can change. Men do not feel called upon to love one par-ticular woman; to make use of feeling. They drift from woman to woman in a carefree migratory fashion dispensing a gay, superficial, facile charm in all directions. The depths of human feeling and tenderness are never explored. Let us have a good time, they seem to say. I am here today and gone tomor-row. Therefore you have a choice. Few women choose to marry. It needs a cer-tain amount of ruthlessness to cajole or force a man into marriage. Thereafter he has to be fiercely hoarded, not someone to love, but an object to possess, like a stack of money, a piece of furniture. Most women are repelled at the thought and never marry, though they have large families of seven or eight fa-therless children and struggle to raise them on a pittance of money they gather here and there. Among the unmarried women are great and strong friendships free of jealousy and envy. No unmarried woman is ever a friend of a married woman. The great gulf is fixed. Things were different long ago when marriages were arranged by parents and elders of the village, but custom and tradition were broken down by taxation and the resultant enforced labor on the mines many miles away from home. Family life and a home are things of the past and for the future there is only continued uncertainty. With all, feeling is sup-pressed and put to sleep. It cannot remain so forever. Under all the gaiety and carefree laughter is a sob and it will need only a small spark to bring the emo-tional life to the surface, into the glare of the daylight. It is not of man's choos-ing but the pattern of life. Man may sleep for just so long then he must awaken to pain, heartbreak, the struggles of ambition, power, achievement.

Kate had a boyfriend; an ephemeral fly-by-night. When he came I would take a walk to the end of the village so that they might have some privacy. That was how I came upon the political meetings held at sunset under a tree in an open patch of land outside the village. A large crowd of people sat on the ground listening intently. In a van with a loudspeaker sat the man, Tao. Drawn by curiosity I joined the edge of the crowd and was immediately caught and captivated by a magnetic spell; lost to myself, while the darkness gathered all round. He could have said anything to us, that the sky was green and cows had six legs and we would have had no resistance to his persuasions. The heavy, deep, rich voice with fine, precise enunciation projected all the force, power and emotional intensity of the man; and yet a withdrawnness, an aloof-ness that seemed to say—You see, I have power to do as I like with you but I cannot because I respect you too much. It was that which created the strong current of trust between the man and his audience and allowed him to take them along with him, unresistingly. He was an artist, using words and plain statistics to project his own inner turmoil making earth and heaven, destiny and independence vivid and real and alive because they are all bound up in the life of man. Any politician can tell you that the country has been prospected and certain areas found suitable for the cultivation of timber and certain areas are to be protected from animal grazing for the cultivation of crops; but few can make plain fact quiver with life. Few have had such a powerful creative intelligence. A man, vividly, passionately alive, awakens all life around him. Strange that he should be one of us and yet a contrast, a new thing, the awakener of deep, hidden suppressed feeling. Such a man, with evil intentions, could cause wreckage and disaster all around him.

I walked home stunned. The whole world had become silent. I could not explain it. Also I could not explain the sudden violent pounding of the heart. Terror-stricken I wished to efface myself for fear that I am alone like the wild animal in the dark of night whose cries go unheeded because its pain is not comprehended. There is an urge to come alive yet an unwillingness to bear the pain of unfulfillment. There is humility too and a child-like need to cling to the blind earth for comfort and protection.

Kate's boyfriend had already left. She was busy cooking her evening porridge but looked up at me sharply and suspiciously. To Kate a woman's primary occupation was sleeping with a man. She was always doing it yet it horrified her moralistic soul. As I seemed unable or unwilling to attract men she had impulsively set me up on a pedestal of virtue. It made her snoop and sniff all the time as though I was hiding a man somewhere!

'Why are you so late? Where have you been?' she demanded.

I told her about the meeting and she plunged into a vigorous tirade against our politics.

'It doesn't make sense', she said. 'It's all nonsense. These two parties are shouting at each other all the time. The one says the other is right of the right and that's supposed to be a bad thing. The other is left of the left and that's supposed to be a bad thing. The people are such fools. They've already decided to support the party of the chiefs. We've been ruled for donkey's generations by the chiefs and we want to chuck them out. Instead we are running to support the party of the rich.'

'They have a good speaker. No one can resist him.'

'I'll tell you something. It's just luck the party of the rich got him. Tao has been the poorest of the poor and now he is the richest of the rich. But the poor don't see him like that. They say he is the prophet come out of darkness to lead them to the light. The party of the rich would get nowhere without him. They sit in their houses the whole day. It's Tao all the time who speaks to us. They say he has to just address a crowd of people once and they can't run fast enough to join the party.'

'Who are you going to vote for?' I asked.

'The party of the rich', she said slyly.

'Then why do you privately favour the party of the poor?'

'A person must have two minds. If the rich think we are going to support them like blind sheep they will sit on our heads. Who may you be voting for?'

'I am not going to vote. I cannot decide matters clearly. Why do you think Tao is such a good speaker?'

'Because he is a simple man. He speaks straight from the heart. Tao is a man whose life is on display in public all the time. He can't hide anything. That is why people trust him so much.'

One night after a little rain has fallen, you awaken to find the earth covered with tender green things. And then, in the heat of the day they die or fall asleep in the parched earth to await the time when life and growth will be theirs again. They wait patiently. But the life force in man is too powerful. It makes the world tumble and fall to pieces about him. I have no courage in this upside-down world. I flee. I would rather efface myself than face the torment of a naked and unashamed desire for an unattainable man with the face of the brooding thundercloud. So, here I drift again in the remote hush and the silence. But the intensities awakened can never be put to sleep again and a spark from any direction can turn the smouldering fire within into a great conflagration.

Prologue from *Love*

by Toni Morrison (USA)

[The women's legs are spread wide open, so I hum. Men grow irritable, but they know it's all for them. They relax. Standing by, unable to do anything but watch,] is a trial, but I don't say a word. My nature is a quiet one, anyway. As a child I was considered respectable; as a young woman I was called discreet. Later on I was thought to have the wisdom maturity brings. [Nowadays silence is looked on as odd and most of my race has forgotten the beauty of meaning much by saying little. Now tongues work all by themselves with no help from the mind.] Still, I used to be able to have normal conversations, and when the need arose, I could make a point strong enough to stop a womb—or a knife. [Not anymore, because back in the seventies, when women began to straddle chairs and dance crotch out on television, when all the magazines started featuring behinds and inner thighs as though that's all there is to a woman,] well, I shut up altogether. [Before women agreed to spread in public, there used to be secrets—some to hold, some to tell.]

Now? No. Barefaced being the order of the day, I hum. The words dance in my head to the music in my mouth. People come in here for a plate of crawfish, or to pass the time, and never notice or care that they do all the talking. I'm background—the movie music that comes along when the sweethearts see each other for the first time, or when the husband is walking the beachfront alone wondering if anybody saw him doing the bad thing he couldn't help. My humming encourages people; frames their thoughts like when Mildred Pierce decides she has to go to jail for her daughter. I suspect, soft as it is, my music has that influence too. The way "Mood Indigo" drifing across the waves can change the way to swim. It doesn't make you dive in, but it can set your stroke, or trick you into believing you are both smart and lucky. So why not swim farther and a little farther still? What's the deep to you? It's way down below, and has nothing to do with blood made bold by coronets and piano keys, does it? Of course, I don't claim that kind of power. My hum is mostly below range; private; suitable for an old woman embarrassed by the world; her way of objecting to how the century is turning out. Where all is known and nothing understood. Maybe it was always so, but it didn't strike me until some thirty years ago that prostitutes, looked up to for their honesty, have always set the style. Well, maybe it wasn't their honesty; maybe it was their success. Still, straddling a chair or dancing half naked on TV, these nineties women are not all that different from the respectable women who live around here. This is coast country, humid and God-fearing, where female recklessness runs too deep for short shorts or thongs or cameras. But then or now, decent underwear or none, wild women never could hide their innocence—a kind of pity-kitty hopefulness that their prince was on his way. Especially the tough ones with two-seated cars and a pocketbook full of dope. Even the ones who wear scars like presidential medals and stockings rolled at their ankles can't hide the sugar-child, the winsome baby girl curled up somewhere inside, between the ribs, say, or under the heart. Naturally all of them have a sad story: too much notice, not enough, or the worst kind. Some tale about dragon daddies and false-hearted men, or mean mamas and friends who did them wrong. Each story has a monster in it who made them tough instead of brave, so they open their legs rather than their hearts where that folded child is tucked.

Sometimes the cut is so deep no woe-is-me tale is enough. Then the only thing that does the trick, that explains the craziness heaping up, holding down, and making women hate one another and ruin their children is an outside evil. People in Up Beach, where I'm from, used to tell about some creatures called Policeheads—dirty things with big hats who shoot up out of the ocean to harm loose women and eat disobedient children. My mother knew them when she was a girl and people dreamed wide awake. They disappeared for a while but came back with new and bigger hats starting in the forties when a couple of "See there, what'd I tell you?" things happened at the shore. Like that woman who furrowed in the sand with her neighbor's husband and the very next day suffered a stroke at the cannery, the grappling knife still in her hand. She wasn't but twenty-nine at the time. Another woman—she lived over in Silk and wouldn't have anything to do with Up Beach people—well, she hid a flashlight and a purchase deed in the sand of her father-in-law's beachfront one evening only to have a loggerhead dig them up in the night. The miserable daughter-in-law broke her wrist trying to keep the breezes and the Klan away from the papers she'd stolen. Of course nobody flat out saw any Police-heads during the shame of those guilty women, but I knew they were around and knew what they looked like, too, because I'd already seen them in 1942 when some hardheaded children swam past the safety rope and drowned. As soon as they were pulled under, thunderclouds gathered above a screaming mother and a few dumbstruck picnickers and, in a blink, these clouds turned into gate-mouthed profiles wearing wide-brimmed hats. Some folks heard rumbling but I swear I heard whoops of joy. From that time on through the fifties they loitered above the surf or hovered over the beach ready to pounce around sunset (you know, when lust is keenest, when loggerheads hunt nests and negligent parents get drowsy). Of course most demons get hungry at suppertime, like us. But Police-heads liked to troll at night, too, especially when the hotel was full of visitors drunk with dance music, or salt air, or tempted by starlit water. Those were the days when Cosey's Hotel and Resort was the best and best-known vacation spot for colored folk on the East Coast. Everybody came: Lil Green, Fatha Hines, T-Bone Walker, Jimmy Lunceford, the Drops of Joy, and guests from as far away as Michigan and New York couldn't wait to get down here. Sooker Bay swirled with first lieutenants and brand-new mothers; with young schoolteachers, landlords, doctors, businessmen. All over the place children rode their fathers' leg shanks and buried uncles up to their necks in sand. Men and women played croquet and got up baseball teams whose goal was to knock a homer into the waves. Grandmothers watched over red thermos jugs with white handles and hampers full of crabmeat salad, ham, chicken, yeast rolls, and loaves of lemon-flavored cake, oh my. Then, all of a sudden, in 1958, bold as a posse, the Police-heads showed up in bright morning. A clarinet player and his bride drowned before breakfast. The inner tube they were floating on washed ashore dragging wads of scale-cluttered beard hair. Whether the bride had played around during the honeymoon was considered and whispered about, but the facts were muddy. She sure had every opportunity. Cosey's Resort had more handsome single men per square foot than anyplace outside Atlanta or even Chicago. They came partly for the music but mostly to dance with the pretty women.

After the drowned couple was separated—sent to different funeral parlors— you'd think women up to no good and mule-headed children wouldn't need fur-

ther warning, because they knew there was no escape: fast as lightening, night-time or day, Police-heads could blast up out of the waves to punish wayward women or swallow the misbehaving young. Only when the resort failed did they sneak off like pickpockets from a breadline. A few people still sinking crab castles in the back bays probably remember them, but with no more big bands or honeymooners, with the boats and picnics and swimming gone, when Sooker Bay became a treasury of sea junk Up Beach itself drowned, nobody needed or wanted to recall big hats and scaly beards. But it's forty years on, now; the Coseys have disappeared from public view and I'm afraid for them almost every day.

Except for me and a few fish shacks, Up Beach is twenty feet underwater; but the hotel part of Cosey's Resort is still standing. Sort of standing. Looks more like it's rearing backwards—away from hurricanes and a steady blow of sand. Odd what oceanfront can do to empty buildings. You can find the prettiest shells right up on the steps, like scattered petals or cameos from a Sunday dress, and you wonder how they got there, so far from the ocean. Hills of sand piling in porch corners and between banister railings are whiter than the beach, and smoother, like twice-sifted flour. Foxglove grows waist high around the gazebo, and roses, which all the time hate our soil, rage here, with more thorns than blackberries and weeks of beet red blossoms. The wood siding of the hotel looks silver-plated, its peeling paint like the streaks on an unpolished tea service. The big double doors are padlocked. So far nobody has smashed their glass panels. Nobody could stand to do it because the panels mirror your own face as well as the view behind your back: acres of chive grass edging the sparkly beach, a movie-screen sky, and an ocean that wants you more than anything. No matter the outside loneliness, if you look inside, the hotel seems to promise you ecstasy and the company of all your best friends. And music. The shift of a shutter hinge sounds like the cough of a trumpet; piano keys waver a quarter note above the wind so you might miss the hurt jamming those halls and closed-up rooms.

Our weather is soft, mostly, with peculiar light. Pale mornings fade into white noons, then by three o'clock the colors are savage enough to scare you. Jade and sapphire waves fight each other, kicking up enough foam to wash sheets in. An evening sky behaves as though it's from some other planet—one without rules, where the sun can be plum purple if it wants to and clouds can be red as poppies. Our shore is like sugar, which is what the Spaniards thought of when they first saw it. Sucra, they called it, a name local whites tore up for all time into Sooker.

Nobody could get enough of our weather except when the cannery smell got to the beach and into the hotel. Then guests discovered what Up Beach people put up with every day and thought that was why Mr. Cosey moved his family out of the hotel and built that big house on Monarch Street. Fish odor didn't used to be all that bad a thing in these parts. Like marsh stench and privies, it just added

another variety to the sense. But in the sixties it became a problem. A new gen-
eration of females complained about what it did to their dresses, their appetite,
and their idea of romance. This was around the time the world decided perfume
was the only smell the nose was meant for. I remember Vida trying to calm the
girlfriend of a famous singer who was carrying on about her steak tasting like
conch. That hurt me, because I have never failed in the kitchen. Later on, Mr.
Cosey told people that's what ruined his business—that the whites had tricked
him, let him buy all the oceanfront he wanted because the cannery, so close by,
kept it unprofitable. The fish smell had turned his resort into a joke. But I know
that the smell that blanketed Up Beach hit Sooker Bay only once or twice a
month—and never from December to April, when crab castles were empty and
the cannery closed. NO. I don't care what he told people, something else wrecked
his resort. Freedom, May said. She tried hard to keep the place going when her
father-in-law lost interest, and was convinced that civil rights destroyed her fam-
ily and its business. By which she meant colored people were more interested in
blowing up cities than dancing by the seashore. She was like that, May; but what
started out as mule-headed turned into crack-brained. Fact is, folks who bragged
about Cosey vacations in the forties boasted in the sixties about Hyatts, Hiltons,
cruises to the Bahamas and Ocho Rios. Truth is, neither shellfish nor integration
was to blame. Never mind the woman with the conch-flavored steak, customers
will sit next to a privy if it's the only way they can hear Wilson Pickett or Nellie
Lutcher. Besides, who can tell one odor from another while pressed close to a part-
ner on a crowded dance floor listening to "Harbor Lights"? And while May kept
blaming Martin Luther King every day for her troubles, the hotel still made
money, although with a different clientele. Listen to me: something else was to
blame. Besides, Mr. Cosey was a smart man. He helped more colored people here
than forty years of government programs. And he wasn't the one who boarded up
the hotel and sold seventy-five acres to an Equal Opportunity developer for thirty-
two houses built so cheap my shack puts them to shame. At least my floors are
hand-planed oak, not some slicked-up pine, and if my beams aren't ruler smooth,
they're true and properly aged when hoisted.

Before Up Beach drowned in a hurricane called Agnes, there was a drought
with no name at all. The sale had just closed, the acres barely plotted, when Up
Beach mothers were pumping mud from their spigots. Dried-up wells and
brackey water scared them so, they gave up the sight of the sea and applied for
a two-percent HUD mortgage. Rainwater wasn't good enough for them any-
more. Trouble, unemployment, hurricanes following droughts, marshland
turned into mud cakes so dry even the mosquitoes quit—I saw all that as life
simply being itself. Then the government houses went up and they named the
neighborhood Oceanside—which it isn't. The developers started out selling to

Vietnam veterans and retired whites, but when Oceanside became a target for people thrown out of work onto food stamps, churches and this affirmative action stuff got busy. Welfare helped some till urban renewal came to town. Then there were jobs all over the place. Now, it's full of people commuting to offices and hospital labs twenty-two miles north. Traveling back and forth from those cheap, pretty houses to malls and movieplexes, they're so happy they haven't had a cloudy thought, let alone a memory of Police-heads. They didn't cross my mind either until I started to miss the Cosey women and wonder if they'd finally killed each other. Who besides me would know if they were dead in there—one vomiting on the steps still holding the knife that cut the throat of the one that fed her poison? Or if one had a stroke after shooting the other and, not able to move, starved to death right in front of the refrigerator? They wouldn't be found for days. Not until Sandler's boy needed his weekly pay. Maybe I best leave off the TV for a while.

I used to see one of them driving along in that rusty old Oldsmobile—to the bank or in here, once in a while, for Salisbury steak. Otherwise they haven't left that house in years. Not since one came back carrying a Wal-Mart shopping bag and you could tell by the set of her shoulders that she was whipped. The white Samsonite luggage she left with was nowhere in sight. I thought the other one would slam the door in her face, but she didn't. I guess they both knew they deserved each other. Meaner than most and standoffish, they have the regular attention that disliked folks attract. They live like queens in Mr. Cosey's house, but since that girl moved in there a while ago with a skirt as short as underpants and no underpants at all, I've been worried about them leaving me here with nothing but an old folks' tale to draw on. I know it's trash: just another story made up to scare wicked females and correct unruly children. But it's all I have. I know I need something else. Something better. Like a story that shows how brazen women can take a good man down. I can hum to that.

George and the Bicycle Pump

by Earl Lovelace (Trinidad)

When he left work, George walked across the road from the printery, paid for an *Evening News* with a dollar bill, and with just a glance at its headlines, folded the paper and put it in his pocket, while Mary, the vendor, whom he had awakened from a snatched moment of slumber, fumbled almost distractedly among the tins and bottles on her tray for the eighty cents change to give him. He watched her gather with merciless patience, one by one, a set of coins from a small biscuit tin next to her stock of cigarettes, then unearth a twenty-five cents piece from below a jar with dinner mints. She was just reaching into her bosom to continue her search when in a fit of mercy George said, 'Give me dinner mints for the balance of the change.'

'You want dinner mints for the change?' she asked, her voice fumbly, appealing, tired, as if the thought, each thought, was a weight to be contemplated before it was lifted; so that George, feeling his own shoulders sag under the burden of her effort, pointed to a bowl of Tobago plums in front of her, 'Look,' he said. 'Give me some of those plums instead.' But his earlier request had penetrated. With one hand poised suddenly above the jar with the dinner mints, she lifted to him a face with a plea for mercy and a promise of tears. 'All right,' he said, quickly, as if wanting to pull back his last request. 'Give me the dinner mints.' And he watched her count again with tireless exactitude the ten cents and twenty-five cents and five cents pieces, while his hand remained stretched out to receive them; and, she didn't look up until she had extracted, from the store of her inexhaustible patience, the number of dinner mints that equalled the value of the money he was owed; and now, she would count them out again, the coins first, then the sweets, as she pressed them one by one into his open palm, so that he found himself wondering if he would ever get away to get to the Savannah to see his team play their football game.

At last it was over. George dropped the dinner mints and change into the same pocket, crossed the street and, hurrying now, went into the lot at the side of the printery, where he had his bicycle parked. As soon as his eyes fell on the bicycle, he saw that, yes, the pump was missing; and it came to him now, with the calm sadness as at a death that, yes, its absence now was to be explained only by theft. 'They thief my bicycle pump,' he whispered.

Seven weeks ago, when the first pump disappeared from his bicycle, George was certain that one of the fellars from the printery had borrowed it and forgotten to put it back. He was furious. Suppose he had a flat?

'Suppose I had a flat?' he asked at the printery next morning. 'You borrow a pump; you mean is such a hard thing to put it back?' And for most of the day he went about the printery with an air of righteousness and injury, lecturing everybody on responsibility and consideration, and it never occurred to him that the disappearance of his bicycle pump might be explained in any way other, other than the one he had theorised, until Marcos, the supervisor and a friend for the fifteen years he was at the printery, and for the two years before when, as young fellars, they both started out at *The Chronicle*, pulled him aside and said to him, 'George, nobody here aint borrow your bicycle pump.'

'Somebody had to borrow it,' he said to Beulah when he got home that evening. 'The pump just can't walk away.'

'They thief your bicycle pump, George,' Beulah looked up from her sewing, her eyes gleaming with the personal triumph she exuded whenever she suspected that he was in the wrong. 'They thief it!' with a sense of victory, as if it was something she had predicted.

'Thief? Thief my pump? You see you. *Your* mind. Thief is the first thing that come to *your* mind.'

Beulah was sewing a dress for her niece who was getting married in Mamoral in two weeks. She held up the garment and bit off a loose end of thread. 'Where you had it?' she asked, the thread still gripped between her teeth. 'Where you had the pump, George?' She had a talent for making his simplest action appear to be the most criminal stupidity.

'I had it...,' George felt like a child. He didn't even want to answer her, 'I had it on the bicycle.'

'You leave your bicycle pump on your bicycle?' She had put down the dress and was looking at him. 'I don't believe you, George.' And with a sigh, she bent her head to her sewing, pressed a foot to the pedal of her foot machine, sending the noise whirring throughout the house. Not another word. She had ended the communication.

But that was Beulah. To her the world outside of Mamoral, where she was born, was a jungle from which her only refuge was the fortress of her house. Here in the city, she kept her windows closed, curtains drawn, doors locked; and whatever business she had with the world outside was transacted through a parted curtain over the open louvres next to her front door. He didn't know how she didn't suffocate inside that house. As soon as he got home from work his first task was to open the windows. As soon as he turned his back, she closed them.

To Beulah, the theft of George's bicycle pump (for she had not doubt that it was theft) was a signal that the criminals of the world were closing in on them, that somehow they had become people marked for further distress, and in that week whenever George went out on the porch to the rocking chair, she locked the front door. He had to knock to get back into the house.

George still held to the theory that someone had borrowed his pump, and that the culprit, not wanting to own up to the responsibility, had found it simpler to keep quiet. As he told Marcos, 'Not everybody have the courage to accept their wrong. A person do one wrong, a little, small inch of a wrong and they frighten to correct it, and that is what start them on the road to crime. But, believe me, Marcos, I wouldn't ask no question. I wouldn't vex, it will just be great if whoever borrow the pump, just bring it back and put it on the cycle. It will be real great.'

'George,' Marcos interrupted, for George was going on and on. 'I tell you already, nobody here aint borrow your bicycle pump.'

George, however, believed otherwise and he expected that any evening he would find the pump back in its place on the bicycle. After two weeks and no sign of the pump, George bought a new pump and fitted it on the bicycle. If he missed this one also, then he would know for sure that the first one was really stolen.

'You still leaving the pump on your bicycle,' Beulah said. 'You shame to walk with it in your hand? You shame to put it in your pocket?'

At the wedding of her niece the previous weekend, with relatives all around and everybody making nearly as much fuss over her as over the bride, she had put on a performance that convinced everybody that she and George were two love birds, and even after they returned to Port of Spain, she had continued to be civil to him. It was that peace that George found himself now straining to keep.

'Is fifteen years I parking my bicycle in the printery. I never walk with no pump. I lock the bicycle, yes; but I never walk with the pump.' He heard himself and was ashamed. He was whining.

'Well, you knows best. Leave it there for them to thief. You rich. You could afford to buy a new pump every week.'

George made for the porch. There on the old rocking chair, he watched the evening grow still and fussy and felt the heat come up and watched the sun set, and he sat in the darkness, not bothering to turn on the lights, waiting to feel so sleepy that when he went into the furnace of a house it would be to go directly to bed. He couldn't enter. Beulah had locked the front door. He began to bang the door. He was real angry. 'But, I right here. I right here, what you have to lock the door for?'

'George, you don't think I see you sleeping there on yourself in that rocking chair. You aint read where they tie up a woman inside her own house and thief all her jewellery. Her husband sleeping on the gallery, and the thief just waltz past him and tie her up and take her jewellery and leave him sleeping there. You didn't read it?'

'Well, is best I go and live in the jail.'

'I don't know about you,' said Beulah, 'but I prefer jail to the cemetery.'

George was really angry. He went back out on the porch, 'and leave the blasted door,' he said.

'Listen, man,' said Beulah, who could always give better than she got, 'Is not I who thief your bicycle pump. Don't take your vexation out on me.'

'Thief?' George tried to laugh. 'Who say anybody thief the pump?'

The next evening he went to get his bicycle, he found that the new pump, the one he had bought just a couple days before, was gone. For a moment, he stood in shock; then, the impulse came over him to steal somebody else's pump, anyone's. There were five bicycles parked in the lot. He went to the first one. There was no pump on it. He turned to the next. Not one of the bicycles had a pump. He felt his body grow chill and a space without bottom open up inside him and he was falling through it.

'I don't have a word to say,' Beulah said when she saw the pump was missing. 'Not a word.'

Out on the rocking chair, George began to wonder about the pumps. Who had removed them? Was it a thief? If it was, on what days did he make his rounds? Was he someone who set out to steal or did he just happen upon the pumps? Who it was that had removed the first pump? Was it the same person who had taken the second one? Was the first pump borrowed and the second one stolen? Or were both borrowed, or both stolen? I wonder, he thought, with a bit of pride, if he doesn't wonder what kind of fellar it is who leaving his pump on his bicycle? I wonder if he know that that fellar is me?

'And by the way, George.' Beulah was standing in the doorway, 'I take out some money from the bank today. We have to put in burglar proofing.'

'Tomorrow,' said George, 'I buying another pump.'

So he had bought another pump. This time, though, he set out to catch the thief, if thief it was. At odd moments he would jump up from his linotype machine and rush outside to the parking lot and his bicycle. At other times with an air of nonchalance, he would steal forth softly. He organised a variety of weapons to be at hand whenever he went into the parking lot. At one point he had hidden a stick, at another, an old hammer with a long piece of pipe iron as a handle. He put stones at definite points. He made a slingshot which he kept in the drawer of his desk. He drew diagrams detailing points from which he might approach the bicycle. He used his lunch hour to patrol the street in front the printery. He studied the passers-by. He noted all strangers who came into the printery. He questioned them. How suspicious everyone looked. Look at them, he thought, as he watched people go by in front of the printery, one of them is the one who thief my bicycle pump.

For four weeks George kept up his surveillance. The slightest sound from outside would send him in a panic to investigate his bicycle. Fellars, noticing this pattern, began to bang things just to watch him jump. Workers started to become suspicious of him. Some thought that he was slacking, others, with more imagination, decided that he was smuggling something out of the printery, though what it was, they couldn't tell. Even Marcos became concerned.

'George,' Marcos said to him, your wife giving you trouble or what? Why don't you take a few days sick leave and rest yourself.'

At the end of the day he was exhausted. Home was no release, and he would sit on the rocking chair and watch the burglar proofing creeping around the house, making it, each day, into more of a prison. He had just begun to relax in the last few days; now, the bicycle pump was gone.

George unlocked the bicycle. He thought that he would be angry. Instead, there was a strange release, a kind of freedom, a peace. Then, rage surged in him, at the world, at the city, at Beulah, at the bicycle. And then he felt sorry for the bicycle and for the world and for Beulah and he thought of the thief. He tried to feel sorry for the thief, to feel superior to him; but, he didn't feel that feeling. He looked around at where he had hidden the stick and the hammer, and he saw the little heaps of stones that he had arranged so subtly as to blend into the lot, and it was for himself that he felt sorry.

George pushed his bicycle out of the lot, no longer hurrying to get to the football game, feeling that in his present state, if he went to the game, he would bring bad luck to his team. It was just a second division team, some young fellars from his part of Belmont, that he had been supporting for the last three years, but, so quietly, so shyly that although the crowds at their games were small and everyone seemed to know everyone else, no one knew him. The only time one of the players noticed him, to his surprise, was last season after they had lost a big game, a final, to John-John. He was making his way out of the Savannah when one of the players, going past him, put a hand on his shoulder and said, 'Hard game, uncle. Hard game!' and went on.

George walked, pushing the bicycle, all the way to the Savannah. At last he came to an empty bench below an overhanging samaan tree. He leaned his bicycle against the Savannah rails and went to the bench, but the scent of urine drove him back and with a sigh and a sense of adventure, he went a little way off and perched on the rails, took out his *Evening News* and began to read. From the corners of his eyes, he saw a young policeman approaching with easy, authoritative, rhythmic steps. Their eyes met, and something in their meeting made George feel a sense of guilt, in need of a defence. He turned back to his newspaper and waited for the policeman to go on. The policeman stopped. He looked at the bicycle. He looked at George. George looked up.

'Why you think they put benches there?' asked the policeman.

'Why they put benches … ?' George didn't know what he was talking about.

'Those rails,' said the policeman. 'They have benches there for sitting down. That is why these rails always breaking down.'

George hopped off the rails. He felt stupid, guilty. He didn't know that he had been committing an offence. Look at that, eh? Harassing me for sitting down on the Savannah rails, and all over the place people thiefing, George thought as he went past a bench with a broken seat to one with the sun shining on it and sat down.

As soon as he began to read his *News*, a fellar came and plunked himself down next to him. He was barefooted, with no shirt under his grimy jacket. As soon as he sat down he put his face in his hands. 'Younger than me,' George thought. 'Mad, maybe.' All this from one glance, and he went back to his paper.

'Gimme one of your cigarettes.' The fellar's glaring eyes were fixed upon him.

'What you say?' An edge was in George's voice.

'I say, Chief, gimme one of your cigarettes, please.'

George was just going to say no when he realised that the fellar was pointing at the cigarette pack outlined in his breast pocket. George took out the pack, removed one cigarette and gave it to him.

'You have a light?' Not 'Chief' anymore, George thought.

George had a lighter, but he didn't want the fellar to touch it, so he lit the cigarette for him and watched him drag greedily on the cigarette, then blow out smoke with a great noise. George hated people to smoke like that. There was a young fellar in the printery who smoked in that greedy, noisy way. Just for that, George never gave him a cigarette. George wanted to get up. He saw the fellar studying him. He hesitated. He didn't want his getting up to make the fellar feel offended.

'What is the headline?'

Relaxed, self-satisfied, smoke issuing from his nostrils, the fellar was looking at him. George held up the paper for him to see, but said, all the same, 'Thieves escape with three hundred dollars from El Socorro gas station.'

'Three hundred? Think the police will catch them?' his tone suddenly familiar.

'I dunno.'

'Most times the police does get tip off and they know just where to look.' With a kind of confidentiality, he added, 'They pay you for tipping off, you know.'

For no reason that he could think of, George said, 'You know they thief my bicycle pump today.'

The fellar grew alert, 'You have a mark on it?'

'A what?'

'A mark. You have a mark on it?'

'A mark? On a bicycle pump?'

'If you don't have a mark on it, then, it not yours, because, then, you see, you can't identify it. When you go and make a report to the police, you have to know what it is you loss, and how you will know if you don't have a mark on it? Whenever you buy a bicycle pump, always put a mark on it.'

To this piece of wisdom, George nodded.

'Everything I buy I have a mark on it.'

George nodded again. Faintly, from behind him, he could hear the roar of a crowd. 'Somebody score,' he said. He was wondering how his team was doing.

'Chief, you have a little change?' The fellar had on his face a confident, expectant look, as if he was asking for fees owed him for his legal advice.

George sized him up, feeling a kind of power, a kind of shame.

'Like they score another goal again,' the fellar said, smiling, his broken teeth coming into prominence, making him look guilty and smug.

But, George was looking at two fellars passing. One had a bicycle pump tucked in at his waist, between his belt.

'Chief, the change,' the fellar said.

George stood up and put a hand into his pocket and came upon the dinner mints he had bought from Mary. To give the dinner mints would, he felt, suggest too great a familiarity, as if they were friends. He felt for the coins, the change from the dollar bill, and he extracted every cent of it from his pocket and he put it all into the fellar's hand, coin by coin, the way Mary had given it to him. Then he went to his bicycle.

People had started to make their way home from the Savannah. George turned his bicycle towards Belmont. At the traffic lights he joined a number of cyclists and pedestrians waiting for the green. And for a moment he felt himself alive, in the thick of things, with the young fellars talking about the game they had just seen, a boy eyeing a girl, mothers with small children, the roar of passing vehicles, cyclists waiting to sprint across the street. A few brave souls, finding the lights taking too long to change, had begun to walk across the road. The traffic stopped for them and the lights turned green and George crossed in the stream of people. He gave his bicycle a little push, then hopped onto the saddle. He took a dinner mint from his pocket and began to take off the paper in which it was wrapped. Beulah was right, you can't leave your bicycle pump on your bicycle. All those people with pumps in their hands and at their waists, all of them was right. He put the dinner mint in his mouth, crumpled the paper and put it in his pocket.

At home, Beulah unlocked the door for him.

'They thief my bicycle pump,' he said.

'You sure they thief it?'

He didn't respond to her irony. He didn't say anything.

'Buy another pump and leave it on your bicycle again,' she said, trying to draw him out. 'They will thief it again.'

'Let them thief it,' he said, as he heard the burglar proofing clang shut behind him, right then thinking that it was cheaper to pay for a bicycle pump than to see the end of the world.

Carnival

by Paulo Colina (Brazil)

Our mouths sewn,
stitch by stitch,
with thin transparent baitline thread
    a slime of spittle, spectacle, an allure.
Shallow hooded figures pale from a fear understood
    but never explained,
a parade, singing that samba
    has no color.
And we brag of our freedom
    in samba songs,
while, at our side,
all the trembling shadows
of all our generations
fight to revive,
in our distracted memory,
the always open wound of our daily
    Ash Wednesday.

We need,
yes,
to hang behind the door
this screwed up fantasy disguise
    of a patience
that sustains a myth
of our feverish asylum
until February next year.

Solstice

by Leda Martins (Brazil)

Not always
were the suburbs of the night
so vast
and the movements of the eyes
so tenuous.

Not always not always
were the signs of pain
so blurred
nor the footfalls
so faint.

The hollowness of the word
enacts the duration of memory
imaginary texture
of a strange and familiar desire.

In the suburbs of the night
my illusions dwell
and on the fringes of the real
a drunken voice hallucinates
slaughtering the intrusion of time.

History is nothing
but fabulation.
Memory is always
an invasion of the void.

And the suburbs of the night
are webbed in the interspace of alleys
in the relics and ruins of the future
in the figures of oblivion
flaring shadows
under the luminaries.

The Son of Oxalá Who Was Named Money

by Mestre Didi (Brazil)

Many years ago, Oxalá had a son by the name of Money, who was very presumptuous and arrogant, to the point of saying to Oxalá, his father and king, in front of many people, that he was as powerful as his father, since he was accustomed to walking with Death and could take her anywhere.

To prove this claim, one day he planned to bring Death however he could, as he had told Oxalá he could in the presence of the whole kingdom.

And so, it occurred to him to lie down at a crossroads. As soon as he came across one, he lay down, remaining quiet and waiting for what might happen.

The people passed by the road, saw him lying there and commented: "Chi! Look how that man is lying there, with his head towards the house of Death, his feet towards the door of Disease, and his sides toward the place of Discord."

After these words were spoken by the people who passed by there and by what he had found out himself, he got up and said: "So, ironically, I know already everything that is necessary to learn and know; my plans are already made." And from there he went directly to the house of Death.

Arriving at her country house, he began to beat on the doleful drums that Death used when she wanted to kill specific people.

He already had gotten a net on the road and was prepared, waiting for Death to come and complain.

And so it passed. Death, hearing the sounds of the drums, arrived very quickly in order to find out who was playing.

The man Money wrapped her in the net and took her to Oxalá with these words: "Here is Death as I promised to bring her before you in person."

Oxalá responded, "Leave here with Death and all of the best things that you can carry from the world because you are the cause of good and of evil. Disappear from here! Take her and you can conquer all of the universe."

And because of this, in the name of Money, all types of crimes continue to be committed.

Billy Green Is Dead

by Gil Scott-Heron (USA)

"The economy's in an uproar,
the whole damn country's in the red,
taxi fares is goin' up ... What?
You say Billy Green is dead?"
"The government can't decide on busin'
Or at least that's what they said.
Yeah, I heard when you tol' me,
You said Billy Green is dead."
"But let me tell you 'bout these hotpants
that this big-legged sista wore
when I partied with the frat boys.
You say Billy took an overdose?"
"Well now, junkies will be junkies,
But did you see Gunsmoke las' night?
Man they had themselves a shootout

an' folks wuz dyin' left and right!
At the end when Matt was cornered
I had damn near give up hope ...
Why you keep on interrupin' me?
You say my son is takin' dope?
Call a lawyer! Call a doctor!
What you mean I shouldn't scream?
My only son is on narcotics,
should I stand here like I'm pleased?"
Is that familiar anybody?
Check out what's inside your head,
because it never seems to matter
when it's Billy Green who's dead.

Chapter 9

Speculation, Spirituality, and the Supernatural

The creative impulse to imagine life in a different world order and reality is a natural expression in the literature of Africa and its Diaspora because racism, inherent in successive global systems of oppression, ranging from enslavement, colonialism, and neocolonialism to negative globalization, has introduced problems that need creative solutions. In addition to being grounded by spirituality, religion, belief systems, and structured ways of living, it has also been natural for people of African descent to imagine a *utopia*, or a better world, and to hope that a *dystopia*, or an undesirable reality, is not at hand to make life even harder. Utopias and dystopias, as literary settings based on speculation of world change, routinely characterize the genre of science fiction, or literature that foresees social change because of futuristic advancements in science and technology. Speculation is closely related to science fiction and the supernatural, and these topics overlap with the belief systems practiced by people of African descent as well as with ideas about magic and superstition. In essence, this chapter helps readers to explore how writers engage topics related to human mortality, immortality, and ideas about alternative realities, including versions of life after death, often found in tales of mystical, or magical, realism.

As products of a modernized society, we often have difficulty imagining what life was like in the past. We rely on history to offer clues, but in our efforts to imagine an authentic version of past human experience, our immersion in the present causes us to take many things for granted. When newly enslaved Africans were brought to the Americas, their first desire was to return to Africa. This seemingly impossible desire, articulated in the folk narratives that spoke of flight back to the homeland after death or of walking on and under water back to Africa, was a dream often satisfied through supernatural belief systems. When this same idea—or "what if?"—was translated into the Back-to-Africa movement of Marcus Garvey, as he envisioned a fleet of ships—The Black Star Line—to take Africans of the Diaspora back to the African homeland, it still embodied notions of speculation and divine intervention. Even the demand for reparations—the political campaign that would require American and European governments to repay people of African descent for the years of exploitation—embodies a speculative consideration that asks, "What would life be like today for people of African descent if they had been treated justly in the past and if racism did not exist?" Many political ideas, including Black leaders' calls for autonomy or separate states or regions, are part of the genre of speculative literature. Whether an ideal world is suggested in Kwame Nkrumah demanding "Freedom, Now!" from the British or Malcolm X demanding territory from the United States, a utopia, or ideal world, to people of African descent is ironically considered a dystopia, or nightmare, to white power structures.

Black literatures also deal formally with science fiction, but the genre's inherent focus on technology and scientific innovation usually appears in the literature of Black writers who live in advanced industrialized societies. However, literary versions of apocalypse can be embellished versions of the types of poverty, natural disaster, environmental imbalance, and nuclear threats that are documented in our actual existence. The themes of space travel, time travel, and the establishment of colonies on other planets are widely documented in Black speculative literature and science fiction. Episodes of traveling backward and forward in time appear in the Black literary tradition within concrete cultural contexts whereby the protagonists experience ancient North African and West African geographies, plantation America, and futuristic urban zones where Black culture thrives. Modern speculative fiction also presents characters who undergo spiritual transformations by reliving the lives and paths of direct and general ancestors as well as those of mythological African figures such as Isis and Osiris.

Black literary characters portrayed as godly, messianic, or prophetic, or as endowed with supernatural powers of omniscience and healing, are also considered a part of this genre. The connection of religion and spirituality with speculation is not an unlikely one. The inclusion in this chapter of an extremely religious speech by Malcolm X is a unique interpretation of speculative literature. This genre is traditionally articulated as speculative *fiction*, but Malcolm X's speech—with its treatment of the topic of "world change"; its elements of religion, spirituality, and ancestor acknowledgment; and its anticipation of God's apocalyptic destruction of the white race because of its evil—suggests that the speech form can serve as speculative *nonfiction*. It is the content, not the setting, that gives the speech its speculative value. It is not surprising that Malcolm X has emerged as one of the most revered Black ancestors of the modern era and as a significant figure of Black cultural mythology. His larger-than-life status sustained in the memory of the global

Black community through written literature is a testament of the relationship between Black cultural mythology and the supernatural.

from *The Palm-Wine Drinkard: And His Dead Palm-Wine Tapster in the Dead's Town*

by Amos Tutuola (Nigeria)

I was a palm-wine drinkard since I was a boy of ten years of age. I had no other work more than to drink palm-wine in my life. In those days we did not know other money, except COWRIES, so that everything was very cheap, and my father was the richest man in our town.

My father got eight children and I was the eldest among them, all the rest were hard workers, but I myself was an expert palm-wine drinkard. I was drinking palm-wine from morning till night and from night till morning. By that time I could not drink ordinary water at all except palm-wine.

But when my father noticed that I could not do any work more than to drink, he engaged an expert palm-wine tapster for me; he had no other work more than to tap palm-wine every day.

So my father gave me a palm-tree farm which was nine miles square and it contained 560,000 palm-trees, and this palm-wine tapster was tapping one hundred and fifty kegs of palm-wine every morning, but before 2 o'clock p.m., I would have drunk all of it; after that he would go and tap another 75 kegs in the evening which I would be drinking till morning. So my friends were uncountable by that time and they were drinking palm-wine with me from morning till a late hour in the night. But when my palm-wine tapster completed the period of 15 years that he was tapping the palm-wine for me, then my father died suddenly, and when it was the 6th morning after my father had died, the tapster went to the palm-tree farm on a Sunday evening to tap palm-wine for me. When he reached the farm, he climbed one of the tallest palm-trees in the farm to tap palm-wine but as he was tapping on, he fell down unexpectedly and died at the foot of the palm-tree as a result of injuries. As I was waiting for him to bring the palm-wine, when I saw that he did not return in time, because he was not keeping me long like that before, then I called two of my friends to accompany me to the farm. When we reached the farm, we began to look at every palm-tree, after a while we found him under the palm-tree, where he fell down and died.

But what I did first when we saw him dead there, was that I climbed another palm-tree which was near the spot, after that I tapped palm-wine and drank it to my satisfaction before I came back to the spot. Then both my friends who accompanied me to the farm and I dug a pit under the palm-tree that he fell down as a grave and buried him there, after that we came back to the town.

When it was early in the morning of the next day, I had no palm-wine to drink at all, and throughout that day I felt not so happy as before; I was seriously sat down in my parlour, but when it was the third day that I had no palm-wine at all, all my friends did not come to my house again, they left me there alone, because there was no palm-wine for them to drink.

But when I completed a week in my house without palm-wine, then I went out and, I saw one of them in the town, so I saluted him, he answered but he did not approach me at all, he hastily went away.

Then I started to find out another expert palm-wine tapster, but I could not get me one who could tap the palm-wine to my requirement. When there was no palm-wine for me to drink I started to drink ordinary water which I was unable to taste before, but I did not satisfy with it as palm-wine.

When I saw that there was no palm-wine for me again, and nobody could tap it for me, then I thought within myself that old people were saying that the whole people who had died in this world, did not go to heaven directly, but they were living in one place somewhere in this world. So that I said that I would find out where my palm-wine tapster who had died was.

One fine morning, I took all my native juju and also my father's juju with me and I left my father's hometown to find out whereabouts was my tapster who had died.

But in those days, there were many wild animals and every place was covered by thick bushes and forests; again, towns and villages were not near each other as nowadays, and as I was travelling from bushes to bushes and from forests to forests and sleeping inside it for many days and months, I was sleeping on the branches of tress, because spirits etc. were just like partners, and to save my life from them; and again I could spend two or three months before reaching a town or village. Whenever I reached a town or a village, I would spend almost four months there, to find out my palm-wine tapster from the inhabitants of that town or village and if he did not reach there, I would leave there and continue my journey to another town or village. After the seventh month that I had left my home town, I reached a town and went to an old man, this old man was not a really man, he was a god and he was eating with his wife when I reached there. When I entered the house I saluted both of them, they answered me well, although nobody should enter his house like that as he was a god, but I myself was a god and juju-man. Then I told the old man (god) that I am looking for my palm-wine tapster who had died in my town some time ago, he did not answer to my question but asked me first what was my name? I replied that my name was "Father of gods" who could do everything in this world, then he said: "was that true" and I said yes; after that he told me to go to his native black-smith in an unknown place, or who was living in another town, and bring the right thing that he had told the black-smith to make for him, then he would believe that I was the "Father of gods who could do everything in this world" and he would tell me where my tapster was.

Immediately this old man told or promised me so, I went away, but after I had travelled about one mile away then I used one of my juju and at once I changed into a very big bird and flew back to the roof of the old man's house; but as I stood on the roof of his house, many people saw me there. They came nearer and looked at me on the roof, so when the old man noticed that many had surrounded his house and were looking at the roof, he and his wife came out from the house and when he saw me (bird) on the roof, he told his wife that if he had not sent me to his native black-smith to bring the bell that he told the black-smith to make for him, he would tell me to mention the name of that bird. But at the same time that he said so, I knew what he wanted from the black-smith and I flew away to his black-smith, then when I reached there I told the black-smith that the old man (god) told me to bring his bell which he had told him to make for him. So the black-smith gave me the bell; after that, I returned to the old man with the bell and when he saw me with the bell, he and his wife were surprised and also shocked at that moment.

After that he told his wife to give me food, but after I had eaten the food, he told me again, that there remained another wonderful work to do for him, before he would tell me whereabouts my tapster was. When it was 6:30 a.m. of the following morning, he (god) woke me up, and gave me a wide and strong net which was the same colour as the ground of that town. He told me to go and bring "Death" from his house with the net. When I left his house or the town about a mile, there I saw a junction of roads and I was doubtful when I reached the junction, I did not know which was Death's road among these roads, and when I thought within myself that as it was the market day, and all the market goers would soon be returning from the market— I lied down on the middle of the roads, I put my head to one of the roads, my left hand to one, right hand to another one, and my both feet to the rest, after that I pretended as I had slept there. But when all the market goers were returning from the market, they saw me lied down there and shouted thus:— "Who was the mother of this boy, he slept on the roads and put his head towards Death's road."

Then I began to travel on Death's road, and I spent about eight hours to reach there, but to my surprise I did not meet anybody on this road until I reached there and I was afraid because of that. When I reached his (Death's) house, he was not at home by that time, he was in his yam garden which was very close to his house, and I met a small rolling drum in his verandah, then I beat it to Death as a sign of salutation. But when he (Death) heard the sound of the drum, he said thus:—"Is that man still alive or dead?" Then I replied "I am still alive and I am not a dead man."

But at the same time that he heard so from me, he was greatly annoyed and he commanded the drum with a kind of voice that the strings of the drum should tight me there; as a matter of fact, the strings of the drum tighted me so that I was hardly breathing.

When I felt that these strings did not allow me to breathe and again every part of my body was bleeding too much, then I myself commanded the ropes of the yams in his garden to tight him there, and the yam stakes should begin to beat him also. After I had said so and at the same time, all the ropes of the yams in his garden tighted him hardly, and all the yam stakes were beating him repeatedly, so when he (Death) saw that these stakes were beating him repeatedly, then he commanded the strings of the drum which tighted me to release me, and I was released at the same time. But when I saw that I was released, then I myself commanded the ropes of the yams to release him and the yam stakes to stop beating him, and he was released at once. After he was released by the ropes of yams and yam stakes, he came to his house and met me at his verandah, then we shook hands together, and he told me to enter the house, he put me in one of his rooms, and after a while, he brought food to me and we ate it together, after that we started conversations which went thus:—He (Death) asked me from where did I come? I replied that I came from a certain town which was not so far from his place. Then he asked what did I come to do? I told him that I had been hearing about him in my town and all over the world and I thought within myself that one day I should come and visit or to know him personally. After that he replied that his work was only to kill the people of the world, after that he got up and told me to follow him and I did so.

He took me around his house and his yam garden too, he showed me the skeleton bones of human-beings which he had killed since a century ago and showed me many other things also, but there I saw that he was using skeleton bones of human-beings as fuel woods and skull heads of human-beings as basins, plates and tumblers etc.

Nobody was living near or with him there, he was living lonely, even bush animals and birds were very far away from his house. So when I wanted to sleep at night, he gave me a wide black cover cloth and then gave me a separate room to sleep inside, but when I entered the room, I met a bed which was made with bones of human-beings; but as this bed was terrible to look at or to sleep on it, I slept under it instead, because I knew his trick already. Even as this bed was very terrible, I was unable to sleep under as I lied down there because of fear of the bones of human-beings, but I lied down there awoke. To my surprise was that when it was about two o'clock in the mid-night, there I saw somebody enter into the room cautiously with a heavy club in his hands, he came nearer to the bed on which he had told me to sleep, then he clubbed the bed with all his power, he clubbed the centre of the bed thrice and he returned cautiously, he thought that I slept on that bed and he thought also that he had killed me.

But when it was 6 o'clock early in the morning, I first woke up and went to the room in which he slept, I woke him up, so when he heard my voice, he was frightened, even he could not salute me at all when he got up from his bed, because he thought that he had killed me last night.

But the second day that I slept there, he did not attempt to do anything again, but I woke up by two o'clock of that night, and went to the road which I should follow to the town and I travelled about a quarter of a mile to his house, then I stopped and dug a pit of his (Death's) size on the centre of that road, after that I spread the net which the old man gave me to bring him (Death) with on that pit, then I returned to his house, but he did not wake up as I was playing this trick.

When it was 6 o'clock in the morning, I went to his door and woke him up as usual, then I told him that I wanted to return to my town this morning, so that I wanted him to lead me a short distance; then he got up from his bed and he began to lead me as I told him, but when he led me to the place that I had dug, I told him to sit down, so I myself sat down on the road side, but as he sat down on the net, he fell into the pit, and without any ado I rolled up the net with him and put him on my head and I kept going to the old man's house who told me to go and bring him Death.

As I was carrying him along the road, he was trying all his efforts to escape or kill me, but I did not give him a chance to do that. When I had travelled about eight hours, then I reached the town and went straight to the old man's house who had told me to go and bring Death from his house. When I reached the old man's house, he was inside his room, then I called him and told him that I had brought Death that he told me to go and bring. But immediately he heard from me that I had brought Death and when he saw him on my head, he was greatly terrified and raised alarm that he thought nobody could go and bring Death from his house, then he told me to carry him (Death) back to his house at once, and he (old man) hastily went back to his room and started to close all his doors and windows, but before he could close two or three of his windows, I threw down Death before his door and at the same time that I threw him down, the net cut into pieces and Death found his way out.

Then the old man and his wife escaped through the windows and also the whole people in that town ran away for their lives and left their properties there. (The old man had thought that Death would kill me if I went to his house, because nobody could reach Death's house and return, but I had known the old man's trick already.)

So that since the day that I had brought Death out from his house, he has no permanent place to dwell or stay, and we are hearing his name about in the world. This was how I brought out Death to the old man who told me to go and bring him before he (old man) would tell me whereabouts my palm-wine tapster was that I was looking for before I reached that town and went to the old man.

But the old man who had promised me that if I could go to Death's house and bring him, he would tell me whereabouts my palm-wine tapster was, could not wait and fulfil his promise because he himself and his wife were narrowly escaped from that town.

Then I left the town without knowing where my tapster was, and I started another fresh journey.

from *The Rape of Shavi*

by Buchi Emecheta (Nigeria)

1
The Bird Of Fire

It was good to rest after such a long drought. King Patayon had thought it was going to carry every man, woman and child away to their ancestors. Evidently this time the ancestors had not been ready to receive them. Even to fifty-year-old, slow-thinking and easy-going King Patayon, descending to the ancestors, however beautiful Ogene the river goddess had said it was, was not a rosy prospect. Not that he distrusted the prophets and priests of Ogene, it was just that nobody had been to the ancestors and back to tell them what it was like. The priests and prophets claimed that the dead ones spoke through them, but King Patayon, indulgently called "the Slow One" by his subjects, sometimes had his doubts. The priests and the prophets were very useful in instilling fears into the minds of the people of Shavi, by adding a tinge of the supernatural to everything. So the King was not going to go out and openly ask the people, "But how do we know the dead really do speak through the priests?" They were doing their work, and he was doing his. And on a day like this, when every-thing was working as expected, why should he complain?

It was blissful to sit with one's advisers, reminisce leisurely about the past, and ponder a little about the future. For the present, there was plenty to eat and the children were in excellent health. The sun was going down in the west, the date palms threw long, spindly shadows, and the palace walls fat, robust ones, as if in competition. Among the shadows, colourful birds sang twitter-ingly in their nests. The palace parrots hopped about in their cages, impatient with the twittering birds. Even the King's bush cat sat lazily by its master, look-ing from one end of the vast palace compound to the other, or stretching and letting out a watery yawn before beginning to lick himself. From the nearby lakes, which had decided the founding fathers to settle here in Shavi, and given them their goddess Ogene, water, and fish, a breeze wafted over the palace walls through the date palms and onto the king and his closest friends, re-clining together in the piazza.

Two of the palace dogs started to bark at the same time, but in that relaxed welcoming tone known to King Patayon, from which he could guess that whatever was approaching was not dangerous. One of his wives perhaps, or one of his many children, or a friend. There was no need for him to stir. He merely changed from resting on one arm to the other, selected another tooth-pick and started to rid the gaps in his teeth of the particles of roasted goat he and his men had eaten for the afternoon meal. He had hardly settled down to this, when he saw six of his chiefs slowly making their way to the piazza. They walked leisurely, looking very dignified, not only because it was a restful af-ternoon, now bordering on early evening, but also because they were chiefs, middle-aged, and, above all, men. Middle age such as theirs demanded dig-nity. They were not ruffled by the barking of the dogs.

The chiefs, as if they were one man, knelt on one knee, moved their white body cloth from their shoulders to their armpits, and bowed their heads. King Patayon smiled, inclined his head in return and motioned them with his hands to get up. He gestured them to their seats, and the chiefs, slowly but with sub-tle calculation, moved, three to each side of the king. They too reclined on the scented skins of animals that had been scattered on all the elevated sitting places built into the inside walls of the palace. Young boys, who worked in the palace as servers and bodyguards, padded in like silent locusts, distributing chilled coco-palm drinks, honeyed bushmeat, nerve-relaxing grass, jenja nuts and eggs. Despite their busy air, not a word was spoken.

King Patayon, known as the Slow One, hated approaching any topic in haste. After a quarter of a century of his reign, his men had come to value this and to accept these long communicative silences as the behaviour demanded within the palace walls. The king knew his men came to the palace for a reason, though he didn't know what it was, but since they were using his own method in approaching the matter, he didn't wish to hurry them. So with them, he changed from reclining on one arm to the other, and gazed at the shadows lengthening along the palace walls.

As the silence was getting longer than usual, Patayon smiled into vacancy. His men had come to complain about something, something embarrassing, so they didn't know how to start. And he wasn't going to help them. The king and his men had sworn with their life blood that no one should oppress or use his position to treat the other subhumanly. They had learnt through their ancestors what it was to be enslaved, and Shavi prided herself on being the only place in the whole of the Sahara, where a child was free to tell the king where it was that he had gone wrong. And the child knew that not only would he not be punished but also that he would be listened to and his suggestion might even be incorporated into the workings of the kingdom. That King Patayon and his fathers before him had been able to do this and still retain their respect and dignity, was always a marvel to other kingdoms around.

Then, as if on cue, one of the men started talking banalities. King Patayon, the Slow, smiled again and joined in the spirit of the game. Then there was a rustle, subtle yet determined, from the part of the palace that belonged to the King's wives. Patayon, who had eight of them, and was about to marry a ninth, knew from experience the rustle of each woman's waist wrap and body cloth. He could tell that that particular nervous rustle was coming from no other than his senior wife, the trouble-maker and great talker, Shoshovi. Now King Patayon was ruffled. For it was one of the prerequisites of respectability in Shavi that a man must be capable of keeping his house in order. The approach of this woman, with her long and rather undignified strides like a man's, spelt trouble. The languid smile disappeared from King Patayon's face and in its place came a fixed grin. He sat up with deliberate slowness, and for once, the stress of ruling over twenty thousand people and of making sure that his family was a model of respectability showed slightly on his face.

The Queen Mother, Shoshovi, did not look at her husband's face. She made straight for the centre of the gathering and knelt in salutation: "I greet you, our King and our owners."

"Get up Shoshovi, you know you're always welcome to come to the gathering of men at any time," King Patayon said cynically.

The King's men noted this, but wore faces so blank that they were almost mask-like.

The King's big cat, Kai-kai, left its master's side and walked slowly to Shoshovi, purring and rubbing its big overfed body against her. She started to stroke him as she got to her feet. She felt like holding the cat for reassurance but it was too big and heavy, so she clasped her hands to her front and looked over the heads of the reclining men. Not that they would kill or harm her if she said something stupid, it was just that in a place like Shavi, people knew so much about each other that shame killed faster than disease.

"My owners," she began, "I invited you to the palace for a purpose. You all know what they say, that women are the softness on which our men recline. But sometimes that softness has gently to give a reminder to our men and our owners. I beg you all to go the heart of the matter, to tell your friend and your King why it is that you are here. For if one's friend behaves badly, one is not entirely without blame. Ogene our goddess says that we are all responsible for each other, and forbids that we should let the communal spirit die and go back to the way our people were forced to live in Ogbe Asaba."

The men all beat their left sides, nodding as they chorused gravely, "Ogene forbid!"

As usual there was a long trembling silence, broken only by Kai-kai's loud purring. Then the King looked at all his men, his eloquent silence demanding explanation from them. His eyes rested on his oldest and most trusted friend, Egbongbele, who shifted from one arm to the other in embarrassment. He coughed and began to speak.

"Our Queen Mother's grievances are not unimportant. For is it not known that if one's women are contented, life will offer one contentment?"

Patayon broke in, coolly, "You are free to get on with it Egbongbele. This is a free kingdom. And sometimes things do happen in one's own home of which one is the last to know. No person in Shavi should be afraid to speak to the King. Even Shoshovi is speaking her mind."

Egbongbele didn't know what to make of this statement, so he delegated the nasty job to a young member of the group who was well known for tactlessness.

"Mensa, stand up and tell the king where he's gone wrong."

A young and over-enthusiastic man, in his early thirties, got up with a jerky energy and spat, "The King must give Shoshovi a cow before taking the beautiful and dutiful daughter of Ayi to be his ninth queen. Shoshovi wants a cow."

Egbongbele now looked very confused and Shoshovi started to wring her hands. Why let the tactless Mensa speak to King Patayon like that? What were these men up to? Trying to amuse themselves at her expense? Trying to trivialize her anger and her pride? "Shoshovi wants a cow", just like that, as if she was a lion hungry for flesh. They were well behaved enough not to laugh, but she knew that they were laughing in their hearts and that her husband, King Patayon, was laughing the loudest behind that noncommittal face. She felt humiliated, ridiculed. To march out of the gathering was her first impulse, but such ungracious behaviour was not expected of the King's wives, to say nothing of the Queen Mother herself. For, being the first wife of the reigning King, having seven younger wives after her, and being the mother of the King's heir, Asogba, was she not the Queen Mother? Her life and position demanded calm and compromise.

Shoshovi had her argument clear in her head, and no amount of ridicule was going to make a thing she had thought out so clearly look and become ridiculous. She stood there, her arms held tight to her front, her head held high, helped by her close fitting ehulu neckband, made from the precious glistening stones found underneath the foot of the hill by the Ogene lakes. Only the king's women were allowed to wear these ehulu neckbands. She had four layers which helped in propping her chin up. A queen was never seen outside her house door without the band. She had to wear it until the day she died. She now concentrated her gaze beyond the palace wall, where the dome of the palace buildings stood in silent silhouette against the sky.

The King's best friend, Egbongbele, was laughing again, this time foolishly. The shame and embarrassment was now theirs, not hers. She had presented her case as befitted the queen mother, and it was left to them to treat it as befitted the King's men. If they had set out to embarrass her, they had misfired. Her determined toughness and calmness were calculated to rattle them too. And she knew that her husband, King Patayon, couldn't help them.

The rest of the kingdom called him "the Slow One" and he didn't encourage people to think of him otherwise, but she, the woman who bore him his first son, Asogba, who had seen him cry when his father King Kofi died, had seen him doubt himself many, many a time, knew that behind that overplayed slowness was a mind that worked very fast and calculated rapidly. She waited.

"Mensa," Egbongbele stood up and began to clarify, "put it rather crudely. What our Queen Mother, Shoshovi, is saying, my King, is that you have forgotten to come to her house and tell her your intention to marry the gentle daughter of Ayi. She said she heard about it from the other queens when she saw the arrangements being made all over the palace, and didn't know what those arrangements were for. It looked as if a new bride was expected, but how come she wasn't consulted? We are now requesting the King to consult her in the proper manner with a well-fed cow."

King Patayon took the trouble to lift the lids of his eyes and look at his wife, Shoshovi. This dry stick of a woman with shrunken breasts! He studied the two bones that held her neck to the rest of her body, which started from each part of her jaw, and dipped themselves into her neck, forming a bony triangle. Her teeth, which were once very white and one of her beauties, now had black gaps between them. She was still thin as previously, but this new juiceless thinness was that of old age, with most of the nerves of her body going crisscross, almost in relief. Why had she become like this? Was it because she was now given to talking to herself in monologues and that whenever she opened her mouth, it was invariably to nag, to criticise? She had made herself unlovable by the bitterness that poured from her mouth.

Patayon didn't like the idea of any of his wives or any member of his household exposing him in this manner. But it would be silly of him to show his hurt. He didn't like the way Shoshovi's case had been given to tactless Mensa to present to the King's friends. Surely Egbongbele could have chosen someone respected in the council of the Elders? It looked as if Egbongbele was making a joke at his expense. If Patayon had not tried his friend of many years, Egbongbele, several times and found him as steadfast and as unmovable as the rocks that guarded the Ogene lakes, he would have doubted his reasons for this undignified behaviour. But he knew that this was a mistake.

Maybe Egbongbele thought he would be pleasing his old friend by ridiculing his troublesome wife Shoshovi, but had forgotten that the people of Shavi said, "If a woman asks you to beat her badly-behaved child for her, one knows that those words do not come from the woman's heart". Only a silly person would take such utterances literally. This shows that one's best friends do not always know one thoroughly. Shoshovi was a troublemaker, but Shoshovi was his first wife, his first queen that his father King Kofi had married for him, and was Shoshovi not the mother of Asogba?

King Patayon's glance involuntarily went to Asogba who was leaning against an egbo tree, chewing something angrily. Like his mother his gaze was directed over the top domes of the palace and into the sky and somehow by this attitude of remote arrogance, he managed to reduce everything being said to a kind of irrelevance. Patayon knew that those eyes looking into distant vacancy missed very little. But how was he to know the way he felt about the treatment his mother was receiving from his advisers? Shoshovi should not have come here to complain about such a domestic issue.

Women! When they are angered, they forget how deeply they have loved. They throw all caution and reason into the empty air. They don't mind who they hurt in their search for justice. Patayon, who had loved Shoshovi, was suffering; Asogba, the son who would supercede him and who was borne to him by Shoshovi, was suffering too. All for what? Simply because he wanted to celebrate the end of a long drought in the way any ruler he knew of would, by taking a new queen. Now troublesome Shoshovi wanted a cow. He had been going to give it to her anyhow on the night of the bride's arrival. But he had been going to make sure that all arrangements were made before he informed her. Now she had found out. Only Ogene knew what trouble she would cook up to make the going difficult for him. He would now have to use more pressure on the parents of the girl—a rather undignified move that would not befit a king. But what was there for him to do? Shoshovi should not have come to the gathering to expose him in this way ...

A big, fast moving cloud suddenly loomed and tore itself from the sky, one minute a cloud, the next looking like an unusually long house, another minute the shape of a bird. It was spinning very fast, faster than any woman's spinning needle. Now it was smoking and coughing, and before the people could think what to do or say, the bird of fire arched and crashed into Shavi, just outside the palace walls, close to one of the Ogene lakes. The ordinary people of Shavi, the king, his men and their wives and children, every living thing, ran and hid.

"What is this? What has landed in our midst?" the people asked each other. "Has the Queen's anger become so great that she's summoned Ogene to send a mysterious bird of fire into Shavi?"

King Patayon gathered his loose body cloth and his wobbly body and ran. He ran in among the egbo trees, the tall cacti, past the palace walls, towards the biggest of the three lakes. There he knelt, his face distorted with fear as he prayerfully addressed the lake. "What is this monster that has descended on Shavi, Mother Ogene and all you goddesses of the lakes? What, or who are they, in that bird of fire? I will give Shoshovi a cow. I promise I will, but please, you ageless mothers, don't terrify your children so," went on King Patayon. But apart from the initial bang, nothing happened. King Patayon prayed himself hoarse. The tranquil Ogene remained calm. The egbo trees stood dignified in their thin stateliness, their stems naked and bare. The cacti shoots stood in humps like little ant hills.

As the air was now quiet, Patayon looked up to see a very curious diffusion of thick smoke melting into the clear blue stretches of sky above his head. The vast desert plain with its patches of cacti shoots lost itself in the horizon, until it met with the gentle incline of the hills surrounding Shavi like huge sentinels.

But neither plains, nor hills, could tell Patayon a thing. Maybe this phenomenon was beyond them, and beyond the Ogene goddesses. For how could Ogene and her sister goddesses, who for centuries had been worshipped and consulted by the people of Shavi in their sheltered desert homeland, dream of a bird that flew with a noise like thunder, a bird that had smoke in its tail, and carried human-like creatures?

Ogene did not answer Patayon. It was beyond her. This was something new, after which things would never be the same again.

2

The Leper Creatures

"Things will never be the same again." Patayon mouthed his thoughts aloud. And because he had said all he could think of saying, he started to listen. He could hear muffled cries of human suffering. When he sniffed, he could smell burning flesh. Patayon got up from his praying and peered in between the groves towards the area of the crash. He saw moving figures that looked very much like human beings, dragging one another from the fire. They were doing what anyone else would have done, but from where Patayon was painfully crouching, he couldn't swear to the fact that they were human. He had seen some animals do likewise.

He altered his position to get a better view. Yes, they looked like people, very much like him and his people of Shavi. But though he was still far from the place of the crash, he could feel that there was something strange about these creatures. Their clothes were odd, their colour frightfully strange, like the colour of lepers, and even their cries were as if somebody was holding their noses, making them emit sounds akin to the ones made by wild things when provoked. Nonetheless, they looked more like humans than animals, Patayon, the slow and dignified, decided eventually. But this was a discovery he was not going to make known until he had heard from his advisers, his priests and his people.

Meanwhile, what was he going to do? Trust that troublesome woman to invoke Ogene to send leprous creatures in a strange-looking bird of fire. He had long suspected that the goddesses of the lakes always sided with women. Shoshovi wanted a cow, and before he could think what to say or do, the impatient goddesses had sent these leper calamities, making funny noises and wearing even funnier clothes. Now everybody in Shavi was going to suffer, simply because of a stupid cow and a woman's jealousy.

Patayon waited, he knew not what for, adjusting and readjusting his body cloth. He shrugged his shoulders again and again, a sign that Patayon the Slow was thinking. He was muttering to himself intermittently, when suddenly a huge pile of leaves slithered up to him. Patayon jumped and shouted, "Ogene, have mercy on us!"

"Oh, father, it's only me," Asogba announced, as he straightened himself, rubbing the camouflage off his body. His usually lop-sided smile was so pronounced that Patayon couldn't tell whether it betokened derision or admiration. If Asogba had noticed that a minute earlier his father had been blaming the goddesses of Ogene for the falling of the bird of fire and was now calling upon them to save him, he didn't show it. He usually behaved likewise. When frightened, he would shout for his mother first, even though he agreed with his father Patayon that most women were created simply to cause men trouble. "I want to go out and meet those people from the bird of fire," Asogba announced in harsh, hushed tones.

The rims of Patayon's eyes had never been so red as they were now. He opened and shut his mouth like the fish in the lakes. He was frightened, and was trying to transmit his fear to this rash son of his. "Are you not afraid, young man?" he asked at last. "Is it not enough that your mother in her anger has invoked Ogene to send us leprous-looking creatures in a strange bird of fire? Now you want to go and bring them into Shavi? Don't they look like lepers to you?"

"Is it like that, father? You mean these people come from our goddesses of the Ogene lakes? I never thought of that. And as for the colour of their skin, they look more like badly washed albinos than lepers to me, because they have no patches, father. I don't think Ogene's finished them properly and maybe she's brought them for our sun to finish them off … I don't know, but I want to find out."

They were both silent, thinking. Asogba flattened himself against an egbo tree, staring and squinting at the place of the crash so as to get a better view. When in thought, his face contorted like his mother's, his brows corrugating in deep furrows that made him instantly look older than his twenty-two years. He would emphasise his contemplative mood by placing a finger over his thin lips as if about to blow a whistle, peering out from dark lashes that looked artificially blackened. Once he had made his mind up, the furrows would smooth themselves out, the lopsided smile would spread across his thin lips, curiously progressing into a near vacant cheeky grin. That grin, sometimes resorted to cover up embarrassment, and sometimes used as a bland senseless gesture, had never ceased to annoy Patayon, first in his wife Shoshovi, and now inherited in an exaggerated way by Asogba.

"It's not funny, Asogba. This is all your mother's doing, and you know it," Patayon snapped.

"Yes, father, but suppose these people are in danger, suppose they're refugees from slavery, like our great, great grandfathers all that time ago? Suppose they need help? Ogene would never forgive us, would she? Remember, father, you taught me that we're all refugees, immigrant strangers on this earth. We come and go like waves, you used to say to me, remember? So, why will you not now let me answer the cries of another set of refugees?"

"Asogba, I didn't ask you not to go," began Patayon, trying to regain his slipping dignity, "only that I have my doubts as to whether those figures are human or not. If they aren't then they have no souls, and why should we pity figures that have no souls, which might be dangerous animals for all we know?"

"Oh, father, I've watched them closely whilst standing behind that egbo tree, and I'm convinced that they've had a very bad accident. It even looks like two of them are dead already. They feel pain, they talk, they walk on two feet. What other evidence do you want them to produce to show that they're human?"

"Asogba, what other human have you seen of that colour? What human have you seen flying birdwise like these ones? These creatures flew in here!"

Asogba was silent and the knowing grin on his face disappeared. His father was right. Only birds or animals of the air flew, not humans as he knew them.

The two men stood facing each other. It was uncommon to disobey a reigning king, and the king, knowing this, was extra careful not to put himself in a corner where any of the people he ruled might be inclined to go against his wishes. And now, to be so challenged by no less a person than his own son! To save face, Patayon mumbled, "I'm not ordering you not to go, but I'm advising you against it, as any other father would advise his son and heir."

There was no other way he could stop his son. The people of Shavi would resort to physical means of persuasion only as a last resort. They believed in talking an evil person out of his bad ways. They also believed that shame kills faster than any disease or physical harassment. Being such a close-knit society, they could leave the wrongdoer to his own conscience. The only punishment given was that of taking a life for a life, and they regarded honour, personal dignity, as life. For, they asked, if one's honour and dignity are taken from one, then what is left of the person? And any one who kills another person, whether in anger or not, must forfeit his own life. This again was as a result of what they had suffered when they were once slaves in King Kokuma's land. So, other than ordering his own son killed, there was no way of getting him to obey. He would leave him to his conscience which would surely prick him as to whether it was right to question a king's authority.

But Asogba's conscience worked differently. For the first time in his whole life, nearly twenty-three years, he was becoming impatient with his father's slow-moving ways. He was beginning to have had enough of this man, who, though his father, was nonetheless so slow, and who because of his younger wives took a kind of negative pleasure in humiliating his mother ...

Suddenly, a piercing shriek rent the desert air. It seemed to make the spindly leaves on the egbo tree quiver and go suddenly brown, and the hair of every human nearby stand on end. Asogba peered through the gap formed by the two naked branches of the egbo trees he had been leaning himself against, and the sight that greeted his eyes made him want to cry.

He faced his father squarely. "That is the cry of a mother. Look, she's carrying her little one, and I think the child is dead or dying. I must go see if they need our help. We must talk about their humanity later."

With that, Asogba padded through the dead twigs and dying shrubs into the open space where the water-coloured bird of the sky had landed.

"Why won't he let one of the palace guards go? After all, he's going to rule," Patayon said aloud, thinking that he was alone and talking to himself.

But he soon stopped as he noticed that the leaves that had been still were moving and egbo trees started to dislodge men from behind them. His men, who had flattened themselves against the trees, apparently hadn't missed a word of the battle before father and son.

"Maybe he needs to show the people of Shavi that he can rule without fear when you're gone, our ruler," Egbongbele felt bold enough to say.

"I'm not going yet, my friend," Patayon retorted.

Egbongbele heard, of course, but acted as if the King hadn't spoken. He turned and addressed the men, "Everyone go back to his egbo tree; you should all have your arrows fully saturated with poison and point them unwaveringly at the place of the crash. That way we will cover our prince, without making him lose face. He should not know of this because going there to face those strange creatures demanded the bravery found only in those of royal birth. We should be proud of him."

The king's men took their places behind the egbo trees, their arrows poised ready to fly, watching every movement that went on in the sandy centre of the place of the crash. They all, including Patayon, felt instinctively that the bird of fire heralded change. Whether good or bad, only Ogene could tell.

from *Midnight Robber*

by Nalo Hopkinson (Jamaica/Guyana/Trinidad/Canada)

Oho. Like it starting, oui? Don't be frightened, sweetness; is for the best. I go be with you the whole time. Trust me and let me distract you little bit with one anasi story:

It had a woman, you see, a strong, hard-back woman with skin like cocoa-tea. She two foot-them tough from hiking through the diable bush, the devil bush on the prison planet of New Half-Way Tree. When she walk, she foot strike the hard earth *bup!* like breadfruit dropping to the ground. She two arms hard with muscle from all the years of hacking paths through the diable bush on New Half-Way Tree. Even she hair itself rough and wiry;

long black knotty locks springing from she scalp and corkscrewing all the way down she back. She name Tan-Tan, and New Half-Way Tree was she planet.

Yes, this was a hard woman, oui. The only thing soft about Tan-Tan is she big, molasses-brown eyes that could look on you, and your heart would start to beat time *boobaloops* with every flutter of she long eyelashes. One look in she eyes, and you fall for she already. She had a way to screw them up small-small like if she angry, just so nobody wouldn't get lost in the melting brown of them, but it never work, you hear? Once this woman eyes hold you, it ain't have no other woman in the world for you. From Garvey-prime to Douglass sector, from Toussaint through the dimension veils to New Half-Way Tree, she leave a trail of sad, lonely men—and women too, oui?—who would weep for days if you only make the mistake and say the words "brown eyes."

But wait—you mean you never hear of New Half-Way Tree, the planet of the lost people? You never wonder where them all does go, the drifters, the raga-muffins-them, the ones who think the world must be have something better for them, if them could only find which part it is? You never wonder is where we send the thieves-them, and the murderers? Well master, the Nation Worlds does ship them all to New Half-Way Tree, the mirror planet of Toussaint. Yes, man; on the next side of a dimension veil. New Half-Way Tree, it look a little bit like this Toussaint planet where I living: same clouds in the high, high mountains; same sunny bays; same green, rich valleys. But where Toussaint civilized, New Half-Way Tree does be rough. You know how a thing and the shadow of that thing could be in almost the same place together? You know the way a shadow is a dark version of the real thing, the dub side? Well, New Half-Way Tree is a dub version of Toussaint, hanging like a ripe maami apple in one fold of a dimension veil. New Half-Way Tree is how Toussaint planet did look before the Marryshow Corporation sink them Earth Engine Number 127 down into it like God entering he woman; plunging into the womb of soil to impregnate the planet with the seed of Granny Nanny. New Half-Way Tree is the place for the restless people. On New Half-Way Tree, the mongoose still run wild, the diable bush still got poison thorns, and the mako jumbie bird does still stalk through the bush, head higher than any house. I could tell you, you know; I see both places for myself. How? Well, maybe I find a way to come through the one-way veil to bring you a story, nuh? Maybe I is a master weaver. I spin the threads. I twist warp 'cross weft. I move my shuttle in and out, smooth smooth, I weaving you my story, oui? And when I done, I shake it out and turn it over *swips!* and maybe you see it have a next side to the tale. Maybe is same way so I weave my way through the dimensions to land up here. No, don't ask me how.

New Half-Way Tree is where Tan-Tan end up, and *crick-crack*, this is she story:

TOUSSAINT PLANET

Quashee and Ione? For true? His good good friend and his wife? Mayor Antonio of Cockpit County stepped up into the pedicab. "What you staring at?" he growled at the runner. "Is home I going."

"Yes, Compère," the runner said through a mouthful of betel nut. She set off, and every slap her two feet-them in their alpagat sandals slapped against the ground, it sounded to Antonio like "Quashee-Ione, Quashee-Ione." He could feel his mouth pursing up into a scowl. He sat up straight, tapping his impatient fingers on one hard thigh. Not there yet? He slumped back against the seat. A trickle of sweat beaded down from the nape of his neck to pool at his dampening collar. *Ione, running a fingertip down the head-back and grinning to see how the touch make he shiver.* Antonio muttered, "What a thing to love a woman, oui?"

The runner heard him. She glanced back over her shoulder. Corded muscle twisted along her back, stretched on either side from her spine to the wings of her shoulder blades. Grinning, she panted out, "What a great thing for true, Compère. Three z'amie wives I have. Woman so sweet, I tell you."

Nothing to say to that. Antonio made a sucking sound of impatience between his teeth. He tapped his temple to alert his earbug; started to identify himself out loud to the pedicab's ancient four-eye, but remembered in time that pedicab runners only used headblind machines. This cab couldn't transmit to his earbug. He sighed, powered the transmission console on manually and selected a music station. Old-time mento rhythms gambolled noisily in the air round him. He settled back against the soft jumbie leather seat, trying to get into the music. It jangled his ears like "Quashee-Ione, Quashee-Ione, eh-eh."

Ione, mother of his one daughter. Ione, that toolum-brown beauty, the most radiant, the loveliest in Cockpit County. When Ione smile, is like the poui trees bloom, filling the skies with bright yellow flowers. A laugh from Ione could thief hearts the way mongoose thief chicken.

Ione and Antonio had grown up neighbours on two wisdom weed farms. Fell in love as children, almost. Time was, Ione used to laugh her poui flower laugh for Antonio alone. Time was, Antonio and Ione were the night cradling the moon.

Maybe all that done now? How it could done?

Antonio tapped the music off. Under his breath, he ordered his earbug to punch up his home. It bleeped a confirmation at him in nannysong, and his eshu appeared in his mind's eye.

"Hot day, Master," grumbled the house eshu.

Today the a.i.* had chosen to show itself a dancing skeleton. Its bone clicked together as it jigged, an image the eshu was writing onto Antonio's optic nerve. It sweated robustly, drops the size of fists rolling down its body to splash *praps!* on the "ground" then disappear. "What I could do for you?" The eshu made a ridiculously huge black lace fan appear in one hand and waved it at its own death's head face.

"Where Ione?"

"Mistress taking siesta. You want to leave a message?"

"Backside. No, never mind. Out." Antonio flicked the music station on again, then nearly went flying from his seat as the pedicab hit a rut in the road.

"Sorry, Compère," laughed the runner. "But I guess you is big mayor, you could get that hole fill up in no time, ain't?"

Runners didn't respect nobody, not even their own mother-rass mayor. "Turn left here so," Antonio said. "That road will take we to the side entrance." And it was usually deserted too. He didn't fell like playing the skin-teeth grinning game today with any of his constituents he might run into: Afternoon, Brer Pompous, how the ugly wife, how the runny-nose little pickney-them? What, Brer Pompous, Brer Boasty, Brer Halitosis? Performance at the Arawak Theatre last night? A disgrace, you say? Community standards? Must surely be some explanation, Brer Prudish, Brer Prune-face. Promise I go look into it, call you back soon. No, Antonio had no patience for none of that today.

Slap-slap of the runner's feet. *Quashee-Ione.* Jangling quattro music in the air. *Quashee-Ione, eh-eh.*

Too many hard feelings between him and Ione, oui? Too much silence. When she had gotten pregnant, it had helped for a little while, stilled some of her restlessness. And his. He had been delighted to know he would have a child soon. Someone who would listen to him, look up to him. Like Ione when she'd been a green young woman. When little Tan-Tan had arrived, she'd been everything Antonio could have wished for.

In a hard-crack voice, the runner broke into a raucous song about a skittish woman and the lizard that had run up her leg. Antonio clenched his teeth into a smile. "Compère!" he shouted. She didn't reply. Blasted woman heard him easy enough when it suited her. "Compère!"

"Yes, Compère?" Sweety-sweety voice like molasses dripping.

"Please. Keep it quiet, nuh?"

The woman laughed sarcastically.

"Well, at least when we get closer to my home? Uh ... my wife sleeping."

---

* a.i. = artificial intelligence.

"Of course, Compère. Wouldn't want she for hear you creeping home so early in the day."

Bitch. Antonio stared hard at her wide, rippling back, but only said, "Thank you."

Antonio knew full well that his work as mayor was making him unpopular to certain people in this little town behind God back. Like this pedicab operator right here.

And like she'd read his mind, the blasted woman nuh start for chat? "Compère, me must tell you, it warm my heart to know important man like you does pedicab."

"Thank you, Compère," Antonio said smoothly. He knew where this was going. Let her work up to it, though.

"Pedicab is a conscious way to travel, you see? A good-minded way. All like how the cab open to the air, you could see your neighbours and them could see you. You could greet people, seen?"

"Seen," Antonio agreed. The runner flashed a puzzled look at him over her shoulder. She made a misstep, but caught herself in the pedicab's traces. "Careful, Compère," Antonio said solicitously. "You all right?"

"Yes, man." She continued running. Antonio leaned forward so she could hear him better.

"A-true what you say. Is exactly that I forever telling Palaver House," he said in his warmest voice. "In a pedicab, you does be part of your community, not sealed away in a closed car. I tired telling Palaver House allyou is one of the most important services to the town."

The runner turned right around in her traces and started jogging backwards. She frowned at him. "So if we so important, why the rass you taxing away we livelihood? We have to have license thing now." Her betel-red teeth were fascinating. "I working ten more hours a week to pay your new tariff. Sometimes I don't see my pickney-them for days; sleeping when I leave home, sleeping when I come back. My baby father and my woman-them complaining how I don't spend time with them no more. Why you do this thing, Antonio?"

Work, he was forever working. And the blasted woman making herself such a freeness with his name, not even a proper "Compère." Antonio ignored her rudeness, put on his concerned face. "I feel for you and your family, sister, but what you want me do? Higglers paying their share, masque camps paying theirs, pleasure workers and rum shops paying theirs. Why pedicab runners should be any different?"

She had her head turned slightly backwards; one eye on him, one on the road. He saw the impatient eye-roll on the half of her face that she presented.

"Them does only pay a pittance compared to we. Let we stop with the party line, all right?"

"But ..."

"Hold on." She wasn't listening, was jogging smartly backwards to the road's median to avoid a boulderstone. Her feet slapped: *Quashee-Ione. Quashee-Ione?* She pulled the pedicab back into the lane, turned her back to him, picked up speed. Over her shoulder: "Truth to tell, we come to understand allyou. The taxes is because of the pedicabs, ain't."

Antonio noted how businesslike her voice had become, how "me" had multiplied into "we." Guardedly he asked her, "How you mean, sister?"

"Is because we don't use a.i.'s in the pedicabs."

An autocar passed in the opposite direction. The woman reclining inside it looked up from her book long enough to acknowledge Antonio with a dip of her head. He gave a gracious wave back. Took a breath. Said to the runner, "Is a labour tax. For the way allyou insist on using people when a.i. could run a cab like this. You know how it does bother citizens to see allyou doing manual labor so. Back-break ain't for people." Blasted luddites.

"Honest work is for people. Work you could see, could measure. Pedicab runners, we know how much weight we could pull, how many kilometers we done travel."

"Then ..." Antonio shrugged his shoulders. What for do? A-so them want it, a-so it going to stay.

The woman ran a few more steps, feet slip-slapping *Ione? Ione?* An autocar zoomed past them. The four people inside it had their seats turned to face one another over a table set for afternoon tea. Antonio briefly smelt cocoa, and roast breadfruit. He barely had time to notice the runner give a little hop in the traces. Then with a jolt and a shudder the pedicab clattered through another pothole. Antonio grabbed for the armrests. "What the rass ... ?"

"Sorry, Compère, so sorry."

"You deliberately ..."

"You all right, Compère? Let me just climb up and see."

"No ..." But the woman was already in the cab beside him. She smelt strongly of sweat. She hummed something that sounded like nannysong, but fast, so fast, a snatch of notes that hemidemisemiquavered into tones he couldn't distinguish. Then Antonio heard static in his ear. It faded to an almost inaudible crackle. He tapped his earbug. Dead. He chirped a query to his eshu. No answer. He'd been taken offline? How the rass had she done that? So many times he'd wish he could.

The woman was *big*, her arms muscled as thighs, her thighs bellied with muscle. Antonio stood to give himself some height over her. "What you do that for?" he demanded.

"No harm, Antonio; me just want to tell you something, seen? While nanny ear everywhere can't hear we."

"Tell me what?"

She indicated that he should sit again. She planted her behind in the seat next to him. Antonio edged away from her rankness. "The co-operative had a meeting," she said.

"Co-operative?"

"Membership meeting of the Sou-Sou Co-operative: all the pedicab runners in Cockpit County; Board of Directors, everybody."

Why hadn't he known they were organized? Damned people even lived in headblind houses, no way for the 'Nansi Web to gather complete data on them. "So you have a communication from your co-operative for me?" he asked irritably.

"A proposal, yes. A discreet, unlinked courier service. Special government rate for you and the whole Palaver House. We offering to bring and carry your private messages."

Private messages! Privacy! The most precious commodity of any Marryshevite. The tools, the machines, the buildings; even the earth itself on Toussaint and all the Nation Worlds had been seeded with nanomites—Granny Nanny's hands and her body. Nanomites had run the nation ships. The Nation Worlds were one enormous data-gathering system that exchanged information constantly through the Grande Nanotech Sentient Interface: Granny Nansi's Web. They kept the Nation Worlds protected, guided and guarded its people. But a Marryshevite couldn't even self take a piss without the toilet analyzing the chemical composition of the urine and logging the data in the health records. Except in pedicab runner communities. They were a new set, about fifty years old. They lived in group households and claimed that it was their religious right to use only headblind tools. People laughed at them, called them a ridiculous pappyshow. Why do hard labour when Marryshow had made that forever unnecessary? But the Grande 'Nansi Web had said let them be. It had been designed to be flexible, to tolerate a variety of human expression, even dissension, so long as it didn't upset the balance of the whole.

But what the runners were offering now was precious beyond description: an information exchange system of which the 'Nansi Web would be ignorant. The possibilities multiplied in Antonio's mind. "The whole Palaver House?" he asked.

"Seen, brother. Some of we did want to extend the offer to you one, oui? But then we start to think; if we putting we trust in only you, what kind of guarantee that go give we? Not to say that you is anything but a honest man, Compère, but this way we have some, how you call it, checks and balances in the deal, right?"

"And what guarantees you offering we?" asked Antonio petulantly.

"Contract between we and you. On handmade paper, not datastock."

"Headblind paper too? How?"

"We make it from wood pulp."

Like very thin composition board, Antonio imagined. Koo ya, how these people were crafty. "And what your terms would be?"

"Some little payment for we services, and reduction of we taxes to the same level as the pleasure workers and them."

Crafty, oui. Turn right away round from paying the government to having the government pay you. Palaver House would have to mask the activity as something else, probably a government-dedicated taxi service. Only the Inner Palaver House could be privy to it, but it ain't have nothing unusual in something like that. Antonio found himself whispering, "We could do it ..."

"Me knows so. You going to come to terms with we?"

"Maybe. You have ahm, a private place where me and some next people could meet with your board?"

"Yes, man." They set a meeting time. She told him the place. "One of we go come and get you. Look smart, partner. You coming online again." She warbled again in impossibly intricate nannysong. Antonio's ear popped. In a voice schooled to convey worry the runner said: "Sorry man, too sorry. It working again?"

"Yes." He was still marvelling at the few minutes he'd been dead to the web. Never before since birth. He chirruped in nannysong for his house eshu.

"Master," said the eshu, "you want me?" No visuals this time. It was capricious sometimes.

"Yes. Something ... malfunction in the blasted headblind four-eye in this pedicab, and I was only getting static for a second. I just making sure you still getting through."

On the screen, the eshu appeared, spat. "Cho. Dead metal." It winked out.

"I name Beata," the woman said. She stuck out a paw. He shook it. Her palm was rough. From work, Antonio realised. How strange.

"Seen." They had an agreement. Silently, she leapt onto the roadway, stepped into the traces and set off again.

They were at the entrance to Antonio's house in minutes. "Here you go, Compère. Safe and sound and ready to ferret out your woman business."

Quashee and Ione? Antonio felt jealousy turning like a worm in his belly. He didn't like the weight of the cuckold's horns settling on his brow. His mind was so worked up, he barely remembered to pay Beata. He got down from the cab and would have walked away, but she hauled it into his road and stood there sweaty and grimy, blocking his path. She poked a bit of betel out from between two teeth with a black-rimed nail. Flicked it away. Smiled redly at him. He threw some cash at her. She caught it, inspected the coin insolently and tucked it into her bubby-band. "Walk good, Compère. Remember what I say."

He was sure he could still smell the sweat of her even though she had jogged off. He opened the white picket gates and walked up the long path towards the mayor house.

This day, Antonio couldn't take no pleasure in his big, stoosh home, oui? He didn't even self notice the tasteful mandala of rock that his Garden had built around the flag pole near the entrance when he first took office. The pale pink rockstone quarried from Shak-Shak Bay didn't give him no joy. The sound of the Cockpit County flag cracking in the light breeze didn't satisfy him. His eye passed right over the spouting fountain with the lilies floating in it and the statue of Mami Wata in the middle, arching her proud back to hold her split fishtail in her own two hands. The trinkling sound of the fountain didn't soothe his soul. Is the first time he didn't notice the perfection of his grounds: every tree healthy, every blade of grass green and fat and juicy. He didn't remark on the snowcone colours of the high bougainvillaea hedge. He didn't feel his chest swell with pride to see the marble walls of the mayor house gleaming white in the sun.

Quashee and Ione? For true?

On the way, Antonio found Tan-Tan playing all by herself up in the julie-mango tree in the front yard. Her minder was only scurrying round the tree, chicle body vibrating for anxious; its topmost green crystal eyes tracking, tracking, as it tried to make sure Tan-Tan was all right. "Mistress," it was whining, "you don't want to come down? You know Nursie say you mustn't climb trees. You might fall, you know. Fall, yes, and Nursie go be vex with me. Come down, nuh? Come down, and I go tell you the story of Granny Nanny, Queen of the Maroons."

Tan-Tan shouted back, "Later, all right? I busy now."

Antonio felt liquid with love all over again for his doux-doux darling girl, his one pureness. Just so Ione had been as a young thing, climbing trees her parents had banned her from. Antonio loved his Tan-Tan more than songs could sing. When she was first born, he was forever going to watch at her sleeping in her bassinet. With the back of his hand he used to stroke the little face with the cocoa-butter skin soft like the fowl breast feathers, and plant gentle butterfly kisses on the two closed-up eyes. Even in her sleep, little Tan-Tan would smile to feel her daddy near. And Antonio's heart would swell with joy for the beautiful thing he had made, this one daughter, this chocolate girl. "My Tan-Tan. Sweet Tan-Tan. Pretty just like your mother." When she woke she would yawn big, opening her tiny fists to flash little palms at him, pink like the shrimp in Shak-Shak Bay. Then she would see him, and smile at him with her mother's smile. He could never hold her long enough, never touch her too much.

Antonio called out to his child in the tree: "Don't tease the minder, doux-doux. What you doing up there?"

Tan-Tan screwed up her eyes and shaded them with one hand. Then: "It ain't have no doux-doux here," the pickney-girl answered back, flashing a big smile at her daddy. Sweet, facety child. "Me is Robber Queen, yes? This foliage is my subject, and nobody could object to my rule." Tan-Tan had become fascinated with Midnight Robber. Her favourite game was to play Carnival Robber King. She had a talent for the patter. "Why you home so early, Daddy?"

In spite of her worries, Antonio smiled to see his daughter looking so pretty. His sweetness, his doux-doux darling could give him any kind of back-talk, oui? "I just come to see your mother. You know where she is?"

"She and uncle taking tea in the parlour, Daddy. Them tell me I mustn't come inside till they call me. I could go in now?"

"Not right now, darling. You stay up there; I go come and get you soon."

Antonio dragged his feet towards the parlour, the way a condemned man might walk to a hanging tree. As he reached inside the detection field, the house eshu clicked on quiet-quiet inside his ear. "You reach, Master," it said. "Straighten your shirt. Your collar get rumple. You want me to announce you?"

"No. Is a surprise. Silence."

"Yes, Master Antonio." The eshu's voice sounded like it had a mocking smile in it. Like even self Antonio's house was laughing at him? Where Ione?

When Antonio stood outside the door, he could hear his wife inside laughing, laughing bright like the yellow poui flower, and the sound of a deep, low voice intertwined with the laugh. Antonio opened the parlour door.

Years after, Antonio still wouldn't tell nobody what he saw in the parlour that day. "Rasscloth!" he would swear. "Some things, a man can't stand to describe!"

Mayor Antonio, the most powerful man in the whole county, opened up his own parlour door that afternoon to behold his wife lounging off on the settee with her petticoat hitched up round her hips, and both feet wrapped round Quashee's waist.

Antonio stood there for a while, his eyes burning. He knew then that whenever he shut them from now on, he would see that pretty white lace petticoat spread out all over the settee; Quashee's porkpie hat on Ione's head; the teasing, happy smile on her face; and Quashee's bare behind pushing and pushing between Ione's sprawled-opened knees.

Antonio never noticed that Tan-Tan had followed him to the parlour door. She stood there beside him, eyes staring, mouth hanging open. She must have cried out or something, because all of a sudden, Ione looked over Quashee's shoulder to see the two of them in the doorway. She screamed: "Oh, God, Antonio; is you?"

Soft-soft, Antonio closed the parlour door back. He turned and walked out his yard. Tan-Tan ran after him, screaming, "Daddy! Daddy! Come back!" but he never even self said goodbye to his one daughter.

Little after Antonio had left, Ione came running alone out the house, her hair flying loose and her dress buttoned up wrong. She found Tan-Tan by the gate, crying for her daddy. Ione gave Tan-Tan a slap for making so much noise and attracting the attention of bad-minded neighbours. She bustled Tan-Tan inside the house, and the two of them settled down to wait for Antonio to come back.

But is like Antonio had taken up permanent residence in his office. Ione took Tan-Tan out of the pickney crèche where she went in the mornings to be schooled: said she wanted some company in the house, the eshu would give Tan-Tan her lessons. So Antonio couldn't come and visit Tan-Tan during siesta like he used to. He had to call home on the four-eye to talk to her. He would ask how her lessons with the eshu were going. He would tell her to mind not to give Nursie or the minder any trouble, but he never asked after Ione. And when Tan-Tan asked when he was coming back, he'd get quiet for a second then say, "Me nah know, darling."

Well, darling, you know Cockpit County tongues start to wag. Kaiso, Mama; tell the tale! This one whisper to that one how he hear from a woman down Lagahoo way who is the offside sister of Nursie living in the mayor house how Ione send Quashee away, how she spend every day and night weeping for Antonio, and she won't even self get out of bed and change out of she nightgown come morning. Another one tell a next one how he pass by Old Man Warren house one afternoon, and see he and Antonio sitting out on the porch in the hot hot sun, old-talking and making plans over a big pitcher of rum and coconut water. In the middle of the day, oui, when sensible people taking siesta!

All the way in Liguanea Town, people hear the story. They have it to say how even the calypsonian Mama Choonks hear what happen, and she writing a rapso about it, and boasting that she going to come in Road March Queen again this year, when she bust some style 'pon the crowd with she new tune "Workee in the Parlour." And Sylvia the engineer to tell she daughter husband that somebody else whisper to she how he see Quashee in the flight yard every day, practising cut and jab with he machète. But eh-eh! If Antonio going to call Quashee out to duel come Jour Ouvert morning, ain't Antonio shoulda been practising too?

What you say, doux-doux? You thought this was Tan-Tan story?

You right. My mind get so work up with all that Antonio had to suffer, that I forget about poor Tan-Tan.

In fact it seemed like nobody wanted to pay any mind to Tan-Tan no more. People in her house would stop talking when Tan-Tan went into a room, even old Nursie. Ione was spending all her days locked up in her room in conference with Obi Mami-Bé, the witch woman. It looked like Antonio wasn't coming back at all at all.

But truth to tell, Tan-Tan wasn't so lonely, oui. She was used to staying out of Ione's way, and playing Robber Queen and jacks with just the fretful minder for company. She liked leaning against the minder's yielding chicle, humming along with the nursery rhymes it would sing to her. She had nearly outgrown the minder now, yes, but it did its level best to keep up with her. Tan-Tan used to play so hard, it come in like work:

"Minder, you see where my jacks gone? I could find the ball, but not the jacks. You think I left them under the settee yesterday?"

"Maybe, Mistress. Make I look." And the old construct would flatten its body as best it could and squeeze itself into tight places to retrieve the jacks Tan-Tan was always losing.

Or, "Minder, let we play some old-time story, nuh? I go be Granny Nanny, Queen of the Maroons, and you have to be the planter boss."

So the minder would access the Nanny history from the web and try to adapt it to Tan-Tan's notions of how the story went.

Tan-Tan had a way to make up tales to pass the time, and like how time was hanging heavy on her hands nowadays, she started to imagine to herself how sweet it would be when her daddy would come to take her away from this boring old place where everybody was sad all the time, their faces hanging down like jackass when he sick. She was going to go and live with Daddy in the mayor office, and them would play Robber King and Queen in the evenings when Daddy finish work, and Daddy would tickle her and rub her tummy and tell how she come in pretty, just like her mother. And come Carnival time, them would ride down to town together in the big black limousine to see the Big Parade with masqueraders-them in their duppy and mako jumbie costumes, dancing in the streets.

Finally, it was Jonkanoo Season; the year-end time when all of Toussaint would celebrate the landing of the Marryshow Corporation nation ships that had brought their ancestors to this planet two centuries before. Time to give thanks to Granny Nanny for the Leaving Times, for her care, for life in this land, free from downpression and botheration. Time to remember the way their forefathers had toiled and sweated together: Taino Carib and Arawak; African; Asian;

Indian; even the Euro, though some wasn't too happy to acknowledge that-there bloodline. All the bloods flowing into one river, making a new home on a new planet. Come Jonkanoo Week, tout monde would find themselves home with family to drink red sorrel and eat black cake and read from *Marryshow's Mythic Revelations of a New Garveyite: Sing Freedom Come*.

But Antonio still wouldn't come home.

This Jonkanoo Season was the first time that Tan-Tan would get to sing parang with the Cockpit County Jubilante Mummers. She and eshu had prac-tised the soprano line for "Sereno, Sereno" so till she had been singing it in her sleep and all. And she had done so well in rehearsals that the Mummers had decided to let her sing the solo in "Sweet Chariot." Tan-Tan was so excited, she didn't know what to do with herself. Daddy was going to be so proud!

Jonkanoo Night, Nursie dressed her up in her lacy frock to go from house to house with the Mummers. Nursie finished locksing Tan-Tan's hair, and took a step back to admire her. "Nanny bless, doux-doux, you looking nice, you know? You make me think of my Aislin when she was just a little pickney-girl. Just so she did love fancy frock, and she hair did thick and curly, just like yours."

"Aislin?" Tan-Tan dragged her eyes from her own face in the mirror eshu had made of the wall. She had been trying to read her daddy's features there. "You have a daughter, Nursie?"

Nursie frowned sadly. She looked down at her feet and shook her head. "Never mind, doux-doux; is more than twelve years now she climb the half-way tree and gone for good. Let we not speak of the departed." She sucked her teeth, her face collapsing into an expression of old sorrow and frustration. "Aislin shoulda had more sense than to get mix up in Antonio business. I just grateful your daddy see fit to make this lonely old woman part of he households afterwards."

And all Tan-Tan could do, Nursie wouldn't talk about it any more after that. Tan-Tan just shrugged her shoulders. Is so it go; Toussaint people didn't talk too much about the criminals they had exiled to New Half-Way Tree. Too bedsides, Tan-Tan was too nervous to listen to Old Nursie's horse-dead-and-cow-fat story tonight. First parang! Nursie had had all the ruffles on Tan-Tan's frock starched and her aoutchicongs, her tennis shoes-them, whitened till they gleamed.

Tan-Tan's bedroom door chimed, the one that led outside to the garden. She had a visitor, just like big people! "You answer it, doux-doux," said Nursie.

"Eshu, is who there?" asked Tan-Tan, as she'd heard her parents do.

"Is Ben, young Mistress," the eshu said through the wall. "He bring a pres-ent for you."

A present! She looked at Nursie, who smiled and nodded. "Let he in," said Tan-Tan.

The door opened to admit the artisan who gave her father the benefit of his skill by programming and supervising Garden. As ever, he was barefoot, console touchpen tucked behind one ear and wearing a mud-stained pair of khaki shorts and a grubby shirt-jac whose pockets held shadowy bulges like babies' diapers. Weeds hung out of the bulgy pockets. He had an enormous bouquet of fresh-cut ginger lilies in one hand. The red blooms stretched on long thumb-thick green stalks. Tan-Tan gasped at the present that Ben was balancing carefully in his other hand.

Nursie chided, "Ben, is why you always wearing such disgraceful clothes, eh? And you can't even put on a pair of shoes to come into the house?"

But Ben just winked at her and presented her with the lilies. She relented, giggled girlishly and buried her nose in the blossoms. Finally he seemed to notice Tan-Tan gazing at the present. He smiled and held it out to her: a Jonkanoo hat. It was made from rattan, woven in the torus shape of a nation ship. "I design it myself," Ben told her. "I get Garden to make it for you. Grow it into this shape right on the vine."

"Oh, what a way it pretty, Ben!" The hat even had little portholes all round it and the words "Marryshow Corporation: Black Star Line II" etched into a flat blade of dried vine in its side.

"Look through the portholes."

Tan-Tan had to close one eye to see through one of the holes. "I see little people! Sleeping in their bunk beds, and a little crèche with a teacher and some pickney, and I see the bridge with the captain and all the crew!"

"Is so we people reach here on Toussaint, child. And look ..." Ben pulled six candles out of a pocket and wedged them into holders woven all along the ring of the ship. "Try it on let me see."

Careful-careful, Tan-Tan slid the hat onto her head. It fit exactly.

"When you ready to go," Ben said, "ask Mistress Ione to light the candle-them for you. Then you going to be playing Jonkanoo for real!"

Nursie fretted, "I don't like this little girl walking round with them open flame 'pon she head like that, you know? You couldn't use peeny-wallie bulb like everybody else, eh? Suppose the whole thing catch fire?"

"Ain't Ione go be right there with Tan-Tan?" Ben reassured her. "She could look after she own pickney. This is the right way to play Jonkanoo, the old-time way. Long time, that hat woulda be make in the shape of a sea ship, not a rocket ship, and them black people inside woulda been lying pack-up head to toe in they own shit, with chains round them ankles. Let the child re-member how black people make this crossing as free people this time."

Tan-Tan squinched up her face at the nasty story. Crèche teacher had sung them that same tale. Vashti and Crab-back Joey had gotten scared. Tan-Tan too. For nights after she'd dreamt of being shut up in a tiny space, unable to move. Eshu had had to calm her when she woke up bawling.

Nursie shut Ben up quick: "Shush now, don't frighten the child with your old-time story."

"All right. Time for me to get dressed, anyway. Fête tonight! Me and Rozena going to dance till 'fore-day morning, oui." Ben knelt down and smiled into Tan-Tan's eyes. "When you wear that hat, you carry yourself straight and tall, you hear? You go be Parang Queen-self tonight!"

"Yes, Ben. Thank you!"

When everything was ready, Nursie fetched Tan-Tan to Ione. Nursie carried the Jonkanoo hat in front of her like a wedding cake, candles and all.

Ione was too, too beautiful that night in her madras head wrap and long, pale yellow gown, tight so till Tan-Tan was afraid that Ione wouldn't be able to catch breath enough to sing the high notes in "Rio Manzanares." She looked so pretty, though, that Tan-Tan ran to hug her.

"No, Tan-Tan; don't rampfle up me gown. Behave yourself, nuh? Come let we go. I could hear the parang singers practising in the dining room. Is for you that hat is?"

"From Ben, Mummy."

Ione nodded approvingly. "A proper Jonkanoo gift. I go give you one from me tomorrow." She put the nation ship hat on Tan-Tan's head, and then lit all six candles.

"Candles for remembrance, Tan-Tan. Hold your head high now, you hear? You have to keep the candles-them straight and tall and burning bright."

"Yes, Mummy." Tan-Tan remembered Nursie's posture lessons. Proper-proper, she took Ione's hand, smoothed her frock down, and walked down the stairs with her mother to join the Cockpit County Jubilante Mummers. The John Canoe dancer in his suit of motley rags was leaping about the living room while the singers clapped out a rhythm.

Tan-Tan was Cockpit County queen that night for true! The Mummers went house to house, singing the old-time parang songs, and in every place, people were only feeding Tan-Tan tamarind balls and black cake and thing—"Candles for remembrance, doux-doux!"—till the ribbon sash round her waist was binding her stuffed belly. Everywhere she went, she could hear people whispering behind their hands: "Mayor little girl ... sweet in that pretty frock ... really have Ione eyes, don't? Mayor heart must be hard ... girl child alone so with no father!" But she didn't pay them any mind. Tan-Tan was enjoying herself. All the same, she couldn't wait to get to the town square to sing the final song of the night. Antonio would be there to greet the Mummers and make his annual Jonkanoo Night speech. For days he had been busy with the celebrations and he hadn't called to speak to Tan-Tan.

At last the Mummers reached the town square. By now, Tan-Tan's feet were throbbing. Her white aoutchicongs had turned brown with dust from walking all that distance, and her belly was beginning to pain her from too much food. Ione had blown out the candles on the nation ship hat long time, for with all the running round Tan-Tan was doing, the hat kept falling from her head. She had nearly set fire to Tantie Gilda's velvet curtains.

Tan-Tan was ready to drop down with tiredness, oui, but as they entered the town square, she straightened up her little body and took her mummy's hand.

"Light the candles again for me, Mummy." Hand in hand with Ione, Tan-Tan marched right to her place in the front of the choir. She made believe she was the Tan-Tan from the Carnival, or maybe the Robber Queen, entering the town square in high state for all the people to bring her accolades and praise and their widows' mites of gold and silver for saving them from the evil plantation boss (she wasn't too sure what an "accolade" was, oui, but she had heard Ben say it when he played the Robber King masque at Carnival time the year before). Choirmaster Gomez smiled when he saw her in her pretty Jonkanoo hat. He pressed the microphone bead onto her collar. Tan-Tan lost all her tiredness one time.

The square was full up of people that night. One set of people standing round, waiting for the midnight anthem. It must be had two hundred souls there! Tan-Tan started to feel a little jittery. Suppose she got the starting note wrong? She took a trembling breath. She felt she was going to dead from nerves. Behind her, she heard Ione hissing, "Do good now, Tan-Tan. Don't embarrass me tonight!"

Choirmaster Gomez gave the signal. The quattro players started to strum the tune, and the Cockpit County Jubilante Mummers launched into the final song of the night. Tan-Tan was so nervous, she nearly missed her solo. Ione tapped her on her shoulder, and she caught herself just in time. She took a quick breath and started to sing.

The first few notes were a little off, oui, but when she got to the second verse, she opened her eyes. Everybody in the square was swaying from side to side. She started to get some confidence. By the third verse, her voice was climbing high and strong to the sky, joyful in the 'fore-day morning.

> *Sweet chariot,*
> *Swing down,*
> *Time to ride,*
> *Swing down.*

As she sang, Tan-Tan glanced round. She saw old people rocking back and forth to the song, their lips forming the ancient words. She saw artisans standing round the Mercy Table, claiming the food and gifts that Cockpit Town people had made for them with their own hands in gratitude for their creations. Every man-jack had their eyes on her. People nodded their heads in time. She swung through the words, voice piping high. The Mummers clapped in time behind her. The she spied a man standing near the edge of the crowd, cradling a sleeping little girl in his arms. He was the baby's daddy. Tan-Tan's soul came crashing back to earth. Tears began creeping down her face. She fought her way to the end of the song. When she put up her hand to wipe the tears away, an old lady near the front said, "Look how the sweet song make the child cry. What a thing!" Tan-Tan pulled the mike bead off and ran to Ione. The nation ship hat fell to the ground. Tan-Tan heard someone exclaim behind her, and the scuffing sound as he stamped out the flame of the candles. She didn't pay it no mind. She buried her head in her mother's skirt and cried for Antonio. Ione sighed and patted her head.

Soon after, her daddy did come, striding into the town square to give his speech. But he didn't even self glance at Tan-Tan or Ione. Ione clutched Tan-Tan's shoulder and hissed at her to stand still. Tan-Tan looked at her mother's face; she was staring longingly and angrily at Antonio with bright, brimming eyes. Ione started to hustle Tan-Tan away. Tan-Tan pulled her hand to slow her down. "No, Mummy, no; ain't Daddy going to come with we?"

Ione stooped down in front of her daughter. "I know how you feel, doux-doux. Is Jonkanoo and we shoulda be together, all three of we; but Antonio ain't have no mercy in he heart for we."

"Why?"

"Tan-Tan, you daddy vex with me; he vex bad. He forget all the nights I spend alone, all the other women I catch he with."

Tan-Tan ain't business with that. "I want my daddy." She started to cry.

Ione sighed. "You have to be strong for me, Tan-Tan. You is the only family I have now. I not going to act shame in front of Cockpit County people and they badtalk. Swallow those tears now and hold your head up high."

Tan-Tan felt like her heart could crack apart with sorrow. Ione had to carry the burst nation ship. Scuffling her foot-them in the dirt, Tan-Tan dragged herself to the limousine that had been sent to the square to wait for them. They reached home at dayclean, just as the sun was rising. Tan-Tan was a sight when Nursie met her at the door: dirty tennis shoes, plaits coming loose, snail tracks of tears winding down her face.

"Take she, Nursie," Ione said irritably. "I can't talk no sense into she at all."

"Oh, darling, is what do you so?" Nursie bent down to pick up the sad little girl.

Tan-Tan leaked tired tears, more salt than water. "Daddy ain't come to talk to me. He ain't tell me if he like how I sing. Is Jonkanoo, and he ain't self even give me a Jonkanoo present!"

"I ain't know what to do for she when she get like this," Ione told Nursie. "Tan-Tan, stop your crying! Bawling ain't go make it better."

Nursie and Ione took Tan-Tan inside to bed, but is Nursie who washed Tan-Tan's face and plaited up her hair nice again so it would not knot up while she slept. Is Nursie who dressed Tan-Tan in her favourite yellow nightie with the lace at the neck. Nursie held to her lips the cup of hot cocoa-tea that Cookie sent from the kitchen, and coaxed her to drink it. Cookie was an artisan too, had pledged his creations to whoever was living in the mayor house. Usually Tan-Tan loved his cocoa, hand-grated from lumps of raw chocolate still greasy with cocoa fat, then steeped in hot water with vanilla beans and Demerara sugar added to it. But this time it was more bitter than she liked, and she got so sleepy after drinking it! One more sip, and she felt she had was to close her eyes, just for a little bit. Nursie put Tan-Tan to bed with the covers pulled right up to her neck, and stroked her head while sleep came. Ione only paced back and forth the whole time, watching at the two of them.

But just as sleep was locking Tan-Tan's eyes shut, is Ione's sweet voice she heard, singing a lullaby to her from across the room.

> *Moonlight tonight, come make we dance and sing,*
> *Moonlight tonight, come make we dance and sing,*
> *Me there rock so, you there rock so, under banyan tree,*
> *Me there rock so, you there rock so, under banyan tree.*

And her earbug echoed it in her head as eshu sang along.

Tan-Tan slept right through the day until the next morning. When she woke up Ione told her irritably, "Your daddy come by to see you while you was sleeping."

Tan-Tan leapt up in the bed. "Daddy here!"

"No, child. He gone about he business."

The disappointment and hurt were almost too much for breathing. Unbelieving, Tan-Tan just stared at Mummy. Daddy didn't wait for her to wake up?

"Cho. Me ain't able with you and your father. He leave this for you." Ione laid out a costume on the bed, a little Robber Queen costume, just the right size for Tan-Tan. It had a white silk shirt with a high, pointy collar, a little black jumbie leather vest with a fringe all round the bottom, and a pair of wide red leather pants with more fringe down the sides. It even had a double holster to go round her waist, with two shiny cap guns sticking out. But the hat was the best part. A wide black sombrero, nearly as big as Tan-Tan herself, with pom-poms in different colours all round the brim, to hide her face in the best Robber Queen style. Inside the brim, it had little monkeys marching all round the crown of the hat, chasing tiny birds. The monkeys leapt, snatching at the swooping birds, but they always returned to the brim of the hat.

"Look, Tan-Tan!" Ione said, in that poui-bright voice she got when she wanted to please. "It have Brer Monkey in there, chasing Brer Woodpecker for making so much noise. Is a nice costume, ain't?"

Tan-Tan looked at her present good, but her heart felt like a stone inside her chest. She pressed her lips together hard. She wasn't even going to crack a smile.

"Yes, Mummy."

"Your daddy say is for he little Jonkanoo Queen with the voice like honey. You must call he and tell he thanks."

"Yes, Mummy."

"You ain't want to know what I get for you?"

"Yes, Mummy."

Smiling, Ione reached under Tan-Tan's bed and pulled out the strangest pair of shoes Tan-Tan had ever seen. They were black jumbie leather carved in the shape of alligators like in the zoo. The toes of the shoes were the alligators' snouts. They had gleaming red eyes. The shoes were lined inside with jumbie feather fluff. "Try them on, nuh?" Ione urged.

Tan-Tan slid her feet into the shoes. They moulded themselves comfortably round her feet. She stood up. She took a step. As she set her foot down the alligator shoe opened its snout wide and barked. Red sparks flew from its bright white fangs. Tan-Tan gasped and froze where she was. Ione laughed until she looked at Tan-Tan's face. "Oh doux-doux, is only a joke, a mamaguy. Don't dig nothing. They only go make noise the first two steps you take."

To test it, Tan-Tan stamped her next foot. The shoe barked obligingly. She jumped and landed hard on the floor. The shoes remained silent. "Thank you, Mummy."

"You not even going bust one so-so smile for me, right?"

Tan-Tan looked solemnly at her mother. Ione rolled her eyes impatiently and flounced out of the room.

Tan-Tan waited till she could no longer hear Ione's footsteps. She went to the door and looked up and down the corridor. No-one. Only then did she try on the Midnight Robber costume. It fit her perfect. She went and stood in front of a bare wall. "Eshu," she whispered.

The a.i. clicked on in her ear. In her mind's eye it showed itself as a little skeleton girl dressed just like her. "Yes, young Mistress?"

"Make a mirror for me."

Eshu disappeared. The wall silvered to show her reflection. Aces, she looked aces. Her lips wavered into a smile. She pulled one of the cap guns from its holster: "Plai! Plai! Thus the Robber Queen does be avengèd! Allyou make you eye pass me? Take that! Plai!" She swirled round to shoot at the pretend bad-jack sneaking up behind her. The cape flared out round her shoulders and the new leather of her shoes creaked. It was too sweet.

"Belle Starr …" said the eshu, soft in her ear.

"Who?" It wasn't lesson time, but the eshu had made her curious.

"Time was, is only men used to play the Robber King masque," eshu's voice told her.

"Why?" Tan-Tan asked. What a stupid thing!

"Earth was like that for a long time. Men could only do some things, and women could only do others. In the beginning of Carnival, the early centuries, Midnight Robbers was always men. Except for the woman who take the name Belle Starr, the same name as a cowgirl performer from America. The Trini Belle Starr made she own costume and she uses to play Midnight Robber."

"What she look like, eshu?"

"No pictures of she in the data banks, young Mistress. Is too long ago. But I have other pictures of Carnival on Earth. You want to see?"

"Yes."

The mirrored wall opaqued into a viewing screen. The room went dark. Tan-Tan sat on the floor to watch. A huge stage appeared on the screen, with hundreds of people in the audience. Some old-time soca was playing. A masque King costume came out on stage; one mako big construction, supported by one man dancing in its traces. It looked like a spider, or a machine with claws for grasping. It had a sheet of white cotton suspended above its eight wicked-looking pincers. It towered a good three meters above the man who was wearing it, but he danced and pranced as though it weighed next to nothing.

"The Minshall Mancrab," eshu told Tan-Tan. "Minshall made it to be king of his band 'The River' on Earth, Terran calendar 1983."

"Peter Minshall?" Tan-Tan asked. She had heard a crèche teacher say the name once when reading from *Marryshow's Revelations*.

"He same one."

The sinister Mancrab advanced to the centre of the stage, its sheet billowing. Suddenly the edges of the sheet started to bleed. Tan-Tan heard the audience exclaim. The blood quickly soaked the sheet as the Mancrab opened its menacing pincers wide. People in the audience went wild, clapping and shouting and screaming their approval.

Tan-Tan was mesmerized. "Is scary," she said.

"Is so headblind machines used to stay," eshu told her. "Before people make Granny Nanny to rule the machines and give guidance. Look some different images here."

The eshu showed her more pictures of old-time Earth Carnival: the Jour Ouvert mud masque, the Children's Masquerades. When Nursie came to fetch her for breakfast, Tan-Tan was tailor-sat on the floor in the dark, still in her Robber Queen costume, staring at the eshu screen and asking it questions from time to time. The eshu answered in a gentle voice. Nursie smiled and had the minder bring Tan-Tan's breakfast to her on a tray.

For two days straight Tan-Tan insisted on wearing her Robber Queen costume. She slept in it and all. Neither Ione nor Nursie could persuade her to change out of it. But she never called Antonio to thank him. Let him feel bad about boofing her on Jonkanoo Night.

Act One, Scene One from *Joe Turner's Come and Gone*

by August Wilson (USA)

CHARACTERS

SETH HOLLY *owner of the boardinghouse*
BERTHA HOLLY *his wife*
BYNUM WALKER *a root worker*
RUTHERFORD SELIG *a peddler*
JEREMY FURLOW *a resident*
HERALD LOOMIS *a resident*
ZONIA LOOMIS *his daughter*
MATTIE CAMPELL *a resident*
REUBEN SCOTT *boy who lives next door*
MOLLY CUNNINGHAM *a resident*
MARTHA LOOMIS *Herald Loomis's wife*

SETTING

August, 1911. A boardinghouse in Pittsburgh. At right is a kitchen. Two doors open off the kitchen. One leads to the outhouse and SETH's workshop. The other end to SETH's and BERTHA's bedroom. At left is a parlor. The front door opens into the parlor, which gives access to the stairs leading to the up-stairs rooms.

There is a small outside playing area.

THE PLAY

It is August in Pittsburgh, 1911. The sun falls out of heaven like a stone. The fires of the steel mill rage with a combined sense of industry and progress. Barges loaded with coal and iron ore trudge up the river to the mill towns that dot the Monongahela and return with fresh, hard, gleaming steel. The city flexes its muscles. Men throw countless bridges across countless rivers, lay roads and carve tunnels through the hills sprouting with houses.

From the deep and the near South the sons and daughters of newly freed African slaves wander into the city. Isolated, cut off from memory, having forgotten the names of the gods and only guessing at their faces, they arrive dazed and stunned, their heart kicking in their chest with a song worth singing. They arrive carrying Bibles and guitars, their pockets lined with dust and fresh hope, marked men and women seeking to scrape from the narrow, crooked cobbles and the fiery blasts of the coke furnace a way of bludgeoning and shaping the malleable parts of themselves into a new identity as free men of definite and sincere worth.

Foreigners in a strange land, they carry as part and parcel of their baggage a long line of separation and dispersement which informs their sensibilities and marks their conduct as they search for ways to reconnect, to give clear and luminous meaning to the song which is both a wail and a whelp of joy.

ACT ONE

Scene One

The lights come up on the kitchen. BERTHA *busies herself with breakfast preparations.* SETH *stands looking out the window at* BYNUM *in the yard.* SETH *is in his early fifties. Born of Northern free parents, a skilled craftsman, and owner of the boardinghouse, he has a stability that none of the other characters have.* BERTHA *is five years his junior. Married for over twenty-five years, she has learned how to negotiate around* SETH's *apparent orneriness.*

SETH: (*at the window, laughing.*) If that ain't the damndest thing I seen. Look here, Bertha.

BERTHA: I done seen Bynum out there with them pigeons before.

SETH: Naw ... naw ... look at this. That pigeon flopped out of Bynum's hand and he about to have a fit.
(BERTHA *crosses over to the window.*)
He down there on his hands and knees behind that bush looking all over for that pigeon and it on the other side of the yard. See it over there?

BERTHA: Come on and get your breakfast and leave that man alone.

SETH: Look at him ... he still looking. He ain't seen it yet. All that old mumbo jumbo nonsense. I don't know why I put up with it.

BERTHA: You don't say nothing when he bless the house.

SETH: I just go along with that 'cause of you. You around here sprinkling salt all over the place ... got pennies lined up across the threshold ... all that hee-bie-jeebie stuff. I just put up with that 'cause of you. I don't pay that kind of stuff no mind. And you going down there to the church and wanna come home and sprinkle salt all over the place.

BERTHA: It don't hurt none. I can't say if it help ... but it don't hurt none.

SETH: Look at him. He done found that pigeon and now he's talking to it.

BERTHA: These biscuits be ready in a minute.

SETH: He done drew a big circle with that stick and now he's dancing around. I know he better not ...
(SETH *bolts from the window and rushes to the back door.*)
Hey, Bynum! Don't be hopping around stepping in my vegetables.
Hey, Bynum ... Watch where you stepping!

BERTHA: Seth, leave that man alone.

SETH: (*coming back into the house.*) I don't care how much he be dancing around ... just don't be stepping in my vegetables. Man got my garden all messed up now ... planting them weeds out there ... burying them pigeons and whatnot.

BERTHA: Bynum don't bother nobody. He ain't even thinking about your vegetables.

SETH: I know he ain't. That's why he out there stepping on them.

BERTHA: What Mr. Johnson say down there?

SETH: I told him if I had the tools I could go out here and find me four of five fellows and open up my own shop instead of working for Mr. Olowski. Get me four or five fellows and teach them how to make pots and pans. One man making ten pots is five men making fifty. He told me he'd think about it.

BERTHA: Well, maybe he'll come to see it your way.

SETH: He wanted me to sign over the house to him. You know what I thought of that idea.

BERTHA: He'll come to see you're right.

SETH: I'm going up and talk to Sam Green. There's more than one way to skin a cat. I'm going up and talk to him. See if he got more sense than Mr. Johnson. I can't get nowhere working for Mr. Olowski and selling Selig five or six pots on the side. I'm going up and see Sam Green. See if he loan me the money.
(SETH *crosses back to the window.*)
Now he got that cup. He done killed that pigeon and now he's putting its blood in that little cup. I believe he drink that blood.

BERTHA: Seth Holly, what is wrong with you this morning? Come on and get your breakfast so you can go to bed. You know Bynum don't drink no pigeon blood.

SETH: I don't know what he do.

BERTHA: Well, watch him, then. He's gonna dig a little hold and bury that pigeon. Then he's gonna pray over that blood ... pour it on top ... mark out his circle and come on into the house.

SETH: That's what he's doing ... he pouring that blood on top.

BERTHA: When they gonna put you back working daytime? Told me two months ago he was gonna put you back working daytime.

SETH: That's what Mr. Olowski told me. I got to wait till he say when. He tell me what to do. I don't tell him. Drive me crazy to speculate on that man's wishes when he don't know what he want to do himself.

BERTHA: Well, I wish he go ahead and put you back working daytime. This working all hours of the night don't make no sense.

SETH: It don't make no sense for that boy to run out of here and get drunk so they lock him up either.

BERTHA: Who? Who they got locked up for being drunk?

SETH: That boy that's staying upstairs ... Jeremy. I stopped down there on Logan Street on my way home from work and one of the fellows told me about it. Say he seen it when they arrested him.

BERTHA: I was wondering why I ain't seen him this morning.

SETH: You know I don't put up with that. I told him when he came ...
(BYNUM *enters from the yard carrying some plants. He is a short, round man in his early sixties. A conjure man, or rootworker, he gives the impression of always being*

in control of everything. Nothing ever bothers him. He seems to be lost in a world of his own making and to swallow any adversity or interference with his grand design.) What you doing bringing them weeds in my house? Out there stepping on my vegetables and now wanna carry them weeds in my house.

BYNUM: Morning, Seth. Morning, Sister Bertha.

SETH: Messing up my garden growing them things out there. I ought to go out there and pull up all them weeds.

BERTHA: Some gal was by here to see you this morning, Bynum. You was out there in the yard … I told her to come back later.

BYNUM: (*To* SETH.) You look sick. What's the matter, you ain't eating right?

SETH: What if I was sick? You ain't getting near me with none of that stuff. (BERTHA *sets a plate of biscuits on the table.*)

BYNUM: My … my … Bertha, your biscuits getting fatter and fatter. (BYNUM *takes a biscuit and begins to eat.*) Where Jeremy? I don't see him around this morning. He usually be around riffing and raffing on Saturday morning.

SETH: I know where he at. I know just where he at. They got him down there in jail. Getting drunk and acting a fool. He down there where he belong with all that foolishness.

BYNUM: Mr. Piney's boys got him, huh? They ain't gonna do nothing but hold on to him for a little while. He's gonna be back here hungrier than a mule directly.

SETH: I don't go for all that carrying on and such. This is a respectable house. I don't have no drunkards or fools around here.

BYNUM: That boy got a lot of country in him. He ain't been up here but two weeks. It's gonna take a while before he can work that country out of him.

SETH: These niggers coming up here with that old backward country style of living. It's hard enough now without all that ignorant kind of acting. Ever since slavery got over with there ain't been nothing but foolish-acting niggers. Word get out they need men to work in the mill and put in these roads … and niggers drop everything and head North looking for freedom. They don't know the white fellows looking too. White fellows coming from all over the world. White fellow come over and in six months got more than what I got. But these niggers keep on coming. Walking … riding … carrying their Bibles.

That boy done carried a guitar all the way from North Carolina. What he gonna find out? What he gonna do with that guitar? This is the city.
(*There is a knock on the door.*)
Niggers coming up here from the backwoods ... coming up here from the country carrying Bibles and guitars looking for freedom. They got a rude awakening.
(SETH *goes to the door.* RUTHERFORD SELIG *enters. About* SETH's *age, he is a thin white man with greasy hair. A peddler, he supplies* SETH *with the raw materials to make pots and pans which he then peddles door to door in the mill towns along the river. He keeps a list of his customers as they move about and is known in the various communities as the People Finder. He carries squares of sheet metal under his arm.*)
Ho! Forgot you was coming today. Come on in.

BYNUM: If it ain't Rutherford Selig ... the People finder himself.

SELIG: What say there, Bynum?

BYNUM: I say about my shiny man. You got to tell me something. I done give you my dollar ... I'm looking to get a report.

SELIG: I got eight here, Seth.

SETH: (*Taking the sheet metal.*) What is this? What you giving me here? What I'm gonna do with this?

SELIG: I need some dustpans. Everybody asking me for dustpans.

SETH: Gonna cost you fifteen cents apiece. And ten cents to put a handle on them.

SELIG: I'll give you twenty cents apiece with the handles.

SETH: Alright. But I ain't gonna give you but fifteen cents for the sheet metal.

SELIG: It's twenty-five cents apiece for the metal. That's what we agreed on.

SETH: This low-grade sheet metal. They ain't worth but a dime. I'm doing you a favor by giving you fifteen cents. You know this metal ain't worth no twenty-five cents. Don't come talking that twenty-five cent stuff to me over no low-grade sheet metal.

SELIG: Alright, fifteen cents apiece. Just make me some dustpans out of them.
(SETH *exits with the sheet metal out the back door.*)

BERTHA: Sit on down there, Selig. Get you a cup of coffee and a biscuit.

SELIG: I been upriver. All along the Monongahela. Past Rankin and all up around Little Washington.

BYNUM: Did you find anybody?

SELIG: I found Sadie Jackson up in Braddock. Her mother's staying down there in Scotchbottom say she hadn't heard from her and she didn't know where she was at. I found her up in Braddock on Enoch Street. She bought a frying pan from me.

BYNUM: You around here finding everybody how come you ain't found my shiny man?

SELIG: The only shiny man I saw was the Nigras working on the road gang with the sweat glistening on them.

BYNUM: Naw, you'd be able to tell this fellow. He shine like new money.

SELIG: Well, I done told you I can't find nobody without a name.

BERTHA: Here go one of these hot biscuits Selig.

BYNUM: This fellow don't have no name. I call him John 'cause it was up and around Johnstown where I seen him. I ain't even sure he's one special fellow. That shine could pass on to anybody. He could be anybody shining.

SELIG: Well, what's he look like besides being shiny? There's lots of shiny Nigras.

BYNUM: He's just a man I seen out on the road. He ain't had no special look. Just a man walking toward me on the road. He come up and asked me which way the road went. I told him everything I knew about the road, where it went and all, and he asked me did I have anything to eat 'cause he was hungry. Say he ain't had nothing to eat in three days. Well, I never be out there on the road without a piece of dried meat. Or an orange or an apple. So I give this fellow an orange. He take and eat that orange and told me to come and go along the road a little ways with him, that he had something he wanted to show me. He had a look about him made me wanna go with him, see what he gonna show me.
We walked on a bit and it's getting kind of far from where I met him when it come up on me all of a sudden, we wasn't going the way he had come from, we was going back my way. Since he said he ain't knew nothing about the road, I asked him about this. He say he had a voice inside him telling him which way to go and if I come and go along with him he was gonna show me the Secret of Life. Quite naturally I followed him. A fellow that's gonna show you the Secret of Life aint' to be taken lightly. We get near this bend in the road …
(SETH *enters with an assortment of pots.*)

SETH: I got six here, Selig.

SELIG: Wait a minute, Seth. Bynum's telling me about this secret of life. Go ahead, Bynum. I want to hear this.

(SETH *sets the pots down and exits out the back.*)

BYNUM: We get near this bend in the road and he told me to hold out my hands. Then he rubbed them together with his and I looked down and see they got blood on them. Told me to take and rub it all over me ... say that was a way of cleaning myself. Then we went around the bend in that road. Got around that bend and it seem like all of a sudden we ain't in the same place. Turn around that bend and everything look like it was twice as big as it was. The trees and everything bigger than life! Sparrows big as eagles! I turned around to look at this fellow and he had this light coming out of him. I had to cover my eyes to keep from being blinded. He shining like new money with that light. He shined until all the light seemed like it seeped out of him and then he was gone and I was by myself in this strange place where everything was bigger than life.

I wandered around there looking for that road, trying to find my way back from this big place ... and I looked over and seen my daddy standing there. He was the same size he always was, except for his hands and his mouth. He had a great big old mouth that look like it took up his whole face and his hands were big as hams. Look like they was too big to carry around. My daddy called me to him. Said he had been thinking about me and it grieved him to see me in the world carrying other people's songs and not having one of my own. Told me he was gonna show me how to find my song. Then he carried me further into this big place until we come to this ocean. Then he showed me something I ain't got words to tell you. But if you stand to witness it, you done seen something there. I stayed in that place awhile and my daddy taught me the meaning of this thing that I had seen and showed me how to find my song. I asked him about the shiny man and he told me he was the One Who Goes Before and Shows the Way. Said there was lots of shiny men and if I ever saw one again before I died then I would know that my song had been accepted and worked its full power in the world and I could lay down and die a happy man. A man who done left his mark on life. On the way people cling to each other out of the truth they find in themselves. Then he showed me how to get back to the road. I came out to where everything was its own size and I had my song. I had the Binding Song. I choose that song because that's what I seen most when I was traveling ... people walking away and leaving one another. So I takes the power of my song and binds them together.

(SETH *enters from the yard carrying cabbages and tomatoes.*)

SETH: Maybe they ain't supposed to be stuck sometimes. You ever think of that?

BYNUM: Oh, I don't do it lightly. It cost me a piece of myself every time I do. I'm a Binder of What Clings. You got to find out if they cling first. You can't bind what don't cling.

SELIG: Well, how is that the Secret of Life? I thought you said he was going to show you the secret of life. That's what I'm waiting to find out.

BYNUM: Oh, he showed me alright. But you still got to figure it out. Can't nobody figure it out for you. You got to come to it on your own. That's why I'm looking for the shiny man.

SELIG: Well, I'll keep my eye out for him. What you got there, Seth?

SETH: Here go some cabbage and tomatoes. I got some green beans coming in real nice. I'm gonna take and start me a grapevine out there next year. Butera says he gonna give me a piece of his vine and I'm gonna start that out there.

SELIG: How many of them pots you got?

SETH: I got six. That's six dollars minus eight on top of fifteen for the sheet metal come to a dollar twenty out the six dollars leave me four dollars and eighty cents.

SELIG: (*Counting out the money.*) There's four dollars … and … eighty cents.

SETH: How many of them dustpans you want?

SELIG: As many as you can make out of them sheets.

SETH: You can use that many? I get to cutting on them sheets figuring out how to make them dustpans … ain't no telling how many I'm liable to come up with.

SELIG: I can use them and you can make me some more next time.

SETH: Alright, I'm gonna hold you to that, now.

SELIG: Thanks for the biscuit, Bertha.

BERTHA: You know you welcome anytime, Selig.

SETH: Which way you heading?

SELIG: Going down to Wheeling. All through West Virginia there. I'll be back Saturday. They putting in new roads down that way. Makes traveling easier.

SETH: That's what I hear. All up around here too. Got a fellow staying here working on that road by the Brady Street Bridge.

SELIG: Yeah, it's gonna make traveling real nice. Thanks for the cabbage, Seth. I'll see you on Saturday.
(SELIG *exits.*)

SETH: (*To* BYNUM.) Why you wanna start all that nonsense talk with that man? All that shiny man nonsense.

BYNUM: You know it ain't no nonsense. Bertha know it ain't no nonsense. I don't know if Selig know or not.

BERTHA: Seth, when you get to making them dustpans, make me a coffeepot.

SETH: What's the matter with your coffee? Ain't nothing wrong with your coffee. Don't she make some good coffee, Bynum?

BYNUM: I ain't worried about the coffee. I know she makes some good biscuits.

SETH: I ain't studying no coffeepot, woman. You heard me tell the man I was gonna cut as many dustpans as them sheets will make ... and all of a sudden you want a coffeepot.

BERTHA: Man, hush up and go on and make me that coffeepot.
(JEREMY *enters the front door. About twenty-five, he gives the impression that he has the world in his hand, that he can meet life's challenges head on. He smiles a lot. He is a proficient guitar player, though his spirit has yet to be molded into a song.*)

BYNUM: I hear Mr. Piney's boys had you.

JEREMY: Fined me two dollars for nothing! Ain't done nothing.

SETH: I told you when you come on here everybody know my house. Know these is respectable quarters. I don't put up with no foolishness. Everybody know Seth Holly keep a good house. Was my daddy's house. This house been a decent house for a long time.

JEREMY: I ain't done nothing, Mr. Seth. I stopped by the Workmen's Club and got me a bottle. Me and Roper Lee from Alabama. Had us a half pint. We was fixing to cut that half in two when they came up on us. Asked us if we was working. We told them we was putting in the road over yonder and that it was our payday. They snatched hold of us to get that two dollars. Me and Roper Lee ain't even had a chance to take a drink when they grabbed us.

SETH: I don't go for all that kind of carrying on.

BERTHA: Leave the boy alone, Seth. You know the police do that. Figure there's too many people out on the street they take some of them off. You know that.

SETH: I ain't gonna have folks talking.

BERTHA: Ain't nobody talking nothing. That's all in your head. You want some grits and biscuits. Jeremy?

JEREMY: Thank you, Miss Bertha. They didn't give us a thing to eat last night. I'll take one of them big bowls if you don't mind.
(*There is a knock at the door.* SETH *goes to answer it. Enter* HERALD LOOMIS *and his eleven-year-old daughter,* ZONIA. HERALD LOOMIS *is thirty-two years old. He is at times possessed. A man driven not by the hellhounds that seemingly bay at his heels, but by his search for a world that speaks to something about himself. He is unable to harmonize the forces that swirl around him, and seeks to recreate the world into one that contains his image. He wears a hat and a long wool coat.*)

LOOMIS: Me and my daughter looking for a place to stay, mister. You got a sign say you got rooms.
(SETH *stares at* LOOMIS, *sizing him up.*)
Mister, if you ain't got no rooms we can go somewhere else.

SETH: How long you plan on staying?

LOOMIS: Don't know. Two weeks or more maybe.

SETH: It's two dollars a week for the room. We serve meals twice a day. It's two dollars for room and board. Pay up in advance.
(LOOMIS *reaches into his pocket.*)

LOOMIS: The girl sleep in the same room.

SETH: Well, do she eat off the same plate? We serve meals twice a day. That's a dollar for extra food.

LOOMIS: Ain't got no extra dollar. I was planning on asking your missus if she could help out with the cooking and cleaning and whatnot.

SETH: Her helping out don't put no food on the table. I need that dollar to buy some food.

LOOMIS: I'll give you fifty cents extra. She don't each much.

SETH: Okay … but fifty cents don't buy but half a portion.

BERTHA: Seth, she can help me out. Let her help me out. I can use some help.

SETH: Well, that's two dollars for the week. Pay up in advance. Saturday to Saturday. You wanna stay on then it's two more come Saturday.

(LOOMIS *pays* SETH *the money.*)

BERTHA: My name's Bertha. This is my husband, Seth. You got Bynum and Jeremy over there.

LOOMIS: Ain't nobody else live here?

BERTHA: They the only ones live here now. People come and go. They the only ones here now. You want a cup of coffee and a biscuit?

LOOMIS: We done ate this morning.

BYNUM: Where you coming from, Mister ... I didn't get your name.

LOOMIS: Name's Herald Loomis. This my daughter, Zonia.

BYNUM: Where you coming from?

LOOMIS: Come from all over. Whicheverway the road take us that's the way to go.

JEREMY: If you looking for a job, I'm working putting in that road down there by the bridge. They can't get enough mens. Always looking to take somebody on.

LOOMIS: I'm looking for a woman named Martha Loomis. That's my wife. Got married legal with the papers and all.

SETH: I don't know nobody named Loomis. I know some Marthas but I don't know no Loomis.

BYNUM: You got to see Rutherford Selig if you wanna find somebody. Selig's the People Finder. Rutherford Selig's a first-class People Finder.

JEREMY: What she look like? Maybe I seen her.

LOOMIS: She a brownskin woman. Got long pretty hair. About five feet from the ground.

JEREMY: I don't know. I might have seen her.

BYNUM: You got to see Rutherford Selig. You give him one dollar to get her name on his list ... and after she get her name on his list Rutherford Selig will go right on out there and find her. I got him looking for somebody for me.

LOOMIS: You say he find people. How you find him?

BYNUM: You just missed him. He's gone downriver now. You got to wait till Saturday. He's gone downriver with his pots and pans. He come to see Seth on Saturdays. You got to wait till then.

SETH: Come on, I'll show you to your room.

(SETH, LOOMIS, *and* ZONIA *exit up the stairs.*)

JEREMY: Miss Bertha, I'll take that biscuit you was gonna give that fellow, if you don't mind. Say, Mr. Bynum, they got somebody like that around here sure enough? Somebody that find people?

BYNUM: Rutherford Selig. He go around selling pots and pans and every house he come to he write down the name and address of whoever lives there. So if you looking for somebody, quite naturally you go and see him …'cause he's the only one who know where everybody live at.

JEREMY: I ought to have him look for this old gal I used to know. It be nice to see her again.

BERTHA: (*Giving* JEREMY *a biscuit.*) Jeremy, today's the day for you to pull them sheets off the bed and set them outside your door. I'll set you out some clean ones.

BYNUM: Mr. Piney's boys done ruined your good time last night, Jeremy … what you planning for tonight?

JEREMY: They got me scared to go out, Mr. Bynum. They might grab me again.

BYNUM: You ought to take your guitar and go down to Seefus. Seefus got a gambling place down there on Wylie Avenue. You ought to take your guitar and go down there. They got guitar contest down there.

JEREMY: I don't play no contest, Mr. Bynum. Had one of them white fellows cure me of that. I ain't been nowhere near a contest since.

BYNUM: White fellow beat you playing guitar?

JEREMY: Naw, he ain't beat me. I was sitting at home just fixing to sit down and eat when somebody came up to my house and got me. Told me there's a white fellow say he was gonna give a prize to the best guitar player he could find. I take up my guitar and go down there and somebody had gone up and got Bobo Smith and brought him down there. Him and another fellow called Hooter. Old Hooter couldn't play no guitar, he do more hollering than playing, but Bobo could go at it awhile.
This fellow standing there say he the one that was gonna give the prize and me and Bobo started playing for him. Bobo played something and then I'd try to play something better than what he played. Old Hooter, he just holler and bang at the guitar. Man was the worst guitar player I ever seen. So me and Bobo played after a while I seen where he was getting the attention of this white fellow. He'd play something and while he was playing it he be slapping

on the side of the guitar, and that made it sound like he was playing more than he was. So I started doing it too. White fellow ain't knew no difference. He ain't knew as much about guitar playing as Hooter did. After we play awhile, the white fellow called us to him and said he couldn't make up his mind, say all three of us was the best guitar player and we'd have to split the prize between us. Then he give us twenty-five cents. That's eight cents apiece and a penny on the side. That cured me of playing contest to this day.

BYNUM: Seefus ain't like that. Seefus give a whole dollar and a drink of whiskey.

JEREMY: What night they be down there?

BYNUM: Be down there every night. Music don't know no certain night.

BERTHA: You go down to Seefus with them people and you liable to end up in a raid and go to jail sure enough. I don't know why Bynum tell you that.

BYNUM: That's where the music at. That's where the people at. The people down there making music and enjoying themselves. Some things is worth taking the chance going to jail about.

BERTHA: Jeremy ain't got no business going down there.

JEREMY: They got some women down there, Mr. Bynum?

BYNUM: Oh, they got women down there, sure. They got women everywhere. Women be where the men is so they can find each other.

JEREMY: Some of them old gals come out there where we be putting in that road. Hanging around there trying to snatch somebody.

BYNUM: How come some of them ain't snatched hold of you?

JEREMY: I don't want them kind. Them desperate kind. Ain't nothing worse than a desperate woman. Tell them you gonna leave them and they get to crying and carrying on. That just make you want to get away quicker. They get to cutting up your clothes and things trying to keep you staying. Desperate women ain't nothing but trouble for a man.
(SETH enters from the stairs.)

SETH: Something ain't setting right with that fellow.

BERTHA: What's wrong with him? What he say?

SETH: I take him up there and try to talk to him and ain't for no talking. Say he been traveling ... coming over from Ohio. Say he a deacon in the church. Say he looking for Martha Pentecost. Talking about that's his wife.

BERTHA: How you know it's the same Martha? Could be talking about anybody. Lots of people named Martha.

SETH: You see that little girl? I didn't hook it up till he said it, but that little girl look just like her. Ask Bynum. (*To* BYNUM.) Bynum. Don't that little girl look just like Martha Pentecost?

BERTHA: I still say he could be talking about anybody.

SETH: The way he describe her wasn't no doubt about who he was talking about. Described her right down to her toes.

BERTHA: What did you tell him?

SETH: I ain't told him nothing. The way that fellow look I wasn't gonna tell him nothing. I don't know what he looking for her for.

BERTHA: What else he have to say?

SETH: I told you he wasn't for no talking. I told him where the outhouse was and to keep that gal off the front porch and out of my garden. He asked if you mind setting a hot tub for the gal and that was about the gist of it.

BERTHA: Well, I wouldn't let it worry me if I was you. Come on and get your sleep.

BYNUM: He says he looking for Martha and he a deacon in the church.

SETH: That's what he say. Do he look like a deacon to you?

BERTHA: He might be, you don't know. Bynum ain't got no special say on whether he a deacon or not.

SETH: Well, if he the deacon I'd sure like the see the preacher.

BERTHA: Come on get your sleep. Jeremy, don't forget to set them sheets outside the door like I told you.
(BERTHA *exits into the bedroom.*)

SETH: Something ain't setting right with that fellow, Bynum. He's one of them mean-looking niggers look like he done killed somebody gambling over a quarter.

BYNUM: He ain't no gambler. Gamblers wear nice shoes. This fellow got on clodhoppers. He been out there walking up and down them roads.
(ZONIA *enters from the stairs and looks around.*)

BYNUM: You looking for the back door, sugar? There it is. You can go out there and play. It's alright.

SETH: (*Showing her the door.*) You can go out there and play. Just don't get in my garden. And don't go messing around in my workshed.
(SETH *exits into the bedroom. There is a knock on the door.*)

JEREMY: Somebody at the door.
(JEREMY *goes to answer the door. Enter* MATTIE CAMPBELL. *She is a young woman of twenty-six whose attractiveness is hidden under the weight and concerns of a dissatisfied life. She is a woman in an honest search for love and companionship. She had suffered many defeats in her search, and though not always uncompromising, still believes in the possibility of love.*)

MATTIE: I'm looking for a man named Bynum. Lady told me to come back later.

JEREMY: Sure, he here. Mr. Bynum, somebody here to see you.

MATTIE: Are you the man they call Bynum? The man folks say can fix things?

BYNUM: Depend on what need fixing. I can't make no promises. But I got a powerful song in some matters.

MATTIE: Can you fix it so my man come back to me?

BYNUM: Come on in ... have a sit down.

MATTIE: You got to help me. I don't know what else to do.

BYNUM: Depend on how all the circumstances of the thing come together. How all the pieces fit.

MATTIE: I done everything I knowed how to do. You got to make him come back to me.

BYNUM: It ain't nothing to make somebody come back. I can fix it so he can't stand to be away from you. I got my roots and powders, I can fix it so wherever he's at this thing will come up on him and he won't be able to sleep for seeing your face. Won't be able to eat for thinking of you.

MATTIE: That's what I want. Make him come back.

BYNUM: The roots is a powerful thing. I can fix it so one day he'll walk out his front door ... won't be thinking of nothing. He won't know what it is. All he knows is that a powerful dissatisfaction done set in his bones and can't nothing he do make him feel satisfied. He'll set his foot down on the road and the wind in the trees be talking to him and everywhere he step on the road, that road'll give back your name and something will pull him right up to your doorstep. Now, I can do that. I can take my roots and fix that easy. But maybe he ain't supposed to come back. And if he ain't supposed to come back ... then he'll be in your bed one morning and it'll come up on him that he's in the wrong place. That he's lost outside of time from his place that he's supposed to be in. Then both of you will be lost and trapped outside of life and ain't no way for you to get back into it. 'Cause you lost from yourselves and where the places come together, where you're supposed to be alive, your heart kicking in your chest with a song worth singing.

MATTIE: Make him come back to me. Make his feet say my name on the road. I don't care what happens. Make him come back.

BYNUM: What's your man's name?

MATTIE: He go by Jack Carper. He was born in Alabama then he come to West Texas and find me and we come here. Been here three years before he left. Say I had a curse prayer on me and he started walking down the road and ain't never come back. Somebody told me, say you can fix things like that.

BYNUM: He just got up one day, set his feet on the road and walked away?

MATTIE: You got to make him come back, mister.

BYNUM: Did he say goodbye?

MATTIE: Ain't said nothing. Just started walking. I could see where he disappeared. Didn't look back. Just keep walking. Can't you fix it so he come back? I ain't got no curse prayer on me. I know I ain't.

BYNUM: What made him say you had a curse prayer on you?

MATTIE: 'Cause two babies died. Me and Jack had two babies. Two little babies that ain't lived two months before they died. He say it's because somebody cursed me not to have babies.

BYNUM: He ain't bound to you if the babies died. Look like somebody trying to keep you from being bound up and he's gone on back to whoever it is 'cause he's already bound up to her. Ain't nothing to be done. Somebody else done got a powerful hand in it and ain't nothing to be done to break it. You got to let him go find where he's supposed to be in the world.

MATTIE: Jack done gone off and you telling me to forget about him. All my life I been looking for somebody to stop and stay with me. I done already got too many things to forget about. I take Jack Carper's hand and it feel so rough and strong. Seem like he's the strongest man in the whole world the way he hold me. Like he's bigger than the whole world and can't nothing bad get to me. Even when he act mean sometimes he still make everything seem okay with the world. Like there's a part of it that belongs just to you. Now you telling me to forget about him?

BYNUM: Jack Carper gone off to where he belong. There's somebody searching for your doorstep right now. Ain't no need you fretting over Jack Carper. Right now he's a strong thought in your mind. But every time you catch yourself fretting over Jack Carper you push that thought away. You push it out your mind and that thought will get weaker and weaker till you wake up one morning and you won't even be able to call him up on your mind.
(BYNUM *gives her a small cloth packet.*)
Take this and sleep with it under your pillow and it'll bring good luck to you. Draw it to you like a magnet. It won't be long before you forget all about Jack Carper.

MATTIE: How much ... do I owe you?

BYNUM: Whatever you got there ... that'll be alright.
(MATTIE *hands* BYNUM *two quarters. She crossed to the door.*)
You sleep with that under your pillow and you'll be alright.
(MATTIE *opens the door to exit and* JEREMY *crosses over to her.* BYNUM *overhears the first part of their conversation, then exits out the back.*)

JEREMY: I overheard what you told Mr. Bynum. Had me an old gal that did that to me. Woke up one morning and she was gone. Just took off to parts unknown. I woke up that morning and the only thing I could do was look around for my shoes. I woke up and got out of there. Found my shoes and took off. That's the only thing I could think of to do.

MATTIE: She ain't said nothing?

JEREMY: I just looked around for my shoes and got out of there.

MATTIE: Jack ain't said nothing either. He just walked off.

JEREMY: Some mens do that. Womens too. I ain't gone off looking for her. I just let her go. Figure she had a time to come to herself. Wasn't no use of me standing in the way. Where you from?

MATTIE: Texas. I was born in Georgia but I went to Texas with my mama. She dead now. Was picking peaches and fell dead away. I come up here with Jack Carper.

JEREMY: I'm from North Carolina. Down around Raleigh where they got all that tobacco. Been up here about two weeks. I likes it fine except I still got to find me a woman. You got a nice look to you. Look like you have mens standing in your door. Is you got mens standing in your door to get a look at you?

MATTIE: I ain't got nobody since Jack left.

JEREMY: A woman like you need a man. Maybe you let me be your man. I got a nice way with the women. That's what they tell me.

MATTIE: I don't know. Maybe Jack's coming back.

JEREMY: I'll be your man till he come. A woman can't be by her lonesome. Let me be your man till he come.

MATTIE: I just can't go through life piecing myself out to different mens. I need a man who want to stay with me.

JEREMY: I can't say what's gonna happen. Maybe I'll be the man. I don't know. You wanna go along the road a little ways with me?

MATTIE: I don't know. Seem like life say it's gonna be one thing and end up being another. I'm tired of going from man to man.

JEREMY: Life is like you got to take a chance. Everybody got to take a chance. Can't nobody say what's gonna be. Come on … take a chance with me and see what the year bring. Maybe you let me come and see you. Where you staying?

MATTIE: I got me a room up on Bedford. Me and Jack had a room together.

JEREMY: What's the address? I'll come by and get you tonight and we can go down to Seefus. I'm going down there and play my guitar.

MATTIE: You play guitar?

JEREMY: I play guitar like I'm born to it.

MATTIE: I live at 1727 Bedford Avenue. I'm gonna find out if you can play guitar like you say.

JEREMY: I plays it sugar, and that ain't all I do. I got a ten-pound hammer and I knows how to drive it down. Good god … you ought to hear my hammer ring!

MATTIE: Go on with that kind of talk, now. If you gonna come by and get me I got to get home to straighten up for you.

JEREMY: I'll be by at eight o'clock. How's eight o'clock? I'm gonna make you forget all about Jack Carper.

MATTIE: Go on, now. I got to get home and fix up for you.

JEREMY: Eight o'clock, sugar.
(*The lights go down in the parlor and come up on the yard outside.* ZONIA *is singing and playing a game.*)

ZONIA:
I went downtown
To get my grip
I came back home
Just a pullin' the skiff

I went upstairs
To make my bed
I made a mistake
And I bumped my head
Just a pullin' the skiff

I went downstairs
To milk the cow
I made a mistake
And I milked the sow
Just a pullin' the skiff

Tomorrow, tomorrow
Tomorrow never comes
The marrow the marrow
The marrow in the bone.

(REUBEN *enters.*)

REUBEN: Hi.

ZONIA: Hi.

REUBEN: What's your name?

ZONIA: Zonia.

REUBEN: What kind of name is that?

ZONIA: It's what my daddy named me.

REUBEN: My name's Reuben. You staying in Mr. Seth's house?

ZONIA: Yeah.

REUBEN: That your daddy I seen you with this morning?

ZONIA: I don't know. Who you see me with?

REUBEN: I saw you with some man had on a great big old coat. And you was walking up to Mr. Seth's house. Had on a hat too.

ZONIA: Yeah, that's my daddy.

REUBEN: You like Mr. Seth?

ZONIA: I ain't seen him much.

REUBEN: My grandpap say he a great big old windbag. How come you living in Mr. Seth's house? Don't you have no house?

ZONIA: We going to find my mother.

REUBEN: Where she at?

ZONIA: I don't know. We got to find her. We just go all over.

REUBEN: Why you got to find her? What happened to her?

ZONIA: She ran away.

REUBEN: Why she run away?

ZONIA: I don't know. My daddy say some man named Joe Turner did something bad to him once and that made her run away.

REUBEN: Maybe she coming back and you don't have to go looking for her.

ZONIA: We ain't there no more.

REUBEN: She could have come back when you wasn't there.

ZONIA: My daddy said she ran off and left us so we going looking for her.

REUBEN: What he gonna do when he find her?

ZONIA: He didn't say. He just say he got to find her.

REUBEN: Your daddy say how long you staying in Mr. Seth's house?

ZONIA: He don't say much. But we never stay too long nowhere. He say we got to keep moving till we find her.

REUBEN: Ain't no kids hardly live around here. I had me a friend but he died. He was the best friend I ever had. Me and Eugene used to keep secrets. I still got his pigeons. He told me to let them go when he died. He say, "Reuben, promise me when I die you'll let my pigeons go." But I keep them to remember him by. I ain't never gonna let them go. Even when I get to be grown up. I'm just always gonna have Eugene's pigeons.
(*Pause.*)
Mr. Bynum a conjure man. My grandpap scared of him. He don't like me to come over here too much. I'm scared of him too. My grandpap told me not to let him get close enough to where he can reach out his hand and touch me.

ZONIA: He don't seem scary to me.

REUBEN: He buys pigeons from me … and if you get up early in the morning you can see him out in the yard doing something with them pigeons. My grandpap say he kill them. I sold him one yesterday. I don't know what he do with it. I just hope he don't spook me up.

ZONIA: Why you sell him pigeons if he's gonna spook you up?

REUBEN: I just do like Eugene do. He used to sell Mr. Bynum pigeons. That's how he got to collecting them to sell to Mr. Bynum. Sometime he give me a nickel and sometime he give me a whole dime.
(LOOMIS *enters from the house.*)

LOOMIS: Zonia!

ZONIA: Sir?

LOOMIS: What you doing?

ZONIA: Nothing.

LOOMIS: You stay around this house, you hear? I don't want you wandering off nowhere.

ZONIA: I ain't wandering off nowhere.

LOOMIS: Miss Bertha set that hot tub and you getting a good scrubbing. Get scrubbed up good. You ain't been scrubbing.

ZONIA: I been scrubbing.

LOOMIS: Look at you. You growing too fast. Your bones getting bigger everyday. I don't want you getting grown on me. Don't you get grown on me too soon. We gonna find your mamma. She around here somewhere. I can smell her. You stay on around this house now. Don't you go nowhere.

ZONIA: Yes, sir.
(LOOMIS *exits into the house.*)

REUBEN: Wow, your daddy's scary!

ZONIA: He is not! I don't know what you talking about.

REUBEN: He got them mean-looking eyes!

ZONIA: My daddy ain't got no mean-looking eyes!

REUBEN: Aw, girl, I was just messing with you. You wanna go see Eugene's pigeons? Got a great big coop out the back of my house. Come on, I'll show you.

(REUBEN *and* ZONIA *exit as the lights go down.*)

from *Black No More: A Novel*

by George Samuel Schuyler (USA)

ONE

Max Disher stood outside the Honky Tonk Club puffing a panatela and watching the crowds of white and black folk entering the cabaret. Max was tall, dapper and smooth coffee-brown. His negroid features had a slightly satanic cast and there was an insolent nonchalance about his carriage. He wore his hair rakishly and faultless evening clothes underneath his raccoon coat. He was young, he wasn't broke, but he was damnably blue. It was New Year's Eve, 1933, but there was no spirit of gaiety and gladness in his heart. How could he share the hilarity of the crowd when he had no girl? He and Minnie, his high "yallah" flapper, had quarreled that day and everything was over between them.

"Women are mighty funny," he mused to himself, "especially yallah women. You could give them the moon and they wouldn't appreciate it." That was probably the trouble; he'd given Minnie too much. It didn't pay to spend too much on them. As soon as he'd bought her a new outfit and paid the rent on a three-room apartment, she'd grown uppity. Stuck on her color, that's what was the matter with her! He took the cigar out of his mouth and spat disgustedly.

A short, plump, cherubic black fellow, resplendent in a narrow-brimmed fedora, camel's hair coat and spats, strolled up and clapped him on the shoulder: "Hello, Max!" greeted the newcomer, extending a hand in a fawn-colored glove, "What's on your mind?"

"Everything, Bunny," answered the debonair Max. "That damn yallah gal o' mine's got all upstage and quit."

"Say not so!" exclaimed the short black fellow. "Why I thought you and her were all forty."

"Were, is right, kid. And after spending my dough, too! It sure makes me hot. Here I go and buy two covers at the Honky Tonk for tonight, thinkin' surely she'd come and she starts a row and quits!"

"Shucks!" exploded Bunny, "I wouldn't let that worry me none. I'd take another skirt. I wouldn't let no dame queer my New Year's."

"So would I, Wise Guy, but all the dames I know are dated up. So here I am all dressed up and no place to go."

"You got two reservations, ain't you? Well, let's you and me go in," Bunny suggested. "We may be able to break in on some party."

Max visibly brightened. "That's a good idea," he said. "You never can tell, we might run in on something good."

Swinging their canes, the two joined the throng at the entrance of the Honky Tonk Club and descended to its smoky depths. They wended their way through the maze of tables in the wake of a dancing waiter and sat down close to the dance floor. After ordering ginger ale and plenty of ice, they reared back and looked over the crowd.

Max Disher and Bunny Brown had been pals ever since the war when they soldiered together in the old 15th regiment in France. Max was one of the Aframerican Fire Insurance Company's crack agents, Bunny was a teller in the Douglass bank and both bore the reputation of gay blades in black Harlem. The two had in common a weakness rather prevalent among Aframerican bucks: they preferred yellow women. Both swore there were three things essential to the happiness of a colored gentleman: yellow money, yellow women and yellow taxis. They had little difficulty in getting the first and none in getting the third but the yellow women they found flighty and fickle. It was so hard to hold them. They were so sought after that one almost required a million dollars to keep them out of the clutches of one's rivals.

"No more yallah gals for me!" Max announced with finality, sipping his drink. "I'll grab a black gal first."

"Say not so!" exclaimed Bunny, strengthening his drink from his huge silver flask. "You ain't thinkin' o' dealin' in coal, are you?"

"Well," argued his partner, "it might change my luck. You can trust a black gal; she'll stick to you."

"How do you know? You ain't never had one. Ever' gal I ever seen you with looked like an ofay."

"Humph!" grunted Max. "My next one may be an ofay, too! They're less trouble and don't ask you to give 'em the moon."

"I'm right with you, pardner," Bunny agreed, "but I gotta have one with class. None o' these Woolworth dames for me! Get you in a peck o' trouble ... Fact is, Big Boy, ain't none o' these woman no good. They all get old on the job."

They drank in silence and eyed the motley crowd around them. There were blacks, browns, yellows, and whites chatting, flirting, drinking; rubbing shoulders in the democracy of night life. A fog of tobacco smoke wreathed their heads and the din from the industrious jazz band made all but the loudest shrieks inaudible. In and out among the tables danced the waiters, trays balanced aloft, while the patrons, arrayed in colorful paper caps, beat time with the orchestra, threw streamers or grew maudlin on each other's shoulders.

"Looky here! Lawdy Lawd!" exclaimed Bunny, pointing to the doorway. A party of white people had entered. They were all in evening dress and in their midst was a tall, slim, titian-haired girl who had seemingly stepped from heaven or the front cover of a magazine.

"My, my, my!" said Max, sitting up alertly.

The party consisted of two men and four women. They were escorted to a table next to the one occupied by the two colored dandies. Max and Bunny eyed them covertly. The tall girl was certainly a dream.

"Now that's my speed," whispered Bunny.

"Be yourself," said Max. "You couldn't touch her with a forty-foot pole."

"Oh, I don't know, Big Boy," Bunny beamed self-confidently, "You never can tell! You never can tell!"

"Well, I can tell," remarked Disher, "cause she's a cracker."

"How you know that?"

"Man, I can tell a cracker a block away. I wasn't born and raised in Atlanta, Georgia, for nothin', you know. Just listen to her voice."

Bunny listened. "I believe she is," he agreed.

They kept eyeing the party to the exclusion of everything else. Max was especially fascinated. The girl was the prettiest creature he'd ever seen and he felt irresistibly drawn to her. Unconsciously he adjusted his necktie and passed his well-manicured hand over his rigidly straightened hair.

Suddenly one of the white men rose and came over to their table. They watched him suspiciously. Was he going to start something? Had he noticed that they were staring at the girl? They both stiffened at his approach.

"Say," he greeted them, leaning over the table, "do you boys know where we can get some decent liquor around here? We've run out of stuff and the waiter says he can't get any for us."

"You can get some pretty good stuff right down the street," Max informed him, somewhat relieved.

"They won't sell none to him," said Bunny. "They might think he's a Prohibition officer."

"Could one of you fellows get me some?" asked the man.

"Sure," said Max, heartily. What luck! Here was the very chance he'd been waiting for. These people might invite him over to their table. The man handed him a ten dollar bill and Max went out bareheaded to get the liquor. In ten minutes he was back. He handed the man the quart and the change. The man gave back the change and thanked him. There was no invitation to join the party. Max returned to his table and eyed the group wistfully.

"Did he invite you in?" asked Bunny.

"I'm back here ain't I?" answered Max, somewhat resentfully.

The floor show came on. A black-faced comedian, a corpulent shouter of mammy songs with a gin-roughened voice, three chocolate soft-shoe dancers and an octette of wriggling, practically nude, mulatto chorines.

Then midnight and pandemonium as the New Year swept in. When the din had subsided, the lights went low and the orchestra moaned the weary blues. The floor filled with couples. The two men and two of the women at the next table rose to dance. The beautiful girl and another were left behind.

"I'm going over there to ask her to dance," Max suddenly announced to the surprised Bunny.

"Say not so!" exclaimed that worthy. "You're fixin' to get in dutch, Big Boy."

"Well, I'm gonna take a chance, anyhow," Max persisted, rising.

This fair beauty had hypnotized him. He felt that he would give anything for just one dance with her. Once around the floor with her slim waist in his arm would be like an eternity in heaven. Yes, one could afford to risk repulse for that.

"Don't do it, Max!" pleaded Bunny. "Them fellows are liable to start something."

But Max was not to be restrained. There was no holding him back when he wanted to do a thing, especially where a comely damsel was concerned.

He sauntered over to the table in his most shiekish manner and stood looking down at the shimmering strawberry blonde. She was indeed ravishing and her exotic perfume titillated his nostrils despite the clouds of cigarette smoke.

"Would you care to dance?" he asked, after a moment's hesitation.

She looked up at him haughtily with cool green eyes, somewhat astonished at his insolence and yet perhaps secretly intrigued but her reply lacked nothing in definiteness.

"No," she said icily, "I never dance with niggers!" Then turning to her friend, she remarked: "Can you beat the nerve of these darkies?" She made a little disdainful grimace with her mouth, shrugged daintily and dismissed the unpleasant incident.

Crushed and angry, Max returned to his place without a word. Bunny laughed aloud in high glee.

"You said she was a cracker," he gurgled, "an' now I guess you know it."

"Aw, go to hell," Max grumbled.

Just then Billy Fletcher, the headwaiter, passed by. Max stopped him. "Ever see that dame in here before?" he asked.

"Been in here most every night since before Christmas," Billy replied.

"Do you know who she is?"

"Well, I heard she was some rich broad from Atlanta up here for the holidays. Why?"

"Oh, nothin'; I was just wondering."

From Atlanta! His home town. No wonder she had turned him down. Up here trying to get a thrill in the Black Belt but a thrill from observation instead of contact. Gee, but white folks were funny. They didn't want black folks' game and yet they were always frequenting Negro resorts.

At three o'clock Max and Bunny paid their check and ascended to the street. Bunny wanted to go to the breakfast dance at the Dahomey Casino but Max was in no mood for it.

"I'm going home," he announced laconically, hailing a taxi. "Good night!"

As the cab whirled up Seventh Avenue, he settled back and thought of the girl from Atlanta. He couldn't get her out of his mind and didn't want to. At his rooming house, he paid the driver, unlocked the door, ascended to his room and undressed, mechanically. His mind was a kaleidoscope: Atlanta, sea-green eyes, slender figure, titian hair, frigid manner. "I never dance with niggers." Then he fell asleep about five o'clock and promptly dreamed of her. Dreamed of dancing with her, dining with her, motoring with her, sitting beside her on a golden throne while millions of manacled white slaves prostrated themselves before him. Then there was a nightmare of grim, gray men with shotguns, baying hounds, a heap of gasoline-soaked faggots and a screeching, fanatical mob.

He awoke covered with perspiration. His telephone was ringing and the late morning sunshine was streaming into his room. He leaped from the bed and lifted the receiver.

"Say," shouted Bunny, "did you see this morning's *Times*?"

"Hell no," growled Max, "I just woke up. Why, what's in it?"

"Well, do you remember Dr. Junius Crookman, that colored fellow that went to Germany to study about three years ago? He's just come back and the *Times* claims he's announced a sure way to turn darkies white. Thought you might be interested after the way you fell for that ofay broad last night. They say Crookman's going to open a sanitarium in Harlem right away. There's your chance, Big Boy, and it's your only chance." Bunny chuckled.

"Oh, ring off," growled Max. "That's a lot of hooey."

But he was impressed and a little excited. Suppose there was something to it? He dressed hurriedly, after a cold shower, and went out to the newsstand. He bought a *Times* and scanned its columns. Yes, there it was:

NEGRO ANNOUNCES
REMARKABLE DISCOVERY
Can change Black to White in Three Days.

Max went into Jimmy Johnson's restaurant and greedily read the account while awaiting his breakfast. Yes, it must be true. To think of old Crookman being able to do that! Only a few years ago he'd been just a hungry medical student around Harlem. Max put down the paper and stared vacantly out of the window. Gee, Crookman would be a millionaire in no time. He'd even be a multimillionaire. It looked as though science was to succeed where the Civil War had failed. But how could it be possible? He looked at his hands and felt at the back of his head where the straightening lotion had failed to conquer some of the knots. He toyed with his ham and eggs as he envisioned the possibilities of the discovery.

Then a sudden resolution seized him. He looked at the newspaper account again. Yes, Crookman was staying at the Phyllis Wheatley Hotel. Why not go and see what there was to this? Why not be the first Negro to try it out? Sure, it was taking a chance, but think of getting white in three days! No more jim crow. No more insults. As a white man he could go anywhere, be anything he wanted to be, do most anything he wanted to do, be a free man at last ... and probably be able to meet the girl from Atlanta. What a vision!

He rose hurriedly, paid for his breakfast, rushed out of the door, almost ran into an aged white man carrying a sign advertising a Negro fraternity dance, and strode, almost ran, to the Phyllis Wheatley Hotel.

He tore up the steps two at a time and into the sitting room. It was crowded with white reporters from the daily newspapers and black reporters from the

Negro weeklies. In their midst he recognized Dr. Junius Crookman, tall, wiry, ebony black, with a studious and polished manner. Flanking him on either side was Henry ("Hank") Johnson, the "Numbers banker and Charlie ("Chuck") Foster, the realtor, looking very grave, important and possessive in the midst of all of the hullabaloo.

"Yes," Dr. Crookman was telling the reporter while they eagerly took down his statements, "during my first year at college I noticed a black girl on the street one day who had several irregular white patches on her face and hands. That intrigued me. I began to study skin diseases and found out that the girl was evidently suffering from a nervous disease known as vitiligo. It is a very rare disease. Both Negroes and Caucasians occasionally have it, but it is naturally more conspicuous on blacks than whites. It absolutely removes skin pigment and sometimes it turns a Negro completely white but only after a period of thirty or forty years. It occurred to me that if one could discover some means of artificially inducing and stimulating this nervous disease at will, one might possibly solve the race problem. My sociology teacher had once said that there were but three ways for the Negro to solve his problem in America," he gestured with his long slender fingers, " 'To either get out, get white or get along.' Since he wouldn't and couldn't get out and was getting along only differently, it seemed to me that the only thing for him was to get white." For a moment his teeth gleamed beneath his smartly waxed mustache, then he sobered and went on:

"I began to give a great deal of study to the problem during my spare time. Unfortunately there was very little information on the subject in this country. I decided to go to Germany but I didn't have the money. Just when I despaired of getting the funds to carry out my experiments and studies abroad, Mr. Johnson and Mr. Foster," he indicated the two men with a graceful wave of his hand, "came to my rescue. I naturally attribute a great deal of my success to them."

"But how is it done?" asked a reporter.

"Well," smiled Crookman, "I naturally cannot divulge the secret any more than to say that it is accomplished by electrical nutrition and glandular control. Certain gland secretions are greatly stimulated while others are considerably diminished. It is a powerful and dangerous treatment but harmless when properly done."

"How about the hair and features?" asked a Negro reporter.

"They are also changed in the process," answered the biologist.

"In three days the Negro becomes to all appearances a Caucasian."

"But is the transformation transferred to the offspring?" persisted the Negro newspaperman.

"As yet," replied Crookman, "I have discovered no way to accomplish anything so revolutionary but I am able to transform a black infant into a white one in twenty-four hours."

"Have you tried it on any Negroes yet?" queried a skeptical white journalist.

"Why of course I have," said the Doctor, slightly nettled. "I would not have made my announcement if I had not done so. Come here, Sandol," he called, turning to a pale white youth standing on the outskirts of the crowd, who was the most Nordic looking person in the room. "This man is a Senegalese, a former aviator in the French Army. He is living proof that what I claim is true."

Dr. Crookman then displayed a photograph of a very black man, somewhat resembling Sandol but with bushy Negro hair, flat nose and full lips. "This," he announced proudly, "is Sandol as he looked before taking my treatment. What I have done to him I can do to any Negro. He is in good physical and mental condition as you all can see."

The assemblage was properly awed. After taking a few more notes and a number of photographs of Dr. Crookman, his associates and of Sandol, the newspaperman retired. Only the dapper Max Disher remained.

"Hello, Doc!" he said, coming forward and extending his hand. "Don't you remember me? I'm Max Disher."

"Why certainly I remember you, Max," replied the biologist rising cordially. "Been a long time since we've seen each other but you're looking as sharp as every. How's things?"

The two men shook hands.

"Oh, pretty good. Say, Doc, how's chances to get you to try that thing on me? You must be looking for volunteers."

"Yes, I am, but not just yet. I've got to get my equipment set up first. I think now I'll be ready for business in a couple of weeks."

Henry Johnson, the beefy, sleek-jowled, mulatto "Numbers," banker, chuckled and nudged Dr. Crookman. "Old Max ain't losin' no time, Doc. When that niggah gits white Ah bet he'll make up fo' los' time with these ofay girls."

Charlie Foster, small, slender, grave, amber-colored, and laconic, finally spoke up: "Seems all right, Junius, but there'll be hell to pay when you whiten up a lot o' these darkies and them mulatto babies start appearing here and there. Watcha gonna do then?"

"Oh, quit singin' the blues, Chuck," boomed Johnson. "Don't cross bridges 'til yuh come tuh 'em. Doc'll fix that okeh. Besides, we'll have mo' money'n Henry Ford by that time."

"There'll be no difficulties whatever," assured Crookman rather impatiently.

"Let's hope not."

Next day the newspapers carried a long account of the interview with Dr. Junius Crookman interspersed with photographs of him, his backers and of the Senegalese who had been turned white. It was the talk of the town and was soon the talk of the country. Long editorials were written about the discovery, learned societies besieged the Negro biologist with offers of lecture engagements, magazines begged him for articles, but he turned down all offers and refused to explain his treatment. This attitude was decried as unbecoming a scientist and it was insinuated and even openly stated that nothing more could be expected from a Negro.

But Crookman ignored the clamor of the public, and with the financial help of his associates planned the great and lucrative experiment of turning Negroes into Caucasians.

The impatient Max Disher saw him as often as possible and kept track of developments. He yearned to be the first treated and didn't want to be caught napping. Two objects were uppermost in his mind: To get white and to Atlanta. The statuesque and haughty blonde was ever in his thoughts. He was head over heels in love with her and realized there was no hope for him to ever win her as long as he was brown. Each day he would walk past the tall building that was to be the Crookman Sanitarium, watching the workmen and delivery trucks; wondering how much longer he would have to wait before entering upon the great adventure.

At last the sanitarium was ready for business. Huge advertisements appeared in the local Negro weeklies. Black Harlem was on its toes. Curious throngs of Negroes and whites stood in front of the austere six-story building gazing up at its windows.

Inside, Crookman, Johnson and Foster stood nervously about while hustling attendants got everything in readiness. Outside they could hear the murmur of the crowd.

"That means money, Chuck," boomed Johnson, rubbing his beefsteak hands together.

"Yeh," replied the realtor, "but there's one more thing I wanna get straight: How about that darky dialect? You can't change that."

"It isn't necessary, my dear Foster," explained the physician, patiently. "There is no such thing as Negro dialect, except in literature and drama. It is a well-known fact among informed persons that a Negro from a given section speaks the same dialect as his white neighbors. In the South you can't tell over the telephone whether you are talking to a white man or a Negro. The same is true in New York when a Northern Negro speaks into the receiver. I have noticed the same thing in the hills of West Virginia and Tennessee. The educated Haitian speaks the purest French and the Jamaican Negro sounds exactly like an Englishman. There are no racial or color dialects; only sectional dialects."

"Guess you're right," agreed Foster, grudgingly.

"I know I'm right. Moreover, even if my treatment did not change the so-called Negro lips, even that would prove to be no obstacle."

"How come, Doc," asked Johnson.

"Well, there are plenty of Caucasians who have lips quite as thick and noses quite as broad as any of us. As a matter of fact there has been considerable exaggeration about the contrast between Caucasian and Negro features. The cartoonists and minstrel men have been responsible for it very largely. Some Negroes like the Somalis, Filanis, Egyptians, Hausas and Abyssinians have very thin lips and nostrils. So also have the Malagasys of Madagascar. Only in certain small sections of Africa do the Negroes possess extremely pendulous lips and very broad nostrils. On the other hand, many so-called Caucasians, particularly the Latins, Jews and South Irish, and frequently the most Nordic of people like the Swedes, show almost Negroid lips and noses. Black up some white folks and they could deceive a resident of Benin. Then when you consider that less than twenty per cent of our Negroes are without Caucasian ancestry and that close to thirty per cent have American Indian ancestry, it is readily seen that there cannot be the wide difference in Caucasian and Afro-American facial characteristics that most people imagine."

"Doc, you sho' know yo' onions," said Johnson, admiringly. "Doan pay no' tenshun to that old Doubtin' Thomas. He'd holler starvation in a pie shop."

There was a commotion outside and an angry voice was heard above the hum of low conversation. Then Max Disher burst in the door with a guard hanging onto his coat tail.

"Let loose o' me, Boy," he quarreled. "I got an engagement here. Doc, tell this man something, will you?"

Crookman nodded to the guard to release the insurance man. "Well, I see you're right on time, Max."

"I told you I'd be Johnny-on-the-spot, didn't I?" said Disher, inspecting his clothes to see if they had been wrinkled.

"Well, if you're all ready, go into the receiving room there, sign the register and get into one of those bathrobes. You're first on the list."

The three partners looked at each other and grinned as Max disappeared into a small room at the end of the corridor. Dr. Crookman went into his office to don his white trousers, shoes and smock; Johnson and Foster entered the business office to supervise the clerical staff, while white-coated figures darted back and forth through the corridors. Outside, the murmuring of the vast throng grew more audible.

Johnson showed all of his many gold teeth in a wide grin as he glanced out the window and saw the queue of Negroes already extending around the corner. "Man, man, man!" he chuckled to Foster, "at fifty dollars a th'ow this thing's gonna have th' numbah business beat all hollow."

"Hope so," said Foster, gravely.

Max Disher, arrayed only in a hospital bathrobe and a pair of slippers, was escorted to the elevator by two white-coated attendants. They got off on the sixth floor and walked to the end of the corridor. Max was trembling with excitement and anxiety. Suppose something should go wrong? Suppose Doc should make a mistake? He thought of the Elks' excursion every summer to Bear Mountain, the high yellow Minnie and her colorful apartment, the pleasant evenings at the Dahomey Casino doing the latest dances with the brown belles of Harlem, the prancing choruses at the Lafayette Theater, and the hours he had whiled away at Boogies' and the Honky Tonk club, and he hesitated. Then he envisioned his future as a white man, probably as the husband of the tall blonde from Atlanta, and with firm resolve, he entered the door of the mysterious chamber.

He quailed as he saw the formidable apparatus of sparkling nickel. It resembled a cross between a dentist's chair and an electric chair. Wires and straps, bars and levers protruded from it and a great nickel headpiece, like the helmet of a knight, hung over it. The room had only a skylight and no sound entered it from the outside. Around the walls were cases of instruments and shelves of bottles filled with strangely colored fluids. He gasped with fright and would have made for the door but the two husky attendants held him firmly, stripped off his robe and bound him in the chair. There was no retreat. It was either the beginning or the end.

Two

Slowly, haltingly, Max Disher dragged his way down the hall to the elevator, supported on either side by an attendant. He felt terribly weak, emptied and nauseated; his skin twitched and was dry and feverish; his insides felt very hot and sore. As the trio walked slowly along the corridor, a blue-green light would ever and anon blaze through one of the doorways as a patient was taken in. There was a low hum and throb of machinery and an acid odor filled the air. Uniformed nurses and attendants hurried back and forth at their tasks. Everything was quiet, swift, efficient, sinister.

He felt so thankful that he had survived the ordeal of that horrible machine so akin to the electric chair. A shudder passed over him at the memory of the hours he had passed in its grip, fed at intervals with revolting concoctions. But when they reached the elevator and he saw himself in the mirror, he was startled, overjoyed. While at last! Gone was the smooth brown complexion. Gone were the slightly full lips and Ethiopian nose. Gone was the nappy hair that he had straightened so meticulously ever since the kink-no-more lotions first wrenched Aframericans from the tyranny and torture of the comb. There would be no more expenditures for skin whiteners; no more discrimination; no more obstacles in his path. He was free! The world was his oyster and he had the open sesame of a pork-colored skin!

The reflection in the mirror gave him new life and strength. He now stood erect, without support and grinned at the two tall, black attendants. "Well, Boys," he crowed, "I'm all set now. That machine of Doc's worked like a charm. Soon's I get a feed under my belt I'll be okeh."

Six hours later, bathed, fed, clean-shaven, spry, blonde and jubilant, he emerged from the outpatient ward and tripped gaily down the corridor to the main entrance. He was through with coons, he resolved, from now on. He glanced in a superior manner at the long line of black and brown folk on one side of the corridor, patiently awaiting treatment. He saw many persons whom he knew but none of them recognized him. It thrilled him to feel that he was now indistinguishable from nine-tenths of the people of the United States; one of the great majority. Ah, it was good not be a Negro any longer!

As he sought to open the front door, the strong arm of a guard restrained him. "Wait a minute," the man said, "and we'll help you get through the mob."

A moment or two later Max found himself the center of a flying wedge of five or six husky policemen, cleaving through a milling crowd of colored folk. From the top step of the sanitarium he had noticed the crowd spread over the sidewalk, into the street and around the corners. Fifty traffic policemen strained and sweated to keep prospective patients in line and out from under the wheels of taxicabs and trucks.

Finally he reached the curb, exhausted from the jostling and squeezing, only to be set upon by a mob of newspaper photographers and reporters. As the first person to take the treatment, he was naturally the center of attraction for about fifteen of these journalistic gnats. They asked a thousand questions seemingly all at once. What was his name? How did he feel? What was he going to do? Would he marry a white woman? Did he intend to continue living in Harlem?

Max would say nothing. In the first place, he thought to himself, if they're so anxious to know all this stuff, they ought to be willing to pay for it. He needed money if he was going to be able to thoroughly enjoy being white; why not get some by selling his story? The reporters, male and female, begged him almost with tears in their eyes for a statement but he was adamant.

While they were wrangling, an empty taxicab drove up. Pushing the inquisitive reporters to one side, Max leaped into it and yelled "Central Park!" It was the only place he could think of at the moment. He wanted to have time to compose his mind, to plan the future in this great world of whiteness. As the cab lurched forward, he turned and was astonished to find another occupant, a pretty girl.

"Don't be scared," she smiled. "I knew you would want to get away from that mob so I went around the corner and got a cab for you. Come along with me and I'll get everything fixed up for you. I'm a reporter from *The Scimitar*. We'll give you a lot of money for your story." She talked rapidly. Max's first impulse had been to jump out of the cab, even at the risk of having to face again the mob of reporters and photographers he sought to escape, but he changed his mind when he heard mention of money.

"How much?" he asked, eyeing her. She was very comely and he noted that her ankles were well turned.

"Oh, probably a thousand dollars," she replied.

"Well, that sounds good." A thousand dollars! What a time he could have with that! Broadway for him as soon as he got paid off.

As they sped down Seventh Avenue, the newsboys were yelling the latest editions. "Ex—try! Ex—try! Blacks turning white! Blacks turning white! ... Read all about the gr-r-reat dis—covery! Paper, Mister! Paper! ... Read all about Dr. Crookman."

He settled back while they drove through the park and glanced frequently at the girl by his side. She looked mighty good; wonder could he talk business with her? Might go to dinner and a cabaret. That would be the best way to start.

"What did you say your name was?" he began.

"I didn't say," she stalled.

"Well, you have a name, haven't you?" he persisted.

"Suppose I have?"

"You're not scared to tell it, are you?"

"Why do you want to know my name?"

"Well, there's nothing wrong about wanting to know a pretty girl's name, is there?"

"Well, my name's Smith, Sybil Smith. Now are you satisfied?"

"Not yet. I want to know something more. How would you like to go to dinner with me tonight?"

"I don't know and I won't know until I've had the experience." She smiled coquettishly. Going out with him, she figured would make the basis of a rattling good story for tomorrow's paper. "Negro's first night as a Caucasian!" Fine!

"Say, you're a regular fellow," he said, beaming upon her. "I'll get a great kick out of going to dinner with you because you'll be the only one in the place that'll know I'm a Negro."

Down at the office of *The Scimitar*, it didn't take Max long to come to an agreement, tell his story to a stenographer and get a sheaf of crisp, new bills. As he left the building a couple of hours later with Miss Smith on his arm, the news-boys were already crying the extra edition carrying the first installment of his strange tale. A huge photograph of him occupied the entire front page of the tabloid. Lucky for him that he'd given his name as William Small, he thought.

He was annoyed and a little angered. What did they want to put his picture all over the front of the paper for? Now everybody would know who he was. He had undergone the tortures of Doc Crookman's devilish machine in order to escape the conspicuousness of dark skin and now he was being made con-spicuous because he had once had a dark skin! Could one never escape the plagued race problem?

"Don't worry about that," comforted Miss Smith. "Nobody'll recognize you. There are thousands of white people, yes millions, that look like you do." She took his arm and snuggled up closer. She wanted to make him feel at home. It wasn't often a poor, struggling newspaper woman got a chap with a big bankroll to take her out for the evening. Moreover, the description she would write of the experience might win her a promotion.

They walked down Broadway in the blaze of white lights to a dinner-dance place. To Max it was like being in heaven. He had strolled through the Times Square district before but never with such a feeling of absolute freedom and sureness. No one now looked at him curiously because he was with a white girl, as they had when he came down there with Minnie, his former octoroon lady friend. Gee, it was great!

They dined and they danced. Then they went to a cabaret, where amid smoke, noise and body smells, they drank what was purported to be whisky and watched a semi-nude chorus do its stuff. Despite his happiness Max found it pretty dull. There was something lacking in these ofay places of amusement or else there was something present that one didn't find in the black-and-tan resorts in Harlem. The joy and abandon here was obviously forced. Patrons went to extremes to show each other they were having a wonderful time. It was all so strained and quite unlike anything to which he had been accus-tomed. The Negroes, it seemed to him, were much gayer, enjoyed themselves more deeply and yet they were more restrained, actually more refined. Even their dancing was different. They followed the rhythm accurately, effortlessly and with easy grace; these lumbering couples, out of step half the time and working as strenuously as stevedores emptying the bowels of a freighter, were noisy, awkward, inelegant. At their best they were gymnastic where the Negroes were sensuous. He felt a momentary pang of mingled disgust, disillusionment and nostalgia. But it was only momentary. He looked across at the comely Sybil and then around the corner at the other white women, many of whom were very pretty and expensively gowned, and the sight temporarily drove from his mind the thoughts that had been occupying him.

They parted at three o'clock, after she had given him her telephone number. She pecked him lightly on the cheek in payment, doubtless, for a pleasant evening's entertainment. Somewhat disappointed because she had failed to show any interest in his expressed curiosity to see the interior of her apartment, he directed the chauffeur to drive him to Harlem. After all, he argued to himself in defense of his action, he had to get his things.

As the cab turned out of Central Park at 110th Street he felt, curiously enough, a feeling of peace. There were all the old familiar sights: the all-night speakeasies, the frankfurter stands, the loiterers, the late pedestrians, the chop suey joints, the careening taxicabs, the bawdy laughter.

He couldn't resist the temptation to get out at 133rd Street and go down to Boogie's place, the hangout of his gang. He tapped, an eye peeped through a hole, appraised him critically, then disappeared and the hole was closed. There was silence.

Max frowned. What was the matter with old Bob? Why didn't he open that door? The cold January breeze swept down into the little court where he stood and made him shiver. He knocked a little louder, more insistently. The eye appeared again.

"Who's 'at?" growled the doorkeeper.

"It's me, Max Disher," replied the ex-Negro.

"Go 'way f'm here, white man. Dis heah place is closed."

"Is Bunny Brown in there?" asked Max in desperation.

"Yeh, he's heah. Does yuh know him? Well, Ah'll call 'im out heah and see if he knows you."

Max waited in the cold for about two or three minutes and then the door suddenly opened and Bunny Brown, a little unsteady, came out. He peered at Max in the light from the electric bulb over the door.

"Hello Bunny," Max greeted him. "Don't know me, do you? It's me, Max Disher. You recognize my voice, don't you?"

Bunny looked again, rubbed his eyes and shook his head. Yes, the voice was Max Disher's, but this man was white. Still, when he smiled his eyes revealed the same sardonic twinkle—so characteristic of his friend.

"Max," he blurted out, "is that you, sure enough? Well, for cryin' out loud! Damned 'f you ain't been up there to Crookman's and got fixed up. Well, hush my mouth! Bob, open that door. This is old Max Disher. Done gone up there to Crookman's and got all white on my hands. He's just too tight, with his blond hair, 'n everything."

Bob opened the door, the two friends entered, sat down at one of the small round tables in the narrow, smoke-filled cellar and were soon surrounded with cronies. They gazed raptly at his colorless skin, commented on the veins showing blue through the epidermis, stroked his ash-blond hair and listened with mouths open to his remarkable story.

"Watcha gonna do now, Max?" asked Boogie, the rangy, black, bullet-headed proprietor.

"I know just what that joker's gonna do," said Bunny. "He's goin' back to Atlanta. Am I right, Big Boy?"

"You ain't wrong," Max agreed. "I'm goin' right on down there, brother, and make up for lost time."

"Whadayah mean?" asked Boogie.

"Boy, it would take me until tomorrow night to tell you and then you wouldn't understand."

The two friends strolled up the avenue. Both were rather mum. They had been inseparable pals since the stirring days in France. Now they were about to be parted. It wasn't as if Max was going across the ocean to some foreign country; there would be a wider gulf separating them: the great sea of color. They both thought about it.

"I'll be pretty lonesome without you, Bunny."

"It ain't you, Big Boy."

"Well, why don't you go ahead and get white and then we could stay to-gether. I'll give you the money."

"Say not so! Where'd you get so much jack all of a sudden?" asked Bunny.

"Sold my story to *The Scimitar* for a grand."

"Paid in full?"

"Wasn't paid in part!"

"All right, then, I'll take you up, Heavy Sugar." Bunny held out his plump hand and Max handed him a hundred-dollar bill.

They were near the Crookman Sanitarium. Although it was five o'clock on a Sunday morning, the building was brightly lighted from cellar to roof and the hum of electric motors could be heard, low and powerful. A large electric sign hung from the roof to the second floor. It represented a huge arrow outlined in green with the words BLACK-NO-MORE running its full length vertically. A black face was depicted at the lower end of the arrow while at the top shone a white face to which the arrow was pointed. First would appear the outline of the arrow; then BLACK-NO-MORE would flash on and off. Following that the black face would appear at the bottom and beginning at the lower end the long arrow with its lettering would appear progressively until its tip was reached, when the white face at the top would blazon forth. After that the sign would flash off and on and the process would be repeated.

In front of the sanitarium milled a half-frozen crowd of close to four thousand Negroes. A riot squad armed with rifles, machine guns and tear gas bombs maintained some semblance of order. A steel cable stretched from lamp post to lamp post the entire length of the block kept the struggling mass of humanity on the sidewalk and out of the path of traffic. It seemed as if all Harlem were there. As the two friends reached the outskirts of the mob, an ambulance from the Harlem Hospital drove up and carried away two women who had been trampled upon.

Lined up from the door to the curb was a gang of tough special guards dredged out of the slums. Grim Irish from Hell's Kitchen, rough Negroes from around 133rd Street and 5th Avenue (New York's "Beale Street") and tough Italians from the lower West Side. They managed with difficulty to keep an aisle cleared for incoming and outgoing patients. Near the curb were stationed the reporters and photographers.

The noise rose and fell. First there would be a low hum of voices. Steadily it would rise and rise in increasing volume as the speakers became more animated and reach its climax in a great animal-like roar as the big front door would open and a whitened Negro would emerge. Then the mass would surge forward to peer at and question the ersatz Nordic. Sometimes the ex-Ethiopian would quail before the mob and jump back into the building. Then the hardboiled guards would form a flying squad and hustle him to a waiting taxicab. Other erstwhile Aframericans issuing from the building would grin broadly, shake hands with friends and relatives and start to graphically describe their experience while the Negroes around them enviously admired their clear white skins.

In between these appearances the hot dog and peanut vendors did a brisk trade, along with the numerous pickpockets of the district. One slender, anemic, ratty-looking mulatto Negro was almost beaten to death by a gigantic black laundress whose purse he had snatched. A Negro selling hot roasted sweet potatoes did a land-office business while the neighboring saloons, that had increased so rapidly in number since the enactment of the Volstead Law that many of their Italian proprietors paid substantial income taxes, sold scores of gallons of incredibly atrocious hootch.

"Well, bye, bye, Max," said Bunny, extending his hand. "I'm goin' in an' try my luck."

"So long, Bunny. See you in Atlanta. Write me general delivery."

"Why, ain't you gonna wait for me, Max?"

"Naw! I'm fed up on this town."

"Oh, you ain't kiddin' me, Big Boy. I know you want to look up that broad you saw in the Honky Tonk New Year's Eve," Bunny beamed.

Max grinned and blushed slightly. They shook hands and parted. Bunny ran up the aisle from the curb, opened the sanitarium door and without turning around, disappeared within.

For a minute or so, Max stood irresolutely in the midst of the gibbering crowd of people. Unaccountably he felt at home here among these black folk. Their jests, scraps of conversation and lusty laughter all seemed like heavenly music. Momentarily he felt a disposition to stay among them, to share again their troubles which they seemed always to bear with a lightness that was not yet indifference. But then, he suddenly realized with just a tiny trace of remorse that the past was forever gone. He must seek other pastures, other pursuits, other playmates, other loves. He was white now. Even if he wished to stay among his folk, they would be either jealous or suspicious of him, as they were of most octoroons and nearly all whites. There was no other alternative than to seek his future among the Caucasians with whom he now rightfully belonged.

And after all, he thought, it was a glorious new adventure. His eyes twinkled and his pulse quickened as he thought of it. Now he could go anywhere, associate with anybody, be anything he wanted to be. He suddenly thought of the comely miss he had seen in the Honky Tonk on New Year's Eve and the greatly enlarged field from which he could select his loves. Yes, indeed there were advantages in being white. He brightened and viewed the tightly-packed black folk around him with a superior air. Then, thinking again of his clothes at Mrs. Blandish's, the money in his pocket and the prospect for the first time of riding into Atlanta in a Pullman car and not as a Pullman porter, he turned and pushed his way through the throng.

He strolled up West 139th Street to his rooming place, stepping lightly and sniffing the early morning air. How good it was to be free, white and to possess a bankroll! He fumbled in his pocket for his little mirror and looked at himself again and again from several angles. He stroked his pale blond hair and secretly congratulated himself that he would no longer need to straighten it nor be afraid to wet it. He gazed raptly at his smooth, white hands with the blue veins showing through. What a miracle Dr. Crookman had wrought!

As he entered the hallway, the mountainous form of his landlady loomed up. She jumped back as she saw his face.

"What you doing in here?" she almost shouted. "Where'd you get a key to this house?"

"It's me, Max Disher," he assured her with a grin at her astonishment. "Don't know me, do you?"

She gazed incredulously at his face. "Is that you sure enough, Max? How in the devil did you get so white?"

He explained and showed her a copy of *The Scimitar* containing his story. She switched on the hall light and read it. Contrasting emotions played over her face, for Mrs. Blandish was known in the business world as Mme. Sisseretta Blandish, the beauty specialist, who owned the swellest hair-straightening parlor in Harlem. Business, she thought to herself, was bad enough, what with all of the competition, without this Dr. Crookman coming along and killing it altogether.

"Well," she sighed, "I suppose you're going down town to live, now. I always said niggers didn't really have any race pride."

Uneasy, Max made no reply. The fat, brown woman turned with a disdainful sniff and disappeared into a room at the end of the hall. He ran lightly upstairs to pack his things.

An hour later, as the taxicab bearing him and his luggage bowled through Central Park, he was in high spirits. He would go down to the Pennsylvania Station and get a Pullman straight into Atlanta. He would stop there at the best hotel. He wouldn't hunt up any of his folks. No, that would be too dangerous. He would just play around, enjoy life and laugh at the white folks up his sleeve. God! What an adventure! What a treat it would be to mingle with white people in places where as a youth he had never dared to enter. At last he felt like an American citizen. He flecked the ash of his panatela out of the open window of the cab and sank back into the seat feeling at peace with the world.

from *Brother Man*

by Roger Mais (Jamaica)

CHORUS OF THE PEOPLE IN THE LANE

The tongues in the lane clack-clack almost continuously, going up and down the full scale of human emotions, human folly, ignorance, suffering, viciousness, magnanimity, weakness, greatness, littleness, insufficiency, frailty, strength.

They clack on street corners, where the ice-shop hangs out a triangular red flag, under the shadow of overhanging buildings that lean precariously, teetering across the dingy chasm of the narrow lane.

Around the yam-seller's barrow, and the tripe-seller's basket, and the coal vendor's crazy push-cart drawn up against the seamy sidewalk, they clack, interspersing the hawking and the bargaining, and what-goes-on in the casual, earnest, noisy, meaningless business of buying and selling; and where the mango-seller sets down her country load.

They clack where the neighbours meet in the Chinese grocery shop on the corner, leaning elbows against the counter with its saltfish odour and the spilled rice grains and brown sugar grains, and amid the dustings of cornmeal and flour under the smirking two-faced scale, waiting for change.

—Mis' Brody's clubfootbwoy get run over ...
—You hear wha' Bra' Ambo say? Say we gwine get nodder breeze-blow dis year yet ...
—Cho Missis, no mind Bra' Ambo, after him no eena Big Massa council ...
—Coal-price gone up since todder day ...
—Ee-ee Ma, him do an' get run over ...
—Oonu lissen hear what' Bra' Ambo say ...

Behind the pocked visage and the toothless grin, behind the wrinkled skin gathered and seamed around the lips and under the eyes, behind the façade of haltness and haleness and cursing and laughter, slander lurks in ambush to take the weakest and the hindmost, and the tongues clack upon every chance.

—Cordy's man get tek-up fo' ganga ...
—Bra' Man show de gospel way ...
—Me-gal still wi' hold wid Bra' Ambo
—Coal price gone up since todder day ...
—Lawd Jesus, po' Mis' Brody ...
—No mind, God is over all ...
—Hush yaw ma', you' mout'-lip favour
—No God do dem t'ing de at all ...

There are sad-faced old ones, and sleek-faced young ones, and all ways in between; and there are those with an accounting of troubles the same and equal to and over and beyond the ones they tell; and there are those too who have missed the accounting, ducking and dodging and putting by for another day; but all, all are involved in the same chapter of consequences, all are caught up between the covers of the same book of living; they look with shuddering over their shoulder past the image of their own secret terror, feeling the shadow of it over them in another's fate.

—Po' Cordy one fe mind de pickney ...
—Lissen good wha' Bra' Ambo say ...
—Cho gwan wid you' Bra' Ambo ...
—Bra' Man know de gospel way ...

—Papacita beat up him gal las' night …
—Is a shame de way dem two de-live …
—Gal waan fo' him an' she get married …
—Hm! Papacita know what 'married' give …

Over washtubs in noisome yards where the drip-drip of the eternally leaking standpipe makes waste in the sun-cracked green-slimed concrete cistern, and under the ackee tree or the custard-apple tree or the Spanish-guava tree or the Seville orange tree behind the lean-to pit-latrine in the yard, they clack-clack eternally telling their own hunger and haltness and lameness and night-ness and negation, like flies buzzing an open unremitting sore, tasting again, renewing, and giving again, the wounds they have taken of the world.

—Flyin' Saucer tek-in Mercedes …
—Cho! A-swing her tail up an' down de street! …
—How she-one manage ketch so-much sailor? …
—Mus' be black-gal somet'ing sweet! …
—Hear dem say-say Papacita de mek eye after Bra' Man gal …
—Mek Bra' Man find out! …
—Hm! Jus' wait bwoy! …
—Massa Jesus! Gwine be hell! …

Night comes down and the tongues have not ceased to shuttle and to clatter, they still carry their burden of the tale of man's woes. It is their own story over that they tell in secret, overlaying it with the likeness of slander, licking their own ancient scrofulous sores.…

ONE

Girlie was idly turning the pages of a magazine when Papacita came in through the door. She did not look up. He closed the door quietly—too quietly—behind him, without taking his eyes off her, came cat-footing across the room.

He noticed that a corner of the page picturing Ingrid Bergman in Koda-color trembled a little between her fingers. Something tickled him at the back of his throat. He wanted to cough.

He said: '*Hm!*' trying to clear it.

She turned the page, slowly, put her other hand up to her back-hair.

He went past her, across to the window overlooking the land, threw it open with a bang, and said, angrily:

'It's like a furnace in here.'

She went on turning the pages of the magazine she held across her knee. She put a finger up to her lips, wet the tip of it with her tongue, raised her eyes slowly to look at him, as though aware of his presence for the first time, saw him without recognition, without change of expression, and brought her eyes back slowly to the page.

He leaned against the window and stood looking at her a moment, shrugged, turned away, went across to the bed, sat down, started pulling off his shoes.

'Lousy bum,' she said, casually, as though she was speaking to herself, just turning her thoughts out to air.

'What's it?' he said.

But when she looked up, quickly, challengingly, ready to get on with it, she wasn't looking at him at all. Her gaze had returned to the thumbed-down page of the magazine she held open across her knees. She put her head a little to one side, and might just as well have been addressing herself to the half-length photograph of Humphrey Bogart.

He pulled off the other shoe, massaged his toes a little, let the shoe fall to the board floor with a clatter, heaved himself over, and rolled into bed.

'All right,' he said, 'might as well get started. I know you're jus' bustin' with things to say. Whyn't I come home las' night, hey? Don't you want to know?'

A little breeze coming through the window fluttered the calendar on the wall.

'Lousy bum,' she said again, almost conversationally, without raising her voice at all.

'All right,' he said, 'but if you want to know it wasn't with any woman I was with.'

'Was a woman you was with I wouldn't care, don't give you'self no fancy airs, could have men friends on the side a-plenty, if I wanted to give you the run-around, I'm tellin' you.'

Ignoring the second part of her statement he said:

'No, you wouldn't care, like hell not you wouldn't, only be scratchin' me eyes out to give you' han's somep'n to do, I guess. Awe, lemme alone.'

'Ain't troublin' you, got somep'n else on you' mind, mus' be. Wasn't a gal you was with, mus' be you was in church.'

'Don't gimme that stuff. I've had about enough of it, always naggin' at a man, don't get a chance to turn.'

'Go to sleep,' she said, 'ketch-up you' strength. You got a hard day before you. Hm! No wonder you too tired to work.'

'If you want to know, honey, was a job Ah was lookin' las' night. A job, see?'

'What kind of a job dat? Night watchman, mus' be. Gwine get meself a job like dat too, you wait an' see.'

'Don't gimme none of you' lip gal. Gimme dat kinda lip Ah up an' slap you down.'

'Slap me down, you try dat again Ah chop you up fine. You know what's good fo' you, you don't even think it, much less talk it, see?'

'Awe, come on, honey. Was only jokin' you. Ah'm gettin' me a job, don't worry. Goin' go to wuk fo' you an' me.'

He patted the side of the bed, slowly, suggestively, with the hand that wasn't holding up his head, said softly, throwing the words at her as he might a cushion or one of those big soft indiarubber balls:

'Come over here. Come on no, honey, come over here.'

'Papacita, you're a big over-grown pickney,' she said, pouting a little with vexation, looking at him sloe-eyed, letting the magazine slide off her lap to the floor, 'you think you can get around me that way, you foolin' you'self. Tell me 'bout the job you was all night las' night gettin' you'self, tell me bout it, eh, why you don't?'

His brows came together ever so slightly, as yet scarcely a frown, as if he was puzzling something out inside his head, trying to make the answer come right.

'The job,' he said, slowly, taking his time, 'Aw, honey, Ah'm keepin' that as a big surprise for you. Yeh, that's what, goin' be a big surprise. Goin' go to wuk fo' you an' me.'

'That shore will surprise me plenty,' she said, the corners of her mouth curling with contempt, 'goin' bust me shore. You get you'self a job, Papa-boy, Ah get meself wings an' fly.'

'All right,' he said, hurt, offended in his pride, 'You don' believe me, hey, you jus' wait an' see. Lissen, the money Ah'll be makin' will take you' lap to hold it in.'

His mouth puckered like a sulky boy's. 'You think Ah'm kiddin', you think Ah'm just' no-good, kiddin' you all the time. Jus' wait, baby, goin' show you somep'm mek you' eyes bung-up wid surprise.'

Her mouth made as though it wanted to laugh but she wouldn't let it.

'Goin' surprise me, don't it, honey? Look, you start me laffin' so soon in the day ...'

'Bitch! Laff no? Why don't you la'ff?'

He said it without heat, without antagonism, a little hurt only, his lips puckered like an obstinate boy.

He said: 'Have a mind to get up an' walk right out on you, you'd deserve it. God damn it! Ah jus' have a mind.'

'You walk out on me honey, where you eat? Walk out on me, eh, why you don' get goin', God hear me, I'd like to see you get up an' start walkin' right this minute. Have a mind is 'bout all you ever do. You think I'm scared of anything you say? Have a mind!'

The skin like parchment around his eyes tightened a little, and let go. And then he came all contrite, all treacle and melting butter again.

'Aw come on over and sit here, will yah, honey? Jus' can't stand to see you takin' on that way.'

2

A small boy trundled an iron hoop down Orange Lane, routed by two scabby mongrels that were going around in circles snifting each other, before him, whistled piercingly a ragged, rowdy tune.

He broke off suddenly, recognizing the tall, rangy man slouching before him up the lane, tried to slink past without the man taking notice of him; but Jennings stopped, took a packet of cigarettes from his pocket, stuck one in his mouth and called the boy.

'Hi Joe,' said Jennings.

Joe looked sullenly at him, grunted, made as though to go on his own way.

'C'mere, Joe,' said Jennings.

Joe stopped, hesitated, looked down at his bare toes an instant, started to cross over.

'You want me?' he said, standing before the tall man, his gaze focusing on the shiny belt buckle at the man's waist.

'What's the matter, Joe?' said Jennings. 'Got somep'n you want to hide? Come on, what you got sticking out of you' back pocket, kid? Come on, show me.'

'Nutt'n, sah, nutt'n, a pass'l, dat's all.'

'Ah, a pass'l. Come on, then, show me what's it you got in dat little pass'l you don't want nobody to see. Eh Joe? Let's have a look at what you got in dat pass'l, eh?'

The boy looked quickly down the street, as though he had in mind to try and make a break for it, brought his gaze back to the tall man's middle, put the thought away. His hand went slowly to the back pocket of his ragged trousers, and brought away with it a folded piece of old newspaper which he handed to the man.

'Open it up, Joe, it's your pass'l, ain't it?'

The boy undid the untidy newspaper wrapping, exposing a slingshot, some pieces of string, and half a penny bullar to view.

'Ain't got nutt'n else on you, eh Joe? Jus' them little things in that pass'l, eh?'

'No, sah, nutt'n else at all; like what, sah?'

'Don't tell me you don't know what I'm looking for, sonny. You tell me a thing like that an' you mek me feel like laffin', an Ah ain't sca'sley had me breakfast, yet, see?'

'Ain't got nutt'n else,' said the boy, sullenly.

'All right, all right, sonny, jus' take it easy now. How about it, Joe, you been passin' any of the stuff around lately?'

'Don't know what you talkin' 'bout,' said the boy, defiantly.

'You don't say that now. I know they been usin' you kids in the lane. Don't you ever pass any of the stuff, Joe? Ever? Now tek your own time to answer. Ah guess you wouldn't want to try kiddin' me?'

'No, sah.'

'That's better. How about it?'

'About what, sah?'

He rubbed the tip of his thumb across the tip of the four fingers of his right hand.

'The weed, don't you know?'

'The weed, sah? Never seen it in me eyes, sah, what it look like? You could tell me, please?'

The man laughed.

'All right, Joe, you're a pretty smart fella. But tell me, don't you know it's against the law to carry around a slingshot, an' Ah could tek you in fo' that?'

'You mean dat, Mr. Jennings, Ah didn't know.'

'Shore is, Joe, an' a smart little chap like you wouldn't want to go breakin' the law an' gettin' you'self into trouble. Now lookit, suppos'n Ah let up on you this time, how's about you'n me doin' a little deal?'

'Do, sah, Ah beg you, don' tek me in. Ah didn't know it was anyt'ing wrong, havin' a little slingshot. Do, Missa Jennings, gi' me a chance dis time.'

'Well, suppos'n you jus' tell me, you know what I mean?'

'Don't know nutt'n, sah, see god, Ah never know.'

Seeing the obvious terror in the boy's eyes, Jennings laughed.

'All right, Joe, no need to get scared. You hear or see anything you let me know?'

The boy gulped, nodded quickly. He was so scared he couldn't speak.

Corporal Jennings, leg-man attached to the famous Flying Saucer Squad, special division of the city police—so called because they went around in fast patrol cars and swooped down without warning and struck without fear or favour, cleaning out dens of vice in the city—laughed as though he was enjoying a good joke, gave a hitch to his pants, patted the boy on the shoulder, and went on up the lane.

3

Cordy was lying in bed with an open bottle of bay rum on the table beside her. Jesmina sat on a stool drawn up close to the bed, and she was massaging Cordelia's hands.

'How you feelin' now?' she said. 'The fever ease you any?'

The sick woman shook her head.

'No. T'ings singin' inside me head, de head feel it goin' bust open any minute.'

She turned her face away from the girl, as though she was ashamed for the other to see her like this, stared blankly at the wall.

'The light. It—it hurt me eyes. Oh Gawd, oh Jesus!'

'Hush! You want me close the window? De fever gone into me eyes—like—like hammers inside me head.'

The girl tried to soothe her.

'If you would try to tek a little tea. You don't tek nutt'n from mornin.'

'Don't feel fo' nutt'n. Nutt'n 'tall. Wish Ah was dead. Lawd Jesus, do mek me dead.'

Jesmina grabbed her wrist, leaned over the bed, put her free hand under Cordelia's face.

'Don't say it, Sis. Hush, do! Is a sin.'

The earnestness in her voice touched something in the sick woman. Her fingers pressed the girl's hand. They were hard and hot, like twigs that had lately been removed from the fire to serve for kindling another day.

She said, in a thin croaking voice: 'Don't leave me, Jesmina. You own sister, flesh an' blood. One mother an' one father, how you can leave me, in this?'

'What you sayin' any at all, Sis? Hush, no mind, don't say them things.'

'Shine,' she said, speaking the single word in a toneless voice.

'Shine?'

And when Jesmina echoed it now, something made the syllable go up at the end, like a singing note.

'Woman trust a man she is a fool, you hear me. Say him love you, no? All him want is somebody work fo' him. Work for him, all a man ever want—an' pleasure him in bed. Like Papacita an' Girlie. Like Jonas an' me.'

Her voice broke weakly at the end, and she started to cry.

Jesmina bit her lip, holding back her own tears.

'Hush, don't talk bitter like that, you know bitter talk like that don't do nobody any good. Hush now, try to sleep.'

'Don't leave me.'

'Hush, no. Who leaving you? Don't 'fraid nutt'n, don't mek nutt'n 'fraid you, don't mek nutt'n fret you, everyt'ing goin' be all right.'

The woman sighed, stretched out her right leg, trying to draw the cover off her—it made her feel so hot. She muttered:

'All dem ever want.'

On the floor by the wash basin against the window a little boy about three sat playing with an empty cotton thread reel on a piece of string.

All of a sudden the sick woman seemed to remember her son. She said, anxiously: 'Where Tad?'

'Tad all right. Playin' on de floor. Don't mek nutt'n fret you, go to sleep.'

'Don't leave him. Bring him, put him 'pon de bed side-a-me.'

'No. Tad quite all right, playin' on de floor. You try to sleep now, try go to sleep.'

The sick woman sighed again. She said, slowly, 'Ah shame fo' walk down de street. De woman stare, dem shame me, can 'most hear dem a-whisper, whisper, *dem tek-up Jonas fo' ganga, hush, see Cordy de a go-long down de street* ... Ah shame, Ah shame, so tell ... man dem never consider 'pon dat, how dem wife wi' shame—jus' wuk she, use she, all dem ever want....'

Jesmina raised her head, patted the pillow, trying to get it cool and soft to the touch. She sprinkled a little bay rum on the soiled pillow-slip, let her head down gently upon it again.

She thought about herself and Shine, and a little cloud of anxiety, dark like the threat of storm, formed on the horizon of her vision straining to look beyond the present. She frowned the thought away, feeling a little guilty. How could she leave her now? Who would take care of her and Tad, now that her man was gone?

Six years for peddling ganga, Lawd, but life was a hard and cruel thing. Six years. Was it God sent it? What kind of God could aim down such a blow upon them, set them asunder six cruel years ... herself and Shine? But it wasn't fair. People were so selfish and unheeding and cruel ... *Don't leave me* ... she bit her lip till she could feel the salty taste of blood, holding in her tears.

4

'Aw come on, honey, come an' sit on de bed,' Papacita urged in a tone that was like warm butterscotch.

Girlie stood by the window, looking out into the lane.

'You don't want any breakfast?' she said.

'You don't worry you'self I will get breakfast.'

'Don't worry meself is right, an' ah ain't worryin'. All de same if you don't stop holdin' up de street corner chattin' to dat little gal Bra' Man tek in off de street, goin' be trouble one of these days, you mark my words.'

'Wha' dat you talkin' 'bout any at all, me holdin' up de street corner wid Minette? You mus' be crazy.'

'Crazy no? Like Ah didn't see you in me own two eyes.'

'Cho, no mind, no bodder wid dat now, come siddung side me.'

She left the window and went across to the door. She said: 'Goin' down to de kitchen, goin' get meself a cup of coffee, you eat breakfast yet?'

'No.'

He wanted to tell her not to give herself the trouble, that he would go down to the kitchen and make breakfast, but she was gone before he could fetch the words out from inside him.

He sat on the side of the bed and lit a cigarette. He had just one left. That would do for after breakfast. After that—Well, perhaps Girlie would be able to find some change in her purse.

He had nearly finished the cigarette when she returned carrying a coffee pot and things for breakfast on a tray. She had to make a noise on the door, using the toe of her shoe, for both hands were full; she had come all the way up the stairs that way.

'Why didn't you call me to help you?'

She brushed past him, setting down the tray on a table.

'Sit down an' have some breakfast,' she said. Else you goin' be hungry later. Got to look a job, Ah'm goin' in town.'

He looked at her, started to open his mouth, but decided it wasn't time to speak. He sat down at the table and started to eat. He was hungrier than he thought. Jeez! He didn't know he was so hungry. The excitement, everything, had put the thought of food clean out of his mind.

Watching her secretly he saw a fly settle on her nose. She didn't even bother to brush it away. She just wrinkled up her nose where its feet tickled her. It buzzed off, and settled again. It did that two or three times, but she didn't stop eating in that mechanical way, didn't take her hand up from the table to brush it off.

Her face seemed to have lost all expression, as though the will to live and laugh had died within her, and nothing mattered any more. He felt hurt, affronted, as though this was a personal accusation, as though it accused him of things he did not feel guilty of inside himself. It made him feel cross.

'What you mopin' about now? Somebody kill you' white fowl?'

'You should ask. Anybody kill me white fowl it would be you; you should ask, yes, an' Ah should leave you to answer you'self.'

He said, with a feeling of sudden contrition, 'No mind, everyt'ing goin' be all right. Jus' wait an' see.'

He scraped back his chair, stood up, went and stood behind her, laid a hand on the top of her head.

'Don't touch me. Lemme alone.'

He turned away, huffed. 'All right,' he said, 'if that's the way it is.'

He went over to the window, leaned an elbow on the sill, looked out over the lane.

'A man come home, an' no little happiness in the house. Nutt'n but naggin', naggin' all de time.'

'Why you didn't stay where you was, why you bodder come home?'

'It wasn't anyt'ing like dat, Ah tell you. Wasn't a woman or anyt'ing like dat at all.'

'You can tell dat to somebody else, maybe they will believe you. What you tek me fo', a first-of-April-born?'

'Was this job Ah was after, anyway.'

'I know; we goin' be rich. Don't mek me laff.'

'All right, you can laff.'

'Ah'm laffin', don't you see?'

'Ah, you mek me sick. No little peace in de home, nuff to mek a man pick-up an' walk.'

He waited, as though to hear her retort to this, but she said nothing, so he went on on his own.

'Goin' get meself outa this, though, you wait an' see, can't stand it any more.'

He saw Jesmina going down the lane. She was coming from the shop with a bottle of healing oil in her hand. He made her a little sign with his hand.

She just raised her head and said: 'How Girlie? Give her howdy fo' me,' and went on quickly down the street.

Girlie looked up from picking at the threadbare tablecloth.

'Who dat?'

He wanted to say, why you don't come an' see for you'self, but he said instead: 'Jesmina. Say to give you howdy.'

And she said: 'Oh.'

She got up, cleared the used breakfast things off the table, started dusting and tidying the place. She hummed a little to herself.

He could see that her anger was cooling, little by little thawing out. She wanted to re-establish the old relationship between them. He was crafty, cautious, made no move to meet her part way; only stood there, looking out through the window, letting things flow through his mind.

'What you doing over by the window?' she said. 'You gone to sleep?'

He grunted two syllables that said nothing at all.

She started singing softly to herself.

She stooped down, picked up some crumbs from the floor, straightened, looked down at the boards under her feet, went behind the door for the broom.

He watched her sweeping, tidying, making the room like new, without letting her know that he was watching her; he watched her every movement, feeling deep down that hunger for her that kept him coming back after every escapade—that deep down hunger that it seemed could never be altogether assuaged.

She was dusting the further end of the room, working gradually over to where he was.

All right, he would smoke that last cigarette now.

He watched her like a cat watching a mouse, without her seeing it. The old passion for her came up inside him, made the inside of his mouth seem dry. He pressed his tongue up against the roof of his mouth, brought down some saliva with it. He cleared his throat gently, tentatively, as though fearful to make the least sound.

5

Brother Man sat at his cobbler's bench before the open window looking out upon the lane. He worked quietly, efficiently, his head bowed over his last.

He was of medium height, medium build. The hair crisped and curled about his head, around his mouth, over his chin. When he looked up from his work his eyes pin-pointed the light, and you could see almost all of the pupils. He had a far-away, searching look, as though the intensity of his being came to focus in his eyes. Many looked away and were embarrassed before the quiet intensity of that gaze.

He had now, as he always did, an open Bible on the stool beside him. He was putting heels to a pair of slippers, and Minette sat on a lower stool, at his feet, blacking a pair of shoes.

Every now and then she stole a glance at him, and went back to blacking the shoes again.

From the yard next door they could hear voices of people, talking, laughing, quarrelling. Beyond they could hear the yam-vendor hawking down the lane.

Brother Man belonged to that cult known as the Ras Tafarites, and some people said he was mad. Others again thought he was a holy man and a healer, and many came to him, secretly, because they feared gossip, to heal their sick, and for advice and encouragement when things were going wrong.

Sometimes when they heard other people abusing and traducing Brother Man, they stood up in his defence, the people who whom he had helped in times of trouble and sickness, but at other times they thought better of it, because they feared what their neighbors might have to say about them behind their backs, lacking the courage of their convictions. Sometimes they forgot, some of these people, that he had helped and comforted them, and healed their wounds. Sometimes they secretly despised him that he cared so little for himself, and so much for others, that he would give what little he had to succour another whose need he thought greater than his.

Minette held up to the light the shoe he was polishing to see how it shone. She sighed and set it down on the floor beside her piece of old newspaper, and took up the other one.

From the yard next door came the sound of someone singing, 'Jesu, lover of my soul....'

She said suddenly, 'What is love?'

Brother Man said, 'Eh? What you say, child?'

'Say what is love? Bra' Man,' she repeated.

She let the shoe rest on her lap and looked up into his face.

He looked at her, earnestly, as though weighing his answer, and presently she let her eyes fall. She took up the shoe from her lap, and started polishing it again.

'Love is everything,' he said, simply. 'It is what created the world. It is what made you an' me, child, brought us into this world.'

And somehow the words didn't sound banal, coming from him. He spoke with such simple directness that it seemed to give new import to everything he said. It was as though the common words of everyday usage meant something more, coming from his lips, than they did in the casual giving and taking of change in conversation, the way it was with other folks.

'Why you ask? You love somebody, child?'

'Yes an' no. I love plenty-plenty people, but none like you.'

He looked at her gravely and said: 'Peace an' love.'

'Why you always say that?' she asked, half closing one eye, as though the better to study his face.

'It is the salutation. It is the way the brothers should greet each other. It is like sayin' good morning, howdydo. But it is more than that too, it is the affirmation of our faith, the Jesus-talk, what you call the way.'

She didn't understand a word of all this. It showed in her face.

'Did Jesus talk it that way, that what you mean, Bra' Man?'

He nodded his head, gravely. 'He give us that word, sister: peace an' love.'

A bird flew smack into the window glass with a dull thud. It fell to the ground outside with a faint cry, stunned with the impact.

Brother Man got up, with a murmured exclamation, went out through the door, and presently came back with the bird in his hand. It fluttered a little, scared, though scarcely conscious, almost dead. A single drop of blood congealing at the side of its beak glowed like a jewel against the dark grey-green of its feathers.

It was going to die, Minette knew it, and she had an instant of impatience and vexation with Brother Man for trying to bring it back, to make it live. She didn't know why she felt this, only knew that it came up inside her, until she wanted to cry out at him, but it stopped in her throat.

She watched him as he stood there, holding the bird in his cupped hand, his head bowed over it.

'Don't trouble you'self over it, Bra' Man,' she said, 'it not goin' live.'

She came up and stood by his elbow, her body just touching his, and felt him move away instinctively, as he did so she knew a sharp pang, savage and strong, and with a surge of exhilaration; but she could not have told what it was all about if somebody had asked her.

'Maybe,' he said, still holding the bird, and looking down at it.

It lay on its side now, and its eyes were shut in death.

'It's dead,' she said.

And she could scarcely hear his whisper, 'Yes.'

But he still held the little dead body cupped in his hand, as though he could not bear to part with it.

'What you goin' do with it?'

And she moved just that breathing space nearer, so that when she drew her breath in, long, the nipple of her breast rested against his arm an instant, and came away with respiration. He stood still, like someone lost in a trance, and as though he was not conscious of her presence.

'What you goin' do with it, Bra' Man?' she said again.

He went and sat down on his stool, let his hand rest on the bench, relaxed his fingers. He sat there looking at the dead bird a longish time, as though in truth he did not know what to do with it. He set it down on the bench, and took up his last again.

She came up, stood behind him, said almost fiercely: 'Why you don't throw it out into the street, what you keepin' it for?'

He looked up at her, and she met his gaze without flinching.

'What's troublin' you, me daughter?'

'Why you want to keep it before you? Why you don't throw it outside?'

'It is one of God's creatures, and it was alive a little while back, and now it is dead, an' it didn't do no harm. Let it rest there, eh?' he said.

And she felt rebuked.

She said: 'I am sorry.'

He put out his hand and touched her arm.

He said: 'Peace and love.'

The Harvard Law School Forum of March 24, 1961

Malcolm X (USA)

Roger Fisher, Moderator

Mr. Malcolm X is a minister of Mosque No. 7, the Nation of Islam, Harlem, New York. Mr. X has agreed to speak to us on *The American Negro: Problems and Solutions.*

Malcolm X

We thank you for inviting us here to the Harvard Law School Forum this evening to present our views on this timely topic: *The American Negro: Problems and Solutions*. However, to understand our views, the views of the Muslims, you must first realize that we are a religious group, and you must also know something about our religion, the religion of Islam. The creator of the universe, whom any of you call God or Jehovah, is known to the Muslims by the name Allah. The Muslims believe that there is but one God, and that all the prophets came from this one God. We believe also that all prophets came from this one God. We believe also that all prophets taught the same religion, and that they themselves called that religion Islam, an Arabic word that means complete submission and obedience to the will of Allah. One who practices divine obedience is called a Muslim (commonly known, spelled, and referred to here in the West as Moslem). There are over seven hundred twenty-five million Muslims on this earth, predominantly in Africa and Asia, the nonwhite world. We here in America are under the divine leadership of the Honorable Elijah Muhammad, and we are an integral part of the vast world of Islam that stretches from the China seas to the sunny shores of West Africa. A unique situation faces the twenty million ex-slaves here in America because of our unique condition. Our acceptance of Islam and conversion to the religion affects us also in a unique way, different from the way in which it affects all other Muslim converts elsewhere here on this earth.

Mr. Elijah Muhammad is our divine leader and teacher here in America. Mr. Muhammad believes in and obeys God one hundred percent, and he is even now teaching and working among our people to fulfill God's divine purpose. I am here at this forum tonight to represent Mr. Elijah Muhammad, the spiritual head of the fastest-growing group of Muslims in the Western Hemisphere. We who follow Mr. Muhammad know that he has been divinely taught and sent to us by God Himself. We believe that the miserable plight of the twenty million black people in America is the fulfillment of divine prophecy. We believe that the serious race problem that [the Negro's] presence here poses for America is also the fulfillment of divine prophecy. We also believe that the presence today in America of the Honorable Elijah Muhammad, his teachings among the twenty million so-called Negroes, and his naked warning to America concerning her treatment of these twenty million ex-slaves is also the fulfillment of divine prophecy. Therefore, when Mr. Muhammad declares that the only solution to America's serious race problem is complete separation of the two races, he is reiterating what was already predicted for this time by all the Biblical prophets. Because Mr. Muhammad takes this uncompromising stand, those of you who don't understand Biblical prophecy wrongly label him a racist and hate-teacher and accuse him of being anti-white and teaching black supremacy. But this evening since we are all here at the Harvard Law School Forum; together, both races face to face, we can question and examine for ourselves the wisdom or folly of what Mr. Muhammad is teaching.

Many of you who classify yourselves as white express surprise and shock at the truth that Mr. Muhammad is teaching your twenty million ex-slaves here in America, but you should be neither surprised nor shocked. As students, teachers, professors, and scientists, you should be well aware that we are living in a world where great changes are taking place. New ideas are replacing the old ones. Old governments are collapsing, and new nations are being born. The entire old system which held the old world together has lost its effectiveness, and now that old world is going out. A new system or a new world must replace the old world. Just as the old ideas must be removed to make way for the new, God has declared to Mr. Muhammad that the evil features of this wicked old world must be exposed, faced up to, and removed in order to make way for the new world which God Himself is preparing to establish. The divine mission of Mr. Muhammad here in America today is to prepare us for the new world of righteousness by teaching us a better understanding of the old world's defects. Thus we may come to agree that God must remove this wicked old world.

We see by reports in the daily press that even many of you who are scholars or scientists think that the message of Islam that is being preached here in America among your twenty million ex-slaves is new, or that it is something Mr. Muhammad himself has made up. Mr. Muhammad's religious message is not new. All of the scientists and prophets of old predicted that a man such as he, with such a doctrine or message would make his appearance among us at a time as that in which we are living today. It is written too in your own scriptures that this prophetic figure would not be raised up from the midst of the educated class, but that God would make His choice from among the lowly, uneducated, downtrodden, oppressed masses, from among the lowest element of America's twenty million ex-slaves. It would be as in the days when God raised up Moses from among the lowly Hebrew slaves and [com]missioned him to separate his oppressed people from a slave master named Pharaoh. Moses found himself opposed by the scholars and scientist of that day, who are symbolically described in the Bible as "Pharaoh's magicians." Jesus himself, a lowly carpenter, was also [com]missioned by God to find his people, the "lost sheep," and to separate them from their Gentile enemies and restore them to their own nation. Jesus also found himself opposed by the scholars and scientists of his day, who are symbolically described in the Bible as "scribes, priests, and Pharisees." Just as the learned class of those days disagreed with and opposed both Moses and Jesus primarily because of their humble origin, Mr. Elijah Muhammad is today likewise being opposed by the learned, educated intellectuals of his own kind, because of [his] humble origin. These modern-day "magicians, scribes, and Pharisees" try to ridicule Mr. Muhammad by emphasizing the humble origin of him and his many followers.

Moses was raised up among his enslaved people a time when God was planning to restore them to a land of their own where they could give birth to a new civilization, completely independent of their former slave masters. Pharaoh opposed God's plan and God's servant, so Pharaoh and his people were destroyed. Jesus was sent among his people at a time when God was planning to bring about another great change. The dispensation preached by Jesus two thousand years ago ushered in a new type of civilization, the Christian civilization, better known as the Christian world. The Holy Prophet Muhammad (may the peace and blessing of Allah be upon him!) came six hundred years after Jesus with another dispensation that did not destroy or remove the Christian civilization, but which put a dent in it, a wound that has lasted even until today. Now, today, God has sent Mr. Elijah Muhammad among the downtrodden and oppressed so-called American Negroes to warn that God is again preparing to bring about another great change, only this time it will be a final change. This is the day and the time for a complete change. Mr. Muhammad teaches that the religion of Islam is the only solution to the problems confronting our people here in America. He warns us that it is even more important, however, to know the base or foundation upon which we must build tomorrow. Therefore, although the way in which Mr. Muhammad teaches the religion of Islam and the particular kind of Islam he teaches may appear to be different from the teaching of Islam in the Old World, the basic principles and practices are the same.

You must remember: The condition of America's twenty million ex-slaves is uniquely pitiful. But just as the old religious leaders in the days of Moses and Jesus refused to accept Moses and Jesus as religious reformers, many of the religious leaders in the old Muslim world today may also refute the teachings of Mr. Elijah Muhammad, neither realizing the unique condition of these twenty million ex-slaves nor understanding that Mr. Elijah Muhammad's teachings are divinely prescribed to rectify the miserable condition of our oppressed people here. But as God made Pharaoh's magicians bow before Moses, and the scribes and Pharisees bow before Jesus, He plans today to make all opposition, both at home and abroad, bow before the truth that is now being taught by the Honorable Elijah Muhammad.

We are two thousand years from the time of the great change which took place in Jesus' day. If you will but look around you on this earth today, it will be as clear as the five fingers on your hand that we are again living at a time of great change. God has come to close out the entire old world, the old world where for the past six thousand years most of the earth's population has been deceived, conquered, colonized, ruled, enslaved, oppressed, and exploited by the Caucasian race. At the time when Pharaoh's civilization reached its peak and his period of rule of the slaves was up, God appeared unto Moses and revealed to him that He had something different for his people. Likewise, God told Mr. Muhammad that He has something different for his people, the so-called Negroes here in America today—something that until now has never before been revealed. Mr. Muhammad teaches us that this old world has seen nothing yet, that the real thing is yet to come.

The Black Muslims who follow Mr. Muhammad are only now making their exit from the old world. The door to the new world is yet to be opened, and what is inside that door is yet to be revealed. The teaching of Mr. Muhammad among your twenty million ex-slaves is only to prepare us to walk out of this wicked old world in as intelligent, pleasant, and peaceful a way as possible. The teaching among the so-called American Negroes is designed only to show proof why we should give up this wicked old house. The roof is leaking, the walls are collapsing, and we find it can no longer support the tremendous weight caused by our continued presence in it. The knowledge of the deterioration and eventual collapse of this old building having come to Mr. Muhammad from Almighty God Himself (whose proper name is Allah, the Lord of all the worlds, the Master of Judgment Day), the Honorable Elijah Muhammad is pointing out these dangerous conditions and future results to us as well as to you who have enslaved us. With proper support and guidance our people can get out of this sagging old building before it collapses. But the support and guidance that we need actually consists of instruction in the origin, history, and nature of the Caucasian race as well as of our own black nation. We must have a thorough knowledge of the true origin and history of the white man's Christian religion as well as an understanding of the Islamic religion that prevails primarily among our brothers and sisters in Africa and Asia. You will probably ask us, "Why, if this old house is going to collapse or go up in smoke, are the Black Muslims asking for some states to be set aside in this country? It's like asking for a chance to retain rooms in a house that you claim is doomed for total destruction!"

God is giving to America every opportunity to repent and atone for the crime she committed when she enslaved our people, even as God gave Pharaoh a chance to repent before He finally destroyed that king, too proud to face his slaves and give them complete justice. We are asking you for a territory here only because of the great opposition we receive from this government in our efforts to awaken our people, to unite them and separate them from their oppressors, and to return them to their own land and people. You should never make the mistake of thinking that Mr. Muhammad has no place to take his followers in the World of Islam. No sir! He is not shut out from the world as many of you wish to believe. All who accept Islam and follow Mr. Muhammad have been offered a home in the Muslim world.

Our people have been oppressed and exploited here in America for four hundred years, and now with Mr. Muhammad we can leave this wicked world of bondage. But our former slave master is [continually] opposing Mr. Muhammad's efforts and is unjustly persecuting those who have left the Christian Church and accepted the religion of Islam. This is further proof that our Caucasian slave master does not want or trust us to leave him and live elsewhere on this earth. And yet, if we stay here with him, he continues to keep us at the very lowest level of his society.

Pick up any daily newspaper or magazine and examine the anti-Muslim propaganda and the false charges leveled against our beloved religious leader by some of America's leading reporters. This only points up the fact that the Caucasian race is never willing to let any black man who is not their puppet or parrot speak for our people or lead our people out of their enslaving clutches without giving him great opposition. The Caucasian slave master has opposed all such leaders in the past, and even today he sanctions and supports only Negro spokesmen who parrot his doctrines and ideas or who accept his so-called advice on how our people could carry on our struggle against his four hundred years of tyranny.

The Christian world has failed to give the black man justice. The [American] Christian government has failed to give her twenty million ex-slaves [just compensation] for three hundred ten years of free slave labor. Even despite this, we have been better Christians than those who taught us Christianity. We have been America's most faithful servants during peace time, and her bravest soldiers during war time. But still, white Christians have been unwilling to recognize us and to accept us as fellow human beings. Today we can see that the Christian religion of the Caucasian race has failed us. Thus the black masses are turning away from the Church and toward the religion of Islam. Furthermore, the government sends its agents among our people to tell lies. [Those agents] make an all-out effort to harass us in order to frighten those of our people in this country who would accept the religion of Islam and unite under the spiritual guidance and divine leadership of the Honorable Elijah Muhammad. Therefore, Mr. Muhammad has demanded that you and your government let us separate ourselves from you right here, into a separate territory that we can call our own and on which we can do something for ourselves and for our own kind; since you don't want these twenty million ex-slaves to leave you and return to their own land and people, and since your actions have proved that the Caucasian race will not receive them as complete equals. Since we cannot live among the Caucasians in peace, and since there is not time enough for us new Negroes to wait for the Caucasian race to be "re-educated" and freed of their racial prejudice, their inbred beliefs and practices of white supremacy, I repeat, "Let our people be separated from you, and give us some territory that we can call our own and where we can live in peace among ourselves."

According to recent news dispatches in daily papers throughout the nation, prison wardens all over this country are unjustly persecuting the inmates who want to change from the Christian religion to the religion of Islam and follow the spiritual guidance of the Honorable Elijah Muhammad. Indeed, these prison wardens even admit that when inmates change from Christianity to Islam, they become model prisoners. Yet despite this, the prisoners are being persecuted and prevented from reading the Holy Koran, the same holy book that is read daily by millions of our darker brothers and sisters in Africa and Asia. When the true facts about this religious persecution are made known in the world of Islam, that strategic area that stretches from the China seas to the shores of West Africa, how to do you think the American Caucasians will then look in the eyes of those nonwhite people there? The very fact that there is a concerted effort against Islam by prison wardens in this country is proof that the American government is trying to stamp out the religion of Islam at home, in a frantic effort to keep it from spreading among her twenty million ex-slaves whom she continues to confine to the lowly role of second-class citizenship. Further proof is the fact that these twenty million so-called Negroes have never been taught about the religion of Islam during the entire four hundred years, since the Caucasians first brought our people here in chains from our African Muslim culture. Yet Islam is, and always has been, the prevailing religion among our people in Africa. Indeed, the American Caucasian, in a last act of desperation, is accusing Mr. Muhammad of not being a true Muslim, and of not teaching true Islam. If the American Caucasian knows so much about true Islam and has suddenly become such an authority on it, why hasn't he taught it to his twenty million ex-slaves before now?

The American Caucasian today also loves to print glaring headlines saying that the orthodox Muslims don't recognize or accept Mr. Muhammad and his Muslims as true Muslims. "Divide and rule" has long been the Caucasian strategy to continue white colonization of dark nations. The American Caucasian actually has settled twenty million black people here in this country by simply dividing us from our African brothers and sisters for four hundred years, converting us to his Christian religion, and by teaching us to call ourselves "Negroes" and telling us that we are no longer African. (I guess he says this because our exposure to this "superior" white culture makes us different, so-called civilized.) Since hundreds of thousands of the ex-slaves here in America today refuse to attend the church of the Caucasians who enslaved us, shun all further use of the word "Negro," and accept Allah as their God, Islam as their religion, and the Honorable Elijah Muhammad as their religious leader and teacher, these American Caucasians are reverting to the old trick of earlier colonialists: divide and rule. They thereby try to separate us from the Muslim world and to alienate us from our people in Africa and Asia who also serve and follow Almighty God, Allah.

There are probably one hundred thousand of what you (whites) call orthodox Muslims in America, who were born in the Muslim world and who willingly migrated here. But despite the fact that Islam is a propagating religion, all of these foreign Muslims combined have not been successful in converting one thousand Americans to Islam. On the other hand, they see that Mr. Muhammad by himself has hundreds of thousands of his fellow ex-slaves turning eastward toward Mecca five times daily giving praises to the great God Allah. No true Muslim in his right mind would denounce or deny this meek and humble little black man, born in Georgia in the very worst part of this country, as a leader, a defender of the faith, and a propagator of the faith, who has rekindled the light of Islam here in the West. His Caucasian opposers have never gotten even one responsible Muslim official to criticize or denounce Mr. Muhammad. They succeed only in getting some jealous, envious little peddler or merchant who migrated here and who wants to be recognized as some sort of leader himself and will therefore accept the Caucasian's bribe of thirty pieces of silver to attack this man of God. How could Mr. Muhammad ever make a trip into the forbidden areas of Arabia, to visit the holy cities of Mecca and Medina, and be welcomed and honored by its most respected religious leaders, the great Imams themselves, if he himself were not recognized as a great religious man, a man of God, doing miraculous works by spreading Allah's name here in the West among the twenty million ex-slaves of America? How could Mr. Muhammad visit the capitals of the Muslim world and be received by its respected leaders, if he were not also recognized and respected as a Muslim leader by them? He visited Al-Azhar, the oldest mosque and Muslim university in the world, and had tea with the Chief Imam, the Grand Sheikh Shaltuat, who kissed him on his forehead in true Muslim fashion. Yet the American Caucasians, hoping to block his success among our people, continue to oppose him and say that he is not a true Muslim.

Again you will say, "Why don't he and his followers leave the house of bondage right now and go and live in the Muslim world?" All of the Nation of Islam can live in the Muslim world tomorrow, but the Honorable Elijah

Muhammad wants justice for the entire twenty million so-called Negroes. You and your Christian government make the problem even more complicated. You don't want your twenty million ex-slaves to leave you, yet you won't share equal justice with them right here. Since you don't want them to leave this country with us, and you won't give them equal justice among your kind, we will agree to stay only if you let us separate ourselves from you right here. Just give us a portion of this country that we can call our own. Put us in it. Then give us everything we need to start our own civilization—that is, support us for twenty to twenty-five years, until we are able to go for ourselves. This is God's plan. This is God's solution. This is justice, and compensation for our three hundred ten years of slave labor. Otherwise America will reap the full fury of God's wrath for her crimes against our people, which are many. As your Bible says, "He that leads into captivity shall go into captivity; he that kills with the sword shall be killed by the sword." This is the law of justice; this is in your own Christian scriptures.

The black masses are shaking off the drugs, the narcotic effect of token-integration promises. A cup of tea in a white restaurant is not sufficient compensation for three hundred ten years of free slave labor. The black masses as represented by the Black Muslims will never be satisfied until we have some land that we can call our own. Again I repeat: We are not asking for territory here because Mr. Muhammad has no place else to take us. But we ask for the sake of the entire twenty million so-called Negroes, twenty million ex-slaves who, despite the fact that the Emancipation Proclamation was issued one hundred years ago, are still begging their former slave master for recognition as human beings. Mr. Muhammad is asking this government to stop toying with our people, to stop fooling them year in and year out with false promises of token integration. Token integration will not solve our problem. This is a false solution, a "token" solution. It is a hypocritical approach to the problem, a tricky scheme devised by you and propagated by your Negro puppets whom you yourselves have appointed as our leaders and spokesmen.

Integration is not good for either side. It will destroy your race, and your government knows it will also destroy ours, and the problem still remains unsolved. God has declared that these twenty million ex-slaves must have a home of their own. After four hundred years among the Caucasians, we are absolutely convinced that we can never live together in peace, unless we are willing to remain subservient to our former masters. Therefore, immediate and complete separation is the only solution. NAACP Attorney Thurgood Marshall has admitted publicly that six years since the Supreme Court decision on desegregation of the schools, only six percent desegregation has taken place. This is an example of integration!

A kidnapper, a robber, an enslaver, a lyncher is just another common criminal in the sight of God, and criminal acts as such have been committed by your race on a mass scale for four hundred years against your twenty million so-called Negroes. It is true that today America professes to be sorry for her crimes against our people. She says she wants to repent, but in her desire to atone or make amends, she offers her twenty million ex-slaves flowery promises of token integration. Many of these downtrodden victims want to forgive America. They want to forget the crimes that you have committed against them, and some are even willing to accept the formula of token integration that you yourselves have devised as a solution to the problem created by your own criminal acts against them. In a court of justice the criminal can confess his crimes and throw himself on the mercy of the court if he truly repents, but neither the criminal nor his victim has any say-so in suggesting the sentence that is to be passed upon the guilty or the price that the confessed criminal must pay. This is left in the hands of the judge. We are living in the Day of Judgment right now. God is the Judge that our American slave master must now answer to. God is striking this country with tornadoes, storms, floods, rain, hail, snow; and terrific earthquakes are yet to come. Your people are being afflicted with increasing epidemics of illness, disease, and plagues, with which God is striking you because of your criminal acts against the twenty million ex-slaves.

Instead of repenting and truly compensating our people for their three hundred ten years of free slave labor that built up this country for you, you buy out the Negro leaders with thirty pieces of silver and have them sell our people your token integration. When one uses a token on the bus or streetcar, that token is a substitute for the real money; token means substitute, that which takes the place of the real thing. Token integration takes the place of the real thing. Two black students at the University of Georgia is token integration. Four black children in New Orleans' white schools is token integration. A handful of black students in the white schools in Little Rock, Arkansas is token integration. None of this is real integration; it is only a pacifier to keep these awakening black babies from crying too loud. According to the above-mentioned rate of desegregation since the decision of the Supreme Court, it will take us another thousand years to get the white man in the South sufficiently "re-educated" to accept our people in their midst as equals. And if the rest of the truth is told, it will take the white man here in the North, West, and East just as long as his brother in the South.

To many of you here at the Harvard Law School Forum this sounds ridiculous; to some it even sounds insane. But these twenty million black people here in America now number a nation in their own right. Do you believe that a nation within another nation can be successful, especially when they both have equal educations? Once the slave has his master's education, the slave wants to be like his master, wants to share his master's property, and even wants to exercise the same privileges as his master while he is yet in his master's house. This is the core of America's troubles today: there will be no peace for America as long as twenty million so-called Negroes are here begging for the rights which America knows she will never grant us. The limited education America has granted her ex-slaves has even already produced great unrest. Almighty God says the only way for America to ever have any future or prosperity is for her twenty million ex-slaves to be separated from her, and it is for this reason that Mr. Muhammad teaches us that we must have some land of our own. If we receive equal education, how long do you expect us to remain your passive servants, or second-class citizens? There is no such thing as a second-class citizen. We are full citizens, or we are not citizens at all. When you teach a man the science of government, he then wants an equal part or position in that government, or else he wants his own government. He begins to demand equality with his master. No man with education equal to your own will serve you. The only way you can continue to rule us is with superior knowledge, by continuing to withhold equal education from our people. America has not given us equal education, but she has given us enough to make us want more and to make us demand equality of opportunity. And since this is causing unrest plus international embarrassment, the only solution is immediate separation. As your colleges and universities turn out an ever-increasing number of so-called Negro graduates with education equal to yours, they will automatically increase their demands for equality in everything else. Equal education will increase the spirit of equality and make them feel that they should have everything that you have, and their increasing demands will become a perpetual headache for you and continue to cause you international embarrassment. In fact, those Negro students whom you are educating today will soon be demanding the same things you now hear being demanded by Mr. Muhammad and the Muslims.

In concluding, I must remind your that your own Christian Bible states that God is coming in the last days or at the end of the old world, and that God's coming will bring about a great separation. Now since we see all sorts of signs throughout the earth that indicate that the time of God's coming is upon us, why don't you repent while there is yet time? Do justice by your faithful ex-slaves. Give us some land of our own right here, some separate states, so we can separate ourselves from you. Then everyone will be satisfied, and perhaps we will all be able to then live happily ever after and, as your own Christian Bible says, "everyone under his own vine and fig tree." Otherwise all of you who are sitting here, your government, and your entire race will be destroyed and removed from this earth by Almighty God, Allah.

from *Parable of the Talents*

by Octavia Butler (USA)

FROM *Memories of Other Worlds*
BY TAYLOR FRANKLIN BANKOLE

I have read that the period of upheaval that journalists have begun to refer to as "the Apocalypse" or more commonly, more bitterly, "the Pox" lasted from 2015 through 2030—a decade and a half of chaos. This is untrue. The Pox has been a much longer torment. It began well before 2015, perhaps even before the turn of the millennium. It has not ended.

I have also read that the Pox was caused by accidentally coinciding climatic, economic, and sociological crises. It would be more honest to say that the Pox was caused by our own refusal to deal with obvious problems in those areas. We caused the problems: then we sat and watched as they grew into crises. I have heard people deny this, but I was born in 1970. I have seen enough to know that it is true. I have watched education become more a privilege of the rich than the basic necessity that it must be if civilized society is to survive. I have watched as convenience, profit, and inertia excused greater and more dangerous environmental degradation. I have watched poverty, hunger, and disease become inevitable for more and more people.

Overall, the Pox has had the effect of an installment-plan World War III. In fact, there were several small, bloody shooting wars going on around the world during the Pox. These were stupid affairs—wastes of life and treasure. They were fought, ostensibly, to defend against vicious foreign enemies. All too often, they were actually fought because inadequate leaders did not know what else to do. Such leaders knew that they could depend on fear, suspicion, hatred, need, and greed to arouse patriotic support for war.

Amid all this, somehow, the United States suffered a major nonmilitary defeat. It lost no important war, yet it did not survive the Pox. Perhaps it simply lost sight of what it once intended to be, then blundered aimlessly until it exhausted itself.

What is left of it now, what it has become, I do not know.

Taylor Franklin Bankole was my father. From his writings, he seems to have been a thoughtful, somewhat formal man who wound up with my strange, stubborn mother even though she was almost young enough to be his granddaughter.

My mother seems to have loved him, seems to have been happy with him. He and my mother met during the Pox when they were both homeless wanderers. But he was a 57-year-old doctor—a family practice physician—and she was an 18-year-old girl. The Pox gave them terrible memories in common. Both had seen their neighborhoods destroyed—his in San Diego and hers in Robledo, a suburb of Los Angeles. That seems to have been enough for them. In 2027, they met, liked each other, and got married. I think, reading between the lines of some of my father's writings, that he wanted to take care of this strange young girl that he had found. He wanted to keep her safe from the gangs, drugs, slavery, and disease. And of course he was flattered that she wanted him. He was human, and no doubt tired of being alone. His first wife had been dead for about two years when they met.

He couldn't keep my mother safe of course. No one could have done that. She had chosen her path long before they met. His mistake was in seeing her as a young girl. She was already a missile, armed and targeted....

FROM *Memories of Other Worlds*

I cannot know what the end will be of all of Olamina's dreaming, striving, and certainty. I cannot recall ever feeling as certain of anything as she seems to be of Earthseed, a belief system that she herself created—or, as she says, a network of truths that she has simply recognized. I was always a doubter when it came to religion. How irrational of me, then, to love a zealot. But then, both love and zealotry are irrational states of mind.

Olamina believes in a god that does not in the least love her. In fact, her god is a process or a combination of processes, not an entity. It is not consciously aware of her—or of anything. It is not conscious at all. "God is Change," she says and means it. Some of the faces of her god are biological evolution, chaos theory, relativity theory, the uncertainty principle, and, of course, the second law of thermodynamics. "God is change, and, in the end, God prevails."

Yet Earthseed is not a fatalistic belief system. God can be directed, focused, speeded, slowed, shaped. All things change, but all things need not change in all ways. God is inexorable, yet malleable. Odd. Hardly religious at all. Even the Earthseed Destiny seems to have little to do with religion.

"We are Earthseed," Olamina says. "We are the children of God, as all fractions of the universe are the children of God. But more immediately we are the children of our particular Earth." And within those words lies the origin of the Destiny. That portion of humanity that is conscious, that knows it is Earthseed, and that accepts its Destiny is simply trying to leave the womb, the Earth, to be born as all young beings must do eventually.

Earthseed is Olamina's contribution to what she feels would be a species-wide effort to evade, or at least to lengthen the specialize-grow-die evolutionary cycle that humanity faces, that every species faces.

"We can be a long-term success and the parents, ourselves, of the vast array of new peoples, new species," she says, "or we can be just one more abortion. We can, we must, scatter the Earth's living essence—human, plant, and animal—to extrasolar worlds: 'The Destiny of Earthseed is to take root among the stars.'"

Grand words.

She hopes and dreams and writes and believes, and perhaps the world will let her live for a while, tolerating her as a harmless eccentric. I hope that it will. I fear that it may not.

My father has, in this piece, defined Earthseed very well and defined it in fewer words than I could have managed. When my mother was a child, protected and imprisoned by the walls of her neighborhood, she dreamed of the stars. Literally, at night she dreamed of them. And she dreamed of flying. I've seen her flying dreams mentioned in earlier writings. Awake or asleep, she dreamed of these things. As far as I'm concerned, that's what she was doing when she created her Earthseed Destiny and her Earthseed verses: dreaming. We all need dreams—our fantasies—to sustain us through hard times. There's no harm in that as long as we don't begin to mistake our fantasies for reality as she did. It seems that she doubted herself from time to time, but she never doubted the dream, never doubted Earthseed. Like my father, I can't feel secure about any religion. That's odd, considering the way I was raised, but it's true.

I've seen religious passion in other people, though—love for a compassionate God, fear of an angry God, fulsome praise and desperate pleading for a God that rewards and punishes. All that makes me wonder how a belief system like Earthseed—very demanding but offering so little comfort from such an utterly indifferent God—should inspire any loyalty at all.

In Earthseed, there is no promised afterlife. Earthseed's heaven is literal, physical—other worlds circling other stars. It promises people immortality only through their children, their work, and their memories. For the human species, immortality is something to be won by sowing Earthseed on other worlds. Its promise is not of mansions to live in, milk and honey to drink, or eternal oblivion in some vast whole of nirvana. Its promise is of hard work and brand-new possibilities, problems, challenges, and changes. Apparently, that can be surprisingly seductive to some people. My mother was a surprisingly seductive person.

There is an Earthseed verse that goes like this:

> *God is Change.*
> *God is Infinite,*
> *Irresistible,*

> *Inexorable,*
> *Indifferent.*
> *God is Trickster,*
> *Teacher,*
> *Chaos,*
> *Clay—*
> *God is Change.*
> *Beware:*
> *God exists to shape*
> *And to be shaped.*

This is a terrifying God, implacable, faceless, yet malleable and wildly dynamic. I suppose it will soon be wearing my mother's face. Her second name was "Oya." I wonder whatever possessed my Baptist minister grandfather to give her such a name. What did he see in her? "Oya" is the name of a Nigerian Orisha—goddess—of the Yoruba people. In fact, the original Oya was the goddess of the Niger River, a dynamic, dangerous entity. She was also goddess of the wind, fire, and death, more bringers of great change....

FROM *Memories of Other Worlds*

Our coast redwood trees are dying.

Sequoia sempervirens is the botanical name for this tallest of all trees, but many are evergreen no longer. Little by little from the tops down, they are turning brown and dying.

I do not believe that they are dying as a result of the heat. As I recall, there were many redwoods growing around the Los Angeles area—Pasadena, Altadena, San Marino, places like that. I saw them there when I was young. My mother had relatives in Pasadena and she used to take me with her when she went to visit them. Redwoods growing that far south reached nothing like the height of their kind here in the north, but they did survive. Later, as the climate changed, I supposed they died as so many of the trees down south died—or they were chopped down and used to build shelters or to feed the cooking fires of the homeless.

And now our younger trees have begun to die. This part of Humboldt County along the coast and in the hills—the local people call these coastal hills "mountains"—was cooler when I was a boy. It was foggy and rainy—a soft, green climate, friendly to most growing things. I believe it was already changing nearly 30 years ago when I bought the land that became Acorn. In the not-too-distant future, I suppose it will be little different from the way coastal southern California was a few decades ago—hot semiarid, more brown than green most of the time. Now we are in the middle of change. We still get a few substantial fall and winter storms each year, and there are still morning fogs in the spring and early summer.

Nevertheless, young redwood trees—those only about a century old, not yet mature—are withering. A few miles to the north and south of us in the old national and state parks, the groves of ancient giants still stand. A few hundred acres of them here and there have been released by the government, sold to wealthy, usually foreign interests, and logged. And squatters have cut and burned a number of individual trees, as usual, to build shelters and feed cooking fires, but the majority of protected ones, millennia old, resistant to disease, fire, and climate change, still stand. If people let them alone, they will go on, childless, anachronistic, but still alive, still reaching futilely skyward.

My father, perhaps because of his age, seems to have been a loving pessimist. He saw little good in our future. According to his writing, our greatness as a country, perhaps even the greatness of the human species, was in the past. His greatest desire seems to have been to protect my mother and later, to protect me—to somehow keep us safe.

My mother, on the other hand, was a somewhat reluctant optimist. Greatness for her, for Earthseed, for humanity always seemed to run just ahead of her. Only she saw it, but that was enough to entice her on, seducing her as she seduced others.

She worked hard at seducing people. She did it first by adopting vulnerable needy people, then by finding ways to make those people want to be part of Earthseed. No matter how ridiculous Earthseed must have seemed, with its starry Destiny, if offered immediate rewards. Here was real community. Here was at least a semblance of security. Here was the comfort of ritual and routine and the emotional satisfaction of belonging to a "team" that stood together to meet challenge when challenge came. And for families, here was a place to raise children, to teach them basic skills that they might not learn elsewhere and to keep them safe as possible from the harsh, ugly lessons of the world outside.

When I was in high school, I read the 1741 Jonathan Edwards sermon, "Sinners in the Hands of an Angry God." Its first few words sum up the kinds of lessons so many children were forced to learn in the world outside Acorn. Edwards said, "The God that holds you over the pit of hell, much as one holds a spider, or some loathsome insect over the fire, abhors you, and is dreadfully provoked; his wrath towards you burns like fire; he looks upon you as worthy of nothing else, but to be cast into the fire." You're worthless. Got hates you. All you deserve is pain and death. What a believable theology that would have been for the children of the Pox. No wonder, some of them found comfort in my mother's God. If it didn't love them, at least it offered them some chance to live.

If my mother had created only Acorn, the refuge for the homeless and the orphaned.... If she had created Acorn, but not Earthseed, then I think she would have been a wholly admirable person.

Space Shuttle

by Gil Scott-Heron (USA)

Space was the place
where at least we thought our dreams were safe;
where yesterdays of youth and innocence and grace
floated somewhere high above the planet's face.
Ah, but the distance has been erased
'cause Uncle Sam is on the case.
E. T. is joining the Arm's Race!
They're up there building some kinda military base.
Rocketing through the atmosphere,
sliding into second gear
while miles below the people cheer
the New Invaders on the New Frontier
… but there are also those who do not cheer
The gravity of their lives appears
and in their eyes flash frozen fears
while rocket sounds are all they hear.

Space Shuttle/raising hell down on the ground!
Space Shuttle/turning the seasons upside down.
Space Shuttle/and all the hungry people know
all change sho' 'nuff ain't progress when you're poor.
No matter what man goes looking for
he always seem to find a war.
As soon as dreams of peace are felt
the war is raging somewhere else.

We must have somehow been disarmed
or lost our heads over false alarms;
undewhelmed and over charmed,
watching the storm clouds from afar.
Exploration, proliferation,
spending more while pockets fill.
Assessments of our investments

drive us on to Overkill.
Practice looks of great surprise
as the Captain Kirk of "Free Enterprise."
Wall Street says "Let's play Defense!"
and "Dollar bills make damn good sense!"
Hail to the new Protectionism!
Let's bring on the new age of Humanism.
We can put the cap on Capitalism!
We've got a giant, mechanical Ray-gunism!
Space Shuttle/raising hell down on the ground!
Space Shuttle/turning the seasons upside down.
Space Shuttle/and all the hungry people know
all change sho' 'nuff ain't progress when you're poor.
No matter what man goes looking for
he always seems to find a war.
As soon as dreams of peace are felt
the war is raging somewhere else.

Space was the rage
so Hollyweird took center stage
and together we wondered whether
we would ever get over the weather.
Things started happening that seemed so strange,
like the whole jet stream is being rearranged:
There was a clear day in L.A.,
a foot of snow in Tampa Bay.
The space shuttle no sooner goes up
than we watch while the Weather Man goes nuts.

Tornadoes and hurricanes,
dead rivers and Acid Rain,
volcanoes ages dead
suddenly just up and lose their heads.
Typhoons, monsoons,
and tidal waves come down from an angry moon.
It's earthquaking all the Goddamn time
and the only common denominator we can find …

Space Shuttle/raising hell down on the ground!
Space Shuttle/turning the seasons upside down.
Space Shuttle/and all the hungry people know

all change sho' 'nuff ain't progress when you're poor.
No matter what man goes looking for
he always seems to find a war.
As soon as dreams of peace are felt
the war is raging somewhere else.

Old folks must have had it right
from the time they saw the first satellite
they said "Some advancements may be good,
but not in God's neighborhood."
Laser beams and moonbeams,
we got peace dreams killed by war schemes,
there's a hole shot through the Ozone layer
that has put the fear back into the atmos-fear.
ICBM, MX, Cruise Missiles,
obsolete today.
Let's spend another billion on The Sergeant York
and then throw that "sumbitch" away.
War is big business without a doubt
so there ain't much chance of peace breaking out.
Underwater, overhead, God we'll all be nervous wrecks
'cause did you hear where they're going next?

Space Shuttle/raising hell down on the ground!
Space Shuttle/turning the seasons upside down.
Space Shuttle/and all the hungry people know
all change sho' 'nuff ain't progress when you're poor.
No matter what man goes looking for
he always seems to find a war.
As soon as dreams of peace are felt
the war is raging somewhere else.

Horoscope

by John Pepper Clark (Nigeria)

So you believe, bastard child,
The moon, as she twines
Her arms to that perfect round,
Can pull the waters
Three-quarter spilled about the earth;

Draw them to bow-bend
At each antipodal end,
And make oceans pound back mountain force?
And will you in self-same breath say the stars,
The stars millions of whom shine
In their own light
More attractive than the sun,
Have not control over the destiny
Of man, this clot of clay
Three-quarters diluted in water?
Vain cynic, believe me, the stars
Even as they in galaxies roll-glow,
Affect our human lot,
Day to day make us ebb and flow;
And though the intricacies of the zodiacs
Be as yet beyond faithful compass
Our individual flux between joy and disasters
Is that interlocking of our souls with the stars.

Chapter 10

Influence, Adaptation, and Structure

By all standards of measure, a chapter on influence, adaptation, and structure could easily offer the longest discussion and contain the largest number of excerpts, for global Black literature has a history and a tradition from which each new writer draws as he or she offers a contribution to the canon. Oral tradition, history, politics, socioeconomic realism, religious texts, Black cultural and world mythology, philosophy, psychology, and the published literature of all national, cultural, and ethnic traditions have liberally influenced global Black literatures and are appropriate for comparison.

As an introductory text, *Literary Spaces* is concerned with the diversity of content and theme rather than with literary theory. This chapter will broadly address influence, adaptation, and literary structure and form. Several standard metaphors, such as the road, the river, and the crossroads, and several musical genres, such as blues, jazz, and percussion beats, are structural foundations of Black literatures. Troupe and Schulte refer to these foundations as "conceptual writing," whereby the "writer no longer relies on the photographic rendering of reality, of the things he sees and perceives around himself. He imposes order on the objects around him, rather than accepting the order established by the objects."[1]

In the essay "Black Internationalism" (1928) early Négritude theorist Jane Nardal offers a format for the process of literary creation for the Black writer, and her description of it addresses influence and adaptation:

If the Negro wants to know himself, assert his personality, and not be the copy of this or that type from another race (which often earns him contempt and mockery), it does not follow from that, however, that he becomes resolutely hostile to all contributions made by an-

---

1. Quincy Troupe and Rainer Schulte, eds., introduction to *Giant Talk: An Anthology of Third World Writings* (New York: Random House, 1975), xliii.

other race. On the contrary, he must learn to profit from others' acquired experience and intellectual wealth, but in order to know himself better and to assert his personality.[2]

Influence is a previous tradition, writer, school of thought, era, or historical event which provides a writer with useful tools and contexts for creating
an original text. Although parts of an author's text reflect one or more sources
that served as inspiration, catalyst, or stimulus, the author's text as a whole is
exclusively his or her own: a new and authentic literary creation. Many authors attribute their choice of narrative style or their use of a specific metaphor
or character type to another influential author. Furthermore, in order for a
writer to develop and perfect his or her craft, he or she can have models, men-
tors, and examples to imitate.

William Shakespeare has been a popular influence on Black writers. Indeed,
Charlotte H. Bruner, in "The Meaning of Caliban in Black Literature Today"
(1976), writes: "Since the formal education in West Africa as started under European domination in certain Gold-Coast countries has continued to be based
on English models, this African awareness of Shakespeare is perhaps not surprising after all."[3] Bruner claims that Black writers have adapted the character
Caliban from Shakespeare's play *The Tempest* to criticize "a common heritage
of forced servitude and enforced ignorance" but that they "reshape this image,
this Black mask, to fit themselves."[4]

In "Studies in Comparative Literature" (1994), Charles Bodunde notes the
perils and processes of source and influence: "Source hunting and influence
tracing in African literature have become areas of scholarship viewed with suspicion because of the negative colouring often attached to them."[5] He adds:
"[A]ll the texts cited are materials of interest to the comparativist whose job
is also to validate the facts of sources and establish whether or not sources are
used creatively. One crucial fact, however, is that in an instance of literary borrowing or influence, the new text must show qualities of independence and
that indebtedness is significant in this regard."[6]

---

2. Jane Nardal, "Black Internationalism," in *Negritude Women*, ed. T. Denean Sharpley-Whiting (Minneapolis: University of Minneapolis Press, 2002), 107.

3. Charlotte H. Bruner, "The Meaning of Caliban in Black Literature Today," *Comparative Literature Today* 13 (1976): 241.

4. Ibid., 242, 245.

5. Charles Bodunde, "Studies in Comparative Literatures,"in *New Introduction to Literature*, ed. Olu Obafemi (Ibadan, Nigeria: Y-Books, 1994), 58.

6. Ibid., 59–60.

As a category, *imitation* is not highly regarded because it indicates a lack of creativity. More important, in a consideration of global Black literature, imitation indicates an oppressive power relationship such as the racism and white supremacy in the periods of enslavement and colonialism, during which writers of African descent were regarded as inferior intellectual beings without a valuable indigenous culture and literature. The earliest published Black writers, such as Phillis Wheatley, imitated white writers because during the 1700s imitation was regarded as an impressive and desired skill. Other early Black writers imitated white literary genres in order to convince white society that they were civilized and were good stewards of the education they had been allowed to receive. Later, imitation thrived in smaller circles of elite writers of African descent who embraced the colonizer's ideas about Black inferiority and sought assimilation through literary imitation.

Adaptation is an author's deliberate structural use of a known source. The new text may offer a different setting, ideology, language, ethnicity or gender of characters, and even an alternate ending, but the general plot and structure remain the same. A successful adaptation—an original interpretation of a previous source—is a testament to the quality of the adapted source as well as to the vision of the new author who breathed a different life into a known story. A well-known example is Aimé Césaire's *A Tempest* (1968), which is an adaptation of William Shakespeare's *The Tempest*. Nigerian playwright and critic Femi Osofisan suggests an additional reason for adaptation: "[T]he urge I feel for adaptation comes from ideological disagreement, when I am provoked to contest some point of view a playwright—usually one I admire—puts forward."[7]

This chapter also addresses structure by including an excerpt from Clarence Major's *Emergency Exit*, which demonstrates a postmodern alternative to storytelling—the interpretation of which is almost like individual-reader detective work. Scholars are in agreement that postmodernism is difficult to define authoritatively; however, in the context of literature, it generally refers to twentieth-century shifts in perceptions of what is considered literary. Postmodernism differs from modernism because it values societal codes, signs, and other stimuli as meaningful information that can enhance a reader's understanding of a text. The inclusion of such stimuli as images, dinner menus, tennis scores, or multiple-choice tests in pages of a literary text permits readers to contribute their responses to these stimuli—

---

7. Biodun Jeyifo, "Interview with Femi Osofisan," *Yearbook of Comparative and General Literature* 43 (1995): 131.

as virtual narrative parts of the text. Postmodern writers use signs and symbols of twentieth and twenty-first century culture to suggest meaning not explicitly written in words. Dramatist Suzan Lori-Parks (USA) uses a postmodern device she calls "Pauses," which permits stage actors (and readers) to include their own reactions, behaviors, and commentary within the action of her plays.

The organization of words on the page is another aspect of structure, and possibly even of postmodernism. Scattered, chaotic, widely or closely spaced, nonpunctuated, or condensed script on a page conveys messages related to the text. Excerpts in this chapter should be liberally compared with selections from previous chapters—a comparison that would also permit intriguing structural analysis. Mustapha Matura's play *Nice*, Simone Schwarz-Bart's play *Your Handsome Captain*, and Octavia Butler's *Parable of the Sower* are appropriate.

Darwin Turner offers the best strategy for this category: "Let Black writers follow Alain Locke's admonition to derive substance and style from their cultural heritage, but let them also have the freedom to borrow where they wish, with the knowledge that, doing so, they expand the Black American literary tradition rather than diminishing it."[8]

---

8. Darwin T. Turner, "Introductory Remarks About the Black Literary Tradition in the United States of America," *Proceedings of the Comparative Literature Symposium* 9 (1978): 86.

from *Emergency Exit*

by Clarence Major (USA)

DEDICATION

To people whose stories do not hold together

> "I mistrust all frank and simple
> people, especially when their stories
> hold together...."

—Ernest Hemingway,
The Sun Also Rises

> " ... if you try to do something different in this country,
> people put you down for it."

—Eric Dolphy

> "Art never seems to make me peaceful or pure."

—Willem de Kooning

Stop: The doorway of life. Take this cliché with ancient roots as a central motif. The practice of carrying the new bride across the threshold stems from a tribal Jewish custom. Its function was complex, full of mystery, and contradictions. A respect for blood (*adom*) as the source of life was at the bottom of it. The tribal Jews were careful not to waste it and considered its loss a sin. Women were creatures who periodically lost, "wasted," blood; therefore, they were born eternally guilty and damned. This male attitude toward the female evolved out of male fear of the mysterious ability of the female to give birth.

There were many other male behavior patterns manifested as a result of this anxiety. One theory has it that all male-oriented civilizations evolved from it. Indications of it are not only observable among tribal peoples today but can be seen in the interactions of people in industrialized societies.

Sacred blood had the power to heal and to protect the ancient Jews from evil. The Blood of the Lamb is both real and symbolic. Animal blood was customarily smeared all along the doorway across the threshold of the Jewish home to keep away evil spirits. As a symbol of goodness and a substance of hope and faith, the ancient Jews practiced this ritual. Because women are eternally guilty of sin they had to be lifted and carried across the threshold and they could not *touch* the doorway. Yet they, the givers of life itself, were the *source* of the symbolism and the ritual. They were the doorway of life.

Some ancient Jews drove their women to the caves in the hills during their cycle as punishment for losing blood. The uterus was perhaps the most mysterious thing among tribal peoples throughout the ancient world. Many other tribes practiced various forms of these rituals of the doorway, the threshold and the cave. Such customs have unmistakable functions and the riddles implicit at their centers speak to the ultimate mystery of life itself. While women were damned—out of fear—they were at the same time the secret object of the profoundest worship. In many tribal cultures men did not realize they had had any part in the birth process.

Emergency Exit. Standing in the blood on the holy threshold right now are so many friends and enemies I'd be up all night trying to remember their names. I see Jean Valjean, Ernest Hemingway, Camille Dumas. And Alice Carroll. Karenina Tolstoy. David Dickens. Slayer Cooper. Gulliver Swift. Henry Thack. Bigger Thomas. Toomer Cane. Nat Gables. Jim Conrad. Cross Damon. Ted R. Tragicar. Harriet Cabin and Portnoy. Gene Autry, Shirley Temple, Spike Jones, Johnny Carson. Jane Brontë. Holden Caulfield. Enrico Caruso, Nelson Eddy, Stephen Foster, Jelly Roll Morton. Johnny Beetlecreek. Doris Catacombs. Mr. Hamlet. Horatio. Ahab. Mr. Ibsen. Dr. Stockmann. Mr. Babo. Oh, Mr. Babo with his razor. Victor Hunch. Dick Herman. John Pilgrim. Anthony Zenda and Black Michael. Charlie Messenger in his yellow wig. The Invisible Man. Stephen Courage and Dan Robinson. There's Hester Prynne, still wearing the curse. And Nog dragging that thing around. The Ginger Man. Steve Saw finding tiny elephants in an old rusty can. Ishtar from upstate. And Sancho Panza stealing the show from Mr. Don. Helga Crane, neither Black nor white. Van Gogh. The Beatles. Stonewall Jackson. Mr. Allworthy and Tom. And Charles Darnay and Catherine Barkley still saying what a dirty trick it is. And Fred Henry still listening. None of them change.

Deruchette Hugo will always be charming. Falstaff and Shylock will remain. Prufrock measures his life. Mrs. Bovary, there in the doorway, cannot get the blood off her underwear. Edmond Dantès counts out his days. Emily Wuther. Charles Ho. H. G. Worlds is still at war. Vivian Grey. Oliver Wake and the Archbishop Thomas Beckett. None of them will ever step away from that spot they occupy on the threshold, their feet stuck in the blood. The Lone Ranger. Raskolnikov. Huck. Walt. King Kong. D. H. It's a crowded place.

Call me Dracaena Messangeana. I don't mind.

"I always knock on wood before I make my entrance."

—Will Rogers,
American Indian

"The threshold of a Mongol's yurt is ... traditionally a sensitive place that involves taboo. The belief among the common people is that to step on the threshold of a yurt is tantamount to stepping on the neck of the owner ... there were reports of foreign emissaries being killed for stepping on the threshold of the royal pavilion as they entered and of guards being placed on either side of the door to lift up and carry foreign emissaries in order to avoid this fate."

—Sechin Jagchild and Paul Hyer,
Mongolia's Culture and Society

The New (Threshold) Law

In the township of Inlet, Connecticut from this day (February 12, 19—) forward, all males (over the age of 21) will be required to lift from the ground, floor or landing or any flat surface made for standing or walking, leading to a door and/or doorway, all females (over the age of 18) and carry such females through, beyond, out of, said doorways, entranceways, exits, across, beyond, thresholds, of all buildings, dwellings, public and private, taking stern and serious care that no physical part of the bodies of said females touch in any manner whatsoever the physical parts of such entranceways, doorways and exits.

Failure to comply with this ruling of the city government will result in arrest and possible conviction; the nature of punishment will be determined by the Civil Court of Inlet, Connecticut. (Punitive Law Number 1026)

Seal: <u>*Rocky T. Mountain*</u>

Mayor

Witness: <u>*James Russell Ingram*</u>

The sky cleared. The backyard is beautiful. I'm sitting here looking through the window at the trees, five of them, and the sky behind them. A long shadow, thick and dark, made by the house covers most of the yard. The December trees beyond the yard are purple. Quickly I write this: "This tree is green with large black limbs. Touch the tree. The fence is uneven. Black lines enclose it, the nails are rust-covered and showing through the rotten wood. I sit on the ground with my back against a woman's back. We sleep this way. Trucks go by on the road, whistling against the long stretch of lonesome highway. The trees down the road are naked, unbearable. This person that is me is reaching out in contradictions. I want to paint my way out of this. Write my way out. This landscape is not for this tree. Fences like this should be in movies, only. My woman should be home in bed. I should be home in bed with her. These trucks should drive on. Drivers who drive on eventually drive through the beautiful forest where Kenneth Patchen sees blue animals."

We go home and play cards. My woman loves to be inside the house, it is the safest place in the world. We throw cards at each other: The Queen of Spades, Seven of Spades, Nine of Diamonds, Six of Clubs, Queen of Hearts, and Four of Hearts.

A storm comes down into the ocean. About certain other things you can't be sure. Like this: a woman comes into the room with a portable TV. She says it's time for Uncle Walter C. She sits the set on my desk. Says let's watch.

Uncle Walter C. says: Today in Inlet, Connecticut sixty-three women were arrested for refusing to be lifted and carried across the thresholds of public buildings. Hours earlier, these and about a hundred other women staged a protest march in front of the Inlet Court House. Inlet, of course, is the town that made international headlines a week ago when it passed a law requiring all men to carry all women across all thresholds at all times. Reporter Jack Pennies talked with the Mayor Rocky T. Mountain this afternoon. Here's his report.

Pennies holds the microphone to the mayor's mouth and the mayor speaks: This law is our attempt to restore moral sanity and honor and dignity to at least this small part of the world! And by god we think we'll win despite those—those *unpleasant* type women out there on the street! We're thinking with this law of the awful failure of marriages, the vanishing family in our society, we're thinking this law will bring back into our lives the kind of stability we all need! Those radical gals out there aren't even aware that this law is for their own good!

Listen: Inlet Research Company reports: purity deep in the psyche racism deep in the psyche cleanliness and proper conduct both deep in the psyche. Facts: Inlet population: eighty-seven point twenty-one percent white, twelve point three percent black, three point seven percent Spanish-speaking and less than one percent other. Fifty percent work in offices handling paper and telephones earning between ten and twenty-five thousand. Eighty percent own cars. Average rent: between one hundred and a hundred and fifty per month many own their own homes. Only nine point seven percent get their hands dirty every day earning less than seven thousand per year. Six percent work at crafts making leather belts. One percent farm. They all own washers and dryers dishwashers air conditioners freezers and two percent own second homes. How do you like them apples.

The Ingram family stands quietly on the stone walkway waiting for Jim's trousers to dry in the sunlight the pants are spread out on a brick wall. Old faded temple on other side. They are in another world. Thousands of tiny windows hand carved figures around each Julie is naked Deborah is thin in a thin gown Jim inspects his pants turns them over. Runs his hands into the left leg then the right his eyes are deep the child watches his father in order to know what to do next.

A cowbell rings in the distance. A Monk prays in a temple. Deborah clicks her tongue against the roof of her mouth. She opens her mouth sticks her tongue out at the temple and the cowbell, she stops and Barbara starts crying.

The Ingram family has gathered together. Jim sits in the hand carved Jacobean chair Barbara wears a golf ball made of gold around her neck Julie has a Deborah Goldsmith paining of one of her ancestors Deborah sits on a wainscot chair. Barbara has brought her fairy lamp with her Julie is working her embroidery frame Oscar is picking his abscesses with a silver pin Deborah scratches his fissures Barbara has an X-ray of a growth in her bladder. Julie is tinkling with the expensive Coalport and Caughley in Jim's hallway. All the doors all the windows are open. Crooks watch from outside. Everything is insured especially the Chippendale antiques and the canted candlestick holder.

I (your narrator) parked my car on the road and went down to say hello to thirty cows eating grass they all came to the fence to greet me. I cut the fence and they stepped across the threshold into the ditch followed me up to the car we went down to the local beer pub and got smashed. The bartender was so delighted he set us up twice. Said all we have to do is vote for his man. I can't remember the guy's name.

Deborah is playing with the ring on her finger. She watches the finger ease up to the opening then she plunges the finger through the ring. She pulls it out with just as much ceremony. It's fun she says her husband continues to look worried it's the same expression he has when he smells something bad like rotten onions.

You finish washing your body and lock the bathroom door. You break down the wall that separates your apartment from the one next to yours. A family is there gathered around a table eating summer food. You dance for them then take up a collection for your services. Under the table surrounded by their feet you sleep dreaming of being lost in one of Goya's paintings.

Julie has turned into an old witch. Sitting on her left shoulder is a demon in the shape of a frog with two horns. The toad whispers into Julie's ear: The researcher is not the one. The frontiersman is not the one. The Black Professor is not the one. Your father's girl friend, Roslyn Carter, is not the one. There is a man whose name is B-sounding with an S-sounding last name who is lusting after you though he has never seen you. Don't see him. Your presence fills his dreams every night. If he were to meet you he'd make you very unhappy. Might even cause your death. Ride your broom and lead a clean life. Think health.

1. In my professional life I am a success. In my amateur life ... ?

2. You girls are no longer my daughters!

3. I love you but you make me sick sometimes.

4. Your father and I told you what we expect of you ...

5. I wish you were dead!

6. No child of mine would talk to me like that!

7. Yuk! Look at you!

8. I wish I'd never been born.

9. Oh, gee, I feel so goooood today! Isn't it a wonderful day?

10. I'm tired of office work.

11. Yak yak!

12. You two are going to be the death of me!

13. You didn't think of your mother and me when you were out running around with your friends.

a. I didn't ask to be born.

b. *I hate you, I hate you!*

c. Why can't we be like other families?

d. You never lift me across the threshold.

e. I love you, do you know that ...

f. Talk to me while we make love, I love to hear you talk to me ...

g. I feel hysterical. Do I seem crazy. I feel crazy.

14. What is it that you want—
    I don't understand you!

    h. Go fly a kite!

15. I wish you'd stop drinking.

    i. I hate you when you lift me
        across the threshold. I hate this
        house, too. And you, too.

16. Would you please listen to me!

17. Hi.

18. I love when you lift me across
    the threshold. Oh, darling, I love
    you soooooo much!

19. So what else is new?

    j. I don't like the food available
        in this country. I'm not at home
        here.

20. I just want problems I can
    handle.

21. Say pretty please.

    k. Kiss.

22. Turn to page two-twenty-two.
    Everybody sing! Two-twenty-two.

    l. Love is a pie.

    m. Mother where are my paper
        shoes?

23. I wish I had been born in
    another time. Say the 20's.

24. Did you look in the attic?

    n. I don't like the taste of myself
        on your mouth and beard when
        we kiss. I know it's a hangup
        but I can't help it.

25. You make me sick but I love
    you. Deep down I always love
    you.

26. I don't want to talk about it
    right now. Tomorrow, okay.

27. Look at the mess you've made
    of your life.

    o. Oh, well.

28. Do you work for the CIA?

    p. Have you seen the painting by
        Morris Hirschfield (1872–1946)
        called "Nude on a Sofa with
        Three Pussies"? Quite an
        accomplishment!

29. My brother doesn't get to
    spend enough time with his
    father. My father is always with
    his girl friend.

30. Nobody loves me.

    q. She's depressed. I hope she
        doesn't kill herself.

There is a serious gap between our ideals and some of our practices ..."

—President Truman

"Backdoor Spending: a term used by opponents of the policy of financing a federal program without going through the normal procedure of making an appropriation...."

—Eugene J. McCarthy,
Dictionary of American Politics

"We keep a horse in the house. Just an old broken down hack we picked up in New Hampshire when I play the piano it tries to tap dance. Thinks he's human." *UPI—Horse kept in house bumps head on kitchen doorway while entering dining room.*

My wife (the narrator's wife) digs in the hillsides for ancient cities she always wears a red raincoat so hunters won't shoot her. Last year she slid down into a mudhole and found herself standing on the tomb of a king who lived six thousand years ago.

The new apartment is full of empty milk cartons Julie walks around naked all day pressing the kittens to her breasts.

Column one page one: husbands *must* carry wives across thresholds through doors maximum penalty for violators.

This cave in the earth is endless. Things warm with tense muscles hide for years in it. The darkness is a darkness full of change. I eat the sunlight drink the sea sunk in it I digest the earth swim deep in my own nervous system, here inside I listen to the poundings of the heart, this strange thing, that surrounds me. I sleep and wake in the blackness and change in it when the beating rhythm changes. It changes when the seasons change which changes when the cave itself changes.

Houses are built the wrong way the walls do not feel like skin or hair. The people in them keep trying to rebuild themselves from scratch. Scraps of ideas won't work.

A threshold is a sill some dwellers think of a threshold as a doorway in fact it is the sill of a doorway the entrance to the house a holy holy place beginning blood of the lamb guilt the exit the whole thing over and over again, again and again.

This living thing hides from the light and drinks little water.

This is a place of inletting where rock stars easily make up songs about one's state of ... when one is let in on the ultimate secret of the "limen" the "threschold" the traskvald" the "threscwald" the ...

Jim and Deborah are standing in the yard together. Her hair is parted down the middle. The expensive rings he gave her are on the fingers of the left hand. Held against her long black dress they shine.

Jim protects me like a father Deborah says. He wears his long grey socks over his ears and down his neck. Sad angry eyes.

The corner of Roslyn's mouth twitches.

Deborah's sister Alla Blake is visiting them at the moment she's jumping from the diving board into the swimming pool she's achieved a fine tan the pink and green of her swimsuit against her body is beautiful. When she dives with both arms up her hair hugs her neck she plunges into the sky.

Sixteen persons at Inlet are listed in *Who's Who in America* but the best known is a short story writer who publishes in New York two of his best known stories are, "Think Health: Eat Your Honey!" and "It Takes Balls to Play Tennis." In the first an old woman carries a horse and a buggy across the threshold of a barn—this is all she ever does. In the second a weak dirty man learns how to be strong and hygienic. The other sixty writers in town are unpublished and unknown they get together and exchange rejection slips.

Barry Sands walks into the room. Julie is sitting at the desk reading. He sneaks up behind her and places his hands over her eyes. Guess who. I can't. I'm your hypnotist, he says. He releases her eyes. Look into my eyes. She turns and looks up into his eyes. Repeat after me. I will always hold a raw potato in my mouth while peeling onions. Julie repeats the words though they mean nothing to her. Barry continues: I am a rabbit who will eventually lay an egg. He listens carefully as she repeats it. I will fall in love with a handsome young Jewish man and live happily ever after. Rather than repeating Barry's word Julie— as though another's voice is speaking through her—says: Pax sax sarax afra afca nostra.

They are bike riding along the path in Central Park and stop and put down the bikes and stretch out on the grass avoiding dog turds. Looking then at the sky Julie speaks in a phony voice. I hope someday you and I can go to Africa together. You'd love Africa, Al. You would like to wouldn't you. He laughs. Certainly. Tries to say certainly like proper people. Sometimes he felt she was simply flaunting the fact that she'd been to Africa twice once as a little girl then later to attend college. Rich niggers from Inlet, Connecticut, going to see the savages no that's not the right image. Returning to one's homeland but Julie Al thinks doesn't see Africa that way. Roots. Boots. Ah so what. Africa might be a place you could dig after all even after Tarzan and white lies. Little white lies. Hello white lies. White lies uneasily on the canvas. Oh it would be so great to see Africa with you Al! She closes her eyes and sees the rolling green hills and the warm storms the rains high in the mountains. Feels herself moving along the street of an East African country the warmth in her African garments. Dark people standing in doorways watching. Al and Julie now on their backs side by side. You know the more I think about it Al says the more appealing the idea is. You mean seeing Africa with me. Yes. She suddenly sat up and threw herself over on him hugging him and kissing his face all over. Over and over. It annoyed him her dramatics but at this point he could live with them her way. Today was Friday and tonight they were going to Inlet to spend the weekend together in Julie's parents' home in Duck Pond while Jim and Deborah were away together on a cruise trying to patch up but not really patch up their cracked marriage. Julie's parents had asked her not to have her boyfriends stay all night while they were away but she was going to do it anyway because this time it was different since Allen Morris was the man she'd spend the rest of her life with. An all night visitor was another matter but Al was special. If mom and dad found out they would have to understand. They'd have the house to themselves. Hello house. Nice and warm inside the word house. Deep inside the house they would plunge deep inside each other. All the way back. They'd have the whole house except perhaps for Barbara who might return home from visiting her best friend a white girl named Nikki. But so what they'd still have privacy and Julie was happy. To her Al looked happy too.

They ride their bikes back to the rental place. On the way Al leads the way through a tunnel. Inside the tunnel an eye follows them. The eye has a voice it says: mirror mirror. Al says huh and Julie says I didn't say anything.

Act I from *Pantomime* from
Remembrance & Pantomime: Two Plays

by Derek Walcott (St. Lucia/Trinidad)

Characters

HARRY TREWE, *English, mid-forties, owner of the Castaways Guest House, retired actor*
JACKSON PHILLIP, *Trinidadian, forty, his factotum, retired calypsonian*

The action takes place in a gazebo on the edge of a cliff, part of the guest house on the island of Tobago, West Indies.

Act One

A small summerhouse or gazebo, painted white, with a few plants and a table set for breakfast. HARRY TREWE *enters—in white, carrying a tape recorder, which he rests on the table. He starts the machine.*

HARRY

> (Sings and dances)
> It's our Christmas panto,
> it's called: Robinson Crusoe.
> We're awfully glad that you've shown up,
> it's for kiddies as well as for grown ups.
> Our purpose is to please:
> so now with our magic wand ...
>> (Dissatisfied with the routine, he switches off the machine. Re-hearses
>> his dance. Then presses the machine again)
> Just a picture of a lonely island
> and a beach with its golden sand.
> There walks a single man
> in the beautiful West Indies!

(He turns off the machine. Stands, staring out to sea. Then exits with the tape recorder. Stage empty for a few beats, then JACKSON, in an open, white waiter's jacket and black trousers, but barefoot, enters with a breakfast tray. He puts the tray down, looks around?)

JACKSON

> Mr. Trewe?
>> (English accent)
> Mr. Trewe, your scramble eggs is here! *are* here!
>> (Creole accent)
> Are you in there?
>> (To himself)
> And when his eggs get cold, is I to catch.
>> (He fans the eggs with one hand)
> What the hell I doing? That ain't go heat them. It go make them
> more cold. Well, he must be leap off the ledge. At long last. Well, if
> he ain't dead, he could call.

(He exits with tray. Stage bare. HARRY returns, carrying a hat made of goatskin and a goatskin parasol. He puts on the hat, shoulders the parasol, and circles the table. Then he recoils, looking down at the floor)

HARRY

> (Sings and dances)
> Is this the footprint of a naked man,
> or is it the naked footprint of a man,
> that startles me this morning on this bright and golden sand.

(*To audience*)
There's no one here but I,
just the sea and lonely sky ...
     (*Pauses*)
Yes ... and how the hell did it go on?

(JACKSON *enters, without the try. Studies* HARRY)

JACKSON
Morning, Mr. Trewe. Your breakfast ready.

HARRY
So how're you this morning, Jackson?

JACKSON
Oh, fair to fine, with seas moderate, with waves three to four feet in open water, and you, sir?

HARRY
Overcast with sunny periods, with this possibility of heavy showers by mid-afternoon, I'd say Jackson.

JACKSON
Heavy showers, Mr. Trewe?

HARRY
Heavy showers. I'm so bloody bored I could burst into tears.

JACKSON
I bringing in breakfast.

HARRY
You do that, Friday.

JACKSON
Friday? It ain't go keep.

HARRY
     (*Gesturing*)
Friday, you, bring Crusoe, me, breakfast now. Crusoe hungry.

JACKSON
Mr. Trewe, you come back with that same rake again? I tell you, I ain't no actor, and I ain't walking in front a set of tourists naked playing cannibal. Carnival, but not cannibal.

HARRY

What tourists? We're closed for repairs. We're the only ones in the guest house. Apart from the carpenter, if he ever shows up.

JACKSON

Well, you ain't seeing him today, because he was out on a heavy lime last night ... Saturday, you know? And with the peanuts you does pay him for overtime.

HARRY

All right, then. It's goodbye!

(*He climbs onto the ledge between the uprights, teetering, walking slowly*)

JACKSON

Get offa that ledge, Mr. Trewe! Is a straight drop to them rocks!

(HARRY *kneels, arms extended, Jolson-style*)

HARRY

Hold on below there, sonny boooy! Daddy's a-coming. Your papa's a-coming, Sonnnnneee Boooooooy!
(*To* JACKSON)
You're watching the great Harry Trewe and his high-wire act.

JACKSON

You watching Jackson Phillip and his disappearing act.

(*Turning to leave*)

HARRY

(*Jumping down*)
I'm not a suicide, Jackson. It's a good act, but you never read the reviews. It would be too exasperating, anyway.

JACKSON

What, sir?

HARRY

Attempted suicide in a Third World country. You can't leave a note because pencils break, you can't cut your wrist with the local blades ...

JACKSON

We trying we best, sir, since all you gone.

HARRY

Doesn't matter if we're a minority group. Suicides are tax-payers, too, you know, Jackson.

JACKSON

Except it ain't going to be suicide. They go say I push you. So, now the fun and dance done, sir, breakfast now?

HARRY

I'm rotting from insomnia, Jackson. I've been up since three, hearing imaginary guests arriving in the rooms, and I haven't slept since. I nearly came around the back to have a little talk. I started thinking about the same bloody problem, which is, What entertainment can we give the guests?

JACKSON

They ain't guests, Mr. Trewe. They're casualties.

HARRY

How do you mean?

JACKSON

This hotel like a hospital. The toilet catch asthma, the air-condition got ague, the front-balcony rail missing four teet', and every minute the fridge like it dancing the Shango … brrgudup … jukjuk … brrugudup. Is no wonder that the carpenter collapse. Termites jumping like steel band in the foundations.

HARRY

For fifty dollars a day they want Acapulco?

JACKSON

Try giving them the basics: Food. Water. Shelter. They ain't shipwrecked, they pay in advance for their vacation.

HARRY

Very funny. But the ad says, "Tours" and "Nightly Entertainment." Well, Christ, after they've seen the molting parrot in the lobby and the faded sea fans, they'll be pretty livid if there's no "nightly entertainment," and so would you, right? So, Mr. Jackson, It's your neck and mine. We open next Friday.

JACKSON

Breakfast, sir. Or else is overtime.

HARRY

I kept thinking about this panto I co-authored, man. *Robinson Crusoe*, and I picked up this old script. I can bring it all down to your level, with just two characters. Crusoe, Man Friday, maybe even the parrot, if that horny old bugger will remember his lines ...

JACKSON

Since we on the subject, Mr. Trewe, I am compelled to report that parrot again.

HARRY

No, not again, Jackson?

JACKSON

Yes.

HARRY

(*Imitating parrot*)
Heinegger, Heinegger.
(*In his own voice*)
Correct?

JACKSON

Wait, wait! I know your explanation: that a old German called Herr Heinegger used to own this place, and that when that maquereau of a macaw keep cracking: "Heinegger, Heinegger," he remembering the Nazi and not heckling me, but it playing a little havoc with me nerves. This is my fifth report. I am marking them down. Language is ideas, Mr. Trewe. And I think this pre-colonial parrot have the wrong idea.

HARRY

It's his accent, Jackson. He's a Creole parrot. What can I do?

JACKSON

Well, I am not saying not to give the bird a fair trial, but I see nothing wrong in taking him out the cage at dawn, blindfolding the bitch, giving him a last cigarette if he want it, lining him up against the garden wall, and perforating his arse by firing squad.

HARRY

The war's over, Jackson! And how can a bloody parrot be prejudiced?

JACKSON

The same damn way they corrupt a child. By their upbringing. That parrot survive from a pre-colonial epoch, Mr. Trewe, and if it want to last in Trinidad and Tobago, then it go have to adjust.

(*Long pause*)

HARRY

> (*Leaping up*)

Do you think we could work him into the panto? Give him something to do? Crusoe had a parrot, didn't he? You're right, Jackson, let's drop him from the show.

JACKSON

> Mr. Trewe, you are a truly, truly stubborn man. I am *not* putting that old goatskin hat on my head and making an ass of myself for a million dollars, and I have already said so already.

HARRY

> You got it wrong. I put the hat on, I'm ... Wait, wait a minute. *Cut! Cut!* You know what would be a heavy twist, heavy with irony?

JACKSON

> What, Mr. Trewe?

HARRY

> We reverse it.

(*Pause*)

JACKSON

> You mean you prepared to walk round naked as your mother make you, in your jockstrap, playing a white cannibal in front of your own people? You're a real actor! And you got balls, too, excuse me, Mr. Trewe, to even consider doing a thing like that! Good. Joke finish. Breakfast now, eh? Because I ha' to fix the sun deck since the carpenter ain't reach.

HARRY

> All right, breakfast. Just heat it a little.

JACKSON

> Right, sir. The coffee must be warm still. But I best do some brand-new scramble eggs.

HARRY

> Never mind the eggs, then. Slip in some toast, butter, and jam.

JACKSON

> How long you in this hotel business, sir? No butter. Marge. No sugar. Big strike. Island-wide shortage. We down to half a bag.

HARRY

Don't forget I've heard you sing calypsos, Jackson. Right back there in the kitchen.

JACKSON

Mr. Trewe, every day I keep begging you to stop trying to make a entertainer out of me. I finish with show business. I finish with Trinidad. I come to Tobago for peace and quiet. I quite satisfy. If you ain't want me to resign, best drop the topic.

(*Exits.* HARRY *sits at the table, staring out to sea. He is reciting softly to himself, then more audibly*)

HARRY

"Alone, alone, all, all alone,
Alone on a wide wide sea …
I bit my arm, I sucked the blood,
And cried, A sail! a sail!"

(*He removes the hat, then his shirt, rolls up his trousers, removes them, puts them back on, removes them again*)

Mastah … Mastah … Friday sorry. Friday never do it again. Master.

(JACKSON *enters with breakfast tray, groans, turns to leave. Returns*)

JACKSON

Mr. Trewe, what it is going on on this blessed Sunday morning, if I may ask?

HARRY

I was feeling what it was like to be Friday.

JACKSON

Well, Mr. Trewe, you ain't mind putting back on your pants?

HARRY

Why can't I eat breakfast like this?

JACKSON

Because I am here. I happen to be here. I am the one serving you, Mr. Trewe.

HARRY

There's nobody here.

JACKSON

Mr. Harry, you putting on back your pants?

HARRY

You're frightened of something?

JACKSON

You putting on back your pants?

HARRY

What're you afraid of? Think I'm bent? That's such a corny interpretation of the Crusoe-Friday relationship, boy. My son's been dead three years, Jackson, and I'vnt had much interest in women since, but I haven't quite gone queer, either. And to be a flasher, you need an audience.

JACKSON

Mr. Trewe, I am trying to explain that I myself feel like a ass holding this tray in my hand while you standing up there naked, and that if anybody should happen to pass, my name is immediately mud. So, when you put back on your pants, I will serve you breakfast.

HARRY

Actors do this sort of thing. I'm getting into a part.

JACKSON

Don't bother getting into the part, get into the pants. Please.

HARRY

Why? You've got me worried now, Jackson.

JACKSON

(Exploding)
Put on your blasted pants, man! You like a blasted child, you know!

(*Silence.* HARRY *puts on his pants*)

HARRY

Shirt, too?
(JACKSON *sucks his teeth*)
There.
(HARRY *puts on his shirt*)
You people are such prudes, you know that? What's it in you, Jackson, that gets so Victorian about a man in his own hotel deciding to have breakfast in his own underwear, on a totally deserted Sunday morning?

JACKSON

Manners, sir. Manners.

(*He puts down the tray*)

HARRY

Sit.

JACKSON

Sit? Sit where? How you mean, sit?

HARRY

Sit, and I'll serve breakfast. You can teach me manners. There's more manners in serving than in being served.

JACKSON

I ain't know what it is eating you this Sunday morning, you hear, Mr. Trewe, but I don't feel you have any right to mamaguy me, because I is a big man with three children, all outside. Now, being served by a white man ain't no big deal for me. It happen to me every day in New York, so it's not going to be any particularly thrilling experience. I would like to get breakfast finish with, wash up, finish my work, and go for my sea bath. Now I have worked here six months and never lost my temper, but it wouldn't take much more for me to fling this whole fucking tray out in that sea and get somebody more to your sexual taste.

HARRY

(*Laughs*)
Aha!

JACKSON

Not aha, oho!

HARRY

(*Drawing out a chair*)
Mr. Phillips ...

JACKSON

Phillip. What?

HARRY

Your reservation.

JACKSON

You want me to play this game, eh?
(*He walks around, goes to a corner of the gazebo*)
I'll tell you something, you hear, Mr. Trewe? And listen to me good, good. Once and for all. My sense of humor can stretch so far. Then it

does snap. You see that sea out there? You know where I was born? I born over there. Trinidad. I was a very serious steel-band man, too. And where I come from is a very serious place. I used to get into some serious trouble. A man keep bugging my arse once. A bad john called Boysie. Indian fellow, want to play nigger. Every day in that panyard he would come making joke with nigger boy this, and so on, and I used to just laugh and tell him stop, but he keep laughing and I keep laughing and he going on and I begging him to stop and the two of us laughing, until ...

(*He turns, goes to the tray, and picks up a fork*)

one day, just out of the blue, I pick up a ice pick and walk over to where he and two fellars was playing card, and I nail that ice pick through his hand to the table, and I laugh, and I walk away.

HARRY

Your table, Mr. Phillip.

(*Silence.* JACKSON *shrugs, sits at the table*)

JACKSON

Okay, then. Until.

HARRY

You know, if you want to exchange war experiences, lad, I could bore you with a couple of mine. Want to hear?

JACKSON

My shift is seven-thirty to one.
    (*He folds his arms.* HARRY *offers him a cigarette*)
I don't smoke on duty.

HARRY

We put on a show in the army once. Ground crew. RAF. In what used to be Palestine. A Christmas panto. Another one. And yours truly here was the dame. The dame in a panto is played by a man. Well, I got the part. Wrote the music, the book, everything, whatever original music there was. *Aladdin and His Wonderful Vamp*. Very obscene, of course. I was the Wonderful Vamp. Terrific reaction all around. Thanks to me music-hall background. Went down great. Well, there was a party afterward. Then a big sergeant in charge of maintenance started this very boring business of confusing my genius with my life. Kept pinching my arse and so on. It got kind of boring after a while. Well, he was the size of a truck, mate. And there wasn't much I could do but keep blushing and pretending to be liking it. But the Wonderful Vamp was waiting outside for him, the Wonderful Vamp and a wrench this big, and after that, laddie, it took all of maintenance to put him back again.

JACKSON

That is white-man fighting. Anyway, Mr. Trewe, I feel the fun finish; I would like, with your permission, to get up now and fix up the sun deck. 'Cause when rain fall ...

HARRY

Forget the sun deck. I'd say, Jackson, that we've come closer to a mutual respect, and that things need not get that hostile. Sit, and let me explain what I had in mind.

JACKSON

I take it that's an order?

HARRY

You want it to be an order? Okay, it's an order.

JACKSON

It didn't sound like no order.

HARRY

Look, I'm a liberal, Jackson. I've done the whole routine. Aldermaston, Suez, Ban the Bomb, Burn the Bra, Pity the Poor Pakis, et cetera. I've even tried jumping up to the steel band at Notting Hill Gate, and I'd no idea I'd wind up in this ironic position of giving orders, but if the new script I've been given says: HARRY TREWE, HOTEL MANAGER, then I'm going to play Harry Trewe, Hotel Manager, to the hilt, damnit. So *sit* down! Please. Oh, goddamnit, *sit ... down ...*
(JACKSON *sits. Nods*)
Good. Relax. Smoke. Have a cup of tepid coffee. I sat up from about three this morning, working out this whole skit in my head.
(*Pause*)
Mind putting that hat on for a second, it will help my point. Come on. It'll make things clearer.

(*He gives* JACKSON *the goatskin hat.* JACKSON, *after a pause, puts it on*)

JACKSON

I'll take that cigarette.

(HARRY *hands over a cigarette*)

HARRY

They've seen that stuff, time after time. Limbo, dancing girls, fire-eating ...

JACKSON

Light.

HARRY

Oh, sorry.

(*He lights* JACKSON's *cigarette*)

JACKSON

I listening.

HARRY

We could turn this little place right here into a little cabaret, with some very witty acts. Build up the right audience. Get an edge on the others. So, I thought, Suppose I get this material down to two people. Me and ... well, me and somebody else. Robinson Crusoe and Man Friday. We could work up a good satire, you know, on the master-servant—no offense—relationship. Labour-management, white-black, and so on ... Making some trenchant points about topical things, you know. Add that show to the special dinner for the price of one ticket ...

JACKSON

You have to have music.

HARRY

Pardon?

JACKSON

A show like that should have music. Just a lot of talk is very boring.

HARRY

Right. But I'd have to have somebody help me, and that's where I thought ... Want to take the hat off?

JACKSON

It ain't bothering me. When you going make your point?

HARRY

We had that little Carnival contest with the staff and you knocked them out improvising, remember that? You had the bloody guests in stitches ...

JACKSON

You ain't start to talk money yet, Mr. Harry

HARRY

Just improvising with the quatro. And not the usual welcome to Port au Spain, I am glad to see you again, but I'll tell you, artist to artist, I recognized a real pro, and this is the point of the hat. I want to make a point about the hotel industry, about manners, conduct, to generally improve relations all around. So, whoever it is, you or whoever, plays Crusoe, and I, or whoever it is, get to play Friday, and imagine first of all the humor and then the impact of that. What you think?

JACKSON

You want my honest, professional opinion?

HARRY

Fire away.

JACKSON

I think is shit.

HARRY

I've never been in shit in my life, my boy.

JACKSON

It sound like shit to me, but I could be wrong.

HARRY

You could say things in fun about this place, about the whole Caribbean, that would hurt while people laughed. You get half the gate.

JACKSON

Half?

HARRY

What do you want?

JACKSON

I want you to come to your senses, let me fix the sun deck and get down to the beach for my sea bath. So, I put on this hat, I pick up this parasol, and I walk like a mama-poule up and down this stage and you have a black man playing Robinson Crusoe and then a half-naked, white, fish-belly man playing Friday, and you want to tell me it ain't shit?

HARRY

It could be hilarious!

JACKSON

Hilarious, Mr. Trewe? Supposing I wasn't a waiter, and instead of breakfast I was serving you communion, this Sunday morning on this tropical island, and I turn to you, Friday, to teach you my faith, and I tell you, kneel down and eat this man. Well, kneel, nuh! What you think you would say, eh?

(Pause)

You, this white savage?

HARRY

No, that's cannibalism.

JACKSON

Is more cannibalism than to eat a god. Suppose I make you tell me: For three hundred years I have made you my servant. For three hundred years ...

HARRY

It's pantomime, Jackson, just keep it light ... Make them laugh.

JACKSON

Okay.

(Giggling)

For three hundred years I served you. Three hundred years I served you breakfast in ... in my white jacket on a white veranda, boss, bwana, effendi, bacra, sahib ... in that sun that never set on your empire I was your shadow, I did what you did, boss, bwana, effendi, bacra, sahib ... that was my pantomime. Every movement you made, your shadow copied ...

(Stops giggling)

and you smiled at me as a child does smile at his shadow's helpless obedience, boss, bwana, effendi, bacra, sahib, Mr. Crusoe. Now ...

HARRY

Now?

(JACKSON's speech is enacted in a trance-like drone, a zombie)

JACKSON

But after a while the child does get frighten of the shadow he make. He say to himself, That is too much obedience, I better hads stop. But the shadow don't stop, no matter if the child stop playing that pantomime, and the shadow does follow the child everywhere; when he praying, the shadow pray too, when he turn round frighten, the shadow turn round too, when he hide under the sheet, the shadow hiding too. He cannot get rid of it, no matter what, and that is the power and black magic of the shadow, boss, bwana, effendi, bacra, sahib, until it is the shadow that start dominating the child, it is the servant that start dominating the master ...

(*Laughs maniacally, like The Shadow*)

and that is the victory of the shadow, boss.

(*Normally*)

And that is why all them Pakistani and West Indians in England, all them immigrant Fridays driving all you so crazy. And they go keep driving you crazy till you go mad. In that sun that never set, they's your shadow, you can't shake them off.

HARRY

Got really carried away that time, didn't you? It's a pantomime, Jackson, keep it light. Improvise!

JACKSON

You mean we making it up as we go along?

HARRY

Right!

JACKSON

Right! I in dat!

(*He assumes a stern stance and points stiffly*)

Robinson obey Thursday now. Speak Thursday language. Obey Thursday gods.

HARRY

Jesus Christ!

JACKSON

(*Inventing language*)

Amaka nobo sakamaka khaki pants kamaluma Jesus Christ! Jesus Christ kamalogo!

(*Pause. Then with a violent gesture*)

Kamalongo kaba!

(*Meaning: Jesus is dead!*)

HARRY

Sure.

(*Pause. Peers forward. Then speaks to an imaginary projectionist, while* JACKSON *stands, feet apart, arms folded, frowning, in the usual stance of the Noble Savage*)

Now, could you run it with subtitles, please?

(*He walks over to* JACKSON, *who remains rigid. Like a movie director*)
Let's have another take, Big Chief.
   (*To imaginary camera*)
Roll it. Sound!

(JACKSON *shoves* HARRY *aside and strides to the table. He bangs the heel of his palm on the tabletop*)

JACKSON
   Patamba! Patamba! Yes?

HARRY
   You want us to strike the prop? The patamba?
      (*To cameraman*)
   Cut!

JACKSON
      (*To cameraman*)
   Rogoongo! Rogoongo!

(*Meaning: Keep it rolling*)

HARRY
   Cut!

JACKSON
   Rogoongo, damnit!
      (*Defiantly, furiously,* JACKSON *moves around, first signaling the camera to follow him, then pointing out the objects which he rechristens, shaking or hitting them violently. Slams table*)
   Patamba!
      (*Rattles beach chair*)
   Backaracka! Backaracka!
      (*Holds up cup, points with other hand*)
   Banda!
      (*Drops cup*)
   Banda karan!
      (*Puts his arm around* HARRY; *points at him*)
   Subu!
      (*Faster, pointing*)
   Masz!
      (*Stamping the floor*)
   Zohgooooor!

(*Rests his snoring head on the closed palms*)
Oma! Omaaaa!
   (*Kneels, looking skyward. Pauses; eyes closed*)
Booora! Booora!
   (*Meaning the world. Silence. He rises*)
Cut!
And dat is what it was like, before you come here with your table this and cup that.

HARRY
   All right. Good audition. You get twenty dollars a day without dialogue.

JACKSON
   But why?

HARRY
   You never called anything by the same name twice. What's a table?

JACKSON
   I forget.

HARRY
   I remember: patamba!

JACKSON
   Patamba?

HARRY
   Right. You fake.

JACKSON
   That's a breakfast table. *Ogushi.* That's a dressing table. *Amanga ogushi.* I remember now.

HARRY
   I'll tell you one thing, friend. If you want me to learn your language, you'd better have a gun.

JACKSON
   You best play Crusoe, chief. I surrender. All you win.
   (*Points wearily*)
   Table. Chair. Cup. Man. Jesus. I accept. I accept. All you win. Long time.
   (*Smiles*)

HARRY

All right, then. Improvise, then. Sing us a song. In your new language, mate. In English. Go ahead. I challenge you.

JACKSON

You what?

(*Rises, takes up parasol, handling it like a guitar, and strolls around the front row of the audience*)

(*Sings*)

I want to tell you 'bout Robinson Crusoe.
He tell Friday, when I do so, do so.
Whatever I do, you must do like me.
*He make Friday a Good Friday Bohbolee;**
That was the first example of slavery,
'Cause I am still Friday and you ain't me.
Now Crusoe he was this Christian and all,
And Friday, his slave, was a cannibal,
But one day things bound to go in reverse,
With Crusoe the slave and Friday the boss.

HARRY

Then comes this part where Crusoe sings to the goat. Little hint of animal husbandry:

(*Kneels, embraces an imaginary goat, to the melody of "Swanee"*)

(*Sings*)

Nanny, how I love you,
How I love you,
My dear old nanny …

JACKSON

Is a li'l obscene.

HARRY

(*Music-hall style*)

Me wife thought so. Know what I used to tell her? Obscene? Well, better to be obscene than not heard. How's that? Harry Trewe, I'm telling you again, the music hall's loss is calypso's gain.

(*Stops*)

---

* A Judas effigy beaten at Easter in Trinidad and Tobago.

(JACKSON *pauses. Stares upward, muttering to himself.* HARRY *turns.* JACKSON *is signaling in the air with a self-congratulatory smile*)

HARRY

What is it? What've we stopped for?
(JACKSON *hisses for silence from* HARRY, *then returns to his reverie. Miming*)
Are you feeling all right, Jackson?
(JACKSON *walks some distance away from* HARRY. *An imaginary guitar suddenly appears in his hand.* HARRY *circles him. Lifts one eyelid, listens to his heartbeat.* JACKSON *revolves,* HARRY *revolves with him.* JACKSON's *whole body is now silently rocking in rhythm. He is laughing to himself. We hear, very loud, a calypso rhythm*)
Two can play this game, Jackson.

(*He strides around in imaginary straw hat, twirling a cane. We hear, very loud, music hall. It stops.* HARRY *peers at* JACKSON.)

JACKSON

You see what you start?
(*Sings*)
Well, a Limey name Trewe came to Tobago.
He was in show business but he had no show,
so in desperation he turn to me
and said: "Mister Phillip" is the two o' we,
one classical actor, and one Creole ...

HARRY

Wait! Hold it, hold it, man! Don't waste that. Try and remember it. I'll be right back.

JACKSON

Where you going?

HARRY

Tape. Repeat it, and try and keep it. That's what I meant, you see?

JACKSON

You start to exploit me already?

HARRY

That's right. Memorize it.
(*Exits quickly.* JACKSON *removes his shirt and jacket, rolls up his pants above the knee, clears the breakfast tray to one side of the floor, over-*

turns the table, and sits in it, as if it were a boat, as HARRY *returns with the machine)*
What's all this? I'm ready to tape. What're you up to?
(JACKSON *sits in the upturned table, rowing calmly, and from time to time surveying the horizon. He looks up toward the sky, shielding his face from the glare with one hand; then he gestures to* HARRY)
What?
(JACKSON *flaps his arms around leisurely, like a large sea bird, indicating that* HARRY *should do the same)*
What? What about the song? You'll forget the bloody song. It was a fluke.

JACKSON

(*Steps out from the table, crosses to* HARRY, *irritated*)
If I suppose to help you with this stupidness, we will have to cool it and collaborate a little bit. Now, I was in that boat, rowing, and I was looking up to the sky to see a storm gathering, and I wanted a big white sea bird beating inland from a storm. So what's the trouble, Mr. Trewe?

HARRY

Sea bird? What sea bird? I'm not going to play a fekking sea bird.

JACKSON

Mr. Trewe, I'm only asking you to play a white sea bird because I am supposed to play a black explorer.

HARRY

Well, I don't want to do it. Anyway, that's the silliest acting I've seen in a long time. And Robinson Crusoe wasn't *rowing* when he got shipwrecked; he was on a huge boat. I didn't come here to play a sea bird, I came to tape the song.

JACKSON

Well, then, is either the sea bird or the song. And I don't see any reason why you have to call my acting silly. We suppose to improvise.

HARRY

All right, Jackson, all right. After I do this part, I hope you can remember the song. Now you just tell me, before we keep stopping, what I am supposed to do, how many animals I'm supposed to play, and … you know, and so on, and so on, and then when we get all that part fixed up, we'll tape the song, all right?

JACKSON

That suits me. Now, the way I see it here: whether Robinson Crusoe was on a big boat or not, the idea is that he got ...

(*Pause*)

shipwrecked. So I ... if I am supposed to play Robinson Crusoe my way, then I will choose the way in which I will get shipwrecked. Now, as Robinson Crusoe is rowing, he looks up and he sees this huge white sea bird, which is making loud sea-bird noises, because a storm is coming. And Robinson Crusoe looks up toward the sky and sees that there is this storm. Then, there is a large wave, and Robinson Crusoe finds himself on the beach.

HARRY

Am I supposed to play the beach? Because that's white ...

JACKSON

Hilarious! Mr. Trewe. Now look, you know, I am doing *you* a favor. On this beach, right? Then he sees a lot of goats. And, because he is naked and he needs clothes, he kills a goat, he takes off the skin, and he makes this parasol here and this hat, so he doesn't go around naked for everybody to see. Now I *know* that there is nobody there, but there is an audience, so the sooner Robinson Crusoe puts on his clothes, then the better and happier we will all be. I am going to go back in the boat. I am going to look up toward the sky. You will, *please*, make the sea-bird noises. I will do the wave, I will crash onto the sand, you will come down like a goat, I will kill you, take off your skin, make a parasol *and* a hat, and after that, then I promise you that I will remember the song. And I will sing it to the best of my ability.

(*Pause*)

However shitty that is.

HARRY

I said "silly." Now listen ...

JACKSON

Yes, Mr. Trewe?

HARRY

Okay, if you're a black explorer ... Wait a minute ... wait a minute. If you're really a white explorer but you're black, shouldn't I play a black sea bird because I'm white?

JACKSON

Are you ... going to extend ... the limits of prejudice to include ... the flora and fauna of this island? I am entering the boat.

(*He is stepping into the upturned table or boat, as* HARRY *halfheartedly imitates a bird, waving his arms*)

HARRY

   Kekkkk, kekkkk,
   kekkk, kekkkk!
      (*Stops*)
   What's wrong?

JACKSON

   What's wrong? Mr. Trewe, that is not a sea gull ... that is some kind of ...
   well, I don't know what it is ... some kind of *jumbie* bird or something.
      (*Pause*)
   I am returning to the boat.

(*He carefully enters the boat, expecting an interrupting bird cry from* HARRY, *but there is none, so he begins to row*)

HARRY

   Kekk! Kekkk.
      (*He hangs his arms down. Pause*)
   Er, Jackson, wait a minute. Hold it a second. Come here a minute.
      (JACKSON *patiently gets out of the boat, elaborately pantomiming
      lowering his body into shallow water, releasing his hold on the boat,
      swimming a little distance toward shore, getting up from the shallows,
      shaking out his hair and hands, wiping his hands on his trousers,
      jumping up and down on one foot to unplug water from his clogged
      ear, seeing* HARRY, *then walking wearily, like a man who has swum
      a tremendous distance, and collapsing at* HARRY's *feet*)
   Er, Jackson. This is too humiliating. Now, let's just forget it and please
   don't continue, or you're fired.

(JACKSON *leisurely wipes his face with his hands*)

JACKSON

   It don't go so, Mr. Trewe. You know me to be a meticulous man. I didn't
   want to do this job. I didn't even want to work here. You convinced me to
   work here. I have worked as meticulously as I can, until I have been promoted. This morning I had no intention of doing what I am doing now;
   you have always admired the fact that whatever I begin, I finish. Now, I
   will accept my resignation, if you want me to, *after* we have finished this
   thing. But I am not leaving in the middle of a job, that has never been my

policy. So you can sit down, as usual, and watch me work, but until I have finished this whole business of Robinson Crusoe being in the boat

(*He rises and repeats the pantomime*)

looking at an imaginary sea bird, being shipwrecked, killing a goat, making his hat *and* this parasol, walking up the beach and finding a naked footprint, which should take me into about another ten or twelve minutes, at the most, I will pack my things and I will leave, and you can play *Robinson Crusoe* all by yourself. My plans were, after this, to take the table like this ...

(*He goes to the table, puts it upright*)

Let me show you: take the table, turn it all around, go under the table ...

(*He goes under the table*)

and this would now have become Robinson Crusoe's hut.

(*Emerges from under the table and, without looking at* HARRY, *continues to talk*)

Now, you just tell me if you think I am overdoing it, or if you think it's more or less what we agreed on?

(*Pause*)

Okay? But I am not resigning.

(*Turns to* HARRY *slowly*)

You see, it's your people who introduced us to this culture: Shakespeare, *Robinson Crusoe*, the classics, and so on, and when we start getting as good as them, you can't leave halfway. So, I will continue? Please?

HARRY

No, Jackson. You will *not* continue. You will straighten this table, put back the tablecloth, take away the breakfast things, give me back the hat, put your jacket on, and we will continue as normal and forget the whole matter. Now, I'm very serious, I've had enough of this farce. I would like to stop.

JACKSON

May I say what I think, Mr. Trewe? I think it's a matter of prejudice. I think that you cannot believe: one: that I can act, and two: that any black man should play Robinson Crusoe. A little while aback, I came out here quite calmly and normally with the breakfast things and find you almost stark naked, kneeling down, and you told me you were getting into your part. Here am I getting into *my* part and you object. This is the story ... this is history. This moment that we are now acting here is the history of imperialism; it's nothing less than that. And I don't think that I can—should—concede my getting into a part halfway and abandoning things, just because you, as my superior, give me orders.

People become independent. Now, I could go down to that beach by myself with this hat, and I could play Robinson Crusoe, I could play Columbus, I could play Sir Francis Drake, I could play anybody discovering anywhere, but I don't want you to tell me when and where to draw the line!

(*Pause*)

Or what to discover and when to discover it. All right?

HARRY

Look, I'm sorry to interrupt you again, Jackson, but as I—you know—was watching you, I realized it's much more profound than that; that it could get offensive. We're trying to do something light, just a little pantomime, a little satire, a little picong. But if you take this thing seriously, we might commit Art, which is a kind of crime in this society … I mean, there'd be a lot of things there that people … well, it would make them think too much, and well, we don't want that … we just want a little … entertainment.

JACKSON

How do you mean, Mr. Trewe?

HARRY

Well, I mean if you … well, I mean. If you did the whole thing in reverse … I mean, okay, well, all right … you've got this black man … no, no … all right. You've got this man who is black, Robinson Crusoe, and he discovers this island on which there is this white cannibal, all right?

JACKSON

Yes. That is, after he has killed the goat …

HARRY

Yes, I know. I know. After he has killed the goat and made a … the hat, the parasol, and all of that … and, anyway, he comes across this man called Friday.

JACKSON

How do you know I mightn't choose to call him Thursday? Do I have to copy every … I mean, are we improvising?

HARRY

All right, so it's Thursday. He comes across this naked white cannibal called Thursday, you know. And then look at what would happen. He would have to start to … well, he'd have to, sorry … This cannibal, who is a Christian, would have to start unlearning his Christianity. He would

have to be taught ... I mean ... he'd have to be taught by this—African ...
that everything was wrong, that what he was doing ... I mean, for nearly
two thousand years ... was wrong. That his civilization, his culture, his
whatever, was ... *horrible*. Was all ... wrong. Barbarous, I mean, you
know. And Crusoe would then have to teach him things like, you know,
about ... Africa, his gods, patamba, and so on ... and it would get very,
very complicated, and I suppose ultimately it would be very boring, and
what we'd have on our hands would be ... would be a play and not a little pantomime ...

JACKSON

I'm too ambitious?

HARRY

No, no, the whole thing would have to be reversed; white would become
black, you know ...

JACKSON

(*Smiling*)
You see, Mr. Trewe, I don't see anything wrong with that, up to now.

HARRY

Well, I do. It's not the sort of thing I want, and I think you'd better clean
up, and I'm going inside, and when I come back I'd like this whole place
just as it was. I mean, just before everything started.

JACKSON

You mean you'd like it returned to its primal state? Natural? Before Crusoe finds Thursday? But, you see, that is not history. That is not the world.

HARRY

No, no, I don't give an Eskimo's fart about the world, Jackson. I just want
this little place here *cleaned up*, and I'd like you to get back to fixing the
sun deck. Let's forget the whole matter. Righto. Excuse me.

(*He is leaving.* JACKSON's *tone will stop him*)

JACKSON

Very well. So I take it you don't want to hear the song, neither?

HARRY

No, no, I'm afraid not. I think really it was a silly idea, it's all my fault,
and I'd like things to return to where they were.

JACKSON

The story of the British Empire, Mr. Trewe. However, it is too late. The history of the British Empire.

HARRY

Now, how do you get that?

JACKSON

Well, you come to a place, you find that place as God make it; like Robinson Crusoe, you civilize the natives; they try to do something, you turn around and you say to them: "You are not good enough, let's call the whole thing off, return things to normal, you go back to your position as slave or servant, I will keep mine as master, and we'll forget the whole thing ever happened." Correct? You would like me to accept this.

HARRY

You're really making this very difficult, Jackson. Are you hurt? Have I offended you?

JACKSON

Hurt? No, no, no. I didn't expect any less. I am not hurt.
(*Pause*)
I am just ...
(*Pause*)

HARRY

You're just what?

JACKSON

I am ashamed ... of making such a fool of myself.
(*Pause*)
I expected ... a little respect. That is all.

HARRY

I respect you ... I just, I ...

JACKSON

No. It's perfectly all right.
(HARRY *goes to the table, straightens it*)
I ... no ... I'll fix the table myself.
(*He doesn't move*)

I am all right, thank you. Sir.
>   (HARRY *stops fixing the table*)
>   (*With the hint of a British accent*)
>   Thank you very much.

HARRY
>   (*Sighs*)
>   I ... am sorry ... er ...

(JACKSON *moves toward the table*)

JACKSON
>   It's perfectly all right, sir. It's perfectly all ... right.
>   (*Almost inaudibly*)
>   Thank you.
>   (HARRY *begins to straighten the table again*)
>   No, thank you very much, don't touch anything.
>   (JACKSON *is up against the table.* HARRY *continues to straighten the table*)
>   Don't touch anything ... Mr. Trewe. Please.
>   (JACKSON *rests one arm on the table, fist closed. They watch each other for three beats*)
>   Now that ... is MY ORDER ...

(*They watch each other for several beats as the lights fade*)

"museum guide" from *Black Girl in Paris*

by Shay Youngblood (USA)

PARIS. SEPTEMBER 1986. Early morning. She is lying on her back in a hard little bed with her eyes closed, dreaming in French. **Langston Hughes was here.** *There is a black girl in Paris lying in a bed on the fifth floor of a hotel in the Latin Quarter. Her eyes are closed against the soft pink dawn. Delicate maps of light line her face, tattoo the palms of her hands, the insides of her thighs, the soles of her feet like lace.* **Jimmy was here.** *She sleeps while small, feminine hands plant a bomb under a seat of a train headed toward the city of Lyon.*

James Baldwin, Langston Hughes, Richard Wright, Gabriel García Márquez and Milan Kundera have all lived in Paris as if it had been a part of their training for greatness. When artists and writers spoke of Paris in their memoirs and letters home it was with reverence. Those who have been and those who still dream mention the quality of the light, the taste of the wine, the *joie de vivre*, the pleasures of the senses, a kind of freedom to be anonymous and also new. I wanted that kind of life even though I was a woman and did not yet think of myself as a writer. *I was a mapmaker.*

I remember the long, narrow room, the low slanted ceiling, the bare whitewashed walls, the spotted, musty brown carpet. To my left a cracked porcelain sink with a spigot that ran only cold water. On its ledge a new bar of soap, a blue ragged-edged washcloth shaped like a pocket, and a green hand towel. A round window at the foot of the bed looked out onto the quai St-Michel, a street that runs along the Seine, a river flowing like strong coffee through the body of Paris. The *quai* was lined with book stalls and painters with their easels and wooden plates of wet fall colors.

I am there again. It's as if I have somebody else's eyes. The Paris at the foot of my bed looks as if it were painted leaf by leaf and stone by stone with tiny brushstrokes. People dressed in dark coats hurrying along the narrow side-walks look like small black birds. Time is still when I look out at the pale, gray sky, down to the silvery river below, which by midmorning will be crowded with double-decker boats filled with tourists. In the river, on an island, I can see the somber face of Notre-Dame cathedral and farther down, an enormous, block-long, turreted, pale stone building that looks like a castle, but which I am told is part of the Palais de Justice, which houses in its basement the Conciergerie, the prison where Queen Marie Antoinette waited to have her head chopped off and the writer James Baldwin spent one night after being accused of stealing a hotel bedsheet. Even the prisons here are beautiful, and everything is so old. Back home you can see the bars on the windows of the buildings and houses, so you know that they are prisons. Sometimes bondage is invisible.

The first time I woke up in Paris I thought I'd been wounded. My body ached that first morning. My eyes, nose, and lips were puffy, as if my face had been soaked in water. My skin was dry and ashy. My joints were tight. When I stretched the full length of my body, bones popped and crunched like loose pebbles in a jar. The dream I woke up with was like a first memory, the most vivid of all the old movies that projected themselves onto the me that was. I woke up with a piece of broken glass clutched in my left hand. There was a small spot of blood on the sheets underneath me.

Before I left home I cut my hair close to my scalp so I could be a free woman with free thoughts, open to all possibilities. I was making a map of the world. In ancient times maps were made to help people find food, water, and the way back home. I needed a map to help me find love and language, and since one didn't exist, I'd have to invent one, following the trails and signs left by other travelers. I didn't know what I wanted to be, but I knew I wanted to be the kind of woman who was bold, took chances, and had adventures. I wanted to travel around the world. It was my little-girl dream.

I woke up suddenly one morning, at dawn. As the light began to bleed between the blinds into my room, the blank wall in front of me dissolved into a colorful collage by Romare Bearden of a naked black woman eating a watermelon. Against the iridescent blue background lay the outline of the city of Paris. The woman was me. This was my first sign of the unusual shape of things to come. By the time I came back to myself I was booked on an Air France flight to Paris. Paris would kill me or make me strong.

In 1924 at the age of twenty-two, Langston Hughes, *the Negro Poet Laureate of Harlem*, author of *The Big Sea*, arrived in Paris with seven dollars in his pocket. He worked as a doorman, second cook, and dishwasher at a jazz club on the rue Pigalle. He wrote blues poems and stories and lived a poet's life. He wrote about the joys of living as well as the heartache.

My name is Eden, and I'm not afraid of anything anymore. Like my literary godfathers who came to Paris before me, I intend to live a life in which being black won't hold me back.

Baldwin's prophetic essays ... *The Fire Next Time* ... *No Name in the Street* ... *Nobody Knows My Name* ... were like the sound of trumpets in my ears. Baldwin knew things that I hoped someday he would tell me. The issues in my mind were still black versus white, right versus wrong, good versus evil, and me against the world.

The spring before I arrived in Paris, the city was on alert. I cut out an article from a news magazine that listed the horrible facts: April 2, a bomb aboard a TWA plane exploded over Athens, killing four Americans; April 5, an explosion in a West Berlin disco killed an American soldier and a Turkish woman, 230 people were wounded; April 15, in retaliation, President Ronald Reagan bombed Muammar Qadaffi's headquarters in Tripoli, killing fifteen civilians. Three American hostages were killed in Lebanon in response. April 17, a British woman was arrested in London's Heathrow airport, carrying explosives planted in her luggage by her Jordanian fiancé, who had intended to blow up a Tel Aviv-bound El Al flight. Terrorism was so popular that there were full-page ads in the *International Herald Tribune* offering hijacking insurance to frequent flyers.

I was no stranger to terrorism ...

I was born in Birmingham, Alabama, where my parents witnessed the terror or eighteen bombs in six years. During that time the city was nicknamed

Bombingham. When the four little girls were killed by a segregationist's bomb at a church one Sunday morning in 1963, I had just started to write my name. I still remember writing theirs ... *Cynthia ... Addie Mae ... Carole ... Denise ...* Our church sent letters of condolence to their families. We moved to Georgia, but I did not stop being afraid of being blown to pieces on an ordinary day if God wasn't looking. I slept at the foot of my parents' bed until I was eleven years old, when my mother convinced me that the four little girls were by now colored angels and would watch over me as I slept. But I didn't sleep much, and for most of my childhood I woke up each morning tired from so much running in my dreams—from faceless men in starched white sheets, from policemen with dogs, from firemen with water hoses. I was living in two places, night and day. In the night place I ran but they never caught me, and in the morning brown angels kissed my face. I woke up with tears on my pillow.

I was no stranger to terror ...

When I was thirteen years old and living in Georgia I was in love with a girl in my class named Rosaleen and with her older brother, Anthony. Rosaleen and I played touching games in her bedroom, games she'd learned from her brother. We never spoke when we were naked and lying still on the carpet waiting for a hand to move an arm, bend a knew, for lips to kiss, for fingers to caress like feathers. We created still-life compositions with each other's pliant limbs, we were corpses, and for a few moments, a few hours, death seemed like something beautiful I wanted for the rest of my life. The fear of being caught heightened the sensations she awakened in me. Once when Anthony was home from college he sent Rosaleen downstairs to watch television, and he and I played the touching games. In Anthony's eyes I was a pretty brown-skinned girl. He whispered a continuous stream of compliments about my strange narrow eyes, my soft, still tender new breasts that filled his hands. He called me "Sugar Mama." His hands were rough, his smell musky and rank. I didn't struggle against the thick fingers that that pushed between my legs, but let the hardness search the stillness inside of me. My feelings about Rosaleen and Anthony created a confusion in me, a terror of choosing. Anthony touched my body, but Rosaleen was the one I wanted to touch me inside. I was afraid to lose Rosaleen, but eventually I did. She got pregnant by a boy she met at the county fair. The baby was sickly and soon died. Rosaleen was sent away to live with relatives in Philadelphia. I never saw her again, but I had been touched by her in a way that would make all other touches fade quickly. After Rosaleen and Anthony I was terrified that no one would ever love me again, that desire was a bubble that would burst when I touched it. Years later I met Leo, who loved my body for a while, then left me when I felt I needed him most.

A bomb can kill you instantly, love can make you wish you were dead.

Within days of my arrival in Paris four separate explosions killed three people and wounded 170. There was an atmosphere of paranoia. The tension was visible in people's eyes. Everyone was suspicious. Every abandoned bag standing alone for more than a few minutes could be filled with explosives set to kill. Anyone could be a terrorist. Bombs were exploding all over the city the fall I arrived, and that made tickets to Paris cheap and suicide unnecessary. I would become a witness. I left my body and another me took over, someone who had no fear of bombs or dying.

It is 1986. I am twenty-six years old. I have 140 dollars folded flat and pressed into my shoes between sock and sole. It is what's left of the 200 dollars I arrived with two days ago. I have no friends here and barely remember my two years of college French. I think that my ticket to Paris will be the beginning or end of me.

In 1948 James Baldwin, author of *Another Country*, then twenty-five years old, arrived in Paris with forty dollars. During the Sixties civil rights movement he led marches, protests, and voter registration drives. His angry, articulate essays on race shocked France and compelled witnesses to action. He was awarded the medal of Legion of Honor by the French government. *I was a witness.*

Josephine Baker arrived in 1935, at age eighteen. She danced naked except for a string of bananas around her waist, sang the "Marseillaise" in beaded gowns, and was decorated by the French government for her efforts during World War II. She created a new tribe in her château with children from every ethnic group. Like the character she played in the film *Princess Tam Tam*, she represented to the French the exotic black, sexually independent woman who could learn to speak French and pick up enough manners to dine with royalty.

I was transformed.

Bricktop arrived penniless and taught Paris how to dance the Charleston. Richard Wright was already a celebrity; he joined the French intellectuals and gave voice to the Negro problem in America. There were others and there will be more. My heroes. They dared to make a way where there was none, and I want to be just like them.

I was born again.

This is the place where it happened, where it will happen again.

For once I slept without dreaming. I woke up when the plane touched down on the runway and heard the entire cabin clap and cheer the pilot and crew for our safe landing. As we taxied along the runway I pulled my small French-English dictionary out of my bag to look up in the phrase section how to take a cab. Across the aisle from me was a young woman who had slept through most of the flight. She was blonde with olive skin and had a long face and pretty features. She wore jeans and a black sweater and held a Museum of Modern Art gift bag in one hand and a large Louis Vuitton satchel on her lap. The satchel looked real, not like the imitations everyone at home wanted. I assumed she was American.

"It's my first time in Paris. What's the best way to get to the city? Is there a bus?"

"We can share a taxi if you like. Where are you going?" Her French accent was a surprise.

"I don't know. I was going to ask the driver for a hotel. I don't have much money."

She looked at me as if I was crazy.

"You don't know anyone?"

I shook my head.

"It will be very difficult to find something not expensive." She pursed her lips and blew into the air, a French gesture I would come to recognize and imitate. She said that the students would be arriving for classes that week.

"Many of the hotels not too dear will be ... *complet*. You understand?"

I quickly flipped through my dictionary and learned that the hotels would be full, no vacancies.

"My name is ... *Je m'appelle Eden.*"

"Delphine. Come," she commanded. We got up and joined the line of passengers exiting the plane. Charles de Gaulle airport was a maze of lines, people talking fast, signs I couldn't understand, and everywhere, guards carrying machine guns and holding fierce-looking dogs on short leashes. Then I began to be a little afraid of what I had done. I didn't know anyone, my French was practically nonexistent, and I had only enough money to last a few weeks until I found a job. But there was no going back. I took a deep breath and followed Delphine to baggage claim. I was relieved to see my duffel bag circle round in front of me. We stood in long, crooked lines in customs. One for citizens of France and several for everyone else. I gave Delphine twenty dollars to change into francs for me. She said she would meet me outside. When she was out of sight I had the fleeting thought that at home I would never be stupid enough to give a stranger money and watch her walk away, but I was in Paris and I was giving myself up to new angels.

When I offered up my passport, the customs officer, who had had a dry, grim expression for all the passengers before me, looked at me, then back at my passport. He scanned my short natural hair, high forehead, slow, sleepy eyes, broad nose, and full lips, as if to make sure the brown-skinned girl in his hands was me. He pushed my passport toward me and startled me by speaking in English. "Welcome to France, mademoiselle. Enjoy your visit."

During the ride to the city Delphine told me that she was a student at the "Science Po," the Ecole des Sciences Politiques, which I later learned was comparable to Harvard. She wanted to be a lawyer and in the current term she was studying English. When I told her I was a writer her eyes grew large and she could not hide her admiration, as if seeing in me something special she had not noticed before.

"I admire the dedication of the artist, but nothing is certain for you. I am not so brave." She looked out the window.

I did not feel brave, there was nothing else I thought I could do or that held my interest in the same way. The taxi was an old white Mercedes with a gray leather interior. The driver looked African and spoke French. We had loaded our bags in the trunk and got inside. Delphine had given the driver an address and instructions in rapid French. We sat in silence looking out at early morning Paris. The cars on the highway seemed to go faster than in the States. I was so tired I kept nodding off. When the taxi stopped on busy rue de l'Université, in front of a photography shop, I opened my wallet and Delphine took out some of the bills she had exchanged for me and added some of her own.

She pointed out the Sorbonne from the foot of the hill before we turned into the lobby of her apartment building. I followed her up four flights of stairs. She opened the door onto a small studio with high ceilings and cream-colored walls that made the room seem much bigger than it really was. Books and a small compact-disc collection lined the longest wall in the small but neat room, a high-tech stereo system and a small TV found space there as well. A bare desk sat in front of the windows, overlooking the street. Two double futons were stacked on top of each other in a corner. The most beautiful feature of the room was the set of tall French windows covered by metal shutters. Delphine opened the windows, letting in the light and noise of the street below. I went to the windows and looked down into the street. I saw a shop displaying cartons of brightly colored fruit, a florist's shop with spring in huge vivid bouquets that brightened the gray morning. She pointed me in the direction of the toilet. The bathroom fixtures were odd and ancient-looking. I did not recognize my face in the smoky gilt-framed mirror above the wide porcelain sink. There were dark circles under my eyes and my hair was so short. It was still me, a new me in a new place ready to begin again. I felt lost. After my father's funeral I felt as if I were drifting inside, as if anyone could disappear. Few things were certain. *My father was dead.*

Delphine made us strong cups of coffee in the tiny red-and-white kitchen area—miniature appliances lined up under tall cabinets. Stale bread crumbs were scattered over the counter, a knife left sticking out of a pot of butter. We added sugar to the coffee and drank it black from heavy yellow bowls.

"What will you do?" she asked, sitting crosslegged on the futons next to me.

"I thought I could look for a job as a secretary or an au pair." I sipped the coffee and felt the caffeine spreading through my chest.

"I have heard the American Church has a place to look for jobs. I can check the newspaper for you. There is a black American writer who is every day at a bookstore close to here. He might help you. I think he is a poet.

Delphine made two phone calls, then we left the apartment to look for a room. Her apartment was in the heart of the Latin Quarter, near the boulevard St-Michel. The streets were filled with people even though it was still early in the morning. Delphine was right, the less expensive hotels in the guidebook were *complet*, and I could not afford the more expensive ones. I could see that she felt pity for me and that she was determined to help me. Perhaps she thought an artist who was destined for a life of poverty needed all the help she could get. It started to rain, and as we were walking along the Seine back to her apartment I saw a hotel with a tiny sign in the window. By some miracle they had one room left, for about thirty-five dollars a night. We were told that it did not have a toilet, I'd have to share one on the floor below, and if I wanted to take a shower it would cost me about three dollars. The shower was in a stone cubicle in the basement. The clerk was a young man who, when he realized I was American, began speaking to me in English. This was a small relief to me, knowing I'd soon be on my own. I agreed without even seeing the room. I only hoped it had a view. It was not far from Delphine's apartment. She helped me carry by bags back to the hotel.

Delphine gave me her phone number and told me to call her when I was settled. She was going away to visit her sister in Lyon for a week until school started. Her cousin Jean-Michel would be in her apartment until she returned and spoke a little English, so if I needed help I was to call him. I reached out to hug her but she leaned only her face toward me. She kissed me on each cheek and wished me *bonne chance*. She was the one who would need the luck. The very next day a bomb was found on a train headed toward Lyon. It was defused and no one was hurt, but it was only the first sign of more danger to come.

Suddenly it was night, and I was far from home and completely alone. The little room at the top of the stairs was not decorated with a chandelier, gold-leafed antiques, and a canopy bed covered in delicate lace as I'd imagined, but I was thankful to have a place indoors to sleep. On the floor at the foot of the bed were my green duffel bag and a black canvas backpack, which contained everything I owned. A tiny book of Bible verses the size of a matchbook, a *1968 Frommer's Guide to Paris* I'd stolen from the public library. I knew all the major attractions by heart. I used the guide as a dream journal, writing between the lines. Between the pages I found poems and movie stubs and photographs. There was the gold pen from Dr. Bernard, three sharp number two pencils, a red Swiss army knife, seven pairs of white cotton panties, two pairs of white socks and one pair of black tights, a navy blue sweater and a pair of black jeans, a fat, palm-sized French-English dictionary, and a new address book with three addresses written in it. On the chair next to the sink, a pair of black stretch pants, a pair of gold hoop earrings, a watch with a thick brown leather band, a green trench coat from a military surplus store, and underneath the chair, a pair of black leather sneakers.

Je m'appelle Eden. Je suis une ... writer." The new me tried to impress a scratched mirror. I couldn't remember the French word for writer. *Ecrivain.* I said other things in French and practiced forgetting my old life.

My mother told me that she found me lying there, like a lost book or a forgotten hat. Found me crying, hungry, wet, and cold, wrapped in newspaper at the bottom of a brown paper bag in the bathroom of a Greyhound bus station. My father confirmed her story.

"*Who am I?*"

"Mama's little girl."

"*Who am I?*"

"Daddy's African princess."

"*How do you know for sure?*"

I discovered that nothing is ever certain. A name, a birthday, an entire life can be invented, and that being so, can be changed. I intended to change all the ordinary things about myself. When I began to write I kept secret diaries, writing between the lines of books my father found in the trash at work. Books on law and economics, typewriter manuals. I wrote about the life I lived in the night place, where I traveled as far as the stars. Before I could speak my father read to me from his found books, sounding out each word as if it were an island, as if either of us understood. Having learned to read so late in life he valued books as treasures of knowledge waiting to be unlocked.

When I was four years old my parents told me that I was an orphan. My parents were orphans too. They found each other in church one Sunday. Hermine was a big-boned, sturdy, pecan-colored woman, with green eyes and gray hair she kept braided and wrapped around her head. She taught Prior Walker how to read the Bible, and in return he worshiped her. He was small for a man, with thick, callused hands, and balding by the time he was twenty-three. She was a seamstress in a blue-jean factory, and he was a custodian at a bank. They were old, like grandparents. Kind and patient, hardworking Christians. They were alone in the world until they found me. Their family, and therefore mine, was the church. We were happy together. They called me Eden. I made dresses for my dolls, but I was more interested in reading books and writing poems than sewing. One summer Hermine and I pieced together a quilt made from scraps of clothes Prior and Hermine had worn out or I had outgrown. She called it the family circle quilt. The center image was three interlocking circles. She cried when it was done and sewed a lock of hair from each of us into three corners of the quilt, and in the fourth corner she sewed a secret. She folded the quilt into quarters and packed it into the cedar chest at the foot of her bed. In winter when it was time for me to go to sleep, she pulled the covers up around my chin.

"When you have a family you can put your baby to sleep under your family circle."

"My baby will have pretty dreams," I said stroking the lines of thread so lovingly handstitched.

"As long as Singer makes sewing machines, we'll get by," Hermine always said. The old machine she had must have been one of the first Singers, made in the late 1800s. She had a new electric model my father had bought her for her birthday, but for the quilt we used the one her mother left her before she died. Hermine told me the same story about how her life began over and over again. At the age of two she had been left on the doorstep of a colored orphanage along with a note and the old Singer sewing machine in its case next to where she lay asleep. This was all she knew, but her life was full of stories she made up as she went along.

The only other family we had was Aunt Victorine, my mother's best friend and mine. On the first Saturday morning of each month she used to take me for blessings to the Church of Modern Miracles, where we both pretended she was my mother. When we were together she called me Daughter and I called her Mother, and that was one of our secrets. Aunt Vic had never married and was childless, and in her way adopted me so that I had two mothers. She had something to do with my wanting to go to Paris. From the time she showed me on a map she drew with a broken pencil on her kitchen wall and told me that black people were free in Paris. Free to live where you wanted, work where you were qualified, and love whom you pleased. At least that was the rumor she had heard. One of her friends in Chicago, where she had grown up, had a sister, an opera singer who went to Paris and married a white man. The opera singer became famous in Europe. According to Aunt Vic the white folks in America didn't want us to know about that kind of living, where a colored person could socialize and marry whom they wanted whether they were white or black, Chinese or Hindu. If she could have chosen, Aunt Vic surely would not have chosen to be a maid for most of her life. She worked two days a week for a rich white doctor in Green Island Hills. That was freedom to her, to choose the life you wanted to live.

"And who would not choose to live well?" Aunt Vic said.

Aunt Vic's stories about Paris had sounded like fantasies. She talked about it as if it were a made-up place. If Paris was a real place, I wanted to go.

"Every day you ought to learn something new, Daughter," Aunt Vic said. I tried to learn new things, and I wrote them down like recipes between the lines of my found books.

I would go to stay with Aunt Vic, who returned me home Sunday morning ready for Sunday school with Hermine and Prior. I slept through most of Sunday morning sermons at the First African Baptist Missionary Church, where the service was orderly, the hymns hushed, and the service short, and nobody cried too loud or shouted that the Holy Ghost had them by the collar. There was no dancing in the aisles. At the Church of Modern Miracles there was a three-piece band—drums, electric organ, and electric guitar—and several ladies in the front row who shook tambourines and their ample hips and tremulous breasts all through the service. People shouted, praised God so their prayers could be heard above the sins of the city, were possessed by the Holy Spirit, who took over their bodies, shaking them with emotion and filling their eyes with tears and their throats with hallelujahs. I could use my voice strong and was put in the young people's choir. Soon I was singing a solo almost every Saturday morning. And Aunt Victorine had me performing at the age of six in juke joints on dirt roads for miles around almost every Saturday night. After midnight, when a juke joint was most crowded, some cigar-smelling man would lift me up onto a table in the middle of the room and somebody else would unplug the jukebox. Sometimes there would be a pianist or a guitar player to accompany me. I would sing songs I'd heard on Aunt Vic's record player. Aunt Vic taught me how to lift the hem of my dress and dance at the end of the song like Josephine Baker and the French can-can dancers who looked so glamorous in the photographs she showed me. The audience would throw handfuls of change and crumpled dollar bills at my dancing feet. I loved the attention. I dreamed about doing the can-can in Paris. If Mama hadn't found out when I was thirteen, I might've become a star on the dirt-floor circuit. Instead I started taking classical voice lesson from a mean old Creole woman who used to be an entertainer. Her long black curls left greasy spots on the collars of her old-fashioned quilted pastel dressing gowns. Miss Candy shouted at me in Creole when I forgot the words to a song. I didn't like her and the lessons didn't last long. Aunt Vic didn't speak to Mama for a long time. She was mad at losing all that income from my singing. And she missed me as much as I missed her. Low lights, Aunt Vic's copper-colored lipstick, and the sparkling dresses she let me borrow to perform in made me dream of a kind of life different from the life I was living. I made maps in my mind that would lead to other worlds.

Aunt Vic loved to be read to. She had grown up in Chicago and still had a subscription to the *Chicago Defender* so she could keep up with the community even though she had left under duress. The circumstances of her leaving the North many years before remained a mystery to me even though I asked her every time she started talking about the old days. Once I got her to admit her leaving had something to do with a man she didn't care to dance with, a gangster who owned the club she worked in. Aunt Vic loved Langston Hughes's Simple stories, which were published in the *Chicago Defender* from 1943 to 1966, Aunt Vic said. His main character, Jesse B. Simple, was everyman, every black man, and she loved him.

"Jesse B. Simple is real, I think that's a real person. I knew somebody just like that back in Chicago. Munro Fish, a sweet-talking jailbird who truly believed that someday he would run for a government office. He had it all figured out just like Simple. Always talking about race."

She had collected all the stories. She cut them out of the newspaper, and every once in a while she would pull them out and I'd read to her. The language was a little salty, but Mama wasn't around to get holy. Simple would talk about having Indian blood, and Aunt Vic would add her commentary.

"Like what Southern Negro don't claim that?" She would laugh. We would start packing our bags when he talked about all the colored people in Harlem. She would start singing about speakeasies and going up to Harlem like we were hearing the story for the first time.

The stories made us laugh and feel like we knew what was going on in the world, and we had a lot of our own opinions about that.

Aunt Vic showed me pictures of her old life as a dancer, the girls who went to France, and Josephine Baker, who was to her a symbol of complete freedom. I made up stories and acted out little dramas for my parents, playing all the parts myself. I wrote sad poems about orphans, and I moved through my life taking pictures with a toy camera, recording things in my mind, writing them down between the lines of other books. One day I made up my mind that I would go to Paris to be free.

When I was thirteen my parents gave me a typewriter, for which they had made many sacrifices. I typed my first novel in fourteen days. I wrote all the stories I knew and made up new ones. I typed them and put them in my library, a small bookshelf next to my bed that my father had made and my mother had painted yellow. By then I was reading in the adult section of the library and was certain after reading Langston Hughes's autobiography, *The Big Sea*, that I wanted to be a writer and feast at the banquet of life. Going to Paris would be an hors d'oeuvre. I kept my thoughts pressed between the lines of biology texts and biographies of dead presidents that no one else ever checked out anyway.

Nice: A Monologue

by Mustapha Matura (Trinidad/Britain)

A prison canteen (tables, chairs etc.). In it a black man in uniform. He is thirty-five to forty years old. He is sweeping/wiping and speaks directly to the audience.

MAN. Wen a come off de boat de customs man was nice ter me, so i was nice back ter him, but a friend of mine who come ter meet me say, boy yer shouldn't be so nice ter dem, dey do' like we, but i say nar man it en so, it en so at all, wen people nice ter yer, you must be nice back ter dem, and if yer want people ter be nice ter you, you must be nice ter dem, but anyhow he say a was foolish an a go fine out, but a was nice ter he so de next day he carry me down ter de exchange dey call it, and de man dey was nice ter me too, so a was nice back ter him, so wen dey give me dis job sweeping out a office, i say tank you ter de man, an he say tank you back ter me but me friend say a shouldn't say tank you ter him, but i say de man say tank you ter me so i say tank you back ter him, an i tell him if yer want people ter say tank you ter you you have ter say tank you ter dem, but he say how a was wrong, but i say nar man, i en wrong i rite, den he say how i stupid, but anyhow a say tank you ter him, so de next night he carry me ter a night club, where dey had some girls dancing with coloured men, de first time a see a white woman dance wit coloured man, and dey en dancing straight an back yer know, dey dancing wit dey bottom all over de place, so i say boy dis is de place fer me, so a went up an ask one a de girls nice fer a dance an she dance wit me an it was a good dance an we had a good time, but me friend pull me aside an say boy, how a go teach yer ter live in dis country wen yer do' listen ter me, yer mustn't be nice ter dem, dey do' want yer ter be nice ter dem, but i say nar man, dat en true because i was nice ter she an she was nice back ter me, but he say de same ting again dat i go fine out, so a miss a dance trying ter fine out, but a en fine out notting, so a went back an ask she ter dance an she say yes an we dance again, but a notice me friend wasn't dancing at all, so a say he must be en feel like dancing or maybe he foot hurting him, so anyhow wen de club start ter close me friend come pulling me saying le we go, le we go, but i say nar man, i go ask de lady ter go home wit she an see wha she say, but me friend say dey do' want we in de house much less in dey bed, he say dey only like ter dance wit we an get hot ter go an heat up de white boys, but i say nar man, dat en true, because i know dat if you heat up someting is you have ter eat it but he say i en know dese woman an i en go get notting off she and dat if a go wit she, in de morning she go cry out an say a hypnotise she an rape she, but i say nar man, it en so if a woman heat you up she heat you up fer a reason, an de reason is because she want you ter burn she, but he say i is a idiot an a go fine out but anyhow a ask she nicely ter come home wit she an she say yes, so a leave me friend outside de club, an me an she went home an had a nice time an in de morning she en cry out an bawl rape or anyting she just say she have ter go ter work an if a does go ter de club often, she go see me again, so i say yes a does go sometimes an a hope a go see she again, an she say she hope so too, so a went outside an a did'nt even know where a was but a ask a policeman nice an he tell me how ter catch a bus back ter me friend's house, boy wen a tell me friend wha happen yer shoulda see de man, de man went mad, de man start ter cuss me an call me all kinda names an tell me a shouldn't ask no policeman notting dat if yer ask dem anyting an dey fine out yer new dey go lock yer up fer someting, but i say nar man, if yer want ter fine out anyting is a policeman ter ask an if yer ask dem nice dey go answer yer back nice but he say a go fine out, but i say how a go fine out he just say a go fine out, but anyhow a was nice ter him so he take me ter de pub wit him, so wen we get inside de pub, i say le me buy de drinks, he say no, a mustn't buy drinks fer people, a must le dem buy de own drinks if a buy drinks fer dem dey go tink a stupid an drink up all me money, but i say nar man, it en so, if yer buy people drink dey go buy yer back a drink, but he say de same ting again how a foolish an how a go fine out, an if a don't hear a go feel, so anyhow dey had a white man stanning up next ter me so a buy him a drink an he buy me back a drink, so a say well if he buy me back a drink, a have ter buy he back a drink an so it go on until me friend say yer see wha a tell yer de man go drink out all yer money but i say nar man, dat en go happen, but anyhow he say he going next door ter de betting shop an wen a ready ter go come fer him, so wen time come fer de pub ter close de white man a tink he name was Fred, Fred tell me he have a bet ter put on, dat he get some tip from some horse's mouth an if a have any money ter put it on it, so we went next door an put on de bet, a notice me friend wasn't looking too happy, so a say wha wrong man, he say he lost all he money, so i say well, look de man just give me a tip an he say ter put all yer money on it, but he say dey en go give no coloured man horse ter back on, because dey en want ter see no coloured man win money,

so i say nar man, because he just put he own money on it, but he say
da is a trick ter fool me, but i say he fool he self because he put more
money dan me, anyhow de horse come twenty ter one so i en do bad
at all anyhow a give me friend a five pound note an we went home wen
we get dey who could be waiting fer we but de girl from de club, de
same girl a meet last night, she say how she pass in ter see if a was
going ter de club later, a musta tell she where a was living, but i say
well if yer going ter de club ter night yer might as well stay here an wen
time come fer we ter go we could go together so she come inside an
me friend say dat if people see she come after work dey go say dat she
working fer me, but i say nar man, dey car say dat, i only meet she last
night how dey go say dat, but he say a go fine out an dat he going an
see a film round de corner, now dat surprise me because i know he
wasn't no theatre man, but a say he must be feeling lonely so anyhow
de girl take off she shoes and start ter clean up de place, an wen she
done she say wha we have ter eat, i tell she notting, she say not ter
worry dat she go round de corner and get someting, so i say da is
awright wit me, so she went, wen she come back de woman cook one
food, pardner a never know white woman could cook so, so a say dat
dis woman is someting boy, an den after we finish eat she take off all
she clothes an say she want de same dat a give she last night, so i say
awright an a give she it an we had a nice time man, wen time come fer
we ter go to de club she say she tired so i say well le we stay here so she
say right she is awright wit she, so da is how we spend de night, i en
even know what time me friend come in, wen he com in i en even hear
im a just feel im trying ter pull de girl in he half a de bed, but she
musta be too heavy fer he, because he give up quick, but in de morning a went ter work an leave she dey wit him so i en know wha happen wen a come back home de night an tell de man wat a nice foreman a had yer shoulda see de man go mad, just like wid de policeman
so ter change de subject, a ask him wha bout de girl if she get out
awright he say yes but a shouldn't tink de foreman nice because de en
nice an dat he job is ter make coloured people work hard, but i say nar
man, dat en true dem have ter work hard too, but he say is a different
kinda work, but i say work is work an if yer working someplace wit
people yer have ter be nice wit dem, but he say how a go learn, an how
de girl leave a message saying how she go be at de club ter night an dat
i must come, so a tell im tank yer, but boy a was feeling so tired i say
i en going ter no club ternight he say, yer see how tired yer is, is because de foreman working yer hard, but i know a was tired fer somet-

ing else, but he say it was de formen so i en say notting, anyhow bout twelve a clock de door bell start ter ring, who it could be but de girl, de same girl from de club, de girl who come home here an cook me a meal, she say she en see me in de club an she come ter see if anyting wrong wit me, but i say nar man, nottin en wrong i just taking a rest da is all, so a ask she if she want ter come in an stay, but she and me friend say de same ting, she say she en want ter stay, an me friend say he en want she ter stay, so a figure dey musta have a row or someting anyhow a put on me clothes an went round by she an we had a good time again, wen a come back from work dat night, me friend say boy, wha yer doing de woman go kill yer, i say nar man, she en go kill me, den he say dem white woman could take more man dan we know so den i ask him how he go feel, if a move out because is me an he was paying de rent, well boy de man went mad again, just like wit de policeman, an wit de foreman, he start ter cuss me an say how a ungrateful, an how is he who look after me wen a first come ter dis country, an is my people beg him ter look out ter fer me, an how now i want ter left him in a lurch, boy a never see a man go so crazy, an den he ask me if a moving in wit de girl, so i tell im a wasn't sure as yet but a was tinking of it, well is den he start ter cuss me, and buse me, well boy wha a could do, but say tank yer fer looking after me but i en want yer ter look after me no more, an a go pack up an leave by ter night, but yer see deep down inside i know he was a nice guy, because he en charge me no rent fer de four days a stay by he, anyhow a move in wit dis girl, well it was awright wen we first start, but den de woman start ter do all kinda a ting like tell me how a mustn't wear sock in bed, i tell she a cole, and how a mustn't wear me pajamas under me clothes, again a tell she it cole, but like she en hear an how i mustn't be nice ter de woman next door, an one set a i must do dis an i mustn't do dis, so i tell she nar man, dat en go happen because fer one ting wen it a cole me en want ter take off no pajamas is den yer go catch cole, but she en listen, she tell me i stupid and i en know bout dis country, an dat de woman next door go believe i after someting because i so nice ter her, but i tell she nar man it en so, is wen yer nice ter people dey go be nice ter you, but den she come like me friend she call me idiot an burke a was going an tell she me name wasn't burke but a was too tired, so anyhow one day wen a come home from work, just as a reach de top a de stairs, who should come outa she door but de woman from next door, so i give she a howdy like a does do anytime a does she, anyhow dis time she ask me if a have a shilling fer de meter, well a tell she i en have no shilling on me but a have one inside on de mantlepiece, she say go in fer it, so i say awright, an a open de door, soon as de woman come in de room, de woman start ter get on, de woman start ter tell me all kinda ting like how i so nice and she like me because i so nice, so i tell she i tink she nice too, an yer no wat de next ting a know is me an de woman having a nice time on de bed, den de woman start ter bawl an groan like she never want ter stop, so me en stop she, de next ting a know is de door bust open and who should come in but, de girl who a living wit, de same girl from de club, well boy a never jump so fast, but it en me she go fer is de woman next door, both a dem start ter cuss one another an row a never know white woman could cuss so much, de girl tell de woman how she is a hoe, an de woman tell de girl how she is a slut, and how she wouldn't push me with a barge pole, and how is me who pull she in de room and give she an aspirin an take advantage a she headache, so boy yer could imagine de fix a in, so right dere an den a say de best ting ter do is go, so whilst both a dem rowing a pick up me bag and put me clothes in it, an as a hit de door, de girl turn round an notice a going, she say wha yer going, a say a going an stay wit me friend, boy de girl start ter cry an break down an tell me all kinda ting like how she love me an she car live witout me an how if a left she go kill she self, well boy dat slow me down, but is wen she tell me she go do anyting fer me den a stop, well by den de woman from next door gone, after a tell she tank you fer coming in, an she tell me tanks fer de shilling, so den de girl tell me how she go look after me an make sure i en have ter work because she know i en like ter go ter work in de cole, well she was right dey, an another ting is she say she go bring enough money fer both a we, well boy wha a could say ter dat, a tell she tanks dat da is awright wit me, an she say awright too as long as a do' leave, well a put down me bag an is den she start ter tell me how she love me an how no man ever please she like how i please she, so anyhow tings start ter go good a went in an tell de foreman tank you fer de job an how a go be leaving soon an he say well how he go miss me an how it was nice having me work fer him, an ting, so pardner tings start ter get good de girl start ter work so hard dat after a while a never get ter see she, she go out ter work an wen she come back she sleep, but i didn't mind so much because everytime she come in she used ter bring in one set a five pound notes a never see so much money in me life, boy a tell yer i'd go outside an spend an spend an de money still wouldn't done, so after awhile a start ter save it, anyhow a didn't mind not seeing she so much because de woman from next door used ter cook me food an bring it in an me an she use ter have a good time, so a couldn't complain too much, now de next ting a know is she too say she want ter go out an work fer me because she could do better dan de girl, an how she have more contacts an she could work harder, so i say awright den give it a try no harm in trying an see if yer like it, so anyhow she look happy wen a tell she dat, but de only ting was worrying me is who go cook me food, because wit both a dem out a go starve, but anyhow a say well if tings turn out so wha a go do, but as soon as a say dat wat should happen but a knock on de door, an who it could be but de landlady she say she come ter collect some rent, so i tell she hold on a minute an le me open de door well she come in de room ter collect she rent but i feel she come in ter look around, so i en say notting because is she place an if she wnat ter look around an see wha going on she have a right ter do dat, anyhow we sit down talking an de next ting a know is how she start ter tell me bout she husband an how bad he does treat she an how he do give she notting so i say well some man like dat an she say how i nice an how i understand an how she feel she could talk ter me, so i say tank you because if people feel dey could talk ter you dey must be like you, so boy we sit down dey talking, all morning an den she say well is lunch time an she have ter go down and cook an how nice it was talking ter me an she sorry how she take up all me time, but i tell she nar man, it en so is awright i enjoy it so den she say how she go make up fer it by bringing some lunch fer me so i say awright den if da is what yer want ter do, do nottin else, so anyhow she bring up de lunch and a must say she cooking wasn't so hot but i tell she it taste nice an she like dat because de next ting she do is ter give me a hug an a kiss, so i say well if yer want ter give me a hug an kiss, i want ter give you a hug an kiss too, well she say she would like dat because is a long time no man hug she an kiss she, not because no man en want ter do it but because she en want any kinda man ter do it, de man she want ter do it must be a nice man, an he must be a kind man an he must understand she well i tell she she right ter want dat an anyhow me an she had a good time man, everyday she used ter cook me food an come up an me an she would have a good time until she husband come home from work den a wouldn't see she but a would know she was dey because sometimes she would start singing, i love you baby, an i need you baby, an sometimes she would collect de rent in de morning an put it back under de door in de evening, so i know she was dere, anyhow one day me an she husband was talking an he say how dat he always wanted ter go ter de West Indies because de people always so happy an nice so i tell im dat if he tink de people so nice over here he should go down dere an he go see how nice dey really is an i even tell him how if he go down dere he could stay with my people an dem an he say how nice dat was an tank me an ting, so after dat me an he was de best a friend an he used ter ask me tings like he hope he wife singing do' bodder me an i know how woman was, i say nar man, i do' mind i like she singing an i glad ter hear people singing, because wen dey do dat it mean dey happy, an i like ter know people happy, an is a funny ting because den he used ter get serious but den he would start smiling again, so he was awright an yer know someting he never used ter take me ter he pub but everytime he come back he used ter bring me a Guinness, yer could beat dat everytime like de sun rise, but a never fine out wha he used ter mean by do kill meself Guinness car kill, but anyhow he was me mate, de first mate a ever had, anyhow yer see how some people could be nice, so one day a buy one a dem Jaguar cars an who a should see crossing de road in front a me, right cross me bonnet but me friend, me same friend who meet me off de boat, so i say wha happening man, how life treating yer, he say not bad he still trying he luck wit de horses an dem but it look like i doing awright, so i say nar man, it might look so but i still paying rent an dat en so good, but he say well a look like a doing better dan he, so a telling him he must be backing de wrong horses, a tought i'd give him a joke an cheer him up yer know, but anyhow he en get no happier so a say i'd buy him a drink like old times, anyhow dat brighten him up a bit, so we went in a pub, wen we get inside de pub, de man start ter tell me he troubles how he was living wit some woman an how de woman take all he clothes an sell dem, an how he en have no money an no where ter live, so i say well boy yer could come an stay by me till tings get fer de better an he fine somewhere of he own, well is den he get bright because de next ting a know is he en finish he beer, de first time a ever see him en finish a whole beer, but anyhow we go home by he an pick up he few tings an a take him round by me, but it hit me dat my girl en like him, so she en go want him sleeping wit we so what a go do, anyhow a know de landlady had a room going spare so a wasn't worried, anyhow wen a get dey a call she aside an explain de position ter she an she say is awright if is a friend a mine, but boy some people de more yer do ter help dem is de more dey let yer down, no sooner dan de man get in de house de man want ter know where all de meters is an wha kinda locks dey have on dem, yer could beat dat, so i say well look man, yer get a room, yer get a food, well take it easy, rest yer body an see how tings go ner, but nar, he say i soft, i en have no brains, i car see further dan me eye, an i en have no business brains, so i say well if is meter yer looking ter teef from he en have no brains, because if yer teef dey go lock yer up, so better dan dey lock yer up, here look some money from we wen yer get a job pay me back, well boy if yer see de man grab de money, no sooner a take de money out me pocket, is was in he hand, so he was awright but de next ting a know is he trying ter pull de landlady in he room, one night de same one who does sing i love you baby, an i need you baby, she say she en give im no cause ter pull she in he room, but i en so sure, yer do know how people does take tings, a mean ter say he hear she singing i love you baby, i need you baby, he must be tink is he she talking bout, yer car blame de guy, so i say well look if is woman yer want why yer do ask dem nice ter give yer a piece he say he do ask no woman fer notten an he en asking no woman nice fer notten wat he want he go take an wen he want a woman he go take she, so i say look pardner it en so it go, dat if he ask he never ter know he might get it, but anyhow he en listen, so de next ting a hear is he go in de woman next ter me room and smelling up all she panties, so i see him an a say ter him look ner man, if is a woman yer want ask me an a go get one fer yer, he say he en want no woman, woman is trouble, now dat start me tinkin because one minute he pulling de landlady in he room an de next he saying he en want no woman so wha he up to, so i say well look here i go give yer some money go an look fer yer own place de man start ter cry an beg me ter let him stay saying i is de only friend he ever had an how i treat him so good an how he shame he try ter take advantage a he position wit me, so i say nar man da is awright, as long as yer behave yer self an he say he go do dat so da was awright yer know wat happen, yer know what de man do wen a tell yer some man bad bad dey bad yer now, de man go down stairs an tell de landlady husband how i an she carrying on but he en know i an he was mate so he come an tell me an we had a good laugh, but en satisfy wit dat he go an tell de police how i living off prostitute not one but two prostitute, an i living off de immoral earnings, well anyhow wen de police come ter see me, de police start ter laugh because he car see how a guy like me could have not one but two woman on de road fer him an he sorry dat he had ter trouble me so much, so i say a sorry dat he had trouble too, because wen people nice ter you, you must be nice back ter dem, so de police leave but de man en sat-

isfy wit dat yer know wha he do, i en know where he get de letter form
from he write me modder an de woman a was living wit back home
an tell dem, wait fer it, he tell dem how, boy some man malicious yer
know, he tell dem how i doing well an how i making a lot of money,
and how i have me own house an ting, well de next ting is dey write
me after all yer car blame dem dey hear dey boy making money so dey
bound ter write, well anyhow dey write me an say how as a doing so
well if a could send fer dem, well wha a go do a say awright, as man,
a have ter send fer dem, after all, a mean ter say so anyhow i went
round de corner an buy a house, an a send fer dem, so all a dem come
me modder de woman a was living wit an me four children, Clarice,
Claudine, Clarissa, an' Claude, move in ter de house round de corner,
a used ter sleep dey nights an tell dem a had a work ter do at de other
house, so tings start ter go good, me modder start ter do some cleaning an me woman start ter take in some washing an make some plans
ter open she own launderette, so who could complain, but boy wen a
tell yer dis life funny it funny yer know so tings start ter go good, wen
de next ting a hear is me friend want ter see me so i say awright, but
he round de corner, yer know, an he en a three penny bus ride away,
nar man de man in Brixton Prison, so a get me forms ter visit wen a
get dey, de first ting de man say is how a doing, so i say yer bring me
all dis way ter ask me how a doing, but he say nar man, dat en what
he want ter see me for, he say he want me ter pay a fine fer him, so i
say well da is awright, how much it is, well he say is only twenty
pounds, it turn out he break a meter an dey charge im twenty pounds
an he couldn't pay so dey trow him inside, so i pay de fine an dey let
im out, but dat en all de man want me find place fer him ter live, so i
say awright, a go do dat a figure prison must a change him, put some
sense in him, so a give im a room in de house me modder an dem was
living in, a figure me modder could keep an eye on him during de day
an i could watch im during de night, an a tell im, a say if a only catch
yer near me meter, is out yer going, friend or no friend, but he say nar
man, dat en go happen, he change, he en go do dat kinda ting again,
how he could do a ting lik dat ter me after a so nice ter him, an how
if people nice ter yer yer must be nice ter dem, so a jump, but den a
say he must be really change a mean ter say, ter hear him say a ting like
dat, an a have ter believe im, after all is a ting i say meself, so a say well
he really learn now, he really get de message, well boy tings start ter
go good, a get me children in a school, me woman open she laun-
drette, an de man en even going near me meters, if he want ter go ter

de WC in de back just not ter pass de meter, de man going through de front door an going round, just not ter pass me meters, da is ter tell yer how good de man get, an he get nice, he get nice ter everybody, he start ter say tank you, ter everybody, an smiling ter everybody, an dat en all he get a job as a nightwatchman in a factory an he even come home an say how nice de foreman is, yer could beat dat, well he beat it, he even get a job fer me modder on de factory bench, so wha a could say ter dat, a could only say well tings like, never say die, an wonders never cease, an when mango ripe it go fall, anyhow dat en all de man even start ter pay me back me money, not in big pieces but a one here a one dere, but dat was good dat shows he was trying, he heart was in de right place, anyhow i stop tinking bout im, but an wen a say but a mean but yer know, one day de man pay me back a five pound note an when a look at de five pound note well a had ter look yer know, because he never pay me back so much, when a look at de five pound note, a see it was de same five pound note a give me wife ter put in de bank fer me, so dat hit me but a figure she must be change some money fer him, so i en worry bout it, but an a say but again yer know, de man start ter pay me back one set a five pound notes, an all a dem is what a give she ter put in de bank so pardner a ask yer wha a go do, what you woulda do if all de five pound note you give yer wife ter put in de bank yer see turning up in another man hand, an is a man yer help, i help de man yer know, tell me what you woulda do, (*Slight pause.*) yer can tink a notten, well i go tell yer what i do or wha i was going ter do, a was going ter go over ter de pub an buy im a Guinness an tell im do kill yer self, but yer know what happen, when a get in de pub, de man in de pub say dey do' serve black people in dis bar i have ter go round, so a hit im, an when a hit im, he fall against a whole pile of boxes an de whole bar mash up, so da is what a in dis prison for, well boy a really learn me lesson, da is de last time a go ever be nice anybody.

A bell rings and the man gets up and walks out singing.

I love you baby
I need you baby.

'Shakespeare winged this way using other powers'

by Dennis Brutus (South Africa)

Shakespeare winged this way using other powers
to wrest from grim rock and a troubled student-
    lad
an immortality outlasting all our time
and hacking out an image of the human plight
that out-endures all facets of half-truth:

here now we hurtle north-east from the westering
    sun
that follows, plucks out from afar
the wingstruts crouched and sunlit for a plunge:

O might I be so crouched, so poised, so hewed
to claw some image of my fellows' woe
hacking the hardness of the ice-clad rock,
armed with such passion, dedication, voice
that every cobblestone would rear in wrath
and batter down a prison's wall
and wrench them from the island where they rot.

    [*Flying to Denmark*]

Leah: In Freedom

by Delores Kendricks (USA)

I run away
                I keep runnin' away
                                they won't let me alone
                                        they won't let me bear
my misery to the river
                and out
                     over the sky
                            or even
                                      under the trees
in moles' holes
                and wolves' caves

and blackberry patches
with my feet
skiddin' and bleedin'
on the thorns
and then it rains
on my run
as quick as my momma's voice
on the slippery road
to freedom
They catch me
all the time they catch me
and bring me back
and whip me
'till I'm blind and deaf
and dumb,
and put me in the cabin
where the blood soak my back
like scaldin' water
and take me out to the fields
and whip me some more.

Oh! the sky is so big!
Ain't it?

The trees are so tall!
Ain't they?

The river's so wide!
Ain't it?

Don't you hear?
Cain't you hear

all that callin', Leah?
Leah's gotta go!

And I run again
all twenty-three years of me
all white and black of me
all the angels in me
and the wings
growing out of my armpits

flapping against my thighs
                    makin' me move
                                    when I can't,
when I don't want to,
                    when my back is so sore
                                    and painful
that every flight
            makes my wings stick to my side sometimes
                                    and keep me slow
and earthbound;
                    all my momma in me
                                    So soon they catch me again
and beat me again
                    That was the last time for that.
                                            I lay here
on the hard floor on my back
                    only place that's soft:
                                    guess it's the flesh,
the wounds that do it,
                    guess it's the salt, too.
                                    So much pain
it don't pain no more
                    only the want of freedom pains,
                                            only the fear
or dyin' before I'm free.
                    Yesterday they took out
                                    one of my front teeth
to identify me
                    in case I 'scape again
                                    and now when I ain't doin'
the housework
                    they put me in an iron collar.
                                            Three days they gives me
three days I got for my wings
                    to heal
                                    but they's bent and dirty
and tattered, need washin'
                    they's not the same
                                    don't round themselves right

somehow.
>I can see the roots of trees now,
>>don't see the tops no more.
The mole and me
>we's on our own.
>>These days I go
>>>to my mistress' room
sew her clothes and cloaks
>though the wounds still breakin'
through my shawl
>and I be sore.
>>She got lots of holes
>>>under her armpits
of her dresses:
>that makes me shiver,
>>think of my momma.
Mistress say, 'good mawnin', Leah'
>(won't look at me)
and tell me about faith
>and Jesus.

Appendix

Sample Questions for Comparative Literary Analysis

The ability to conceptualize a concise and well-organized research or essay question is an art form as well as proof that a reader can identify the multiple relationships among different literatures. The following sets of questions are offered as a guide to readers for formulating their own questions. For optimum comparative analysis, most questions require an examination of three writers, texts, characters, themes, ideas, issues, gender constructs, and/or geographies. In addition, Chapter 1, Chapter 2, and the brief introductions to the remaining chapters contain numerous observations and quotations about the nature and tendencies of Black literature. Students are encouraged to analyze and debate these ideas in their writing exercises while drawing from the diverse samples of Black writing as evidence to support their arguments.

While many questions address themes and concepts introduced in the titles of Chapter 3 through Chapter 10, naturally in their responses to the questions below, students should address authors' use of literary conventions that enable the creation of successful and stylistic literature. In addition, students should review the "Suggestions for African-Centered Literary Analysis" (see Chapter 2, pp. 50–51) as a reminder of how this volume aims to challenge readers to broaden the scope and application of Black literature beyond traditional conventions.

Part 1 — Questions Ordered by Chapter

Chapter 3
Nationalism and Identity

1. How are European influences, whether viewed through the lens of colonialism (*Song of Lawino/Song of Ocol*), of Americanism ("The Woman from America"), or of hierarchies of skin color (*Passing*) responsible for elements of conflict in the lives of people of Africa and the Diaspora?

2. Explore global visions of "Africa" using three different genres of literature (e.g., the short story "A Song for the Parade," the traditional narrative *Song of Lawino/Song of Ocol*, and the poem "The Mighty Three.")

3. What roles do race and culture play in the construction of identity according to the novels *Desirada, Passing,* and *The Autobiography of an Ex-Colored Man*?

4. How does literature transmit the significance of the community's influence on national identity according to the poem "Meta-Score," the novel *Desirada,* and the short story "A Song for the Parade"?

5. Based on readings of the poem "The Mighty Three," the short story "A Song for the Parade," and the novel *Desirada,* explore the significance of "historical legacy" in the process of identify formation.

6. Critically explore literary responses to Pan-Africanism based on readings of "A Song for the Parade," "The Mighty Three," and "The Woman from America."

7. Select and analyze three texts that offer diverse sketches of "coming of age" in Africa and the Diaspora.

Chapter 4
Gender Contexts and Complementarity

1. Critically explore the strengths and weaknesses of Black male characters in the short story "Man of All Work," the play *Your Handsome Captain,* and the novel *The Fisher King.*

2. Explore how literature offers unique visions of womanhood according to the short stories "Girl," "Everything Counts," and "Man of All Work."

3. Select representative texts from three different genres to explore the relationship between race and gender.

4. Explore the gender-related themes of marriage, infidelity, and parenting in the short story "Man of All Work."

5. Critically explore the intersection of class and gender in the poem "Althea from Prison," the short narrative "Girl," and the novel *Woman at Point Zero.*

6. How does the novel *Woman at Point Zero* illuminate the issues of gender, economics, and religion that challenge North African women?

Chapter 5
History, Justice, and Politics

1. Critically explain how literature is a vehicle for historical exploration based on an analysis of the speech "Liberia: Its Struggles and Its Promises," of the play *Tragedy of King Christophe*, and of the poem "Revenge."

2. Explore global Black writers' regional treatments of the theme of justice in the novel *Pastrana's Last River*, the short story "Nineteen Thirty-Seven," and the novel *The Spook Who Sat By the Door*, representing Ecuador, Haiti, and the United States, respectively.

3. Explain the power and structure of poetry, including symbolic representation, metaphor, understatement, etc., to reveal how it is an ideal form for offering subtle political commentary.

4. Critically analyze race and politics in the African world through a comparative critique of the narrative prose selection "My African Friend," the poem "Let me say it," and the novel *The Spook Who Sat by the Door*.

5. How do African writers create and preserve images of human dignity amidst political injustice according to the novel *Pastrana's Last River*, the poem "Ndzeli in Passage," and the prose narrative "My African Friend"?

Chapter 6
Black Cultural Mythology

1. How does nonfiction literature in the form of the speech or essay, as seen through "In the Spirit of Butler" and "Toussaint L'Ouverture of the Haytian Revolutions," contribute to Black cultural mythology?

2. Critically explore the realism of the hero dynamics in the novel *Dreamer*, the speech "Toussaint L'Ouverture and the Haytian Revolutions," and the poem "For Chief."

3. What techniques does poet Laini Mataka use to mythologize and memorialize African American heroes and legends in her poems "Were You There When They Crucified My Lord," "George," and "freedom's divas"?

4. How do the poems "George Schuyler Again," "Bicentennial Blues," and "Fairy Tales for a Black Northeast" expose the antihero of Black cultural mythology?

5. Critically explore the Black Nationalist theme of resistance in three representative works.

6. Select three representative works to highlight how the variables of society and race influence Black writers' visions of Black cultural mythology.

Chapter 7
Autobiography and Personal Narrative

1. Critically explore the regional variations of Black male experience offered in Paul Robeson's *Here I Stand*, Wole Soyinka's *Aké: The Years of Childhood*, and Albert Memmi's *The Pillar of Salt*, which represent the United States, Nigeria, and Tunisia, respectively.

2. What testimonies about women's gender roles and constructs do the works "Nadine," *All God's Children Need Traveling Shoes*, and *Soul to Soul* share?

3. Explore the theme of religion/spirituality in *Here I Stand*, *Aké: The Years of Childhood*, and *All God's Children Need Traveling Shoes*.

4. Compare and contrast the variables of being African and Jewish according to Albert Memmi's *The Pillar of Salt* and Yelena Khanga's *Soul to Soul*.

5. To what extent does an African heritage influence dominant themes about identity in the narratives of Paul Robeson, Yelena Khanga, and Maya Angelou?

6. Critically analyze the confessional nature of personal narratives based on three representative texts.

7. Based on critical readings of "Nadine," *The Pillar of Salt*, and *All God's Children Need Traveling Shoes*, to what extent can personal narrative function as a tool of empowerment for readers?

Chapter 8
Community, Folk Culture, and Socioeconomic Realism

1. Based on critical readings of the short story "The Lesson," the novel *Xala*, and the folk narrative "The Son of Oxalá Who Was Named Money," explore how the authors creatively used different genres to offer unique approaches to conveying society's economic issues.

2. Critically explain how the short story is effectively used to present regional variations of socioeconomic realism in "The Lesson," "Village People," and "George and the Bicycle Pump," representing the United States, South Africa, and Trinidad, respectively.

3. Critically explore the themes of community, folklore, and economics in Toni Morrison's novel *Love*.

4. What sense of community emerges from a comparative analysis of the poems "Solstice," "Carnival," and "Billy Green is Dead"?

5. Analyze the themes of labor, gender, and society in the short story "The Lesson."

6. Select and analyze three representative texts that reveal unique regional folk interpretations of labor and work.

7. What is the relationship between gender, economics, and community in the novel *Xala* and the short story "Village People"?

Chapter 9
Speculation, Spirituality, and the Supernatural

1. According to Malcolm X's speech at the Harvard Law School forum, August Wilson's play *Joe Turner's Come and Gone*, and Octavia Butler's *Parable of the Talents*, critically explore how each author suggests the distinction between spirituality and religion.

2. Compare and contrast the central speculation—or "what if"—of *Black No More*, *The Rape of Shavi*, and *Midnight Robber* and how this central speculation influences the plot of each novel.

3. What is the relationship between Black literature and science and technology according to the poem "The Space Shuttle" and the novel *Black No More*?

4. Critically analyze how Caribbean history is central to the future organization of the Caribbean community in Nalo Hopkinson's *Midnight Robber*.

5. Critically explore how politics, religion, and history influence Malcolm X's apocalyptic vision of world order in the speech delivered at the Harvard Law School Forum.

6. Compare and contrast the fine line between the supernatural and religion as seen in *Joe Turner's Come and Gone* and *The Rape of Shavi*.

7. Select and analyze three representative works that could sustain a debate about the values of simplicity, human awareness, spirituality, and other traditional values versus modernity, technology and scientific advancement.

Chapter 10
Influence, Adaptation, and Structure

1. Compare and contrast the unique structural elements introduced by the novel *Emergency Exit*, the play *Nice*, and the novel/fictional travel narrative *Black Girl in Paris*.

2. How do the play "Pantomime," the novel/fictional travel narrative *Black Girl in Paris*, and the poem "Shakespeare winged this way" offer interpretations and adaptations of formerly established literatures?

3. Critically explore how the play *Nice*, the poem "Leah: in Freedom," and the novel *Emergency Exit* offer innovative structural uses of words and language.

4. Select three representative works and evaluate them according to their models in order to show how Black literature makes creative use of world literary traditions.

Part II — General Questions That Transcend Chapter Organization

Readers should begin to categorize works of literature into groupings that go beyond chapter organization and delve into more unique and diverse aspects of literary analysis and criticism on the basis of individual interest.

1. Critically explore the relationship of music and song to the global Black literary tradition based on three of the following works: the play *Joe Turner's Come and Gone*, the play *Your Handsome Captain*, the memoir *All God's Children Need Traveling Shoes*, the novel *Love*, and the short story "A Song for the Parade."

2. Which three works from this collection offer the best models of the credo of Africana Studies, which is to "create knowledge and inspire behaviors that will increase the life chances and life experiences of people of African descent, in particular, and of humanity, in general"?

3. Critically explore the nature of the global Caribbean experience based on three of the following works: the novel *Desirada*, the science fiction novel *Midnight Robber*, the play *Nice*, the short story "George and the Bicycle Pump," the novel *Brother Man*, the short story "Nineteen Thirty-Seven," the short narrative "Girl," and the novel *The Fisher King*.

4. According to the short story "A Song for the Parade," the novel *The Rape of Shavi*, the short story "Everything Counts," and the traditional narrative *Song of Lawino/Song of Ocol*, what is the nature of African modernism?

5. Select and critically explore three works that offer positive representations of Pan-Africanism in literature.

6. Select and critically explore three representative works that demonstrate either the extreme diversity or the homogeneity of the global African experience.

7. Select and critically explore three representative works that demonstrate the function and role of European characters in Black texts and Black life.

8. Write a well-developed essay that critically analyzes three of the most surprising or least known aspects of global Black identity conveyed in literature.

9. What is the nature of and challenges of translation based on your comparison of the original versions and translated versions of works such as *Your Handsome Captain* (French), *The Pillar of Salt* (French), *The Tragedy of King Christophe* (French), *Desirada* (French), *Soul to Soul* (Russian), "Meta-Score" (Portuguese), "Carnival" (Portuguese), *Pastrana's Last River* (Spanish), *Woman at Point Zero* (Arabic), and *Song of Lawino* (Luo)?

10. Select and critically explore three representative works whose political, sociological, and psychological themes, plots, conflicts, and resolutions are based on race.

11. Comparatively explore the language/linguistic issues presented in three of the following sources: Mustapha Matura's *Nice*, Roger Mais's *Brother Man*, Derek Walcott's *Pantomime*, and Toni Cade Bambara's "The Lesson."

12. Select and comparatively analyze three sources from different genres that permit a formal analysis of the authors' strict use of basic and advanced literary devices.

13. Select and comparatively analyze three sources suitable for analysis based directly on the "Suggestions for African-Centered Literary Analysis."

14. Select and comparatively analyze three regional literature selections that permit a sophisticated treatment of symbolism.

15. Critically explore the literary, social, and spiritual treatment of themes related to elders, aging, and ancestors in several of the following texts: Toni Morrison's *Love*, Nelson Estupiñan Bass's *Pastrana's Last River*, Buchi Emecheta's *The Rape of Shavi*, Bessie Head's "Village People," and August Wilson's *Joe Turner's Come and Gone*.

16. Identify and critically explore three selections for which the presence of, or lack of, music-dance-song in the narrative's plot, conflict, and/or setting is pivotal to the text's effectiveness.

17. Select and critically explore a set of texts from a single geography of Africa or the Diaspora.

18. Compare and contrast competing versions and visions of the meaning of "home" found within both fiction and non-fiction texts.

19. Identify and analyze the diverse mythologies documented in Black writing.

20. Examine and debate a scholarly quotation or observation from Chapter 1, Chapter 2, or the introductions to Chapter 3 through Chapter 10 using diverse examples from Black writing to support your ideas.

About the Author

Christel N. Temple, a native of Richmond, Virginia, is a literary historian and cultural critic whose innovative work spans Afrocentric studies, history, and literature. She is associate professor of Africana Studies at the University of Maryland, Baltimore County (UMBC). She holds a B.A. in History from the College of William and Mary, and an M.A. and Ph.D. in African American Studies from UMBC and Temple University, respectively. Professor Temple's articles and essays appear in Africana Studies journals such as *The Journal of Black Studies*, *The International Journal of Africana Studies*, *Africalogical Perspectives*, and the *CLA Journal* of the College Language Association. Professor Temple is also author of *Literary Pan-Africanism: History, Contexts, and Criticism* (2005). She is currently completing companion volumes, *The Theory of Black Cultural Mythology* and *The Black Cultural Mythology Reader*.

Index